Pra

"Pentecostalism is the fastes today, and nowhere is this more obvious than in Nigeria. The interactions of African and foreign missionaries brought about the fascinating, vibrant and sometimes controversial movement that is Nigerian Pentecostalism today. The biography of a key player in the formation of this movement, Sydney Elton, is presented for the first time in this eminently readable and historically sound book. Abodunde has done the world of Pentecostal studies a great service in this fine account."

—Allan Anderson (University of Birmingham),
author of *To the Ends of the Earth: Pentecostalism and the Transformation of World Christianity*

"Ayodeji Abodunde has written the definitive biography of Sydney Elton, the single most influential Pentecostal missionary to Nigeria. Abodunde's biography also draws on a plethora of new sources to explain Elton's successful missionary career that spanned several Pentecostal movements and fifty years of Nigeria's history. . . . While many scholars write about aspects of these Pentecostal movements—working within certain accepted typologies and chronologies—Abodunde's book refreshingly takes a look at continuities between these movements over time through the lens of Sydney Elton. This is an excellent book and an important read for scholars of African Christianity, Pentecostal Studies, and Global Christianity."

—Adam Mohr (University of Pennsylvania),
author of *Enchanted Calvinism*

"How Can I find a few words to write about this big comprehensive book about my father? Not that I need to say much, the book is comprehensive! It covers so much of what happened in Pa's lifetime, the things which happened to other people, and so many things he was involved in. It tells the story of what happened since he came to Nigeria in 1937 and till he passed on in 1987. . . . Enjoy reading it. You will learn and be blessed."

—Ruth Elton,
Daughter of Sydney and Hannah Elton

"Ayodeji Abodunde's *Messenger* is an exhaustive biography of an 'ancestor of holiness Pentecostalism in Nigeria.' . . . The book is well-researched, well-written, informative, and thought-provoking. The author is sympathetic but not uncritical, raising substantive issues on the civic and moral role of Nigerian Pentecostalism, and the bigger issue of the future of Nigeria (Africa) as a new emerging centre of gravity in the shifting contours of world Christianity. The book will spontaneously attract and interest scholars, students, religious practitioners and all other stakeholders interested in mapping the complex provenance and changing dynamics of Pentecostal Christianities, and engaged in the wider discourse on contemporary Pentecostalism in the Nigerian spiritual marketplace, albeit its local-global challenges and impact."

—Afe Adogame (Princeton Theological Seminary), author of
*The African Christian Diaspora: New Currents and
Emerging Trends in World Christianity*

"This book is a remarkable achievement. Written in lucid and erudite style, it examines the life of the British Pentecostal missionary, Sydney Elton, whose ministry had such a significant impact on the church in Nigeria. . . . Drawing on a wide range of sources, Abodunde provides us with a detailed account of Elton's life and ministry, while at the same time presenting us with a comprehensive history of Nigerian Pentecostalism up until the late 1980s. Skilfully interweaving eyewitness testimony and scholarly accounts with sermon extracts and correspondence, Abodunde demonstrates how the different phases of Elton's ministry were closely connected to critical moments in the history of this important movement. . . . Abodunde's book is full of insights and interesting historical detail. It will be an invaluable resource for those interested in the history of Nigerian Christianity and especially its Pentecostal and Charismatic expressions."

—Richard Burgess (University of Roehampton),
author of *Nigeria's Christian Revolution: The Civil War
Revival and Its Pentecostal Progeny (1967–2006)*

MESSENGER

ALSO BY AYODEJI ABODUNDE

A Heritage of Faith: A History of Christianity in Nigeria

MESSENGER

Sydney Elton and the Making of Pentecostalism in Nigeria

AYODEJI ABODUNDE

PIERCEWATERSHED

LAGOS

MESSENGER
Copyright © 2016 by Ayodeji Abodunde

Published in Lagos, Nigeria by Pierce Watershed
19, Town Planning Way, Ilupeju, Lagos

For information, e-mail:
piercewatershed@gmail.com
sales@piercewatershed.com
+234 902 914 9486
+234 902 358 7348

First edition, 2016

ISBN 978-978-949-765-2

To D

Thank You.

"Christianity was never designed to be comfortable but revolutionary. It had to be completely revolutionary if it had to succeed in changing men, saving them, meeting their needs and thus changing conditions and nations. . . . Jesus used no violence but He was the true revolutionary."

—Sydney Elton

CONTENTS

A MOST UNUSUAL EXIT

It would seem that the steady stream of visitors who came to Ilesa in the days following the death of Sydney Elton shook the dust from their feet as they departed for their homes. When news of Pa's death initially filtered around the country, a deep sense of loss pervaded many Christian circles, particularly Pentecostal groups—a titan had passed on. Dying at eighty, after fifty unbroken years of ministry in Nigeria, Elton was the missionary (Pentecostal or otherwise) who had laboured the longest in the country since Thomas Birch Freeman, the great Methodist pioneer, stepped down in Badagry on September 24, 1842.

Elton's career stands out not only for its longevity but also for its impact: the careers of only a few individuals have been as consequential in shaping Nigeria's Christian landscape in its more than 170-year history. It was as a result of Elton's impact, first on the Pentecostal movement that began in the early 1930s, and later on the charismatic movement which took off in the late 1960s, that hundreds flocked to Ilesa when they heard that he had passed on. A whole generation had drunk from this well of inspiration at one time or the other and it was only fitting for them to identify with him in death as much as in life.

So why did Elton's memory fade as quickly as the visitors left? Within a few years he was all but forgotten in Pentecostal discourse. To hear those who knew him speak, one would think he was a contemporary of Mary Slessor rather than a man who still breathed in the harmattan of 1986—his memory had suddenly become so distant. It was a most unusual way for a leader of such stature to exit the scene. How did this happen? How did a generation find it convenient to forget him so easily?

The gradual distancing from Elton and his message by a generation whose attention had once been riveted by it had begun years before Elton's death, as his message began to assume dimensions that the charismatic movement he had helped nurture became uncomfortable with. Elton's message significantly shifted gears in the last years of his life to what a significant number considered high-sounding theology that did not have any immediate applications to what the church was then experiencing. Others were irked by his continuous denouncing of many of the practices that had emerged in some streams of the movement; it looked like Elton had turned his back on the baby he had helped bring to life.

Elton continued to give himself tirelessly to most of those who had embraced his message in the sixties and seventies, and his invitations to meetings were still considerably many, at least for his age; but most people now embraced only the part of Elton they considered non-threatening. Ironically, Elton believed these were his best years and would not exchange them for any of the previous decades; he believed it was at this time that he entered into the fullness of his calling; he believed the wine he served at this stage was the finest. But had he been speaking beyond his time, so that the church was genuinely unprepared for what he had to say, or had he brought a word crucial for the times but unacceptable to the church because of a conflict of interests? Or was it both?

One thing is certain, Elton did not die popular. But then, those who had really known him at the different stages of his ministry wouldn't have been surprised—Elton was never popular. Elton was only popular with those who could receive the message he had to deliver at any point in time. And his message to the church at any given time was a function of what he believed God was presently saying and doing. So much did he build his ministry on what he believed God was *saying* and *doing*, that it is interesting to see how his missionary career continually morphed in its fifty-year span as a result of this. Elton was always ready to abandon whatever he had previously been involved with to become a part of what he believed God was presently doing on the face of the earth. He always made it clear that he was more concerned with what he perceived was God's current focus than with what other people were thinking. Till the end of his life, he despised stale water and was always in pursuit of God's unfolding plan. This life principle is embodied in a question which he consistently asked and which his protégés became very familiar with over many years: "What is God doing in the earth today?"

Elton was a restless soul. It can be a daunting task for any biographer to keep track of his thinking because he so constantly and easily (or so it seems) changed allegiances, forged new ones and associated with new acquaintances from the time he landed in Nigeria in 1937 until he passed on in 1987. His visionary leaps frequently caused crises in his relationships, which made many conclude he was unstable in his commitments. It would seem Elton had the unique gift of evoking loyalty and animosity in equal measure. To be sure, it took a lot of bravery to be very close to him for more than a decade, but then, this was only so because of his ability to continually discern new frontiers in the plan of God and then stake everything to participate in its establishment. Elton's commitment to God and the establishment of His kingdom in Nigeria in his days was fierce, daring, and unmatched. In many ways, Pentecostal Christians in Nigeria and Africa are heirs of his vision—a prophetic vision that significantly shaped Nigeria's spiritual landscape for five decades; a prophetic vision that is still unfolding today, and whose full potential is yet to be tapped.

Indeed one would be hard pressed to find a preacher who took the designation "missionary to Nigeria" more seriously than Elton did. Although Elton came to Nigeria as just one more missionary of the Apostolic Church with headquarters in Penygroes, Wales, he soon came to believe, to really believe, that he had been *sent* to Nigeria, so much so that if he had not come on the platform of the Apostolic Church, he would still have come, that he would not have been sent to any other place but Nigeria, because he had an assignment to fulfil—a divine assignment, divinely packaged for the nation called Nigeria. Elton was so conscious of his role as God's messenger to Nigeria that a casual observer could not be blamed for judging it to be extreme or bordering on self-aggrandisement.

Elton considered himself a messenger who had been sent to a nation destined to play a crucial role in God's end-time plan. He approached this assignment with an almost extreme sense of responsibility, working as if any failure on his part had the potential to jeopardize God's intention for the nation. He saw himself and his mission as enormously crucial to the spiritual destiny of Nigeria. This created in him an emotional attachment to the country; indeed, it is clear he had psychologically shed his British citizenship at some point. He declared in 1982, "I want to warn you, and serve you notice, that I'm going to have my interest in Nigeria, whether you like it or not. I may be a white man, but this is where my inheritance is. God has . . . brought me to Nigeria, and I've been here these forty-five years, and nobody will take me back to a place where I've got nothing. This is where I've got it all. Here! And there are ten thousand people already in heaven, because I'm here and there's another ten thousand waiting to go with me. Yes, my inheritance is here and more than that, I've put my feet in enough soil in Nigeria for me to say, that's mine, that's mine!"[1] This grave sense of mission, expressed in different hues throughout his career, underlies everything he did, and it is only from this perspective that we can truly understand and appreciate his ministry of half a century in the country.

For fifty years, Elton continuously challenged a nation by his radical spiritual outlook. In the 1950s, he spearheaded on a national scale the first wave of modern-day mass revivals in the country. In the 1960s he provided the platform for some of the leading figures in the global Pentecostal movement to have a major influence on the direction of Nigeria's Christianity. Beginning in the late 1960s, he embarked on an ambitious project of training the next generation; he sought them out wherever they could be found, especially in universities and colleges, and encouraged them with every resource at his disposal to lay hold of their destiny in God. He envisioned a spiritual army of young Nigerian Christians boldly marching through the nation establishing God's government everywhere they went. Battling not a few conservative forces on his way, he stopped at nothing to ensure that a generation clearly understood its place in God's plan and had the courage to pursue it. This resulted in a massive spiritual shift that defined Christianity among young people in the sixties, seventies and eighties, and directly led to the emergence of the charismatic movement in Nigeria.

Elton's emphasis on the importance of the power and the gifts of the Holy Spirit to the present-day ministry of the church was perhaps the single most important factor in the emergence of the charismatic movement in Nigeria. Elton pioneered systematic teaching on the operation of the gifts of the Spirit and the practical application of these gifts in the lives of Christians in Nigeria through his seminars on the subject on university campuses, through one-on-one and small group meetings at his base in Ilesa, and through teaching on the subject in churches and conferences around the country. Virtually all the Christian leaders who were influenced by Elton agree that one of the greatest legacies he bequeathed to their generation, and by extension to the nation, was laying the foundation of their understanding and practical application of the gifts of the Holy Spirit—both by teaching and impartation. This legacy played a significant role in equipping a generation of Nigerian youth for the Christian ministry as church leaders, missionaries, Christian educators, and Christian workers in all spheres of spiritual endeavour.

When Pentecostalism was still struggling to be recognized as a valid tradition in Nigeria's Christianity, Elton had seen its emergence on the global stage and called on Nigerian Pentecostals to prepare to take the gospel to the ends of the earth. He unrelentingly prophesied that Pentecostal Christianity in Nigeria would lead a spiritual revival in Africa and the Western nations that would usher the church worldwide into the glory that has been reserved for the last days. To borrow a phrase from historian Ron Chernow, Elton was "the messenger from a future that we now inhabit."[2]

Perhaps Elton's greatest legacy to Nigerian Christianity was the vision he cast for the future. He spent the last ten years of his life articulating what the church would look like at the end of the age. He believed the church at the close of the age would be so radically different in outlook than what obtained in his day, and that only a courageous generation would dare to make a transition to this new and final phase of God's programme. Elton saw a daring generation of Nigerian and African Christians who in the last days would lead global Christian thought and experience. Elton believed he was called to prepare the way for that generation, that he was called to point the way to the future.

Elton carried the DNA of a warrior: a spartan life, a courageous spirit, a fierce devotion. He dared to go to new places in the Spirit, even when no one else would follow. He was a frontiersman, always feeling for what might lie ahead, always reaching for what had yet been unexplored, always thirsting for what God might still have in stock. Figuratively speaking, Elton lived in tents throughout his life, ever ready to move at the first scent of a new move of the Holy Spirit.

Any comprehensive biography of Sydney Elton must also necessarily be a study of the historical development of Pentecostalism in Nigeria. Therefore, this book is as much a history of Pentecostalism in Nigeria as it is a biography of Elton. The generosity of archivists, librarians, and individuals in different parts of the world has turned up a trove of previously unused and unpublished documents, which have made possible a major reconstruction of the history of the movement. The result, I hope, is a fresh and inspiring perspective.

By the time Elton died in 1987, his ministry and collaborations had completely reshaped Nigeria's spiritual landscape. But so much has happened since then. If Elton were alive today, he would no doubt look at the landscape with some ambivalence. One is safe—judging from the overwhelming body of evidence in Elton's writings in serial publications and books, his taped sermons, his surviving letters, and from interviews with those who were close to him—to conclude that if Elton were to assess today the movement he played so large a role in shaping, his reaction would be a re-enactment of Ezra 3:10-13:

> Now when the builders had laid the foundation of the temple of the Lord, the priests stood in their apparel with trumpets, and the Levites, the sons of Asaph, with cymbals, to praise the Lord according to the directions of King David of Israel. They sang, praising and giving thanks to the Lord, *saying*, "For He is good, for His loving kindness is upon Israel forever." And all the people shouted with a great shout when they praised the Lord because the foundation of the house of the Lord was laid.
>
> Yet many of the priests and Levites and heads of fathers' *households*, the old men who had seen the first temple, wept with a loud voice when the foundation of this house was laid before their eyes, while many shouted aloud for joy, so that the people could not distinguish the sound of the shout of joy from the sound of the weeping of the people, for the people shouted with a loud shout, and the sound was heard far away.

Elton would be exultant; but he would also be depressed. He would rejoice; but he would also cry. At no other time—when the foundations of Pentecostal Christianity in Nigeria are being vigorously shaken, and when both the church and the nation are in desperate need of a new breed of visionary and courageous leadership—does Elton's prophetic vision; his commitment to generational succession; his devotion to the highest standards of Christian living; his ideas about the church's role in social transformation; his thoughts on moving from a church mind-set to a kingdom mind-set; his unrelenting cry against the denominational spirit; and his pursuit of revival and the full release of the operation of the gifts of the Holy Spirit hold greater significance for our collective spiritual experience.

Elton's life and ministry bore all the fruits of an apostolic ministry of biblical stature and his story can stir us to seek the restoration of a truly apostolic Christianity and ministry in our day. The burden he carried till his dying days—a Nigerian church walking in the fullness of her spiritual calling—still lives with us. We can follow the pathways he pioneered in the Spirit and cry out for the outpouring of the latter rain he so desperately sought.

This biography is a study of the life, ministry and theology of the man who believed he had an apostolic message for the church in Nigeria and who stopped at nothing to deliver it. Gordon Lindsay's comment about Elton when he visited Nigeria in 1971 was spot on: "Rev. Elton is indeed an apostle to Nigeria. For a third of a century he has faithfully carried on the work through peace and war. Missionaries have come and gone, but his steady labours have borne abundant fruit."[3]

ONE

"FROM SHREWSBURY TO AFRICA"

Daniel Knight Elton, Sydney Elton's paternal grandfather, was born in 1840,[1] in Willenhall, a small English town situated between Wolverhampton and Walsall, with a population of about eight thousand in 1844.[2] Census records show that in 1841, Daniel was living in the same house with Amelia Elton, twenty, and Louisa Elton, fourteen, in St Margaret, Leicester; we cannot establish his specific relationship to them through the records.[3] In 1861, Daniel was living with his grandmother, Hall Phoebe, a seventy-seven-year-old widow; by this time he was employed as a lock maker.[4] In later years, he filled his occupation as "rim lock maker"[5] (1881) and "lock manufacturer"[6] (1891). The 1851 *History, Gazetteer and Directory of Staffordshire* records that Willenhall's "inhabitants are mostly employed in the manufacture of locks, keys, bolts, latches, chafing dishes, gridirons, currycombs, etc. It is said that more locks, of all kinds, are made here than in any other town of the same size in England or Europe."[7] One source quotes 340 lock makers in Willenhall in 1855, mostly in small workshops.[8] By 1881 Daniel had his own small workshop, which employed six men and a boy.[9]

In 1884 Daniel and his wife, Eliza, gave birth to their sixth son, Ernest. In the 1891 census, Ernest is registered as a "scholar"[10] (a word which was then in popular use for school children); he was a rim lock maker by the time he was seventeen.[11] Whether or not he was ever in his father's employ is not certain, but it is highly probable. Between 1901 and 1906 Ernest changed occupation to become an engine fitter, which he maintained until his death in 1925.[12] On May 26, 1906, Ernest Elton married Edith Annie Baker at the St. Mary's Church, Bushbury, a suburb of Wolverhampton.[13] On April 16, 1907, eleven months after their wedding, their first son, Sydney Granville Elton, was born.[14] He would be followed by two others—a girl, Marjorie, born in 1909, and a boy, Maurice, born in 1911.[15]

The Eltons' family life in Wolverhampton was one of constant change and painful experiences. When Sydney Elton was born, the family lived in 22 Owen Road, Wolverhampton;[1] by 1911 the family had moved to 43 Sherwood Street; in 1916 the family had moved again, to 31 Church Road, Bradmore—a suburb of Wolverhampton.[16] In 1916 Edith died of pulmonary tuberculosis at thirty-four.[17] Ernest Elton remarried after Edith's death, giving birth to one more son, Ronald.[18] (From later family stories by Sydney Elton's daughter, Ruth, it does not seem that there was any cordiality between her father and his siblings and their stepmother and her son, Ronald.[19]) In 1925 Ernest Elton, in the presence of his son, Sydney, also succumbed to pulmonary tuberculosis after battling it for three years; he was forty-three.[20] Elton himself was at some point diagnosed with the disease. In later years when an X-ray of his chest was taken at the University College Hospital, Ibadan, the doctor detected that he had once come down with tuberculosis[21]—the traces could still be seen in the X-ray. After their father's death, Elton assumed responsibility for Marjorie and Maurice.[22]

There are only two extant pictures of Elton taken while he was still in Wolverhampton. Both pictures were taken around the same period—one is dated 1926, and the other, as written on the photograph, was taken when he was eighteen going on nineteen. Both are classic portraits of the adolescent Elton. The 1926 photo, marked "IOM 1926," where Elton is wearing what seems to be a bathing cap, looks like a holiday snap. Elton most likely had this photo taken while holidaying on the Isle of Man in 1926. (The Isle of Man is a small island in the Irish Sea, which has long been a popular holiday destination for English people, situated roughly midway between Liverpool and Belfast.) In the second photograph taken at West Park, Wolverhampton, situated on the western side of the town, Elton is wearing a "straw boater" (hat) and smart clothes, and posing with a walking stick; it was then in vogue to dress this way when strolling (or boating) in the park.[23] We do not have any other records of the years of the Elton family in Wolverhampton.

Elton relocated to Shrewsbury with his siblings, about forty-five kilometres from Wolverhampton, sometime between 1926 and 1928. It has been suggested that the strained relationship between Elton and his stepmother might have contributed to this move.[24] But one still wonders why Elton decided to leave a bustling town with good opportunities like Wolverhampton for the more rural Shrewsbury. Shrewsbury is a town in the historic county of Shropshire, one of England's most rural and sparsely populated counties.[25] Shrewsbury is most famous for being the birthplace of Charles Darwin, whose seminal work, *On the Origin of Species* (1859), laid the foundation for the theory of evolution by natural selection and brought about a revolution in the life and earth sciences and in modern thought in general.[26]

When exactly Elton arrived in Shrewsbury cannot be determined from available records. But his conversion (like the rest of the Elton family, he was a non-church goer), which took place in Shrewsbury, gives us the closest idea of the time he arrived there. We know from Elton and one other source that he committed his life to Jesus Christ in 1928. When he was asked in a 1982 interview how long he had been a Christian, he responded that he had been "serving the Lord for fifty-four years."[27] That would put the year of his conversion at 1928. We have another indirect reference from one of his very rare mentions of his activities as a new Christian: "When I first studied the Tabernacle in 1928 and in 1930, over fifty years ago, I was concerned mainly with enjoying the glories of the beauty of the Lord Jesus Christ."[28]

But the most direct reference we have is from a report in 1966 by Carole Lindsay, daughter of Gordon Lindsay, following a trip to Nigeria, where she wrote, "In 1928 he [Elton] had a conversion experience, and from that day on his uppermost thought was to give himself to the Lord's work full-time."[29] We can conclude that Carole Lindsay's record is reliable, considering that the Lindsays (Carole was on this trip with her father) got this information directly from Elton. Since this conversion took place in Shrewsbury, we can safely say that he was already settled in this town by 1928, and probably a little earlier. Even though his name does not appear in the 1928 directory of Shrewsbury[30] (his name first appears in the 1931 directory—the directories were not printed annually) we know he was already there by this time.

This 1928 conversion experience took place at 3 Nelson Place, Havlock Road, which also happens to be the first residential record we have of Elton in Shrewsbury.[31] The house, a bread-and-breakfast lodging, belonged to one Mrs Polly Palmer who frequently rented it to travellers, or other people who needed a place to stay for short periods.[32] Living with Mrs Palmer at this time was her niece, Hannah Cartwright. Hannah, a devoted Christian and at the time a member of the Plymouth Brethren, frequently preached to lodgers, but she had become discouraged because the discussions mostly ended in arguments, and she decided to no longer engage them in "gospel talk." She, however, failed to abide by her decision when Elton moved in. We don't know whether Elton argued with her or not, but in the end he opened his heart to the gospel message and committed his life to Jesus Christ. He also joined her in attending the Brethren Church.[33]

In the town's 1931 directory, Elton is registered as a wireless engineer[34]—this matches his 1930 wedding certificate.[35] On the 1934 birth certificate of his daughter, he is registered as a radio and electrical engineer. There are a number of pointers to the fact that Elton started out in life not as a wireless engineer but as a schoolteacher, perhaps while still in Wolverhampton, though there is no hard evidence to support this. On two occasions when Elton briefly mentioned his work as a schoolteacher, the context makes it difficult to determine whether he was talking about his pre-Nigeria years or referring to his work as principal of the Apostolic Church's teacher training centre in Ilesa in the 1940s.[36] The closest thing we have to proof that he worked as a schoolteacher before coming to Nigeria is Carole Lindsay's 1966 report: "Missionary Elton had been educated as a school teacher. After some years in this profession, he turned to radio and worked as a radio engineer and announcer for ten years."[37] Again, because her report was from a direct interview with Elton, it has a lot of credibility.

We know from Ruth Elton's recollection that her father once interned with the Rolls Royce Company, where he trained to become a salesman.[38] Whether or not he eventually worked for the company is not certain. It was probably after this that he trained as a wireless engineer. From Ruth we also know that he was once in the employ of Medlicott Brothers, "radio, electrical and television engineers and service agents,"[39] who had their main office on Mardol Street, Shrewsbury. In a printed documentary of the town produced in the late 1950s, Medlicott Brothers were the only radio and television engineers advertised.[40]

All of Elton's pictures from this period reveal a dapper young man with an unmistakable sense of style. He was fairly tall, with an assured poise and a confident pose. He was a natty dresser and a natural charmer. He usually wore the look of a young man who was thoroughly enjoying the present, but who remained sensible about the future. He had definitely achieved some level of financial comfort, considering he already had a car in his early twenties, and could afford to rent a three-storey house, which by all accounts was very comfortable.

Elton sometimes talked about his inheritance from his father which seems to have been substantial. Once referring to it he said, "When my father died there was a will . . . and I inherited. I was his first born and I inherited quite a bit of property."[41] This likely contributed to his early comfortable status. (Elton may have been referring to this inheritance when he mentioned years later that he continued to draw a personal income even after he became a missionary: "I was sent out by a missionary society, by a missionary church, and I was given an allowance. . . . In 1937 that allowance in English money was £7.15 per month. That was my allowance, and I had to live on that. Of course I couldn't live on that; fortunately I had a little income of my own."[42])

It is not surprising that a warm relationship developed between Elton and Hannah Cartwright since they stayed in the same compound (though Hannah shuttled between Aunt Polly's house and her parents' place) and attended the same congregation. What is daring, however, is that they decided to get married, considering that there was a difference of thirteen years between them—Hannah was then thirty-six and Elton twenty-three.[43] But this was not completely strange to the Cartwright family; Hannah's mother, Elizabeth, was five years older than her father, John.[44]

During this period, John and Elizabeth worked for a retired military officer (an English nobleman) who lived on an estate that was called The Trench, located somewhere between Shrewsbury and neighbouring town, Wem: John was a butler and Elizabeth housekeeper. As butler and house-keeper, the Cartwrights had catered to nobility all their working lives.[45] Also, part of the Cartwright family lore is that Hannah's mother once cooked a meal which was eaten by Queen Elizabeth the Queen Mother.[46] Hannah had an older brother, John Thomas, who gave her the pet name "Ciss" immediately she was born; many extended family members also fondly called her by this name. Aunt Polly called her "Cissie." From all indications, this family of four was a free-spirited, close-knit and happy one.

Sydney Elton and Hannah Cartwright were married on April 22, 1930 at the Brethren Church, in Castle Fields, a suburb of Shrewsbury.[47] A newspaper (most likely the *Shrewsbury Chronicle*, a weekly community newspaper which had been published in the town since 1772) report described the wedding of Sydney and Hannah in classic small town (Shrewsbury had a population of 32,372 in 1931[48]) tabloid fashion. The telling of the story showed as much determination to inform the public as to titillate the minds of young girls and unmarried ladies, giving them gossip material for some time. With the header "Elton-Cartwright,"[49] the gist of the wedding began thus: "At Hebron Hall, Clive, on Tuesday, Miss Hannah Catherine Cartwright, only daughter of Mr and Mrs T. Cartwright, The Trench, Wem, was married to Mr Sydney Granville Elton, Shrewsbury, eldest son of the late Mr and Mrs E. Elton, Wolverhampton." The bride, "who was given away by her father, was dressed in blue georgette, with beige hat, and carried a Bible." She was attended by two bridesmaids, "Miss Grace Smith, Shrewsbury, and Miss Peggy Cartwright, niece of the bride, who were attired in lemon suede georgette and pink suede georgette respectively, with picture hats. Miss Smith carried a bouquet of pink carnations, and the younger bridesmaid a basket of primroses." And finally, "the bridegroom's brother, Mr Maurice Elton, carried out the duties of best man, and the officiating pastors were Mr T. Cartwright (uncle of the bride) and Mr W. H. Clare. Miss Bullock, Shrewsbury, was at the organ. After the reception, which was held at Hebron Hall, the newly married couple left for a tour of North Wales, the bride travelling in a Lido blue coat with hat to match." This was enough fantasy for anybody who needed one. No reporter could resist the temptation to excite the community in this fashion.

In a small town like Shrewsbury, whose residents fondly called themselves Salopians (this is from Salop—an old abbreviation for Shropshire—the former name of the county; the name was changed to Shropshire in 1980 but residents are still referred to as Salopians[50]), most people would know the couple or at least one of them, which made the story all the more interesting. Ruth Elton recalls one interesting anecdote of her parents' honeymoon: their car broke down on the way and the new bride had to push while Elton tried to get the engine to start.

The newlyweds most likely moved into 83 Belle Vue Road after the wedding. Belle Vue Road is about ten minutes walking distance from Havlock Road, where Elton lived until the wedding. The house was a large three-storey building, and Ruth Elton remembers that it was always full of people. One of those living there at the time was Grace Smith, Hannah's bridesmaid; she was then apprenticing as a seamstress with Hannah, and doubled as a housekeeper. When Ruth was born Grace took up the role of nanny also. Marjorie, Elton's younger sister, also lived in this house. She also was a seamstress, and one imagines the dressmaking trio at 83 Belle Vue Road, sharing space and machines, trying to meet delivery deadlines. Marjorie died of pulmonary tuberculosis on June 3, 1934, at the age of twenty-five. (The early deaths of Elton's closest family members proved a false omen of his own later long and mostly healthy life.) The Cartwrights, Hannah's parents, also lived at Belle Vue House for a period. On September 7, 1934, a girl was born to the Eltons—she was named Ruth.[51]

As she did with his career, Carole Lindsay again bequeaths to us an interesting insight into Elton's early spirituality. She records that after his conversion "the only thing he knew to do was to start where he was. Day after day he and his wife passed out tracts and testified to all who would listen."[52] Also, Okey Onuzo, a protégé from the early seventies, remembers Elton talking about his involvement in "aggressive witnessing" in his early days as a Christian. Elton would tell stories of walking round the park, "wearing placards: in front—'I am a fool for Jesus;' and at the back—'Whose fool are you?' "[53] Here and there over the years, Elton himself dropped hints of his formative period as a Christian. As seen earlier, he mentioned studying the tabernacle of Moses in 1928 and 1930. In two other instances, he connects his early spirituality and the study of the Tabernacle: "The Tabernacle is one of the most wonderful pictures in the Bible and I spent some months in 1928 and again in 1930 studying the book of Exodus, and studying the object lesson to build the Tabernacle. I actually built a model of it."[54] And elsewhere: "I want to talk to you about a most wonderful subject I personally enjoy following—the Tabernacle in the wilderness. In the year 1928, I had a course of studies on the Tabernacle and in 1930 after I was married, I spent six months building a model and studying every detail of the Tabernacle. I can assure you I was thrilled and I never lost my joy and pleasure at studying the Tabernacle."[55]

The study of the Tabernacle would become a lifelong obsession for him. He was convinced that the Tabernacle revealed God's redemption plan for man from Adam till eternity and that to understand it was a crucial step to grasping both the principles and timeline of God's prophetic programme. "God instituted the principles of the Tabernacle and it is one of the greatest and most wonderful studies of the Old Testament,"[56] he frequently taught. Disagreeing with Christians who considered the reading of the Old Testament unnecessary, he preached that it was God's "picture book of principle."[57] "As we study and use the Old Testament we are to look for the principles that God has instituted and laid down; and use those principles as guidelines for our own lives and future. God's principles do not change; therefore, we are quite safe in studying the Old Testament for those principles. We can use the Old Testament stories and illustrations as our guidelines and as the subject for our messages to encourage people to go on to perfection."[58]

And furthermore: "Many people today will not regard the Tabernacle as being important, they say, 'They are only shadows.' That's quite right; they are shadows, but very important shadows, because as 1 Corinthians 10 says, 'These things are written for our examples, for our learning, that we might study what they mean.' And when God does a thing, He does it properly with a very special meaning. In addition, let me remind you that when God took Moses up into the mountain to talk to him, He showed him a pattern of a tabernacle in heaven and told him to copy it. The architect and designer of the Tabernacle is God; therefore, it must be important. I want to study its meaning and importance, and especially its relevance in these days, because it has a meaning for the end times and especially for the manifestation of the sons of God in the end time."[59]

These studies were done while he was with the Plymouth Brethren. Elton, in later years, would at every opportunity credit his love and devotion to the Scriptures to his Brethren heritage. Once, while speaking of this heritage, he specifically mentioned the strong commitment of the Brethren to the Scriptures: "Towards the end of the last century a body of people arose who were very astute Bible students. They are known in England and in some parts of America as the Plymouth Brethren. We are very familiar with them. I was born again, baptized in water among the Plymouth Brethren. Much more important, we were married there too, in the Plymouth Brethren. Now, I know quite a little bit about them. They are an excellent body of people."[60]

Elsewhere he referred to his involvement in Christian service while in Shrewsbury, which was most likely when he was still with the Brethren. "Before I became a minister or perhaps I should say, before I became a missionary, before my wife and I ever made arrangements to come out to Africa, we used to go into the street of our home city; going into the slum and finding those who are drunkards. I have rescued many a man lying in the gutter, drunk, soaked in rain, and rain water as he lies helplessly in the gutter. And we have taken him home, taken him to his family and in some cases we have got him to bed and let people there to take care of him. I have helped many a drunkard home. That was our work and we went from house to house ministering to widows, ministering to the poor, providing all sorts of advice and help; and they came to us for advice."[61]

The Apostolic Church opened its doors in Shrewsbury in 1929. It took over a chapel on Belle Vue Road located by the Nonconformist Cemetery, which, according to the town's directory, had earlier been used in 1922 by the Salvation Army.[62] The Apostolic Church, which grew out of the Welsh Revival of 1904 to 1905, was at the forefront of the Pentecostal movement in Britain from the latter part of the 1910s.[63] Its founder, Daniel Powell Williams, was converted in Penygroes, Wales, under the ministration of Evan Roberts in December 1904[64] and was baptized in the Holy Spirit with the evidence of speaking in tongues in 1909 when he encountered, while on a holiday, a group of Christians who had received the experience.[65] In 1910 he became part of a Christian group in Penygroes, but when the group split in 1911 as a result of arguments about the present-day manifestation of the Pentecostal gifts, Williams emerged as the leader of the Pentecostal group.[66] About this time, he became acquainted with W. O. Hutchinson, the pastor of the Apostolic Faith Church, Bournemouth, England, which was founded in 1907; it was the first Pentecostal church in Britain.[67]

Hutchinson's church "had a strong emphasis on the prophetic predictive word by which a number were called into ministry and sent out by this means. They taught that God would restore the offices of apostle and prophet back to the church."[68] In 1911 Williams affiliated his group with Hutchinson's growing network of churches, and it subsequently became the Apostolic Faith Church in Penygroes.[69] In 1914 at the London Convention of the church, he was ordained as the apostle of the Apostolic Faith Churches in Wales.[70] In 1916, as a result of a major disagreement with Hutchinson, he led most of the assemblies in Wales to break away from the Apostolic Faith Church and founded the Apostolic Church.[71]

From its inception, the major doctrine of the Apostolic Church which distinguished it from other Pentecostal churches was its strict belief in the government of the church by apostles and prophets.[72] It has been noted that "the Apostolic Church followed the teachings of its parent body—Hutchinson's Apostolic Faith Church—in emphasising the place of prophecy as opposed to preaching cast in the prophetic mould. Apostolics laid stress upon the importance of the spoken word in tongues, interpretation and prophecy in accordance with their own reading of Acts 2 and 1 Cor. 12. The importance of the 'Ascension Gifts' was highlighted; thus the scriptural designations of Ephesians 4:11—'apostle,' 'prophet,' 'evangelist,' 'pastor' and 'teacher'—became the titles of recognised offices in the church. This application was not regarded as an innovation as it was believed that it was laid down in the New Testament for all times."[73] Between the years 1917 and 1922, the Penygroes church united with three Pentecostal groups in Glasgow, Hereford, and Bradford, and the church continued to experience remarkable growth.[74]

A missionary council was created in 1922 and from this time "as a result of invitations and Missionary Board initiatives,"[75] the Apostolic Church began planting churches in many overseas countries. In September 1931, D. P. Williams, his brother W. J. Williams, and the vice president of the church, Andrew Turnbull, visited Nigeria at the invitation of the leadership of the Faith Tabernacle Church in Nigeria, and, after an agreement was reached, the first missionaries of the church arrived in Nigeria in 1932 as the first Pentecostal missionaries in the country.[76]

The Eltons joined the Apostolic Church in Shrewsbury, which was within walking distance of their house, most likely in 1931 or early 1932.[77] There is little information about their activities in this local assembly as there are no records from the church and Elton hardly ever gave details about this period. The most significant information we have from Elton is that he became an elder there.[78] The earliest document we have of the Eltons' connection with this assembly is an April 1935 letter from one T. Davies (most likely a staff of the church's literature department in Penygroes) to Elton and his wife: "This is a letter of thanks for favours bestowed. Also a business one—Bro. Elton will find the book ordered enclosed, with invoice. I had promised to write Bro. Ricketts, so it was better to enclose the whole together."[79]

The "Bro. Ricketts" mentioned in the letter was the pastor of the Shrewsbury assembly during the period the Eltons were members. Elton first received prophetic revelation about his call to Nigeria while serving in this church.

I know what it means to be called and ordained by prophecy. I can remember and I have a record in my office of a prophecy which came in our own house in England in November 1932. . . . One evening we had visitors, we had a company of the Lord's servants amongst us. And one of them was a prophet, another one was an apostle and when we knelt down to pray, well after midnight, the Lord began to speak; I have a record of what he said on that day. And five times in that prophecy, the laying on of hands is mentioned.

The Lord specifically told me that He had laid his hands upon me and He said: "My hand is upon you and if I say this many times, I would have you to know when I repeat my word it is for those to take notice of what I declare—upon my servant, my hand is upon him. And I will do many things. I will give him a ministry unto others. The ministry of the Lord." . . .

I know the responsibility that came upon my head when the word of the Lord went out over me in that 1932. And I have been very conscious that the Lord has been with me, safely carrying through his promise of 1932, but I had to constantly look back and remember the word of the Lord to me and His command to me regarding my ministry and my service in Nigeria.[80]

One frequent visitor to Ilesa remembers that Elton permanently kept a copy of this prophecy on a particular spot on his table, and when asked why, he replied that he never wanted to forget what had brought him to Nigeria.[81] Elsewhere, Elton relates another significant experience that happened two years later: "I was called to active service on July the 14th, 1934, in my own bedroom, where the Lord spoke to me and told me he was sending my wife and I—he was sending us to Nigeria. He gave me certain signs and certain evidences which were confirmed; and I waited and told no one except my wife."[82]

At a meeting of the church's Council of Apostles at its general headquarters in Penygroes, Wales, in 1936, Elton was called by prophecy to be a missionary to Nigeria. Speaking of this many years later, he recalled: "Forty apostles met in a certain place. . . . They met and they were considering what to do about the great call of God and the revival in Nigeria. There were four prophets there as well as forty apostles. . . . And the prophets took no part in the council, took no meeting of any kind. They were there in touch with God. And eventually one of them moved forward and began to speak: 'Hear ye my voice, let my will be known unto you . . .'" He then went on prophesying for a while and in the middle of it said, "Send my servant Elton to Nigeria."[83] At the same hour this prophecy was given in Penygroes, a similar prophecy was given by a member of the church in Nigeria. According to Elton: "I was called by two prophets separated by three thousand miles at the same hour to be an apostle. . . . In England a council was meeting and a prophet was used by God, 'Separate and ordain my servant Elton as an apostle.' In Lagos, Nigeria, in a council meeting there a prophet said 'I want you to know my servant Elton is an apostle among you,' an hour after it was said in England."[84] "Then I got a telegram to say, please telephone and I knew what that meant. I got on the telephone and the president of the church said 'come down' . . . and I said, 'I am coming, sir.' "[85]

He travelled to Wales to meet the council and when he got there he was told, "Brother Elton, you are called over to Nigeria." The always confident, almost cocky, young Elton straightaway replied, "That's not new, I know that."[86] He was then given his brief: He was required to spend two years to see what it was like and then return to say goodbye to his wife and child. This instruction meant he was to proceed to Nigeria alone, without his family. (The missionary council took this decision on health grounds—they were not sure if three-year-old Ruth could survive the harsh tropical climate.) Elton's reaction to this decision reveals the independent streak he always possessed: "That's not God. . . . You are wrong; [but] I will go,"[87] he told the council. One can imagine how shocked the council would have been at the young man's audacity. Elton never took instructions without scrutiny, and this kind of episode would repeat itself time and again over the coming years. Hannah Elton was totally uncomfortable with the decision of the council to have Elton leave her and Ruth behind. Elton recalled that his wife "did not agree, and that's putting it mildly; she did not agree and the Lord spoke to her and told her, 'Write the vision, make it plain, it is yet for an appointed time, though it tarries wait for it.' "[88]

From Ruth we learn of how her parents had romanticized about missionary work even before they were married.[89] After Elton's conversion he had read a book on the life of Mary Slessor, the famous Scottish missionary who laboured in Calabar for twenty-eight years until her death. This story left a deep impression on him. During their honeymoon, he read the story of C. T. Studd, the missionary to China, while Hannah devoured that of Slessor. Elton had always sensed a call in his spirit to Africa and especially Nigeria, and when he shared this with his wife, she recalled a revelation she had received of being a missionary to Africa. (When Ruth was born in 1934, she was given a doll which her mother named "Calabar," almost certainly after the title of the Mary Slessor biography she read during her honeymoon.[90]) So strong was the sense of the call that Hannah had a severe bout of depression when she was not allowed to travel with her husband. "God's will was that I should be with him; I knew that,"[91] she would say many years later. She prayed continually about this, reminding God that she also had the call, and God repeatedly confirmed this until a door was opened about four months after her husband left.

Elton was privileged to closely interact with the first generation of British Pentecostals, and this interaction played a major formative role in his early Pentecostal experience. His many emotive references to first-hand encounters with leaders whose ministries witnessed mighty demonstrations of the power of God reveal something of the impact these experiences had on him. In one reference to the strong prophetic atmosphere in which he was nurtured, he said, "I have been in meetings where apostles and prophets have been there and the Lord had spoken through prophets to call men into ministry, to go to new places. And they had no idea who He was talking about. And the minister-in-charge, the apostle-in-charge has had to stand up and say, 'Is there anybody by the name . . . ?' And the man concerned would have to stand up and say, 'That's me.' They didn't know who he was; they'd never met him before. I knew someone who was chosen under the same circumstance. He was my special friend and he came to Nigeria before I did. He's dead now. But you see we knew what that ministry was and when I came to Nigeria, I knew what I was going to face. We didn't come in order to lay empty hands on empty heads."[92]

Elsewhere he noted, "Way back in the 1930s I knew of the ministry of apostles and saw men who were undoubtedly apostles, they were not big political people . . . they were not big business people, they were spiritual leaders who exercised spiritual government. I met those people, I saw them. I saw and listened to them and heard how God spoke to them. For God not only spoke in prophecy to His body, [His] church, in edification, exhortation and comfort as it is explained in 1 Corinthians 14, but [we] also exercised government."[93]

Throughout the course of his missionary career in Nigeria, he would refer again and again to the powerful prophetic encounters he had during the 1930s: "I can tell you that those prophecies and those laying on of hands have imparted to me a very grave responsibility and a sense that I knew I was in the will of God and that I had to stir it up and not neglect the gift. I think I can say that those experiences of the 1930s have kept me steady and have kept me in the way of God right to the very present time."[94]

On February 17, 1937, Elton recorded in his diary: "Farewell Shrewsbury, 7:30 p.m." and noted that he had been presented a gift of £52.30.[95] This was most likely the day he was sent forth by the church, because he didn't leave Shrewsbury until three days later. On Saturday, February 20, a very emotional Elton left Shrewsbury for Bradford; he wrote in his diary: "Last sight of home for 2 years!! Very severe struggle at parting. Last saw Ciss & Ruth & Grace warming on Doorstep & later through window in rain. Very downhearted."[96] On the twenty-first he recorded, "A good day in Bradford. Feeling better but would like to be at home!" On the twenty-third: "Shopping in Bradford." Later in the evening of the 23rd, at 7:30 p.m., Elton was ordained into the ministry of the Apostolic Church.[97]

He sailed for Liverpool at 4:00 p.m. on February 24 and from there travelled to Nigeria on an Elder Dempster ship. (Elder Dempster Lines was the main shipping line serving West Africa during this period; it "operated three liners on a scheduled service to Ghana and Nigeria."[98]) His diary entries from February 24, when he left Liverpool, to March 6, when he first stepped down in Africa, help us feel the pulse of this first-time missionary, and the fascination with which he experienced each day:

February 26: Still sea sick. Spent one hour on deck. Felt really ill. . . . Jmc [short for James McKeown, his fellow Apostolic Church missionary to the Gold Coast, who was also on his first tour] is [a] godly man. Great help. *February 27*: Still, ship rolls badly. A very bad stretch of rough weather. Nearly half [of the] passengers ill. All the ladies [ill]. Spent nearly three hours out of cabin. But glad to get back. Had all meals in cabin. Only oranges and bread and milk. *February 28*: Up to breakfast. Felt better. . . . Sea calmer. Weather improving. . . . Letter to home.

March 1: Dropped anchor Madeira, 6 p.m. Felt very much better. Pretty place. Portuguese selling chairs, etc. Sailed 12 noon. Letter home. *March 2*: Up 6 a.m. Dropped anchor 7 a.m. . . . Went ashore. Spanish. Franco. Indigenes. No sign [of] gospel work. Very interesting place. 3 hours ashore. Terrible beggars. Sailed 12 noon. Much warmer. (133 km. to Freetown.) *March 3*: At sea all day. Beautiful. Thoroughly enjoyed warmth. Sunburnt. Red. Had several interesting talks with passengers. Registered salvations. 'Our God how wonderful thou art.' *March 4*: Changed to grey Humids. Warm. At sea all day. Wrote Ciss. *March 5*: Warmer. Sunburnt. Read . . . Genesis. *March 6*: Very warm. Docked Freetown. Went ashore. Land. Walked round Freetown. Africa at last. More at home than Las Palmas. Sailed 4 p.m. Sing-song among pass[engers]: Sat. night: very enjoyable.[99]

Elton greatly admired the spiritual consecration of "Jmc," with whom he bonded within their short period together. McKeown seems to have provided fresh inspiration for Elton as he looked forward to his own assignment. On the day McKeown got off the ship, Elton wrote in his diary: "Accra. Jmc bravely goes forward in sent boat. Very sorry to lose him. His task is big but he tackles it in confidence. A godly, brave & yet simple man. Message in reading today: Deut.—'Underneath are the everlasting arms.' Amen. We have proved it."[100] Even though they were pioneering in different countries, it is remarkable how the careers of Elton and McKeown would take a very similar turn in later years.

Elton's ship docked in Lagos on March 11, making him the seventh[101] missionary of the Apostolic Church in Nigeria. He was welcomed by George Perfect (one of the pioneer missionaries) and J. A. Babatope (the church's leading Nigerian minister in the Ilesa Area) in Lagos. He arrived in Ilesa on March 15, after a twelve-hour trip by rail from Lagos to Osogbo and then by lorry from Osogbo to Ilesa.

He immediately got to work once he arrived at his base. After he was given a "grand reception" on the sixteenth, he embarked on a school inspection the next day. He visited the *Owa* (king of Ilesa) on the eighteenth and thereafter put his observations to paper: "Visited Owa. . . . Dirty palace. Ornamented like Egyptian old man." Some days later he was "off to Efon." His activities on most days involved studying, preaching, leading a prayer meeting or Bible study, meeting with the church's leaders or attending choir practice. He reported at the mission's school at 9:00 a.m. on most days.

He had only been a few days in Ilesa when he began to seriously long to hear from home. He wrote on the nineteenth, after a visit to the post office, "No letter yet from home!!" But he was able to write the next day: "Letter from Ciss. Posted 3/3/37." A sampling of his diary entries during this period reveals Elton spending hours writing home and also desperately looking forward to letters from Ciss and also occasional letters from friends and also his pastor, W. Ricketts: "No letter. Letter to Ciss"; "No letter. . . . One month since I left England. Possible another 11 before I see Ciss and Ruth"; "Letters arrive 7 p.m. Letter written 16/3/37. Ciss' cat missing"; "Writing letters. . . . Letters to W.R., Mrs Davies., H. Cousen"; "Letter from Ciss"; "Writing letters. A.M. letter to Ciss"; "No letter from Ciss"; "Great news. A parcel from Ciss. Cake. Choc[olate]. . . . What a thrill. [A great day]"; "Writing letters etc. all day. Wrote Ciss 10 pages. . . . Thoughts mostly on home"; "Long 16 page letter to Ciss"; "Writing letter all day. 12 pages to Ciss"; "Finished letter to Ciss. 30 pages. . . . 88 pages of writing in 4 days. 42 to Ciss. Great expectation in replies."

Once, after picking up letters from Ciss and another friend from the post office, he described the mails as "streams in desert." On some other days, however, the entries reveal a melancholy, almost depressed Elton, who could not be consoled with mere letters: "Dark days. Ciss and Ruth will surely come," he wrote on April 8. About three weeks later: "Letter from W. R. [his pastor] & Grace [Smith]. The cry of any little girl [Ruth], 'I haven't got a daddy'!! Felt very bad."

Elton made much progress in his first few weeks at his station. "I am glad that I have followed the pillar [reference to the pillar that followed Israel] to Nigeria" he wrote on April 8. And then two days later: "Resting today. Had a good read. Some studying. Plenty of visitors. I feel I am winning the heart of the people." But at other times he felt overwhelmed and had to cast himself afresh upon God's grace. He wrote on April 3: "Pastor Perfect went to Ibadan. Left now to face tremendous work. Feel very incapable. God will have to be my all." Another day he wrote, "Feeling the absolute incapability of humanity doing God's work. J.C. [Jesus Christ] is all."

After some months in the country, Elton sent a letter to the missionary headquarters in Bradford, informing them that some white Methodist missionaries had their children with them and that they did not have any health problems. The committee which had initially disapproved, on health grounds, of Elton's wish to take his family with him, now reluctantly decided to allow them to go to Nigeria, stating in its minutes of May 24, 1937, that "with regard to the going out of Mrs Elton and Ruth and after giving careful consideration to Pastor S. G. Elton's two letters of 19th April and 10th May where he states that he would take the complete responsibility of this move and quotes several instances of young children being out there, we agree to the sending out of Mrs Elton and Ruth"[102]

Elton recorded in his diary on May 7, "Letter from Ciss—has decided definitely to bring Ruth. I am glad. She is God's gift to both of us." After many weeks of preparation, Elton wrote on July 12: "Ciss should be in Bradford"; and on the thirteenth, "Ciss' last day in G.B. [Great Britain]." On the fourteenth: "ACCRA [the name of the ship] SAILS. Liverpool. With Ciss & Ruth. My thoughts are full. Hurry up Accra." On the fifteenth: "Have read all 22 letters of Ciss. I would like to express my thought but I feel too full." Ciss and Ruth arrived on July 29: "Accra docked 11 a.m. Ciss & Ruth both well. Ruth knew her daddy. All pleased to be together again!"

On the front page of an illustrated Bible for children which the Sunday school department of the church presented to Ruth on her departure were the words:

Presented to Ruth Elton
From
The Superintendent & Teachers of the Shrewsbury Apostolic Sunday School
"Jesus took a little child"
From
"Shrewsbury to Africa"[103]

TWO

THE "WRETCHED TABERNACLES"

Elton arrived in Nigeria on the eve of a crisis. This crisis was the result of a breakdown in a relationship that had begun with great promise seven years earlier, between the mission he came to represent and its Nigerian partner, and Elton would find himself right in the storm's eye.

In September 1931, the leaders of the Apostolic Church in the United Kingdom visited Nigeria at the request of the leaders of the Faith Tabernacle churches scattered around the country. The roots of the Faith Tabernacle movement can be traced to the quest by a small group of Anglican Christians in Ijebu Ode to practise Christianity in a way that they believed was more in line with the Scriptures than what obtained in the Anglican community of which they were a part.

In July 1918, "Daddy" Ali, the elderly sexton of the St. Saviours Anglican Church, Ijebu Ode, had a dream in which he saw the St. Saviour's congregation divided into two—one part was in darkness and the other in light; the section in darkness was the larger of the two groups.[1] He was told in the dream that the first group was in darkness because they were not prayerful.[2] Ali believed this was a timely message for the congregation and immediately went to discuss it with the minister of the church, Rev. S. J. Gansallo. Gansallo, without much thought, dismissed this as the product of too much sleep. Ali was hurt that Gansallo made nonsense of the dream and decided to keep it to himself. But not long after this, he had the same dream. Now sure that this had to be a divine message, he bypassed

Gansallo and discussed with other key leaders in the church—J. B. Sadare (the churchwarden), E. O. Onabanjo, D. C. Oduga and E. O. Olukoya.[3] The response from these men was encouraging, and a decision was taken to start a prayer band to intercede for the church.

Once the group started meeting, other members of the church joined, and soon the group could boast nineteen members. For a while the group's meetings were held in the church hall after the Sunday service, but because of an increase in prayer requests, it was shifted to Monday nights. With time, J. B. Sadare (later J. B. Esinsinade) emerged as the leader of the group.[4]

During the influenza epidemic that ravaged the country from 1918 to mid-1919 (an offshoot of the worldwide pandemic that began in the closing months of World War I, lasting from March 1918 to June 1920) members of the prayer group regularly gathered in front of the church building on Sundays to worship and pray.[5] The epidemic resulted in about 500,000 deaths,[6] and about fifty to eighty per cent of the population was infected.[7] The disease was introduced into Nigeria by "passengers and crews who arrived via ship from overseas"[8] during this period. In an attempt to contain the spread of the virus in Nigeria, the government ordered the closure of all public buildings: schools, places of religious worship, and government offices. Gansallo locked up the church building in compliance with the government's order and went to his village. Many of the church's members interpreted Gansallo's action as desertion. "In contrast," the Rev. S. A. Phillips, a school headmaster, "led a procession of church members about the town praying for deliverance from the epidemic. The prayer group, following Phillips' rather than Gansallo's example, intensified their efforts during the epidemic."[9]

While this was happening in Ijebu Ode, there appeared on the already excited spiritual scene a prophetic young lady named Sophia Odunlami.[10] She was a member of the Anglican Church and a primary school teacher in Isoyin, a village near Ijebu Ode. Her actions and physical bearing painted the perfect apocalyptic picture. She was definitely the strangest spiritual figure that Ijebu Ode had witnessed up until that time.

Odunlami, who was then only nineteen years old, said she had seen a vision where she was told to instruct everybody in the Ijebu Ode area who had been infected by the influenza virus to store the water from the rain that would fall on a particular day.[11] Anybody who took a bath with the water would be healed of the disease. She also heard a voice that told her: "I shall send peace on this house and to the whole world. The World War is ended."[12] Odunlami said she had been instructed by God to warn Christians to desist from using medicines of any kind, eating kola nut, taking alcoholic drinks or palm wine, using charms, excessively adorning the body, and violating the Sabbath.[13]

She travelled throughout Ijebu land and also reached Ibadan preaching this message, and large crowds gathered to hear her wherever she went. Zechariah 14 was the most prominent theme in her sermons—the perfect match for her apocalyptic image.[14] It was not long, however, before she began experiencing persecution from her immediate community as a result of her strange outlook, and it became difficult for her to continue for long as a solo prophetess. Historian Harold Turner writes of Odunlami's experience: "She began to have experiences of inspiration by the Holy Spirit, as she claimed, although such an unusual experience in the Anglican community was interpreted by some as devil-possession, and by her father as madness."[15]

Odunlami told her pastor, Rev. I. B. Ogunmefun, about the vision of the rainfall. According to Robert Mitchell, a historian of the Faith Tabernacle movement, "Word of her revelation subsequently travelled to the prayer band in Ijebu Ode, which sent for her. Addressing the whole congregation after an evening service, she told them that rain would soon fall and that the water from it should be used with faith for healing. Her message made a profound impression upon the anxious assemblage. Many used the water from the subsequent rain and testified of its effectiveness. No one was more impressed than the prayer band members who regarded her vision as a confirmation of the earlier vision of 'Daddy' Ali. She was invited to join the group."[16]

In 1917, David Ogunleye Odubanjo, a clerk with the colonial government in Lagos, came across a booklet, *The Seven Principles of Prevailing Prayer*, at a friend's house.[17] Odubanjo had just been transferred to Warri and was there to say goodbye. He was fascinated by the title: the idea that anyone could know how to consistently have their prayers answered was totally strange to him.[18] Determined to probe further, he borrowed the booklet and took it with him to Warri. Once he settled at his new station, he sent a letter to the publisher—Ambrose Clark, pastor of Faith Tabernacle Church, Philadelphia—requesting more of their publications. Clark responded with a generous number of tracts on various topics on the Christian life.[19]

After some time studying and applying the teachings in the publications, Odubanjo experienced a spiritual transformation. He was particularly moved by 2 Peter 1:7–8—"and in your godliness, brotherly kindness, and in your brotherly kindness, love. For if these qualities are yours and are increasing, they render you neither useless nor unfruitful in the true knowledge of our Lord Jesus Christ"—and felt his heart overwhelmed by love. He then made a pledge to God that if He blessed him with sixty pounds, he would resign from his government job and take the message of healing and prayer as the solution to all problems—the major themes in the publications from Ambrose Clark—to his friends and family in Ijebu Ode.[20] Through a succession of events he was soon flush with cash, having up to 120 pounds.[21] But keeping his pledge proved more difficult than he anticipated; the security of his government job was too tempting to let go.

He decided to test the waters by taking a leave of absence in 1919, so he could travel to Ijebu Ode for evangelistic work. If his first attempts at preaching failed, then he would return to his job; otherwise, he would resign and devote his life to preaching the gospel. The immediate response to his ministry in Ijebu Ode was encouraging, so he returned to Warri, resigned, packed his belongings, and relocated to Ijebu Ode. Sometime after he arrived there, he reconnected with an earlier acquaintance, D. O. Segun, and decided to preach the gospel to him. But Segun was by now a committed Christian and also a member of Esinsinade's prayer group; and he invited Odubanjo to attend one of the group's meetings.

From the first day Odubanjo attended the prayer group's meeting, he knew he had found the comradeship he had long desired. Likewise, after he gave his testimony, the group immediately identified him as a potential leader. He is said to have spoken about divine healing in a way that completely mesmerized his audience.[22] This was definitely a result of Odubanjo's voracious reading of literature from Faith Tabernacle Church in Philadelphia on healing and on other aspects of Christian growth. After he finished speaking, the members were unanimous about the fact that Odubanjo was ahead of them in spiritual understanding, and almost immediately they decided to make him leader of the group. J. B. Esinsinade was also in complete agreement.[23] Taking such an important decision so quickly may now be considered highly improbable—Mitchell believes this was likely "an oversimplification of what actually happened"[24]—but it was very possible within the very volatile spirituality that the group was known for. Depending very much on the leading of the

Holy Spirit, the group sometimes took crucial decisions without much deliberation, once they were sure they were divinely inspired.

The group was first named "Precious Stone Society," and later renamed "Diamond Society" in July 1920,[25] to formalize its existence and give it greater recognition within the church.

Ambrose Clark continued to send large quantities of Faith Tabernacle publications to Odubanjo, which he then circulated to members of the group. Soon, the members were writing to Ambrose Clark themselves, asking questions about the teachings they did not understand. *The Sword of the Spirit* particularly began to enjoy a very wide readership. One of the early readers describes the influence of this magazine: "*Sword of the Spirit*, the official organ published by the Faith Tabernacle Congregation in U.S.A. was regularly sent to us. Several copies of this magazine and other tracts published by them containing deeper spiritual truths of the Bible were freely sent to us, which were also freely distributed to members within our fold and outsiders. In fact, we were not using the Bible as [much] as we were using the 'Sword of the Spirit.' "[26]

In 1921, Odubanjo took up a new appointment with the government in Lagos due to a major financial misfortune; Esinsinade therefore resumed the leadership of the group in Ijebu Ode. During his first year in Lagos, Odubanjo gathered a sizeable number of people to start a second branch of the society. When the Lagos branch celebrated its first year anniversary, Odubanjo sent the group's photograph to Clark. In his excitement Clark published it on the front page of the following issue of *The Sword of the Spirit*. The photograph was labelled "The Diamond Society of Faith Tabernacle, Lagos, Nigeria."[27] Soon after this, particularly through the spread of this issue of the magazine in Nigeria, the Diamond Society group became more widely known as Faith Tabernacle group.

Mitchell explains how the society evolved into a distinct spiritual group separate from the Anglicanism which they were a part of and how this evolution eventually led to a parting of ways with the church: "Since the Society required its new members to abstain from the use of both traditional and modern medicine, it differentiated itself from the Anglican congregation of which it was still a part. There was no conscious antagonism toward fellow Christians or the pastor, but as they immersed themselves more and more deeply in their type of Christianity, they developed a form that was more rigid and demanding than the Anglican persuasion and which eventually led to a clash with the church authorities."[28] He continues: "About half their rules covered behaviour and attitudes which would be considered as prohibited for Christians in any part of the world: adultery, envy, polygyny, bribery, hatred, and so forth. Eight more involved traditional practices, some of which were already proscribed by the mission churches—such as sacrifices and going to *babalawos* for divination. Others involve prohibitions peculiar to the Diamond Society, such as the rule against participating in so-called 'contributions societies.' Twelve of the rules were puritanical, defining as immoral dancing and drumming, debt, drinking, cigarettes, cards, gambling, 'interest in money,' not keeping the Sabbath, 'too much ornament,' and chewing kola nuts. Finally there were rules against the use of medicine and 'getting into company with non-Christians.' "[29]

A major turning point in the relationship of the society with the Anglican Church came in 1922 when several children who were baptized at St. Saviour's Church died. From studying *Sword of the Spirit* and the Scriptures, the members had earlier come to the conclusion that baptism was meant only for those old enough to publicly confess Jesus Christ as their Saviour. After praying and seeking counsel from Clark, they concluded that the recurring deaths during child baptism was a warning from God to the church to desist from the "unbiblical practice" of infant baptism.[30] Gansallo was incensed when they communicated this to him and refused to further entertain what he believed was plain fanaticism. When the group successfully convinced parents to boycott the baptizing of their children, Gansallo appealed to the bishop of Lagos, Melville Jones, for help. Jones visited Ijebu Ode and held a meeting with the leaders of the society. The main points of discussion were their stand on infant baptism and divine healing. He wanted them to take a more liberal stand on the issues, but they rejected this appeal as being against the will of God. He left without being able to convince them.[31]

Jones later sent Bishop Isaac Oluwole, his assistant, to meet with the leaders and reiterate Jones's position. When they refused to shift ground, he wielded the big stick; he instructed all the members of the society who were in the employ of the church to leave the group or risk losing their jobs. Some, afraid, left the group; the others were sacked.[32] The members of the society withdrew their children from the CMS schools in protest of this high-handedness, and opened a school where the children were tutored by some of those who had been relieved of their jobs. This marked the transition of the group from a society within the Anglican Church to an independent church. This was formalized on January 22, 1922, of which date the Society recorded: "It is a day noted for the separation of the Diamond Society from the C.M.S Church, brought about by the persecution from the said C.M.S members, St. Saviour's Church, Ijebu-Ode."[33] The Nigerian group officially affiliated themselves with the Faith Tabernacle Church, USA, in 1923 and from then became Faith Tabernacle Church, Nigeria.[34]

The Faith Tabernacle Church (FTC) in Lagos continued to grow, and new branches were also opening in several parts of the country. Many members were in the employ of the government as clerks, railway workers, post and telegraph workers, and school teachers, and when they were transferred from their station to other parts of the country, they started branches of the church to cater to their spiritual needs. In this way, branches of the church were opened around the country. Usually they were small churches with a very strict holiness doctrine. Most members lived very austere lives, denying themselves of most conveniences. They were generally looked upon with pity by other churches and members of the community in general, who wondered why they had chosen such a wretched life. Beginning in Ijebu Ode and gradually around the country, they came to be known as *"Ojiya Tabanako,"* a Yoruba phrase which, literally translated, means "Wretched Tabernacles."[35] It became commonplace in Ijebu Ode to mock an antagonist by saying he or she was wretched like a "Tabernacle."[36] Odubanjo's uncle, Alli-Ige Oduwole, a wealthy businessman in Ijebu Ode, often derided him for choosing to remain poor when he could easily be very rich if he decided to join him in his business. Whenever Odubanjo visited from Lagos, his uncle would make jest of his dressing, alleging that he had perfected the art of masking his hunger by "using his belt to hold his waist."[37] He also taunted Odubanjo by saying that his white collar was in fact a "neck holder," designed to prevent him from "talking too much" and so making sure he "got hungry less frequently, since he had nothing to eat most of the time."[38]

Another major twist in the history of the movement occurred in 1925, when Clark was accused of adultery by the leadership of the church in Philadelphia. He was initially suspended from the pastorate; when he tried to regain control of the leadership after only a short period, he was firmly resisted, resulting in him leaving to start a new church, called First Century Gospel Church.[39] He tried hard to win back the loyalty of former subordinates, including the Nigerian branch of the Faith Tabernacle, but failed. Though some members of the Nigerian church, in solidarity with him, left to start a Nigerian congregation of the First Century Gospel Church, the effort soon petered out.[40] The leaders of the FTC in Nigeria appealed several times to the leaders of the FTC in America and Pastor Clark to reconcile, but all the efforts were unfruitful. In 1928, the American FTC leadership responded with a letter which the Nigerian leaders considered uncharitable and dismissive of their opinion.[41] Miffed by this response, the Nigerian leadership sent a nineteen-page reply, reemphasizing their position on the issue.[42] This fiasco ended the decade-long relationship between the Faith Tabernacle movement in Nigeria and the Faith Tabernacle Church in Philadelphia.

Odubanjo immediately began eagerly seeking a new foreign partnership for the church because of the many challenges the FTC in Nigeria was experiencing as a small, independent church in a colonial dispensation. They needed foreign affiliation to bolster their image and push back the frequent bullying they experienced from the government and the mission churches. In the past, they had requested missionaries to be sent to them by the FTC in America, but Pastor Clark had replied saying, "We are trying our very best to send a suitable man to see you; but it seems a difficult problem to solve, as our men here are very active, engaged and absolutely needed; but we must try to get you help and to find a suitable man soon. Kindly pray to this end."[43] Nobody was ever sent. Odubanjo was soon in touch with a certain Faith and Truth Temple Church which was headquartered in Toronto, Canada. This led to a brief relationship; they sent a missionary team to Nigeria in 1929, but nothing tangible resulted.[44]

• • •

BY 1930 THE TOTAL MEMBERSHIP of the FT movement in all the branches across the nation was just about one thousand, "gathered in small pietistic congregations."[45] One of its largest congregations, the Ilesa church, had only 120 members in 1930. The major leaders of the Faith Tabernacle movement in 1930 were David Odubanjo, in Lagos; J. B. Esinsinade, in Ijebu Ode; Isaac Akinyele, in Ibadan; J. A. Babatope, in Ilesa; Samuel Adegboyega, in Ebute Metta; S. A. Mensah, in Kaduna; and E. G. Macaulay, in Zaria.

When, in July 1930, a revival broke out in Ilesa through the ministry of

Joseph Ayo Babalola, a Faith Tabernacle member, the leaders believed their persevering stand on divine healing for over a decade had been divinely vindicated. Samuel Adegboyega, one of the FT leaders and a later historian of the church, said that by 1930 the church had been praying fervently, "accompanied with fastings [*sic*] for the period of seven years"[46] in anticipation of a mighty revival. As Harold Turner perceptively observes, "By 1928 the Nigerian Faith Tabernacle Church was beginning to query the Philadelphian restriction of the manifestations of the Spirit, and was earnestly seeking revival and fuller power. . . . The revival they sought was to come through the most famous and charismatic prophet figure in the aladura movement, Joseph Babalola."[47] The healing revival brought a major refreshing and reinvigoration to the Faith Tabernacle churches—membership swelled and new churches were opened. Thousands visited Ilesa week after week, witnessing hundreds of miracles of healing. It was the most powerful revival the nation had witnessed up to that time. The revival, which began at the Faith Tabernacle Church, Oke Oye, Ilesa, during a national congress of the leaders of the church, was initially sparked by the resuscitation of a dead boy after Babalola offered prayers.[48]

The most enduring image of Babalola, who was still a young adult of twenty-six years at the time, is that of a generally affable prophetic figure, "clothed in shorts and cotton shirt, with Bible and bell in hand."[49] Historian John Peel, after giving only a slight variant—"clad in white shorts and shirt, with Bible and hand bell"—rounds up that Babalola "by all accounts, was modest and cheerful."[50]

Joseph Babalola was born on April 25, 1904, at Odo Owa, near Ilofa.[51] His parents were members of the Anglican Church. After some years of formal education—he left school after completing Standard 4 around 1924—and after serving as an apprentice on a number of jobs, he got an appointment in 1928 as a steamroller driver with the Public Works Department (PWD) at Osogbo. That year, he had his first encounter with the supernatural while working on the construction of the new Igbara Oke Road. He heard an audible voice which instructed him to leave his job and go on a six-day fast. He afterwards had a series of supernatural experiences which included angelic visitations. More periods of fasting followed and eventually, when he began his ministry in Ilofa, his hometown, miracles, signs, and wonders accompanied his message.

In 1929, Babalola was introduced to the leaders of the Faith Tabernacle

Church in Ibadan by a friend who "came from the same Ilofa district and who was now a member of Akinyele's Faith Tabernacle Church."[52] After listening to his story, they concluded he had received a genuine call from God and decided he needed to share his testimony with the top leadership of the church in Lagos. In November 1929 he was introduced to the Faith Tabernacle leaders in Lagos, where he gave the testimony of his call. "The whole congregation was held in a six-hour suspense as Babalola . . . described the events that led to his call and early ministry."[53]

Babalola also indicated his intention to join the church. His testimony was received with great joy, and the leadership requested that he be baptized. After Babalola sought God's counsel about this step, he accepted and was baptized by J. B. Esinsinade.[54] Before his departure, "a missionary offering consisting of new clothing and money was contributed towards the furtherance of his ministry."[55] Odubanjo visited Babalola in Ilofa shortly after this to witness first-hand his evangelistic outreaches; he recorded in his diary in 1929: "Since the days of the Apostles, I have not met with any man of his type who has direct dealings and intercourse with the Holy Spirit."[56]

In July 1930, Babalola was invited by Odubanjo to a congress of the leaders of the church in Ilesa, on July 9 and 10, 1930. It was here that the now famous "1930 Revival" was ignited. During one of the sessions, a dead boy was carried past the venue of the congress. When Babalola heard the commotion from the burial procession, he excused himself from the meeting and requested that the corpse be brought to him. "After about ten minutes of prayers, the dead boy came back to life. As a result of this spectacular miracle, sick people rushed to Babalola for prayers for healing of different ailments. About two hundred people came for healing during the first week. Many came back to testify of their recovery; these were responsible for spreading the news of the healing miracles. By the third week of the revival, about a hundred lepers, sixty blind people and fifty lame and crippled persons had been healed, along with several others healed of diverse sicknesses and diseases. The revival meetings which had been conducted beside a house up until this time had to be moved to a more spacious place. The new venue was an open space near a hill called Oke Oye on the outskirts of Ilesa."[57]

In the following weeks, Ilesa experienced an unprecedented number of visitors, who trooped into the town day and night to experience the spiritual revival and miracles. The British assistant district officer in charge of Ilesa, in a letter to his superior in Ile-Ife, wrote of the events which he witnessed: "Recently I have been spending much time in road work on the Ijebu-Ijesa road and I have been very struck by the extraordinary numbers of people, mostly women, who are pouring into Ilesa and returning laden with bottles of holy water. There are very many aged cripples among them. . . . It is the same on the other roads, and the market is chock-a-block with lorries which have brought passengers in from a distance."[58]

H. L. Ward-Price, the Resident of Oyo Province from 1931 to 1936, a very keen observer of the peoples and cultures of Yorubaland, wrote in his memoirs what he personally witnessed of the revival: "The main item in his [Babalola] programme was that if anyone would bring water to his meetings he would bless it, after which it would cure almost any sort of sickness. Crowds swarmed to him from near and far. The price of empty beer bottles in which to carry water to be blessed rose from a half penny till they cost a strong man's daily wage; bottle-shops sprang up by the score; the rail-way trains were full of pilgrims, and the old-established missions were temporarily denuded of their adherents. With tears running down their cheeks, disciples of Joseph told me they had been cured of blindness, elephantiasis, leprosy, and other ailments. A group of people assured me that he had raised a child from the dead in their presence. He was not encouraged by the Administrative Officers; but any Negro who does anything out of the ordinary never is."[59]

One of the closest observers of the revival, Henry Dallimore, the Anglican archdeacon in charge of Ekiti District, wrote in a January 1931 article in the CMS' *Western Equatorial Africa Church Magazine*:

Great interest was aroused some nine months ago by the appearance of a man of striking personality and of real sincerity. . . . Joseph Babalola, a C.M.S. member, gave out that he had had a vision and had heard God call him to pray and preach, there was nothing new in his announcement; but it was soon evident that he had both personality and power. He was instrumental in carrying conviction to the hearts of thousands, causing them to cast away their idols, and to express a desire to learn of God in Christ. People flocked to him from all quarters, and the crowds became ever denser as rumours of remarkable miracles worked by him spread about the country. It was said that he even raised the dead. . . . I was much impressed with Joseph Babalola, by his humility, his simplicity, and his belief in his mission: and also by the awe and reverence in which he was held by the vast crowds. The scenes along the roads leading to the town where he was then working, gave one a vivid picture of what must have happened along the roads of Palestine in the days of our Lord. The blind, the lame, the sick, the leper, all were there, and occasionally there was the dead body being borne to him. . . . At the meeting place were crowds hanging on his words, even seeking to touch his garment.[60]

News of the revival spread around the country. The *Nigerian Daily Times* of August 28, 1930, recorded: "A 'Prophet' is said to have put up an appearance at Ilesha, whose power of healing by prayer has been testified by many who have been healed. Two well-known figures in Ibadan who have nearly lost their sights have completely recovered; pilgrims mostly consisting of lames, blinds, deafs and all kinds of invalid [*sic*] are crossing Ilesha everyday by motors to receive this wonderful healing."[61] Babalola's fame spread round the country and also beyond its shores. One missionary on board a ship to Nigeria from England wrote of how he was approached by a "young lady-missionary" with whom he had become acquainted during the trip. She "presented him, during the course of a conversation, with a type-written letter, and asked him to read it." He found, to his amazement, that it "contained an account of the remarkable activities of a certain prophet Babalola and a pastor by the name of Babatope. Wonderful miracles were attributed to them."[62]

A letter was published in the Jersey (UK) *Morning Post* in 1931, written by a CMS missionary working in the Igbira district:

> My dear Jersey Friends,—I am so sorry to have left you for so long without a letter, but the demands made by the work on one's time and strength have been so insistent there has been no time for letter-writing.
>
> During the last three months most remarkable things have been happening in this district. We have had miracles, a mass movement, and a martyrdom. It has been like living in the time of the Acts of the Apostles . . .
>
> The cause of these amazing events is a young Yoruba prophet [Joseph Babalola] whom the Lord "took" when driving a steam-roller. God's call came to him in the midst of his work. He gave up his lucrative job and started preaching. Literally thousands of people flocked to hear him, and hundreds have confessed their sins of witchcraft. Thousands have publicly burned their idols; even Mohammedans have been converted and given up their rosaries. All these people are now clamouring for Christian instruction.

In the Bassa country, on the other side of the Niger, the preaching of this young prophet has achieved more in three weeks than the C.M.S. in seventy years. The entire heathen population have given up the idols and are pouring into the church! Our little handful of CMS agents are overwhelmed by the situation. In each village there are from 100 to 300 people all clamouring for instruction in the Christian religion. The head chief of this district, who is a Mohammedan, offered to build Miss Ritsert and myself a house and school free of all cost to the C.M.S. if only we would go and settle among them. The attendance at the Sunday morning service at Kpata rose from 70 to 500, the next Sunday to 800, and the following to 1,000; yet, as I write, this town has no teacher! It would only take 12 pounds a year to place one there. Oh, you people at home who live in the midst of such spiritual luxuries, have you no crumbs to spare for these starving souls out here?[63]

In the following weeks and months, other healing evangelists were raised within the movement. Some of them were Daniel Orekoya, Peter Olatunji, Emmanuel Omotunde and David Babajide. Babalola and the other healing evangelists focused on stirring the faith of the people to believe in the miraculous. Unlike the Faith Tabernacle leaders, these evangelists did not teach the biblical principles of healing in any systematic way; they rather relied on the operations of the healing gift of the Holy Spirit, which many of them were strongly endowed with. Crowds came to the revival meetings expecting a stirring message by Babalola or some other evangelist, perhaps Olatunji or Orekoya, followed by singing and prayers and then specific instructions to the sick and oppressed as a means of receiving a cure for their ailments. By far the most prominent of these instructions was the application of water which Babalola had prayed over to the part of the body which was diseased.

The activities of these evangelists and the methods which they employed generated a lot of controversy, first with many of the established churches and then with the colonial government. On the one hand, many church leaders were first surprised and then became uncomfortable, and even angry, by the massive followings of these unlettered men; they had never seen such a sudden and massive response to the gospel message. On the other, the government was clearly uncomfortable at how whole towns and villages fell under the sway of the evangelists: the colonial authorities generally treated religious matters as delicate, but they were doubly wary of anything that smacked of extreme enthusiasm or fervour.

The government's immediate response was to allow the evangelists' activities to go on unhindered while keeping a close watch on them. However, the official position soon changed to one of hostility due to three factors: pressure from some of the mission churches who were fast losing members (in terms of membership, the revival was a mixed blessing for the mission churches—while some experienced an explosion in numbers, others quickly lost a large percentage of their members); complaints from traditional rulers and local chiefs that the presence of the revivalists was instigating unrest in their domain; and reports of the activities of crooks who impersonated Babalola and were going about tricking people to part with their money and also stirring up the populace to revolt against the payment of tax to the government.

One official noted that "The Wesleyan Mission [in Ilesa] feels its continued existence is threatened and there is no doubt that considerable defections have already taken place both from them and from the C.M.S."[64] He noted also that many crooks, who were impersonating the healing evangelists to make money, were "going about the country making disparaging remarks about the missions and drawing attention especially to the fact that they have to be supported by money. Part of their appeal is that the new 'religion' is a free one."[65] The secretary of the Southern Provinces, writing to the Resident of Oyo Province, also noted that "Babalola himself is a quiet responsible man who confines his activities to the teaching of his own creed and takes no part in any form of political agitation."[66]

The government embarked on a crackdown on the activities of the evangelists in the form of arrests; refusal of applications to buy land for building churches; and the denial of many other civic rights. The most famous of the arrests made by the government was the imprisonment of Babalola for six months in 1932 after he was accused by a woman of compelling her to drink a concoction to force a confession out of her of being a witch.[67] Even though Babalola was clearly innocent, such accusations, which were then rife, provided the government with the legitimacy they desperately sought to shut down genuine leaders of a movement which they were uncomfortable with, but had nothing concrete against.

As the revival spread from Ilesa to many parts of the country, "it brought a new force and vitality to the once small FT churches, scattered round the country."[68] It transformed a hitherto small and isolated community into a large movement. "The FT churches were not only strengthened from within; new leaders who were raised directly through the revival strengthened the churches from without. As they travelled round the country their natural base was the FT churches which reaped the benefits of their ministry of signs and wonders. As an example, the Faith Tabernacle Church membership in Ilesa rose from sixty to two thousand during this revival."[69] Also, all the Faith Tabernacle leaders worked diligently to promote the revival in their various locations: David Odubanjo in Lagos, J. B. Esinsinade in Ijebu Ode, and Isaac Akinyele in Ibadan. However, unlike Babalola and the other healing evangelists, they travelled to other places only as the need arose; they primarily worked from their locations. Some other FT leaders stayed in Ilesa to help as the work greatly increased.[70]

Even though Babalola was a Faith Tabernacle member, there were thousands of converts who acknowledged him as their leader but who did not have any sense of connectedness to the Faith Tabernacle movement. Some of them remained in the mission churches; some joined local FT churches; others were not connected to any church; they only recognized Babalola as their spiritual leader and lived from revival meeting to revival meeting. Most of them had only a faint idea about the Faith Tabernacle movement. However, because Babalola himself had submitted to the leadership of Faith Tabernacle, they were indirectly yoked to the movement.

Nevertheless, two streams emerged from the revival—the Faith Tabernacle stream with David Odubanjo as leader, and the healing revival stream, which had Joseph Babalola as leader. Both streams were connected by their faith in divine healing. However, Odubanjo was the overall leader of the movement, effectively shepherding the two streams. The FT leaders were bound with Babalola and the other healing evangelists in all the trouble they went through. Many of them suffered as much as the healing evangelists; they also had to bear the burden of those who were persecuted every step of the way. Babalola travelled to Lagos several times to confide in the FT leaders and to find a solution to the problems he and the other healing evangelists were facing. The FT leaders were also a crucial source of funds for many of the evangelists. The movement was continually troubled by the authorities, hounded from place to place, constantly living on the edge of collapse. There was hardly ever any breathing space, and the situation soon became overwhelming for everyone involved.

The FT leaders believed the only way out of their dilemma was to form a partnership with a foreign church organization, preferably of British origins, whose doctrines, especially on the new birth and divine healing, was in agreement with theirs. Sometime in 1930, Odubanjo serendipitously came across a magazine, *Riches of Grace*, published by the Apostolic Church in Britain, with missionary headquarters in Bradford.[71]

After studying its contents, he began corresponding with the leaders and received more of the church's literature. From studying these publications, he became convinced that the Apostolic Church was the answer to the church's partnership dilemma. First the Apostolic Church was of British origins. This was a great advantage as regards their relationship with the government, since Nigeria was a British colony. One of the leaders had noted that "the British government under whose colonial regime we were was not favourably disposed to our relationship with America which was regarded as a lawless country at that time."[72] Second, the church believed in divine healing. The church's belief in the baptism of the Holy Spirit with the evidence of speaking in tongues also excited Odubanjo, who had been seeking for truth about the present day Pentecostal experience of speaking in tongues and the manifestation of spiritual gifts as early as 1922.[73] It is not certain how he came about this quest, since the Faith Tabernacle Church in Philadelphia did not believe in speaking in tongues and even vehemently opposed it—in 1919, the church published a tract, "The Modern Pentecost or Tongues Movement,"[74] in which it rejected the teachings and practices of the Pentecostal movement. Odubanjo read and corresponded widely, and it is not unlikely that he had come across materials published by any of the Pentecostal groups which were then spreading the Pentecostal message around the world.

Odubanjo was a true Berean Christian, and even though he had a high regard for Pastor Clark's teachings, he believed the Bible had the final say on all matters. Therefore, if any teaching seemed not to be representative of the Bible's position, he usually kept on seeking until God's position on the matter became clear to him. Clark's position on the baptism of the Holy Spirit with the evidence of speaking in tongues did not dissuade Odubanjo from further seeking the truth about the experience. After studying the literature from the Apostolic Church of Britain, which taught that baptism in the Holy Spirit with the evidence of speaking in tongues was still for the modern-day church, he began teaching it to the Lagos congregation. In the words of Adegboyega: "After reading and studying the Apostolic Church literatures on the above subject (Baptism of the Holy Ghost with signs following) and after listening attentively to the inspiring teachings on the same subject from the Holy Scriptures by . . . Pastor D. O. Odubanjo, we all decided to hold revival tarrying meetings for the Baptism of the Holy Ghost. . . . Odubanjo conducted the revival tarrying meetings in the year 1930, at Lagos. It was in these meetings that two of our brothers . . . received the Baptism of the Holy Ghost in a wonderful way speaking in tongues and prophesying."[75]

The belief in the doctrine of the baptism of the Holy Spirit and the other Pentecostal experiences by the Apostolic Church thoroughly excited the FT leaders, who thereafter became optimistic about the possibilities of a partnership with them; a letter was sent to Bradford in this regard. In September 1931, D. P. Williams, the founding president of the Apostolic Church; Andrew Turnbull, the vice president; and Williams Jones Williams, the leading prophet, visited Nigeria. Their arrival on the twenty-third of that month was met at the Apapa wharf in Lagos by an overjoyed crowd who had been eagerly praying for and awaiting their coming. The crowd was made up mainly of Faith Tabernacle members of the Lagos (Lagos Island) and Ebute Metta assemblies; however, delegates from other branches across the country were also in attendance.

That same evening, a welcome service was organized for the visitors at the Lagos Assembly at 51, Moloney Bridge Street.[76] There was excitement and great anticipation in the air as hundreds of members gathered at the welcome service in readiness for the blessings which they had prayed the visitors' coming would bring. They were not disappointed. Samuel Adegboyega, one of those present, recollected this experience: "It was a great day of great rejoicing and happiness to us. It was to us as if our fetters had been broken. We were jubilant as slaves emancipated from bondage. The service was filled with the manifestation of God's power."[77] Odubanjo reported that in one of the evening meetings during the first week, "the power of the Holy Spirit was so tremendously felt that some men and women in the Church were swept off their feet and baptised with the Holy Spirit. Some of them wept and floods of tears rolled down their cheeks, rejoicing and praising God at the same time."[78]

The first week's meetings were so successful that the leadership decided to give wider publicity to the second week's meetings. The meetings were "advertised in the local papers" and handbills were printed which were distributed "in offices and shops, also to friends and acquaintances." Odubanjo reported that as a result, "many prominent people in the town who never in their life would have stepped into our church, known as a Holy Ghost movement in Lagos,"[79] came. He continued: "Never in the history of this country has there been such a spiritual awakening. The result of the campaign seems to be sweeping everything before it, and hundreds of people crowded into these meetings each night with the hope that they might receive full salvation and healing. All denominations crowded into our twin halls—Catholics, Methodists, Baptists, members of African native churches, professional men of all types and calibre."[80]

One Lagos newspaper reported: "Never before has Lagos witnessed such scenes as those which are now daily taking place in this Revival and Divine Healing Campaign; every night hundreds seek salvation from sin and baptism of the Holy Ghost; many who have been prayed for and anointed have testified to the healing power of Christ in their body. The morning prayer meeting in their [the Europeans'] residence at Yaba has been crowded daily by men and women from Lagos, Ebute Metta and Agege districts, seeking salvation for soul and body. That the days of miracles are not past is being proved every morning and evening in these meetings since the Revival started."[81] During the two weeks of meetings in Lagos, it was reported that "nearly 400 souls have been saved and we prayed for over 800 for divine healing."[82]

The team visited Ijebu Ode, Abeokuta, and Ibadan, where many great testimonies were also reported. Their plan to visit Ilesa, Kaduna, Owo, and Efon Alaye was stopped by government officials. The meeting in Ibadan, which was attended by the largest number of representatives from the assemblies around the country, was the most important. It was attended by Odubanjo, Babatope, Babalola, Akinyele, Adolphus Hanson (who later became one of the most prominent leaders in the Ibadan district), and several other key leaders. It was at this meeting that the decision was made by the Nigerian leaders to form a partnership with the Apostolic Church of Great Britain. As the Apostolic Church leaders reported of the meeting: "Yet here, in this pagan region, in this Moham-medan city, did the climax of our journey come sooner than was antici-pated, when Pastor Babatope and Brother Joseph Babalola and others formed their decision to be henceforward one with us and to cooperate with us in the Apostolic Church, having now heard us, which made it possible for them to judge our standing in Christ. We had a glorious time in Ibadan, the Lord working most mightily. In an Officers' meeting, when approximately 40 percent were present, it was decided that we should return to Lagos to meet representatives of the Church from various parts."[83]

Subsequent events would, however, test the true understanding of the phrase "to be henceforward one with us." Thomas Napier Turnbull (Andrew Turnbull's son), a major historian of the Apostolic Church, writing about thirty years after, maintained that at the end of the two weeks of meetings, "the African brethren were so satisfied with the discussions that they unanimously decided to join the Apostolic Church."[84] A more plausible understanding of the agreement is offered by Samuel Adegboyega, who still maintained fifty years later, despite having parted ways with the original Faith Tabernacle leaders, that the agreement was regarded by both parties as an equal partnership—a mutual cooperation.[85]

In discussions with government officials, the Britons repeatedly gave the assurance that they would make sure the movement, which would now be under their effective control, adhered strictly to the state's laws. After one such meeting with Turnbull and the Williams brothers, J. W. Garden, the assistant police commissioner at Ibadan, wrote to his superior, the resident of Oyo Province: "They came to my office at my request yesterday. . . . They informed me that they had been sent to Nigeria to coordinate the various faith healing movements and to assist and uplift the followers of the Faith Tabernacle. . . . They were to meet Babalola with a view to absorbing him and his followers into the Apostolic Church provided Babalola accepted their teaching."[86]

Garden was reporting a few days later, "After arriving in Ibadan they did not leave the town but had a series of meetings with the heads of the various churches and sects including Babalola and Babatope. The proposal is to absorb Babalola and his followers in[to] the Apostolic Church and to establish churches in Ibadan, Ilesa and elsewhere under European pastors."[87] The district officer for Ife and Ilesa wrote in 1932 that George Perfect had promised that "local activities would have adequate European supervision,"[88] which essentially meant the Europeans would regulate the activities of the Nigerian leaders. Perfect also promised that "no persons without reasonable educational qualifications would be placed in positions of responsibility"; that "no teaching inimical to Government or the established missions would be permitted"; and that "no propaganda with a view to winning adherents from other missions would be permitted."[89]

Even though the promises made to the government by the Apostolic

Church's delegates were done with the best intentions—to save the movement from further harassment and possible shutdown by the government—the fact that they did not present this front to the FT leaders would later come to haunt the movement. (But, given the circumstances—the overwhelming pressure the FT leaders and healing evangelists were facing from the government at the time—it is doubtful that they would have raised any objections had they been privy to the details of the discussions between the Apostolic Church's delegates and the colonial authorities.)

When the Apostolic Church delegation returned to Lagos, they spent two weeks deliberating on the doctrines and practices of the Apostolic Church: "Church government, gifts of the Spirit, healings, doctrinal themes, institutions both medical and educational, polygamy, family life, the qualifications of leadership, the constitution of the soul—emotional, moral and intellectual—ordinations of the church, baptism, marriage, communion, membership, etc."[90] The last major function the Apostolic Church leaders performed before leaving Nigeria was the ordination of seven FT leaders as pastors. Ambrose Clark had previously ordained these leaders by proxy, sending accreditation letters recognizing them as pastors of their local FT congregations.

Some days before the ordination, the Apostolic Church team wrote that the seven leaders were going to be "honourably and respectfully ordained,"[91] a not-too-discreet slight of Clark's proxy ordination. When the leaders of the Faith Tabernacle Church in Philadelphia, who by now had only a rather casual connection with Nigeria, were informed of this new relationship, they were "strongly and vehemently"[92] opposed to it. But by then their opinion mattered next to nothing; they were only informed as a matter of courtesy—for old friendship's sake. On November 15, 1931, at Moloney Bridge Street, Lagos, seven leaders of the Faith Tabernacle Church were ordained into the pastoral office. They were J. A. Babatope, David Odubanjo, S. A. Mensah, Isaac Akinyele, J. B. Esinsinade, Samuel Adegboyega, and E. G. Macaulay.

The FT leaders submitted to ordination by the Apostolic Church leaders so they could be recognized by the government and not because they were submitting to their spiritual authority. Even though the FT leaders had always sought foreign partnership, they had nevertheless remained fiercely independent and protective of the revelation they had received from God. They were always careful to make sure that the move of God in their midst was never contaminated. As Harold Turner noted, "The Nigerian interpretation of the relationship, as recalled by one of the leading members of the time, was rather different: Faith Tabernacle could see how a European might help to deal with the opposition they had met, and as the Apostolic Church was understood to be Pentecostal and to believe in divine healing it was invited to assist. When its missionaries came they asked the Nigerian church to affiliate, meaning to become one and the same in everything; the latter objected to such a relationship and agreed to have fellowship with the British church, to be known by the same name, and to share their doctrines, but to keep the Nigerian property [movement] separate."[93]

After the deliberations, the Faith Tabernacle leaders decided to adopt the name "Apostolic Church," as they had done a decade before in the case of Faith Tabernacle, Philadelphia.

During the deliberations in Lagos, the FT leaders requested that the Apostolic Church send missionaries to continue from where the leaders had stopped. Anybody they were sending had to be a man "full of the Holy Ghost, a gentleman, cheerful, sympathetic, unassuming, level headed, law abiding, non-fanatic, and lowly in nature like yourselves; yea a spiritually devoted and elderly-mannered man with thorough education, a graduate if possible, a good revivalist, a good speaker and preacher, and one that makes himself accessible to all people making no difference in his treatment in account of colour. Such are the qualifications of the man suitable for our need as Africans."[94]

After the departure of Turnbull and the Williams brothers, two missionaries were sent—Idris Vaughan and George Perfect. Vaughan and Perfect arrived in Nigeria on June 2, 1932, to great expectation by the Nigerian church. They immediately rolled up their sleeves to work, and the ensuing cooperation resulted in significant progress for the Nigerian movement in terms of less opposition from the government, schools started, and most importantly, the blessings of the Pentecostal outpouring.

The work also spread more rapidly, and by 1933 the new mission was divided into four administrative units initially designated as "centres," but later renamed "areas" in 1936: these were Ilesa, Zaria, Lagos, and Calabar. Vaughan and Perfect were joined by three others within the next four years—Cyril Rosser, Noah Evans, and Vivian Wellings. The missionaries sent back home glowing reports of the annual conventions, of new churches opened, and of revival breaking out in church meetings, and especially of a great working partnership with the Nigerian leaders; these were frequently published in *The Apostolic Herald*.

The arrival of the Apostolic Church's missionaries marked the formal beginnings of Pentecostalism in Nigeria. The ministries of these missionaries, and those that would join their ranks in the following years, witnessed mighty demonstrations of the power and gifts of the Holy Spirit.[95] According to one report, "The nine gifts of the Spirit and their proper use, correct method of tarrying for the Holy Ghost baptism, liberty, prayers in divine worship and in prayer meetings . . . divine guidance by the word of the Lord through prophetic ministry, singing of joyful choruses, clapping of hands, scriptural dancing and jumping and shouting of Hallelujahs,"[96] were being experienced in meetings (with audiences ranging from hundreds of people to about two thousand) throughout the country. Reports of revival fires poured in from everywhere. The years 1932 to 1940 saw great outpourings of the Holy Spirit, which laid the foundation for the decades that followed. The movement was then in its infancy, routinization and institutionalization would later set in, but in those early years, heaven came down. One woman who received the baptism of the Holy Spirit in her kitchen recounted her experience thus:

I feel sure that you will rejoice with me that, what I have been so hungrily seeking, has been given me. My feeling is now one of entire joy. . . . This morning at about 5:30 I awoke conscious of complete happiness. I felt as if a "Presence" was near. So strong was this that I lit the candle. I had never felt so utterly safe and happy in my life. A few minutes passed, then something made me rise, though this was a full hour before my usual time. I came quietly downstairs and commenced to lay the fire. Again I felt that I was not alone—I was compelled to cease what I was doing, and sat down. . . . Prayers came from me without any effort of mine. I felt glowing, and my whole being vibrated. It was glorious, unforgettable and indescribable. Words rushed from my lips, bubbling and spitting forth in a gush. These words were meaningless to me though I am convinced they were words of exaltation and glory.

Then after a brief pause, I praised my Saviour with long, rich and fervent sentences—I could not restrain myself—nor would I, if I could. I felt supremely happy, on fire, and my humble kitchen was hallowed and transformed. . . . I shall never cease to thank God, the Son and the Holy Ghost for the supreme joy and love manifested not only around me but so deep within me.[97]

Samson Odunaike (one of the early leaders of the Faith Tabernacle) in his 1945 book, *The Path of a Master Christian*, writes of his own experience in 1937:

> It was in the Apostolic Church in Kaduna on that memorable Friday night (25th June, 1937). We assembled, as did the disciples in the upper room, waiting for the Baptism of the Holy Ghost. As soon as we knelt, a Great Light overshadowed me. Presently, I saw myself in different attire. All my degradation, unrighteousness, hypocrisies came to light at once. It seemed as if I was turned inside out, so I cried, "Lord, have mercy on me." But the Light was descending lower and lower until I began to feel as though in the proximity of a fire. Again, I cried, "The Fire of God";—"Oh people of God pray that I may not be consumed." It was a marvellous visitation—I rolled, screamed, I wept. Many passers-by and neighbours were pleading "Lord have mercy." After an interval of warm-hearted prayers the Light withdrew, but still under irresistible compulsion, I began to rehearse my open and secret sins, being temporarily unconscious of the presence of men, women and children. After this I began to weep. I was brought under a serious conviction of the Holy Ghost.[98]

We also get some of the most beautiful glimpses into the early days of the Pentecostal movement in Nigeria from the writings of George Perfect. Speaking of how the baptism of the Holy Spirit spread around the country before the mid-1930s, he said that "in a comparatively short time after the first tarrying meeting began, there were hundreds baptised in the Spirit, and tarrying meetings were being held from time to time in most of the assemblies. Although no actual record was or could have been kept of the number baptised in the Spirit, it must be well within the mark to say there were thousands, many also manifesting gifts of the Spirit; of healing, prophecy, tongues and interpretation of tongues."[99]

Perfect recorded that in many districts, it was shocking to the believers when, in many cases, the first people to receive the baptism of the Holy Spirit were new converts and backslidden Christians who had just rededicated their lives to God, only then followed by the older believers. Of course, this was not the rule, but it happened so frequently as to be noticeable to the leaders in many districts. Perfect recalled a conversation with Babatope, the Nigerian leader in the Ilesa Area, after one of the tarrying meetings. Babatope unburdened his heart to Perfect that he did "not understand this work," that he had "men and women amongst my members who are old and faithful Christians, and they are not receiving the baptism in the Spirit, although they pray much and earnestly. But there are many women there who are speaking in these wonderful foreign languages of which they know nothing, and they have only just given up their idols and jujus, and hardly know yet how to worship God at all."[100] Even Babatope had not received the baptism at this time!

The same thing was happening in Lagos. "We had in the meetings African pastors and elders, and other Christians, both men and women of long experience, men and women who had proved their faithfulness to God through years of trial and difficulty. . . . But these were by no means the first to enter into the promise," wrote Perfect. "While they were still waiting upon God, boys and girls in their teens, with scarcely any knowledge of God or His ways, were the first to be filled with the Spirit, and to speak in tongues."[101] As a result of this situation, Perfect wrote, "Those who were critical of the work were quick to make use of this fact. 'If,' they said, 'the work was really of God, why was not the Spirit given to the leaders?'—men who had been for years proved amongst them for their integrity and consistent spiritual life. 'These women and children are being deceived,' the critics declared. But the leaders as a whole did not say anything like this. They were encouraged by what they saw and heard, to press on, and God has answered their prayer of faith."[102]

Even though Odubanjo saw people receive the baptism in his house—"We reached church again on Friday evening, some fifteen minutes before time for the meeting to begin, and found a young woman speaking freely in tongues as she sat in her seat. She and another young woman and a boy had received the Spirit the previous day in Pastor Odubanjo's house,"[103] Perfect wrote in 1933—and both Adegboyega and himself saw scores of people baptized in the Holy Spirit in their respective assemblies, and rejoiced at the outpouring, it was not until late 1933 that they were baptized in the Holy Ghost and spoke in tongues.

In the August 1935 issue of *The Apostolic Herald*, Cyril Rosser gave a report of the 1935 Easter convention in Lagos: "When the Convention did begin the atmosphere was electric . . . the Spirit did indeed come down as he came on that day of Pentecost at Jerusalem. . . . Several strangers, visiting the meetings for the first time, were deluged with the power of God and began like many of the others in the congregation, to speak in tongues as the Spirit gave them utterance. One outsider in particular was amazed at what had happened and quickly noised the fact abroad insomuch that many others came to verify his account, and to enquire more specifically into the matter. In this way churches are founded here and the work is growing accordingly."[104] Speaking further, he said, "The Holy Spirit came down in mighty sweeping power, rousing some people into songs of praise, filling others with volumes of tongues and charging and pervading all with the divine Pentecostal power. It was 10 p.m. before the crowd finally broke up and began to make tracks for home, many with extreme reluctance, although they had been there since 6 0'clock in the morning!"[105]

While the glowing revival reports were being published, strains began to appear in the relationship between the Apostolic Church's missionaries and the Nigerian leaders. First, there was the leadership tussle between the missionaries and the Nigerian leaders about who was responsible for major decisions—the missionaries or the former FT leaders? The Nigerian leaders felt they had been gradually edged out of leadership, with all the control firmly in the hands of the Europeans. Who was responsible for controlling finance? Who was in charge of posting workers? Also the issue of the care of the missionaries became thorny—were they to be permanently sustained by offerings from the Nigerian congregations, or was Bradford to assume more responsibility for their support? It eventually became clear that there was a leadership tussle between the Ebute Metta assembly on the mainland, the seat of the European superintendent, and the Lagos assembly on the island, the seat of Odubanjo, the de facto leader of the Nigerian movement.

From the time the first missionaries arrived in 1932, the Ebute Metta assembly became the seat of the Lagos Area superintendent—usually a European—who, according to the constitution, was the president of the council of the church, while the Lagos assembly, located on Lagos Island, retained its place as the seat of the most senior Nigerian leader of the church, Odubanjo. The battle that would follow reflected a fundamental leadership rivalry between *Lagos* and *Ebute Metta*. With time, the loyalties of the church's leaders and assemblies around the country became divided between these two assemblies. Another major development was the gradual—and eventually, sharp—polarization of the Nigerian leadership.

All was not well with the movement. Yet, as serious as these problems were, the major litmus test for the relationship would eventually revolve around, first, the operations of the healing evangelists, and then, most importantly, the interpretation and application of the truths about divine healing.

· · ·

THE IMMEDIATE BACKGROUND TO ELTON being sent as a missionary to Nigeria was the request in 1936 by the church's council for "missionaries as superintendents for the new Areas"[106] which were created in 1936. Perfect, who left Nigeria in 1935, was reassigned to the country as the superintendent of the Lagos Area; Idris Vaughan remained the Calabar Area superintendent; A. Taylor was sent to the Zaria Area; and Elton was sent to take charge of the Ilesa Area. According to the church's constitution, the area superintendents were not to report to the Lagos Area superintendent, who was the president of the Nigerian council; they were to report directly to the International Missionary Committee in Bradford.[107]

The Lagos Area, with the headquarters at Ebute Metta, covered the towns and cities in the western area of western Nigeria: Ijebu Ode, Abeokuta, Ibadan, and Sagamu being the major ones; Zaria Area with headquarters in Kaduna covered all northern towns and cities: Jos, Kano, Minna, and Zaria were the largest; Calabar Area covered southern and eastern Nigeria: Calabar, Creek Town, Port Harcourt, Ikot Ekpene, Umuahia, and so on. Ilesa Area covered towns and cities in the eastern area of western Nigeria, which was divided into Ilesa district, Ekiti district, Yagba district and Gbedde district.

The Elton family spent the first three years in Ilesa in Babatope's residence at Oke Odo. The family moved in 1940 only when the mission house at Oke Oye was completed. Elton's immediate responsibility was to coordinate the growth of the revival in all the centres in the Ilesa Area; tend to the existing churches and lead the planting of new ones; and train new leaders to manage the rapidly expanding work. Remembering his earliest days in Ilesa and the immense scope of the work he was faced with, he said, "The fire of revival spread throughout the whole country, and I was sent out to look after that revival—180 church groups consisting of many thousands of souls—with only four trained African workers to help me. I lived with 49 Africans in an African house until my wife and daughter joined me in 1937. In one town alone we baptized eight thousand people. That is the size of the task we had in those days. There were over five thousand people in my welcome service."[108] He also travelled extensively with Babalola and Babatope on evangelistic campaigns, and was involved in the regular large open-air crusades at Oke Oye.

He soon settled well into this new role, which demanded long trips to the revival centres in the Ilesa Area, which was very large, and Elton had hardly landed in the country before Perfect began soliciting a car for him: "To be independent of the African drivers and their lorries will be of very great help to our missionaries. In the Ilesha area, the needs of the work will call for frequent visits by Pastor Elton to different parts of the Area, which is large and widespread. . . . To be able to run his own motor in his visiting will save him very much time and inconvenience, speeding up his work and making his travelling very much less of a trial than it would otherwise be."[109] Elton was the first missionary Perfect would make such a case for.

Before the mission got a car, Elton had to "walk on the roads visiting the villages of Ijesha land"; many times he walked between "ten and fifteen miles a day every day, for a whole week."[110] Once, he had to "Journey in pouring rain to Ise"; on another occasion, "Journeyed to Ilara. 2 hrs wait by roadside"; and at another time, "Back to Ilesha; walked in hot weather."[111]

Elton's photographs of these trips provide us some of the most valuable insights into the early phase of his work in the country. There is a picture, taken in 1940, of Hannah and Ruth leaning on the missionary vehicle, a Chevrolet Kilton, on their way to Ekiti. After he had just got the car in 1938, Elton rejoiced that "we have got the long expected car" and said, "It has already proved a very big help to us, for we have just returned from a tour of some of the most distant districts from Ilesha, the tour lasting nearly three weeks and covering many hundreds of miles."[112] Elton spent weeks travelling with his family visiting these towns and villages. Hitherto Hannah and Ruth had "never been able to go on tour because of the problem of travelling with Ruth in an African lorry," which was "not an altogether enjoyable experience of a European at any time."[113]

At the back of another photograph he wrote, "Taken by Pastor Perfect on our arrival at Ise. There had been a rain storm and we were wet through, hence our dishevelled appearance. Pastor Babatope is standing with me. Taken just outside the house where we stayed. I am wearing a grey tunic shirt and I am holding the clasp of my belt in my hand. Note the mud wall at the back of us. The natives had hastily thrown their clothes around them." Another photograph shows Hannah and Ruth posing with the king of Sabongida Ora and his deputy. (Missionaries in the country since the mid-nineteenth century had adopted the policy of befriending traditional rulers as a major strategy for penetrating their territories.)

Elton's diary entries give us an insight into his early labours. Within the first few weeks in Ilesa, he had the responsibility of organizing the church's convention, which had "5,300 present." "A great day," he afterwards recorded, "I wept at sight of African eager faces. What a joy to J.C. [Jesus Christ]."[114] He had regular administrative tasks, such as appointing a school manager and attending school board meetings. He was also frequently preaching. His favourite themes included "Calvary"; "the Person of the H.S. [Holy Spirit]"; "Redemption by blood"; "How shall we escape?"; "Praying always"; and "Justification."

Once, after a sustained period of work, his health broke down. "Rest, all day. Tired after heavy 14 days," he wrote on April 24, 1937. And after that, things generally went downhill, with only brief periods of respite. "Rested afternoon till 3 o.c. & then off to Igbogi for B.S. [Bible study]. Heat Stroke. Ret[ire]d very ill. . . . No good. Result of respiral [sic] exhaustion & heat." The next day: "Still felt ill and unwell. [Met with] students at 10 o.c. but rested for remainder of day. . . . No strength or desire for food. Just rest." The following day: "Resting all day. Felt very much better." But this was quickly followed by, "A very nasty attack. [Watch lowering of vitality]." On the twenty-ninth, he was "still feeling weak. Resting from teaching all day." But on the thirtieth, he "felt better in morning & so went to Igbogi by cycle at 4 p.m." But then another relapse: "Bad all day again. Igbogi effects." On May 2, he "rested all day—not going out at all. Being taught to be still & listen to God. The value of intimate fellowship & prayer with God." The next day he was "still feeling weak." Two days after, he was "feeling much stronger. 2 ½ hrs lecture to workers. 2nd coming of Christ." By the next day, he was "well again and at school 9 o.c." But he promised himself to thereafter "take things steady." He had kept the whole ordeal to himself: "No mention of sickness to anyone except G.P. [George Perfect]."

The origins and development of the work in Ilesa and the surrounding towns owed much to Babatope's leadership, the man with whom Elton would work in close and cordial relationship for fourteen years until Babatope's passing in 1950.[115] Babatope, while speaking at the Apostolic Church convention in Bradford in 1937, recalled his pioneering work: "Well, we started praying to the Lord in July, 1924, and by that time we were seven in number. And until 1930, we continued growing in number to be about 120. By that time, the Lord raised up a certain young man called Joseph Babalola (who is well known to all the missionaries who have been amongst us). This man is a very mighty man of God in praying and preaching. He came to us in July, praying and preaching, and within two months our church members, from 120, had grown to more than 2,000."[116]

As a result of the revival, new churches sprang up throughout Ijesaland such that by May 1931 there were twenty-four churches under Babatope's leadership. The fame of the Ilesa (Oke Oye) assembly spread around the country and beyond, eventually eclipsing for some years that of any other Nigerian congregation of the church. When Perfect and Vaughan visited the Oke Oye church in 1932, they "met with a congregation of two thousand or more."[117] Perfect and other later missionaries, like Rosser who arrived in 1934, visited Ilesa frequently and sometimes stayed for extended periods, but Elton was the first fully resident missionary of the church in the town.

From July 1930, Babalola and his co-evangelists marched throughout the Ilesa Area—Efon Alaye, Owo, Ibadan, Ijebu Ode, Akure, Benin, Ilofa, Yagba district, Ekiti towns and Akoko towns—stirring up whole towns and cities with the power of God. As Perfect, who spent a lot of time with Babalola, aptly described it, after his encounter with God on the Igbara Oke Road, "[Babalola] went into a secret place and fasted for seven days. When these had expired he burst in upon the world with a flaming message, scorching the consciences of the people, bidding them eschew their idolatry and witchcraft and pointing them to Christ, the Saviour."[118]

When Babalola's ministry exploded, many young men who were converted at the time earnestly prayed to be endowed with the same measure of power that was evident in his life, and many received the power to preach and heal. They fanned all over the country, stirring waves of revival, small and big. Perfect wrote, "And now, young natives who had received the Lord felt moved to become revivalists to their brethren in the absence of European instructors. What revivalists! The Spirit-filled African revivalists ARE revivalists with a capital ARE. They get white-hot with the fire of God. So it was with these young preachers. They set Nigeria on fire. And thus was founded the Spirit Movement, as it was called, of which Joseph Babalola was the central personality."[119]

Many of these evangelists, like Babalola, were semi-literate or illiterate young men, but they were so filled with the Spirit of God that both literate and illiterate stood in awe as they ministered in the power of God. Perfect described one of these evangelists in Ibadan, one of the "men whom the Spirit Himself had raised up and empowered": he was "an unlettered man, of little previous Christian experience, who, if he had appeared before an English audience, would have caused a shout of laughter at the grotesque efforts he made to clothe himself in European dress. But this man was being used by God in miracles of healing, and to the salvation of hundreds. He was one of God's princes."[120]

Unfortunately, many of these evangelists had rougher experiences with the government and the mission churches than Babalola did. Babalola was the most prominent figure, and the authorities, apart from the six-month imprisonment, were reluctant to harass him; but his co-evangelists were free food for the hawks. Suspicious government officials, rankled kings and chiefs, and disquieted missionaries were determined to curb the movement. And if the government couldn't get at the movement through Babalola, because of his overwhelming popularity, it could successfully target his protégés. It was simply a case of giving the dog a bad name so as to be able to hang it.

The evangelists were harassed everywhere they went; many were beaten, jailed and publicly humiliated in any way that satisfied the lust of their persecutors. The healing evangelists also had the local authorities—kings and councils of chiefs—to combat. While some welcomed them, others vehemently opposed them. The kings and chiefs, custodians of culture, were often offended at the way Babalola and his men made nonsense of their most cherished traditions. Since ancient times, these kings and chiefs had used the fear of idols and gods to force their subjects into submission. Now, overnight, they were stripped of the psychological and spiritual sway they held over the people.

Those who listened to Babalola's message and embraced it were no longer afraid at the mention of judgment from idols and local gods—they were free. This threatened the status quo, and many local custodians of tradition were disturbed by the developments. Those who had congregated around Babalola's message therefore became outlaws in many communities. The kings and chiefs justified their opposition to them by labelling them rebellious citizens, disrupters of the normal life and culture of their communities.

The difficulties experienced by these evangelists was further compounded by Babalola's impersonators, who went about preaching against the payment of tax to the government and making statements which the government believed was capable of causing unrest among the populace—usually a sore spot with colonial authorities. The authorities, sometimes mistakenly, but often deliberately, lumped the healing evangelists and the impersonators together and clamped down on their activities. The government convinced itself and wanted everybody to believe that all "*aladuras*" were the same and were supposed to be suppressed for the benefit of the public. But government officials knew this was not so.

(In 1930 the appellation "aladura" became the most used for all the prophetic and evangelistic figures who went from town to town holding revival meetings; it lumped together all groups and persons which had emerged up till then, including the Cherubim and Seraphim movement, the Church of the Lord [Aladura], Babalola and his colleagues, and the hundreds of independent preachers who were not affiliated with any group.)

Even in the sometimes riotous religious ferment of the late 1920s and early 1930s, the authorities could usually discern those who were the troublemakers, but their official policy was shaped by their hostile attitude to indigenous Christian initiatives, especially one that stirred whole communities, and their close rapport with the missionaries of the established churches who were jealous of the movement's success.[121] (One official wrote in 1932: "The established missions are unrelenting in their hostility to the new movement, partly on religious grounds, and partly from the fear of losing yet more adherents."[122])

Of all the preachers that were making statements capable of causing unrest, Josiah Ositelu, founder of the Church of the Lord (Aladura), was particularly notorious, especially because he was one of the most charismatic and also had one of the largest followings. His 1931 pamphlet in Yoruba, *Awon Asotele Ohun Ti yio Bere si Sele, Lati inu Odun 1931 Lo, ati bi Odun Mefa si I*, translated, *The Words of Prophecies of Things to Happen from the Year 1931 Onwards and for about the Next Six Years*,[123] gave the authorities concern about the potential trouble that could arise if the Aladuras were left unchecked. One government official wrote, "Previous to that meeting, I had sent to Mr Brice Smith, as I had also sent to Captain Ross a copy of a book of prophecies in Yoruba, called 'Awon Asotele' by [Prophet] Woli J. Ositelu of Ijebu-Remo. Both Mr Brice Smith and myself were, and still are, of the opinion that many of the prophecies if preached or read literally will cause unrest among the African population, especially in the bush areas. . . . At the conference at Ibadan on 13th Sept. with Crown Counsel I gave a fairly accurate translation of the paragraphs which in my opinion are likely to cause unrest and with these translations you agreed. I also explained how the Aladura movement had been responsible for the unrest which culminated in the anti-Tax riots at Iddo and Akure [Ekiti Division, Ondo Province]."[124]

Ositelu's teachings and prophecies became so much of an embarrassment to Babalola and his colleagues that he (Babalola) had to denounce him and his ministry to save his colleagues and himself from the government's wrath. In a letter to J. W. Garden, the secretary of the Southern Provinces noted, "Babalola blames the pamphlet for much of the agitation. He says that it has been in circulation for some eight months in large numbers and is sold by persons representing the printer. It has nothing to do with him and he condemns its contents as bad."[125] Garden noted in one correspondence, "Babalola the founder of the Aladura movement repudiates the preaching of Ositelu and is now touring Ondo Province trying to counter the anti-government preachings."[126]

Babalola and his men gladly suffered these troubles, confident that they were suffering for the cause of Christ. They were, however, bewildered when they began to notice a certain aversion to some of their practices by their European partners. This was the real beginning of troubles for the movement. Even though Perfect, Vaughan, and the other missionaries were excited about the ministry of Babalola and the other evangelists, they were uncomfortable with many of their methods. Though they initially concealed their disagreement, they eventually began to voice their discontent about practices such as the use of water which had been blessed through prayer to heal the sick.

Vaughan, speaking in later years about the pioneering work in Yorubaland, revealed the prevailing thought among the missionaries: "Naturally in taking over such a great body there were many difficulties, such as preconceived ideas and doctrines that are not Scriptural, and, perhaps, because of that we might say that the Yoruba side of the work is the hardest side, and the missionaries have, perhaps the greatest problems to face on that side."[127] Writing to the district officer of Ekiti Division in 1937, Perfect said, "I note what you say on the question of the 'holy water.' I am afraid this may be the difficulty, but I think the only one, but am hoping, in view of the stand already taken at Efon, that we shall be able to get Ikere to follow suit. I can assure you that all our missionaries will be only too glad to see this thing stopped."[128]

The Apostolic Church's missionaries were clearly more comfortable with the conservative spiritual outlook of the early FT leaders like Babatope, Odubanjo, Akinyele, and Adegboyega, but they could also not deny that the healing evangelists—Babalola, Orekoya, Babajide, and Olatunji—had been the soul of the movement since 1930. From about the mid-1930s, some of the FT leaders—specifically the Ebute Metta leaders—began to side with the missionaries on the methods employed by the prophets. Adegboyega, who was one of those who became uncomfortable with some of the practices, mentions that there "was also a misunderstanding amongst us as leaders of the church in respect of continuous use [of] so-called holy water for healing of the sick." He continued, "It was admitted by us all that when God raised up . . . Babalola the evangelist and . . . D. O. Orekoya, the use of water was instrumental in wonderful healing of the sick as commanded them by the Lord. But it was afterwards a common practice by unscrupulous and so-called prophets to wear short knickers and jumpers over it, with bells in their hands as well as sticks, rods and all such materials alleged to have been blessed and sanctified through prayer by people to conduct services for healing and deliverance through the use of so-called holy water in bottles or in containers, which the people were asked to bring to their revival meetings by these so-called prophets."[129]

But it is doubtful that the hostility that some of the Nigerian leaders displayed towards the evangelists' methods was only as a result of the use of the same methods by crooks who were impersonating Babalola and his colleagues; they definitely had been influenced over time by the European missionaries' views. As Adegboyega noted, "We were against this practice which was noticeable and prevalent in our church at that time. Some of us who were church leaders at that time strongly advocated putting embargo on such unscriptural practices for performances of signs and wonders. There were others who felt that the practice should be tolerated and not wholly eradicated. Therefore we who advocated against such practices were branded and accused as being too strict, rigid and quenchers of the Spirit. This also resulted in fomentation of trouble in our midst."[130] The ambivalence in Adegboyega's statement is loud—while admitting the divine origins of the healing evangelists' methods, he also calls for an embargo on it. This ambiguousness, however, had nothing to do with

Adegboyega's character; it was only a sign of the times, for the following years proved to be a period of great controversies and contradictions.

Also, the revivalists were not aware that when the Apostolic Church leaders visited the country in 1931, one of the assurances they gave to the colonial authorities was to curb some of the excesses of the healing evangelists. When the pioneer missionaries arrived in 1932, this understanding was reaffirmed in their discussion with the authorities. So, while the Apostolic Church's missionaries themselves were clearly uncomfortable with some of the healing evangelists' practices, they also had a responsibility to fulfil the promise they had made to the colonial authorities, who saw them as coming to take over the movement. The colonial authorities, assuming the European church was firmly in charge of the movement, expected the missionaries to enforce the conditions of their 1931 agreement.

As the colonial authorities pressured the European missionaries, they in turn pressured the healing evangelists. The healing evangelists believed their partners had no right to pressure them; after all, they were their *partners* and not their *persecutors*; they had come to help them, not oppose them. The missionaries had a really difficult job pacifying both parties. Their presence in the country prevented the government from clamping down on the movement—they were seen as the stabilizing factor against the excesses of the revivalists. They were well aware of this and did not want to violate the government's trust. On the other hand, they knew they had come to serve the revival movement—the only reason they were in the country at all was because they had been invited by the FT leaders and the revival leaders. They were in the country to do the work of the ministry.

The Apostolic Church's missionaries had to continually reassure the government and the native authorities that the movement meant well, that they were not out to foment trouble, and that they were willing to cooperate with them as much as possible to keep the revivalists in check. This was the only condition on which the movement was given land to build churches and schools and to hold evangelistic meetings in many communities. Elton wrote in one diary entry in 1937: "Good hope of Akoko chiefs being persuaded by D.O. [District Officer] to give land."[131]

In what was later known as the "1936 agreement," the Apostolic Church's missionaries and the revivalists (grudgingly) acceded to a set of rules laid down by the kings and chiefs of many communities to ensure the continued activity of the revivalists in their communities. This set of rules, which was originally drafted by the king of Ijero for his own town, was later adopted by the rulers of other communities. The 1936 agreement stated:

1. That the members are of good behaviour
2. That they do not interfere with adherents of other missionary bodies
3. That no meetings are held during the hours of darkness
4. That the use of holy water is abandoned
5. That the leaders of the church take strict measures to check immoral practices and any kind of witch-finding among the congregation
6. That any new adherent is brought before the Ajero.[132]

But sticking to the rules turned out to be more problematic than anticipated. The problems did not go away, because they were often complex and different in each locality, and the motives of the actors were often cloaked. For instance, the revivalists continued to challenge the third and the fourth rules about holding meetings "during hours of darkness" (which they thought was ambiguous), and the use of "holy water." As the district officer of Ekiti Division wrote in June 1937, "The Ikere Council inform me that the use of 'Holy Water' has not been abandoned."[133] In a separate letter another official wrote, "I might add that they [the conditions in the agreement] have all been accepted by local leaders of the church except that relating to holy water to which they demurred."[134]

The application of water that had been prayed over by the healing evangelists to diseased parts of the body to effect a cure was the most prominent, and also the most contested, practice. From the early days of the healing revival at Oke Oye, it had become the strongest symbol of God's power to heal. It was difficult for the healing evangelists to comply with the ban on the use of holy water for three reasons: they believed it was a product of divine revelation; there were thousands of testimonies of its effectiveness; and they dreaded that they would undermine the people's faith if they abandoned the practice.

In an interview with Henry Dallimore, Babalola offered an interesting insight into his continued use of holy water. Dallimore wrote: "[Babalola's] method was to call people to confession of sin, and to the surrender of idols, and he would then preach to them and pray for them.

He . . . asked them to bring water with them, and this he blessed, and the people went away with the impression that this water would cure all ills. Many cures were reported, and the water came to be termed 'the water of life.' Joseph Babalola told me . . . that as far as he was concerned the water had no significance. He simply allowed the people to bring the water, and to hold the belief that, after blessing, it had . . . powers, in order that he might get the people to come and to listen to his preaching, and thereby throw away their idols and accept the Gospel teaching. The water could at least do them no harm. I need hardly say, however, that in the minds of the people the water was wholly significant."[135]

The government and some traditional rulers and chiefs banned the use of holy water for health reasons. The way "blessed water" was applied in drinking, bathing, and washings of other kinds, was considered hazardous to the health of the public. In some cases, the water used was fetched from the Oke Oye stream or any other stream or river near a revival ground. This was applied—in drinking or washing—on the spot. Hundreds or thousands of people, depending on how large the revival meeting was, would besiege a river or stream to collect water to be prayed over. Usually there were large numbers of diseased people, including lepers and many with contagious diseases, who would cluster around a stream at once—collecting water or even washing on the spot. This, the authorities feared, could lead to an outbreak of disease.

A European visitor to one of the revival towns reported to the Resident of Akure: "For example, if anyone is ill of pneumonia, small-pox; the former is likely dangerous to be exposed to cold, and cold water is the medicine for this in Efon; small pox, the latter, should be isolated and instead of this, cold water is the cure and whereas cold water is highly dangerous in some stages of the disease, and the Aladura's cure is solely and practically cold water. . . . I beg and think that it is high time for the Authority to step in and see that a check is put for the benefit of Efon town and the neighbouring districts."[136] One official wrote, "The Aladuras agreed with the above [conditions in the agreement] but wished to have the provision re: 'Holy Water' modified. The Ajero [king of Ijero], quite rightly in my opinion, says that the use of holy water is highly dangerous in cases of small-pox and other skin diseases, and does not wish it in his district."[137]

THREE

HEALING WARS

Even though Elton's posting to Ilesa was the product of a prophetic word, sending him there was still a huge step of faith and a practical decision by the council in Bradford. (Even when the missionary council was posting based on prophecy, it did not ignore practical considerations. An example was the decision not to allow Elton's wife and baby to follow him initially. So even though Elton was called by a prophetic word, the council would still have ratified it after a consideration of all the peculiarities of the individual and the specific mission field.) We must pause at this point to ask why the leaders in Bradford made the decision to send young Elton to the core of the revival.

Most of the church's missionaries who had served in Nigeria up till then, and also the newly appointed superintendents, were veterans of the church's mission work. George Perfect and Idris Vaughan had been leaders in the Apostolic Church since the early days—Vaughan was one of the first to be called out into the full-time ministry of the church in 1921, and Perfect was one of the founders, in 1917, of the church in Bradford, which alongside three others, formed the Apostolic Church;[1] Noah Evans, who came to Nigeria in 1934, had spent eight years in France;[2] Cyril Rosser, who also arrived in 1934 and who became the Lagos Area superintendent after Perfect, was one of the first members of the church in Wales in the mid-1920s;[3] Vivian Wellings, who came in 1936, was then the secretary of the international missionary council in Bradford and was one of those who drafted the church's *Guiding Principles*.[4]

In stark contrast, the highest office Elton had ever held was that of an elder in his local assembly in Shrewsbury.[5] In fact, he said that when his name was mentioned through prophecy in Penygroes in 1936, many of the leaders wondered who he was. "God had spoken in prophecy and said, 'Send my servant Elton to Nigeria.' And some of them [the council of apostles] said, 'Elton, who is that? Do you know anybody named Elton?' I was not a pastor in the church; I was nothing."[6] We know that Elton must have been rated very highly in his local assembly, however, because the church's leadership was searching for "key-men of proved and tried maturity"[7] for the position of superintendent for the newly created areas. The only-thirty-year-old Elton was one of the "key-men of proved and tried maturity."

It is also significant that he was sent to take charge of the Ilesa Area, which was the "largest Area in the Apostolic work in Nigeria"[8] and also the fortress of the healing evangelists. Did they notice, after discussions with him in Penygroes, a fierceness and determination that was needed to sort things out in the troubled spot? While we may not have definite answers to these questions, it seems that Elton was sent to Ilesa with specific instructions to settle things down. From Elton's tone, it is very possible that a major focus of the 1936 meeting where he was called to Nigeria—"Forty apostles met in a certain place. . . . They met and they were considering what to do about the great call of God and the revival in Nigeria"[9]—was to resolve the issues surrounding the activities of the healing evangelists. That such a delicate assignment was entrusted into his hands says a lot about Elton's character.

Because Elton was the superintendent in charge of the area that served as the base for the healing evangelists, he was responsible for communicating to the evangelists both the displeasure of the European missionaries with what they considered to be the obstinacy of the revivalists on certain issues and also the demands of the government and native chiefs. This onerous task required Elton to constantly battle on two fronts—convincing and appeasing both the healing evangelists and the colonial officials.

An October 1937 letter by Elton to the district officer, Ekiti Division, gives us a clue about his earliest mediation attempts with the government: "I know that you have had a lot of trouble with the churches in your area and for that reason I would particularly like to meet you, but I can assure you that we are doing all that is in our power to establish them on a peaceful and proper foundation. You will, I know readily appreciate that it is no small task, particularly having in mind the largeness of the congregations in some places and the difficulty of changing ideas and customs that have been firmly established for many years, but we are definitely finding much improvement, so we trust that you will help us and if at any time you have any difficulties or matters relating to the Apostolic Church in the Ekiti country I should be glad if you will communicate direct with me and I will try and help you."[10]

On the part of the healing evangelists, one of Elton's most famous struggles was in trying to communicate what he believed to be a more biblical interpretation of Joseph Babalola's use of physical elements—specifically a rod, a hand bell and a bottle of water. Babalola said he had been shown in a vision at the onset of his ministry to carry them as instruments through which God's power would be manifested wherever he preached. He interpreted this vision literally, and throughout his ministry carried a rod and prayed over water for the healing of sicknesses and diseases. But Elton told Babalola that the physical elements he was shown were symbolic—the iron rod represented his authority and the bottle of water signified the level of his anointing.[11]

Babalola's lieutenant, David Babajide, while discussing the events of the 1930s with a group of evangelists in 1977, specifically recollected that Elton had told Babalola that the vision he had been shown (Babalola thrice saw a bottle of water: the first time, it was filled up to half; the second time to three-quarters; and finally, it was filled to the brim) was not a divine directive to start to pray on water for healing; rather, it was representative of the increasing levels of the power of the Holy Spirit he could operate in if he continued in purity, holiness, love and humility.[12] Elton himself frequently repeated this in discussions with many of his protégés.[13] Elton argued that the practice of blessing water encouraged many to place their faith in "holy water," rather than in the word of God.

The revivalists countered saying that the practice had come by revelation, and Elton was to face his business, which was to teach new converts the basic doctrines of the Bible.[14] This infringement on what the revivalists considered a divine mandate was completely unacceptable to Babalola and the other prophetic figures who became embittered towards Elton and his colleagues, who were increasingly perceived as a hindrance, rather than a help, to the move of God in their midst. "*Mefoyinbo,*"[15] which means "we don't want the whites," became their war cry.

Travelling with the revivalists afforded Elton the opportunity to observe what he believed were lapses in the revival. According to him, the emphasis was only on miracles, healings, and the destruction of charms, amulets, and other occult materials of idol worshippers, without an equal emphasis on sound teaching from the Scriptures. Speaking in later years, Elton revealed some of his innermost thoughts about the developments at the time: "For those of you who are not aware of my background, let me spare a few precious moments. I came into this country forty-five years ago and I was sent to take over a revival that had happened; a revival which had very, very little gospel in it. It was a revival against juju medicine. . . . I was sent out by a group of Pentecostal churches in Europe who believed in justification by faith, baptism by water, [the] second coming, baptism of the Holy Ghost with signs following and a manifestation of divine government in the church today."[16] Elton further noted:

I want to issue a note of warning in case I don't get a chance to do it again. The evidence of miracle is no proof that you're in the will of God. No proof! You may be able to heal; you may be able to do miracles, but that's no proof that you're in the will of God. The proof that you're in the will of God is that you are doing the will of God and the work of God in the days of God. And I have . . . had to work it all out for myself.

When I first came into this country I came up against this problem, because I came to take over the revival where there were many miracles. Many miracles! And yet I was present amongst those people and I saw the miracles done by people who were living in immorality and I said, "You can't do that Lord. You can't do that!" I wept many nights and said Lord, "You can't do that." The Lord turned to me and said, "*You* will do it then." That was a very good reply, "*You* go do it then." God can use a man and God is using men in Yorubaland and they are doing miracles. They are performing healings and yet their lives are completely corrupt. Why? God will honour the preaching in the name of Jesus; He can dispose the channel when He wishes and God help the channel that doesn't realise that. There are men that are so used to miracles that they get to a situation where they can do without God and that's dangerous.[17]

This statement is crucial to our understanding of Elton's thinking. Contrary to the general feeling by many of the revivalists that Elton exhibited a determined opposition to their ministry, he was in fact concerned that the movement should not derail. The way he went about addressing his concern, however, was another matter, which definitely played some role in obscuring his true intentions. It is possible that Elton was not empathetic enough to appreciate the battles that both the early Faith Tabernacle leaders and the later healing revivalists had fought to preserve the spiritual truth they had received.

Elton was a prophetic type, and his major concern was to set the erring straight; he could hardly identify with their struggles and emotions. Also, he was then young and brash and most likely too opinionated to be a successful peace broker and reconciler. No matter how well intentioned he was, it was perhaps *his* fault that the healing evangelists did not feel he was on *their* side, even though he really believed he was on their side and that all he was doing was in their best interest.

Dealing with the crisis often wore Elton out. He was almost certainly referring to the toll the pressure was taking on his spiritual and emotional wellbeing when he wrote in his diary on June 23, 1937: "I feel as tho[ugh] my heart has turned to stone. A dangerous condition. I will give myself with renewed vigour to the work. It shall not suffer. I would like to wipe out the memory of the past 4 months."[18] Perhaps this aggravated his yearning for Ciss. He bluntly confessed the next day: "Letter started to Ciss. Words are useless things! Have decided hereafter that I will not allow desires to express."[19] The feeling of despair had not abated by the third day, and he must have been playing with the idea of returning to the UK after he had had a meeting with some of the healing evangelists when he again divulged his thoughts to his diary: "Feel I cannot go back."[20]

Several months later, he was still battling to put out fires on several fronts. Once during a trip to the assemblies in the Ekiti Area, he complained to his diary: "Ekiti Bad. Blessing of water, etc."[21] He recorded in his diary on November 25: "Saw D.O. [District Officer] re: Efon [Alaaye]. Service at 5:30 p.m. J. B. [Joseph Babalola] spoke. D. O. O. [David O. Odubanjo] present. BAD."[22] A few weeks after, he was still writing, "Afraid of J. B. [Joseph Babalola] and water. Water problem bad."[23] And a few days later: "J. B. [Joseph Babalola] arrived at night. Promises settlement of agreement."[24] Elton must have felt overwhelmed by the constant need to intervene on behalf of the healing evangelists while not being able to control their activities.

Despite acrimony about the methods and practices of the revivalists, there was continued cooperation between all parties for the furtherance of the move of God in the country. What pushed the already precarious situation to a point of no return was an issue that the Nigerian leaders considered sacrosanct. It had defined the Nigerian movement since its early days; it had brought them into conflict with the Anglican authorities and had led to their eventual expulsion from the church; it had cost them ridicule in society, opposition and terrible persecution from the government, and the lives of loved ones—it was the doctrine of divine healing.

The interpretation of faith in divine healing as total, complete trust in God for the healing of all sicknesses and diseases, without recourse to medicine—any kind of medicine, Western or traditional—was non-negotiable to the Nigerian leaders. They had been so careful to make their position clear in any intending partnership that when, in 1931, after they had made initial contact with the Apostolic Church in Britain, they later heard "rumours" that they were not totally committed to the doctrine of divine healing "without the use of medicine; a doctrine which we members of Faith Tabernacle Congregation in Nigeria warmly embraced, taught and practised since 1918,"[25] they sent a cablegram to the International Missionary Council of the church in Bradford cancelling the invitation they had earlier extended to them. The cablegram read, "DON'T COME FOR YOU DON'T BELIEVE IN DIVINE HEALING."[26]

A congress of the FT leaders—Esinsinade, Odubanjo, Akinyele, Babatope, Macaulay, Mensah, Adegboyega, and others—was held in Ijebu Ode in early 1931, shortly after the cablegram had been sent, to discuss the issue. There, Isaiah Sakpo, a prophet recognized in the movement, but who was not a part of the deliberations, came to the meeting place as led by the Holy Spirit and prophesied to the leaders that it was the will of God that the representatives of the Apostolic Church visit and that the FT were to refrain from preventing them. As Adegboyega recalls, "The prophetical ministry was so clear, inspiring and convincing that Pastor D. O. Odubanjo . . . took it down word for word . . . and copies [were] distributed to the church leaders who attended the conference."[27] Shortly after, even without a further word from Nigeria, the Apostolic Church replied the cablegram: "WE ARE COMING, DIVINE HEALING A THING MOST SURELY BELIEVED."[28]

Perhaps no other story better illustrates how seriously the Faith Tabernacle movement took the issue of divine healing than its short-lived relationship with the Faith and Truth Temple Church with headquarters in Toronto, Canada, after its partnership with the Faith Tabernacle of Philadelphia came to an abrupt end in 1928. Odubanjo, who had continued his search for foreign partnership after the fallout with the FT of Philadelphia, got information about the Faith and Truth Temple Church sometime in 1928, most likely through their pamphlets. (Odubanjo was always investigating about churches from around the world, especially by acquiring tracts and pamphlets. Historian Robert Mitchell quotes a letter by Akinyele to Odubanjo in 1930, after the latter had sent Akinyele some pamphlets to investigate: "I received the cards and pamphlets with thanks. . . . I cannot yet form any opinion but my advice is that we should be slow indeed to adopt any foreign method, there are hundreds of them. We are just coming into contact with them . . . we should be careful of *imitation*, we should strive to be *original* ourselves."[29])

Odubanjo began corresponding with their leader, one E. O. Crawford;[30] and when, in 1929, Crawford said he was sending some missionaries to the French-controlled Upper Volta (present-day Burkina Faso), who would pass through Lagos, Odubanjo asked that they be his guest. The leader of the crew, C. R. Myers, arrived in Lagos with his wife, a little daughter, and two other missionaries in 1928. Unfortunately, disaster struck shortly after the team arrived in Lagos—the missionaries who accompanied Myers became gravely ill and because the FT doctrine forbade doctors and medicines, they did not get any medical help, and eventually both of them died. Adegboyega describes the situation:

> But with deepest regret we have to relate that one of the . . . missionaries, in person of Revd. Ralph Curlew, died in the midst of us without the use of medicine. It was a sad experience indeed. The incident was reported to the government. . . . Not very long [afterwards] . . . their secretary, Miss [Daisy] Crawford also died without the use of medicine. Then we became cynosure of all eyes as fanatic [*sic*] people. In reply to our critics we made them to understand that we believe the word of God on its face value as it is written in the Holy Writ and that we obey the command of our Lord Jesus Christ with complete faith in His prevailing name and meritorious blood shed on Calvary's cross for health and deliverance of His redeemed people from sickness, diseases and all infirmities.
>
> One Rodent Inspector of Police who was sympathetic with us kindly advised us that to avoid similar sad occurrences in future, more especially in areas where burial could not be allowed without medical certificate, it would

be better and more advantageous for us to call in a doctor for consultation and examination if it was observed that the condition of any of our sick people was becoming seriously critical unto death. According to him, this would make it possible and easy for us to obtain medical burial certificate in case of death without undergoing the crucial process of post mortem experience. He told us further that although we might not use medicine for healing in the act of doing the will of God by prayer of faith, yet by consulting for necessary examination before death, we would have covered requirements of the law for burial purposes in the areas concerned. And this principle we agreed to follow.[31]

Left with only his wife and daughter, a devastated Myers pleaded with the leadership of the Lagos FT to give him two men who would accompany him to the Upper Volta (present-day Burkina Faso). Two men were chosen and, in addition, money was contributed by the Lagos and Ebute Metta assemblies for the trip. But the trip was a disaster. Myers' wife, who was pregnant, became very ill and later died in a hospital after giving birth to a boy; the Nigerian brethren who accompanied them found their way, in the most unpleasant of circumstances, back to Nigeria without Myers. When Myers eventually was able to come back to Nigeria, he encountered problems with the immigration office and was not allowed to re-enter the country without a guarantor. When he sent a message to the leaders of the Faith Tabernacle, they declined to stand for him. One of the reasons for their action was that Myers had taken his wife to the hospital against their stated position.[32] As Harold Turner puts it, "The Faith Tabernacle members in Lagos felt that he [Myers] had deceived them in sending his wife to hospital and not relying entirely on faith."[33] Such was the unyielding stand of the Faith Tabernacle on the issue of divine healing.

The 1938 crisis started when, during one Bible study in Lagos, Perfect, the Lagos Area superintendent, in answer to some questions about divine healing, made certain statements which raised doubts in the hearts of the members about his true position on the issue. When Odubanjo returned (he had been on a trip outside the city), he was informed by the members that Perfect had made some statements "which were capable of making the Saints lose their complete faith in God for healing of the body without the use of medicine" and that if "Perfect was not checked in time, such continuous ministry of his could weaken and jeopardise our doctrine on Divine Healing,"[34] Adegboyega was later to write.

As Adegboyega recounts the story, after Odubanjo had been briefed about the situation, he approached Perfect "to enquire from him the fact of the allegation. It was during this time that hot arguments and altercations which were decent and indecent began to come out of their mouth against one another."[35] Odubanjo informed the leaders in Lagos about the development, and a meeting was called by the "joint presbyteries of Lagos and Ebute Metta assemblies" to hear "from the mouth of Pastor Perfect, his views concerning divine healing as alleged." At the meeting, which was fully attended, Perfect was questioned about his position on the issue; to the consternation of the elders, he "said it was wrong to say that doctors and medicines were bad and evil in themselves." Further, "he said they were good in themselves. That it depended on how people made use of them. He also said that it was not wrong for people to use anything natural that might be termed drugs or medicines to protect themselves from being sick."[36] Perfect was asked to produce his argument in writing so that the presbytery could thoroughly study and debate it.

Perfect found himself in a tight position and had to walk a thin line. Because of the susceptibility of the European physical constitution to the tropical climate, he and his colleagues had been using quinine as a prophylactic since the time they came into the country, a preventive measure against malaria. (This was standard precaution for all Europeans who came to Africa during the late nineteenth and early twentieth centuries.) They did not see this as a violation of their faith in divine healing: they believed that using anything that could prevent illness while living in a harsh climate was acceptable. However, in agreement with their Nigerian counterparts, they never resorted to drugs in the event of illness, they trusted only in prayers for recovery. But the missionaries also made it clear that even though, on their own part, they trusted entirely in prayers for healing, they were not against doctors or medicines, and that if a believer's faith was weak, there was nothing wrong in seeking medical help.

The missionaries were aware of their Nigerian counterparts' firmness on the issue of divine healing, but were convinced that their own position on the subject was completely scriptural, and that any seeming difference on the subject could only be superficial, that is, on the non-essentials, and definitely not the fundamentals. They assumed that in the event of a major debate over the issue, they could agree to disagree. But they could not have been more mistaken; they obviously had not counted on the diehard stance of their Nigerian partners that they later encountered.

In his response, Perfect was clear about the position of the missionaries, however, considering the sensitivity of the issue, he framed his answers with the intention of dousing the brewing tension; this unfortunately resulted in a long-winded and convoluted argument.[37] He ended by saying, "It is however a question of 'trust' or 'seeking to' either flesh on the one hand, or the Lord on the other. To voluntarily go to the doctor or make use of medicine etc, is to depart from our trust in the Lord." The only exception he said was for the man "who, laying helpless in his sickness finds a doctor brought to him by other people or a child who is under obedience to his parents, and takes medicine in obedience to them, has no need to depart from the Lord in his own heart and will."[38] Perfect, who was otherwise theologically sound, had to subject himself to so much muddle in his attempt to placate the Nigerian leaders.

When the Nigerian leaders read through Perfect's thesis, they decided to state their position in writing. "With reference to the above, we as a church do not teach that doctors and medicines are wicked and evil in themselves; but we do teach that the use of medicine is the world's way of obtaining healing, it is the way of unbelievers and it is diametrically opposed to God's way which is healing by supernatural divine power. The institution [medical science] is therefore unscriptural,"[39] the elders began. They emphasized that throughout the Bible God unequivocally declared "Himself as the Healer of His people," and therefore "He is the Physician to whom all His people should go for healing." Point by point, they sought to demolish Perfect's arguments.

For instance, to Perfect's statement that "we have no scriptural grounds for teaching that it is wrong to use such good things as God has given us for the protection of our bodies from getting sick," the elders responded that if the "good things" meant "medicines, drugs, quinine and other human remedies" then "we have no scriptural ground (not even a verse in the Scriptures)" that defends such a position, because "healing has definitely been promised through the atoning blood of our Lord and Saviour Jesus, as it is an incontrovertible fact that deliverance is greater than attack, so we believe that it is axiomatic also that the greater (divine healing) includes the less (divine protection)."[40]

To put the unfolding crisis into perspective, it is important to reiterate the fact that both the Apostolic Church's missionaries and the Nigerian leaders firmly believed in divine healing, and outstanding miracles of healing were consistently accomplished through the ministries of both groups. The crisis was, therefore, not over the basics of divine healing, but over one clause, just one clause, the insistence by the Nigerian leaders that faith in divine healing required total rejection of all medicines and doctors. They equated hospitals and medical science with idolatry, and concluded that it was sinful and tantamount to idolatry, for a Christian "to go to doctors for healing."[41] It was over this clause that the partnership that laid the foundation of the Pentecostal movement in Nigeria would eventually founder. As Harold Turner notes, "They [Faith Tabernacle leaders] had strong faith in divine healing and were consistent in their rejection of all medicines, both native and Western, and though all the overseas churches they dealt with also believed in faith healing, these did not carry it so far as to reject Western medicines and hospitals."[42]

At the July 1938 convention of the church held in Lagos, the Nigerian elders met with Perfect, Wellings, and Elton to discuss the issue; they "faced them with these facts with [a] definite promise that a letter would be sent through the president to the missionary committee in England."[43] The letter to the missionary committee in Bradford noted that "Pastor Perfect said that a believer in the Lord Jesus could use medicine, drugs and other human remedy as protection from being sick but should not use such remedies when he is actually sick, and he was informed that the statement was weak and absurd and scripturally groundless." The letter went on to state six points which articulated the position of the Nigerian leaders on the doctrine of divine healing and why they so vehemently rejected any hint or suggestion to the contrary. The "Wretched Tabernacles" would fight to their last breath to see to it that divine healing meant absolute trust in God for healing without recourse, absolutely no recourse, to any other remedy.

The first point stated that "the use of medicine, drugs, quinine or human remedies, either for protection or healing of the body in this country will only lead our people back to idolatry and will absolutely remove their confidence and trust in Christ as Saviour and Healer." The second, third and fifth points warned of a similar consequence, with the third saying that many people in the denominational churches in West Africa, "where converts have been allowed free use of medicines, drugs, quinine and other human remedy, either for protection or for healing for the body" had become "disgusted with Christianity as if there is no virtue therein and the power in the blood is trifled and nullified." The fourth point admonished that "if faith is once assassinated by the bad example of the leaders, it is impossible, humanly speaking, to resuscitate it." The sixth point: "That it is understood, however, in case of serious sickness, that a doctor may be called in for examination of the patient in compliance with the law of the country but this does not sanction the use of medicine, etc, by such a patient and should be done, in the first instance in consultation with the elders."[44]

Understanding the sixth point is crucial to understanding the stand of the Nigerian leaders. In the case of "serious sickness," a doctor could be called in by the permission of the elders; but this was not for the purpose of administering medication. It was just to satisfy the requirements of the law—so that the church could obtain a medical burial certificate without any hassles in the event of death—as they had been advised during the Myers fiasco. The sick person—adult or child—was still prohibited from taking any medication; if the person did not recover by faith in divine healing alone, then the person would die.

Studying documents from the early days of the Nigerian movement, particularly correspondence between Philadelphia and Lagos, there is overwhelming evidence that the inspiration behind this extreme stand on divine healing was Ambrose Clark. Clark's teachings largely shaped the movement in its first decade—his letters contained detailed instructions on how the Nigerian leaders were to apply the Scriptures to practically every aspect of life. As one early member noted, "Our unshakable stand today in matters of faith in divine healing, holiness and how to trust God wholly for all things by faith in the Lord Jesus Christ in answer to prayer, depends largely on the inspirational teachings inherited from Faith Tabernacle Congregation [Philadelphia] and our experiences in the past."[45]

Clark's teachings were, in the main, orthodox, but his views on certain subjects bordered on the extreme, and many of his instructions on divine healing can best be described as disturbing. One of Clark's letters to the Nigerian Faith Tabernacle leaders in the early 1920s sheds light on this point:

In response to a person dying without a physician: the same rule is in force in this country [America] as in your own. We do not believe in calling in a physician under any circumstances when a person is living. When a death occurs, the family notifies the undertaker and before he can get a permit to bury the dead person, a physician's certificate must be obtained. As no physician was attending the person who died, the official sends a physician to examine the dead body and to learn the circumstances of the death and they issue the necessary certificate. No one can be held responsible for the death of an adult person who has died without medical aid, any more than they could hold a person responsible for a member of their family committing suicide. In the case of children, the officers try to hold the parents responsible. Many years ago, they tried to make trouble if a child died without a doctor's attention, but as we placed all things into God's hands, we were delivered from every difficulty, and have been spared from all trouble since then. We are sure God will protect your interests there, as you take a stand to go through with Him regardless of the cost.[46]

Clark also encouraged the Nigerian movement to reject vaccination for their children. In a letter written most likely in early 1921, Odubanjo asked Clark about the church's stand on vaccination. Lagos had been ravaged by an epidemic and the government required all citizens to be vaccinated. This conflicted with Clark's stand on using medications and the leaders were unsure of how to respond to the government's directive.[47] Clark replied with the following instructions:

In response to the vaccination, I would state, we are firmly convinced that it is not scriptural to have it done. It brings us into the same position that the Hebrew children were in in the 3rd chapter of Daniel, where they were told to bow down to a human plan for blessing and protection and if they would not do it, there was only a fiery furnace left for them. They took their stand and refused to bow down, or trust in that golden image, and God delivered them and made the king—whose favour and pleasure they thought they would lose—give them better positions and bestow great favour upon them. We trust you will be strengthened, by God's grace to take the same stand for vaccination; and those who have been done [*sic*] will ask God to forgive them for this act, which they, no doubt, did in ignorance, and God will forgive them. As you refuse to have this done, in the future, you will find that God will greatly bless your firm stand to trust Him alone and refuse to submit to any law, or command, of men, which conflicts with God's Word and plan. We have taken this stand here and God has given us the victory unto the present time.[48]

Even though the Nigerian FT leadership cut ties with Philadelphia in the late 1920s, rejected Clark's opposition to the Pentecostal movement (Clark labelled it a "demoniacal manifestation"[49]), and were to a large extent diligent in judging his teachings with the Scriptures while the association lasted, somehow, they never reviewed his teachings on divine healing.

The letter to the missionary committee in Bradford included a two-point resolution "passed at a special conference of all pastors, elders and representatives of the Apostolic Church in Nigeria convened at the Lagos Chapel, commencing from the 25th to the 28th of July 1938, in which 40 members were present with a vote of the 40 as a whole" which stated that "any European Missionary of The Apostolic Church who by sacrifice, has already been here in West Africa, or is coming out to west Africa, should by the grace of God, be able as God's Spirit-filled believer by faith in the atoning work of Grace through the blood of our Lord and Saviour Jesus Christ, to adapt himself or herself to the standard of teaching of divine healing as taught and preached in the church, without the use of drugs, medicines, and quinine, either for protection or for healing of the body, under any circumstances whatsoever" and "that any such European missionary should not under any circumstance, teach or advise any member of the church or inquire contrary to Mark 16:17, 18 and James 5:14 to 16."[50]

According to historian John Peel, in a 1938 issue of *The Apostolic Herald*, Elton wrote about the ongoing debate, thereby throwing into the open the issues which had previously been discussed only in high circles.[51] If he had kept quiet, he would not have been Elton. In the meantime, the situation became tenser. For some time in 1938, Perfect and the other missionaries became personae non gratae in many districts of the church. Perfect wrote that "through a misunderstanding, I and the rest of our missionaries were debarred for several months from visiting the work in Ibadan and district."[52]

On receiving the letter from the Nigerian leaders, the Bradford committee requested the "opinion of the European Superintendents on the Nigerian Field."[53] When this had been received and processed, the committee drafted two documents: "A Reply to the African Pastors of the Apostolic Church in West Africa" and "A Concise Statement on the Question of Divine Healing."[54] These were sent under "seal of secrecy to Pastors C. H. Rosser, V. Wellings, I. J. Vaughan and S. G. Elton, missionaries on the Nigerian Field." Perfect was back in the UK by this time and was part of the team that prepared the documents. The recipients were instructed "carefully to peruse the contents of the reply and to let the

Committee have in time for the General Council meetings now in progression, their comments and suggestions on the same."[55] The committee relied on the response from the missionaries to prepare a final draft which was ratified by the church's council in the UK.

The response of the area superintendents and the missionaries was unanimous in its conclusion—they believed in divine healing, but an individual was free to resort to medicine if he or she felt the need for it; and also, they could not stop using quinine.[56] But the conclusion was not really the issue in contention—the missionaries' stand on divine healing had not changed—it was the wording of the reply that was in contention—how to say what they had always believed but without seeming to say it; how to say that they were in agreement with the Nigerian leaders on divine healing without saying that they were not in total agreement with them on divine healing.

Apart from the more general conclusion, Elton and Rosser (who had by now become superintendent in Lagos) had major recommendations for the committee. The recommendations of Elton and Rosser stand out both for their length and their differing approaches about the form that the reply should take.

Elton's recommendations insisted on the re-wording of some phrases in the reply to preclude any ambiguity. He believed the reply had to be less diplomatic and more straightforward, so that the committee's position would be very clear, once and for all. Elton's nature abhorred ambiguity! Elton suggested a replacement of indirect expressions with more pointed statements. For instance, in responding to one point, Elton stated, "Delete first paragraph of answer and substitute: 'We agree that failure on the part of any child of God to attain and maintain the divine standard of any aspect of truth tends to weaken the witness and testimony concerning those truths. Yet as in conversion and sanctification, so in divine healing, we cannot enforce faith or it ceases to be faith, but, conscious of our human failings we should encourage all to press forward to attain the goal of divine Perfection.' "[57]

Elton wanted no pretence; he wanted the church to face up to what it truly believed and not in any way continue to try to circumvent the issue. There was to be no sugar-coating; to continue to be diplomatic was to only prolong the evil day.[58] Elton thought one statement that suggested that the missionaries had been almost perfect in their conduct to be pointless: "Delete words 'and have thus far proved themselves amongst you as men of God sound in doctrine and practice, even though two have been nigh unto death and one has died.' This statement opens the door for personal indictments against any missionary and is not necessary."[59] And on and on Elton went.

Rosser, on the other hand, wanted a more diplomatic reply. The goal of the reply must not be to prove a point—because there was no point to prove—it had to be deliberately targeted at prolonging the discussion until hopefully there was a solution. "I fear that in the critical eyes of the brethren here at Lagos, your reply will not be accepted in its present form. You begin very well by crediting their belief upon the point in question, but in your later remarks you are inclined to draw back what you have said. Again, your language will not be new to them for they have heard it all before. Therefore you will be in danger of being accused by the more acute minds here of being persuaded by those who have been on the field and among them, instead of giving . . . your conviction as a body,"[60] he noted.

Rosser also cautioned against making any statement that could give the impression that the Apostolic Church in the UK was more concerned with the more sublime issues of the Christian life, and cared less about a more minor issue like divine healing: "I note with baffling interest the prophecy on Page 73 [that] Healing is not Perfection. That to me is only part of the whole truth. In that light I would be right in saying that the Incarnation, Atonement, Baptism of the Holy Ghost etc. is not perfection in their individual application to us, but each of them is a perfect truth and have their part to play in perfecting us."[61] "With all this in view," he concluded, "I cannot help but make a humble suggestion that will to my mind save the position, and that is, that you condense your remarks into a framed minute and not to answer categorically like you have done."[62]

In a bid to pacify the Nigerian leaders, the Bradford committee went as far as trying to prove that quinine was not medicine. (Rosser had written to the committee: "I for one cannot accept their [the Nigerian leaders'] assertion that it is strictly speaking medicinal. If the truth were known concerning its composition, we may find that it is possibly vegetable after all, some dispenser would probably help you to find this out, and if such is vegetable then it would be an invaluable defence for our policy."[63]) The committee obtained "an analysis of quinine from Messrs Richardson and Jaffe, the Public Analyst for the City of Bradford and the West Riding of Yorkshire."[64] We do not know whether the committee found the report useful or not.

In the reply from Bradford, which came in July 1939, a year after the letter from Nigeria was sent, the missionary committee tried its best to calm frayed nerves—it both defended its missionaries and also praised the Nigerian leaders for their devotion to God's word. While the committee was "convinced that in principle we are in full agreement with our African brethren in their declared stand for the truth of divine healing," it was however "not in agreement with their attitude towards those who fail to seek the Lord for healing or having done so do not experience healing and, because of this, turn to the use of medicines, drugs, quinine or other remedies." The ideal was for a Christian to live in divine health, but if a Christian was not yet walking at that level of faith, he or she was not to be harassed because of it. "It is the inestimable privilege of every believer in Christ to claim deliverance from sickness should he be thus stricken, and there is not only absolute power in God to heal but absolute provision . . . for it in the redemption purchased by Christ to restore such an one without recourse to any human aid whatever. But we feel that to adopt an intolerant attitude to those unable to rise to the highest course, or to those who are not healed, must be discouraged and discontinued. Thus it has ever been our endeavour to preach the highest standard of truth in regard to divine healing but to permit liberty of action to all."[65]

With regard to its missionaries' use of quinine, the committee made the point that its missionaries did not violate the Nigerian church's stand on divine healing; they only used quinine because of the peculiarities of the climate—excessive heat, mosquitoes, and other harsh conditions which the European was not accustomed to; when in their homeland, these missionaries did not need and did not use quinine. The committee explained, "It is acknowledged that those living in extremes of climate are especially endowed by nature with power to resist diseases which are prevalent in their particular climate. There is therefore a greater inherent tendency to sickness for those travelling to different climates, whether polar or tropical. Whilst admitting that God is able to keep in good health or heal sickness in all climates, it is obvious that it is a much greater test of faith for Europeans visiting tropical climates when they know of the great risks, than for Africans living in Africa. Therefore it becomes a matter of personal responsibility as to whether some means should or should not be adopted to assist the body to counteract the diseases to which it becomes specially subjected as the result of living in a climate to which it is not naturally accustomed."[66]

As such, the missionaries truly abided with the stand of the Nigerian leaders: they did not use drugs; quinine was for the peculiarity of the climate, the same way the Nigerian leaders, if they were to work in Europe would need "heavy raincoat, heavy over-coat and heavy woollen suit to prevent against attack of cold weather as well as taking of hot beverages to keep the body warm."[67]

The committee submitted its own resolutions: (I) "That divine healing is only one of the many aspects of the truth of the gospel of Christ for which we as a church are taking a definite stand in these days of apostasy"; (II) "That no aspect of truth must be emphasised by us to the exclusion or detriment of others equally as important in their location"; (III) "That all European missionaries of the Apostolic Church proceeding to West Africa, or any other country, should by the grace of God so live as to prove themselves sound in doctrine and practice on all fundamental principles including divine healing"; (IV) "That as a council in this country we appeal with all earnestness to our African brethren with whom God has brought us into contact in these last few years, that together, as those who have received the Vision of the Church, through whom God is going to make known His manifold wisdom, we should endeavour to keep the unity of the Spirit in the bonds of peace and thus cooperate with God to bring about His divine purposes."[68]

There was a flurry of activity around the country, "meetings upon meetings by a cross section of the leaders of the church,"[69] to decide how to respond to the reply from Bradford. While deliberations were still on-going before the Nigerian council sent its August 1938 letter, Sakpo, a respected prophet from the Ebute Metta assembly, gave a word from the Lord to the council. According to Adegboyega, "The Lord spoke through Pastor I. G. Sakpo that the letter decided to be written to the Missionary Committee, Bradford, England, was according to His will. And that if the Missionary Committee refused to agree with us on our stand on divine healing, that should be the end of our affiliation with them. But that if they agreed with our decisions, we should continue with them."[70] The council was unanimous in their acceptance of this prophetic counsel. The stand of the Nigerian leadership was, therefore, very clear before the letter was sent. But by the time the reply came, the leadership became polarized.

After one major congress (held after the Bradford reply came), a committee of seven was formed to look into the issue and advise the council. According to Ademakinwa, "This reply [from Bradford] brought about certain arguments. Some people wanted them [the Nigerian council] to act according to Prophet Isaiah Sakpo's prophecy to separate from the Britons; but the others wanted the whole issue explained to them again. A committee of seven was chosen to decide."[71]

Unfortunately, the great movement that had started with a handful of saints who formed the nucleus of the first Precious Stone group in Ijebu Ode in 1918, which had gone through many changes and phases of partnership and which by 1940 had become a vibrant nationwide movement, could not reconcile the differences that had begun to threaten its unity since the mid-1930s. Sides were taken, friendships broken, insults traded, blame passed, and eventually the house did not stand. By April 1940, the centre could no longer hold, and the great split occurred—the first split in Nigeria's Pentecostal movement. This split did not happen at once; it occurred in phases. There are indications that the issues at play in the breakup were not strictly based on the interpretation of the doctrine of divine healing; sectional loyalties definitely played a role.

The first group to break away from the partnership mainly included the healing evangelists and their loyalists—Joseph Babalola, Peter Olatunji, David Babajide, and J. A. Medaiyese—who had long been suspicious of the European missionaries.[72] This was after a major October 1939 meeting in Ibadan, attended by Odubanjo, Akinyele, Babalola, and other leaders. In leaving, they declared, "We cannot go back to Egypt the second time."[73] Odubanjo wrote to Elton after this that a section of the Nigerian leadership had formed the "Nigerian Apostolic Church."[74] Most of the churches in the Ilesa Area pitched their tents with them.

The leaders from Ebute Metta (Sakpo included), and many of the leaders in the Ilesa, Calabar, and Zaria areas, concluded that the letter from Bradford was in agreement with their stand on divine healing—that it didn't contradict the August 1938 letter. Adegboyega wrote that "when the reply of the Missionary Committee came, after examining it thoroughly, we leaders of Ebute Metta Assembly unanimously agreed to be loyal to The Apostolic Church vision in the country, whatever happened, because the Missionary Committee in England did not oppose our stated convictions."[75] The Ebute Metta leaders (made up of those who had earlier sided with the missionaries on the practice of the healing evangelists) had now come to see eye to eye with the European missionaries: they now believed that the strict interpretation of divine healing that they had all the while held on to was extreme.

The Elton family had travelled to the UK in April 1939 for their first furlough. They were still away when Babalola and his men left. Babatope, whose loyalty Idris Vaughan said was "tested to the utmost"[76] in the 1940 split, wrote in March 1940 that "in the absence of Pastor Elton, Satan worked hard to jeopardise the glorious work established here, but we praise God that 'He is able' and we, the Apostolic saints, are now marching on to victory. Jesus is our Captain, Hallelujah! Before we the supposed Apostolics here were not really Apostolic. We were semi-Apostolic, but God has wrought wonders in our midst."[77] The crisis had reached feverish heights by the time the Eltons returned to the country in November 1939. In January 1940, Elton wrote to the district officer, Ekiti Division:

In certain places however—such as Efon Alaye—Ijero—Ikere—and Ara we were constantly finding the leaders rebellious and wanting their own way and not willing to accept European supervision but merely to use us as a cloak to protect them from the Government. Particularly was this in the matter of the use of "holy water," and in spite of our teaching and instructions and the various agreements with the Government authorities, they still refuse to forsake this and other such practices.

These leaders, headed by Joseph Babalola of Efon, Pastor J. A. Medaiyese of Ikare, J. A. Olutayose (the leader of the emigration from Efon to Ife in 1936), Pastor J. F. Ekundayo of Efon, Pastor D. Fakunmi of Ilawe and Pastor J. B. Owolabi of Akure have refused any further assistance and have formed a church of their own called the Nigerian Apostolic Church, and are urging their people to reject European supervision and advice. Joseph Babalola claims the right of freedom to act as he feels led even though contrary to the agreements made with the authorities.

In view of such actions I have written to the following churches in Ekiti [Efon Alaye, Ara, Erio, Igede, Ilawe, Ijero, Ikoro, Ado Ekiti, Ilogbo, Ikere, Akure, Ondo, Iwaji Ido Ajinare] asking for their decision as to whether they still desire to belong to the Apostolic Church. In some cases they have agreed to do so, but it would appear that there is a big division of opinion and a danger of an uproar.

I have closed all the schools temporarily and I should be glad if you could help by bringing the question before the various Ekiti town councils, so that the congregations may be allowed to decide for themselves.[78]

Odubanjo, Akinyele and some of the early Faith Tabernacle leaders still held out some hope that a solution could be found. This hope would not last long. There was a major separation soon after: most of the churches in the Lagos and Zaria Areas remained under Odubanjo's leadership. Only four congregations in the Lagos Area, which had sixty churches; five in the Zaria Area, which had thirty churches; and almost all the churches in the Calabar Area chose to remain under the leadership of the European missionaries and the Nigerian leaders who sided with them (Adegboyega, Babatope, J. U. Udom and E. O. Ene).[79] The assemblies which chose to stay under the leadership of the European missionaries retained the name "the Apostolic Church." The churches which rallied under the leadership of Odubanjo, Akinyele, and Babalola were renamed Christ Apostolic Church (CAC). Esinsinade had left the movement in 1933 because of what he called the high-handedness of the Europeans; he thereafter focused on rebuilding the original Precious Stone Church in Ijebu Ode.[80]

Because Elton had the hapless task of managing the fallout from the split in its most volatile areas—the disputes about the ownership of property, the battle to retain the loyalty of individual congregations, and the struggles with the authorities, during which Elton had to constantly disassociate himself from the activities of the evangelists—he would be remembered by many of the evangelists in the years that followed the split as the European missionary who gave them the most trouble. This was especially so in the case of the church's property and the adherence to the 1936 agreement.

Once, when the district officer of Ekiti Division wrote to Elton saying that "I have received a complaint from the Alaye of Effon that the members of the Apostolic Church at Effon held meetings from 11:30 p.m. onward on the nights of 28th and 29th February, 1940. I have, therefore, to invite your attention to my letter . . . of 1936, and to ask for an assurance that breaches of the conditions on which the use of the land is granted will not recur,"[81] Elton distanced himself from the group. "I very much regret the occurrences complained of, but I would refer you to my letter of 18th Jan. 1940 where I outlined the position in regard to the Apostolic Churches in Ekiti. In the case of Efon the leaders have definitely refused European supervision and it is they who have committed the offence complained of. They now refuse to agree with the conditions laid down in your letter of . . . 1936."[82]

In fact, as late as 1949, the leadership of CAC still had an on-going battle with Elton. One of the sections of the minutes of the church's General Executive Council meeting of June 16, 1949, titled, "Warning to Pastor S. G. Elton," reveals the feelings of the CAC leaders: "The General Executive Council asked the Secretary to inform Pastor Elton that what transpired in his meeting with their General President, Pastor I. B. Akinyele at Ibadan has been reported to them and to warn him concerning the sphere of our Mission upon which he was encroaching. The secretary should also write the Apostolic Church Authority at Oke Oye to warn Pastor Elton over the disturbances he has been causing in our Area. Copies of this letter of warning should be sent to the Education Officer, Benin Province and to the Education Officer, Ondo Province. The District Officer and the Resident should be served each with a copy."[83]

Elton always praised the healing revival as one of the greatest things that had ever happened to Christianity in Nigeria. Publicly acknowledging this in Penygroes in 1939, he said, "The story of the Ilesa Revival is a lovely one—an illustration of how God used the weak and uncultured to bring to birth one of the greatest revivals in Africa."[84] In fact, decades later, and even till he died, Elton kept telling the story of the revival with excitement.

But he always believed that the healing evangelists' focus on the miraculous was unbalanced with regard to other realities of the Christian experience. For many years after these events, Elton continued to lament that the healing revivalists would not submit to the discipline required to attain greater heights of spirituality—he regretted that they were so held under the sway of the gifts of the Spirit, which truly operated mightily in their lives, that they were oblivious to the need for any other spiritual input. All through his missionary career, Elton amply demonstrated by his ministry and teachings that he was a staunch advocate of divine healing and the supernatural manifestations of the Holy Spirit, but he was always uncomfortable with extremes. And he believed that the healing revival had some extremes which ordinarily would not have been an issue if only the leaders were open to teaching and correction.

But despite these initial animosities, Elton and the key figures of the revival—particularly Joseph Babalola and Isaac Akinyele—would later work closely together. In fact, as will be seen, by the early 1950s, Elton had become one of Babalola's staunchest supporters, and it can be said with some latitude that, in a sense, Babalola embraced his spiritual leadership.

FOUR

"WHY THE HALO?"

Beverly Wells, an American missionary who served with her husband under Sydney Elton from 1961 to 1962 and from 1967 to 1970, gives us one of the most vivid descriptions of the Eltons' family life in Ilesa. Beverly and her husband, Delbert, had to live with the Eltons for four months when they first arrived in the country, because their accommodation was not ready.[1] Though the Eltons had been in the country for more than twenty years before the Wells came to live with them, Beverly's descriptions are still relevant for the early years, because the Eltons' family routine was fairly stable. Aside from her description of the house, which had changed, every other thing was as it would have been in the forties and fifties. Even Job Uwalaka, the cook who had been employed by the family in the late 1930s, was still around.

The first thing the Wells' quickly learned, but which they obviously enjoyed, was taking tea twice a day. Beverly remembered with childlike excitement the "piping hot tea served to us in our room"[2] early in the morning. Later in the day came another serving, but this one involved the whole household. Everyone would stop what they were doing and have a little chat while sipping their tea, which was usually accompanied by "tiny tea-time sweets."[3] The cakes and pastries (which could be filled with lemon curds, dried fruits, or flaky crusts), prepared only by Hannah and Ruth, were really delicious; this, of course, was no surprise: Hannah came from a line of expert chefs. These short communal periods were usually one of the highlights of the day.

Beverly was also forced to adapt to the very scheduled life of the Eltons. Every activity was timed: bathing, using the washing machine, and even having tea. Though at first uncomfortable with this somewhat regimented living, Beverly quickly realized it was necessary in order to get things done in an environment where a lot of things were makeshift. One example was the "washing machine." It was a "square wooden box set on a metal frame. It contained a large crank-type handle in the middle of the top of it and a wringer."[4] It was unlike any other she had seen before—of course it was a contraption of the Eltons, possibly with Job's technical help. To wash their clothes, they would "boil the water on the propane gas stove, pour it into the wooden basin, add Omo soap . . . and turn the handle backward and forward about 100 times to agitate."[5] This was done weekly. To get the best wash results for white materials, they would first boil the clothes on the stove before washing and "then hang in the sun to whiten them."

The Eltons dressed for dinner every evening in strict keeping with British culture. All guests had to join them in this. The table was usually set with lovely linen and silverware Hannah had brought with her from Shrewsbury. After dinner everyone would sit in the living room and listen to the BBC broadcasts; usually the men were more interested in this than the ladies.[6] Elton never missed listening to the BBC World News at 9:00 p.m. He considered it very important to keep track of what was happening everywhere in the world at any given time. His knowledge of current affairs and history was vast and he was very good at matching this with Bible prophecy.

Bode Akintade, a protégé of Elton for many years, was always amazed as he listened to him connect eschatology and world events. "He did not have a television; he only owned a transistor radio. But Pa Elton knew what was happening around the globe at any time. He would say, 'This happened in Germany after World War II, then it happened in Britain and now this is what will happen in Nigeria.' He connected these events seamlessly and never failed to hit target. When Pa Elton told you how something would turn, you either agreed or disagreed—but it was only a matter of time; it happened as he had prophesied. He projected into the future by his knowledge of the past and the present and it produced tremendous results."[7]

Akintade was spot on in this observation. We see an example of this in one 1984 sermon: "Economically the world is in a terrible mess; no one knows the solution to the problem of inflation. I heard a speaker the other day say that the great economists in America, in Harvard, and Yale Universities have ceased trying to predict the future. President Carter and later President Reagan called his economic advisers together and asked them to come up with a solution to the economic situation of America. Because if America can get it right economically, the rest of the world has some hope. There is no solution. And you must prepare for that in your mind and in the working out of your budget. You must prepare for that in Nigeria. We haven't seen anything in inflation yet; it will go through the ceiling. Money is going to be very little, practically with no value in Nigeria in the near future. Not this year and not next year, but very soon."[8] On Sunday evenings, the radio would be tuned to Billy Graham and other Christian programmes. This was usually a spiritually refreshing time.

Beverly and Hannah would sometimes take strolls in the evening. This was always a good opportunity for Beverly, then in her twenties, to learn about missionary life from an old hand. They were sometimes accompanied on these outings by Sue, Hannah's dog, a black cocker spaniel, and less frequently by the ginger-coloured Judy, Ruth's dog.[9] Many evenings were also spent in needle work of all kinds: knitting, crocheting, tatting, and embroidery. Female visitors, usually wives of missionaries, also participated in this craft, in which Hannah and Ruth were experts. Hannah had been a professional seamstress back in the UK and Ruth had been introduced to sewing when still very young. Ruth has kept one of her practice cardboards from that time.

Job Uwalaka did much of the cooking and was responsible for purchasing food items from the market. Once every week, the cold store (as it was called) opened for business. This was a store that brought in a truck with perishable foods such as "cheese, butter and some meat imported from European countries."[10] All the Europeans, and some Nigerians living in Ilesa, would congregate on that day to make their purchase and then wait until the next week when the store would open again. These supplements to the local food were a big blessing to the Europeans living in Ilesa. It saved them the trouble of travelling to Ibadan just to be able to purchase their favourite European foodstuff every now and then. Less frequently, the truck would bring into town rare foods like apples and chestnuts (mostly during the Christmas period), causing a lot of excitement in the white community.[11]

The Eltons feature in several photos of all-white Christmas parties organized by the European community in Ilesa. One taken in 1940 has

Ruth and Jane Hunter (a girl who was about two years younger than Ruth and whose father was a doctor at the Wesley Guild Hospital) beside Father Christmas holding a bag of gifts; standing beside them is Reverend Nelson Ludlow; behind him is a maid carrying baby Peter Ludlow; Elton and his wife are watching with delight in the background. The picture was taken in the Ludlows' compound. Nelson Ludlow, a Methodist missionary who arrived in Ilesa in 1932, worked there till 1946 before he was transferred to work in other parts of Nigeria. The Ludlow family were well acquainted with the Eltons during this period. A December 1947 picture shows Elton dressed up as Father Christmas for that year's celebration. Another photograph which was most likely taken ca. 1952, labelled "Christmas afternoon tea," shows Andrew Pearson and his wife and baby; missionaries of the Apostolic Church—R. Brunt, J. Kirkwood, C. T. Morris, A. H. Lewis and their families; two unmarried ladies, and Ruth and Hannah.

From the time Hannah Elton arrived in Ilesa, she became heavily involved in "women's work." She has been duly credited by one of the Apostolic Church's historians as "one of the forerunners in this type of work."[12] The "women's work" is described: "Domestic training instruction is also given by the wives of our missionaries in various areas. The indescribable conditions in which women live, work and rear their children were obviously among the major problems to be solved. So the women were taught the simplest ways of cleanliness, cookery, nursing, sewing, care of children and such-like hygiene."[13] Hannah would make an interesting remark in later years about how difficult it was to break ground: "My first job after I was here a short while was to help to train the women, because they didn't know anything about training. And the pastor and the men said, 'She wouldn't change our women.' And when I talked to the women about the men, they said 'well you won't change our men.' But in a few months' time, the men were coming, begging me to take their wives. They had seen the change in the women that had been trained. So the big difficulty was that the women were not trained. . . . They enjoyed church, but their homes were still not what God intended."[14]

Hannah was following in the steps of contemporaries like Joyce Ludlow, Nelson Ludlow's wife, who arrived in Ilesa five years before her and in 1935 set up a Home Craft Centre which "made a distinctive contribution to girls' education."[15] The centre taught "a whole new 'enlightened' way of life" which ranged from "hygiene to reduce infant mortality to new home craft skills, as well as marketable qualifications."[16] Knowing that the

Eltons and Ludlows enjoyed a good relationship, it is most likely that Joyce's experience and expertise (she was a medical doctor) would have rubbed off on Hannah. Hannah made such a great impact on the lives of many women in Ilesa during her first two years that when her family was to go on furlough in 1939, the women trooped out to testify of what God had done through her. One of them said Hannah had taught her how to love her husband and children.[17] Despite tremendous success in this work, Hannah always made it clear that her first assignment was to look after her husband, to make sure he fulfilled his call. Thus, when the missionary committee in Bradford directed her to serve fully as a missionary alongside her husband and send reports on all her activities like every other missionary, she objected, insisting that she was in Nigeria primarily to ensure that her husband succeeded in his work. Hannah could be just as stubborn as her husband if she thought a directive was not right.

For his part, Elton was always clear-eyed about missionary work. While there was no doubt that he was one of the most courageous and competent missionaries on the field, he never pretended that it was not a very challenging task. "It has often been very embarrassing to have to listen to the many flattering statements made about missionaries, especially when they are missionaries from Africa," Elton once said in response to the prevailing stereotype about missionaries labouring in the continent, which was often revealed in statements like, "My, it must be wonderful to be a missionary."

"People always seem stirred by stories of God's dealings with our African brethren and seem to regard the poor missionary as a hero. I have often mused in my heart . . . 'if only they knew what it feels like!' "[18] In an article titled "Why the Halo?" Elton debunked the myths associated with the call: "At the risk of stripping missionary life of some of its glamour, I want to try and tell you what it *does* feel like to be a missionary," he began.[19] "It is certainly a wonderful call and a very big honour, but a missionary soon realises that he is just the same person on the foreign field as he was in the homeland. . . . Whilst in the homeland, in the midst of the excitement and thrill of the 'call,' everything seems wonderful and you look forward to your new sphere of service vowing that you are going to begin a new life for the Lord. But the trouble starts as soon as you step aboard the ship. When it is known that you are a missionary (and this is quickly discovered), you are looked at and questioned by the 'old coasters' [Europeans who had been in Nigeria for some time—mostly government officials and businessmen—majority of whom were opposed or apathetic to Christian missionary enterprise] as to why you need to 'upset' the heathen, who are far happier without your interference."

The situation was not very different when the missionary finally arrived at his station: "On the mission station you find that here more than anywhere else, you are a 'marked man.' You very likely find yourself amongst those whom you would never have chosen as fellow-workers, and who would certainly have never chosen you!!! You miss the friendly atmosphere of the Homeland services; you long for some of the old friends to talk to; you betray your home-sickness by constantly worrying why the mail has not arrived; and then you begin to pity yourself. Self-pity is a ruthless foe and needs strong handling, especially during those first few years when homesickness is so often acute, and the sea that divides you from loved ones seems cruelly vast and separating. You speedily realise that you are not the 'strong hero' that many in the homeland think you are. As you begin your mission station life, you soon discover afresh your weaknesses and failings, forgotten perhaps in the whirl of events since leaving the homeland."[20]

Character issues were real and not to be taken for granted; it could be the making or breaking of a missionary's career: "If you are of the 'bossy' sort, you may rebel against having to be taught how to be a missionary. You do not realise that missionary life is entirely different from any other kind of work in the old country and no matter how experienced you may be in the work 'at home,' yet you have to begin all over again to learn to be a missionary. At home, you were the 'leader,' now you have to be the learner. That needs grace and still more grace. If you are of a submissive nature then you are inclined to lose your individuality and to slip gradually into a comfortable rut, letting others do the work. If you are of an enthusiastic temperament you may be asked to work with a colleague who is reserved and who dislikes your enthusiasm and energy. If you are of the quiet sort, your colleague may be just the opposite and his enthusiasm and energy tries and tires you. And remember, there are so many days and hours that have to be spent together and whatever your temperament, you will be certain to find plenty of opportunities for self-discipline and grace, to seek to acquire that wonderful quality of being 'easy to live with' which so many of us seek after but so sadly lack."[21]

Then there was the climate, *that* tropical climate, which tried every white man, even the strongest of them: "Then there is the climate to be faced and, in West Africa, this is a very big problem. Unconsciously it takes its toll and you soon find that you cannot be as energetic as you were in the home-land. The heat and humidity tend to make one irritable, over-sensitive and touchy, and the devil sees to it that you get abundant chances of taking offence. He also tries to make mole hills seem mountains, and small and petty misunderstandings that in normal life would have been laughed off, now assume mighty proportions and can quickly cause tension and even division between colleagues. Brooding over real or imaginary slights is fatal and may easily wreck a missionary's career. You are often called upon to do things that you consider unnecessary; to walk long distances through the sweltering bush; to endure long 'palavers' and seemingly endless discussions so that you have to go without food or drink for perhaps six or seven hours—and still to keep sweet!"[22]

Overcoming the language barrier was hard work: "Further there is the problem of the language, which demands endless patience and endurance. You are faced at the beginning with a crowd of dark skinned kindly people who greet you with long strings of words of welcome, while you stand helplessly before them, just longing to say something but being unable to say anything beyond a badly worded 'Thank you.' "

Even more discouraging were the long months or sometimes years of labouring and waiting before the spiritual fruits would come: "Sometimes the work is hard and there does not seem much response to your advice and instruction but you must learn that only the Holy Spirit can move men and change hearts and that He is at work in the unseen. . . . Somehow things seem entirely different from what you dreamed when you were called; there is no big sweeping revival immediately you arrive; the people listen carefully to all you have to say but are slow to take any action."

"But perhaps the greatest of all trials to a young missionary is loneli-ness," wrote Elton. "To be sent to a part of the country where there is no European fellowship and where you get the mail only once or twice a week. Where there are no shops, no newspapers, no radio, no callers except the constant stream of needy people calling for your patient attention; where the food is strange and mostly 'native,' and not too plentiful. Then comes the test. Then the new missionary discovers he is not a hero but just a weak needy child of God. Tears are often ready to fall and, unless he is careful, the missionary is tempted to give it all up and ask to be recalled."[23]

When Elton was sure that he had given a more realistic perspective of missionary life in Africa, sufficient to disillusion friends and well-wishers at home, he was careful to make the point that despite the challenges, serving as a missionary on the continent was a noble assignment and he would not for any reason trade places with anyone in the homeland. He assured prospective missionaries that the article was not to scare them or make them change their minds; it was to prepare them for what they would experience. "But do not forget the Master," Elton began rounding off, "He it is who has called and He knows all the pathways, and it is then we can prove His words: 'Lo, I am with you always.' " "The missionary then learns that it is not by power but 'by My Spirit' that the Lord is building His Church, and that human effort, however able and directed will not replace the work of the Holy Spirit. Have I been too pessimistic? Are you [more] discouraged now, [than] when you felt led to offer yourself to the Lord for the foreign field? May I just conclude by one word? As time goes by and the period of adjustment passes and you look back over the years of service and learning on the field, then you feel happy and glad that it was not otherwise, for you have learned much of the Lord by the way. Whilst missionary life seems to be one constant battle, yet, let me emphasize this also, it is wonderfully satisfying and I would not willingly change places with anyone in the homeland now. But why the halo? To Him be the glory for His patience and kindness, perseverance and love to the poor missionary. It is but our reasonable service to render our bodies, our minds, and our whole lives to Him."[24]

Every missionary looked forward to furloughs. They were times of resting and recuperating; reuniting with family and friends; and going round churches to tell stories of trials and give testimonies of triumphs, which was equally a psychological booster and a powerful tool for raising support for the work on the mission field. Ruth remembers the family going around speaking in several churches around the UK during their 1939 furlough.

One of the high points of this trip was when Elton stood before the crowd at the Apostolic Church International Convention at Penygroes to give a report of his first term as a missionary to Ilesa: "I am grateful for three reasons to be able to stand before you tonight. Firstly, on my own account; secondly, on behalf of Ilesa; thirdly, on your account; that, you may be fully enlightened of the tremendous opportunity and need in that part of Nigeria. On my own account I am grateful that the Lord has preserved, protected and spared our lives, through the past two years whilst living in Nigeria. These years have been two of the happiest and the healthiest of my life and it has been a great privilege and honour to have been allowed to see what God has been doing in Ilesa."[25]

The first article Elton sent back home for publishing in *The Apostolic Herald* after his arrival in the country in 1937 was titled "Kings Shall Fall Down before Him."[26] It was a clear call of his apostolic spirit; it was a hint of that overcomer theme that would dominate much of his theology. Elton's mind was fashioned to conquer territories. Throughout his time as superintendent, the Ilesa Area was the most influential centre of the Apostolic Church's work in Nigeria. In a letter of appeal to the members of the church in the UK while on furlough in October 1939, Elton said, "I am sure that never before in the history of the Apostolic Church have we been given such a wonderful opportunity of spreading the Gospel, as that existing today in the big Ilesha Area of Nigeria."[27]

Once, describing the fervency of the Ilesa church, Elton wrote: "Ilesha has been the scene of much rejoicing during the past three months. To begin with, there was the annual Easter Convention. This was attended by many thousands of people, representatives coming from all the different areas in Nigeria and it was a time of great joy and happy fellowship. . . . The people are hungry for the truth. Often when someone was speaking on the glorious truths of the Gospel, one of the truths would strike the congregation like a flash of discovery, and all the people would interrupt him, rising to their feet and starting to sing one or other of the familiar Apostolic choruses in Yoruba, accompanied by stamping of bare feet, clapping of hands and swaying of bodies. It was indeed a wonderful experience to see so many coloured people gathered together and rejoicing in the God of their salvation."[28]

At the beginning of 1940, there were four congregations in Ilesa town—Oke Oye, Oke Igbogi, Oke Iro and Oke Eso—with a total membership of about four thousand. The Ilesa Area had about one hundred and seventy churches, "many of them with congregations of over 1,000."[29] After the 1940 split, the scope of the work was greatly reduced. Elton, who had formerly led close to two hundred churches, was now left with the four assemblies in Ilesa and some assemblies in the Yagba and Ekiti districts.

From his base at Oke Oye, he, alongside the leaders in the other parts of the country, started to rebuild the Apostolic Church in Nigeria from the remnant that the fire had left. By 1942 the Lagos Area had twenty-five churches and stations under its care; the Ilesa Area one hundred and twenty-five churches; the Calabar Area over three hundred churches, and the Zaria Area three churches.[30]

For the Ilesa Area, this was a pretty amazing recovery. The only area which had more churches than the Ilesa Area, the Calabar Area, had been untouched by the crisis of 1940; it had about the same number of assemblies in 1942 as it did before the crisis. Elton was truly determined to make "kings fall down before Him." Writing in the January 1940 *Herald of Grace* about the church's recently concluded convention, which had "Peace" as its theme, he declared, "But there is one realm with which we cannot declare peace, the realm of the powers of darkness. We are committed to a life-long struggle with them and particularly in Nigeria are we aware of the reality of the struggle."[31] He reported in April 1944: "The last two years in Ilesa has [*sic*] seen some big changes. They have been years of consolidation, teaching, training, but today in Ilesa there exists a stable Christian body of people, who are gradually assimilating apostolic truths and showing a desire to conform to God's high standards of faith and living."[32]

As the work expanded, Elton never failed to cry out for more labourers—European missionaries and Nigerian pastors and evangelists—to join in the field of harvest. Once, obviously overwhelmed by the need for more workers, he made an appeal in *The Apostolic Herald* for more people in the United Kingdom to volunteer as missionaries:

Yet still He calls. Thank God for those who have heard His call and whose souls have been filled with joy in working with Him. There are many, but too few to meet the growing needs, even in our own church. It is the privilege and responsibility of the saints in the homeland to see that these needs are met. . . . The enemy is very, very busy, the time is very short; opportunities are slipping away. Let us rise and in prayer seek to know the Will of God for each one of our lives. He calls; He knows the needs and can supply them all. The men and women He needs for His work on the mission fields are just ordinary human beings, plus dominating unselfish devotion to Himself, wrought by the Holy Ghost.

It may mean death, but what of that? It will mean privation and isolation, but for how long? It will mean suffering and weariness, but what is that compared with the joy of walking and working with the Master? I would venture to say that no one has really known the depths of surrender until he has experienced these lessons. But the joy He gives . . . none but His loved ones know! That is the vision and challenge of Ilesha. The Master waits; the unsaved wait; the seekers wait; and we who have answered wait for more help. Will you give it? A lot may depend upon it. But be assured of this, that whatever happens, God is going to find someone to send to the waiting multitudes. By His grace we will go forward—even to death—and the people shall hear the Gospel; he shall be glorified and Jesus shall reign.[33]

Nevertheless, Elton gave more priority to the training of Nigerian leaders. "Whatever else the Apostolic Church in Ilesa does and leaves undone, we must give *our best* to the training of these [Nigerian] workers. A missionary can do more for Africa and Christ by preparing Africans to go out and preach the Gospel than he can possibly do by going out into the villages himself with the Gospel,"[34] he wrote in 1945. In addition to travelling to various towns to supervise the work of the mission, Elton's other major focus when he arrived in Ilesa was to lead the church's Bible school, which had been started by Babatope.

Giving the background to this early thrust of his ministry in Ilesa, Elton wrote: "It is just over seven years since the Lord raised up Joseph Babalola in the Ilesa district and used him to proclaim the Gospel. His fiery message attracted eager crowds; literally thousands turned from idols to serve the living God. It soon became apparent that something must be done to instruct those who had been converted. Pastor Babatope felt that this was the work God had called him to undertake."[35] Babatope, he continued, "began teaching the people the Scriptures, but as the numbers grew he found it impossible to deal with the problem alone. On Sundays, so vast were the masses, who gathered to hear the Word that it was often necessary for three speakers to address different sections of the crowd at the same time. As a result of this preaching, many assemblies grew up quickly around Ilesa. Then the difficulty arose as to teachers and leaders. Pastor Babatope thought the best thing was to set about training several young men. This he did and it was out of this that the Ilesa Bible School originated. After a period varying between 12 and 18 months, these young men were sent out to take charge of various out-stations."

Elton took over leadership of this school when he arrived in Ilesa and immediately brought his passion for leadership training to bear on the task. Babatope, testifying of Elton's early days in the country, spoke about his devotion to this aspect of the work: "About 90 assemblies are thirsting to have good leaders, trained leaders in the Apostolic Church. We do not have them. They have left the churches and idols, but do not know how to serve God. Pastor Elton, whom you sent to us, has seen this need, but what he has done is to preach to the young men to tell them to sanctify themselves and give themselves to the Word of God. We have got about 80 young men whom now Pastor Elton is teaching, day and night, preparing them to meet the need, for the need is very great."[36]

A typical day at the Bible school, which ran for five days a week, began at 5:00 a.m. with an exhortation from the Scriptures lasting for an hour. The students then dispersed to reassemble at 9:00 a.m. in the school's compound for another hour of Bible instruction. English, Yoruba and Arithmetic were taught for the rest of the morning. The afternoons were spent in private study before one more address from the Scriptures during the evening prayers. When the Friday lessons were over, the students were sent to different outstations "for practical experience."[37]

The staff was usually made up of Elton and other pastors, who were mostly European missionaries. We do not have any record of the curriculum at the Ilesa school, but Cyril Rosser's much smaller Bible school at Ebute Metta gives us an idea of the Ilesa curriculum. The course at Ebute Metta was divided into General Studies, "which covered a large field of study in character, method, and discipline, the doctrine of the Church being particularly dealt with."[38] There were twenty-eight lessons in all: Homiletics dealt with the basics of sermon building and had twelve lessons; the remaining sixteen lessons were divided between Simple English Studies, mainly a "treatise upon tricky words that sound alike but mean something totally different. Nouns, verbs, adjectives . . ."; and Scripture text placing, which "took the form of drafting certain scriptural principles in opposition to the modern and sceptical views generally met by every Christian."[39] The Scofield Study Bible was the preferred reference Bible at the school. In addition to the Ilesa school, Bible training centres were set up in several districts to cater for the ever-growing number of pastors and evangelists. As an example, when the missionary house at Aiyeteju in the Yagba district was built, Elton and his family would usually go to spend about three weeks there, to train the workers.

In 1945 the church opened its government-approved teacher training centre called "Elementary Training Centre"[40] in Ilesa, and Elton was the pioneer principal. According to Elton, "We set up our own teacher training centres with government approval and I was privileged to be the principal of my own training centre for the first six years—the only Full

Gospel training centre in all of West Africa—from which we sent out hundreds of trained teachers to minister in the day schools of West Africa."[41] His role as pioneer principal again lends credence to his educational training because, according to the advertised vacancy for a new principal in the July 1950 issue of *The Apostolic Herald*, any applicant had to possess "a degree or a teaching diploma," because only "a man with one of these qualifications will be accepted by the Government of Nigeria."[42]

We learn from Edgar Parkyns, who became principal after this advertisement, that the teacher training centre was entirely a result of Elton's vision and planning. "These problems were foreseen and met by the wise policy of instituting our own Teachers' Training Centre, and our educational scheme is sound, healthy, and proportionate to the work. The Africans are very conscious that their happy state in this connection is entirely due to the wise planning of the Superintendent [Elton], in the establishment of a training centre."[43]

In a letter to the chief inspector of education for Oyo Province in 1946, the Resident wrote about Elton's activities concerning the school: "With reference to your unnumbered confidential letter of the 20th March, so far as I can ascertain there are no political objections to the granting of assistance to a school belonging to the Apostolic Church at Ilesa. This church is well established at Ilesa and holds substantial grants of land, and no complaints about the church have been made to the District Officer, Ife. Mr Elton who is the chief pastor in the area has perhaps some peculiar ideas, but he is an enthusiastic member of a number of local committees and his conduct has not been the subject of any complaint. No political or educational objections appear to have been raised to the opening of an Elementary Training Centre by this church."[44] Elton was writing in 1952, "The students in the Teacher Training section include representatives from Government-sponsored Schools as well as from the Salvation Army, Assemblies of God and our Eastern areas of Nigeria. You will therefore realise that the Centre wields a big influence in many ways."[45] The training centre must definitely have been making a major contribution to the educational advancement of Nigeria for it to have merited the visit in 1951 of Nigeria's governor-general, Sir John Stuart Macpherson.[46]

In addition to itinerating throughout the Ilesa Area, Elton was responsible for the training and coordination of the work of the many missionaries who were serving under him: Donald McGill, who arrived in Nigeria in 1942; J. G. Brown, 1943; J. Kirkwood; H. L. Copp, 1945; Cecil Morris,

1948; Vernon Wood; Eric Williams, 1951; Vera Allan, Roger Brunt; A. H. Lewis, and some others.[47] He was also very involved in strengthening the national leadership: "I have been the instrument, the channel in Nigeria to call and ordain dozens of apostles—from Calabar to Kano and Kaduna to Lagos."[48] In 1949, Rosser, who had been in Nigeria for fifteen years, the greater part of which he had served as the European superintendent in charge of the Lagos Area, left Nigeria permanently.[49] Rosser's departure made Elton the most senior European superintendent in the country. "I was number one superintendent for the whole of Nigeria,"[50] said Elton.

After their first furlough in 1939, the Eltons next travelled to the UK in 1944.[51] Ruth has vivid recollections of the trip. World War II was in its final years, and they had to travel on a troop ship which moved in a convoy. The missionaries on board regularly held services with the padre, and during service one morning, with the congregation singing the hymn "Eternal Father," their accompanying battle ship, a destroyer, began firing at what was most likely an enemy submarine. Ruth remembers praying several times that God would surround their ship with a mist to prevent enemy ships from attacking them.[52] The family safely arrived in Liverpool on March 16. Elton tried to return to Nigeria after a few months but couldn't, because most commercial ships were busy in the war effort. He eventually secured a place on a troop ship which departed from Liverpool sometime after June 1945.

Ruth remembers that her father "was on the water when the end of the war was declared."[53] Hannah and Ruth stayed back in the UK because they couldn't secure seats on any ship. During this period Ruth was enrolled in a private school in Shrewsbury; they later joined Elton in Nigeria in 1946. The family went on furlough again in 1948[54]—only Elton and his wife returned in November of that year; Ruth stayed back to attend secondary school. Elton and Hannah travelled again to the UK in April 1950,[55] during which time they enrolled Ruth in a technical college to specialize in the arts and in dress making. Elton alone returned to the country in August.

We have a surprising entry in the July 14, 1949, minutes of the missionary committee meeting in Bradford: "Pastor Elton is stressing the need and reiterating his appeal for a relief superintendent as he feels his strength is waning and he will not be able to remain indefinitely in Africa."[56] About two years later, in referring to a similar letter Elton had sent to them, the committee minutes recorded: "There is one statement in his [Elton's] letter which is rather veiled concerning his future and we would like the secretary to ask Pastor Elton if he can clarify this statement in the near future."[57] About three months later, one of the missionaries in Ilesa mentioned in a letter that "Syd's [Elton] talking of resigning from being Schools Manager."[58] Was Elton simply getting tired of Africa, or was he experiencing a burnout after so many years on the field, or was it a sign of dissatisfaction with the state of the denomination that he was a part of? Elton had a deep reservoir of endurance, and in light of the saga that would unfold just a few years down the line, it is more likely that his "waning strength" was more a symptom of an underlying dissatisfaction rather than a real burnout.

FIVE

RAIN

B y the late 1940s, the glory days of the healing revival were beginning to fade into a distant memory. Also, the avalanche of Pentecostal outpourings of baptism in the Holy Spirit; manifestations
of the gifts of the Spirit; and the spontaneous revival that had marked the
previous decade had come down to a trickle. These phenomena had
become the exception rather than the norm. It was common talk among
many missionaries of the Apostolic Church in Nigeria that the work had
degenerated into a routine and that there was the need for a new outpouring. Cecil Morris, one of the missionaries in Ilesa, hinted at this situation
in a January 1951 article published in *The Apostolic Herald* (*TAH*): "It is
very noticeable that in the main, spiritual values change with the second
and third generations of most denominations, and often with the change
comes a deterioration of spiritual life and power. This is clearly seen in
missionary work, and, where it has taken place, sad indeed has been the
result."[1]

Using the analogy of an organization that had lost its *raison d'être*,
Morris warned that the church was dangerously drifting in a similar
direction: "A firm of repute once installed a very complicated system of
keeping accounts. Sometime afterwards a member of the directorate was
asked how business was. 'Oh,' he said, 'we have had to give up business to
attend to the new system.' "[2] "There are many varied ways of approach to
the presentation of the Gospel," he continued. "What succeeds in one
country fails in another; but whatever the manner of approach may be, it is

but subsidiary and not the substance. Therein, it seems to me, lies our most subtle temptation."[3]

As Elton would complain in later years, the focus of the church had shifted from the pursuit of the presence of God to merely managing an institution: "In the 1930s, God tried and broke through [in] the new revival. . . . It was the revival where healing became recognised and known as being from God. Thousands of people received healing and many of the Pentecostal churches were started because of the healing revival. But, the healing revival turned inwards and became a denomination and the healing power largely evaporated. . . . It turned inwards and it began to die and it will continue to die as long as mankind gets his hands on it, and turns it inwards to build a commercial system for himself."[4]

Articles published in *TAH* by the missionaries of the Apostolic Church in Nigeria during this period show a longing for revival in the church's mission in Nigeria. "We are constantly praying for a mighty revival, and rightly too, for it is sorely needed,"[5] wrote E. L. Derry from the Calabar Area in January 1951. Vernon Wood, reporting of the church's Yagba convention held in late 1951, said, "The Lord promised that 1952 would be a year of real revival but unless His servants were prepared and yielded to Him the revival would sweep by them. His servants must come down from their exalted positions and bow to Him."[6]

The title of a long poem by Vera Allan, another missionary in Nigeria, published in December 1951, was "Rain On Mown Grass,"[7] with the theme Scripture being "Surely the people is grass" (Isaiah 40: 7) and "He shall come down like rain upon the mown grass" (Psalm 72: 6). Cecil Morris wrote in late 1952 or early 1953: "The showers of God's Spirit are greatly needed in organised Christianity. Speaking generally, the people of God seem very hard and unbending, and there is a notable absence of deep conviction and repentance of heart. There is a dryness, too, in many services; and the unction of God's Spirit is not upon the preaching of the Word—at least, not as it ought to be, considering our noble heritage. May I suggest one sure remedy to meet the urgent need? We need the showers to fall upon us."[8] Leila Williams, based in Ilesa, wrote in November 1951, "There seems to be an air of expectancy everywhere as revival is promised for 1952."[9]

The Pentecostal movement around the world was also experiencing a major slowdown at this time. In fact, it had begun about a decade earlier. There was a general feeling among Pentecostals that the previous decade was characterized by "spiritual dryness and lack of God's presence."[10] One historian describes the general mood in Pentecostal circles during this period: "In the third quarter of the 1940s the modern Pentecostal movement was over 40 years old and much of its denominational life had become ritualised. The former spontaneity and manifestations of the gifts of the Holy Spirit had often become lost in regular church life and relegated to a theoretical status. From the mid-1930s there was a spiritual hunger and many longed for a revival of the energy accompanied by signs of the Holy Spirit's presence which had characterised Pentecostal life at the beginning of the century."[11] Wrote one commentator likewise, "In the hearts of all those hungry for God was a cry for a fresh visitation. Those in the ministry as well as those in the pew felt a deep and longing hunger for more from heaven. There was an acknowledgment from many in the ministry and also from those in official positions to this effect."[12] Pentecostal giants like John G. Lake frequently expressed deep concern at what they considered to be the "institutionalization and denominalization of the Pentecostal movement."[13] It was into this atmosphere that what came to be known as the Latter Rain Revival of 1948 broke out.

On February 12 and 13, 1948, a revival started in North Battleford, Saskatchewan, Canada, among Bible school students at the Sharon Orphanage and Schools who had been waiting on the Lord for an outpouring of the Holy Spirit.[14] Ern Hawtin, one of the faculty members at Sharon, recounts the beginning of the outpouring: "Some students were under the power of God on the floor, others were kneeling in adoration and worship before the Lord. The anointing deepened until the awe of God was upon everyone. The Lord spoke to one of the brethren. 'Go and lay hands upon a certain student and pray for him.' While he was in doubt and contemplation one of the sisters who had been under the power of God went to the brother saying the same words, and naming the identical student he was to pray for. He went in obedience, and a revelation was given concerning the student's life and future ministry. After this a long prophecy was given with minute details concerning the great things God was about to do. The pattern for the Revival and many details concerning it were given."[15]

In the days that followed, there were manifestations of God's power and the gifts of the Holy Spirit, which included healing and prophecy. Many also immediately received specific gifts when hands were laid on them to equip them for the ministry to which they had been called. Hosea

6:1-3 provided much inspiration for the revival: "Come, let us return to the LORD. For He has torn *us*, but He will heal us; He has wounded us, but He will bandage us. He will revive us after two days; He will raise us up on the third day that we may live before Him. So let us know, let us press on to know the LORD. His going forth is as certain as the dawn; and He will come to us like the rain, like the spring rain watering the earth."[16]

News of the Canadian outpouring spread, and people flocked to these meetings from all around North America. Afterwards, the main leaders of the Sharon movement began to receive invitations to speak all over North America. Historian Richard Riss offers an explanation about how the movement spread so quickly and widely: "One of the distinctives of this Latter Rain movement, which took place exclusively within Pentecostal circles, was that it involved a resurgence of the operations of the gifts of the Holy Spirit that had become, to a large extent, dormant among many Pentecostals who believed in the miraculous gifts, and who were anxious for manifestations of them in their midst. It was this thirst for the operation of the gifts of the Spirit that may be helpful in explaining the rapid expansion of the movement within a very short time. Also very important in contributing to widespread revival was what was reported by participants to have been a deep sense of the 'presence of God' at various meetings that sprang forth within the movement very quickly. This sense of God's presence, usually accompanied by widespread repentance and 'brokenness' before the Lord, was not limited to Latter Rain circles, but characterized the entire mid-twentieth century evangelical awakening of which the Latter Rain movement was only a part."[17]

Riss notes that "the Latter Rain paralleled the Pentecostal movement of the early twentieth century in its zeal for the miraculous, its excitement about the imminent return of Jesus Christ, its repudiation of formal religious organisation, and its enthusiasm for the presence of God which, it was felt, was to be manifest in the Latter Rain outpouring of God's Spirit."[18] Another writer comments on the early development of the revival: "It is important to remember that the Latter Rain was birthed out of a desire for the Pentecostal movement to continue in accuracy. 'Discouraged by waning spiritual fervour and the relentless institutionalisation and professionalism of North American Pentecostalism, they viewed their early history as merely having set the stage for a greater event and opted once again to believe that in their day, the restoration of apostolic power would be realised.'"[19]

A major emphasis of the Latter Rain Revival was the laying on of hands for the baptism of the Holy Spirit and the impartation of spiritual gifts. Previously, Pentecostals had mostly spent hours, days, or even weeks "waiting on God" in prayer—usually described as "tarrying"—for the baptism of the Holy Ghost. The laying on of hands for the receiving of the baptism was a new practice, hitherto unknown in most Pentecostal circles. Other major emphases were the laying on of hands for revealing a believer's place of ministry in the body of Christ and for imparting and activating the gifts of the Holy Spirit; the restoration of the offices of prophet and apostle to their place in the ministry of the church; unity of the body of Christ in line with the prayer of Jesus in John 17 (with a major focus on the rejection of human organization and denominational structures); restoration of all that the church had lost as a result of disobedience and rebellion—Nehemiah and Ezra became the models for this restoration; the revelation of body ministry—all believers, as opposed to a few clergy, were to become active in the work of the ministry, since all Spirit-filled Christians were gifted by the Holy Spirit; the mainstreaming of the deliverance ministry and the demonstration of extraordinary signs and wonders; and extravagant, Spirit-led praise and worship in place of the often cold, formal singing in most Pentecostal circles.[20]

These emphases often found expression in the establishing of "local churches [non-denominationally connected] worldwide, supporting missions and missionaries, founding Bible schools and training institutes, and providing accredited correspondence courses."[21] At that time, many ministers "left mainline Pentecostal denominations to follow the deeper things of God, the gifts of the Spirit with manifestations, and the healing and prophetic gifts."[22] Many were drawn to the Latter Rain revival because they saw in it a restoration of the early fire that had characterized the first two decades of the Pentecostal movement, something which had become lost in most Pentecostal denominations.

One of the leaders of the Apostolic Church in the UK, who grew up in the early days of the Pentecostal movement in what he described as an "almost semi-revival state where the movings [sic] of the Holy Spirit were real, were miraculous and were almost normal with us,"[23] testified of the revival that "this is like what it used to be."[24] As historian Bill Hamon has written, "The Latter Rain Movement, with its doctrine of laying on of hands for anything other than deliverance and healing brought about a revolution within Pentecostal circles. It affected the Pentecostal organisations in the same way that the Pentecostal Movement affected the Holiness Churches, the Holiness Movement affected the Protestant Churches, and the Protestant Movement affected [the] Catholic Church. In the 1950s as much difference could be found between a Latter Rain Christian and a Pentecostal Christian as between a Pentecostal Christian and a Holiness Christian."[25]

This revival was received as a genuine move of God by some of the leaders of the Apostolic Church in the US and the UK. One of them, Cecil Cousen, one-time member of the International Missionary Council, organized several revival meetings in the UK, which stirred up Pentecostal churches and brought a fresh release of the Spirit, and which several believers who had yearned for a fresh outpouring of the Spirit in the church embraced wholeheartedly.[26] Cecil Cousen and his wife visited Nigeria ca. 1948.[27] No records reveal a later visit.

The meetings in the UK witnessed "weeping for the condition of the church followed by a fresh revelation of the person and lordship of Jesus Christ which resulted in great demonstrations of the power and presence of God."[28] Apart from Cecil Cousen, some of the other leaders at the forefront of the revival in the UK were Arthur Wallis and David Lille.[29] Cousen first came in contact with the pioneers of the movement in Canada in 1949 when serving as a pastor of the Apostolic Church in Hamilton, Ontario.[30] Later, he and George B. Evans, pastor of the Apostolic Church in Toronto, visited Bethesda Missionary Temple in Detroit, Michigan, and Elim Bible Institute, Hornell, New York—two major centres of the Latter Rain revival in America. They returned to their churches with the spirit of the revival.[31]

Afterwards, they invited Thomas Wyatt, Carlton Spencer, and other key figures in the revival to hold a convention in Toronto in 1950.[32] Cousen reported of this meeting in a letter: "We announced it as a 'Latter Rain' Convention [they use the word 'Conference' here] and invited a Dr Thos. A. Wyatt as our guest speaker. I can best describe him to you as Pastor Andrew Turnbull and D. P. Williams rolled into one. Never have I known such a man of God. He is mighty in the depths of the word [in essentially Apostolic topics] as D. P. and a mighty man of faith and healing and miracles, as humble and loveable a man as ever one could wish to meet."[33] "After this meeting many of the pastors of the Apostolic Church were invited to speak at Latter Rain meetings, including Cousen and Evans, Fred C. Poole, Frank Warburton and T. Kenneth Michell."[34]

Cousen fully embraced the teachings and manifestations, and in 1951, he and Fred Poole went to the UK with cheering news of the revival: "The people accepted the Latter Rain ministry with open hearts. . . . People were baptised in the Spirit, many were healed and filled with the Spirit and demons were cast out, and the blessing of the Lord was there. There is a very definite move of the Spirit right over the United States and many parts of Canada: we are convinced that we are on the verge of a mighty REVIVAL that will sweep not only this continent but flow over to the uttermost parts of the earth. It surely is an outpouring of the Latter Rain, and how we needed it! We had got so barren and dry. In spite of all our teaching there was practically no progress, but bless His Name, He has sent the RAIN, bringing fresh life."[35]

In spite of this, at the 1951 General Council meeting of the Apostolic Church in Britain, "there was a form of stalemate between those favouring the Latter Rain movement and the leaders of the Executive."[36] After a word of prophecy, however, Cousen was granted permission by the council to go wherever he wanted to hold meetings promoting this new revival. Peter Hocken, historian of the charismatic movement in Britain, in his seminal work, *Streams of Renewal*, notes that "this permission had no precedent and was not allowed for in the Constitution of the Apostolics. It allowed Cousen and [Philip] Rhodes [his partner] to have further success in their preaching of revival with Pentecostal fire."[37] Arthur Wallis, who became one of the most prominent figures in the charismatic movement in the UK, relates his experience of Cousen's ministry: "At one of David Lille's conventions at Exeter I first heard tongues, interpretation and prophecy, and had an instinctive witness that they were genuine. A speaker that came quite often to those early conventions with a strong message on faith, healing and deliverance was Cecil Cousen."[38]

News of this revival had reached Nigeria by 1951, and the Apostolic Church's missionaries in Nigeria were abreast of Latter Rain news from the UK and America. The church's missionaries, like Elton, Cecil Morris, Vernon Wood and Edgar Parkyns, followed news of the revival with excitement. In fact, there were plans as early as 1951 for a major Latter Rain team to visit Ghana and Nigeria. As the minutes of the May 24, 1951, missionary committee in Bradford recorded: *"Pastor Poole's letter re Pastor C. Cousen's going to the Gold Coast and Nigeria.* THAT we are in perfect agreement with the going out of Pastor C. Cousen to meet the party from USA who intend visiting the Gold Coast and Nigeria, and we ask the Secretary to write to Pastors F. C. Poole, J. McKeown, S. G. Elton, D. C. Hopkins and C. Cousen, pointing out that we believe that contact with our missionaries with the party cannot fail to bring blessing to our already prosperous work, but at the same time we ask him to point out the possible dangers in these countries, particularly in respect of the imparting of Gifts and the receiving of the Holy Spirit because of the extreme element so prominent in our African brethren."[39]

In a letter from June 26, 1951, Leila Williams (a missionary stationed with her husband, Eric, in Ilesa under Elton, from 1951 to 1953) wrote, "We have heard that sometime a delegation is coming to Nigeria from America—LATTER RAIN—so we'll be having a revival. We don't know who is coming."[40] The planned visit, which most likely was initiated by the American team, did not, however, materialize until about two years later. There was definitely communication between Elton and the revivalists in North America by early 1952. The April 29, 1952, minutes of the missionary committee in Bradford, under the heading "Pastor Elton: Copy Letter to Pastor Poole," recorded that "we note that the Secretary has received from Pastor Elton a copy letter of one he has sent to Pastor Poole in reply to his, concerning the visit of the delegation to the Ilesha Area. The content has been duly noted."[41]

Letters from Eric and Leila Williams to their children give us glimpses of the general mood among the missionaries concerning the revival. "We received news from Hereford [UK] about the weekend when Pastor Poole from USA was there. (He is an Apostolic pastor but interested in the LATTER RAIN movement which is happening in America.) Everyone was thrilled. The meetings didn't finish in the evenings until 10.30 – 11. Many young people received the baptism in the Holy Spirit, and a little dumb girl was delivered and spoke! There was such rejoicing,"[42] Leila wrote on July 6, 1951. She wrote on August 22, "At the Penygroes convention, I believe the majority of people had great blessing from 'latter rain' pastors. Vernon [Wood] of course is full of latter rain and it hurts him if anything is said against it. He is a real humble Christian and his one aim is to get all the students saved and baptised with the Spirit. Two who were opposed to the baptism at one time have recently been baptised."[43] Her letter of October 25, 1951: "It seems that Syd [Elton] and Vernon [Wood] have been talking 'latter rain,' and during a week's devotional meetings of all the African pastors prior to the convention, have been preaching it and came full of expectancy."[44] Eric Williams wrote on April 17, 1952, "We are still waiting for revival. We hear we are likely to have a visit from Latter Rain folk from America and Canada later in the year, so it may be they will be used to promote revival."[45]

In May 1952,[46] Elton travelled on furlough to the UK to join Ruth and Hannah, who had been there since April 1950. By the time he arrived, they had been attending some of the Latter Rain meetings and had embraced it as a new move of the Holy Spirit. The meetings were "different,"[47] Ruth remembers. Elton immediately joined his family in attending the meetings. Ruth has noted that upon attending the meetings, her father identified this new outpouring as the revival which God had showed him was coming.[48] According to the story, Elton had a vision around 1951 of a coming revival in which he saw the name of an American who would be involved in it; the vision also indicated that the revival would spread to Nigeria. Sometime later, Joseph Banji, a member of the Apostolic Church in Ilesa, had a similar dream and came to Elton for interpretation. Elton saw this as a confirmation of his earlier vision and, therefore, was all the more on the lookout for a new outpouring in the church. We have a confirmation of this from a sermon Elton preached in 1955: "Four years ago, the Lord began to tell us in prophecy through Africans that He was going to send 'a team' from America and that He was going to pour out rain on us. They did not have at that time any idea of what God was doing in America, but the Lord said He was going to send the 'latter rain' upon us out there and a wonderful spirit of expectancy covered the whole nation."[49]

Elton participated in many of the Latter Rain meetings in the UK. He was also at the August convention of the church in Penygroes, where there was a major emphasis on the Latter Rain revival.[50] Ruth recalls that there was a clearly discernible difference between the preaching of the Latter Rain and non-Latter Rain ministers at the convention. Cousen and Elton were both speakers at the convention. The Eltons spent at least a full weekend in the Cousens' house in Bradford—Cousen, Philip Rhodes, and Elton spent a considerable part of the time in discussions about the revival.[51]

Elton recalled how the revival, marked by brokenness and repentance, transformed his ministry and that of several leaders: "When the priests weep between the porch and the altar, the congregation will follow you. But until you begin to weep, the congregation won't weep. And that's where [the place of brokenness] God will begin. I saw it happen in the lives of myself and my friends—God broke us."[52] He continued: "[In] 1952 I went to England. I had worked in Nigeria as a missionary for fifteen years then. . . . I saw what God was doing. I wasn't concerned with the miracles—we had seen more miracles in Nigeria than they had ever heard of. It wasn't the miracles I saw. I saw God break men, break men. Men . . . many of them well-known clever preachers; I saw God break them. And they got on the ground and they wept, wept, asking God for forgiveness. Forgiveness for what? Dead works. Dead works. And I was one of them. Fifteen years as a missionary, then I went home to England to begin again, repenting from dead works."[53]

Edgar Parkyns (Elton's colleague in Ilesa) was also at the convention. His retelling of the events to an audience decades later captured the mood of those days. "In those grand days, many of us were stirred by the news of revival in America which went by the name of Latter Rain; it was a real move. . . . We heard about these things and longed for them. And coming back to England to the great convention in . . . Penygroes, oh, our hearts were stirred when we saw three of our brethren from America, ministering with tears. I had never seen it before. . . . All the Pentecost I had seen was all the shouting kind; in fact you had to shout to get anywhere. And to see these men ministering with tears about the love of Jesus and their rediscovery of Him, made my whole heart reach out for God. Together with some others who were particularly missionary personnel, we asked that hands might be laid upon us so that our ministry should be strengthened. . . . Praise the Lord, what a difference it made when, not only I, but others, went back to the mission field and we found out that God was working with us in a new way and our hearts were thrilled in a new way. And one of the Africans said to me, 'Sir, What's happened to you?' I said, 'What's the matter?' He said, 'You are different.' I said, 'How?' He said, 'You are full of the Holy Spirit.' I said, 'Wasn't I before?' He said, 'Well, yes, but . . .' Thank God. Something real had happened."[54]

The Eltons left the UK for Nigeria in August 1952. On their way back to Nigeria, the ship docked in Takoradi (Ghana) to drop off some passengers, and Elton was able to have a lengthy discussion about the revival with James McKeown, the fellow missionary with whom he had travelled to Africa the first time, in 1937.[55] It is possible that McKeown, who had embraced the revival by this time, first came in touch with it through his brother, Adam McKeown, who had been a missionary of the Apostolic Church to the Gold Coast (Ghana) from 1945 to 1948, and as a pastor of the Apostolic Church in Canada, was already a prominent leader in the revival in North America by 1952.[56] The discussion between Elton and McKeown included arrangements for hosting North American Latter Rain revivalists in their respective countries.[57]

In the final months of 1952, there was a heightened level of expectation for revival in Nigeria. When it was confirmed that the Latter Rain team would be visiting in early 1953, many of the leaders hoped the team's ministry in the country would be used by God as an instrument to spark the long-awaited revival. Joy Williams, daughter of Eric and Leila Williams, who had relocated to Nigeria, wrote in a January 7, 1953 letter: "Do you know that the Latter Rain people are coming here from the USA in February? They are spending five weeks in Nigeria. We are looking forward to them coming."[58] On January 31, 1953, Eric Williams wrote, "We are anticipating a visit from the Latter Rain folk shortly, consisting of a trio: Dr Wyatt, Pastor Fred Poole and Pastor Adam McKeown. They were expected in the Gold Coast this weekend, Fred Poole having flown there via England. Yesterday he was to have flown from England to Accra in the Gold Coast, and the other two were flying direct from USA. They will stay there three weeks and then we expect them in Nigeria. Pastor Elton went to Lagos yesterday and booked a large independent hall so that others outside the Apostolic Church may be attracted. We don't know the full programme but expect they may stay five weeks, covering Calabar and Ibo areas, also Lagos, Ilesha, Kabba areas—and possibly Zaria area as well. We are certainly hoping for a great blessing and I hope we shall see and experience something of it before we return home to England."[59]

In February 1953, a high-powered team of leaders in the Latter Rain revival from North America, led by Fred Poole, arrived in Nigeria. They were many, but the main leaders were Thomas Wyatt, Fred C. Poole, Adam McKeown (James McKeown's brother), Raymond G. Hoekstra, and Stanley M. Hammond. Thomas Wyatt (mostly called Dr Wyatt by his associates), the pastor of Wings of Healing Temple in Portland, Oregon, was at the forefront of the movement in North America. A meeting hosted by Wyatt in February 1949, which had George Hawtin and Milford Kirkpatrick as guest ministers and which was attended by "90 preachers from almost every part of North America,"[60] is frequently referred to by Latter Rain historians. Though the team to Nigeria was led by Fred Poole, most likely because of his position within the Apostolic Church denomination, Thomas Wyatt was the key revivalist. Fred C.

Poole, "a major figure in the Latter Rain revival,"[61] was the pastor of Gospel Temple in Philadelphia, a congregation within the Apostolic Church fold; for a time he was the superintendent of the Apostolic Church in the US. Poole's influence within the Latter Rain movement was significant.

David Schoch, a participant at one of the Latter Rain conventions in Los Angeles in 1950 gives us a vivid description of the ministries of Fred Poole and Adam McKeown: "Pastor Fred Poole from the Gospel Temple in Philadelphia, the main speaker, was speaking on the last night of the convention. He preached until midnight, but it wasn't because of a long-winded sermon. God was so sovereign that Brother Poole would make a statement, and the people would stand and begin to worship until worship was the predominant thing. Then Brother Poole would make another statement, and people would just get lost in worship again. A prophet from Ireland named Adam McKeown was in the congregation on the morning that the Lord spoke to us. Pastor Poole was speaking. There were about a thousand people in that morning service. The word of the Lord came to this Irish prophet, who began to call different ones by name and he set them into office. I didn't know this man and he didn't know me, but God knows who you are. All of a sudden the word of the Lord came, and he called my name. He didn't even mispronounce it."[62]

"When we received word from Dr Wyatt ... and Rev. Fred Poole ... that they were coming," said Elton, "we were all excited. We made big preparations and planned visits to as many large centres as possible."[63] Wyatt recorded of their arrival in Lagos, a few hours after concluding a major two-week gospel campaign in Ghana: "We found a large delegation waiting at the airport, headed by Pastor S. G. Elton. This man had also been in Africa for 16 years and had done a wonderful work in bringing salvation to thousands."[64] Elton was meeting Wyatt for the first time, but Fred Poole had been his "colleague in England 25 years previously."[65]

Hours before the team arrived at the airport in Lagos, an excited crowd had gathered at the church where the first meeting was scheduled to hold, so much so that it was difficult to get near the church. Joy Williams, who was part of the delegation that welcomed the team at the airport, recalled that "even at 3 pm the church was full, the front being crowded with sick people who lay on the floor—a most pathetic sight. The meeting didn't begin until 7 pm. People who couldn't get into the church sat outside, and were able to hear everything because of the amplifiers. Electric light was also taken outside."[66]

Four hours later, Wyatt was at Ebute Metta to preach the evening service. "At 7 p.m. that Monday night," Elton vividly recollected, "we fought our way through the crowd gathered outside the church building. We pressed our way through a hot, steaming crowd inside the building to the speakers' platform. There we were, about ten white men on the platform. Many of the government officials had come to hear this wonderful message. There was no form or ceremony about the service, for there were too many people trying to get in."[67] During Wyatt's sermon, a significant miracle occurred: a paralyzed Muslim beggar was completely healed. Wyatt had commanded him to get up and walk, and at that moment he stood up and began walking. It caused such uproar, and the news of the miracle went all round Lagos.

We have the most detailed account of the highlights of this visit from the awkwardly titled booklet, *Black Magic and Jungle Prophets,* the printed version of the talks Elton gave on Wyatt's radio programme in America in 1955. Elton's vivid description of this miracle and other happenings during the service that opening night is moving:

Directly in front, near the platform were the sick, the lame, the blind and the people who couldn't get into the seats. God was gracious to us and gave us a miracle at the very beginning of our campaign, and I have never seen an equal since. Lying on three seats at the front was a young man of Nigeria who had fallen from the top of a five story building while he was working several years before, breaking both legs and injuring his spine. He had been in the hospital for more than three years, had undergone thirty-three operations and had been turned out as incurable by the specialists. Since that time he had spent much money on ju-ju and witchcraft. He was brought through that pushing crowd and laid on three chairs with his crutches by his side.

Dr Wyatt was speaking on faith . . . and though he was tired, the need of these people seemed to draw strength out of him. As he ministered, he said, "We are going to pray for you all in a few minutes, and when we begin to pray, I want you all to not merely pray that God will heal you, but if you believe that God can do it and is doing it, get up and do something and know that God has done something. And you, young man," said he, pointing out to the man lying there, "Begin to do something." The young man didn't wait any longer. He began to put his faith into action. With all eyes watching him in amazement and some consideration, he got to his feet and began to wobble about unsteadily. Those near him rushed to his aid, but he waved them aside and within two minutes, to the astonishment of all, he was dancing and praising God! He was very soon on the platform pulling off his clothing to show the steel brace that was around his waist, taking it off and waving it in the air.[68]

"If you have ever been in a revival when something like that happened, you know what was the result. There was no question of law and order after that. The revival turned into a riot," Elton continued. "Thousands of people outside tried to get into a space only large enough for the 500 inside. Our great concern was to save the lives of the people who were inside. It was no question of laying on of hands for healing, but of laying on of hands to keep them out. We had to push them out. We fought our way to hold back that great pressing crowd that pushed to get in. All sorts of things were happening. Blind people were suddenly healed. I remember one sister pressing her way through the crowd of people to the platform. Throwing herself at the feet of Mrs Wyatt, she cried out, 'I can see! I can see! I can see!' "

The organizers feared that people would be trampled to death in the "wild excitement as the waves of healing virtue swept over the people and God worked mightily all over that vast crowd."[69] It took a lot of effort to get Wyatt and the team out of the building, but they were eventually smuggled out. Joy Williams' eyewitness account was as intense as Elton's; she concluded her report saying, "It was impossible to restore order, so we had to close the meeting. It was a great pity the delegation didn't stay in Lagos then, as the next night the church was packed and they had to send the people away."[70]

The *Daily Times* of February 17, 1953, under the caption "Apostolic Church Delegates Arrive in Lagos from U.S.A." reported, "Delegates of the Apostolic Church, U.S.A., led by Pastor Poole, President of the Church, arrived in Lagos recently. On the eve of their arrival, a revival meeting was held at the Apostolic Church, 92 Cemetery Street, Ebute Metta. After the meeting, preaching by Pastor Poole followed and there were divine healings. Later, the delegates left for Ilesha and Ibadan for further gospel and divine healing campaigns."[71]

Close to twenty thousand people attended the second crusade, which was held the next day in Ilesa. The building could not hold the crowd; the church had to be turned into a "place where sick people could rest," and they had to "knock out the end of the building so we could speak to the great crowd outside."[72] The Ilesa crowd, like those which the team would encounter again and again around the country, had an unusual expectancy. Wyatt recounts the Ilesa experience: "The day meetings began with a prayer service at five o'clock in the morning. It had rained the night before, but hours before daylight the people came, several thousand in number, and prostrated themselves on the wet ground, and continued for hours in mighty travailing and prevailing prayer until the preaching service at nine o'clock."[73]

Elton described one of the phenomenal occurrences during the week-long meetings in Ilesa: "The team ministered in many places, to many people until everyone was exhausted! We were crowded out of churches into athletic fields. We saw hundreds of people baptised with the Holy Spirit in single services. Practically all of the teachers in training, including the staff in my teacher-training institute, were baptised with Holy Spirit in one service! I never saw such a sight in my life. Here were school teachers training for their degrees baptised with the Holy Ghost, the whole crowd of them. They were beautifully speaking in tongues and glorifying God. Many of those teachers have gone back to places where there are no missionaries and no churches. These school teachers have taken the Gospel where missionaries can't go."[74]

Joseph Babalola participated in the Ilesa crusade and was given the platform to pray during one of the services. Wyatt had been briefed about Babalola, and he was intrigued by his encounter with him during his time in Ilesa. Wyatt afterwards expressed a desire to "bring this man to America just as soon as we can raise the necessary funds and arrange an itinerary of meetings."[75] This never happened. However, more important is an observation about Babalola by Wyatt which perhaps lets us into an aspect of Babalola's life previously not told. After recounting a little of Babalola's story, which he definitely got from Elton, he concluded, "In a little while, his fame spread through the country and thousands came and were healed, but the authorities put him in jail for several months until his spirit was broken. When he was released, he did some preaching, but had lost his power. While we were there, he came and was restored to the place of power he formerly enjoyed and when he left, he was taking about 100 preachers into the jungle to wait on God that there might be a complete restoration to the church of all the Bible benefits and blessings."[76]

Did the heavy persecution which followed the 1930 revival and persisted for much of the 1930s, his six-month imprisonment in 1932, and the crisis which eventually led to the parting of ways with the Apostolic

Church disillusion Babalola, wear him out, and cut short the life and potency of the revival? Was Babalola a broken man by the 1950s, only a shadow of his former self? Did the distant memories of the 1930s come alive afresh in the Latter Rain revival? While his ministry continued through the 1940s and '50s, did he always long for a restoration of the glory days of the 1930s?

Invitations poured in from all over the country for revival teams to be sent. Isaac Akinyele, the FT leader in Ibadan, and who had now become *Olubadan* (king of Ibadan), travelled to Ilesa with his entourage to request that a crusade be held in his city. (It is notable that during the revival, Elton and many of the leaders of Christ Apostolic Church worked together, and that they enjoyed a good relationship in the years that followed. This is attested to by his collaborations with Babalola during this period; Gordon Lindsay also wrote in 1971 that Akinyele was "a close friend of the Eltons."[77] We are not sure whether this reconciliation took place before the revival or whether it was the revival that brought it about.) More than fifteen thousand attended the one-day event in Ibadan. From there, the team travelled to Lagos for one more meeting. From Lagos the team took a plane to Calabar, where they were received at the airport by about four thousand people. The following report by *The Nigerian Daily Standard* of February 23, 1953, captures the experience:

> Throughout the week, people received their sight, the cripple walked, and the dumb and deaf spoke and heard. Diverse diseases were cured, not by medicine, but by the Divine visitation that fell on the people. Rev. Wyatt traced the various elevations of faith in Christians and compared them with (1) The faith of a Ruler that had a child sick; (2) The woman with the issue of blood; (3) The Centurion who only asked Jesus to speak and his servant would be well. . . . [Some of those] who gave testimonies of themselves before the microphone were:
>
> Titus Ukpong of Ikot Ante suffered from paralysis—now cured. Madam Iquo Udo Edel of Edgerly Road, Calabar, who for many years was suffering from blindness—now cured. Atim Ekpo Efiong of Nyo Hopika, whose right eye for over ten years was dead and blind—now cured. Okokon Udo of Uruan in Uyo Division who was suffering from deafness and dumbness—now completely cured, and speaks quite well.[78]

Elton said, "The revival went on and spread and spread. It shook the native preachers. It shook the missionaries too. After we had been labouring there 16 years, we certainly had an awful jolt. What had we been doing for all these years? We had seen some revivals, but this was bigger than we had ever seen before, and it was much bigger than we could ever hold. We had telegrams from all over the country, from villages hundreds and thousands of miles away appealing for teams to go to them. The newspapers reported that there was an attendance of two million people in these meetings within one month after the arrival of the team from America. We don't know how many tens of thousands were converted, or how many were healed—it doesn't matter. We saw God on the move and that is what we wanted."[79]

Speaking decades later about this nationwide sweep, he remembered, "I have spoken many times for many weeks to thirty, forty, fifty thousand people. I saw a hundred and fifty churches born in six weeks."[80]

By invitation of Bishop A. W. Howells, a Briton and the administrator of the Lagos Diocese of the Anglican Church, they next went to Christ Church, Marina, where they addressed clergy from many denominations who were gathered at the bishop's request. (Wyatt had by this time returned to America.) The *Daily Times* of March 5 reported: "The Right Reverend, A. W. Howells, Administrator of the Lagos Diocese, has kindly agreed to invite Dr Poole, leader of the Evangelists of the Latter Rain Movement and his team now touring Nigeria, to the Cathedral Church of Christ, Lagos, today, March 5, at 7 p.m., when it is expected that there will be a demonstration of healing by faith, it was announced yesterday."[81] After this meeting they were offered the service at the cathedral the next evening. "So the team went to the largest cathedral in West Africa with only thirty-six hours' notice," Elton later wrote. "When we arrived, there were more people outside than inside, and they called out the whole police force of Lagos (several hundred men) to govern the crowd." The paralysed man who had been healed at the Ebute Metta church gave his testimony. It must have been a stirring moment when he turned round and pointed out "the doctors who had operated on him, as many of them were sitting among the prominent people in the choir loft."[82]

After his departure, Wyatt began sending teams of evangelists to hold campaigns, albeit smaller ones, but for longer periods, in different parts of the country. The evangelists worked closely with the leaders of the Apostolic Church in the country who were fully committed to promoting the revival. Wyatt and his team returned to Nigeria in November, and large healing crusades were again conducted. The *Nigerian Tribune* of November 20, 1953, gave headline coverage to the Ibadan crusade under the caption—"Blind for 5 Years Healed Last Night":

A woman who claims to have been blind for the past five years stood up on the rostrum of the Ibadan Race Course last night and announced to a large gathering that she could now see. She distinguished a Black Bible from a white sheet of paper and was able to know a red wrist strap from both.

Alice was one of the many people who claimed to have been made whole after prayers at the Race Course at the instance of three American evangelists who arrived in Ibadan this week. The three evangelists were Dr Thomas Wyatt, Messrs Hockstar and Saunders. They are guests of the Apostolic Church Mission who organised an open air prayer meeting for healing the diseased and the afflicted.

A man said he had been blind for 30 years but yesterday at the Race Course he saw. Elizabeth Adejoke had palsy. Yesterday she said she had been healed through prayer at the Race Course. Sarah Ajayi said she had been lame for 30 years but she was healed yesterday at the Race Course.[83]

For the Ibadan meetings, Wyatt and Raymond G. Hoekstra were joined by Erskine Holt (dean of Thomas Wyatt's Bible school in Portland, Oregon), Max Wyatt (Thomas Wyatt's son), Paul Shaver, and Paul Cannon. "Thousands" are reported to have attended and "great healings and miracles happened nightly."[84] Max Wyatt recalled that in one meeting in Ibadan, "hundreds received the baptism of the Holy Spirit and the numbers attending the meetings ran into the twenty-thousands!"[85] After leaving Nigeria, Wyatt and Hoekstra travelled to Accra, where they held similar meetings. They returned home after a week. Erskine Holt and Max Wyatt stayed back in the country for a month, after which they left Shaver and Cannon to continue the meetings around Nigeria.

In 1954 another team comprising Fred Poole, Stanley Hammond, and Adam McKeown held a major crusade in Warri. This was at the request of the *Olu* (king) of Warri, who personally visited the Eltons' home in Ilesa "to insist that the American revival Team visit Warri."[86] (The *Olu* was at the time attending the Western Region House of Chiefs in Ibadan, and had been enthused by the reports and eyewitness accounts of the impact of the 1953 crusades in several parts of the country.[87]) Writing in

1954, Elton remarked, "We arranged to go and we knew that the Lord had a wonderful treat in store for us. We had been having good crowds in all our campaigns this year (and we have already held three campaigns this year) but we knew that Warri would be different because it is right in the centre of a great dark tribe; ju-ju is everywhere and the king says his people are living in darkness."[88]

The crusade was hosted by the *Olu* and Felix Okotie-Eboh, a prominent politician. Five thousand people attended the first meeting, which was held on "a large cleared piece of bush." When Elton began to pray before his sermon on the first evening, a major miracle occurred. "We have noticed that the Lord has seemed to give a real sign at the beginning of most campaigns by a real miracle and thus gathering the big crowds,"[89] Elton later remarked. This miracle was of a hunchbacked boy who suddenly began shouting from the back of the congregation, "It is gone, it is gone, it is gone."[90] This caused great commotion, and by the time he made his way through the thick crowd to the front, it was discovered that the hunch had disappeared and his back straightened. That marked the end of the meeting, as people burst into praise and "many people followed him down the road." By the next day, the crowd exploded. The numbers grew until the crowd averaged fifteen to twenty thousand each day before the campaign was a week old.

"I have rarely seen such eagerness or hunger for God as we saw in Warri," Elton remarked after the crusade had ended. "The people would not leave the place and would gather for the morning meeting at 9 a.m. and stand for three or four hours in the sun, eagerly expecting the Lord to heal them all, and when the meeting ended they would sit around in the shade waiting for the 5 p.m. meeting. Great crowds of sick folk came and it was pitiful to see their eagerness and hunger. Blind, lame, lepers, and diseased of all sorts and conditions and the Lord healed in every meeting."[91] Another major miracle occurred on the fifth evening of the campaign. A big thunderstorm broke as the team arrived on the campaign ground, where thousands had already gathered. The crowd was standing about two to three inches in water, and the team found it difficult to get out of the car; Elton got to the platform "by jumping over large pools." They then asked the crowd "to lift their hands and pray that the Lord would stop the rains." "He did," said Elton, "almost before we had finished praying, the rain ceased and we began our service. After that we became known as the magicians. Can you wonder?"[92]

Decades later Elton told the same story more colourfully: "I have stopped storms in campaigns, saying, 'Hold on rain; don't come yet.' It didn't happen always; there have been quite a number of failures, but we have done it sometimes. I remember it in Warri, there was a great crowd of 25,000 standing with their feet disappearing in pools of water; they couldn't see their feet; they were standing in water, 25,000, waiting for the blessing of God and it was pouring with rain and we stepped forward and said, "Let's stop this rain." 'Lord, we stop it now in the name of Jesus,' we declared, and it did; and we went on with our meeting. That was for the crowd, not for me; I was under a shelter so it didn't matter about me. That was the crowd and the crowd from that time on would say, 'These are miracle men; they talked to the rain and it stopped.' "[93]

The Latter Rain revival provided fresh inspiration and reinvigoration for Christian witness all over the country. For those who were around in the 1930s, it was rain after a period of drought; for those who did not experience the move of the thirties, it was Christianity come alive. Samuel Odunaike (son of Samson Odunaike, author of *The Path of a Master Christian*, and one of the young men who joined Harold and Faye Curtis, the pioneer missionaries of the International Church of the Foursquare Gospel in Nigeria, in 1955, and who later became the first indigenous general superintendent of the Foursquare Gospel Church in Nigeria), personally witnessed how the revival marked the transition from the cold formality to a new vibrancy during this period of Nigeria's Christianity:

By Independence, 1960, the Lord had started moving in Nigeria. I may find it difficult to place my fingers absolutely on a cause and effect of what gave rise to the revival, but one of the significant things that I could place my finger on that was responsible for the change from this laissez-faire and decay in the church and society then was the visit of the Latter Rain evangelistic team which came to Lagos. I believe it was in February 1953. That team was led by the late Dr Thomas Wyatt. It held revivals in the Apostolic Church. . . . The crusade was supposed to last for one week, but it eventually lasted for three weeks, before it was rounded off.

Now, that meeting meant a lot of things to various people, but I think one of the most significant things about it was that it demonstrated beyond any shadow of doubt that miracles are for today. In the days of Babalola I heard that there were miracles, but I [had] never seen one, so this was a different thing for me. What I had been reading about in the Bible, [I now saw] right before my eyes. . . . That revival blew my mind in several directions, and I believe it also affected other people the way it affected me. If a bomb blasts, the splinters go in different directions; that is the only way I can describe what happened with the visit of the Latter Rain team to Nigeria. But the number of young people who caught the vision as a result of that revival must have been countless.[94]

SIX

CRISIS

Sometime in 1953, the revival experienced a major hitch from a crisis that had international and local dimensions. At the international level: although the revival had initially been favourably received by the leadership of the Apostolic Church in the UK, Latter Rain revivalists soon ran into trouble with the section of the leadership that favoured the status quo and therefore vehemently opposed the revival.

The earlier open-mindedness towards the revival had been born out of the desire for reform by a section of the church. Notably, one of these reformers was W. J. Williams (brother of D. P. Williams), one of the church's founders. However, his voice—and that of others calling for reform—is said to have been silenced.[1] One historian has noted that "whereas it is but *possible* that Apostolics—with their intense evangelistic code, Pentecostal theology, devotional life-style and strictly observed ministerial order—have made an impact upon the mainstream churches, it is certain that by the years 1937 to 1950 the Apostolic Church had lost much of its initial fervour. Ministerial hierarchy, Area committees and other organisational paraphernalia had assumed a degree of importance disproportionate to their effectiveness in promoting the Christian gospel. . . . It appears that rules and regulations had almost become reasons for the Church's existence. There were many who thought that the introduction of a Constitution pandered to those whose approach was rigid as it appeared to induce an attitude of mind which cared more for the manner in which things were done than for the actual tasks performed. . . .

Loss of zeal was a symptom of the consolidating and denominationalising process within Pentecostal churches in general and the Apostolic Church in particular."[2]

The top hierarchy of the church's leadership was particularly irked by the fact that the revivalists were emphasizing a more independent form of church organization as opposed to the very rigid structure of the Apostolic Church; the latter, coded in the phrase "divine government," had become the hallmark of the church over the years. The Latter Rain emphasis on independent local assemblies in line with the New Testament pattern, free of overwhelming denominational control, was the very antithesis of the Apostolic Church's structure.

In embracing the revival, Cousen said, "God showed me, too, how sectarian I had become, in conjunction with the rest of the Apostolics who thought they were *the people*. They had the vision and very much looked down on everybody else. God also opened my eyes to the blinding, crippling nature of our church organization with its central government. And I repented."[3] Cousen also referred to the early hints of opposition during revival meetings in the UK in 1951: "People were baptised in the Spirit, many were healed and filled with the Spirit, and demons were cast out, and the blessing of the Lord was there, and instead of a few dozen, there were a few hundred people. . . . A lot of the pastors (of the Apostolic Church) were open, and were prayed for, and were changed. But behind the scenes the powers that be, especially the Executive, which was led by a very strong man by the name of Pastor Hugh Dawson . . . believed in the Apostolic Church as such, and especially in divine government."[4]

After several days of discussing the revival at the quadrennial meeting of the General Council of the church in Bradford in May 1953, the anti-Latter Rain faction of the leadership was able to convince the council to take certain steps guaranteed to checkmate the further influence of the revivalists—particularly that of the non-Apostolic Church ministers—within the Apostolic Church fold. According to historian Kingsley Larbi, "The conclusion of the meeting, to the amazement of some, was that the Latter Rain 'abused the privileges granted them in condemning both in public and in private, our recognised Church Government in the Apostolic Church.' "[5]

First, the anti-Latter Rain group secured an amendment to the constitution, "to make sure that no-one from outside the Apostolics ever again visited their work without approval of home base."[6] Second, all fifty-four council members present were asked to "reaffirm allegiance to the Church Tenets and Constitution."[7]

All those present reaffirmed, except Cecil Cousen and James McKeown. Cousen and McKeown had no problem with the tenets, but declined to reaffirm the constitution, which would have stopped them from participating in any other move of God or spiritual ministry outside of the Apostolic Church's programme. James McKeown's biographer, Christine Leonard, writes that "the Apostolics had very strict central control. The sect has been called 'The most authoritarian and hierarchical structure in British Pentecostalism.' It was rare for an outsider to be allowed to speak to Apostolic meetings, rules and regulations covered every eventuality. The UK Apostolics seem to have become bound by their own constitution. Into this situation, Cecil Cousen and his friends tried to bring the freedom of Latter Rain."[8] McKeown, says Leonard, "stood and quietly said that he felt the amendments were unscriptural, so he could not, out of a pure conscience, subscribe to them."[9] Cecil Cousen on his own part said, "I thoroughly accept the tenets of the Apostolic Church, but I cannot accept the constitution as it is at present administered in the United Kingdom."[10] There and then, both of them were forced to submit their ordination certificates. ("Between 1950 and 1953, about a dozen British pastors left the church over the Latter Rain issue."[11])

Before this council meeting, the president of the Apostolic Church, Hugh Dawson, is said to have "addressed the question of Apostolic Church involvement with Latter Rain. He conceded that the Apostolic Church appeared to have departed from its original belief and stood in need of renewal but he was not convinced that renewal should include Latter Rain teaching."[12] The decision of the council in the UK reverberated to the church's missions around the world.

James McKeown wrote to one of his colleagues in Ghana after the council meeting: "I am sure by this time you will have learned both from official and unofficial sources that there was a show down in Council on the Apostolic Church interpretation of Latter Rain and Latter Rain interpretation of the Apostolic Church with the result that Pastor Cecil Cousen and I had to hand over our ordination certificates and from that moment we were no longer . . . ministers of the church. This will have far reaching effects on the Gold Coast. . . . We left the council in the Spirit of the Master and we will walk in that Spirit."[13]

When news of the Bradford decision reached the leadership of the church's council in Ghana, a meeting was immediately convened. The chairman of the council, a Ghanaian, opened the meeting by saying, "We are not to stay at one stage of our spiritual journey. The Apostolic Church came to enlighten us to some extent, the Latter Rain vision has been higher so despite what people both in this country and abroad say, we must go on to higher realms of power and glory in the Name of the Lord."[14] The Gold Coast Council took the decision to stand behind McKeown. Its resolution, which was sent to "the Missionary Committee, Bradford, James McKeown in Northern Ireland, the missionaries at the Gold Coast, Superintendent Missionaries in Nigeria and 'responsible authorities in the Gold Coast,' " read, "Council unanimously behind you [James McKeown]."[15]

There were two other British missionaries in the Gold Coast at this time—Albert Seaborne and Stanley Hammond—Seaborne pitched his tent with Bradford, while Hammond stayed with the Gold Coast Council's decision. Seaborne rallied his immediate constituency and retained a following for the Apostolic Church. But most of the assemblies went with McKeown and the Gold Coast Council, who now assumed a new name, the "Gold Coast Apostolic Church,"[16] as opposed to the former name connected with Bradford, "the Apostolic Church in the Gold Coast." Two missionaries—Cyril Rosser and Vivian Wellings—were sent from Bradford to convince the Ghanaians to change their minds. They had some level of success in winning back the loyalty of some of those who had joined McKeown, but they were not able to win back the majority. The church under McKeown later changed its name to Church of Pentecost (CoP) and went on to become the largest Pentecostal denomination in Ghana. ("In 1989 the Ghana Evangelism Committee published a survey of churches where the CoP was found to be the largest with regards to church attendance in Ghana. A further survey in 1993 revealed that CoP had become the biggest protestant church in Ghana. Later in 2001, the *Operation World* church statistics confirmed this position."[17])

In Nigeria, most missionaries had initially embraced the revival and promoted it in their various areas, but they then became sharply polarized over reaffirmation. As in the UK, the missionaries in Nigeria were required to sign a letter of reaffirmation that would prevent them from any present or future relationship of any kind with the Latter Rain revival or any other spiritual ministry outside the Apostolic Church.

Some of the missionaries submitted to the council's decision and signed the document, but others were not ready to give up what was generally acknowledged as a move of God on the altar of denominational loyalty. Sydney Elton, Cecil Morris, Edgar Parkyns, Roger Brunt, and Anna Ungermann refused to sign the document.[18] Vernon Wood (an American), the principal of the Elementary Training Centre in Ilesa, delayed signing for almost two years.[19] He was able to do this because he had come to Nigeria as an educator and so did not pose an immediate threat on the field, and anyway, the council would have had a very difficult task finding an immediate replacement for him. But they kept on putting pressure on Wood until he could no longer keep his neutrality. There are clear indications that many who reaffirmed were either not sure whether or not they had taken the right decision, or were not pleased that they were forced to go against their conscience. Thus, an atmosphere of suspicion continued to prevail, even among those who had reaffirmed, as to who might still be harbouring any sympathies towards the revival. Some of those who had initially reaffirmed could not sustain their earlier decision and later left the field dissatisfied, never to return.

Parkyns, describing the situation years later, said, "But after all that excitement and all those wonderful experiences [of the revival], I had to leave the Apostolic Church. . . . They put a constraint upon us which I couldn't relate to. They wanted me to confirm without any reservations whatsoever, my faith in the Apostolic tenets and practices. And I thought, my, I've got reservations to a lot of them. . . . And I said, 'Please let me continue, I want to serve the Lord . . . but don't ask me to make a declaration like that.' But it had been passed in committee and that was it, and so eight of us missionaries found ourselves outside the organisation."[20] Parkyns left Nigeria in December 1953. He returned to the country in 1960 as an independent missionary to Mid-Western Nigeria, and would afterwards play a significant role in the launching of the ministry of a then still unknown young evangelist named Benson Idahosa.

The confusion also spread to the Nigerian leaders. Most of them had welcomed the revival at the initial stage, but when the reaffirmation issue came up, many became unsure of how to respond. The Nigerian leaders were not required to reaffirm, but there was a fierce battle for their allegiance among the missionaries. For instance, Samuel Adegboyega, who had joyfully welcomed the initial team and who had interpreted for Wyatt at the first service in Lagos, made a 180-degree turn.

Elton and other Latter Rain enthusiasts found themselves on a collision course with some Nigerian leaders and the missionaries who reaffirmed. This resulted in a major struggle for the direction of the church—pro-Latter Rain or anti-Latter Rain. The arguments for and against the revival resulted in a major crisis in which leaders and local assemblies took sides. Months of acrimonious engagements between the missionaries followed. The situation became so precarious that at one point there were fears that the work of the Apostolic Church in Nigeria would collapse.

Elton was the undisputed leader of the Latter Rain group, and the crisis came to revolve around him. Not only was he the most senior superintendent in the country, his longevity on the mission field had earned him unrivalled influence among the assemblies in the country. Other missionaries were in awe of his influence, and so, even when they were on the opposite side of the Latter Rain debate, they knew they could not match his influence with many of the local assemblies and leaders, particularly in the western part of the country. There was an intense bid among the missionaries on either side of the argument for the allegiance of the local pastors in their area. But with the passing months, apprehension grew that Elton was going to succeed at converting the Apostolic Church work in Nigeria over to the Latter Rain movement.

At the height of the crisis, Rosser and Wellings were sent by the leadership of the church in the UK to address the problems. Writing home after they arrived in Nigeria, Rosser and Wellings said, "Seeing our African and European friends at Lagos again was an inspiration indeed. Pastors Elton, Adegboyega, Odunaike, Sakpo, together with Mr Silas Williams, and our host, Mr Wild, were all at the Customs' Shed awaiting our arrival. . . . That there are difficulties to be settled we cannot deny, but we are the more confident that what God has established among us needs very little settling in our own hearts, and we therefore believe that when we come together, there will be little remaining for us to settle, other than a re-affirmation of our faith in the things God has been so gracious to reveal unto us. . . . So, dear friends, in our first letter to you in the homeland after our departure, we are hopeful for a true and lasting settlement of all differences and difficulties. . . . There is no denying the untold blessing that has followed in the train of the Delegation from America, and no one wishes to detract from this, and we now seek to make possible such blessing to continue among us in true Apostolic fashion."[21] By "true Apostolic fashion," Rosser and Wellings meant "within the confines of the denomination."

Ruth Elton believes that the council sent Rosser and Wellings to Nigeria because they had been in support of the revival in the UK and believed they were in the best position to talk Elton out of it. In fact, Rosser and Elton attended Latter Rain meetings in the UK together. "Wellings too had been so much supportive of it [the revival] in the beginning."[22] However, when the council in the UK decided against the revival, they yielded to the council's decision. "We thought that because of his agreement with Pa before, he was chosen to come and talk to Pa and the others here, because he had formerly been supportive of it. So they thought that now they'd get him to talk to them; so he and Wellings came. Then, at that time, they put out the letter to reaffirm the missionaries' obedience to the council in the UK,"[23] Ruth recalls.

As the crisis hung over the church for months like a dark cloud, the tension and arguments brought the worst out of many missionaries. Letters written by the Williams'—who had reaffirmed—and who were now stationed in the Calabar Area during this protracted struggle, reveal the confusion that prevailed. The Williams' were, of course, writing from a thoroughly biased viewpoint. And it seems that they had not been very fond of the Eltons even before the Latter Rain crisis. (In reading their letters, one cannot but come away with the feeling that they had a long-standing dislike for the Eltons.) Even though their letters are skewed against the revival—and against Elton in particular—and were sometimes short on fact and high on emotion, they are a generally good source of anti-Latter Rain missionary gossip.

Leila Williams wrote in September 1953, "The Latter Rain delegation are making another journey to Ilesha next week but it looks as if Syd [Elton] is getting away with all that area, except the Bible School. He declines to go home. We understand that the Morrises are also waiting for a while before returning."[24] And also that same month: "Some say Vernon isn't coming back, while others say he is and is going to live with the Eltons. . . . I believe the Brunts are now Latter Rain and are returning home."[25] Eric Williams wrote on October 8: "Cecil's [Morris] position regarding Latter Rain is not really clear yet, but I'm hoping he will decide to stay with the church"[26]; Leila wrote the following day: "I don't want to open the subject to Ivy [Morris] as we are living together and don't want any unpleasantness."[27]

Leila wrote on October 25, "I heard a whisper that an American delegation of nine men are on their way over here and this may be the reason why Cecil [Morris] is waiting—and no-one can stop them flooding the place, either. The Nigerian Pentecostal Fellowship will welcome them. I guess we shall all have to pack up—or fight them—hopeless! It's turned out to be just a battle against the Apostolic Church. Oh well, God is still on the throne!"[28] And on November 3: "Regarding the Latter Rain, we hear such lots of things and all come from the one source—Ilesha. Eight different events have happened all proving God is on their side—etc, etc. The pastors here all seem to be absolutely Apostolic but will welcome the Latter Rain delegation. Cecil is, of course, in an awkward spot and I think he is hoping for something from them. If he remains Apostolic and finishes this tour, that's the end for him—unless he is ordained as a pastor at home. Syd is certainly getting all his own way now and influencing everybody."[29]

Joy Williams also wrote on November 3: "We have heard that Edgar Parkyns has withdrawn his reaffirmation, and the position with the Morrises is touch and go. These people don't realise it, but in most cases the personal element comes into the decision, and it is really a question of which is going to be to their best advantage—or so we feel. If we wanted any proof about this Latter Rain not being the genuine thing, the fact that they are working in such an underhanded manner would, I think, give us this. Fair play to them all, I think our missionaries genuinely believe that Latter Rain is an additional blessing, and it is obvious that Syd has completely prejudiced them against the Apostolic Church so that their grudge is against the church rather than the Latter Rain. It's a dreadful muddle."[30]

Leila wrote on November 16: "There is certainly nothing to stop the delegation coming here though. It's a worrying position for Eric, but I don't think he's bothered. At the moment these people are thoroughly Apostolic. It's horrible. It's just Syd working against the church and trying to make the European missionaries think they are big noises and so influence them. It's nothing but plotting, scheming, intrigue, etc."[31]

Joy wrote on November 30: "We have heard that the Americans have given Pastor Elton five hundred pounds, so maybe he is going to pay the Morrises a salary; or perhaps the Africans in the Ilesha area are going to pay him. Brunts will be on the way home now having done only twelve months! Miss Ungermann is Latter Rain and has resigned but she really comes under Denmark. Syd Elton has resigned. As far as we know Joe Kirkwood is standing firm but he is due home in the new year. Then in Calabar the Ashwoods' position is not clear. Pastor Hopkins has arrived back but I personally, from a talk we had with Mrs Hopkins when we met her accidentally at Aba the other week, think he has Latter Rain leanings. She definitely said they wanted Latter Rain, and when the delegation went to Calabar before, no ill effect was the result but the church has been more Apostolic since. She said they think they can have Latter Rain in our church. So just what is their hope, we don't know. The Derrys returned from furlough recently and Lewis came last week to collect the things he had left here. As the Morrises were here, we had no private talk with him but Leila managed to whisper: 'Are you Latter Rain?' He said: 'I don't know; I must go carefully.' "[32]

The crisis dragged into 1954. Rosser's report in March that year shows that the argument still centred around understanding the revival as a blessing for the denomination that needed to be kept within "the mould the Lord has given to us," as he put it. "We have repeatedly received letters from some in the Homeland, asking us to give them news of what is going on. They hear so little and know much less. Consequently, I want to free myself of this burden and to let you know all I know. Until recently, there has been little indeed to report about, but progress makes her own road and erects her own signposts toward her ultimate destination. . . . Just as God is 'Fitly framing us together in Christ,' so also ought we to be relevant in vision to fit every other blessing the Lord sends, within the over-all framework of the Divine Order the Lord has given to us as part of His Church. 'Latter Rain' unquestionably comes from God, and is a blessing we as a Church have accepted, though we are not prepared to accept everything that comes with it. The Lord shows me quite clearly that it can be contained, yea, must be contained within the framework of what the Lord has already given to us. If all would see this, then reconciliation upon this aspect of progress can be attained. . . . White-hot metal is dangerous out of control, but run into moulds, it is shaped into all manner of useful articles. Don't scare about blessings. Keep them within the mould the Lord has given to us."[33]

Even though Rosser said the church was open to the revival, this was not entirely the case; such words were used more to douse tension than to actually engage with the revival. Of course, the church was not opposed to the scriptural promise of "latter rain," and this was what it referred to in any further show of sympathy in discussions about "latter rain" after the May 1953 council meeting. The church was not opposed to latter rain, but it was definitely opposed to the Latter Rain revival that began in

Canada in 1948, and had banned it within its fold since May 1953. So there was dishonesty in Rosser giving the impression that the church was not opposed to the revival. It was convenient to say the church was not opposed to *latter rain* while it was opposed to the on-going Latter Rain revival—it made it easy to wriggle out of any argument or commitment. Rosser had to be this diplomatic to win the hearts of the Nigerian leaders and assemblies.

Rosser's and Elton's concepts of embracing the revival were totally divergent. Elton was not content with a vague idea of latter rain. He wanted the church to go the whole hog with the Latter Rain revival that originated from North Battleford, Saskatchewan, Canada, and which had spread to different parts of the world. Elton was hoping that the church would see the fact that God was doing something new and that it was in its best interest to move forward. He wanted the church to see this was its God-given opportunity for reform, its chance to stay relevant with God's programme, rather than just continuing to exist as a denomination. Elton was trying to get the church to see that the work had degenerated into a routine and desperately needed the fresh outpouring that had come in the form of the Latter Rain revival. "As the years passed, men attempted to build four walls around the revival, just as they have always tried to do in the past, and the fire began to die down, for God cannot be contained or restrained within four walls anywhere, anytime,"[34] Elton expressed his disappointment. Elton was pained that the leadership of the church did not see what he was seeing. Baring his thoughts about the situation in later years, he said:

> When the revival occurred in the 1930s, we turned round and drove the people into churches and sat down to teach them and teach them and teach them, and we have never ceased teaching them. We did not realise then, that you can teach a person a small amount of truth and then they should go out and put it into operation, and then come back for more teaching. Instead of which we kept them as church members sitting them and helping us to maintain a system which we were building up and losing the anointing of God.
>
> The Holy Spirit was gradually pushed out of leadership, and man-made leaders took over, establishing constitutions, establishing commercial rules and regulations, particularly concerning money and authority and position. It became a great big business. Education which was necessary came in and all sorts of additional things came in, without the power of the gospel as the basis.

So the revivals of the 1930s failed: they brought in a large number of people but they failed to establish the authority of the Lord Jesus Christ over every-thing in life.[35]

Edgar Parkyns, in a reply to Joy Williams' questions about his thoughts on the revival, brilliantly captures the thoughts and mood of the pro-Latter Rain group led by Elton.[36] To the question of whether or not he believed "that there should be an end-time revival before the Day of the Lord?" Parkyns answered, "Yes." "Can it legitimately be called LATTER RAIN?" asked Joy. "Yes," said Parkyns, "see T. B. Barratt's book written twenty years ago." To the question "Will the truth of Apostles and Proph-ets be a feature of that revival?" Parkyns again said, "Yes. I believe that every great truth will be manifest in a new, big way. Pentecostal truth, no longer confined to Assemblies [of God]. Healing truth, no longer con-fined to Elim [Pentecostal church]. Faith truth, no longer confined to WEC [Worldwide Evangelisation Crusade]. Evangelical truth and missionary truth ... everything."

When Joy asked how it would affect existing denominations, Parkyns answered that "the effect will be similar to that of the Pentecostal revival but more drastic. You may remember Mrs Penn-Lewis's reaction to the 'tongues' movement. She knew so much of the Holy Spirit's power yet she, and many other fine Christians, became bitter. If this move is from God, IF it must be worldwide, and IF the time is short, any denomination which is too narrow in its rules and organisation to hold it must either reject it or be revolutionised or even disrupted by it. If the wine is new it will burst any wine-skin that has lost its elasticity."

Parkyns' answer to Joy's question, "Is the Apostolic Church in that danger?": "Judge ye. But remember that the Lord often warned us through prophecy that if we continued to fail to grasp that which He had for us, He would raise up another people. If His coming is near and we have failed to carry His vision to His people through being over-occupied with our own security, not willing to go to the Cross as a denomination, perhaps He has begun to fulfil that word."

"But if the movement is from God, will it not be free from fault?" asked Joy. "No," said Parkyns, "the end-time net will be full of fishes, good AND bad. . . . Make NO MISTAKE about THAT. We have been warned." To her question, "How may we know if the movement called LATTER RAIN is the real thing?" "Not by the opinions of men," said Parkyns, "nor only by signs and wonders. By their fruits ye shall know them. If in the lives of individuals we recognise in the spirit the deep, sweet fruits of love, joy, peace, meekness, etc, we shall know. The other test is: is the Lord Jesus being given His rightful place?"

"When I was first drawn to Pentecost," Parkyns continued, "what sweet, heavenly oneness we found as we loved and worshipped the Lord! But other good Christians, once my patrons, cut me dead. So the Lord who gives peace and love also brings a sword . . . and a Cross." "Have you ever read the Church Fathers?" asked Parkyns. He continued, "They fairly disciplined and organised the church until the Holy Spirit was unable to move. Every move of the Spirit has ended the same way. Like the Wise Men of Gotham who built a wall round the cuckoo to try and retain perpetual spring, we have built our walls around the Holy Spirit, and He, being grieved, has spread His wings and departed. Walls of creed, walls of organisation, walls of committees. We desired security and achieved sterility. Why not launch out into the deep this time? If the Holy Spirit is moving in a sovereign, worldwide manner, let us have sufficient faith not to try and cage Him. His methods are men. He desires freedom of move-ment found in the Book of Acts. I believe that if we launch out we shall find ourselves swept along in currents that are too strong for us. Isn't that horribly risky? . . . Yes. Faith always looks risky. Let go and let God . . . ! And let us pray that our own Fellowship may not be too hard to yield to the hands of the Potter. The condition of the heart is even more important than the condition of the doctrine."

Were Elton and the other champions of the revival naïve to believe they could reform the church from within? Were they simply being idealistic in pushing for change when the odds were stacked against them?

The Ilesa and Kabba areas were the hottest battle grounds, with loyalties torn in different directions. The districts and assemblies in the two areas were always ready to follow Elton's leadership, and if he had wanted to lead them out of the Apostolic Church to form another denomination, it seems he would have succeeded, but Elton was tired of denominations and denominationalism. Elton was not ready to go the way of James McKeown. Elton lingered in the church, soldiering through many tough months, hoping that the Apostolic Church, at least in Nigeria, would see his perspective.

The Kabba Area actually severed its connection with the Apostolic Church in 1953.[37] The influence of the Latter Rain movement on the

Kabba Area was strong because of Elton's relationship with its leaders over many years. Kabba Area was initially a district under the Ilesa Area; it was much later that it became a separate area with its own superintendent. Many of the leaders in this area were trained by Elton and easily became devotees of the revival. The decision by the Kabba Area leadership to leave the Apostolic Church did not originate from Elton. There were other skirmishes here and there. For instance, when there was a contention ca. 1954 over the superintendence of the Igbo Area, Elton and the Latter Rain revivalists were fingered as the trouble makers. Idris Vaughan, who was in charge of the area until he went for furlough, insinuated that there was a conspiracy between Cousen and Elton.[38] Vaughan accused them of colluding to impose a "Latter Rain pastor" as the superintendent while he was away. When Cousen's wish prevailed, Vaughan refused to return to Nigeria.

Despite his determination to keep the fire of the revival burning in the Apostolic Church, Elton was not willing to take or sanction a step as drastic as had been taken in Ghana. Months after refusing to reaffirm, he was still in the church, which resulted in a stalemate—he was neither in nor out—but he obviously could not sustain this position indefinitely. Despite several attempts at finding a resolution to the crisis, it had not abated by the middle of 1954. Elton's mind was made up about the revival—he would go on promoting it. He resigned his appointment sometime in mid-1954. The missionary committee meeting in Bradford recorded in its minutes of June 16, 1954, "We ask the secretary to write Pastor Elton notifying him that in the light of his letter of resignation, we have appointed Pastor Rosser to relieve him. We ask the secretary to write to the general secretary asking him to send a letter to Pastor Elton stating that he is no more acknowledged as a member of the Apostolic Church."[39]

Rosser had by now temporarily relocated to Ilesa and was living next to the Eltons at one of the mission houses in Oke Oye. The Eltons did not vacate Oke Oye immediately because they were beloved by the congregation, which wanted them to stay. Ruth recalls, "My father [was] at Oke Oye and the people of Oke Oye said, 'No, stay, don't go,' and he said, 'Yes, but I must go out, this is Apostolic, and I am not reaffirmed; this must be Apostolic, so I must get out. But don't you [members of the Apostolic Church] leave the Apostolic Church."[40] But the loyalty to Elton in Ilesa was really strong; therefore, against his counsel, many of the leaders in Ilesa led sections of their congregation out of the Apostolic Church. "He

[Elton] told the Apostolic not to divide, but some of them said, 'Well, we want that revival, and the Apostolic Church doesn't support that revival; we want it, so we cannot stay inside with the restrictions against the revival.' So they left the Apostolic Church, Oke Oye, and became then the Apostolic Gospel Church, Oke Iyin. So my father said, 'Well, I'm not your leader; you are not getting out to follow me. If you want to get out, that is your business, not mine.' They said, 'No, we want to get out, we are standing on ourselves.' But at times, my father and those people [worked] together. They brought some evangelists for my father to train and he trained them and sent them."[41]

There were splits in other assemblies also. The Apostolic Church had six major assemblies in Ilesa at the time. Pastors led sections of their congregation out of the Apostolic Church to form churches that either became affiliated to the newly formed Apostolic Gospel Church or that remained independent. As Ruth recollects, "In the Apostolic Church Igbogi, most of the congregation got out and left and built a shed in some ground they found nearby in their area, they became Ikoti, but Igbogi with the building was still there with few members. . . . Then Oke Iro did the same thing: they left Oke Iro Apostolic Church and became Oke Iyin Apostolic Gospel Church. And I think probably Ikoyi did the same thing. . . . In many churches around Ilesa Area, this move went on. It wasn't Oke Oye but many of the other branches all around Ilesha Area I should think; they had breakaways you can say, which became the Apostolic Gospel Church."[42]

It is noteworthy that on the eve of the visit of the team from America in February 1953, Elton had tried to resign. The February 3, 1953, minutes of the missionary committee meeting in Bradford under the entry titled "Pastor Elton's offer of resignation," stated, "We have passed this on to the General Secretary, as requested, but, as a committee, we cannot entertain the thought for a moment."[43] Why did Elton want to resign just before the arrival of Dr Wyatt's team? Had he made up his mind—based on the stories of the revival and his personal experience of it while on furlough in 1952—that he wanted to be free to give his full attention to furthering its cause? Or did he feel he could no longer endure what he considered to be a loss of vision in the Apostolic Church and wanted to get out as fast as possible, so he could be available for any opportunities that would open up either through Wyatt's team or elsewhere?

Ruth Elton believes the former to be the reason: Her father had seen the

LEFT. The thirty-year-old Sydney Elton in Shrewsbury, taken February 3, 1937, three weeks before his departure for Nigeria.

BELOW *(left)*. Elton's mother, Edith Elton, died of pulmonary tuberculosis at thirty-four.

BELOW *(right)*. Elton's father, Ernest Elton, was an engine fitter in Wolverhampton.

ABOVE. Elton's younger brother, Maurice.

RIGHT. Elton in 1926. This photo, labelled "IOM 1926," was probably taken on a visit to the Isle of Man.

The young and fashionable Elton in a hat and smart clothes with a walking stick, at West Park, Wolverhampton, taken when he was "eighteen going on nineteen."

Elton's younger sister, Marjorie, died of tuberculosis in 1933.

One of the earliest photographs of the
dapper Elton in Shrewsbury.

Elton's future wife,
Hannah Cartwright, most
likely in her twenties.

Elton playing at seaside in the UK.

Shrewsbury, a town of less than 40,000 people in the 1930s. It was here that Elton recorded his first major milestones in life.

ABOVE *(left)*. Aunt Polly, Hannah Cartwright's aunt, and owner of the bread-and-breakfast where Elton was converted and met his future wife.

ABOVE *(right)*. John and Elizabeth Cartwright, Elton's parents-in-law.

BELOW. Wedding of Sydney Granville Elton and Hannah Catherine Elizabeth Cartwright at the Brethren Church, Clive (near Shrewsbury), 22 April 1930. The couple are flanked by the bride's parents.

Elton with mother-in-law in Shrewsbury.

Elton in his car in Shrewsbury, ca. 1930.

Ruth, the only child of the Eltons, born in 1934, in Shrewsbury.

Elton and Ruth in Shrewsbury.

The Apostolic Witness Band (youth group) of the Shrewsbury Apostolic Church. Elton is standing in the middle on the back row.

A newly-arrived Elton on a trip with J. B. Babatope to Ise Ekiti, one of the mission's outstations.

Hannah, during the early years in Ilesa.

Elton with Ruth, cutting bananas in Ilesa, ca. 1938

The Elton family in full Yoruba attire, Ilesa, late 1930s.

Hannah and Ruth on the Yagba road during a mission trip, 1940.

Ruth was usually the cynosure of all eyes wherever they travelled for mission work. Most of the natives were seeing a white baby for the first time.

Hannah and Ruth with the king of Ora and his deputy.

J. A. Babatope, one of the key leaders of the Faith Tabernacle movement. He was Elton's closest ally in the Ilesa Area.

David Odubanjo was responsible for coordinating the activities of the Faith Tabernacle movement nationally from the early 1920s. His leadership was significant in the early growth of the movement, its interface with the healing revival from 1930, and eventually, in the emergence of the Pentecostal movement in Nigeria.

ABOVE. Job Uwalaka served the Eltons as cook from the late 1930s until the 1960s.

RIGHT. Elton was a frequent caller at the post office in Ilesa. Letters from home—from family and supporters—were crucial to the wellbeing of any missionary.

At the young age of twenty-six, Joseph Ayo Babalola became the central figure in the healing revival that shook western Nigeria beginning from July 1930.

Ambrose Clark, pastor of Faith Tabernacle Church, Philadelphia, provided guidance—-through literature and by correspondence—for the budding Faith Tabernacle movement in Nigeria in the first half of the 1920s.

Noah Evans, George Perfect and Idris Vaughan—all of the Apostolic Church, Britain—were the first Pentecostal missionaries in Nigeria.

D. P. Williams, W. J. Williams and A. Turnbull, leaders of The Apostolic Church in Britain, with the leaders of the Faith Tabernacle Church, in Lagos, 1931.

Ruth and Jane Hunter (her father was a doctor at the Wesley Guild Hospital in Ilesa) beside Father Christmas, 1940; standing to their right is Rev. Nelson Ludlow of the Methodist Mission; Elton and Hannah look on with delight in the background.

Hannah teaching knitting to a women's class in Ilesa.

The Eltons on furlough in the UK, ca. 1945.

The Eltons on a ferry to Calabar in 1941.

Elton playing Father Christmas, 1947.

Elton and Hannah, and A. H. Lewis and his wife, with the Bible school students at Oke Oye.

The Eltons in Shrewsbury, 1948.

Students of the Apostolic Church Training Centre completing their course in December 1949, with Elton (principal) and Edgar Parkyns (deputy principal).

revival coming and had made up his mind to be a part of it and wanted to be free of any encumbrances. "My father had already resigned before they had to sign [the reaffirmation] because he said to himself that he must not be apostolic *only*, he should be interdenominational."[44] It is definitely curious that he would want to leave a few days before the arrival of the American team, considering he was the chief organizer. Whatever his reason for wanting to leave, the leadership did not want to entertain his request at the time. In retrospect, maybe they should have let him go then.

The one written statement that we have that is closest to an official position by the church reveals the extreme bitterness of the leadership towards Elton's action; it fingered him as the major culprit in the Latter Rain saga. It is contained in a short biography of Samuel Adegboyega, published by the church after his death in 1979: "Pastor S. G. Elton who was then the Missionary Superintendent for Ilesa Area was the principal agent who organized and spearheaded the Latter Rain Movement to come to Nigeria to undermine and to destroy the established doctrinal principles and practices of The Apostolic Church laid down by his counterpart expatriate missionaries in West Africa. He wilfully decided to do this in defiance to the authority of The Apostolic Church International Missionary Council who sent him to Nigeria as a missionary, thereby stabbing his master at the back. The battle was so fierce at that time that the International Missionary Council in United Kingdom sent one of their ablest Leaders in person of Pastor C.H.G. Rosser and another representative to visit West Africa with a view to reconciling the situation arising from the havoc done by Pastor Elton."[45]

The church noted that the revival "resulted in the breaking away of some members and assemblies from the Apostolic Church in Nigeria and in Ghana where they had also conducted similar Revival campaigns," and that if not for the "timely intervention of late Pastor Adegboyega who waded into the crises with the help of the grace of God under Divine Guidance, the whole structural work of the Apostolic Church in Nigeria and in Ghana would have been torn into pieces. . . . The upheavals and the unfavourable atmosphere created by the after-effect of the Latter Rain movement episodes almost rocked the foundational work of the Apostolic Church in Nigeria and in Ghana into a state of oblivion."[46] After praising the Lord for blessing Adegboyega with the "wisdom, patience, courage and steadfastness" through which he was able to "restore the Divine Order and Government in The Apostolic Church, its principles and Practices," the leadership went on to portray Elton as a rebellious leader: "Today, Pastor S. G. Elton, now resident in Nigeria, somewhere in Ilesa, is no more in The Apostolic Church despite all efforts to make him re-trace his steps."[47]

Elton once gave a slightly different picture of his departure. After relating how the enemy had opposed him over the years through "storm after storm, tornado after tornado and [had] failed," he said, "And since we moved out of the church which was my ministry for sixteen years—I left them because God said, 'I have got a bigger ministry for you.' The prophetic word as I left was: 'Don't you deter or delay my servant Elton; I have got a bigger job for him and it will cover the whole country and beyond.'"[48]

It may at first look like one of the parties was attempting to manipulate historical facts, but when we look closer we find that both parties were square. Most likely the prophecy to Elton was given at the Oke Oye church, which was totally supportive of his role in promoting the revival and which was equally very sympathetic throughout his ordeal with the national leadership. So he would have been sent off with a buoyant prophecy at the local assembly in Ilesa. But this was in total contrast to the mood of the officials at the national level.

Elton was disappointed with his colleagues for exalting denominational allegiance above what they all believed was a move of God. He was angry that they had all acknowledged it was a fresh outpouring of the Holy Spirit and had all participated in it, only for them to later buckle under denominational pressure. "Those people heard what God said; those people accepted the vision, until it conflicted with their own rules and regulations and threatened the authority of their own established leaders. And then the established leaders rejected that light. They preferred their own way; they preferred to stay as they were,"[49] Elton lamented. He believed they had missed the opportunity to lead the church in Nigeria into the next phase of God's programme.

Also referring to this episode many years after the events, Elton said, "In 1954 . . . God told me, I want you to move out, and in prophecy He told me what to do. At that time I was number one superintendent for the whole of Nigeria for a big church; the leading church at that time of the Pentecostal mission/work. And in that church we all sat there when God was speaking to us, and telling us what He was going to do for Nigeria, what I am telling you today, some of it. Pouring out of the former and the latter rain and moving on to deal with the whole of Nigeria; and God challenged us all then and said, 'It's yours if you will go forward.' And He said what will happen, 'I will move my servant Elton out,' and it was the Nigerians who prophesied it. Not I. I knew what God was going to do, but they prophesied it. And when the issue came and I moved on, they said, no. We are staying inside our four walls; we are staying inside our church because that's what the constitution says."[50]

It is remarkable that in the official history of the Apostolic Church worldwide, *What God Hath Wrought*, written by T. N. Turnbull, the son of Andrew Turnbull, the first vice president of the church, Sydney and Hannah Elton are missing. Turnbull's book, which was published in 1959, featured Nigeria prominently, recognizing it as one of the most fruitful mission fields of the church; it also listed the names of all the European missionaries who had ever served in the country up till that time. Elton was one of the finest missionaries of the church and was the most senior European superintendent in the Apostolic Church, Nigeria, at the time of his leaving. Turnbull was definitely well acquainted with Elton. His omission was, therefore, too glaring.

Elton had been one of the most celebrated missionaries of the church, and his reputation back home had become legendary, but as he would reflect many decades later, he knew that he was in danger of becoming blinded by success, a sure indication that he would not be willing to move into the next phase of God's programme. He was, therefore, willing to walk away from all his achievements and if need be, start all over again. He had no delusions that it would be a painless process, but he was resolute about laying it all on the altar in order to move on with God. "I built churches. I opened churches: [between] 4,000 and 5,000. I built schools; I built a college. I built and built and built," Elton would remark many years after the crisis. "And my authorities in England, when I used to go home to England, they [would] point to me and say, 'You see that man? He opened 150 churches in one [month]; that's more than all the churches that we've got in England. And he opened them in one month. He's got a teacher training college; he's got sixty schools; and he's a proprietor. He's a member of the proprietor's council for education in Nigeria. He's a permanent member of the syllabus committee to work out the syllabus for all schools. That's a man!' I could ask for anything I wanted and I almost [certainly] could get it. I said I wanted more missionaries, and they said, 'How many?' What do you want? . . . I was the number one man. One day I met the Lord Jesus in a new way and I repented. Repented? Of what? Repented of being so successful."[51]

After Elton resigned, he was pressured to vacate his accommodation on the mission compound in Oke Oye, but he stayed a while longer due to the insistence of the church members that he should not leave. But eventually, Rosser and Wellings came around and forced his eviction from the house. Joy Williams describes (almost gloating to herself) the awkward situation in the days just before Elton's departure from the mission compound: "At present the Eltons are still living in No. 1 house. The Rossers and Morrises are sharing No. 2 house, and Vernon and his wife are in No. 3. Imagine the atmosphere! Pastor Rosser said Eltons are really acting very courteously to him but he doesn't feel they have as much spiritually as they had prior to Latter Rain. Morrises are now anti-Elton and anti-American regarding non-organisation, and Cyril is hopeful they might reaffirm now. Cyril thinks Vernon might even reaffirm in time but at present his position is different as he is engaged mostly on the secular side. Cyril doesn't think Eltons will return to UK but go to some other place in Nigeria. We are glad we are not in Ilesha!"[52]

Joy Williams' statement that the "Morrises are now anti-Elton and anti-American regarding non-organisation," is incorrect. In fact, Cecil Morris was one of the staunchest supporters of the revival and worked closely with Elton in promoting it. When Rosser arrived in Ilesa, he tried to win over many of the missionaries, and because of Rosser's accommodating tone towards the revival, Morris felt he could work with him. So he began to cooperate with Rosser and was for a time not active in promoting the revival with Elton, but he remained very close to the Eltons. Ruth recalls that the reason why Morris decided to work more closely with Rosser was because of financial support. Since the missionary allowance of all those who did not reaffirm was withdrawn, and he wasn't sure of how he would support himself, he decided to go along with Rosser, since he claimed not to oppose the revival.

In fact, Morris' closeness to Rosser is better understood in light of a story Morris told the Eltons at the height of the crisis. Rosser and Morris had been driving in the car, and Rosser suddenly said he was so fed up with what was going on in the Apostolic Church and that he would almost like to drive the car to the bush and end his life.[53] "From what C. T. Morris said," recalls Ruth, "Cyril Rosser in his heart knew the revival was from God . . . [but] he had reaffirmed to obey the council which the Apostolic Church believed was absolutely next to God. So how could he change? He had reaffirmed and obeyed everything. What could he do? But in his heart he believed in the revival. I believe that."[54] Rosser's internal crisis about the situation made it easier for Morris to work with him. Ruth remembers that Morris "was for it [the revival], and he came out of the Apostolic Church for the revival in support of my father until he had no financial support, so he went back to help a bit; I think hoping that he would calm things down and make peace until about six months later [when] they supported him back to the UK. Getting to the UK, he couldn't do anything; he couldn't cooperate with them, and he left the Apostolic Church, UK."[55] That financial support was always an issue for Morris throughout the crisis is adequately confirmed in the minutes of the missionary committee meetings in Bradford.

Elton was replaced by Eric Williams. The Eltons temporarily moved to a newly completed building in Imo, at the time a suburb of Ilesa. This building, which was then arguably one of the most elegant in the town, was owned by one Olaitan, a native of Ilesa. The connection was made by a mutual friend, Adetunji, a mechanic, who was very close to Elton; he had for many years complained about the Eltons' accommodation at Oke Oye and had often talked about getting him a more befitting place. He was only too glad to link Elton with Olaitan when he was ejected from Oke Oye. The Eltons lived in Olaitan's house for two years.[56] A 1954 picture of Elton and Hannah standing at the balcony of this house shows them looking into the horizon and laughing. Were they looking into the future that was beckoning?

The decision to leave the Apostolic Church mission while remaining in Nigeria was a major step of faith for the Eltons. Telling the story many years later, no doubt with some nostalgia, Elton did not in any way attempt to downplay the precariousness of the situation—God had to come through for them or they were going to become the laughingstock of many who thought they had made a foolish decision by leaving the mission: "I remember the day, more than thirty years ago, when my wife and I submitted our resignation from any salaried job," he began. "We told our leaders who were visiting us from England that we would now no longer require any salary. We had finished. We had no income in this country. We had no farm. We had no food in our stock room. But we knew God was leading us."[57]

In a very rare display of emotion, which further reveals how deeply he felt about the situation, he talked about how two leaders from England (Rosser and Wellings) "who had just left me, who had accepted my resignation and walked away, drove away after being my guests and eating my food in my house; they drove away, leaving me, knowing that I had no source of income, and they hoped that I would soon after pack up and leave Nigeria."[58] "For months no money came in," recalled Elton, "We came down to our last five pounds. I had no farm, I had no business. My wife prayed, 'Lord if we have done the right thing, today in the post there will be a letter from someone in England who is sending us money who has never sent us money before.'"[59] One can therefore imagine their excitement when they went to the post office "and in the post box was a letter from a person we had never heard of before." Enclosed in the letter was a cheque and a part of the letter read, "We feel that you are possibly facing a crisis and are in need, so we are enclosing a cheque which we hope will meet your need whatever it is." Elton remarked, "Now, they didn't know what I was facing, and they didn't know what I was going to go through." The money was substantial enough to buy him "a car for transport as an independent person." As he later said, "I moved out in faith, believing God would provide and He did so."[60]

Leaving the Apostolic Church released Elton into his most fruitful years of ministry in Nigeria. For the first few years, he became primarily occupied with organizing Latter Rain meetings in different cities around the country. Before organizing any revival meeting, Elton requested all participating Pentecostal churches to work together in the interest of the gospel and organize the meeting as a joint fellowship. For the first time, denominational walls were broken as churches around the country cooperated. Elton, though a member of the Apostolic Church, had always been interdenominational in his Christian world view.

Through the revival, new opportunities for ministry opened everywhere, even to the Christ Apostolic Church members and ministers whom he had previously been unable to reach because of the 1940 split. Joseph Babalola recorded in his diary on February 3, 1953, that he received a letter from Elton.[61] On June 25, 1954, Babalola recorded that "we went for baptism service by the seaside for 167 people. Pastor Elton came from Ilesa."[62] Again, on the twenty-seventh: "Morning baptism service for 248 people. Thanksgiving service in the evening. The white men [Elton and his team] went to three villages."[63] The baptisms took place in Sapele, a town where Babalola did a lot of ministry work. Timothy Obadare (who founded the World Soul Winning Evangelistic Ministry in 1975, and subsequently became one of the most successful evangelists in the history of the Christ Apostolic Church) was one of the people who were significantly impacted by the revival. Christ Apostolic Church historian, Christopher Oshun, writing of the beginning of Obadare's ministry, says that "his first experience of Pentecostal baptism was in February 1949"; he had "made his first spiritual debut within the [Christ Apostolic] Church" by 1952; and "when in April 1953 two expatriate Pentecostal missionaries, Brother Poole and Dr Wyatt, visited Ilesa, Obadare as a young man recognised in them proof of a Pentecostal ministry. Desirous to make this his own, he entered into a week of retirement at the end of which he was filled with Pentecostal power."[64]

For some years there was close and frequent collaboration between the Latter Rain leaders and teams in Nigeria and Ghana. James McKeown visited Ilesa a couple of times. Joy Williams wrote on March 22, 1955, "James McKeown was here all the week though, and every night he and Pastor Elton visited one of our six churches in Ilesha."[65] One of McKeown's circular letters, describing the situation in Ilesa, read, "Three assemblies in Ilesa are for God and three for Bradford!"[66] McKeown was again in Ilesa in August 1955 to speak in Latter Rain campaigns.[67] In 1955 Elton and Wyatt were trying to help McKeown found a magazine in the Gold Coast.[68] Stanley Hammond and his wife relocated to Nigeria around 1954 to work with the Eltons. He was very much involved in the running of the Bible school associated with the revival.[69] When the Eltons travelled on furlough in 1955, Hammond was put in charge of the work.[70] At one time about a dozen "Gold Coast people" were at the Bible school in Ilesa.[71]

The Eltons travelled to the UK sometime in 1955. Elton alone then travelled to the US from Manchester, arriving in New York on August 25.[72] He went on an extensive tour of the United States, meeting with many preachers. He was the guest of Dr Wyatt in Portland, Oregon, where he preached "over the Wings of Healing and Global Frontiers international radio broadcasts."[73] He appealed to Christians in America: "I have made this trip to England and to America for more teams. The need is terrible. We must help the tribes who are crying for help *now*. Dr Wyatt met many of the leaders of 7 different denominations, all pleading for more teams. They want more literacy and agricultural teams to go in and help follow up the preaching of the Gospel. Dr Wyatt made some big promises that will require the help of many and must be backed by a tremendous faith in God. We are training and sending *African* teams under Global Frontiers to tribes where missionaries cannot go because our bodies cannot endure the climate—the Africans can. 20 cents per day will provide them with food. God has brought us face to face with the need and with the responsibility."[74]

The Eltons returned to Nigeria from this trip in November 1955.

In the 1950s, whenever the Eltons travelled to the UK, they visited Dean House Christian Fellowship in Bradford, a local assembly founded by Cecil Cousen after he left the Apostolic Church. Dean House became a centre from which the renewal was propagated. Cousen, writing about the genesis of the fellowship, said, "It will be sufficient for the reader to know that God visited us personally with Deliverance and Restoration. Thereupon we began immediately, in faith, to rebuild our spiritual temple. Unfortunately, however, such a ministry was unacceptable in certain quarters and so Christian Fellowship came into being as an independent local assembly and a centre somewhat similar to the pattern of Antioch in the book of Acts. Already many have joined us locally and many others have visited us from the British Isles and other countries—all for one reason, they long for a new move."[75] "It was a good evangelical place,"[76] Ruth still remembered decades later.

Until the end of his life, Elton would never again trust huge denominational structures to be faithful with the move of the Holy Spirit.

SEVEN

"THERE IS A RESPONSIBILITY UPON ME"

On February 16, 1935, one Rev. G. G. Danby George, writing as "a Representative of the Apostolic Faith, Corner Six Burnside Street, Portland, Oregon, USA, in Nigeria,"[1] from Aba, to the district officer in charge of Ahoada, in the Eastern division of the country, reported that he had opened mission stations in "Ubeta Ikpafia Clan under Uribe Native Court." In this letter, he requested permission to open a school in one of these stations in response to the converts' zeal for an educational institution. It is interesting that though Rev. Danby George was generally accurate in his information about the Apostolic Faith Church in Oregon, whose headquarters was then located at NW Sixth & Burnside Street, it is doubtful that he was at any time officially commissioned by the church to go to Nigeria. It seems his missionary adventure was a personal initiative.

One cannot but come to this conclusion considering that in the annals of the Apostolic Faith Church's missionary expansion, neither he nor the mission stations he established are once mentioned.[2] The church established by Timothy Oshokoya in Lagos in the year 1944 is regarded as the beginning of the Apostolic Faith Church's work in Nigeria. If the lack of recognition for Danby George's "pioneering work" was an oversight, then it was a most unfortunate one. But given the fastidious way the Apostolic Faith mission went about its business, this was very unlikely; in all probability, George, though a member of the church, came to Nigeria on his own; perhaps with the knowledge of a few brethren, but not in any official capacity. Records show that Danby George was still in Nigeria in 1946;[3] whether he was still around long after is not certain. By 1946, he not only had oversight of the mission stations, he was also addressing letters as "The Manager, Apostolic Faith Schools, Olokuma—Ahoada."[4]

Danby George's independent, one-man operation was representative of the pattern along which the earliest Pentecostal missions in the eastern part (at the time comprising south-eastern and south-southern Nigeria) of the country developed—with the exception of the Assemblies of God, the Apostolic Church and the Church of Christ, all foreign Pentecostal organizations. Many of the eastern Pentecostal churches were isolated operations for many years after their founding, their leaders often lacking the training and resources necessary to fulfil their stated mission. Most of the founders were Nigerians who had come across foreign or local Pentecostal literature and were zealous to replicate such experiences; others were Christians in the older denominational churches who had at one time or the other briefly been under the informal tutelage of foreign Pentecostal missionaries like Danby George. These men, often with little education, secular or spiritual, but with much spiritual zeal, were simply trying their best to establish something for God.

It was to this region and its small indigenous and independent Pentecostal churches that Elton devoted much of his energy in the first few years of becoming an independent Pentecostal minister. The early history of the Church of the Nazarene in Abak, one of the churches Elton adopted in this region, illustrates the prevailing situation of these churches. Sometime in the 1940s, a Nigerian Christian, Jeremiah Ekaidem, while serving with the Allied Forces in North Africa and Europe during World War II was given a tract with the name and address of the Church of the Nazarene in the United Sates by a crewman of a merchant marine ship which docked in Lagos.[5] (The Church of the Nazarene was founded in 1908 from the merger of a number of Wesleyan-Holiness churches.[6]) Ekaidem was deeply moved by the message of the tract, and once he returned home he shared it with the members of his church in Abak, but the leadership rejected his attempt to introduce the Church of the Nazarene's emphases to the congregation.

In 1946, Ekaidem, along with some other members of this church, left to start a new church and a school which they named "Church of the Nazarene."[7] During the next few years, they corresponded with the headquarters of the church in the US in Kansas City, Missouri. In 1951 the general superintendent of the church visited Nigeria during a tour of the church's missions in Africa, but he was not able to make contact with the Nigerian assembly due to communication problems. The church soldiered on as best as it could, and when an opportunity to be a part of something bigger opened up, they were willing to come under Elton's wings.

The Light Bearers Mission in Aba was another example. In November 1952, the leaders of this group, which had affiliated itself with a Pentecostal church in the US, Light Bearers Church of Enid, Oklahoma, were requesting a permit from the Officer in Charge, Immigration Office, Lagos, for the American pastor to visit. "We are ministers of the Light Bearers Mission, an interdenominational church springing up in Nigeria and affiliates with the U.S.A. The Superintendent, Rev. J. E. Jeter of Enid Oklahoma, sent us Church Charter as an authority with which we are carrying on God's work in the said Mission. The Church Charter was registered at Port Harcourt. At the moment Rev. J. E. Jeter wants to visit us to see how our mission work is going on."[8] Of the Light Bearers Mission, the senior district officer, Aba Division, wrote in an official letter in 1953: "This body is a revivalist sect, connected with a parent body in the United States of America, though the American body has no control over the local one. The local organisation is an entirely African controlled concern. They have four small churches in this Division."[9]

After leaving the Apostolic Church, Elton began operating in the country under the name "World Christian Crusade."[10] This name was jointly chosen by Elton and Cecil Morris.[11] For a time, Elton and Morris worked together closely in promoting the revival, but Morris did not stay much longer in the country; after returning to the UK, he went on to have a thriving ministry which spanned a number of European countries.[12]

Through the platform of World Christian Crusade (WCC), Elton was able to secure what was then called a missionary quota, which meant that he had government approval to invite missionaries—in this case Latter Rain evangelists—to work in the country. In a 1956 letter to the permanent secretary, Ministry of Internal Affairs, Enugu, Elton explained the mission of World Christian Crusade: "We have been requested to inform you of our desire to work in Eastern Nigeria and to explain our policy and the purpose of this movement, particularly in connection with Eastern Nigeria. The World Christian Crusade is a non-denominational and non-sectarian movement associated with many independent groups of churches in U.S.A. and we do not seek in any way to commence new churches but rather to work with, and render the very much needed assistance to, many of the indigenous and smaller denominations in Nigeria who are not represented on the Christian Council of Nigeria."[13]

He also made it known that the mission had a staff strength "in Nigeria of around twenty, mostly Americans." He made sure to emphasize the diversity of skills and professional qualifications of this group: "Some are mainly missionaries of many years' experience in overseas work, others are trained educationists, and others have medical training and experience." Elton was also pleased to let the secretary know that they had "been invited into Eastern Nigeria by the leaders" of the denominations among whom they planned to conduct ministry. He mentioned six churches: in Ikot Ekpene—Light and Life Assemblies and African Apostolic Church; in Uyo—Associated Pentecostal Assemblies of the World and Pentecostal Assemblies of Nigeria; and in Abak—Church of Nazarene and Wings of Healing.[14]

Elton brilliantly diagnosed the condition of these churches and their leaders, and strategically positioned himself to transform them into vibrant, dynamic Pentecostal churches. This would require a complete overhaul of their structures, the systematic training of their leaders, and a certain level of oversight by Elton. Elton engaged both his personal resources and the loose but potent machinery of the Latter Rain movement to accomplish this burning passion. In line with this, he noted in his letter to the permanent secretary: "Some of these groups have adopted the titles of our American organisation without actually joining them but they have all expressed a desire to co-operate with us and with one another, in an endeavour to raise the standard of Christian experience and living conditions of the people."[15] If arrangements were satisfactorily concluded, they were going to open two Bible training centres—one at Ikot Ekpene and the other at Uyo. This would be housed in "temporary rented buildings, to train church catechists for the above mentioned groups."

Most likely Elton first came across the leaders of these churches during the Latter Rain revivals conducted in the region in 1953 and 1954. Once he became free of his commitment to the Apostolic Church, these churches became a major focus of his ministry. Apart from the ones mentioned in Elton's letter, some of the other Pentecostal churches in the region were Christ Pentecostal Mission, which had ten branches with a total of 450 members; United Apostolic Church, which had three branches and a total of 480 members; Independent Apostolic Church, which had two branches with a total of 2,464 members; and Pentecostal Holiness Church, which had nineteen branches with a total membership of 1,391.[16]

In the 1950s and 1960s, there were scores of such groups scattered around the region.[17] Elton founded the Nigeria Christian Fellowship (NCF)—which served both as a network of churches and a ministerial association for the small independent churches in this region—through which he could more easily coordinate his outreach to them. David du Plessis, who toured the region with Elton in 1958 observed: "Thus, one finds many smaller indigenous Pentecostal movements throughout the country. The terms *Apostolic Church* and *Pentecostal Assemblies* are popular and are contained in one way or another in the name of these movements, which have recently formed the Nigeria Christian Fellowship in Eastern Nigeria."[18]

To fulfil his grand plan for these churches and the region at large, Elton engaged evangelists from churches in the Latter Rain movement in America in short-term missionary service, which lasted two years on the average. Many Latter Rain leaders in America who were in constant touch with Elton regularly fed him young men and women who had been trained in their churches and Bible schools and who were eager to put their training to use in foreign mission fields. Ruth, who worked closely with her father during this period and who managed the office whenever Elton travelled, remembers that "one time we had twenty missionaries from America. They would come for a few months preaching, holding revivals and crusades."[18]

These evangelists were fiery young men and women in their late teens and early twenties, who were able to match Elton's energy and enthusiasm. Under Elton's direction, they invaded the region, and eventually, every part of the country, spreading Pentecostal fires and sowing seeds that would become major Pentecostal missions in later years. The groups of young men and women who came to work under Elton were called "invasion teams."[19]

Harold Alcock came in February 1954.[20] In October 1954, Grace and Claude Stran, Bill Zigler and Purvis Lane (later joined by his wife, Thelma) arrived in Nigeria. Joe Bass and Jackie Evans, both eighteen-year-old young men, arrived in 1955. Then there was Herbert Stevens; Harold Brown; Marjorie Nixon; Jean Schlappi; Delbert and Beverly Wells; Dale

Collins and his wife; Edgar Powells; the John Cookes; the Ted Patmores; the Edward Urbancsoks; the Joseph Sabos; Eurmal Scarborough; Maxine Dargel; Dean Jeche; Earl Leasure; Paul Mueller; and many others. Many of these missionaries were trained at the Bethesda Bible Training Institute in Portland, Oregon, founded by Thomas Wyatt.[21]

Surviving letters by these evangelists give us a picture of the Pentecostal revival that was blazing across the country. In one of her letters back home, Grace Stran wrote, "Visited four villages today and ministered. . . . The results were amazing! . . . As we drove to our destination, everywhere on the road men, women and children waved their hands and called out to us 'Hallelujah!' . . . In one village 81 women signed their names to a request that I return and instruct them in whatever I felt led. They long for deliverance. This is God's time—and He does have a plan—for the deliverance of the woman particularly in Africa. . . . Many of our congregations number into the thousands. My husband and I have moved to Benin City, considered spiritually the darkest place in Africa. To date no great revival has ever been held here. Today we find God is preparing hearts and people seem to desire something from God. We are making preparations for a large campaign. Every day last week we spent with the pastors and workers and the response was good—something definite is being accomplished."[22]

Herbert Stevens wrote in one letter, "We rejoice that all the area around the city of Sapele (within a radius of about 30 miles) has been reached with the message of God's LOVE for the first time, and they have seen demonstrations of His miracle working power. . . . Recently a whole village, including the ruling juju witch doctor, forsook their idols. Upon our word that the idols were dumb and dead, they took sticks and beat them into an unrecognizable rubble."[23] Harold Brown wrote:

Brother Elton and I went way into the jungle to a village to minister. There was only a trail leading into it. We must have had 1,500 [people] out, anyway. I think nearly everyone stood for salvation. There really is a need for workers here.

Last week we held meetings at Efi. There are a lot of good reports of healings which took place. Some blind people received their sight. It was wonderful to see the people take off their juju. One man was carried to the service and during the message God touched his body and made him completely whole. One night we had all the sick fenced in by bamboo and we laid hands on them.

The next night we received many wonderful testimonies. This place is completely turned upside down. When we came home riding in the back of the truck we received more cheers and hallelujahs than if it were the Queen. These really are lovely people. After we came home and had our supper we heard them going past the rest house still singing and praising God.

Last Sunday we went to the leper colony in Ilesa—open door. My, what a need. They are starved spiritually. Hope to return to them soon. . . . We were out to a new village Friday night, the largest crowd yet for one village. When the Lord said to pray for labourers, He must have been looking to the people of Africa as they are perishing for lack of someone to tell them about the Lord. Yesterday, Herb [Stevens] ministered in the Baptist church. I was going to a village but got rained out. We both went to two villages and on the way home we had to minister again in two other villages as the people see us go by and know we have to return that way so every village gathers, waiting, for our return. When I got home I didn't want to eat but went right to bed. We were preached out.[24]

Stanley Hammond wrote back home, "The campaign at Iwaraja is enlarging with many people saved and healed. Jackie Evans and I minister in each meeting."[25] And Purvis Lane: "I was amazed to see the hunger of the people to hear the Word of God. I saw many turn from their juju and fears. We are ministering in the villages and also preparing for a mass meeting. We are very happy with the cooperation from local ministers, and people. Harold Brown, Bill Zigler and myself had a meeting with Olu, King of Warri, and some of the ministers, as we are making plans to have a mass meeting there next month."[26] John Cooke, who was then twenty years old, wrote to his mother in 1956:

Dear Mom. We have just finished a five-day meeting in Ikot Ubo. I am very tired, but rejoice over the great work accomplished in these few days. Never have I seen so many people so anxious to hear the Gospel of Jesus Christ. For some, it meant walking many miles—some stayed on the grounds even between services lest they miss something. These neglected people are awakening to a new hope.

It is late, but the atmosphere is still hot and humid. The others are retiring for the night but I wanted to get this letter written, since tomorrow will be another very busy day. Tonight's meeting still lingers in my mind, and as I write I re-live many scenes that speak of souls being born into the Kingdom of God and of the hope that has been kindled in the hearts of the people. A once-dead nation is coming to life—eternal life!

Whatever were my feelings as I said good-bye to you and the folks at Wings of Healing that December morning when the Caravan left for Africa, I am more than rewarded. I feel so unworthy to have a part in this great revival that is sweeping this area. It is a difficult field of labour, in the natural, but the spiritual revival that is sweeping thousands into the Kingdom of God puts something in my heart that makes me want to spend the rest of my life ministering to those who have never before heard of the Gospel of Christ.

We Began in Abak: A village four miles from Abak was selected for the first big campaign. In Ikot Ubo, there are two main churches and they were very cooperative. Meetings were planned for every morning and evening for five days. The morning meetings averaged about 750 in attendance. The first evening we had better than 2,000 in attendance. They brought an insane man to the service bound hand and foot. When we prayed for him, he was instantly delivered and leaped for joy. The next night we had over 6,000, which shows you how fast the word spreads when God performs miracles.

Crowd Doubled: The third night the crowd had more than doubled, and some of the African ministers said they counted over 14,000. That night we prayed for a blind man whose sight was immediately restored. We learned later that his nephew is chief of Ikot Ubo and the chairman of the Abak district schools. Later, this chief stood up in one of the services and publicly thanked us for coming to his area and stated that he was sure much progress and good would result among the people. . . .

All Manner of Sickness Healed: Over 16,000 people attended the last night of the campaign, to climax what has been the greatest experience of my life. People again testified that they had been healed of all manner of diseases and illnesses. Arms and legs were straightened, blind eyes were opened, the deaf could hear, and many sick and afflicted found health and deliverance. One old man who had been badly crippled with arthritis and had big ugly knots on his joints, was instantly healed and knots vanished. The joy of these people as they come in contact with the goodness of God cannot be described. We found ourselves crying and laughing with the people. . . . [26]

Delbert Wells first heard about Elton while attending the Bethesda Bible Institute in Portland, Oregon. [27] (Wells had previously served in Nigeria in 1957 under another mission but had no knowledge of Elton until this time.) While there, Wells met an American group who introduced him to the work of the World Christian Crusade in Nigeria.[28] He decided to work with World Christian Crusade, and in 1961 he came to Nigeria with his wife, Beverly. After landing at the Kano Airport, they took a flight to Lagos, from where they were picked up by Elton, who drove them in his car to Ilesa. Their work for a few months mainly involved running a small Bible training for local evangelists who ministered in small villages all around western Nigeria.

Delbert and Beverly Wells returned to the US in 1962 and then came back to the country in 1967, but were stationed in Uyo this time. Their work was with Life and Light Apostolic churches, one of those mentioned in Elton's 1956 introductory letter. The leader of this church, which had many branches scattered in small villages all over the East, was S. U. Ekpo, who lived in Oron, a neighbouring town. From their base in Uyo, Delbert "travelled almost daily to the nearby villages to teach Bible School [and] have training sessions for the pastors and evangelists."[29] There were "over 300 indigenous churches to work with,"[30] Beverly remembered, and Delbert preached every Sunday at one or two of these churches. Where did the Wells get the students for the Bible school? Elton sent letters to his "fellowship of churches in the East" (the NCF network of churches) stating that "there would be a Bible school beginning for potential pastors and evangelists."[31] Once the letters were received, information spread by word of mouth and the students gathered from far and near. The students received teaching in the mornings and went out to evangelize in the afternoon. The school lasted for three months and then the students had another three months of practical work; this ended a session; another session would then commence for the next six months. During their three terms in Nigeria, Delbert and Beverly Wells trained over five hundred evangelists and pastors in eastern and western Nigeria.[32]

Like Thomas Wyatt, Dale Young—the pastor of a church in Caldwell, Ohio, active in the Latter Rain movement—was also involved in sending missionaries to Nigeria and raising financial support for many others who were not connected to his ministry, but who were willing to come to Nigeria to serve under the World Christian Crusade. He organized a support network for the missionaries under Elton with a monthly stipend of five pounds.[33] Around 1963, Glen Reeves, his wife and two children, came to Nigeria through Young's connection; they worked mainly in the Ikot Ekpene area for close to two years, after which they returned to the

US. Ruth Elton fondly remembers Reeves and his wife: "They were quite tall. Reeves's legs hung over any bed he slept on!"[34]

Elton was heavily involved with the invasion teams as they moved across the country; records show that Elton was on these trips for weeks at a time. One letter, dated December 17, 1955, from the Resident of Calabar Province to another government official about Elton and his team, reported that a "team of missionaries—leader, Elton, from Ilesa—now touring division under the auspices of World Christian Crusade."[35] From all indications, it seems they were still around by January 30, 1956.[36]

Elton developed a Bible correspondence course for the NCF network of churches, titled *Special Ministers' Course for Nigeria.*[37] The twelve-lesson course had a booklet devoted to each lesson. Each lesson ended with questions to which the students had to supply answers "clearly and neatly written on ruled paper. Leave a margin of one inch, on the left hand side of the paper for the Tutor's remarks and two lines between each answer."[38] Each student had an enrolment number so that Elton could "keep track of their progress." Students' answers to the questions in the studies were to be sent to "World Christian Crusade Bible Course" in Ilesa. If they desired to have the correct answers to the questions from him they were expected to enclose a "stamped addressed envelope." This course was perhaps the most important tool in the training of the local evangelists and pastors throughout that region. Thousands of pastors and evangelists enrolled for this course.

Elton's efforts through the Bible school programmes and correspondence course represent the largest individual effort towards laying the foundation of Pentecostal doctrine in eastern Nigeria outside denominational boundaries. In the 1950s, the Apostolic Church and the Assemblies of God were the only Pentecostal organizations involved in Bible schools and correspondence courses in this region; these were, however, strictly denominational. Elton was the only one in this region reaching out to the non-denominationally affiliated indigenous Pentecostal churches with specialized Pentecostal Bible training.

When the overall impact of the work of these missionaries/evangelists on the development of the Pentecostal movement in eastern Nigeria can be fully assessed, the result will definitely be staggering. The Latter Rain missionaries also worked extensively in other parts of the country. Elton had a vision that the "full gospel" would be taken to every nook and cranny of Nigeria within a short period of time, resulting in a completely

"Christianized" nation. Elton envisioned a nation where all traces of idolatry, or "jujuism," as he frequently called it, would be completely rooted out, a nation where the name of Jesus Christ would be exalted throughout the land. (So determined was Elton, in conjunction with Wyatt, to make and keep Nigeria "Christian" that they started printing two magazines to counter Communist literature that was then flooding the country.

The mission of one of the magazines, named *Our Freedom*, was stated thus: "Under the supervision of Global Frontiers, natives in Ilesa, Nigeria are working six days a week printing 'Our Freedom,' a publication carrying a Gospel message of deliverance for their people and a strong counter-action against false communistic propaganda. More than seventy thousand copies are printed in the native language monthly in addition to ten thousand copies each month in the English language."[39]) Elton wanted the whole of Nigeria blanketed with the Pentecostal message: He wanted the existing indigenous Pentecostal churches to become equipped to confront the spiritual darkness that prevailed in many parts of the country and for the Pentecostal message to be taken to areas where it was previously unknown. Elton, like an army general marshalling his forces in strategic warfare, was intent on "taking" Nigeria for Christ—nothing less was satisfactory. Elton believed this was possible, and from the mid-fifties, he threw his whole energy into it. He wrote to Wyatt in April 1955:

Dear Dr. Wyatt:

Already we are being pressed by several districts about the [Invasion] Team's visits. We hope to be able to send a Team to the North (Kabba) Province as soon as possible after our return from the East. We are opening a Bible School in Sapele at once so this will not give much time or leave many persons available for Team visits. It is therefore essential that you try and send more personnel as soon as you are satisfied they are trustworthy. Ibadan is pressing for a Team as soon as possible, but this must be an experienced Team.

We shall need Teams for the East to follow up our visit there.

I am also reminding you about the question of help toward the maintenance allowance of the nondenominational African Teams we are building up. We shall be able to send out at least THREE Teams very soon and your promise to try and place this need before the people in the U. S. A. has stirred up things here, and the Team members are eagerly awaiting the results. We shall easily be able to build up African Teams if you can help us on the question of maintenance allowance for a limited period.

Yours in the conflict, and victory of His will,

(signed) S. G. Elton.[40]

Under Elton's coordination, invasion teams moved swiftly and power-fully across the country—one of the most remarkable grassroots Pentecostal initiatives in Nigeria's history was underway! It was a whirlwind of a movement. One Solomon Akintola, writing on behalf of a group of evangelists who had been set ablaze by this nationwide revival, appealed to Wyatt in 1955: "I have been preaching this wonderful Gospel since the beginning of last year. I have been going from town to town and from village to village. But Nigeria is a very big nation; therefore many evangelical teams are needed. The Lord has placed it in my heart to save Africa for Him before the communists come in. I determined to do it. I say in my heart, 'How can I endure to see the evil that shall come unto my people?' Or how can I endure to see the destruction of my kindred? I say I cannot, and I will not endure it. I thank the Lord that the move is on! Many prophets who have been hidden in the caves are now rushing out. I see this everywhere I go; and this is the reason why I asked for great help from you Americans. People know Africa to be a dark continent, but it will now be called a pool of blessings to all nations."[41] S. U. Ekpo from Ikot Ekpene, writing in the same vein, said:

I am one of the members of the African Teams in Ikot Ekpene District that attended Bible School in Ilesha. . . . Ever since our return from Ilesa, I have [had] no rest. The arrangement was that Pastor Elton and the Wings of Healing Teams should visit us for more . . . work preparing for the big healing campaign in October or November this year. We are looking forward to hearing from them by a telegram informing us to expect them. They have to go to the North Province first before they come to the East Province. This may cause a little delay.

I have been meeting different Local Councils and spoke to them about Jesus. The people are stirred up waiting for deliverance. I have so many invitations from various groups wishing to hear from me after returning from the Bible School. On arriving at my station here in Odoro, Ikpe, one Akpan Uso Akang was reported to be very seriously ill. I went to visit him without rest. He was hopeless, but upon calling upon Jesus' Name, this man was made whole and is now going on well in his business. Hallelujah! God is moving indeed.[42]

For about ten years beginning from 1953, the second great wave of Pentecostal outpouring swept the country. A sense of urgency and anticipation concerning what God was about to do pervades Elton's writing during this period:

Nigeria needs a revival—a great spiritual awakening in every town and village—which will cause men and women to turn to God and accept His salvation and way of life. God is ready—He is waiting NOW for His people to fulfil the necessary conditions. God has promised a MIGHTY HOLY GHOST REVIVAL SOON and we believe we shall see it.

You can begin NOW to prepare for this revival by gathering your people and preparing them to be willing to meet God's conditions for a spiritual awakening. . . . The people of God must repent and make a full confession of all sins. Name them before God and plead forgiveness for each one.

Let the people of God make full restitution for sin wherever possible. Ask God to show you how. Urge the people to dedicate themselves to do God's will in their daily lives. Claim the baptism of the Holy Spirit and refilling daily.

Pray for revival and arrange for aggressive open air meetings in your villages. Let every Christian be encouraged to witness for Jesus Christ. Arrange for every house in your community to be regularly visited. Pray for those that are sick and encourage faith in Jesus Christ.

Be fearless in your opposition to sin and all the works of Satan. Attack the powers of darkness and they must yield to Jesus Christ.

Time is short—people are perishing.

Our Motto: Revival in Nigeria in our time.[43]

The 1950s marked the beginning of the integration of Nigeria's Pentecostalism into global Pentecostalism. Hitherto, the Pentecostal movement in Nigeria had been recognized primarily through the activities of the major Pentecostal denominations that were working in the country—the Assemblies of God, the Apostolic Church, and the Apostolic Faith Church—but now a significant traffic was launched beyond denominational boundaries. And Elton's interaction with Pentecostal leaders and groups from around the world, perhaps more than any other factor, made the greatest contribution in spotlighting Nigeria on the global Pentecostal map. Elton was fast gaining the reputation—both by providing information to foreign Pentecostal groups and journals and through his partnerships with many foreign Pentecostal leaders—as the go-to person for an understanding of developments in the Pentecostal movement in Nigeria.

As an example, Elton began sending reports of Pentecostal revival in the different parts of the country to *Pentecost* in 1954. *Pentecost*, a magazine dedicated to reviewing "world-wide Pentecostal missionary and revival news," was edited and published by Donald Gee, one of the most widely respected Pentecostal leaders of the twentieth century. *Pentecost* was one of the most widely read Pentecostal papers in the mid-twentieth century—it was highly regarded for its thoroughness, its avoidance of sensationalism, and because of its editor's stature in the Pentecostal world. One of Donald Gee's first biographers, writing of his editorials in *Pentecost*, said they were "the most openly honest and perceptive pages in all Pente-costal literature."[44] Gee's history of the Pentecostal movement, first published in 1949, is still a classic.

In the December 1957 issue of *Pentecost*, Gee published the report of a survey of Pentecostalism in Nigeria, titled, "Nearly 200,000 Pentecostal People in Nigeria." The report, sent in by David du Plessis, stated, "Until a few weeks ago the figure [of Pentecostal Christians] for Nigeria stood firm at 51,000, being the figures for Assemblies of God, Apostolic Church of Wales and a few others. Then last week I received a report from Eastern Nigeria. . . . You will notice this comes from the Nigeria Christian Fellow-ship, and it was under cover of their official letter."[45] As stated by du Plessis, the survey report was sent by the Nigeria Christian Fellowship, the organization founded by Elton.

Elton hosted David du Plessis when he later visited Nigeria. Du Plessis, who arguably played the frontline role in the emergence of the charismatic movement that swept the denominational churches beginning from the 1950s, visited Nigeria in January 1958.[46] He came to Nigeria from Accra, where he attended the assembly of the International Missionary Council (IMC). He was invited to the assembly as a consultant because he was then perhaps the most popular Pentecostal in the world, especially among the traditional Protestant churches, which were still largely closed to the Pentecostal movement. Du Plessis was conducting a study on the statistics of "world-wide Pentecostal adherents" for a global Pentecostal directory, and he wanted to have a first-hand assessment of the development of the movement in many countries. Elton took him round Nigeria.

Du Plessis reported after the trip: "In the three states (East, West and North) of Nigeria I found no less than thirty-five indigenous movements. As near as we could ascertain they have a total of over 1,700 churches with a membership of 170,000 in a nation of 30,000,000. Besides these churches the Pentecostal missionary societies have a combined total of about 1,000 churches with about 100,000 adherents. The Holy Spirit is moving upon the nation and great revivals are in progress. In the North the Moslems are taking over with a very aggressive programme. Whether Christ or Mohammed will win out depends on how far Christians will 'work with God' in His move to stir the nation by the Spirit."[47] This was the first comprehensive statistical analysis of the Pentecostal movement in Nigeria. According to the final report released by du Plessis, with approximately 170,000 Pentecostal Christians, Nigeria had the sixth largest Pentecostal population in the world, coming behind the United States of America, Brazil, Indonesia, Chile, and South Africa.

Du Plessis's report noted the growing interaction between Nigerian and foreign Pentecostal organizations: "Appeals from the Nigerian brethren for help and fellowship from overseas movements are constantly reaching the Pentecostal leaders in other lands. Thus, there has been more and more cooperation between American movements and those in Nigeria. Recently, the Apostolic Faith Mission of South Africa sent a representative to Lagos to accept one of those indigenous movements into fellowship."[48] The indigenous movement which the representative of the Apostolic Faith Mission of South Africa had been sent to accept into fellowship was the then budding "*Ijo Irapada*,"—"Redeemed Church"—founded in 1952 by Josiah Akindayomi. The partnership with the South African organization did not last long though, and after a series of name changes in the 1950s, the church eventually settled for the name Redeemed Christian Church of God.

In March 1956, *Pentecost* published a photograph of the leaders of the "Christ Apostolic Church of Nigeria," which had been sent to the magazine's publisher by David Odubanjo.[49] The report noted that "African ministers of this denomination are entering British Pentecostal Colleges for further training."[50] In 1959 Peter Akinyele, Isaac Akinyele's son—he had graduated from the International Bible Training Institute (IBTI), a Pentecostal training centre in the United Kingdom which had been founded just after World War II by Fred Squire, one of the notable Pentecostal evangelists of the time—spoke at the seventh annual convention of the International Full Gospel Business Men's Fellowship in Los Angeles.[51] In 1955 the IBTI had "an interesting group of students from various lands, including Greece, Spain and Nigeria."[52]

At the 1958 International Missionary Council assembly in Ghana, Max Warren, the general secretary of the Church Missionary Society from 1942 to 1953, discussed Nigeria's Pentecostalism: "Only the other day, in Ibadan, I was talking with a number of Anglican missionaries and discussing the very rapid progress of the Pentecostal sects in Nigeria. There has been notable progress, demonstrable to the point that when you travel you see the innumerable churches which carry the name of one or other of the Pentecostal groups. I was enormously encouraged to hear missionaries say that, for all their disagreement with much that was being said and done, the fact remained that they were bringing men and women out of paganism to Christ; to a Christ who was saving men and women from the fear of atheism. That was a most encouraging judgement by a group of Anglican missionaries, who one might expect to be biased against the Pentecostal expression of the faith."[53]

W. V. Grant, one of the more prominent healing evangelists in America in the 1950s (he was vice-president—Gordon Lindsay was president—of The Voice of Healing organization for six years), visited Nigeria to conduct an evangelistic campaign in 1962.[54] These were heady days for the rapidly expanding indigenous Pentecostal movement, and Nigeria began to feature more and more in global Pentecostal discourse.

It seems that it was during the early- to mid-fifties—especially during the first three years after his exit from the Apostolic Church—that Elton caught the vision, or at least the beginnings of it, that would permanently bind his heart to the plan of God for Nigeria. After the initial fervour of the revival, he could easily have returned to the United Kingdom like his colleagues and become involved in a church or some other interdenominational organization, or even launch an organization of his own.

Why did Elton choose to remain in Nigeria? While we may not have a direct answer, what seems clear is that it was during this period that he first began to sense that he was a messenger to a nation destined to play a crucial role in God's end time programme.

His message to his audience in America in 1955 reveals the heart of a man whose mind was made up; a man who had embraced a call that was beyond him; a man who had submitted to a cause that would drive him till the end of his life. His message to his American audience was a message of identification: identification with Nigeria and with the purpose of God for Nigeria.

"There are forty million of my African brethren in Nigeria. Next year they will be offered self-government by the British, and rightly so [Elton was referring to the proposed self-government for the regions, decided at the 1954 constitutional conference in London]. Most of the Nigerian colony will accept self-government. This will produce both opportunities and problems. Global Frontiers must take advantage of this wonderful opportunity—now! It may be too late in two years' time. This is why I am here," Elton announced.

> I had planned to go back to Nigeria without coming to America, but I am glad I didn't, for I want to tell you of the terrible need of my people in their ignorance and superstition, in their ju-ju and witchcraft. You cannot convince and convert the Africans by mere book knowledge—they have seen supernatural manifestations. They know that ju-ju and witchcraft are satanic, but what is their alternative when sickness comes? They know of nothing as powerful as the witchcraft and ju-ju, and even though they know it is satanic, at least it is supernatural. It is not superstition—it is the power of the devil really at work. It is the opposite of the manifestation of the kingdom of God—and it is real.
>
> You cannot convince the Africans with a creed or a doctrine, but when they see God at work, as they have in the last three years, they throw all their ju-ju away. I have seen great piles of their idols and charms as they have turned from ju-ju and placed their faith in God. The power and manifestation of ju-ju and witchcraft is far stronger than the ordinary orthodox religion, but it is not to be compared to the power of God as it is manifested in the Global Frontiers campaigns we have seen and in which we have participated. We are training and sending out African teams under Global Frontiers to tribes where white missionaries cannot go because our bodies cannot endure the climate. There are many millions of Moslems there that we cannot reach as yet because we do not have enough teams.[55]

Then he ended with words that would define his life for the next three decades: "There is a responsibility upon me and a burden upon my heart. I bring that responsibility and that burden to you. What will be your response? They are crying out for help. What can you do? I am laying that burden on your shoulders. Will you make it? I know you will. May God bless you in advance."[56]

Elton was changing. He was beginning to see things differently. He was beginning to see himself not as just another *missionary*, but as a *messenger*.

EIGHT

PARTNERSHIPS

As part of the 1960 independence celebrations, the government of the Western Region invited over sixty people who had in some measure contributed to the progress of Nigeria to be its guests in an elaborate ceremony in Ibadan. Of these, more than twenty were missionaries or representatives of missionary organizations, which had laboured in the country for decades. Christian missionaries played a major role in Nigeria's pre-independence development through their pioneering role in education, healthcare and vocational training. T. D. Rennie, who was then the president of the Apostolic Church in the United Kingdom, was privileged to be invited to be a part of the celebrations.[1]

As it did for all the other invitees, the government footed his travel expenses (from the UK) and hosted him in Ibadan, where he participated in the public ceremonies to mark the celebrations. The educational work of the Apostolic Church in western Nigeria, for which the church was invited to the celebrations, was to a large extent developed by Elton. Concerning his years as leader of the Apostolic Church's largest network of educational institutions in Nigeria, Carole Lindsay wrote that "Rev. Elton had 350 teachers working for him. Some of these teachers later became minsters in the newly independent government."[2] But, of course, Elton had by this time moved on.

Elton greeted Nigeria's independence with great hopes for the new nation. He seemed to be aware, probably from close observation and analysis of events pre- and post-independence, and through prophetic insight, that many battles, spiritual and physical, would be fought for the soul of the nation. Elton saw a great future for the new nation and believed it would take a collective responsibility, again spiritual and physical, to build it. And throughout his ministry, he was prescient most of the time with regard to the direction in which Nigeria was heading.

Elton was not in the country during the Independence celebrations. He travelled to the UK sometime in 1960; from the UK, he travelled to the US and most likely spent the whole or much of September there. He travelled back to the UK and then returned to Nigeria before the end of the year. The trip lasted about six months in all. This was his second and last visit to the United States of America and also his last trip outside Nigeria.

Apart from the fact that he was busy with the work in Nigeria, there was another reason why he never again left the shores of the country: sometime in the 1960s, he got wind of a plot to permanently expel him from Nigeria. The plan was to deny him re-entry into the country whenever he travelled abroad.[3] He therefore stayed put. Elton had those who loved him almost to an extreme, but he also had his fair share of detractors. Later speaking of this plot, he said, "Many people have tried to move me out of Ilesa— [but] I am still there—including the government that was under the control of the white people before 1960; they tried to move me, and I am still there. I move when God's finished. When God moves me out, I will gladly go. But let them try until then, they won't succeed because I know who sent me there."[4] He confirms this in a 1982 interview: "I haven't been out of this country for over twenty-two years now, and I don't have any intentions of going."[5]

Elton's purpose for his second United States trip was to make contact with a number of notable leaders in the Pentecostal movement: to intimate them about his work in Nigeria and secure support. During this trip he made significant contacts that would become a major doorway for human, financial and material resources from the global Pentecostal movement to flow into Nigeria. This would forever change the landscape of Nigeria's Pentecostalism.

This trip marked the beginning of a major development in Elton's ministry in Nigeria. He became more open to a wide variety of partnerships and collaborations to further his work in the country. There is one curious entry in the delegates list of the thirteenth assembly of the Christian Council of Nigeria (CCN) tagged "Kaduna 1962."[6] The list, divided into four sections—officers, representatives of member churches, observers and visitors—has Elton's name in the visitors section.[7] What was Elton, the only Pentecostal preacher at the assembly, doing at a meeting of Anglicans, Methodists, Presbyterians, Baptists, the Qua Iboe Church, Sudan United Mission congregations, and other mainline Protestant churches? Did he want to have a sense of the vision and general direction of Christian leaders in the country, or was he there to network with the members of the largest umbrella body for Protestant Christians in Nigeria at the time?

From his 1956 letter to the permanent secretary of the Ministry of Internal Affairs in Enugu in which he stated his intention to bring under his wings "many of the indigenous and smaller denominations in Nigeria who are not represented on the Christian Council of Nigeria," it is clear that he highly regarded the CCN. While we may never be sure of his reason for going to Kaduna, his participation at the assembly confirms a direction which his ministry had taken by the beginning of the 1960s—a willingness to work with a wide variety of leaders and organizations to multiply his effectiveness.

The most prominent of Elton's foreign collaborations were with the organizations of two leading American Pentecostal evangelists, Gordon Lindsay and T. L. Osborn, and with Gospel Revivals Inc, a major American evangelical group.

In November 1961, Gordon Lindsay—the publisher of *The Voice of Healing* magazine, which chronicled and promoted the ministries of the leading evangelists in the healing revival in America beginning from 1948, and later the founder of the internationally renowned Christ for the Nations Bible Institute in Dallas, Texas—initiated a programme called the "Native Church Crusade."[8] After travelling overseas to conduct crusades for many years and also discussing with missionaries working in different parts of the world, Lindsay came to the conclusion that for the revival which was then breaking out in several parts of the world to be sustained, strong native churches had to be built wherever pioneering evangelistic efforts had been successful.[9] (Lindsay, more than any other person—perhaps with the exception of the South African David du Plessis—had been responsible for promoting the healing revival that had swept across America and the Pentecostal revival that was then sweeping across many nations through the work of Pentecostal missionaries. He also strongly promoted the overseas crusades of American healing evangelists.) It was not sufficient for an evangelist to go into a new territory and win converts—a local church had to follow. In the absence of this, the missionary's or evangelist's work bore little lasting fruit.

He noted that a lack of missionaries on one hand and of trained nationals on the other, problems which had previously slowed the task of harvesting the nations for Jesus Christ, had been surmounted, but sadly, these gains did not amount to much if there were no church buildings where the hundreds and thousands that were being converted could worship. The great harvest of souls was taking place in areas where the new converts were so poor they couldn't afford to put up a place of worship—the lack of a defined physical space to congregate often led to a total loss of the work in a short time.

In explaining this vision, Lindsay noted that "The *Native Church Crusade* is a simple plan by which any American family can sponsor the building of a native church in a foreign missionary field and thus have a vital part in fulfilling Christ's command to evangelize the nations. . . . While it is always good news to hear of new evangelistic efforts on the mission field, the facts are that unless some kind of shelter or church is built to take care of the converts, the work is to a great extent lost, just as it would be lost here in America, unless there is provision made for a place for the people to worship."[10]

The Native Church Crusade, founded to address this need, required American families to adopt a native church anywhere around the world with $250 and above.[11] This amount, $250, was enough to put up a modest building in most developing countries, even though larger building projects required more. "*For the cost of a refrigerator, a washer, an electric stove!*"[12] a family could sponsor a native church, Lindsay pleaded. The response to this appeal was generous, and the plan became wildly successful. In the first year, 388 church building projects were completed or embarked upon; in the second year, seven hundred; and by 1964 they could take on one thousand building projects.

We don't have any record of Elton's first contact with Lindsay, but it is most likely that Elton contacted him after reading about the plan for building native churches in *The Voice of Healing*, which had a global circulation. Lindsay himself mentioned that "The Voice of Healing magazine goes out to thousands of missionaries and workers in the foreign lands keeping them informed of our activities. In turn our office keeps in touch with the field."[13] We have the first reference to Elton's relationship with Lindsay's organization in the January 1963 issue of *The Voice of Healing*, where Lindsay mentioned that "Word came recently from a missionary in Nigeria who, together with a team of evangelists, is seeking to spread the Full Gospel message in the Afenmai district, which is largely pagan or Moslem. This district is undeveloped and conditions are primitive, but most villages are hungry for the gospel—except for where the Moslems have taken hold first. In the last two years a dozen churches have been established, many have been healed, and the open air services continue to attract large crowds even in the Moslem towns."[14] This "missionary" was, of course, Elton, as later issues of the magazine would reveal.

Gordon Lindsay visited Nigeria most likely for the first time in April or May 1963. Reporting this trip in his magazine, he wrote, "At dusk we came in for a landing at the airport at Lagos, where Brother Elton and his daughter Ruth had come to meet us. The following day we spent several hours in conversation over the needs of this great country. . . . Evangelization of Nigeria is at an advanced stage in comparison to other countries, but scores and perhaps hundreds of congregations have no building. Without regular services there is grave danger of losing the results of years of labor. The Native Church Crusade must step in and provide shelters for these people. Brother Elton with his devotion to the field and his many years of experience is perhaps the most fitted man in Nigeria for the task of handling the great responsibility of choosing the congregations which are ready to be sponsored by the crusade."[15] In the August 1963 issue, Lindsay wrote, "S. G. Elton is in charge of the work of Nigeria. He is doing a great work among the Mohammedan villages. We have just approved dozens of projects which Brother Elton will be supervising."[16] The article then reprinted Elton's latest report:

> We sent an evangelist into the totally Moslem area of Agaie, Nigeria one and a half years ago, and he now has a congregation of 40 – 50 good converts, but they are facing severe persecution because of the Moslem traditions and hatred of Jesus Christ. However, the converts are ready to suffer and are determined to have a church. They have created a temporary shelter and will provide all the labour, build the walls, etc., but they need help for the roofing and the cement. This is the only Christian witness in an area of many miles.
>
> The evangelist in Etsugaie, Nigeria, began work in the Nupe tribe land in January of 1962. This is an area totally Moslem. Government leaders and

emirs are fanatical Moslems. Nevertheless, the Lord has blessed and a good company of converts now meet and are anxious for a proper church. I am recommending this work in Nupe as a splendid Native Church Crusade project. It is the only Christian witness in this area.

Fagbore is a village near Ilesa, Nigeria. There was no church and no Christians there prior to January 1962. About fifty converts have built a temporary grass shed. Now they have secured a plot of land, and the local congregation will provide all the labour, doors and windows and walls. I am appealing for aid to complete the roof and for the concrete for the floors and walls.

The small congregation in Ikuehi, Nigeria are converted Moslems. They have suffered much persecution. They erected a temporary building, but opposers burned it down, so they have erected this new building. It has completely drained all their resources, and if it is not cemented before the advent of the rains, then the whole building may collapse. It is a very fine effort and the saints have done well. It is the only Gospel witness in Ikuehi.

Obehira is a completely Moslem town and this effort is the only Gospel witness. Started in 1961, it is a good group. They have had great difficulty in securing a plot, and they were given a piece of sacred ju-ju land on top of a hill. The Christians accepted the challenge, and erected a building. However they do not have any funds left to cement the building against rains nor to lay a concrete floor.[17]

Elton had hundreds of evangelists under his care who were regularly opening up new areas to the gospel. They received stipends for their sustenance, part of which came from T. L. Osborn's organization, but they lacked funds to build churches whenever they had been able to gather a congregation. The Native Church Crusade was therefore a godsend, and Elton was quick to make the most of the provision made available by the plan. Many leaders who enjoyed financial support from Elton, especially in the first few years of the life of their church or parachurch ministry, often wondered how he managed to support so many ministries at the same time, and often for many years. Elton could not bear to see people who were genuinely labouring to expand the work of the kingdom hindered by finances. He often went out of his way to raise funds for many budding organizations around the country even though most of the time the beneficiaries had never discussed their financial difficulties with him.

"God has provided me with enough to meet my personal needs; He provided me with enough to meet the needs of many others and at one stage a few years ago He was providing monthly enough funds here to enable me to meet the bare necessities of at least 500 Nigerian evangelists in this country,"[18] Elton once said. "Every month money came in, some-time from sources I didn't know from where they came and that money was distributed, not abundance, but enough to enable them to have enough food and it was distributed to men and women who were working in unreached areas and many hundreds of churches have been begun and established in this country, many churches have been built as the result of our distribution of money which God had brought into our hands."

Elton made the point that his discipline in matters of personal finance and his faithfulness in disbursing the funds that were committed into his hands by others played a crucial role in the sustained growth and influence of the ministry's outreach for decades. "I had to learn how to handle money. I had to learn how to handle my own money," he said. "I can tell you that there was a time in my experience where I came down to the last five pounds—it was pounds in those early days—the last five pounds in the bank, but I have never had less than five pounds. God has always supplied my needs. I have handled large amounts at times, as much as 30,000 dollars on one cheque alone, but I had to distribute that honestly and faithfully and I did so at once, because it was for a definite project. But people learned that they could trust me and so they gave me money for other projects in Nigeria." He continued, "Since that time, hundreds of men and women have been moved by God in various parts of the world to write and send me money. I get letters from all over the world writing and telling me of what God has told them."[19]

Under the Native Church Crusade programme, missionaries were expected to "carefully evaluate their fields" and inform Lindsay's organiza-tion about "their most urgent projects—projects which have reached the stage where with help there is a practical certainty of the project being completed."[20] These applications would then receive further evaluation, and if accepted, were assigned to sponsors in the United States. The story of a church in Upogoro, a village located in the hills around Okene, is a classic example of how Elton approved a congregation to be a beneficiary of the fund. There had never been any Christian witness in the village until 1963, when an evangelist preached there and led a small group of women and two men to the Lord. Elton later visited this group, most likely on the invitation of his daughter, who was superintending the evangelists working in the area. "When I first saw this group," he wrote, "their number was so small. They gathered amid much opposition and mocking from the rest of the town Moslems. They had only a small grass-roofed shed without walls in which to meet. But they knew God, and they stood firmly for Him."[21]

The group persisted and even grew amid heavy persecution and after a while decided to build a permanent place of worship. They saved money and were able to get the foundation laid. Then they saved again for another year until they had enough to build the walls. When they were told about the Native Church Crusade, they immediately appealed for funds to complete the building. "Their joy knew no bounds when they were told they would get roofing sheets and some cement to complete the church," Elton reported. "Now they have a real church building—the only one in the area—and it stands as a testimony to the power of God and the determination of His people. It also shows the Christian love and fellowship of our friends in America."

One cannot fail to notice how Elton's heart connected with the group when he met them—"their number was so small. They gathered amid much opposition and mocking from the rest of the town Moslems"—just as a father connects with a child. Elton deeply cared about the group and immediately adopted them into his family and was willing to sacrifice everything to make sure they prospered. The Upogoro story is repeated hundreds of times with groups across the country. To these groups who were struggling and had no support or encouragement outside of themselves, Elton became the father to the fatherless. Each new group he met had a special place in his heart.

By 1965 Elton had secured funds to build ninety-five churches in Nigeria,[22] second only to Mexico's one hundred and ninety-six among the fifty countries where the Native Church Crusade had built churches. Elton wrote in 1965:

> To every careful observer of world events it is clear that we are all heading up for a crisis and international upheaval. If this is evident in the Western countries of the world, then it must be expected that Africa too will feel the same effect and this we are seeing in some nations of Africa now.
>
> In Nigeria we are facing our first National Federal Elections since independence was secured in 1960, and if what we are experiencing now is any indication of the shape of things to come then the future of Nigeria is bleak. Thuggery rules instead of democratic government; political parties engage young

out-of-works whose only qualities appear to be the ability to wield a matchet [*sic*] or heavy stick; and many are beaten up daily. The president of Nigeria, in a nation-wide broadcast, warned the nation that if the present condition continues then the events of the Congo will be child's play to what will happen in Nigeria.

Yet in spite of all this the gospel is going on and the demand far exceeds the supply. We press into new areas every month. . . . We may have only about five years left in West Africa in which to freely preach the gospel and so we are redoubling all our efforts to quickly reach as many as possible while we have a chance.[23]

When he said as a result of the situation, "we are redoubling all our efforts to quickly reach as many as possible while we have a chance," he meant every word of it. Elton would run, really run with the message, as if he actually had just five years left.

In July 1966, Gordon Lindsay and his daughter, Carole, visited Nigeria again to see the churches their partners in America had helped to build; by this time the number had increased to 110. "This is a land in which The Voice of Healing has a major interest," Lindsay wrote in his report of the trip. "We regard Rev. S. G. Elton as the key man in this country, although there are other excellent missionaries, some of whom it was our pleasure to meet."[24]

By 1971, 156 churches had been built.[25] This was huge. In addition to the large number, the geographical spread of these churches says a lot about how the programme brought about a major leap in the growth of Pentecostalism in the country. It ushered in the era of mass planting of small, independent Pentecostal congregations in areas that had never had a Christian witness. In many of these areas, Pentecostalism became the first form of Christianity the natives came in contact with—a major departure from the past decades, in which the traditional mission churches were usually the pioneers.

• • •

SOMETIME IN THE EARLY 1960s Elton approached Gospel Revivals Inc., publishers of *Herald of His Coming*, one of the most popular evangelical magazines of the twentieth century, with the offer of coordinating the distribution of the magazine, which was devoted to promoting spiritual revival in the church, in Nigeria.[26] *Herald of His Coming* was first published in 1941 in Los Angeles, California, by Willard C. Moore and his wife Sarah Foulkes Moore, who served as editor and associate editor respectively. The Moores had been "greatly burdened for revival in the church worldwide."[27] Letters of testimony from readers published in the magazine show that Nigeria was one of the countries *Herald of His Coming* had reached into within the first five years of publication.[28] We have additional evidence of this in one of Elton's early writings, sometime in the mid-1950s, in which he directed his Bible school students to "read carefully the article in the *Herald of His Coming* of April 1954 which is entitled 'The Authority of the Believer.' It will be sent free if you write Box 113, Ilesa."[29]

From Ruth Elton we learn that her father's decision to work with the Moores as their agent in the country was informed by the haphazardness which plagued the magazine's distribution in the early days, and his desire to focus it for greater impact.[30] The earliest correspondences between Elton and the Moores are now lost to history. (Elton is still fondly remembered at Gospel Revivals Inc. for signing his letters "Brother S. G. Elton."[31]) We, therefore, do not have information on how the partnership developed. But information printed in the magazine indicates that he and the Moores were in correspondence about publishing *Herald of His Coming* in Nigerian languages in the early 1960s. In the May 1963 edition of the magazine, the Moores wrote, "For those who have Nigeria on their hearts: the Lord brought us into contact with a missionary overseer for the work of the Herald in the Yoruba, Efik, Hausa and other languages of Nigeria. This is to be a faith work as the Lord sends in amounts designated for these Heralds. The needs are stupendous with large areas of Africa still to be covered with Heralds as well as Salvation Heralds."[32] Elton's later correspondence also shows he had initiated the partnership: "When I first offered to help in this work I had no idea it would grow so rapidly."[33]

Elton's broad plan to grow the magazine's ministry in Nigeria began with its reproduction in Nigerian languages: coordinating the distribution of the international English edition sent from the United States came only after this. From his letters, it is clear that Elton set up a committee, most likely in Ibadan, to oversee the project. "I was able to meet with many leaders again during the Easter meetings," he wrote in one of his letters published in *Herald of His Coming*, "and we have agreed to your suggestion that salvation sheets shall be published first and the ordinary Herald magazine to follow." He continued, "As a result of our meetings we have had a number of articles translated into Yoruba and sufficient for a four page sheet. The paper will be called 'Ona Igbala' (Way of Salvation). We propose that at least 20,000 shall be run off as soon as funds are available."[34] According to this plan, the four-page salvation sheets, called Salvation-Herald, which was essentially a compilation of excerpts from the main magazine, were to be the easy-to-read evangelism-focused precursors to the fully reproduced editions in the Nigerian languages. These tracts were to be printed in English and also translated into four languages—Yoruba, Efik, Igbo, and Hausa.

By October 1963, twenty thousand copies of the Yoruba Salvation-Herald, *Ona Igbala*, had been produced.[35] Elton reported about the progress being made: "We are making a definite system of distribution for Ibadan. I spent some time last week in Ibadan, a city of 500,000 people and thousands of 'Ona Igbala' have already been distributed by university students and eager Christians in small indigenous groups."[36] To promote the work he made major trips to eastern and northern Nigeria in 1963. "I have visited northern Nigeria twice and find that the English paper is greatly in demand because most of the literates read English and wish to read a simple paper in that language. We have printed 30,000 of a simple 'Way of Salvation' in English. . . . These are in great demand both in the North and East Nigeria [*sic*] where we are distributing and mailing large numbers."[37] The English paper was also being mailed to schools and colleges in western Nigeria.

According to Elton, by 1964 the work had "exploded almost and swamped us completely in the office." He wrote enthusiastically to his partners in the US, "I am afraid all our efforts to maintain a proper mailing list have been swept aside by the tremendous demand for literature. It may interest you to know that we are now sending literature into more than 1,500 different towns and villages in Nigeria and the demand grows rapidly."[38] He definitely had every reason to be so excited: by the end of 1963, two issues of the Yoruba Salvation-Herald, totalling forty thousand copies, had been printed, and a third issue of thirty thousand copies was ready to go to print.[39]

Christian leaders in Ibadan were also requesting at least twelve thousand copies of the paper monthly.[40] Three issues of *Ipe fun Isoji—Call for Revival*—the main Yoruba edition of *Herald of His Coming*, had been produced and another was in the press; the first edition of *Hanyan Ceto*, the Hausa *Salvation-Herald*, was in print; the mailing list of the English *Herald of His Coming* was growing by the day.

During the last three months of 1963, Elton and his staff handled "nearly 88,000 pieces of mail"[41] for all the different papers. The projection for 1964 was higher: "*Ona Igbala*, the Yoruba salvation paper: 30,000 monthly for three months, rising to 50,000 about mid-year. *Ipe Fun Isoji*, the Yoruba Call for Revival: 20,000 for months January to March, each. Then it is felt we shall need 30,000 each month thereafter. *Way of Salvation in English*, four-page sheet: 30,000 for January–March, 1964."[42] Elton rounded up his 1963 report with great excitement, "Now trust that I have not overburdened you with too many details or caused you any additional burdens. Also hope that our growth has not put too big a strain upon your finances. Please do not hesitate to 'put the brake' on us if you are unable to find the finances. The Lord has been good to us and we are all thrilled very much with the prospects of rapid increases in 1964. The Lord be praised and we know His word will not return void!"[43]

Between March and May 1964, a total of 150,000 copies of the different papers were produced. In July, 200,000 copies were produced. "At the moment we are struggling to get all this into the mail and out into the hands of the readers. The daily response is full of encouragement and the staff are happy to do all they can to get it out daily. We are averaging 10,000 papers in singles daily for this month,"[44] Elton wrote a few months later. The vernacular and English Salvation-Heralds were also being sent to Ghana: "We still get a large number of requests from Ghana for all our vernacular and English [Salvation] heralds and we are able to meet the need at present. But the need is likely to grow soon and we shall then have to print off a larger number of English 'Way of Salvation.' These are wonderful days of opportunity and we are anxious to see that His Word and Gospel is spread over the whole country."[45] The office in Ilesa now had a staff of six men "working many hours daily in getting the present Nigerian heralds into circulation. Our printer has had to increase his machine facilities and the Post Office has had to increase its staff. There are many days when we close the office doors at night (often ten o'clock) and feel very tired *in* it but never tired *of* it."[46]

The testimonies that regularly poured in from several parts of the country more than compensated for the sacrifice the *Herald* staff put in all-year-round. Two of such letters:

May God bless you and your ministry. Amen. We thank God that more lost souls are now converted. We see that the Heralds of His Coming are helping us to win lost souls for Christ. We are hearing from their testimony that on the day they read the African Herald, the Almighty Father speaks to them in heart. Since that day some people begin to come to church and they begin to testify to the people how they found their salvation. I shall be very grateful if you can continue to send the Heralds to me and if you are going to send them, please send up to 300 Ona Igbala and 300 Ipe Fun Isoji. . . . We are praying for you. Greet all saints for me.[47]

I am greatly delighted to receive Ona Igbala and also Ipe Fun isoji. We have longed for such spiritual food for many years and now the Lord has heard our prayer. May the Lord bless you as you seek to lead many into His kingdom. Please I want you to know that these papers are being mightily used by the Holy Spirit and we are seeing many souls changed because of this ministry. In our Bible classes we use these papers to instruct the people and God is using them greatly. I beg you to send me up to one hundred of each paper every month because we are now using it as a sword to deal with the works of Satan. . . . I myself wish to thank you for the spiritual food because I have now been revived and encouraged to go on to know the Lord and serve Him with my full heart. God bless you.[48]

By 1965 the office at Ilesa was receiving a monthly supply of 2,500 copies of *Herald of His Coming* from Los Angeles for mailing in Nigeria, but this was a far cry from the 14,000 names who wanted their copy of the magazine every month. "This leaves 12,000 requests unsatisfied,"[49] Elton noted sadly. He requested that the Los Angeles office urgently increase the supply to 15,000 copies monthly. A little later he wrote to notify them that the requests had jumped to 25,000 "and . . . we are only now receiving 5,000 monthly. We are worried what to answer the many who write asking why they do not get their Herald. The demand still grows here."[50]

By the middle of 1965, the breakneck speed at which the work of printing and distribution had progressed for more than a year was suddenly brought to a halt. Los Angeles was having a difficult time with its finances and was temporarily unable to foot the bill for the ever-expanding work. After appeals to readers in the US, some money was raised and printing re-commenced, but things were not quite the same after this for the earlier steady support became more and more infrequent.

There were occasional bursts of joy at the release of funds, which allowed printing to recommence, only to be followed by sustained periods of dryness. "With great rejoicing we were able to forward to S. G. Elton sufficient funds to print another issue of the four vernacular Heralds in Nigeria, after months of delay. These tens of thousands of copies coming off the press will soon be consumed—and pleas will come for more—more!"[51] and "God has given the *Herald of His Coming* and Herald International in Africa an abundantly fruitful ministry. Yet at this time, the Herald International work in Africa is at a virtual standstill for lack of finances"[52] are two letters written a few months apart in 1966.

"I have spent time in eastern Nigeria, where the demand for Herald is almost unbelievable," Elton began positively in one of his letters during this period, but the news quickly went downhill: "I regret to have to report that we have been forced to close both our offices and centres in Uyo and Ekpoma, as we could not find money for the staff. We should now have to handle the mail from these areas in the Ilesha office."[53] And then, "We have stopped all printing, awaiting your further instructions to re-start. We are not sparing any effort in our attempt to get more support internally."[54]

Publication picked up sometime after, but it is doubtful if it ever attained the pre-1966 peak. The Nigerian Civil War, which began in July 1967, also disrupted printing and distribution plans. The effect of the war was most felt in the shutdown of postal services in the affected areas and the shortage and sharp rise in the cost of newsprint immediately after the war. Despite the difficulties, Elton's commitment to getting the gospel message to every part of the country kept the work going. He was clearly making the best of a very challenging situation when he wrote: "But we are grateful to the Lord for His provision so far and we look to Him for the further provision and working out of His purposes. It is likely to become increasingly difficult in this country to keep the Gospel and the Message going out as formerly due to rising costs and currency problems."[55]

At some point after the war, mails between Los Angeles and Ilesa became difficult to sustain. "Since we were having extreme difficulty contacting Bro. Elton by mail, we had no assurance that the packages of Heralds we were sending him were reaching him. It was thought best to discontinue sending because of lack of funds on hand to do so,"[56] wrote the Los Angeles office. The last letter from Elton to Los Angeles was received in 1974.[57]

• • •

THE PRINTED MEMENTO OF DAISY Osborn's meeting with the king of Ilesa, which took place sometime during the Nigerian Civil War of 1967 to 1970, gives us a spectacular view of foreign Pentecostal evangelistic foray into Nigeria in the sixties, seventies, and eighties. This photo documentary, titled *The King and I*, was produced for the supporters of the T. L. Osborn Evangelistic Foundation, to solicit financial contributions for the Osborns' work around the world and especially in Nigeria and Africa.[58] Daisy was received by the king at an elaborate and very public welcome ceremony complete with "a welcome speech, dozens of introductions, songs, photographs . . ."[59] and then the official oration by the king. Overjoyed by this reception, Daisy Osborn expressed her elation at her acceptance by the community: "I felt I had been accepted by the Yoruba Tribe in Ilesa, Nigeria as I emerged from the palace of His Highness, the *Owa* [the king's traditional title] of Ijeshaland, fully clad in tribal array."[60] The king was equally excited about this meeting. The *Owa* was already very familiar with T. L. Osborn's ministry for many years, firstly because of his 1957 crusade in Ibadan, which created no small stir throughout western Nigeria, and secondly through Osborn's books, one of which he had read. The king's speech, which would have pleased Daisy to no small degree, was just the kind of message that moved the hands of the ministry's supporters.

"I have heard many wonderful things about your husband. . . . And I have looked forward to meeting him face to face today. I learned a few days ago that he could not personally visit our country at this time, but we thank him for the demonstration of his love by sending you, his wife to us,"[61] were the king's opening words. He talked about how "when Mr Osborn was in Nigeria years ago, news reached my ears of his positive preaching and I heard of miracles which brought healing to multitudes of my people. I purposed in my heart to see this man whom everyone had come to love and respect. We are waiting for his return to our country because we are suffering very much these days and the situation of our land is very grave. Mr Osborn can help heal our nation with his gospel of peace and love."[62] The *Owa* continued for a while, lavishing praises on Osborn, and then mentioned that he had recently read his widely popular book, *Soul Winning*. He then requested the book to be published in "our Yoruba language," saying, "My people are ready for the teachings in this book." He thanked her for the resources she distributed to the locals at the occasion, which included fifty bicycles "and other assistance . . . to our suffering brothers" and promised that "your generosity will be reflected by our own Christian brothers." He ended with a plea for T. L. Osborn to visit the country as soon as he was able.

After praising the king's Christian example in glowing words, Daisy Osborn said, "The king and I became good friends and my husband and I pray that we may be permitted to return to Nigeria's millions in more great campaigns." She then appealed to her readers: "You may never see Nigeria in person, or visit the Ijeshaland king in his palace, but you can provide tools for evangelism in native languages to proclaim the KING OF KINGS to the unreached everywhere."[63] The message could not have been better delivered to supporters and potential supporters—the Osborns were masters in the art of communicating their passion, and they didn't fail to deliver on this occasion. The documentary featured many photographs of the event, but one face which clearly stood out, sitting beside Daisy Osborn and third from the king's right, was that of Sydney Elton. Though missing in Mrs Osborn's telling of the event, he was the facilitator of the meeting—the Osborns' gateway into the heart of the Ijesa kingdom.

T. L. Osborn had visited Nigeria for the first time in 1957, to hold evangelistic crusades in Lagos and Ibadan. The crusades were immense and represented the second major wave of modern-day mass evangelistic meetings in the country after the Latter Rain meetings of 1953 to 1954. The 1957 meetings were in turn followed by Billy Graham's 1960 crusades. The 1957 Lagos crowd, which congregated at Rowe Park Grounds, Yaba, was indeed massive.[64] (Samuel Odunaike interpreted Osborn's sermon for the Yoruba audience in Lagos.[65]) Osborn wrote in his diary about the third night of the Lagos crusade: "How can I record what I saw tonight? I've already used every word I can think of in writing about the first two services and I still have failed to describe it. Nearly 40,000 souls were massed together on the Rowe Park grounds. It was a tremendous night. . . . After praying with them to be saved, I prayed for all of their sick in a great mass prayer. When I had finished, an ocean of praise swelled up from the multitude. The platform was overrun with people pressing to tell of the miracles God had performed on their bodies."[66]

The same was the case with the Ibadan meetings, which were held at the

Race Course. (The Race Course hosted so many major Pentecostal revival programmes where hundreds of miracles were reported to have taken place that one newspaper called it the "modern pool of Bethesda."[67]) The Osborn team went to Ibadan at the "personal invitation" of the Pentecostal *Olubadan*, Isaac Akinyele, who "every day . . . left his official responsibilities to direct the meetings, which began at 4:00 0' clock."[68] "As I walked up the steps of the platform at the Race Course in Ibadan, Nigeria," Osborn wrote, "I struggled to control my emotions. I was cordially received by His Highness the King of Ibadan and a platform full of fine Native Pastors; but the thing that moved my heart was a field of hungry people engaged in a spontaneous mixed uproar of praise to God, because a man of God, an anointed 'Revivalist' had come to their city; he would preach to them God's Word; they would be shown the way to be saved; he would pray for their sick and they would be healed. They never tried to conceal their joy. We wept and shouted together!"[69]

There were reports of many outstanding miracles,[70] but the healing of Karimu, a crippled man who was a very popular beggar in the city, was by far the most sensational. Decades later, many remembered it as the high point of Osborn's 1957 meetings.[71] Karimu, who had been crippled for more than thirty years, came to the meeting at the invitation of Isaac Akinyele. "I regularly visited the King's Court and asked help from him. He was a good kind man, and a known Christian. He always gave me something. He told me about a revivalist whom he said was a true man of God and who was a personal guest of the king . . . and the king had given him the Race Course to conduct his teachings,"[72] said Karimu after the miracle had occurred. "The King commanded *me to go at once*! He told me the revivalist began his service at 4:30 p.m. and ordered me to go quickly and listen and believe."[73] The testimony of Karimu's healing, which shook the city, is still wonderful to read.[74]

When Karimu got to the platform, he didn't need to say much: almost everyone knew Karimu, the beggar. When he lifted his rubber pads and wood blocks with which he formerly moved around for everyone to see, the crowd went wild! "So much rejoicing broke out in the crowd that the Revivalist lost control of the people and they had to dismiss the multitude."[75] Karimu was rechristened Cornelius by Daisy Osborn. The documentary video of the 1957 crusades, titled *Black Gold*, became one of the most widely distributed videos in the history of T. L. Osborn Evangelistic Foundation. So excited was Osborn about the results of the crusade, which gave a major boost to his then budding international evangelistic outreach, that the stories from the Nigerian crusades were told and retold for years in the ministry's magazines. In the introduction to the video *Black Gold*, Osborn opened with the lines "Our mission to Nigeria was to proclaim that Jesus Christ, who healed the sick, who blessed the poor, and who set the captives free is the same today as He was in the Bible days! We went to Nigeria in search of lost souls . . . lost African souls, and it was in them that we found . . . Black Gold."[76] In the decades that would follow the 1957 crusade, as a result of his staggering contribution to the cause of evangelism in Nigeria, Osborn would become the foreign evangelist to have the greatest influence on the development of Pentecostalism in Nigeria.

Elton's first and only visit to the T. L. Osborn Evangelistic Foundation in Tulsa, Oklahoma, was during his September 1960 trip to the US. One of the pictures of this visit show him boarding the plane from Caldwell, Idaho, to Tulsa, most likely on his way to the Osborn Foundation head-quarters. It is not certain if he met Osborn himself; however, he would have sufficiently communicated his vision to any official he was oppor-tune to speak with in a way that made his visit there worth the effort. Elton's point of engagement with Osborn's ministry was a programme Osborn had initiated in 1953 to train and sponsor native evangelists around the world to carry out the work of evangelizing their respective countries.

In 1953 Osborn founded the Association for Native Evangelism (ANE), which was "established for the sole purpose of raising and distrib-uting funds for the assistance of proven, recommended and capable native evangelists and preachers, to get them into full-time ministry, who otherwise, would not be able to give their full time to the work of spread-ing the Gospel."[77] Osborn wrote in the July 1953 issue of *The Voice of Healing* magazine: "For the past five years we have carried the Gospel in eleven different countries to as many thousands of heathen souls as we could possibly reach, but we have not been able to do enough. Although we shall continue to do our part both at home and abroad, we have come to realize that missionaries alone can never accomplish this task. Mission-aries are needed to train native workers, but *the real task of world-evangelization rests almost entirely in the hands of the natives!*"[78]

It is not unlikely that Elton approached Osborn on the basis of the information in the booklet *Native Evangelism*, published by the ANE, which gave details of "how missionaries may secure this assistance for natives under their supervision"[79] or through *The Voice of Healing* magazine. He had already built a platform—a network of independent native missionaries and evangelists all over Nigeria—that Osborn's programme could build on.

In 1960 Osborn's organization began sending money for the upkeep of evangelists under Elton's supervision.[80] As Osborn's agent, Elton was responsible for training the evangelists, who were then to go to a village where there was no church to preach and plant a church. These evangelists were paid seven pounds a month from the money sent from the United States.[81] At the end of each month, each evangelist was expected to submit a report of his work during that month, which was then forwarded to Osborn's headquarters. This financial support was for a year or two at the most, by which time the church was expected to be self-supporting. The evangelist would then move on to a new area. These evangelists were trained for a few weeks, four weeks at the most, and then sent to target areas Elton had identified. Under this programme, evangelists were sent all over the country.

By 1967 Osborn's magazine, *Faith Digest*, was reporting that "Rev. Elton has personally supervised 57 native missionaries and seen over 70 new self-supporting congregations raised up through Native Evangelism in the past eight years."[82] Elton was to write in later years, "Over 500 evangelists have been under my own personal care in Nigeria, preaching the gospel in unreached areas and that work is continuing today."[83]

In collaborating, Osborn and Elton launched one of the most powerful evangelism thrusts in Nigeria's history. So much did Osborn and Elton's vision meld that *Faith Digest* reported that "Elton, a tireless worker . . . has been a hearty 'exploiter' of the Osborn Native Evangelism Programme. 'Exploiter' has come to be a sinister word that is badly loaded, whereas, in fact, it beautifully describes anyone who TAKES FULL ADVANTAGE OF THE BENEFITS OFFERED."[84] If the Lindsay-Elton partnership released the greatest number of independent indigenous Pentecostal missionaries and church planters yet at that time in Nigeria's history, and in the process ushered in a new era in the Pentecostal movement, the Osborn-Elton partnership released the largest number of independent, indigenous Pentecostal evangelists.

The Osborn-Elton partnership also ushered in the era of the individual Christian who boldly moved all over the country with tracts, megaphones, radiophones, and other evangelism tools to win souls for Christ. Christians all over the country joyfully embraced the call to win souls.

Elton's collaboration with Osborn's ministry was integrated into the former's overall strategy to cause a revival of soul winning and personal evangelism to engulf the country. Elton wanted Christians everywhere to be actively engaged in preaching the gospel. This strategy involved training full-time evangelists and also training everyday Christians to be effective soul winners. Several people knew Elton for different things, but if there was one thing "everybody" knew him for, it was evangelism. Peter Daniels, an expatriate teacher who arrived in Nigeria in 1969, remembers Elton regularly visiting Benin City in his pickup truck to deliver tracts weighing up to a quarter of a ton.[85] Mike Oye, the first travelling secretary of the Scripture Union in Nigeria, used tracts from Elton as a major evangelism tool as he visited secondary schools around the country. According to Oye, he was always in Ilesa to get "loads and loads"[86] of tracts, which he distributed to students.

Soul winning had always been at the core of Elton's mission, and in attempt to further its cause in the country, he started an organization in the early seventies called "Soul-winners Unlimited Nigeria"[87] (SUN). The mission of the new organization: "A new company has been started called SOUL-WINNERS UNLIMITED NIGERIA. God himself is the founder, chairman, and Managing Director, but He is inviting all His blood bought people in Nigeria to become His partners in this wonderful business. . . . To take the Gospel of His dear Son . . . the Lord Jesus Christ, to all the untouched and unreached areas of Nigeria within the next three years."[88] Before the formation of SUN, Elton had been training and sending evangelists to different parts of the country, but he obviously sensed the need to formalize the structure for greater effectiveness and also to solicit local partnership in accomplishing the vision. "This is Nigeria's wonderful opportunity to join in PARTNERSHIP WITH GOD,"[89] he wrote concerning the newly formed body.

Under the umbrella of SUN, Elton started "Schools of Evangelism"[90] in several states of Nigeria, which lasted for one to two weeks. This was mainly targeted at students and young people; they were trained in "witnessing, soul-winning and the deliverance ministry."[91] He said, "Satan is being challenged by this new group of young Christians all over the world and God is using them mightily in many places."[92] The schools were run for free; the students were given "a small range of text books" at no cost. Large numbers of youth were turning out for these schools, and there was a special arrangement for students during holidays. He wrote in 1977: "During university vacations, there are hundreds of groups of young people gathering for schools of evangelism to train in the work of the Lord. We estimate there are at least fifty thousand young people in camps for this purpose right now. We keep in touch with them all by mail and regular newsletters, magazines, and books."[93]

In 1974 alone, 10,000 students were trained in these "schools of evangelism, Bible training camps and Bible schools"[94] across the country. An excited Elton reported, "This is the way God is moving among the young people of Nigeria today. Young people are eager to know more about God and they want to know as much as possible of the 'new vision,' the 'new move' of God for these crisis days." He continued, "These camps have been led by many undergraduates and student leaders who have of themselves tasted of the 'power of the age to come,' and who have learned how to preach the gospel to the unreached and who have been filled with the Holy Spirit and therefore have a burning urge to go into action for the Lord Jesus for the unsaved. Many of these camps have been 'fasting' camps where the students have completely dedicated themselves to the giant task ahead."[95]

Elton's passion for Nigerians to take up the responsibility of evangelizing the nation comes out brilliantly in these words: "We are expecting the Lord to lay a heavy burden on the hearts of many Nigerians, who have the means to support these volunteers. . . . We are doing our part . . . calling men and women to move into the revival and bear the responsibility God is putting upon us. We are sending literature to anyone who needs it. We are training the volunteers."[96] "We are training them; teaching them how to face the enemy and overcome him and to establish new groups of Christians, who will then be trained in this 'last day's message of revival' to become soul winners."[97] And again: "The great un-evangelized of Nigeria CAN be reached in our day: if we ACT and dedicate ourselves and means to the greatest job on earth. The great mass of those in darkness and in bondage can be reached IN OUR DAY, if the Christians of Nigeria will realise their duty and opportunity and ACT."[98]

Elton and his team were regularly training evangelists in the five Bible schools he was running across the country. He noted that "these volunteers spend a short period [in] intensive 'commando' training and are then sent out into un-opened areas with the Gospel."[99] It was his vision that these groups would eventually grow in spiritual stature to "apostolic" teams like those in the book of Acts. Elton had great expectations for these evangelists: "Evangelists! And I don't mean a man who's just going from village to village, I mean people who are governmental, whom we know. They are people who can lead a crowd of ten, twenty, thirty thousand, hold them and produce signs and wonders, and who do not have to get a whole band of people praying for them. I have told those whom I have trained, you have not got anywhere near where you should get, until you can stand in a meeting and say, 'You, get up and walk.' And the man will get up and walk. That's governmental. That's an evangelist. But if you ought to pray for two days and two nights, okay! You're learning, but you are nowhere near it. When you point a finger and use authority, your word will cause that man, that blind man to open his eyes; that lame man to walk."[100] He then went on to outline an apostolic plan to capture Nigeria:

Are all your family saved? This is your first responsibility, before dreams of large crusades and huge crowds or even mass open air meetings. Have you claimed deliverance for every member of your family?

Has every house in your town or village and quarter been visited and do they all know you are a Christian? You may not be able to conduct a service in every house or even preach to them, but they will listen to your testimony and that is what the Lord Jesus said you must be . . . a witness.

Have you a supply of tracts and literature for all who enquire and need advice? Send to us for some and carry some tracts everywhere with you. Make every single tract do a big job. . . . Use it as an entry for your testimony.

Gather Christian friends . . . to pray and discuss how your people can be trained and reached with the Gospel.

How great is your faith for your own community? Your school . . . business . . . colleagues . . . villages . . . church? God has placed you just where you are now so that you can testify of this salvation to them.

Set yourself, with your group if you have one, the task of checking the spiritual situation in every village or quarter of your town or district. Make a note of every church it has and then you will find those places which have never heard the Gospel.

Time is short and we do not have many years left now . . . Now is the time for action.[101]

By the 1970s, Elton was clearly overstretching himself to train and sponsor evangelists and further the cause of evangelism in the country, so he began to cry out for Nigerians to collaborate with him in this vision. Many of the trained evangelists were ready to go but could not, because of financial constraints. He wanted Nigerian Christians to sponsor these waiting evangelists to different fields.[102] Once, appealing for support for the various evangelistic initiatives, he wrote, "All these projects are being undertaken by FAITH that the Lord desires them and will provide both men and money to put them into operation. But we do not wish to claim exclusive right to this PLAN or VISION and will welcome all whom the Lord will call to work with HIM and ourselves as partners. You are being invited to share with us in this wonderful work."[103] In a 1974 New Year greeting card which carried a photograph of Elton, Hannah, and Ruth, and which had "Greetings to our Nigerian Partners" written in front, he thanked everyone for their prayerful remembrance of the work in Nigeria and then went on to present to them their hopes for the year and solicit prayers. One of these read: "Please continue to remember us in over 250 independent World Christian Crusade evangelists, working in mainly new areas in Nigeria and in over 20 different languages."[104]

The new soul winner as released by the Osborn-Elton movement was thoroughly Pentecostal. They did not just preach that Jesus saved—they told their audience that Jesus was healer and miracle worker, that He could baptize with the Holy Spirit, and that He could make the new convert an effective soul winner for the kingdom almost immediately. Testimonies by Christians who were working out this new dimension of evangelism in their lives began to pour in from all over the country from the beginning of the 1960s. "I am happy to report that many were healed when I used the message from your tracts and books that I received. One woman who was an idol worshipper heard the message and surrendered all of her idols and jujus to be burned,"[105] somebody testified in 1963. Wrote another person in the same year: "I am happy to let you know that many were healed when I used the messages from your books *3 Keys to the Book of Acts*, *Healing from Christ* and *Faith's Testimony*."[106]

Also in 1963 wrote another excited Christian, "It has been a wonderful month. We have rejoiced daily as we have seen the wonderful works of God shaking this native tribe. Many have been healed and changed. Every day we see those who are eager to know this wonderful blessing which God is now pouring out."[107] One beneficiary of Osborn's books and magazine in Abat-Eket wrote in 1966, "I am an evangelist, a regular reader of your FAITH DIGEST. A year ago I was ill at the point of death. I had to attend so many hospitals where I spent much money and was told by doctors that I wouldn't survive the illness. A friend gave me your book entitled HEAL-ING THE SICK and a copy of your FAITH DIGEST. As I read them, I was able to claim God's promise and immediately I was healed by God!"[108] From Calabar in 1970: "I have the pleasure to thank you for receipt of four parcels of T. L. Osborn's books for our Bible students. God is moving wonderfully in this school."[109]

Osborn's organization introduced revolutionary evangelism methods to global Pentecostalism, one of which debuted in Nigeria in 1965. The project, tagged the "Nigerian Tools Invasion"[110] was the recording of Osborn's "big ten sermons and miracle films" in six Nigerian lan-guages—Efik, Hausa, Igbirra, Igbo, Nupe, and Yoruba—into tapes played by a portable "transistorized battery-operated loudspeaker tape-deck." The "miracle film" was usually a documentary which allowed "the viewer to witness first-hand an Osborn Miracle Crusade, complete with the call to accept Christ and the prayer for the sick."[111] The captivatingly titled *Black Gold* recording from Nigeria, *Java Harvest* from Indonesia and *Filipino Passion* from the Philippines, were classic examples.

The recordings in the different languages were done "back in the bush in Ilesa"[112] where they "converted a tin-roofed storage shed into a make-shift recording studio by stacking bales of Osborn native language tracts as sound-baffles"; a second recording "studio" was set up simultaneously in the open air. The workshop team leader, Lonnie Rex, led the "inside" recordings while Jerry O'Dell, Osborn's son-in-law, was in charge of the open-air studio, both assisted by "a small corps of Nigerian interpreters, Spirit-filled bilinguals." The project, conducted under Elton's supervision, witnessed many interesting moments; Jerry O'Dell and Lonnie Rex "shared the rigours of bush life—hand laundry and bathing from a 5 gallon can—with Rev. and Mrs S. G. Elton."[113] Later, in the early 1970s, Elton started a tape ministry with these translated messages:

A NEW TAPE MINISTRY FOR THOSE POSSESSING A TAPE PLAYER
It is now possible for all Christians possessing a tape recorder or player, to minister the gospel to their friends in their own homes, by borrowing tapes recorded in the following languages by Evang. T. L. Osborn. By this means it is possible to sit and listen to the finest gospel messages without even moving out

of the home. If you have a Tape player, or Tape recorder, using 3 ¾ speed of tape, then we can loan you a set of Brother Osborn's tapes free (please send postage) for a week's listening, in the following languages: English, Yoruba, Ibo, Efik, Hausa, Nupe, Igbira. We are also planning to open a studio to make another twenty language tapes in Nigerian and Dahomian languages.

Remember, it is the duty and the call of every born-again child of God to witness. You may not be able to preach but you can witness and one way in which you can effectively do this is to use a tape recorder or player with proper tapes, giving the full gospel and witnessing of the saving power of the Lord Jesus. WATCH OUT FOR MORE NEW WAYS BY WHICH YOU CAN WORK FOR THE LORD IN THE NEAR FUTURE. THE LORD IS MOVING ALL OVER NIGERIA IN THESE DAYS. BE SURE YOU ARE A PART OF THAT MOVE. THIS CAN BE YOUR NEW MINISTRY.[114]

The "tools" were paired with another major Osborn innovation—Mobile Evangelism Units, MEUs. The MEU initiative, at different times dubbed "Combine Soul-Harvesters," "Go-Ye Mobiles," "E-VAN-gelism," and "World Action on Wheels," was a programme which equipped "large van-type vehicles with Osborn 'tools for evangelism' in the natives' own dialects" for "Full Gospel" missions who were willing and able to operate them in the unreached areas of a country. In many villages and towns in Nigeria in the sixties and seventies, you were likely to come across a Mobile Evangelism Unit. Each MEU, described as a "soul winning centre and Bible School on wheels" comprised "a large van-type vehicle; crusade films in the local dialect; film projector, stand and loudspeakers; giant 7 1/2'x10' rubber aluminium screen; portable gasoline generator for supplying electricity in remote areas; Lingua-Tape Units (usually six); sets of BIG TEN sermon tapes; and ONE MILLION tracts in the dialect."[115]

The most important item on each Mobile Unit, however, was "a mimeographed and hand-stapled Operator's Manual" written by T. L. Osborn, called "Tool's for Evangelism Handbook." The handbook, designed to be read by operators of the mobile units, was described as "a manifesto of missionary revolution! . . . Written from a heart that burns with a passion for souls, T. L. Osborn's TOOLS MANUAL is a blueprint . . . an exciting mixture of the old and the new, blending the use of modern 20th Century tools with the message and the methods of apostolic Christianity."[116] According to the handbook, after a village or town had been chosen, an ideal location—a marketplace, park, or plaza—was to be found where the Miracle Films "can be projected, nightly, for two or three weeks." "Using the Mobile Unit as a hub for their activity, the workers fan outward into the surrounding community, distributing Osborn tracts, ministering from house to house with the Sermon Tapes, announcing the time and place of the public film showing that evening."

As night falls and the curious crowd gathers, the missionary or national preacher announces that what they are about to see on film is the power of God in ACTION. He explains that this is not a film for entertainment; it is a documentary of an *actual* Osborn crusade. No actors were used, no scene was staged. Then he gives a short message about one of the miracles of Jesus, identifying it with what the Miracle Film audience is about to see. He tells them that Jesus is alive today, that the film is PROOF that He will do for them—NOW—the same things that He did for people in Bible days. The worker then tells them that he will give them further instructions at the end of the film and will pray for Christ to heal them and to forgive their sins.

The turn of a crank, and, the powerful electric generator comes to life. Scenes from another land begin to flash upon the giant screen. Then the hubbub of the crowd subsides as they hear their own dialect coming from the loudspeakers. The Osborn tools are speaking *their* language, where *they* live, giving *them* PROOF that God is alive—and that He cares for THEM!

When the film ends, an appeal is made for souls to accept Christ. Many respond. And the MEU team remains in the same spot night after night, showing the same films, preaching simple messages from the life of Jesus, praying for the sick and for sinners, asking for volunteers to open their homes and provide places for follow-up meetings to teach new converts more about the promises of God.[117]

This was the experience in village after village, town after town, and city after city throughout Nigeria in the sixties and seventies. In this way, by December 1967, four-and-a-half million tracts in five Nigerian languages had been distributed across the country.[118] (It is possible that Osborn's tracts have been the most widely distributed in Nigeria's Christian history. In 1973 alone, Elton was "arranging for the printing of tracts by Evang. T. L. Osborn—1,000,000 in English, 1,000,000 in Ibo, and 1,000,000 in Yoruba."[119] The numbers printed in the mid- to the late seventies topped that of the previous years.) As reported in the *Faith Digest* of December 1967, "Like the BOAT, the English built 'Thames' truck, Mobile evangelism Unit is equipped with Osborn 'tools for evangelism.' It is hard to imagine the impact of the MEU on jungle villagers who never saw electric lights before, much less a moving picture. The Miracle Films, with their crystal clear message of Salvation, are available now *in six major Nigerian languages*. Nothing of this size was ever attempted or achieved before in the history of West African Evangelism. The Nigerians responded with great faith to T. L. Osborn's personal platform ministry during the great 'Black Gold' Crusade. Now, hearing him preach on tape and film, reading his tracts and studying his books, thousands more are finding Christ and peace within."[120]

In December 1967, Josiah Adefidipe, the MEU's Nigerian supervisor (working under Elton) wrote in *Faith Digest* about the MEU campaigns after one outing in Olodi Apapa (Lagos) which "yielded over 200 conversions": "The remarkable thing about it is that some of these people are searching us out at our lodging place, and when they see our MEU they come right in to inquire, 'What shall we do to be saved?' Those inquiries keep us busy by day before we go out to the open air campaign at night."[121] Adefidipe wrote elsewhere: "We go round in the MEU gathering the people to come and watch Osborn's free miracle films produced in our own language. We [usually] have a large attendance. We then relate the T. L. Osborn sermons on tape—BLIND BARTEMEUS and others. After this we show JAVA HARVEST FILM. One night 20 people were converted. The following night 30 people gave their hearts to the Lord."[122]

Virtually every evangelist of note who emerged during this period was in one way or the other connected with Elton. Evangelism heavyweights like J. K. Solomon of All Nations Disciples for Christ Evangelistic Ministry; Timothy Iyanda, who founded Go Ye Evangelistic Association; Timothy Obadare of World Soul Winning Evangelistic Ministries; and scores of others continually drew inspiration from Elton's devotion to evangelism and evangelists. It would seem that Elton had lit a fire of evangelism at his Ilesa base that never went out; and evangelists continually trooped there from every nook and cranny of the nation to refuel their own fire. Others who were not previously committed to evangelism in any serious way left Ilesa deeply convicted—never again would they take this all-important issue lightly. "Whenever you get to his house, you would feel the impact of heaven. Each time I went there, I always come back with revival [fire] concerning evangelism. He didn't usually talk about anything [except] the gospel of our Lord Jesus Christ,"[123] one evangelist said, recalling his visits to Elton in the seventies.

The Osborn-Elton partnership reached its high point in the mid-seventies with the School of Evangelism that was organized in Benin in December 1974 and the mass crusades held across the country from that year on. The partnership effectively ushered in the third wave of mass evangelistic crusades in the country (after the crusades of the 1930s and 1950s). Isaiah Oke, an evangelist in Ilesa who came under Elton's mentorship from the late sixties, recalls being summoned to a meeting in Ilesa sometime in 1974, where Benson Idahosa, who had also been invited by Elton, was in attendance. Elton informed them that Osborn wanted to visit the country to hold a crusade; he then drafted them into the planning committee.[124] Benin was chosen as the host city. Much of the initial pre-crusade planning was done in Ilesa; however the arrangements required frequent trips to Benin. Later, the bulk of the groundwork moved to Benin.

Amos Aderonmu, another evangelist who had been working closely with Elton, said that "in December 1974 when T. L. Osborn came to Nigeria to organize a crusade in Benin City, Pa Elton was an instrument in bringing him. He told me, 'Amos, I want you to be a part of the pre-crusade team for the main crusade.' They brought four land cruisers for the crusade; he assigned one to me, assigned me a driver, and we went around the midwestern state, preached, advertised the crusade."[125] Oke recalled decades later, "I was with Elton when we welcomed him [Osborn] at the Lagos International Airport."

The Osborns prepared their best for this meeting and actually prayed it would be their greatest ever. For this visit, Daisy Osborn, who was the forerunner for the Osborn crusades, visited the country most likely in November 1974, with instructions to "meet with the church and government leaders of Nigeria." Her reconnoitring activity was described in *Faith Digest* thus: "In her pre-Crusade role, Daisy is literally, T. L.'s eyes and ears, always sensitive to the Spirit's guidance as she steers preliminary activities toward a successful mission. Her God-given ability to detect difficulties and to perceive ways to circumvent them saves Mr Osborn from making fruitless and time-consuming trips. In this way, each partner's investment is wisely administered, each gift accomplishing its maximum in evangelism."[126]

After spending some time in Nigeria, Daisy sent the following cable-gram to the Osborn Foundation headquarters: "NIGERIA WIDE OPEN/MUST MOVE QUICK/HIGH GOVERNMENT OFFICIALS FAVOR NATIONWIDE MEETINGS/HUNDREDS PREACHERS & CHURCHES MAKE CRUSADE PLANS/BIGGER THAN KENYA/PARTNERS MUST PRAY & RALLY FOR BIG HAR-VEST/MAKING LARGE COMMITMENTS HERE BY FAITH/DETAILS FOLLOW/ALERT PARTNERS FOR SACRIFI-CIAL ACTION/LOVE DAISY."[127] Big plans were made: "Nothing on this magnitude has ever been done before, and its influence is sure to spread throughout Africa and the world."[128] The Nigerian crusades would be the biggest ever, with "THE LARGEST GOSPEL 'TOOLS' AIRLIFT YET"[129] in the history of the Osborn crusades. And, as it turned out in 1974, it was.

The highlight of the event was the one-week school of evangelism that was held immediately after the crusade at the Lawn Tennis Court of the Ogbe Stadium. At Elton's invitation, the school of evangelism was attended by evangelists, church leaders, students, national youth corps members, and Christian workers from around the country. "It was filled up with people," Aderounmu recalls. There were actually seven thousand preachers and Christian workers in attendance.[130] This was the biggest and most strategic national evangelism mobilization that the country had ever witnessed. Referring to the crowd that attended the one-week meeting, T. L. Osborn said, "The cream of the crop . . . a new breed of Christian activists with a positive approach to all-out evangelism that's destined to sweep not only Nigeria, but on beyond her borders and into nations abroad!"[131]

Six hundred lingua tape units, fourteen complete film evangelism units, a fleet of mobile vans, and tons of literature were distributed to Christian workers around the country after the meeting. John Ladega, another evangelist who worked closely with Elton in organizing the crusade, remembers how they had to move many of the evangelism materials from Benin to Ilesa. These included Toyota Jeeps, which were given out round the country for missionary work along with projectors, films of Osborn's crusades, books, audio tapes, small playing machines, generators, horn speakers, and several other evangelism tools. Elton was solely responsible for the distribution of these evangelistic tools to evangelists working all over Nigeria.

There is a consensus among preachers, evangelists, and Christian leaders and workers around the country who have been actively involved in evangelism since the sixties and early seventies that the 1974 School of Evangelism was the most significant turning point in the history of evangelism in Nigeria; that it was responsible for catalysing the greatest evangelism thrust in Nigeria's Christian history.

"Rev. Elton . . . [cooperated] with Dr. T. L. and Dr. Daisy Osborn in helping them to cover many of the details required to assure the setting up of and successful conclusion of Osborn Global Crusades of Faith and Miracles in several cities of Nigeria. . . . In our dealings with Rev. Elton, we knew him as a friend and dedicated servant of the Lord Jesus Christ,"[132] the staff of Osborn Ministries International would remember nearly four decades later.

NINE

LAST-DAYS MESSENGER

S taff of Gospel Revivals Inc., publisher of *Herald of His Coming* magazine, recall that "about the last correspondence we had from Brother Elton, he informed us that because of the 'tremendous demand and the revival in so many areas, we had to turn and produce our own Nigerian *Herald of the Last Days* . . . which is exclusively Nigerian and deals with Nigerian problems.' "[1] This letter from Elton was received in 1974.

Why did Elton make this significant shift, letting his relationship with Los Angeles go dark and transitioning to what would become his flagship publication? Why did he abandon *Herald of His Coming* and the Nigerian Salvation-Herald papers, considering the enormous impact they were making? While he had the highest regard for the message published by the thoroughly Evangelical *Herald of His Coming*, he nevertheless believed there was the need for a widely circulating, independent Pentecostal paper that could deal with issues that *Herald of His Coming* would not discuss. Elton wanted his own *Pentecostal* magazine to promote the cause of revival across a wide spectrum of the body of Christ. The gift of a printing machine he received from a friend after the war most likely helped him in this direction.[2]

The first issue of *Herald of the Last Days* (*HOLD*) is revealing of Elton's motivation in starting the paper: "But before He can return . . . there must be a mighty revival which will reassert the power of the Gospel and restore the church to its proper place, and for this revival there must be also a mighty revival of the miraculous and in the development of the ministry of deliverance over sin . . . sickness . . . evil powers . . . poverty . . . fear, and all that raises itself up against the authority of the Lord Jesus. This ministry has been committed to the Church and this magazine will seek to stimulate the faith of those whom the LORD has called to minster and to enable them to minister properly and to demonstrate to the whole world of men and spirits that the Lord Jesus Christ is indeed the LORD and that He has given His church . . . and His people, the power to deliver and to prepare for His coming, to set up the promised kingdom of heaven on earth. So we feel there is a need for a magazine of this type."[3]

Also, by the beginning of the 1970s, Elton began to perceive himself not just as a prophet who operated in the church ministering to the needs of individual believers, but as a prophet sent to call Nigeria into her prophetic destiny. He wrote: "While there are many good preachers of the Gospel, and there are some champions of the Faith once delivered to the saints, we are greatly in need of prophets who will boldly declare . . . 'Thus saith the Lord . . .' We at Herald of the Last Days believe that God is speaking to us and that He has something special to say to us. . . . We believe we are a VOICE (and there are many others in many different countries today) calling the Lord's people who desire to hear the Voice of God calling."[4]

"These are exciting and thrilling days," Elton wrote in one of the early issues, "God is moving in the world in a new way. . . . God has never moved in this way since the day of Pentecost and it is full of excitingly wonderful prospects. . . . I seriously appeal to all Christian leaders to seek the face of God and to read their Bibles to see how far the Lord would have them to move forward with Him in this way at this time. Be patient with those who have seen the plan of God and are anxious to move forward with Him."[5] To give this kind of direction and vision to the church in the nation, Elton needed his own paper.

Even though Elton registered to operate in the country under the name "World Christian Crusade," his use of this name became a mere formality in subsequent years. Herald of the Last Days, the name of his flagship publication, became the de facto name for his ministry. Elton never officially declared it, but it is unmistakably written over all he said and did. Elton's choice of a name for this magazine—and ultimately, his devotion to it—lets us into his very heart: in *Herald of the Last Days* we come to see him in full prophetic bloom.

From the first issue, he left no one in doubt that he was a messenger sent to prepare the church for its final and finest hour. "We are living in the closing days of this age . . . when men's hearts are failing them for fear as they look to prevailing world conditions and the seeming inability of the world's leaders to deal with the situation. We are also living in days of declension in the church when the truth is not being preached and people are disillusioned as to the value of the Gospel. We are living in days when many Christians are deeply concerned about events and the lack of power in the Christians and the growing power of evil everywhere. Hence this magazine . . . and its title . . . HERALD OF THE LAST DAYS."[6]

The grand theme that ties all the articles in *HOLD* together is that of the emergence in the last days of a glorious church that would walk in the fullness of Christ's power and character; that would demonstrate unyielding resolve and courage in the battle against the greatest onslaught of evil the world had ever known; and that would bring to a close the church age and usher in the kingdom age. "The glory of the last days is the glory of the Church,"[7] Elton loved to proclaim.

> The Lord Jesus Himself is coming again . . . to be united with His triumphant Body. That event draws very near now. But the Bible leads us to believe that when He comes it will be to rapture a "glorious" Church, triumphant and victorious. It is certain that at the moment His Church is not a victorious or glorious Church. But when the promised revival comes, that will restore the Church to her promised glory and so she will be raptured at the peak of her glory.
>
> It is certain that the Lord's return will not be to remove a defeated church or even a disgraced church. So we can expect a wonderful future and experience soon for the church. We are now beginning to see the early moves of the Lord to revive His church again. The Holy Spirit is moving again and the gifts are being restored with the increase of signs and wonders and the demonstration of the miraculous, as experienced in the early church.[8]

The eighth issue of *HOLD* was released in 1972[9] and the thirty-ninth and last issue (by Elton) in 1978.[10] (Two final issues were published in the mid-eighties by some of his close protégés, but Elton had no input in these except for an editorial in the last one, and even this was published posthumously.[11]) We do not have dates for any other issue. However, considering the frequency with which they were released, it is safe to assume the first issue was released ca. 1970. The first issue set the tone for the style of the magazine—a twelve-page paper with several short teachings on a variety of Pentecostal truths. The first issue, for instance, contained six teachings, which carried titles such as "God's Move Today in Nigeria," "Soul Winning—Our Supreme Task," "According to Your Faith," and "The Work of Demons." The size of the magazine was doubled from the thirty-first issue, and this was sustained till the final release.

Elton stated clearly early on in this new venture, "We, at HERALD OF THE LAST DAYS, are not a church and do not speak for, or represent, any particular church, or revelation and we do not have any members and we shall never become a church."[12] Rather, "H.O.L.D. seeks to minister to Christians of all churches and to enlighten on the MOVE OF GOD IN NIGERIA TODAY and the Christian move in the world." The editorials of the later issues of the magazine usually stated that it was the "Voice of the Move of God in Nigeria."[13]

From the first issue, Elton warned prospective readers that the magazine would not "play with words or spare anyone . . . it will be strong meat for the hungry but it will also liberate and challenge many and call upon them to get up and dedicate their lives to HIM whom we serve and love."[14] He further declared, "If you think you dare expose yourself to ideas which are not traditional, if you think you are capable of 'thinking new' without turning to condemn normal concepts; if you think you are big enough to make an honest re-assessment of your church and Christian attitudes . . . then go ahead and expose yourself to the challenge contained in this magazine and see what happens. But you are warned before you start to read . . . God will expect a response to his commands and challenge."[15] He also wrote, "We, at Herald of the Last Days, believe that God is speaking to us and that he has something special to say to us, and you, and realize that the message is revolutionary and therefore costly, and likely to be unacceptable to many church leaders."[16]

On the one hand, the articles in the magazine were targeted at introducing revolutionary teachings to "enlighten all Christians in all the denominations, so that they may be prepared for the (coming) revival, that it may not overtake us unprepared."[17] On the other hand, it addressed specific on-going debates, especially as they touched on developments in Pentecostal Christianity in the country. He greatly hoped the magazine would shape the thinking of a new generation along the lines of what he termed the "NEW MOVE." "We are in the closing days of this Age, at the end of the dispensation of grace and God is about to usher in the dispensation of the Kingdom Age. . . . So God has to take steps to prepare the world, and the church, for this momentous event. And this is the 'NEW MOVE' which God is starting these days all over the world."[18]

Elton rejected the notion that the church already knew everything there was to know and already walked in the fullness of God's plan. "It is firmly stated by many Christian leaders that there can be no further new revelation as we now have the completed revelation in the Bible," he noted with objection. "But we must also acknowledge that there have been several distinct and different revelations from God during the past 100 years. These revelations produced some of the leading denominations existing today. They were formed as a result of those revelations. God has steadily restored new Bible truths in stages as His people can absorb and accept them. It proves there has been a gradual process of unfolding revelation. IT CONTINUES TODAY."[19]

When *HOLD* appeared on the scene, it was truly revolutionary because of its content and the bold style with which it dealt with issues. Elton was not careful to avoid offending religious people; he was troubled about the state of the church and he did not hide it. Nothing pained his heart more than the weak state of the church, which, according to him, disqualified it from being able to govern the earth the way God intended. He was, therefore, blunt about the need for a new order to shake things up and bring about the much needed change. "Oh, that our church leaders would only read their Bibles and open their eyes to see what God is doing today and thus save themselves the embarrassment of finding that the power of God is now with a new group of believers who are ready to exercise faith and produce the results . . . even if they are not ordained and have not been trained in our Bible training colleges."[20]

Elton regularly denounced the prevailing spiritual apathy and believed *HOLD* had a special role, much like that of Simeon in the New Testament (Luke 2:25-32), to open the eyes of the church to see what God was doing. "No matter how difficult may seem the spiritual condition in the churches; we believe that God is moving again by His Holy Spirit in these last days. . . . We at Herald of the Last Days feel honoured as we realise that God has revealed Himself to us and given us a vision for these last days . . . and we are determined to cast aside every hindrance and to give everything we have to spreading this Vision and share it with all whom the Lord has called and to endeavour by all possible means to hasten that coming and fulfilment by sending the Gospel to everyone in Nigeria so that the Vision can be brought to pass in our day."[21]

"This magazine desires to help YOU to understand this 'new move' of God so that you may not be found opposing God to your own hurt,"[22] he declared. In what was a direct reference to the prevailing situation of the day, he noted concerning the ministry of Simeon: "Real faith was at a low ebb in Israel when the Lord Jesus was born. There was plenty of religious activity, but the real, spiritual essential value was very small indeed. The conditions were bad. Yet this old man, this visionary, had the faith to utter a prophecy concerning Israel, directing the thoughts and attention of all to that BABY—'Thy salvation, which Thou hast prepared before the face of all people . . . the glory of Thy people . . . Israel.' "[23] "So today, when conditions are similar in Christendom, we at the Herald of the Last Days proclaim that there is hope for the people of God today. God has not forsaken His Church. There is a promise of revival; of renewal, of victory. The way of blessing is the same today as in the time of John the Baptist . . . repentance and unreservedly seeking the Lord Jesus Himself." He then turned to the leaders: "That repentance should begin with the ministers . . . 'Let the priests, the minsters of the Lord, weep between the porch and the altar, and let them say, spare thy people, O Lord . . .' "[24]

Elton believed that the articles in each issue of the magazine were not just meant to be seen as good biblical teaching; each one was a call to action that required a definite response. The final piece at the back of each issue was usually a column titled "Now Is the Time for Action," which challenged Christians to be fully engaged in the process of establishing God's purpose in Nigeria. The following is the call to action at the back of the third issue:

Herald of the Last Days desires to awaken, shock, enlighten and CHAL-LENGE its readers. We have no desire to entertain passive readers. We must get something done because the situation demands urgent action NOW. So we CHALLENGE YOU.

WE CHALLENGE ALL CHURCHES

To repent as all minsters are called to do in Joel 2:12-17. Study the truths in this magazine and seek the face of the Lord and then awaken the congregations. Faith in the Word of God provokes action. Then every church should seek the Lord, as did the early church in Acts 4:29-30.

WE CHALLENGE ALL EVANGELISTS

To realise the burden of the lost and to find out the districts where there is no Gospel. Do not try to revive existing churches while others perish because they have never heard the Gospel once. Step out in faith and the Lord will confirm your faith by signs and wonders.

WE CHALLENGE ALL YOUTH

Remember the Lord Jesus said "You (th) must be my witnesses" (Acts 1:8).

Do not rest until everyone in your company knows about the Lord Jesus ... be on fire for the Lord Jesus. Do not be content to listen to sermons ... or be in the choir ... be a fighter and a deliverer for the Lord Jesus to the needy and sick.[22]

Despite the many challenges the church was grappling with, Elton was optimistic about the immediate future: "Because we believe that there is a 'true church in Nigeria today and that God has a plan and purpose for that 'true church' in the very near future, and that there are many young Christians who are anxious to obey God rather than men, and who earnestly want to know where they can serve the Lord, then we want to reveal what the Bible says about that 'true church', and God's plan for it and all who are part of it."[26] Elton said, "All over the world today the Lord is raising up men and women with the New Vision of what he can do in them and of the end-time revival which will demonstrate His Lordship and authority. We are dedicating this magazine to YOU."[27] Those who were ready to embrace this new vision—who were ready to explore new possibilities in God, who were ready to risk everything for a new spiritual adventure, who were willing to press into deeper things of God—had to love God and His purpose enough to risk everything to lay hold of His present plan. "God will strip away from us all that hinders a clear Vision of His Son—attachments which demand first loyalty."[28]

Having a "New Vision"—a vision of what God was about to do—was the gateway into God's present purpose, Elton taught. Without a new vision, the church would quickly lose focus and stagnate. The vision "represented the transition from the old order, dispensation and system, to an entirely NEW MOVE."[29] To access the mind of God, the believer's spiritual sight had to be elevated and fixed on Him. Using Simeon as a type, Elton explained, "He [Simeon] was daily found in the Temple—daily expecting the fulfilment of the Vision. His was an active faith, as indeed all faith must be. It kept him walking with God. It made him a man of prayer. We must have a motive for maintaining our prayer life, otherwise it becomes mechanical and routine. Prayer is maintained in strength by vision. His faith in the Vision produced patience in the midst of the external pressures of the growing failure and corruption of the organised religious worship of his days. The vision absolutely controlled and governed his life. He lived for nothing else. Yet there was no outward sign of any move of God. That is the most testing of all in the Vision and demands great faith in God's Word and promises. I have no doubts that Simeon experienced the same doubts and assaults on his faith that many are experiencing today in relation to the NEW VISION for the end time."[30]

There was bound to be a separation between those who could *see* and those who could not—between those who were willing to move on with God and those who would resist the new move. "God is revealing a NEW MOVE to meet new conditions today in the whole world. God is moving again now, and many church leaders are troubled as they see some of the wonderful things the Lord is doing and it is sad to say that some leaders are seeking to ban such operations and to try to stop this 'new move'. . . THAT IS IMPOSSIBLE."[31] But then he adds, "In what way will it affect existing denominations? Are we about to witness a spate of new breakaway churches, and the start of another new denomination to add to the strife now existing between churches? . . . NO, NO. God never moves to cause division and strife. It is we who refuse to move with God and open our eyes to His Word and plans for His work and the re-establishment of his authority and kingdom on the earth as promised."[32]

Elton made sure to "emphatically state that" the new vision or move "is NOT the time for a new denomination or sect, drawing Christians into another internal fight with the resulting strife and bitterness, but God is speaking and is saying something SPECIAL to us today."[33] No doubt Elton long grieved over the 1953/54 misunderstanding. He would in later years frequently refer to the needlessness of such divisions if only man learnt to cooperate with what God was doing. His later writings show that he was always careful to make sure that his actions, occasioned by his response to the move of God as he saw it, were not interpreted as a deliberate attempt to cause division in any church.

"Let us tell you what God has spoken about to us," Elton wrote in one issue. The first was that "God is definitely drawing the attention again of His people to the Person of His Beloved Son: Our Lord and Saviour

Jesus Christ." God was refocusing attention on the "name, work and glory that belongs to HIM [Jesus Christ] alone." He warned, "So many other 'things' are creeping into the churches, and Satan is seeking to divert the faith of Christians away from the Saviour—Jesus Christ. . . . So we believe God is drawing special attention again to the LORD JESUS CHRIST. God is saying, 'Thou shalt have no other Saviour for any of your needs, other than My Son Jesus Christ.' "[34]

The second thing God was saying was that "the organised church is not fulfilling the Great Commission—'Go ye into all the world and preach the Gospel unto all creatures . . .' and thus is delaying the return of the Lord Jesus to His rightful place in this world. The church is concentrating too much on internal developments, ministry appointments, special revelations which have taken the place of Evangelism. Money has also assumed far too great a place in our church services, resulting in spiritual death and declensions which has put the Lord outside His own church."

God was also saying that the "great battle of the Ages is near—the conflict between God and Satan, and God needs His people to be ready for this conflict. They [God's people] are NOT [ready]: hence the urgent calls now coming to those who will hear HIM."

The fourth thing was that "God will find His own people—He will gather them as He has done so often—even though only a remnant." But God was well able to use this remnant to "thrash the evil powers—to prove the Lord has indeed bought and produced a 'Master race' who today can, and will, stand and use their blood-bought authority to overcome the powers of evil and prove the power of the Full Gospel today—to all peoples, in all places, and under all circumstances." Lastly, the end of the age was near and God was "going to remove His church; but before He can do so He will demonstrate to all—in heaven and hell—that the Gospel is still the power of God unto salvation; which will demonstrate and bring deliverance to all who call upon the name of the Lord." Elton concluded, "We at HERALD OF THE LAST DAYS believe all we have printed in this issue and we are seeking by every possible means to translate it into action. We accept that light brings responsibility and that God has revealed many of His plans to us. But we also know that light can kill—light ignored or not obeyed will force God to leave us out of any further revelations. We mean to press forward."[35]

Elton devoted much space in *HOLD* to emphasizing the need for the church to embrace the supernatural ministry of the Holy Spirit. "I believe the puny programmes offered by modern churches have had their day of greatest success, and that they will do nothing more but continue to fade into obscurity as a mighty army of living witnesses appears upon the horizon of this closing Gospel age,"[36] he declared. He fervently preached that the good news had to be proclaimed "with proof, with evidence" and that "fancy sermons and elaborate discourses have no place, and draw no audience in this day of miracle evangelism. There is no place for such in the ministry of the Holy Ghost."[37] "The work of God can only be successfully carried out by the Holy Spirit and therefore we will need the fullness of the Holy Spirit if the job is to be successfully completed."

The church's message had to be with evidence; our gospel with proof; and our preaching with demonstration. A gospel that was not accompanied with the demonstration of the power of God only massaged the soul. "Ah, church awake, arise, shake thyself, Go forth, Preach the Truth, Proclaim this Gospel of the kingdom,"[38] Elton cried. And again: "It is this Gospel of the Kingdom, being preached in the power of the Spirit of God, confirmed by signs and wonders and divers miracles, that is bringing to pass some of the greatest world-wide evangelistic triumphs in history today."[39] He chided, "Our sleeping Church cannot produce miracles. . . . They sing about miracles, preach about them, pray for them but do not really expect any. So they cannot produce any. But it will take a mighty wave of the miraculous to convince this unbelieving world of the gospel, and to awaken and challenge a dead church."[40]

"How can we prove that Christ is indeed risen from the dead, according to the Bible, if there are no miracles done in His Name?" he asked. "Our arguments will not prove it to the satisfaction of the heathen. The theologian cannot prove it. Miracles in His Name alone will prove it."[41] "Where there are true believers, devils are cast out and the sick are healed in Jesus' Name; the works of Christ are manifest. . . . Wherever Christ's healing power has been allowed to heal the people, multitudes have gathered. We've proven that multitudes still follow Christ when they see his miracles on the diseased. Theologians tell us that the days of miracles are past—that healing for the sick is no longer necessary in the Church. What are the results of this theory? False cults which have offered healing have flourished everywhere. A healing church has always been, is, and always will be a church which draws the people to hear the Gospel—an evangelising church."[42]

Elton argued, "If we do not have the supernatural in Christianity, we have nothing left to offer the heathen except a religion—and true Christianity is not a religion. . . . All normal men crave the supernatural. They long to see the manifestation of the power of God. People are even willing to excuse extravagances and individual fanaticism if they can find God working today. . . . The heathen do not want to hear excuses for not being healed or comforted by promises that all will be better when they reach heaven. They want to taste and enjoy the benefits of the Gospel which Jesus preached and was given to the disciples to preach also."[43]

The outpouring of God's Spirit at the end of the age, he said, "will be the same in character as the one on the day of Pentecost . . . but it will be world-wide and it will be poured out on ALL FLESH. It will create a tremendous world-wide revival and prepare for the return of the Lord Himself. It will sweep away denominational barriers and will overflow denominational walls and men everywhere will be seeking salvation and the Lord . . . and it will be accompanied by supernatural wonders and miracles . . . far greater than those of [the] Day of Pentecost."[44]

Elton coined a phrase to articulate the position of the Scriptures concerning the last days: "These wonderful crisis days." He frequently used this phrase to express the opportunity the church had to exercise its dominion before the rapture. Describing this opportunity, he wrote:

Men everywhere are aware that something is amiss with the life and activities of the church in Nigeria. We have a form of religion but no power. For the average Christian life has lost its meaning, its joy, and there is no shout of praise in the soul. Moral and spiritual decline has fallen very low and already we are seeing the terrible signs in our society which speak of the last days. Standards of decency in public and private are debased and sacredness of home and family is forsaken. THE CHURCH MUST CARRY MOST OF THE BLAME FOR THIS STATE OF AFFAIRS.

Yet there are also signs of a great spiritual awakening in many places and particularly among the youth of the land. Hundreds are getting converted and are seeking to know more of the real Christian way of living. It is for this that we send out this issue of Herald of the Last Days. It is dedicated to the young people of Nigeria who are stirred and excited by the prospect of tasting the wonderful life of a Christian; of realizing the wonders of the New Birth and fullness of the Holy Spirit and of service for the lord Jesus, in these wonderful but crisis days . . . if they are crisis days . . . they are also days of wonderful opportunities . . . to lead others into salvation and life in its fullness.[45]

"We are determined," he also said, "to continue to publish *Herald of the Last Days* to stir and awaken young Christians to the challenges of these wonderful crisis days."[46] And again, "These are CRISIS DAYS. These are harvest days. These are vital days for every Christian."[47]

"As we are pressed with the nearness of the coming of the Lord and the existing conditions in the church and the world," he wrote, "we are deeply concerned that the Lord's people are so indifferent to the situation."

It is possible that our repeated appeals and cries about the serious and critical situation may arouse some opposition among church leaders and members who maybe feel that we are being alarmist. But things are serious and someone must "Blow a trumpet and sound an alarm." There is far too much comfortable, easy going Christianity which does not awaken sinners or bring conviction but merely pleases the enemy, Satan. Empty forms and hollow ceremonies and services are causing many to be lost and there is no evidence of the miracle working God of Elijah in our midst.

Yet He is not dead; He is alive and waiting to support any man who will step out of the normal formal church organisations and call upon the people of God in Nigeria with Elijah's words. Many will say that the days of miracles and such interventions by God are past. This is simply not true. Never have we needed a miraculous intervention more than we do now—with thousands going to hell and never hearing the Gospel that can rescue them. God is looking today for Elijahs. Men who will listen to the call of God in the quietness of their own souls, and who are willing to give up everything . . . EVERYTHING . . . and step out with souls aflame, to move among the churches and Christians to awaken them. . . . Men need to believe what God says in His Word instead of trying to analyse every word to find special small points of doctrine. The Gospel which is preached in many churches today is too calculating, too analysed and too philosophical. No wonder people fail to find God today.[48]

The last days would witness the greatest release of evil that man has known, but God was ready to meet "this onslaught from Satan with a group of MEN who were formerly Satan's slaves, but whom He has redeemed and filled with his Spirit and whom he is now training to deal with this 'mystery of iniquity' and the coming onslaught of evil, and to prepare the world for the coming of the real World Ruler—God's Own

Son—His appointed King and Judge, the Lord Jesus Christ."[49] The church, Elton preached, was supposed to be on the offensive against Satan and his host. "Prayer meetings should be attacking centres—directing authoritative prayer against the plans and devices of the enemy."[50] God's people were supposed to be "attacking the enemy and delivering men and women from the kingdom of darkness."[51] He once wrote, "We declare our intentions and policy, even though it will probably provoke reprisals from the Deceiver. . . . We intend to recruit many 'overcomers' who will dedicate themselves to this great Battle of the Ages."[52]

Elton believed that one of the "important functions" of *HOLD* was to "instruct many, so that revival can be carried on properly and Satan defeated BY US. This is not the time for sitting down in churches listening to sermons—this is the time for ACTION. We must go out and attack the enemy wherever we can find him and prove WE HAVE THE POWER TO CHANGE LIVES."[53] Again: "We ought to stand in prayer and intercession and FIGHT Satan and his hosts as they attempt to possess people, as they try to bring sickness and defeat and failure. We are to challenge everything Satan is attempting to do today in the lives of the Lord's people."[54]

Another issue to which Elton regularly spoke was the need for the church to own the purpose of God. He believed the body of Christ to a large extent had failed to realize her critical role in the fulfilment of God's plan. Many in the church assumed that the ultimate responsibility for the fulfilment of God's eternal plan rests on God's shoulder and that they were only required to live good Christian lives and watch God do His work on earth. In contrast, Elton argued, God was waiting on the church to establish His kingdom on the earth. As long as the church refused to rise to the occasion, the purpose of God would remain unfinished. In describing the progression of the spiritual life, peaking at the stage he refers to as mastery, Elton identifies four stages—slaves, children, sons, and rulers.[55]

A sign that one had attained the levels of sonship and "rulership" was the level of commitment to the execution of God's plan on earth—how much an individual had come to embrace God's burden for the earth. The heart of a son throbbed with the passion of the father. "Thy kingdom come, thy will be done on earth as in heaven," was the prayer of the mature Christian. A sense of partnership defined the mind-set of the church walking in its calling. "We are co-workers with God," was the creed of the ascending church. "Christians think they are honouring God in their trust in Him, when they say, 'there is nothing we can do about the future. God will work out His will, regardless of what I do.' But such is often the thinking of Christians who wish to escape responsibility of taking action or making decisions, which will determine their own future,"[56] wrote Elton.

"In many of our seemingly pious prayers, we humbly beg God to undertake to do what He has commanded us to do. It is true we need His guidance, power and wisdom, but He needs us as His only means of carrying out His programme," said Elton. "We should not hand the responsibility back to God. It is our responsibility. We now have the right to minister and work with His AUTHORITY over all His enemies and, as He overcame, so we too will overcome. The Lord exercised His authority by commanding all other powers and authorities to submit and obey Him. He spoke words—words of life and power and authority. We must do the same. As we keep in fellowship with the Holy Spirit we become His vessels, His voice, His hands, to express his authority. . . . It is not a question of praying for the Lord to do it. We are the Lord's militant army and, under the leadership and control of the Holy Spirit, we must accept the responsibility for these operations and pray, and declare war on Satan's strongholds and take action."[57] In articulating the effect on the ministry of the church of such a shift in thinking, Elton remarked:

God also looks for men and women today who refuse to let the world situation and the increasing operations of evil force them into silence and acceptance of an expected tribulation and to fold their arms in passive acceptance. We are not prepared to accept the woeful story of the terrible situation in the world and churches. We are not looking or waiting in despair for the second coming of the Lord as the only hope of escaping the coming tribulation, for ourselves only. We see the "falling away" in the churches, but we also see the thousands of new young converts who are being filled with the Holy Spirit and who face the unbelieving world and backslidden church and yet "We are well able to go in." The world is rapidly moving into judgement, but we are still alive and still here and we know it is not the will of God for any to perish and that there are whole tribes in Nigeria who have not yet heard the gospel or had the chance to repent and be saved and so we boldly pray, "Do not come yet Lord. Give us a few more years and we will give ourselves to taking the gospel to them." . . . We are not begging to be "raptured" and so leave Satan to take over this world. We are truly citizens of heaven and the kingdom of Heaven but we also have a God-given burden for this world and its people. It belongs to our Heavenly Father and His divinely appointed King is waiting to return to take up His kingship here. We know that we are in God's will in desiring the salvation of the unreached in Nigeria and we believe God is allowing us time to do this. We refuse to be passive acceptors of existing conditions. We have a God who can change those conditions and the faith that we can do it. We must begin to understand God's plan for these days and realise we can be a vital part of that plan if we choose to dedicate ourselves to God.[58]

Christians had to become "vessels of recovery,"[59] as Elton liked to phrase it. "The Lord Jesus has finished the work of redemption and now He has committed into our hands the power to overcome the powers of Satan in nearly every realm. It is now for us to attack the kingdom of darkness; it is now for us to overcome the evil one and his works; AND WE CAN DO IT."[60] God would use men, "converted and saved by his grace and power, to conquer Satan and recover the whole world."[61] He wrote, "We are God's soldiers in His army of liberation;"[62] and also, "The battle of the Ages is God's battle, but we are His representatives, and we shall win."[63]

"Many Christians are aware of the backsliding in the church and the growing evil in the world and they are praying that the Lord will come quickly and remove His people from it all. But that would be admitting that Satan has won and that God had to remove His people in order to save them from Satan. We believe that God has another plan. He has sufficient faith in His redeemed channels and 'vessels of recovery' to entrust them with the task of withstanding Satan and his plans. God has more faith in us than we have in Him. He knows we can win, in spite of our weaknesses and failures."[64] Believers were supposed to develop "a passion for God. A passion for God's people; for God's honour; for God's Name; for God's temple and city."[65] He wrote, "That is the purpose of the present move of the Holy Spirit throughout the land. God is moving and calling out those whom He can trust to carry this revival; and most of those whom He is calling are laymen and young people."[66]

According to Elton, "God does not want employees. He wants travailing sons." God does not want His children to just be "experts in Biblical exposition or criticism"; God wants "those who have a passion for souls and His Name."[67] He urged the church: "Heavenly responsibility rests upon us today to carry on the war against the enemy and we have no right to throw the responsibility back upon God."[68] And again: "The Lord therefore calls upon every one of His people to be 'good soldiers' and to go forth in His strength and power against the foe. Every child of God is called to be a 'fighter' and take part in the 'warfare' raging now."[69] There had to be "a radical change of mind and attitudes among our church leaders. We have been carried and cared for as babies for far too long and we can never expect to be regarded as mature Christians, or even part of the church militant, until we assume this vital responsibility."[70]

"Heavenly responsibility rests upon us today to carry on the war against the enemy and we have no right to throw the responsibility back upon God. As we find the will of God when we seek Him, then our full responsibility is to 'speak the word of authority' and that enables God to work. He delights in responding to Words of Command from His children when they are spoken in faith and in His Will and against the powers of darkness. We are 'co-workers' with God in this battle,"[71] Elton wrote. And also: "The Lord's soldiers must be fully committed to Him and ready to submit, without questioning, to His command and count everything they possess as being loaned to them for His work and service. They must be ready to endure hardship. They must be ready to count their life not dear in order to serve the Lord Jesus. It is the responsibility of these 'chosen soldiers' to enforce the victory of our Captain. It is His victory we proclaim and assert in Satan's face constantly. In the Name and with the authority of the Lord Jesus, we challenge Satan's reign and right to hold people in bondage and we set them free in His Name. We proclaim the gospel of full deliverance."[72]

Elton bemoaned the fact that the gospel "has been buried beneath a church which has become more and more worldly and money conscious, and which has clearly shut the Lord Jesus outside His Own church (Rev. 3:20). In these days the church on earth has acquired wealth and property and influence and has become part of the worldly system, to the extent that it cannot be separated from the world or its systems. Satan has done a fine job of taking over the task of managing the church and it now no longer represents the mind of God."[73] Because of the prevailing situation, God had to "intervene if He is to complete His task of producing a church 'glorious, pure and powerful' for His Son, who purchased it with his own blood on Calvary's Cross. We are sure that God will never allow Satan to boast that he has completely spoilt the church and destroyed its power and made it useless to God. God must have a 'spotless, pure and powerful' Body to represent Him on earth in the last days, in order to use that Body to demonstrate the mighty power of God and sweep the powers of Satan and evil spirits to demonstrate the power of the Cross and Holy Spirit to deliver men and women, and change them, and make them what He means them to be."[74] God had to "make some drastic changes and sweep the church with a great Holy Spirit revival which would accomplish His purposes in the last days. We are preparing for that Holy Spirit-sweeping revival NOW."[75]

"There is no time for petty sermons for these days," said Elton. "We must speak the truth, we must call forth repentance, we must call upon our leaders to examine ourselves, we must call for the priests to fast and repent and weep for their failures in these last days. In these last days, there's going to be a big change in the quality and style of the ministry, the teaching that's going forth to the church, awakening it and calling it to gather together, for special purposes. The trumpets are sounding, and you will find the prophetical ministry is likely to cry out with this and bring this to our notice. Let us look for this, let us expect this and let us detect in it the call from the Holy Spirit to awaken to these last days' season."[76]

There are far too many Christians who, although they have been saved, yet they have not gone on to follow the Lord and [instead] have a superficial experience of salvation. It is feared many of these will fall by the wayside in the coming conflict or be left behind when the Lord comes again. They have a mental acceptance of salvation which does not stand the strain of demon pressures and worldly temptations.

It is those who have experienced a deep conviction of sin and have forsaken all known sin, and hate sin, who will be further tested and trained and equipped by the Holy Spirit for these last days of conflict. So there will be more emphasis upon deep and real CONVERSION in these last days. The Holy Spirit MUST use men, but those men will be men of conviction and changed men. Let us not seek for mere show of hands but seek the genuine Holy Spirit's conversion so that real changed men and women are ready for further training and equipping by the Holy Spirit.[77]

Elton devoted much space in the magazine to the subject of revival. "The Lord is also speaking to His church to awaken her from her slumber and slothfulness and worldliness. It is the plan of God to come for a glorious church, 'not having spot, or wrinkle, or any such thing; but that it should be holy and without blemish.' There has been such a decline in the spiritual values of the church that it is hard to believe that it is really God's intention to revitalise and awaken and purify His church, but it is His plan still. It is equally hard to understand how God will manage to accomplish that task, but he will do it and, because of the fact that it is nearly time for the next Age to begin, that work will be a quick and drastic operation."[78]

"As we see the awful condition of the churches today and the sins of 'Christian people' we may be led to despair of ever seeing a true spiritual revival in the world. But the Apostle Peter, moved by the Holy Spirit, states that the revelation of the prophet Joel in Joel 2:28—'It shall come to pass afterward, that I will pour out my Spirit upon your flesh . . .' —is indeed for these last days and that it was only partially fulfilled at the day of Pentecost. The great outpouring is still ahead of us."[79] But Elton noted that "it would also seem that this event is taking place NOW. The Holy Spirit is moving and filling many Christians, especially young men and women, for the service of God."[80]

The worldwide revival would not be "a denominational revival. It will probably start outside the denominations but it will also flow into the churches and thousands will call upon the Name of the Lord and be saved. It is possible that some denominations will fiercely oppose this last day's revival, feeling that they have the Holy Spirit and that all converts should join their churches. God is never tied to denominations and will ignore this spirit of sectarianism."[81]

A major feature of the revival would be "a restoration of the Gifts of the Holy Spirit to the church. God has never withdrawn them, but the Church has neglected them and they have stopped [being] exercised."[82] The revival would witness "a restoration of the mighty power of the Holy Spirit filling the Lord's people, especially the new converts. There will be a restoration of the powers of healing and the power of God to heal in many different ways." The church would also see a restoration of the "operation of the supernatural, with God speaking through human channels to His people, in prophecy and the gift of tongues . . . a restoration of God's use of dreams and visions especially with the young people. There will be a greater use of women in the ministry." The body of Christ would also experience "a restoration of true spiritual PRAISE and WORSHIP . . . and there will be a wonderful restoration of the glory of God in His church." He said, "This world-wide revival has already started in many lands, and we believe it has started in Nigeria and will spread all over the world."[83]

"There are many attempts to 'stir up' revival, [to] shout it down, [to] dance it into action," noted Elton, "but these efforts are not of the Holy Spirit; they are man-made and of the flesh and will not bring in the long promised revival." He continued, "The true revival will cause men to fall on their faces and cry for forgiveness, [to] call for God's mercy—it will not be a revival of shouting and dancing and entertainment. It is also clear that the beginning must be made by the 'priest, the clergy, the ministers' of the altar; who will have to fall on their faces and ask for cleansing and pardon. Then the revival will spread to the congregations and then to the people outside. It will affect the whole country, the whole world. . . . Souls will be saved in their thousands—drawn to realise the power of God as they see the many demonstrations of the healing and delivering power of God manifested by Spirit filled believers whenever the people gather. Denominational barriers and names will not matter in those days. People will gather where the Spirit of the Lord is at work in His latter day power."[84]

"Today, Satan laughs at the efforts of the church and is quite satisfied that time is spent in organisation meetings, councils, discussion. He does not respect or fear our groups, men's meetings, fine organs or even brilliant preachers (however well-intentioned they may be)," wrote Elton. But "they do not interfere with his plans or attack his kingdom. Satan does not worry very much about some of the many all-night prayer meetings held. They are often without purpose or objective; or devoted to selfish, personal motives. But Satan is very upset and always reacts when Holy Spirit filled men and women gather (even though only in small numbers and groups) and who know how to wage spiritual warfare against Satan. Christian history is full of examples of men who did not fear even mighty church organisations but did great things for God by prayer and faith and the power of the Holy Spirit. Prayer and faith can do anything that God can do because God prays through His people. What wonderful power Peter and John manifested in Jerusalem when faced with severe opposition from Church leaders and persecution from government authorities. Some were imprisoned and beaten. . . . We have become used to and satisfied with a second rate Christian life and have accepted another spiritual standard apart from the Holy Spirit."[85]

A study of "the life and actions of the Lord as stated in the four gospels" shows that "His actions and life [were] really daily attacks on the 'usurper' kingdom of darkness and a revelation of what God wanted to establish on earth."[86] The Lord never "had any doubt of His Father's WILL for Him and His work. He attacked the forces of and authorities of the kingdom which had deceitfully taken over God's kingdom on earth, because of the failure of Adam and his handover of the authority of the kingdom to SATAN. The Lord expressed in His life and ministry His complete mastery and authority over all the evils that Satan had introduced into his kingdom so we can be sure that kingdom will be re-established on earth. . . . There is a choice given to the Lord's people NOW on earth and in this time and Age, to recognise this programme of God and become a part of it. This will mean complete dedication of ourselves and all we possess to Him and to recognise that all our talents and possessions MUST be dedicated to His service Now and for the Future Kingdom."[87]

Elton repeatedly emphasized the great need for the right heart posture to any new move of God. Believers could either humble themselves and receive what God was revealing, or they could resist and become mockers and be left behind. They could choose to stick to tradition or jump into the river of God's revelation. They could decide to be stuck in the past or joyfully move into the unfolding plan of God. "The healing of the blind man [John 9] was an advance in the revelation of God of that time, and an opportunity and a challenge to all followers of God to move forward with that new revelation. Instead of advancing, the majority refused and rejected the new light and revelation. That miracle challenged them: *The living Christ or a dead tradition.* This is a principle of all new revelation or light, which must be applied in these days of so many confusing doctrines and teachings, all claiming to be of God."[88]

Blessing and revelation forces people to decide; it's going to force you to decide as you listen to this [message] what you are going to do in response to what the Holy Spirit is now saying to you. You can accept it and accepting it will require action, a repentance and a change of your life and a change in your decisions and your dedication. That is certain in these last days. But if you decide to delay action and are not prepared to give heed to what the Holy Spirit is saying, it will bring judgement; not only will it bring judgement, but you in your turn, even though you are a believer, will join a growing body of people who will be hostile to those who are moving forward in obedience to the word of the Lord. And you will begin to persecute that which is moving forward. It has been experienced right through the Christian Church.[89]

"Every new revelation from God will exalt and glorify the Lord Jesus," wrote Elton. "Old traditions will be tested, and where found inadequate, they must be abandoned, and loyalty to the Lord Jesus Himself will have to be regarded as the real test. It is also a spiritual principle that spiritual development depends upon obedience to revelation and light already given. God will not give further new light until we have obeyed light already given. It is to be regretted that rejection of light and revelation often produce bitterness, hatred and fierce opposition and persecution by the rejectors against those sincerely following the new revelation. Light brings death as well as life, if light is refused. Pharisees, who claimed to be in the light of God, became blind when they refused God's new revelation. So it is today. There are many of God's servants now spiritually blind because they have rejected the light and revelation of God's present day move."[90]

The earliest issues of *HOLD* were a fitting prologue to the 1970s—they challenged the status quo and watered the ground for the revival that was about to break out all over the country. The magazine eventually became the most widely read and consistently circulated Pentecostal magazine in Nigeria throughout the seventies. We do not have an estimate of how many copies were printed over the course of the magazine's life—the closest we get is that by 1974 Elton was printing twenty-five thousand copies monthly[91]—but it became a staple for a whole generation and revolutionized Christian expression among young people in the country. Its content and style came to symbolize the spiritual battles of the seventies.

TEN

"WE ARE AT WAR"

From the late 1960s to the end of the 1970s, Christian student groups in Nigeria's institutions of higher learning became the arena of fierce battles between Pentecostals and Evangelicals. Until the late 1960s, Pentecostalism as a distinct expression of the Christian faith was virtually unknown in Nigeria's higher institutions. Protestant, Roman Catholic, and Evangelical groups dominated the spiritual landscape. A quick history of the Evangelical groups in Nigeria's tertiary institutions is necessary, since it was from this base that the charismatic movement among students, the subject of this chapter, emerged.

Evangelical witness in Nigeria's post-secondary institutions came about as a result of the activities of expatriate teachers in Nigeria's secondary and post-secondary institutions who were either members of the Scripture Union (SU) or former members of the British Inter Varsity Fellowship (IVF). "At one stage there were nearly 200 members of the British Graduates' Fellowship active in Nigeria alone, many of them in secondary and tertiary education."[1] They were encouraged by IVF-Britain's executive to get "students together for prayer and Bible study; leaving the initiative in the hands of the students, except for the jobs they hadn't the time to do."[2] Usually, "on a Sunday afternoon these men invited students, many of whom had had their secondary school education in mission schools and some of whom were Christians, to their homes for a Bible 'reading.' This was followed by questions, discussion, prayer, tea and biscuits. Some of these students were converted. Spontaneously on their own initiative they banded together, formed Christian Unions and applied for recognition as student societies."[3]

The Ibadan Varsity Christian Union (IVCU), which was founded in 1961;[4] the Evangelical Christian Union (ECU) of the University of Ife, which was founded in 1964;[5] the University College Hospital, Ibadan, Fellowship, which started ca. 1955;[6] the Fellowship of Christian Students at Ahmadu Bello University, Zaria, and in several other institutions in northern Nigeria, all owed their founding to the activities of IVF lecturers.[7] Evangelical student work at the Lagos University[8] and the University of Nigeria, Nsukka,[9] owe their founding to the Scripture Union—but after interactions with students from IVF-initiated groups from other schools, they shed their initial Scripture Union affiliation and became independent evangelical student groups and thereafter developed along IVF lines.

A 1967 report of the Christian student work at the University of Nigeria, Nsukka, stated: "Through the providential transfer of a number of Christian students from Ibadan, Ife and Zaria to Nsukka, a firm foundation is being laid for an effective evangelical witness in this university. The Christian students are very much aware of their responsibility in this respect, and the witness of the small Scripture Union group already in existence on the campus has been completely reorganized. A constitution with a definite evangelical basis is being drawn up by leaders;"[10] and of the Lagos University: "Their small group was encouraged to receive news of Christian Unions in sister colleges and to realize that they also face difficulties similar to their own. The group was formed last November [1966] from a small informal gathering of Scripture Union members for prayer and Bible discussion."[11]

The fire of evangelicalism swept through the campuses in the 1960s. One report from the IVCU in 1966 stated, "Many freshmen are showing interest in the activities of the Union. While we pray that they may see their need for the Lord and decide for Him, we thank the Lord that some already know Him and are prepared to live for Him. At fortnightly Saturday squash parties, we will be hearing speakers on 'Live issues: Sex, Race, and Church Union.' The student-led service on Sunday evenings plan to use themes from different metaphors in St. John's Gospel. We have all seen the need for personal evangelism in the campus and we are going to concentrate much on this through His grace."[12] The University College Hospital Fellowship reported, "We are thankful for many who attended welcome squash parties at both the nurses' hostel and the clinical students' hostel. Many of the Christian students teach in the Sunday School on the hospital site. The Sunday School has outgrown the building in which it is held. Christian films are shown monthly to students, and outsiders are invited. The nurses' prayer fellowship is growing."[13] And from the University of Nigeria, Nsukka: "The Christian Fellowship . . . meets every Sunday between 5 p.m. and 6 p.m. when we have our regular Bible studies. The discussions often extend to 7 p.m. because of the enthusiasm shown by the members. They obviously demonstrate that pleasure derived from their oneness of fellowship in Christ."[14]

The Inter-Varsity Fellowship (IVF) had worried in 1955 that "there were only about a dozen universities in black Africa, many of them very small; and no evangelical Christian Unions anywhere. An unbiblical theology prevailed; liberal student groups already existed and many people in the universities were determined to prevent the emergence of separate evangelical groups."[15] This concern had disappeared by the 1960s. Evangelical books and speakers dominated the spiritual discourse among many groups. Some of the books by renowned Evangelical preachers and theologians that were widely read by students were *Basic Christianity* (John Stott); *Consistent Christianity* (M. C. Griffiths); *Authority* (Martyn Lloyd-Jones); *Prayer* (O. Hallesby); *Your Money Talks* (Tom Rees); *Screwtape Letters* and other Lewis books (C. S. Lewis); *Principles of Conduct* (John Murray); *Pilgrims' Progress* (John Bunyan); and *Absolute Surrender* (Dwight Moody).[16] Also, world-renowned evangelical speakers like John Stott,[17] Billy Graham,[18] Skevington Wood,[19] and David Bentley-Taylor[20] visited Nigerian universities in the sixties—further stoking the Evangelical fervour. By the late 1960s, a solid evangelical base had been established in Nigeria's colleges and universities, and it was not long before the Nigerian movement was incorporated into the global evangelical movement.

In 1947, the International Fellowship of Evangelical Students (IFES) was formed by the Inter-Varsity Fellowship bodies from several countries, including Britain, the United States of America, Australia, Canada, France, and Holland to provide "fellowship and encouragement"[21] to the global evangelical student movement. In 1958, the Pan African Fellowship of Evangelical Students (PAFES) was formed, with the same vision as IFES, but specifically for the promotion of the evangelical cause among students on the African continent.[22] PAFES was founded by IVF-affiliated expatriates who were working as staff in different universities on the continent. Christian Union groups from Ghana and Kenya were the first to join PAFES, followed by groups in Liberia, Sierra Leone, Zimbabwe, and Nigeria.

The first West African PAFES conference was held in Winneba, Ghana, in 1962. Kayode Adesogan, one of the pioneers of IVCU, remembers the event this way: "Delegates from the University of Ibadan, and the three Nigerian Colleges of Arts and Science and a few other Nigerian institutions constituted the Nigerian contingent to the conference. It was a memorable gathering that brought much thrill, fellowship, sharing and deep exposure to sound biblical truths. Many friends were made; faiths were strengthened; and virtually all of us who attended agreed that the conference was not only worthwhile but would have to be held regularly."[23] The Lagos University Medical School and Teaching Hospital Fellowship sent five delegates to the 1965 PAFES West Africa Conference in Ghana,[24] and by 1967 the ECU of the University of Ife had joined.[25] IVCU hosted the 1966 PAFES West Africa Conference.[26]

The need for the formation of a national evangelical group in Nigeria was mooted around the mid-sixties. Ironically, the first "recorded major contact"[27] of university students with the Pentecostal movement, as documented by historian Matthews Ojo, was at the preparatory conference towards the formation of this group, later to be known as the Nigeria Fellowship of Evangelical Students (NIFES).[28] Elton was the main speaker at the conference, held in Ilesa from August 31 to September 4, 1967, which also featured Gottfried Osei-Mensah, the travelling secretary of the Pan African Fellowship of Evangelical Students (PAFES), and some other evangelical leaders.[29] Elton's message to his audience, which comprised the representatives of Christian Union groups from several institutions of higher learning in the country, was centred on the Pentecostal experience of the baptism of the Holy Spirit.[30] Knowing that Elton was a Pentecostal preacher, his invitation by the committee (which comprised students from the participating institutions) to be the main speaker at a conference which had the formation of an evangelical fellowship as its main goal seems odd. However, when placed in the context of the time, this was not strange.

Elton was only one of a number of expatriates who were regular speakers at students' meetings. Tony Wilmot, a British Christian businessman who pioneered evangelical work among students in Africa in the mid-1950s;

John Dean of the Fellowship of Christian Students in northern Nigeria; Jane Sutton of the Scripture Union in Ibadan; secondary- and post-secondary school lecturers like Alan Rees, professor of Chemistry at the University of Ibadan, who played a significant role in the formation of the Ibadan Varsity Christian Union in 1961; and missionaries of the Sudan Interior Mission were regular faces among campus groups. Christian students developed a close relationship with these speakers—who were fondly referred to as "senior friends"—beyond their sessions on campus. They visited their homes for further spiritual mentorship, for counsel on personal issues, and also hung around them for the wisdom they dispensed about life in general.

In the mid-sixties, Elton fell into this category—in this regard, he was not different from Wilmot or Sutton or Dean. John Dean distinctly remembers "meeting him and hearing him speak on one occasion . . . in the early seventies in Ibadan at a student 5:00 p.m. service."[31] Even though Dean had "limited knowledge of Mr Elton," he had "the very highest regards for him and his ministry." Elton's teachings on the campuses during this period focused on the popular themes of Christian growth and deeper spirituality, and to a lesser degree, on the Pentecostal themes of the baptism in the Holy Spirit and the manifestations of the gifts of the Spirit. It was in this context—as a well-known campus speaker, rather than as a Pentecostal preacher—that he was invited to the Ilesa conference.

The content of his message at the Ilesa conference was, however, overwhelmingly Pentecostal. Elton even showed a Pentecostal film (most likely one of T. L. Osborn's "docu-miracle" films) to drive home the message—to the dismay of many attendees.[32] Many of the participants, who comprised student groups other than the Ibadan and Ife student communities which Elton frequently spoke to, were uncomfortable at the direction in which Elton took the meeting.[33] Many of the Ife and Ibadan students, except for those who had been privately exploring the issue, were also taken aback at Elton's threatening push into this uncharted water. A disagreement ensued between those who were more disposed to his message and those who felt the Pentecostal emphasis was extreme and unhealthy. The brewing conflict did not, however, immediately boil to the surface. It remained simmering for about two years on the different campuses until the 1970 PAFES West Africa conference at Ijebu Ode.[34]

In the meantime, despite the initial setback at the Ilesa conference, Elton continued to propagate the Pentecostal message among students at every opportunity. Elton, a Holy Ghost preacher through and through, would never compromise his Pentecostal beliefs and preferred to go only where he could preach "his message." While preaching at the Chapel of Resurrection of the University of Ibadan (UI) in 1971, he told the story of how he declined an invitation from his close friend, Bishop John Falope, a notable Anglican priest and strong supporter of the evangelical revival among university students, to preach in his parish.[35] When Falope asked why, he replied, "If I come, I will split your church down the line into two, you will take half and I will take the other half."[36] That made the point. "I am friends and want to be friends with every one of them [non-Pentecostal churches and groups] and if they will invite me into their churches to preach this vision, I will go. But I know what will happen. It will divide. It's bound to do. Light divides. When you bring light there will be those who will say, 'Yes, we accept;' there will be those who will say, 'No, we reject.' . . . It's bound to happen. It will happen throughout the whole of Nigeria,"[37] Elton would say in later years.

The excitement generated by Elton's teaching at the Ilesa conference led many students into a further search about Pentecostal doctrine. Christian Union groups at the universities of Ibadan and Ife, led by those who were anxious to get a better grasp of the issues which Elton had discussed, continued to invite him to speak at their programmes. In 1969, Elton preached at an IVCU programme where he again emphasized the baptism of the Holy Spirit and as a result some of the students received the experience and began speaking in tongues.[38] In late 1969, "As a result of the enthusiasm generated by Elton's teachings . . . the leaders of IVCU . . . invited . . . [the] pastor of the Assemblies of God, Mokola, Ibadan . . . to give a series of talks on the baptism of the Holy Spirit. After Pastor Kashibu's ministration some of the students claimed to have received the baptism of the Holy Spirit and were said to have spoken in tongues as well. Because there was not much understanding about it, the majority of members in IVCU rejected the experience, but months after Pastor Kashibu had come and gone, there was still discussion between the executive of IVCU who were in favour of the Pentecostal experience, and the majority of members who were against it."[39]

Afterwards, the Pentecostal group at the University of Ibadan started weekly meetings that came to be known as the Tuesday Fellowship, to promote Pentecostal teachings and manifestations.[40] During one January 1970 meeting, many of the leaders received the baptism of the Holy Spirit and spoke in tongues.[41] As one observer was later to describe this experience:

> On one of the University Campuses, there was a group of students seeking God's face day in day out on specific days of the week and the glory of the LORD descended on one Tuesday prayer session. . . . The brethren in the prayer room burst into tongues of unknown languages. It was the beginning of a great move of God on the campuses of our higher institutions. A generation of Bible-believing, truth-honouring, full-gospel-preaching, and Holy Spirit-filled young Christians were emerging.[42]

This was the prelude to the Ijebu Ode conference. The first indication that trouble lay ahead during the September 1970 conference were the nightly meetings held after the general evening sessions by a group that was devoted to exploring Pentecostal teachings and manifestations. These meetings created the impression among other participants that the "Pentecostals" believed the teachings and fellowship at the general sessions had become inadequate to meet their yearning for a more vitalized spirituality.[43] Even though this group did not congregate during the day, many of those involved in it were known to most of the participants at the conference. As the conference progressed, however, these issues became more heatedly debated and sides were taken—one group emphasising the need for Pentecostal teachings and manifestations and the other saying that it was an unnecessary distraction. When the messages of the two main speakers at the conference—David Bentley-Taylor from the UK and Mike Oye, who became the first indigenous travelling secretary of the Scripture Union, Nigeria, in 1966—repeatedly clashed, the situation, in the words of one participant, became "nasty."[44]

David Bentley-Taylor, a famous missionary to China under the China Inland Mission (later Overseas Missionary Fellowship), had been at the meeting at Harvard in 1947 where the International Fellowship of Evangelical Students (IFES) was founded. He had gone on to play a leading role in IFES and was its regional secretary for the Arab world from 1967 to 1974.[45] Having such a much sought-after speaker at the Ijebu Ode conference was a big score for the organizers. Oye, a Pentecostal Christian, had become acquainted with Elton in the 1960s. Recollecting Elton's influence, he said, "Most of those who were dynamic in the SU revival often invited Elton to speak in some of our meetings. His teachings had a lot of influence on many of us. I became like a personal friend—like a small boy—to him. I would go to his house, and because of my zeal to preach the gospel I would collect thousands of pamphlets and tracts, particularly that of T. L. Osborn and Gordon Lindsay. I would sit with Pa Elton and we would discuss deep things of the Spirit. He also gave me ancient books to read and return. That helped me in my faith very much."[46]

Throughout the conference, Mike Oye repeatedly emphasized the need for the Pentecostal experience in all his messages; Bentley-Taylor became embarrassed and asked why the organizers had invited him when they were clear about the direction they wanted the meeting to go.[47] Though the leadership tried to salvage the conference, the cleavage had become irreparable. Thus 1970 became a watershed year—both the January IVCU outpouring and the later Ijebu Ode episode set the stage for the emergence, among Christians in Nigeria's higher institutions, of two distinct groups—the Pentecostals and the non-Pentecostals—tongue-talkers and non-tongue-talkers. The Pentecostal fire spread to many campuses, and by 1972 the movement had acquired great momentum. Elton had successfully lit a fire which would eventually engulf the whole nation.

Elton wrote in the early 1970s that "the subject of the baptism of the Holy Spirit is causing much study and reasoning all over Nigeria at this time because the Holy Spirit Himself is moving again in revival and many young people are being filled with the Holy Spirit in a special way."[48] He dedicated a section in the second issue of *Herald of the Last Days* to the baptism of the Holy Spirit, which was widely circulated among the students. He also deliberately engaged in teaching, on the campuses, and also outside the campuses, specifically targeted at spreading the Pentecostal experience. He was also the major source of books by Gordon Lindsay and T. L. Osborn, which contained much scriptural exposition and personal experiences of the Pentecostal outpouring.

Elton acknowledged this new spiritual outpouring as the beginning of the charismatic movement in Nigeria: "We have been writing in previous issues of H.O.L.D on the new move of God in Nigeria which is being called the 'Charismatic movement' or 'Charismatic renewal' and trying to examine the present position and results and to advise on future moves."[49] He again hinted at the on-going events when he wrote, "Many Christians in Nigeria are experiencing a new blessing in their lives and it is revolution-ising their witnessing and Christian lives—it is the baptism of the Holy Spirit and the resultant daily fullness of the Spirit."[50] He went on to talk about the controversies that were trailing this new move: "But it is also creating many problems and questioning."[51] Also, "Neither do we wish in this issue to deal with the *controversial topic* of 'speaking in tongues' as this will need a separate special article to itself."[52]

While many Christian leaders were fighting this experience, Elton was going in another direction; he declared enthusiastically ca. 1973, "The church needs this Holy Spirit revival. . . . The church members in many churches are hungry and eager for the real revival . . . and God is preparing a company of His men and women whom He has called out of ritualism and sectarianism and whom He has filled with His Spirit in these crisis days in readiness for the Harvest . . . and they are now being prepared in secret places for those days. . . . This is the reason for the tremendous increase among Christians of the baptism of the Holy Spirit."[53] He also wrote that "it must be emphasised that this new outpouring of the Holy Spirit is worldwide and God seems to be filling many hungry hearts with His fullness and this is especially true of the young Christians who are tired of the existing routine system of church worship and services, and demand and seek reality and the power of God. . . . We thank God for what we are seeing today in Nigeria and many other countries in the world, in the renewal of spiritual power in their lives and we are sure this flow and outflow will increase, so we desire to help and advise those who are receiving this wonderful experience and power."[54]

Students from virtually all the campuses were regularly visiting Ilesa to learn about Pentecostal doctrine. A Holy Ghost baptism quest was in the air. "Nearly every day we get letters or visitors seeking advice and guidance on these wonderful new experiences,"[55] wrote Elton.

The Tuesday group at the University of Ibadan, which became a ma-jor force for the propagation of the Pentecostal message among Ibadan students and students in other campuses around the country, was started by four members of IVCU—Biola Adeniran (IVCU president in 1970), William Ifode, Wilson Badejo, and Gbenga Adeya. The four of them were residents of Azikiwe Hall on campus and regularly met to pray. As Biola Adeniran remembers, "We usually met to pray together. Brother Ifode was the one coordinating us. We just wanted to [be closer] to the Lord and see how we could bring the gospel to the campus. We were not really much satisfied by what was being done in the orthodox churches, and we wanted to get deeper with the Lord. We had times to pray and fast together. . . . The IVCU didn't really embrace this wholeheartedly as at that time, but . . . we motivated people to [join us in] the prayer meetings. That's how the Tuesday prayer meeting started. The four of us were meeting on Tuesdays and then others joined us. . . . That was how some of the brethren in IVCU who wanted to know more about the Holy Spirit started having time together with us."[56]

In 1970, the foursome founded a new group called the World Action Team for Christ (WATC). "The Tuesday meeting was to really emphasise on the need of being born again, repentance from sin and also receiving Holy Ghost baptism so as to be able to have the power to serve the Lord. But we did not limit it to prayer . . . we really wanted to use it as a platform for evangelising the community and also to carry out evangelism to different campuses."[57] They decided to organize "retreats from time to time, from one city to another." The first retreat, tagged "Congress," was held in Agbor in 1970, at the Agbor Girls' High School. It was attended by university students from around the country. Many Pentecostal ministers were invited to speak, including Samuel Odunaike, William Kumuyi, and Mike Oye. "It was a wonderful time," recalls Adeniran, "and I remember the message that Odunaike preached on Holy Ghost baptism; and God really opened the eyes of many people to know about the deeper experience we can have in the Holy Spirit. As at that time there wasn't much understanding about Holy Ghost baptism . . . but the ministration opened the eyes of many people and I can remember many people got into the experience at that time."[58] Subsequent conferences were held in Port Harcourt, Owerri, and Ibadan. Elton was the main speaker at one of the conferences.

In the mid-1970s, members of the Tuesday fellowship would routinely go into the streets, and to the school of the deaf and dumb in town, and call the deaf and dumb and the lame; they would bring them to the campus and pray for them. There were many testimonies of healings.[59] Many students particularly remember Abraham Adenigba, a mathematics student with a first-class brain, who was mightily used in the miraculous. "Abraham Adenigba was a phenomenon,"[60] one student recalls. "He was a very dynamic brother, very charismatic and very gifted,"[61] remembers another student. Adenigba went "from one campus to the other teaching Pentecostal doctrines to Christian students."[62] There was a deep hunger among the students to experience the power of the Holy Spirit and to see the restoration of the miraculous. This thirst conditioned their spiritual disposition and made them easily distinguishable from other Christian students. This disposition earned them the epithet "holy rollers."[63] Stories of the outpouring in Ibadan spread around the country.

"The first time we learnt about speaking in tongues and interpretation, it was actually from Papa Elton," recalls Bunmi Oni, an ECU member in the early seventies, "because he came once, and I think he saw the energy and enthusiasm, and at one point he started to speak in tongues and then after it, he sort of interpreted, and it brought such comfort, so much so that we then thought, 'We must, we must, we must be able to do that,' and before we left [school], we started having such things in our fellowship. There would be tongues and there would be somebody else that would interpret, and it was such a powerful, powerful thing. . . . We started experiencing [it] . . . routinely in the fellowship in the ECU. But a lot of that was the mentoring from Papa Elton."[64]

In a 1973 holiday letter to his colleagues, the president of the ECU wrote concerning the manifestation of the Holy Spirit in the fellowship: "We sincerely thank the Lord of harvest—the Holy Spirit—for His manifestation last session in baptism, healings, miracles, demonic deliverance and casting-outs, etc. . . . I would wish to say some things however. Let there be no inferiority complex, even to being ashamed or timid to share the Bible with filled brethren. The infilling does not make us 'superlatives' as it were—normal Christian life brethren. Let there in the love of Christ, be NO Holy Ghost club within the group."[65] He also mentioned reading "the newsletter of [another] Christian group. God has moved mightily among them too."

Whenever Elton visited the campuses, he would teach on the baptism of the Holy Spirit and the manifestation of the gifts of the Spirit and thereafter ask for those who wanted to be prayed for to be filled. After one such meeting at a Sunday evening ECU service in 1973, where Elton requested those who desired the baptism of the Holy Spirit to wait behind for prayers, many received the Pentecostal experience with the immediate result being "intensified evangelism and missions in the villages around the campus. On the campus itself, there were more activities in the fellowship sub-groups and open and bold witnessing in rooms, dining halls, and even to lecturers."[66] For the 1973 orientation programme for freshmen, ECU had "two main talks—a squash and two film shows:

HOLLAND WONDERS and JAVA HARVEST cine miracle films—a T. L. Osborn production. Pastor Elton has promised the two film strips."[67]

Ikechukwu Utah, a student of the University of Ife in the early 1970s, vividly recalls Elton's life-transforming teachings at the Sunday evening fellowship meetings in the foyer of the Agriculture department. From five in the evening, as the sun began to set, the fellowship would open with a session of worship; then there would be a period of quietness when prophecy, tongues and interpretation, and other forms of revelatory gifts were allowed to flow. After a period of watching the students move in the manifestations of the Holy Spirit, Elton would then take the stage.[68]

Bill Isaacs-Sodeye, a senior lecturer in medicine at the University College Hospital, Ibadan, in the mid-seventies, recalls Elton's teachings on Sunday afternoons at a lecture room in the department of zoology. "Papa Elton was the first to teach properly the biblical Holy Spirit. He would talk for about an hour, then people would ask questions, then there would be ministrations. . . . It was a discipling process. You see, he [did] not just teach us, he imparted unto us [spiritual] authority. . . . I can picture Papa Elton just sitting there as though he wasn't there, as though he was seeing God."[69] Isaacs-Sodeye and some of the medical students who were close to Elton would often travel to Ilesa to have some time of fellowship with him.

One of these students was I. K. U. Ibeneme, who later started the famed Faith Clinic in Ibadan; he became one of the most mightily used of God in the area of deliverance and miracles in the eighties and early nineties. Others were Okey Onuzo ("I used to go to Ilesa a lot. I could wake up in the morning at 5:00 a.m., go to Ilesa, arrive there at 6 or 6.30 a.m. and return for lectures,"[70] recalls Onuzo) and Femi Soetan—both leaders in the Pentecostal movement. "When you saw Papa Elton," recalls Isaacs-Sodeye, "he was usually lounging in a chair, and he would be turning around. He would be talking to you like he was not the one talking. It wasn't [just] that he sometimes prophesied, but that he was always . . . in the Spirit."

Many leaders—local and international—contributed to the growth of the movement in its early days. The fire was being sparked on virtually every university campus in the country. Jim Hodges, who led a Christ for the Nations Institute team to University of Nigeria, Nsukka, in 1975, during Freda Lindsay's (Gordon Lindsay's wife) visit to Benin, wrote of the visit: "Then while the Luminaries [the team] prayed for the sick, I went to a nearby classroom to pray for believers to be filled with the Spirit. At midnight the Holy Spirit fell and some 75 were baptized by Jesus and spoke in new tongues!"[71] Pentecostal meetings and outreaches by American evangelists like Morris Cerullo (in Ibadan) and Arthur Blessitt (at the University of Ife) in 1973, and that of Nigerian evangelists like J. K. Solomon, were usually attended by many students in their thirst for the infilling of the Holy Spirit. The ministry of Benson Idahosa played a significant role in these early days and hundreds of students flocked to Benin in the 1970s for the myriad programmes organized by Idahosa's ministry, usually held at either Idahosa's church or the university.

Idahosa was young and on fire, and many students were moved by his vibrancy and testimonies. It was difficult not to be enchanted by him. He preached the message on the baptism of the Holy Spirit with an unusual forcefulness and succeeded tremendously in leading many university students into the experience. Niyi Beecroft, who was at a time the vice president of ECU, remembers one of Idahosa's visits to the University of Ife in early 1974.[72] After the Sunday meeting, Idahosa announced that those who believed they would be baptized in the Holy Ghost were going to have the experience. The next day, the students who responded to his call gathered at one of the streams on campus and were baptized in water. As they came out of the water Idahosa would immediately lay hands on them to be baptized in the Holy Spirit. Many of the students were immediately baptized in the Holy Ghost with the evidence of speaking in tongues.

Beecroft had been seeking the Holy Ghost baptism and so he attended this by-the-stream service, but he did not experience the infilling. His quest continued. Sometime later he went to the University of Benin for a presentation with the ECU drama group. After the programme, Idahosa invited the leaders of the group to lunch at his house. Beecroft was initially reluctant to join in the eating, because he was fasting in anticipation of receiving the baptism of the Holy Spirit. But Idahosa told him not to worry and just eat. After the meal, Idahosa began praying. "You needed to see Idahosa flowing with God, as big and tall and massive [as he was]," Beecroft recalls. "He then laid . . . hands on me and I spoke in tongues."[73]

As popular as it was among students, the "new move" did not go down well with many of the evangelical leaders who had a major stake in Christian work in post-secondary institutions, and it was fiercely resisted. Most important was the opposition of the three major evangelical blocs in the country—the Scripture Union, the Fellowship of Christian Students (FCS) and the Nigerian Fellowship of Evangelical Students (NIFES). The budding movement brought about deep convulsions in evangelical circles around the country, especially among young people. By the early 1970s, opinion was sharply divided as to the relevance and specific interpretation of many Pentecostal manifestations. Controversies raged everywhere and emotions ran high: eventually leaders and groups were forced to take a stand, for or against, if they were to satisfy the yearning of their immediate constituencies, who demanded quick decisiveness on the issue.

The opposition by most evangelical leaders was based on two factors. First, they were generally very uncomfortable with any manifestation of the Holy Spirit that was not acceptable within the prevailing evangelical interpretation of the baptism of the Holy Spirit. Manifestations of the Holy Spirit such as speaking in tongues; operations of the gifts of the Holy Spirit, like prophecy or healing; and emotional expressions in worship were considered weird and therefore best avoided. Christians were supposed to focus on the fruits of the Spirit and not distract themselves pursuing after gifts and manifestations. "There was tremendous opposition from the evangelicals . . . and the argument at that time was that the times of such manifestations were gone. Number two, that it wasn't really important—that what you just needed to do was to become born again and then go to heaven,"[74] recalls one of the students who embraced the outpouring.

Kayode Adesogan also describes the evangelical stance at the time: "In the 1960s, members of the Christian Unions were quite sober. It was rare to clap in some fellowships when singing choruses. Emphasis was on the wordings of a song and application. More attention was therefore given to the fruit of the Spirit rather than the gifts."[75] Simeon Ifere, in his history of NIFES, *God's Response to Nigeria,* quotes a NIFES president of that era on the issue: "Before the second half of the seventies, we mostly heard of books on 'Does God Answer All Prayers?'; 'What to Do When Your Loved One Dies' instead of those on 'Power' and 'How to Meet God.'"[76] A report by one participant at a PAFES Training Course in 1968 best sums up the evangelical attitude towards the doctrine of the Holy Spirit: "Our Bible studies in 1 and 2 Timothy urged me not to waver in faith and doctrine, and reassured me of the faithfulness of God. Discussions on Christian literature made me realize the need of reading Christian books other than the Bible as an aid to spiritual growth. Another talk which helped me was the one on the Holy Spirit. I had the assurance that the Holy Spirit was in me and that it was not necessary for me to speak in tongues as a sign of being filled with the Holy Spirit. It taught me not to be over-anxious to receive any specific gift but to wait on the Lord and receive with thanksgiving what He wished to give."[77]

Kola Ejiwumi, the first travelling secretary of NIFES, wrote in 1972: "There is a perennial problem that faces groups in the Fellowship. This is raising the issue of the person and work of the Holy Spirit to the point of controversy. There are small but vocal and undoubtedly zealous splinter groups in one or two groups. We are praying for the love, wisdom and courage to deal with this problem in a way to bring forth the richness of fellowship and effectiveness which the Lord desires to give us."[78]

IFES historian, Pete Lowman, writing about this crisis from the NIFES angle, notes that "there were serious problems. Throughout the early 1970s the Nigerian groups were torn by disagreement over the charismatic issue. . . . Over the next couple of years the crisis reached their height."[79] Lowman continues: "Two unfortunate results were the alienation from the national body of certain groups that had come to see tongues as the 'one thing needful,' and also the distancing of student leaders from senior friends who would have been their advisers. This could manifest itself in disagreement over secondary matters in which no fundamental doctrinal issue was involved—clapping, for example, or repetition of choruses. In some cases senior friends had perhaps not succeeded in 'incarnating' themselves within the prevailing campus culture. One experienced Nigerian leader felt that difficulties arose not because they disagreed with the Christian books popular on campus, but because they had not even read them. The generation gap could be worsened by the occasionally remarkable arrogance of student leaders who were convinced that God had begun a 'new thing' with them, and hence they had nothing to learn! Too often relationships no longer existed where advice and discussion would go deeper than polite conversation."

The second reason for the opposition from evangelical leaders and groups was the extreme teachings and practices that developed just a few years into the life of the charismatic movement among students. As is the case with any new movement, extreme teachings and practices began to circulate, which many zealous Christians naively swallowed. Of the numerous examples, the most widely embraced were Franklin Hall's teachings, which found their way into student charismatic groups and other groups in the country from about 1973. Hall, an American evangelist, whose ministry became popular with the publishing in 1946 of his book, *Atomic Power with God through Prayer and Fasting*, made his first and only visit to Nigeria in 1975, but he had been preceded by the popularity of his books. He came to Nigeria by invitation from some of those who had embraced the teachings in his books.[80]

Hall's teaching on fasting and prayer was initially popular among many of the healing revivalists in America in the 1940s and '50s. Many embraced it as a revolutionary teaching, testifying that it had transformed their lives and ministries. One of the testimonies published in one of the editions of the book was by T. L. Osborn, who remarked concerning Hall's teaching: "We were happy to let you know that we feel our lives have been revolutionized by fasting and praying to Jesus. It was by reading your books that we were enabled to go into many days and weeks fasting and praying. Both my wife and I have had many deep fasting and prayer experiences. My life was so changed that God began using me in the healing ministry. As I began to exercise the ministry of praying for the sick, more and more folks were healed."[81]

In his classic on the mid-twentieth century healing revival in America, *All Things Are Possible*, David Harrell Jr. quotes one of the observers of the early revival years: "Every one of these men [the healing evangelists of the 1950s and 1960s] down through the years followed Franklin Hall's method of fasting."[82] Hall advocated long periods of fasting—ranging from ten to sixty days—as a key to spiritual breakthrough. Hall's ministry never attained the popularity of the famous healing evangelists, but his teachings on this subject became widely practised.

However, as years passed, his teachings became more and more skewed with what he claimed to be new revelation from the Scriptures. These teachings, usually a patchwork of confusing "spiritual" phrases, varied over a wide range of subjects and had titles such as "The Return of Immortality," "Body-felt Salvation," "Faith Treatments," and so on. Even his teaching on prolonged fasting, which initially enjoyed wide acceptance, was eventually rejected in most circles. Most of these teachings, which had no basis whatsoever in the Scriptures, gradually isolated him from the mainstream of Pentecostalism in America. Even Gordon Lindsay, a man who would not normally run from a good fight and who put himself on the firing line for many of the healing evangelists, had to eventually pull all advertisements of Hall's books and meetings from *The*

Voice of Healing magazine when he could no longer defend his teachings and practices. Lindsay believed that "Hall ruined his influence because he became obsessed with particular doctrines and refused to use common sense to balance his views."[83]

It is difficult to comprehend why many young Nigerian Christians found his teachings fascinating. Obviously they were unaware of the controversies that trailed his ministry or his isolation from America's mainstream Pentecostalism. Had they been aware, it is very doubtful they would have received his message with such enthusiasm. They had been thrilled by the news and testimonies that were being released from Hall's ministry headquarters, but were oblivious to the fact that the buzz was entirely restricted to Hall's diehard devotees. Many Nigerian Christians, especially university students, who were in pursuit of the manifestations of the Holy Spirit were not discerning enough and thus became prey to Hall's eerie ideas. These teachings were first introduced into the country by some members of the Tuesday fellowship about 1973.[84] As later revealed in some of Hall's books, his teachings found one of the most fertile grounds in Nigeria.[85]

One of Hall's more bizarre teachings which became widespread in the country was that the salvation of man's soul was only half salvation and that for man's salvation to be complete his body had to be converted, an experience which he termed "body-felt salvation." According to Hall, "The atonement which provides the two fold salvation originates not from the cross only, where He shed His blood, but also from another tree. The whipping post tree is where His wonderful body was beaten for an express purpose. His beaten body substituted, and paid for, our body. His blood, after His body was first beaten and broken at the whipping post, was shed more completely and fully at the cross. This was for our sins and had to do for the inner man, called our soul."[86] This body-felt salvation, which Hall claimed could be "received at our meetings everywhere," could be experienced by "impartation, by the laying on of hands . . . by imparting by the gift of faith the Holy Ghost fire upon those who would believe." It was capable of shielding a Christian from many natural laws and processes. Thus, anyone who received this body-felt salvation would never get physically tired again, would never fall sick again, would be shielded from earthquakes, riots and wars, and even overcome physical death.

The reception of this salvation, he claimed, was usually accompanied by certain physical experiences, some of which are described in the following testimony: "This blessing comes upon our body just exactly as it was taught. As we continued attending these meetings, the wings of healing, cloven tongues like fire, began baking deeply upon our flesh. Each and every service it became more deeply imbedded, making the substance of our Lord and Savior a part of our body. It eventually poured all over us. The Suntan of healing righteousness, called Holy Ghost fire by John the Baptist burned out, consuming all of the chaff of toxemia (Adamic sickness) leaving our body with salvation upon it."[87] In the caption of a photograph of his visit to Nigeria in 1975, published in his book, *The Return of Immortality*, he gave an example of one of the manifestations of this phenomenon in his own life: "In Lagos, Nigeria, West Africa, Brother Franklin Hall (Helen looking down) receives gift from native at [St.] Jude's Church. Brother Hall's light colored jacket is seven years old and has never been pressed or cleaned or aerated in 7 years, since new, yet it has been worn repeatedly in many overseas countries and regularly in all crusades everywhere (excepting one). It has been on more than 200 airlines in travels. It has no spots, stains, discoloration or body odors anywhere on it or inside it—similar to the children of Israel's clothes under the Glory, Immortality Cloud of Fire Power."[88]

Hall preached that it was wrong for believers to close their eyes when worshipping as it could hinder their faith. Christians were supposed to practise what he called "open-eye worship," approaching God just like they would a friend and saying, "Hello, Jesus," because God loved it. In line with his teachings, many students in the universities began to claim they could see Jesus Christ during fellowship meetings—that by anointing their eyes with eye salve according to the book of Revelation, they could see Jesus physically. "During fellowship meetings some people who had fasted and gotten high in the Spirit would claim to see Him [Jesus] and would wave into the air as a sign of greeting Him."[89]

Many students, following Hall's teachings, began to practise the rapture. In discussing the Franklin Hall crisis, Pete Lowman writes, "The consequences of this alienation [of student leaders from senior friends] became apparent when far more bizarre teaching swept the campuses in 1975–1976. One popular speaker taught that the Rapture was so close that believers could hope to participate in it right now. Several reputable sources relate how at conferences students could be seen 'jumping up and down, practising the Rapture, trying to fly.' Soon the idea spread that running backwards might bring about translation to heaven, and on at least one notable occasion a whole group spent part of their conference running backwards around a room. Another widely-used speaker taught that, after having received the baptism of the Spirit, the believer should expect the 'baptism of fire,' after which he would never physically die and his clothes would never physically die and his clothes would never wear out. [Half the leadership of one of NIFES' largest groups went over to one of these teachers, including the president and vice-president.]"[90]

Some students were also always trying to physically "smell Jesus"[91] during fellowship meetings or during their personal devotion. Another of Hall's pet teachings was on UFOs (unidentified flying objects), which he preferred to call UHOs (unusual heavenly objects) or IHOs (immortality heavenly objects).[92] He believed that preachers who taught against UFOs were ignorant. According to him, "Some of these great and unusual heavenly signs and wonders UFOs or UHOs are the Immortal Chariots of Fire. Some are the last day outpourings of the Immortality Light and Fire of the Baptism of the Holy Spirit. Some ministers are sick in their bodies today. Some have come under severe judgment of God. Some folk are even in their graves ahead of time because they have dared to speak things derogatory concerning the Holy Spirit and His Fireworks. The author without any exaggeration has seen the Miracle Substance come down as a great and mighty UHO object, and attend with blessings to many sincere and loving, Jesus folk."[93]

The purported manifestation of IHOs in Ilorin and Lagos were some of the major highlights of his visit to Nigeria in 1975. Hall's record of this visit contains some fantastic stories.[94] Another trend that became popular in the country was "fasting meetings," or conferences organized based on Hall's recommended pattern. Such fasting conferences were organized in several countries, at his encouragement, as a way of propagating his teachings on the subject. In early 1975 (before Hall's visit), a major fasting conference centred on this teaching was organized at the University of Ife.[95]

Prior to the Ile-Ife meeting, a fasting conference had also been organized at the University of Benin by students who were followers of Hall's teachings.[96] All those who attended the meetings fasted continuously for the five days during which the meeting lasted. In the quest for spiritual power, students frequently fasted for weeks, some up to forty days, taking only water. Sometimes these fasts resulted in some damaging health problems—some never fully recovering[97]—and in at least one case, it resulted in death.[98] Some of these extreme cases resulted in embarrassing situations for Christian groups and their patrons. Students who had not prepared for tests or exams expected to pass supernaturally. After one divine healing meeting, some students went back and smashed their glasses, only to discover that they couldn't see the board in class the next day.[99]

An incident at an IVCU meeting in 1975 reveals how bad things had become. Tony Wilmot (arguably the most influential expatriate evangelical leader in the history of evangelicalism in Nigeria) had been invited to speak about the Holy Spirit. He made some remarks about speaking in tongues and the baptism of the Holy Spirit which did not go down well with some of Franklin Hall's devotees. A certain brother who had come to the meeting anticipating what Wilmot would say immediately stood up and prophesied that within seven days the judgement of God would fall on Wilmot.[100] (Previously there had been teachings that anyone who opposed Hall's teachings would have the judgement of God fall on them within seven days.)

Another American preacher whose influence proved devastating to the emerging movement was Neal Frisby. Frisby, pastor of the Capstone Cathedral in Phoenix, Arizona, proclaimed that the return of Jesus Christ was imminent and that at the rapture, Jesus was going to descend in Arizona. Many of the students who believed this prophecy abandoned their studies—this was particularly so at the University of Ife—and travelled to Arizona to wait for Jesus' return.[101] One student remembers how these Frisby devotees went around collecting money from other brethren in the fellowship, so they could have enough to pay their airfare to the US: "They were fleecing us. They would say, 'Brother, let me have some money.' We didn't know they were collecting money from us so that they could travel to Arizona. They said we were Egypt; just like Israel looted Egypt, they looted us."[102] Scores of students abandoned their studies and left for Arizona. "It was an epidemic,"[103] says Yinka Ayankogbe, a student of the University of Ibadan in the mid-seventies. Many parents whose children were caught in the web arrived at the campus bewildered, weeping because of the tragedy that had befallen them. Some of William Branham's heretical teachings, which surfaced towards the end of his life, and which were sustained by a cultic following after his death, also caused major problems.[104]

In light of these strange teachings, experiences, and upheavals which were fast gaining ground among many groups in the country, it is not difficult to be sympathetic to the position of the SU, FCS, and NIFES, who at every opportunity feverishly countered anything that had to do with the charismatic movement. More so, in some instances when things went out of hand (like when a young lady died after fasting for about fifty days[105]), *they* had to bear the brunt of the anger of parents and the public because the young people involved were members of either the SU or NIFES groups; and the public believed they were the ones responsible for such extreme practices. One observer recalls that when students left the University of Ife for Arizona, "Everybody was checking everybody out of Scripture Union; everybody thought it was Scripture Union."[106]

Evangelical leaders around the country were therefore on a mission to exonerate themselves and also to save an emerging generation from self-destruction. The Scripture Union was one of those that led in taking a definite and public stand against this new movement. The following is an advertisement by the SU in the *Daily Times* of August 6, 1973:

> We are aware of and gravely concerned about the recent wave of emotionalism, wrong teachings, over-enthusiasm, disrespect to traditions of the church, and various fanatical activities of certain evangelical groups which are erroneously attributed to SU. This leads to a misrepresentation of the aims and the objectives of the Scripture Union.
>
> The SU does not encourage members to abandon their jobs, forsake their studies, or leave their homes, in defiance of parents, with the claim that they have been called by the Spirit to full time evangelism without adequate training, maturity and experience. The SU does not encourage its members to be indifferent to the activities of their churches. The SU does not baptise and so it is opposed to members engaging in controversies or sacred church ordinances. While we believe fully in the operation of the Holy Spirit, we have nothing to do with the fanatical displays of tongues, healings, and legalistic fasting.[107]

The Fellowship of Christian Students, Ahmadu Bello University, Zaria, also published a tract "for Born Again Christians" titled "Body-Felt Salvation??? Beware, It Is False."[108] In July 1977, Bola Akande, a Scripture Union leader, delivered a paper at a Scripture Union Training Course in Benin City titled "An Issue Paper on False Teachings."[109] These were only some of the many efforts targeted at nipping these wide spreading heresies in the bud. Hall's teachings "created quite a big problem among those who had embraced the Charismatic outpouring and provided a major argument for those who had denounced the movement."[110]

With time, however, some of the believers within the charismatic camp began to entertain doubts and even express concern about the teachings. One of the members of the Tuesday group who had been one of the greatest advocates of Hall's teaching received a revelation that they were false. He thereafter went from room to room to warn those who believed it to desist from it![111] Some other charismatic Christians also claimed to have received revelation warning them against Hall's teachings. Specifically, a prophecy was sent to western Nigeria by some brethren at the Ahmadu Bello University, Zaria, warning Christians against Hall's teachings.[112] However, these feelings of discontent were limited to a few people—most still followed the teachings up till the time Franklin Hall himself visited Nigeria in July 1975.

Many of those who attended Hall's meetings at Mapo Hall, Ibadan were disappointed. Much of the hype that had been generated by his books and the reports from his ministry was discovered to be unreal and unfounded. In the words of one of the participants, "the meetings were dry."[113] Many of those who had been ardent followers of his teachings were disillusioned. A special meeting of the Tuesday group was called immediately after the conference, with the purpose of re-examining many of Halls' teachings. The participants were allowed to voice their opinion of the teachings in light of the meeting they had just attended. All the key issues were raised one after the other, and the brethren were told to go back and search to see if the teachings were in line with the Scriptures.

This marked a crisis point in the charismatic outpouring on the campuses. Hall's teaching gradually faded out, but overall, it had been a bitter experience that many regretted had happened at all. The Tuesday fellowship also gradually faded out, but by this time it had successfully introduced the genuine teachings and experiences of the charismatic movement into the main body of IVCU and other campus groups around the country. By the mid-seventies, the major charismatic groups had seen the heresy in the teachings of Franklin Hall, Neal Frisby, and William Branham, become disillusioned, and moved away from them. But authentic charismatic teaching and practices had come to stay. After the confusion, there was calm and stability. "By 1977 Kola wrote that 'after two to three years of upheavals in most groups there is a greater determination to maintain the unity of the Spirit in the bond of peace' and 'many genuinely spiritually-gifted students have been able to minister freely and effectively,' "[114] writes Lowman.

Many evangelical leaders, however, never forgave these students' mistakes. In combating the excesses, most evangelical leaders threw out the baby with the bathwater—even when the heresies had become a thing of the past, the charismatic outpouring was never embraced.

Referring to this fierce opposition some years after the crisis, Elton wrote, "When the revelation of the baptism of the Spirit was first preached, it was received eagerly by the converts and many were filled with the Spirit. But the teaching was strongly opposed by many church leaders because they did not realise the growing importance of the ministry of the Holy Spirit in these last days. Even some evangelical Christian leaders openly opposed the teaching. But this did not stop or even delay the progress of the ministry of the Holy Spirit, until today there are literally many thousands of Holy Spirit baptised believers in many churches all over Nigeria. The doctrine of the baptism of the Holy Spirit is no longer a hotly disputed truth."[115]

Against the tide of popular opinion, Elton became a staunch supporter of the activities of the Tuesday group. One early member of the group recalls Elton's role: "Pa Elton was our spiritual father. He was a simple, straightforward and loving Christian father. His publications really helped us. He allowed us to learn, to make mistakes; he stayed at the rear and allowed you to move on. Sometimes he came around to speak at the Tuesday Fellowship meetings."[116] In his *HOLD* articles, Elton sparingly emphasized his points with italics, but his response to the opposition of the evangelical groups constitutes his longest use of italics: "*Despite unbelief, these gifts have never been withdrawn by God. Many who wish to oppose 'tongues' refer to 1 Cor. 13:8. 'Whether there be tongues, they shall cease' and they insist that 'tongues' have already ceased. But Paul is here referring to the time when 'that which is perfect is come,' v. 10. When 'prophecies shall fail,' and 'knowledge shall vanish away.' It is when that which is perfect is come that (that) which is in part shall be done away with. We have not yet reached this point and until that time comes . . . (when prophecy and knowledge shall also be done away with) we shall still need to speak in tongues.*"[117]

Elton stated elsewhere: "May God have mercy on those who are opposing the miraculous new move of God today in Nigeria. May their blind eyes be opened so that they can find a new revelation of Jesus Christ and . . . follow Him;"[118] and again, "Each new move of God in blessing has from experience been opposed most severely by the people of the last move of God. I can tell you this having experienced fifty years inside the Pentecostal movement. I can tell you that the severest persecution of the Pentecostal movement was from the evangelicals who, [though] born again, baptised in water, were not prepared to accept the new revelation of the baptism of the Holy Ghost. And we experienced a great deal of opposition mainly from the evangelicals who said the baptism of the Holy Ghost is demonic."[119]

Elton was not unaware of the excesses and extreme elements that were creeping into the emerging movement (and even in the Tuesday fellowship), but his response was always to correct the problems while strengthening the pursuit of the genuine. He was focused on establishing Christians in the manifestations of the Holy Spirit; he was never afraid of extremes, which he believed proper teaching would take care of. A member of the Tuesday fellowship remarked that Elton "counselled without quenching the fire."[120] He would preach, "You have got to know your Bible. You have got to know your Bible from Genesis to Revelation so that when a prophecy is coming you can immediately determine whether or not it is from God."[121] Another Tuesday group member recalls, "The Lord used him greatly, because we were very young; we didn't understand much; we didn't understand many things. But God used him to enlighten our eyes to know the importance of holiness and living a right life. Because when young people come together . . . there may be some excesses, but God used him to open our eyes."[122]

One of the students at the vanguard of the outpouring recalls, "Apart from teaching and instructing, Elton also tried to mentor and keep us in line, away from excesses. He taught biblical, spirit-filled life."[123] "Elton was operating above the crisis,"[124] another observer aptly commented. Says another perceptive observer: "Looking back now, it was really a counter move from the enemy to discredit the work of the Holy Spirit. But Pa Elton [helped us remain] steady; he was a rallying point to deepen our knowledge of the miraculous; and he taught a lot [on] leadership."[125]

Fred Adegoke, who was initially based in Ilorin, one of the major strongholds of Franklin Hall's teachings, before transferring to the University of Ibadan, recalls that at the peak of Hall's popularity in Ilorin, some of Hall's disciples, who also respected Elton, wanted him (Elton) to come to Ilorin to preach at a meeting where Hall's teachings were being propagated, but he declined the invitation. He obviously refrained so as not to lend any modicum of credibility to Hall's teaching. "Pastor Elton was a stabilizing force during the Franklin Hall crisis; he corrected the error that was there. Because I remember a lot of the brethren who got involved in those teachings also respected Pastor Elton; they knew him and they were in touch with him, in spite of their involvement with Hall. They still kept their relationship with him. In fact they organized meetings and wanted Pastor Elton to minister side by side with [Hall's disciples]; Pastor Elton did not come. But they had respect for him; but he kept telling them that these things were excesses and [that] these things were not right,"[126] recalls Adegoke.

> But for him [Elton], the casualty that we had would have been much more. Because a lot of brethren went into some excesses, some fasted until they hurt themselves, some left school. God used Pastor Elton at that time to mitigate the wrong teaching and keep us all on track. . . . I can remember some of the meetings he held with us on campus and some of the CSSM [Christian Students' Social Movement] meetings, where he made reference to some of the excesses. He talked about William Branham—how the man was mightily used of God and how he deviated. He brought out some very powerful lessons for us. And many times he talked about these excesses and helped to stabilize us. You know, our minds were young and impressionable. We wanted anything exciting, and a lot of us would have been swept away out of zeal, because it was very appealing to every young person. Because of the power and respect he had, he was a stabilizing force and that whole wind of false doctrine could not go too far, because a person like Pastor Elton was there. He was a reference point; many who got confused rushed to him; many people who out of innocence picked up these wrong doctrines would rush to him, and he gave a balanced [view] that kept us on track. . . . He [Elton] never for once got mixed up. His teaching was straight and clear. His teachings were never muddled up at all like these other [ones].[127]

Through several media, particularly in an article which he published ca. 1973 and which was widely circulated, Elton aimed to help believers avoid any pitfalls on their path to operating in the gifts of the Spirit. He admonished, "God has given the gifts as weapons to be used by the Holy Spirit for the edification and encouragement of the Church and the fighters, and therefore it is dangerous when the gifts are used for personal benefit or internally in the Church only. The gifts must not be used as 'toys' in Church services or for internal consumption and benefit only. They are not given for entertainment . . . but for battle equipment. It is unwise to meet privately or in secret prayer meetings merely to encourage the use of the Gifts. They should be operated in public and be subject to control by spiritual leaders whom the Lord has given to the church."[128]

When many students were leaving the university at the height of the crisis, Elton visited the campuses several times to warn against such rashness. "When young people started leaving campus . . . Pastor Elton would grieve and come to the campus and say, 'God can't open the door for you to come to university and change His mind. Stay and get all the learning; God will need all the dedication; stay and get your education.' I heard him very clearly; he would lament. But those to the extreme would say he [Elton] was Babylon,"[129] recalls Ikechukwu Utah. Another student remembers it this way: "There is one important sermon that he preached when we were in UCH; because there was a lot of passion and enthusiasm for the work of God, and many people were feeling that God was calling them to fulltime work, they were abandoning their studies. . . . I cannot forget the message he preached in UCH; he said, 'If God has called you to the university, He cannot change His mind mid-way; you should finish your course and then go to the next thing God is calling you to do.' "[130]

Elton himself was misunderstood a number of times. Sam Olofin remembers one Wednesday meeting in the early seventies at the University of Ibadan where Elton preached on the subject of the end times and during the message spoke about what the attitude of believers was supposed to be on a number of issues, marriage included, in light of the fact that the end times were already here. "At the end of that meeting—the following week—people started breaking up their relationships,"[131] Olofin recalls. He particularly remembers a brother and sister whom he knew were engaged who informed him that they had broken the relationship. When he asked them what the problem was, they replied that Elton had said that the end times had come and so it was no longer time for marriage. "I went there on Wednesday, that wasn't what he said; you are taking it out of context," Olofin told them. But as was the case with many who went off on a tangent, they had made up their minds based on a misinterpretation of a particular teaching and would not change their minds, even when confronted with the facts. Even when Elton came back to the campus a week or two later (after he had been told what some students were doing after his message) and said they were doing the wrong thing—"That's not what I said you should do,"[132] he told them—they did not listen.

Despite the excesses and the opposition, Elton staunchly stood behind anyone who was sincerely pursuing this new move of the Spirit. There were extremes, but on the whole, a great move of God which was revitalizing the church was underway and Elton considered it a tragedy to miss out on it. As one student of the University of Lagos in the mid-seventies would recall four decades later, "He [Elton] taught on the gifts of the Holy Spirit like I have not heard anyone teach before him or since. He was convinced that it was impossible for the church to function as intended without the manifestation and free operation of the gifts of the Holy Spirit. . . . His greatest legacy, in my opinion, was the introduction of the baptism in the Holy Spirit into Nigerian Christianity."[133] Even when the issue of fasting became hotly contested and resulted in a lot of embarrassing situations when it was taken to the extreme, Elton did not shy away from publicly encouraging the pursuit of the genuine:

A new day is dawning in the spiritual life of Nigerians. The slumbering church is awakening and many young Christians are asking the meaning of fasting. It is a day of spiritual renewal. There are searchings [sic] and enquiries, burdens and longings for a manifestation of real spiritual power and many are prepared to pay almost anything to secure it. The Holy Spirit is stirring in the hearts, creating desires for power and the ability to deliver men and women.

FASTING will play a very big part in this awakening. The truth of fasting is being sought so that we may secure the gifts of the Spirit and be partners with God in His program of deliverance, and that a mighty revival of spiritual power may sweep over Nigeria, with signs and miracles in these last days. . . . In these days of revival, evil forces which have lain dormant in some human beings are being forced to reveal themselves and men can only be delivered by sustained authority acquired through prayer and fasting.[134]

He was willing to live with the stigma of the excesses if only he could get much of the church to embrace the genuine. He expressed this position very clearly in one of his teachings:

Not long ago I was going to a certain place and a few days or so before I went I felt a burden within me and wondered what it meant. Eventually I went into that place and when I got there, they said, "You're due for a meeting in half an hour." Oh! Alright! As I walked into that meeting an anointing came upon me, then did I recognize the reason for the burden and what I've got to say. They said, "Your subject is this", but I took no notice. I stood up and began to talk and that settled that problem. They'd got a problem that they didn't tell me and I dealt with that problem and didn't know what it was.

You will come to that stage too. You will come in and a burden will be upon you. But at any time in any meeting when you feel a burden, an anointing on you, and the Lord is talking to you, let it go. I'll tell you what it will be. "Behold I' m with you." That's the first word and you're safe, because that's in the Bible. "I will never leave you nor forsake you." You're quite safe. "I will go with you, hearken to my voice." So far no problem; and then the tap turns off. You say, "What do I do next?" Start again. You are here and a message comes in five or six sentences, [and then] runs dry, you start all over again and repeat it. That's baby prophecy; but a mother likes to hear a baby call, "Baba!" Therefore don't despise the day of small beginnings. . . . But for goodness' sake, when you feel an anointing on you and you're going to prophesy, prophesy, even if it's foolish. You come to us, "A bruised reed will He not quench." We will take care that you are not crushed. That's our job. We will come along side and say, "You did well, next time, tell you what to do." We've got to encourage; we've got to develop that. [135]

Beginning from the early seventies, Elton was at the forefront of systematically teaching the revelation and operation of the nine gifts of the Holy Spirit to audiences around the country through his books, magazines, and conferences. [136] Emphasizing that these gifts were crucial to the success of the church's ministry, he declared, "It must also be realised that there are nine different gifts and not just speaking in tongues and prophecy. We need the whole nine to overcome the forces of darkness and all baptised in the Spirit believers should expect the other gifts to be developed in them. Every new convert should be taught the importance of the commands of the Lord (Matt. 28; Acts. 2) and be made to realise that every believer, (no matter how young they may be) is expected by the Lord to be a witness and an active soldier in the war against the forces of darkness and to seek the baptism in the Spirit and expect to be used by the Holy Spirit. There must be no more complacency and sitting at ease in Zion!! We are at war." [137]

Under his mentorship and encouragement, believers in campus groups and churches around the country boldly moved into the charismatic outpouring and began operating in the gifts of the Spirit. His no-holds-barred treatment of this subject generated a lot of excitement. "Prophecy was strong in those days,"[138] recalls Emeka Nwankpa, ECU president from 1972 to 1973. His teaching created an atmosphere where believers had the liberty to operate in and also judge prophetic messages. Elton frequently used his own personal examples to train and encourage his audience to boldly move into these gifts: "A man came to me the other day and said, 'There are times when I'm in a meeting and I feel a tremendous anointing upon me. What am I to do?' 'Ask the Lord to give you a message and open your mouth and let it go,' was my reply."[139] "But you say, what if it's wrong?" Elton asked, pre-empting his audience. "Yes! I've been in that situation too, and can remember the first time I prophesied many years ago. And when I prophesied, I wanted to get under the seat and crawl out. What a fool! I've prophesied . . . hundreds of times since then and I never feel any bigger now. Good! Good! You've got to step out in faith that it is the Lord speaking through you."[140]

Elton was excited when believers manifested the gift of prophecy. On many occasions, when a word of prophecy was given about an individual in a programme and there was an argument as to whether it was accurate or not, those involved would pack themselves into a car and drive to Ilesa—several times late in the night—and Elton would never turn them back. He would sit down and listen to the opposing sides; when he had given his opinion, the side which believed it had been vindicated would give themselves a thumbs-up. All of them would then drive back to Ibadan or Ile-Ife that night.[141] During one meeting at the Ibadan Polytechnic in 1981, a prophecy was given concerning one of the participants. Some of the attendees travelled to Ilesa to confirm whether the prophecy was accurate or not. After telling Elton what happened, he told them they were six months late, the prophecy had already been given months before in the United States of America.[142] Such was the atmosphere that had been created—it allowed the prophetic gifts and ministry to blossom.

Elton had written in his book on the gifts of the Spirit: "True prophecy grows and develops in an atmosphere of peace, encouragement and understanding and we must watch out for young channels and develop them. All spiritual gifts grow and mature with exercise."[143] It was in this spirit that he said during one of the meetings with young people in March

1984, "I wasn't in the meeting this morning, but I was made to understand that prophecy flowed. I was informed that while that prophecy flowed, one of our brethren present was named as an apostle. We welcome it, but there's going to be no ordination service tonight, because this is not a church and is certainly not an organization. This is a body of people where we recognize that God has something right and can express His mind and doesn't consult us in many cases. And if He has called an apostle, then I promise that all the experience and ability that I've got will be placed at his disposal to enable him [to] rise to that position, because he is not an apostle yet . . . and we are going to help that man reach his call."[144] Elton was always encouraging any move to develop spiritual gifts and calling in the emerging generation.

Many of those who began operating in the gifts of the Spirit were more encouraged to do so because Elton himself mightily demonstrated these gifts and gave many testimonies of his experiences. Once, talking about how in the last days, "we shall see a revival in the miracle ministry to convict unbelievers, confirm believers and bring judgement to scoffers," Elton gave an example of the operation of "the miracle ministry" in his life: "I have had occasions in the past where I have stepped forward and claimed that authority and bound men and women, not spirits. I bind spirits every day. But I bound men and women who were causing havoc to the church of God. I have bound them and stopped them operating. That is my authority, yet I have to be very careful because it is also the authority of every believer,"[145] he said. "In one case, a wealthy business man in western Nigeria defied God's law and the leadership of the church, took another brother's wife as his own. After much advice and many warnings, he was eventually handed over to Satan for action (1 Cor. 5:5). He laughed and continued his defiance. Within a year he was taken dangerously ill, allegedly poisoned by the very wife he had stolen, and although he cried out for repentance, he died in agony."[146]

Elton's ability to discern God's plan for individuals was remarkable. Even when he was meeting people for the first time, he spoke forth the gift God had placed in them; when, where, and how it would be used; and the pitfalls they had to watch out for. Many recall how Elton just had the ability to see through people. Many testified that when they stood before him, his eyes looked so penetrating; they felt he could view, as though with an X-ray machine, all that was in their hearts—and many times he did.

For many it was the norm to confess all their sins and plead the cleansing power of the blood before they went to see Elton; they knew if there was any known sin in their lives, he would identify it. Time after time, as people stood before him, he would reveal things they had done, and he was usually accurate. Paul Nwachukwu (one of the leaders of the Pentecostal revival in eastern Nigeria after the civil war), describing Elton's prophetic ministry, recalled:

> He was a prophet, and he preached with a lot of symbolism. This made a lot of people misunderstand him. Sometimes, during a service, as the people filed out to give their offering, he would say, "Seventy per cent, seventy per cent," or "sixty per cent, sixty per cent," signifying the number of those who would make it.
>
> Also he could suddenly look at someone and say, "That man is not with you." I would argue that he was my right-hand man, but Pa would laugh, and later, true to his words, that man would stab you in the back and move out just like he said. At a time, he asked me, "What about the pastor in Umuahia?" I replied that he was doing wonderfully well. He laughed and said, "That man is not with you." The amazing thing is I never told him we had any pastor in Umuahia. I replied saying that he was a faithful man. He then laughed and kept quiet. I later found out it was true![147]

"When I go to Benin City and I stand in front of the congregation there, quite a number of people used to tremble," Elton once said of the impact of his prophetic gift on his audience. "I would go in as a lamb to the slaughter, and I would open my mouth and begin to talk to the point. And because I could prophesy, they would say, 'That man is a prophet.' "[148]

For a decade, the articles in *Herald of the Last Days* represented the most systematic, consistent and robust teaching of what is now popularly known as "New Creation" realities and established a whole generation in these truths. Typical titles of articles in the magazine include: "Claiming Your Rights"; "The Authority of the Believer"; "Your Inheritance"; "Signs, Wonders and Miracles"; "According to Your Faith"; "The Wonders of Faith"; "We Are the Master Race"; "What Is the Purpose of the Healing Ministry?"; "Faith that Demands"; "Full Deliverance"; "How to Deal with Demons"; "Power for Today"; "Healing for Today"; "How to Get Divine Guidance"; "God's Way of Prosperity"; "The Way to the Throne"; "Concerning Spiritual Gifts"; and "From the Cross to the Throne."

Throughout the seventies, thousands of Christians around the country first came into the full revelation of the foundation truths of the charismatic movement through Elton's teachings. By the time the books and tapes of Kenneth Hagin, Kenneth Copeland, and the Word of Faith teachers began to be distributed widely around the country beginning from the late seventies and early eighties, Elton's teachings had already laid a solid foundation.

Virtually everyone who became a leader in the charismatic movement in Nigeria beginning from the early 1980s was directly influenced by Elton's teachings on the baptism and empowerment of the Holy Spirit while they were students in Nigeria's higher institutions. Tunde Joda at the University of Lagos, David Oyedepo at the Kwara State College of Technology, Ilorin, Bayo Famonure at the University of Nigeria, Nsukka, Francis Wale Oke at the University of Lagos, Emiko Amotsuka at the University of Ibadan, the founders of Christ's Ambassadors Evangelistic Team at the Ibadan Polytechnic, and scores of others. And, as will be seen shortly, when they began to found independent charismatic churches and parachurch ministries, he was also there for them.

"Pa S. G. Elton is probably one of the best things that happened to Christianity in Nigeria. As a matter of fact, if there is anyone who brought the real gospel apart from just church-going kind of Christianity to Nigeria, I think it is Pa S. G. Elton. He was the one who taught those things about the gifts of the Holy Spirit, Holy Ghost baptism, five-fold ministry, and so on and so forth,"[149] says Enoch Adeboye, who became the general overseer of the Redeemed Christian Church of God (RCCG) in 1981, after the passing of the church's founder. Adeboye continues on Elton's influence on his life:

> To me, when you talk about a missionary par excellence, a man who sold his life completely into the work of missions, Pa Elton is a very prominent example. I think before he died, he hadn't been back to Britain for several years, because he said, "What am I going there to do?" And in one of our intimate moments, he said to me, "My son, I will contest Ilesa with you when Jesus returns. I am going to tell the Lord that this is where I spent most of my life; where I did most of my work, and this is my heritage."
>
> Papa S. G. Elton knew the word of God and taught it with simplicity; with candour. . . . He was a great instrument of God in the life of many people, including myself. I visited him towards the end of his life every two weeks, and

I [used to] spend only one hour. And you can be sure we were not talking politics; we were not talking business. We were discussing the Lord Jesus Christ.

I remember he said once that he regretted that he didn't meet me earlier in his life, and I regretted that I hadn't met him earlier either, but I thank God the last days were profitably used, and I think it's on record that the last major meeting that he had in 1984 or 1985 was on this [RCCG] camp ground. . . . He slept in our little house and we had time for fellowship together, and I remember that his last sermon brought every one of us back to the altar—general overseer, pastors, everyone. We all came back to the altar to cry before God and rededicate our lives to the Almighty God. So nobody can truly write the history of either Pentecostalism, or full gospel as it were, in Nigeria and leave Pastor S. G. Elton out of it. He was a tremendous influence not just on individuals, but on the church of God as a whole.

S. O. Ogedengbe, who joined RCCG in the early seventies (he and Adeboye were the first university graduates to join the church, and they became very close friends from that time), confirms Elton's influence on RCCG in the early and mid-eighties: "In 1985 when we wanted to start the School of Disciples, Adeboye and I came to Papa, and he [Elton] said, 'That is a move in the right direction.' There was nothing that we were doing in the RCCG that we didn't make known to Papa."[150]

Emiko Amotsuka, one-time president of Ibadan Varsity Christian Union and founder of Koinonia Ministries, is generally acknowledged to have played the most pivotal role in the emergence of the Word of Faith movement in Nigeria.[151] He recalls going to Ilesa to discuss with Elton the vision God had given him when he was launching out: "After the Lord gave me the vision of the ministry I am involved in today, I went to share with him in Ilesa. He was ecstatic; he was excited; he was very enthusiastic. That was a great encouragement to me, a kind of confirmation that I was on track. For a young man who was trying to find his way in ministry to have an old man like that give such endorsement was a tremendous boost and encouragement. After that, he made available everything he had to me. Every major step I wanted to take in ministry, I went to discuss with him. He was somebody I could go to bounce off my ideas on and depend on his wisdom and experience of age and many years of success in ministry, and that saved me a lot. . . . He had a high-speed duplicating machine which he made available when I wanted to start reproducing tapes of foreign ministers who had given us permission. I would take master tapes to him in Ilesa and he would copy them and label and I would go back to collect them and he never took a penny from me. Anything he could do to help me in my early days of ministry, he readily did. He was a tremendous backbone to me in my early days of ministry."[152] Amotsuka continues:

S. G. Elton was an apostle; he operated very much in the office of an apostle, and so the gifts of the Spirit moved in and out; he moved in and out of the different gifts of the Spirit. . . . The word of knowledge was very much in operation in his life, especially as he met with people one-on-one—in counselling and in one-on-one discussion. . . . He had a lot of insight into people's lives. Of course, the word of wisdom also was there. And healings and deliverances were all a part and parcel of his ministry as well. He was a man who walked mightily in the miraculous. . . .

He did teach a lot on the gifts of the Spirit. Some of his magazines and his books were on the gifts of the Spirit. As a matter of fact, in the years in which he was involved with us in the fellowship on campus, they were the periods in which the controversy still raged over the baptism of the Holy Spirit, the gifts of the Spirit, whether they were for today or whether they were past. S. G. Elton did a lot of teaching in these areas; he helped to establish the heart of people a lot in these areas. . . .

He laid a very strong emphasis on the fact that God was going to move very mightily in these closing hours of the end times. He laid emphasis on the end-time move of the Spirit of God. So, being under him, you would sort of get stirred up concerning moving with God in the end times. . . . You knew that your life wasn't just for you to live for yourself. You lived in the reality of the fact that there was a move of God and you wanted to prepare yourself to be a part of that. And, as a result, a lot of Christians who were on campuses in those years . . . are very active in kingdom work today either as full-time ministers or as part-time ministers. People from that generation are people who had a clear sense of the hand of God on their lives and that they had a responsibility to serve God in whatever vocations they found themselves. This was one of his legacies, I would say, to let you know that your life was for a purpose, especially in these end times.[153]

Olubi Johnson founded Scripture Pastures Christian Centre in Ibadan in 1984, one of the first charismatic churches in the country. He recalls that his first contact with "Pa Elton was not physical, it was through a tape. I was in England, Imperial College, when I was studying for my masters, and I had gotten born again in 1979. . . . One of my friends who was a Christian, who had been a Christian when we were in UI, gave me Pa Elton's tape; that was my first contact with Pa Elton. I will never forget [the message]; he preached from the Beatitudes." Johnson worked with Amotsuka for some time in the early eighties and recalls that "initially, I didn't know Pa Elton personally, I just used to go with Brother Emiko and just sit outside; of course, I was introduced—as a young man that just came from England and who had dedicated his life to the Lord; he [Elton] said he was impressed. Then after a while, I used to go and see Pa Elton. I would just go and see him in Ilesa and ask his advice before we started Scripture Pasture, and I think after we started Scripture Pasture, I must have gone one or two more times."[154]

> Brother Emiko was close to Pa Elton. . . . I don't think there was anybody back in those days who was not close to Pa Elton. Majority of the ministers at that time, if not all—particularly the young ones in the university—would go to Ilesa for counsel, for direction. . . . Pa Elton was the conduit through which God brought in what I would call the revelation knowledge of faith, the gifts of the Spirit, to the church with clear accurate knowledge of the Scriptures. Because there had been a lot of stuff before, but there was a lot of confusion—all of Franklin Hall and all of that—but God used Pa Elton . . . to bring clear light. So we could distinguish between what was false and what was true, and that now established the churches.[155]

When Francis Wale Oke, founder of Sword of the Spirit Ministries (which was pioneered in Ibadan in 1983), one of the earliest charismatic ministries in the country, visited Elton to share his burden for God's work a few years before the ministry started, he recalls that Elton "really got excited about this." "Lord, keep your hand upon Francis. Shield him from the adversary. Wherever he goes, let the anointing speak for [itself],"[156] Elton prayed. Elton became a major influence in Wale Oke's life and ministry from his days in the university and was one of the speakers at the early editions of the ministry's Holy Ghost Convention, which "was arguably the most popular gathering of the Charismatic movement in Nigeria for almost a decade"[157] until the mid-nineties.

Paul Jinadu, a former pastor of the Foursquare Gospel Church in Ibadan, who founded New Covenant Church in 1985, which has grown to become one of the frontline charismatic churches in Nigeria and in the United Kingdom, regularly visited Elton in Ilesa. Elton was the speaker at the inaugural service of New Covenant Church.[158] William Kumuyi, founder of Deeper Life Bible Church, visited Elton in Ilesa.[159] David Oyedepo, who founded Faith Liberation Hour Ministry in 1982 (which metamorphosed into Winners Chapel), visited Ilesa.[160] In the seventies, Elton was a regular speaker at meetings of the Foursquare Gospel Church, and many in that generation of the church's leadership, like Samuel Odunaike and James Boyejo, were influenced by Elton's teachings.[161] Odunaike and Boyejo frequently visited Elton in Ilesa.[162]

Elton played one of the most influential roles in the emergence of the charismatic movement in the orthodox churches. Throughout the seventies he fervently prayed and prophesied that God would raise an army of young people in the older (traditional) churches to start a revival that would reawaken them and cause them to seek God for what He was doing in the present. Many young believers who embraced the move of the Holy Spirit in the seventies and eighties stayed in these churches where they were members because Elton encouraged them to do so.

His reason for this was that revival was coming to these places and that God needed vessels to ignite it. He counselled, "Stay where you are converted and there manifest the power of the new life, until they say they don't want you, and then Jesus Christ will receive you."[163] Elton frequently prophesied about the role of young people in the "wonderful move of the Holy Spirit" in the last days and that "channels for these gifts of power are now being prepared, anointed and trained in readiness for the big increase in calls from traditional churches for assistance in handling the tremendous revival which will bring many thousands into the kingdom of God, and into the churches."[164]

One regular caller at Ilesa recalls that "Anglican priests who were touched by God [i.e. the Pentecostal baptism in the Holy Spirit] went to see Elton."[165] Raphael Okafor (one of the first people to receive the Pentecostal experience during the post-civil war revival in eastern Nigeria) remembers Elton challenging many of them that the churches they called dead were soon going to experience revival.[166] When Okafor returned to the country after studying overseas, he was made SU travelling secretary, and later the general secretary; afterwards, he became a minister, and then a bishop, in the Anglican Communion. This is the story of scores of leaders in the Anglican Communion of Nigeria. Their Pentecostal experience continues to be a revitalizing force within the Anglican Communion of Nigeria.

In the same vein, Elton's vision has had an equally significant impact in the Roman Catholic Church in Nigeria through the Catholic Charismatic Renewal movement. Elton was thrilled about news of the Charismatic Renewal movement in America in the 1970s and wanted the same experience for Roman Catholics in Nigeria. He wrote with excitement: "In America alone there are over 10,000 house meetings of Charismatic Roman Catholics. They gather in fellowship, they talk, and they give their testimonies. Those who have gifts among them and those whom God has put His hands upon are the leaders."[167]

When, in the late 1970s, many Roman Catholic students in higher institutions in western Nigeria who had embraced the Charismatic Renewal began to sense that a mighty outpouring of the Holy Spirit was coming to the Roman Catholic Church in Nigeria, it was to Elton that they turned for clarity and counsel. In prayer, they had received a prophetic word which they interpreted to mean they were to form a national students' movement of Catholic Charismatics in Nigeria's higher institutions. Elton "confirmed that God meant what he said, and encouraged them to take it seriously. Pastor Elton's confirmation of the prophecy dispelled every iota of doubt in their mind that God was leading them.... The wise counsel they received from Pastor Elton helped the students to determine what future direction they were to take to actualize what God had told them."[168]

Encouraged by Elton's confirmation, they boldly reached out to students in higher institutions across the country and as a result, in 1981, the National Catholic Charismatic Students (NCCS) was inaugurated.[169] Within a short time, the NCCS emerged as the most vibrant force within the Catholic Charismatic Renewal movement in Nigeria—it completely transformed a hitherto cautious movement into a blazing fire that within a decade brought hundreds of thousands of Roman Catholic adherents in Nigeria into the Renewal. According to Cosmas Ilechukwu, one of the leaders of the Renewal at the University of Ife in the late 1970s, and later founder of Charismatic Renewal Ministries, "certain external and internal factors facilitated the awakening among the Catholic university students in the 1980s. The external influences included the spirit of revival within the global Catholic Church, and the role played by Pastor S. G. Elton who was around to counsel and encourage."[170]

After conducting extensive research among the first generation of charismatic Christians in Nigeria in the early eighties, Matthews Ojo, in his ground-breaking PhD thesis on the movement, concluded, "He [Elton] is the 'father' of the Charismatics."[171]

ELEVEN

REBELS

Sydney Elton is credited by many historians and scholars of religion in eastern Nigeria as being the "link between the two major strands of intensive revivalist and Pentecostal activity in Nigeria in the two periods/strands, 1914–1939 and 1967–1975."[1] Church historian Ogbu Kalu articulates it thus: "Three sources have been canvassed for the modern outburst of Pentecostalism in the 1970s which widened into a great variety with the years: (a) University students of Ibadan and Ife. After they graduated, they intensified their commitments. Other institutions of learning picked up the 'vibration.' As they went on National Youth Service, they spread the Pentecostal influence into the nooks and crannies of the nation; (b) Secondary students from the Scripture Union. This group benefited from the ministry of Bill Roberts, a British Travelling Secretary of the Scripture Union, 1958–1968. He inspired the young men connected with the Civil War spirituality which turned into a revival in the immediate aftermath of the Civil War; (c) Unclassified flares such as Idahosa who just started to 'happen.' This factor increased in the 1980s and 1990s as Pentecostalism took diverse forms. The career of one man of God—Sydney Granville Elton, linked the three groups to the earlier outpouring of the Holy Spirit."[2]

The revival that broke out in eastern Nigeria during the civil war of 1967 to 1970 was in the beginning an evangelical revival, which had its roots in the Scripture Union (SU) work in several eastern towns before and during the war. The revival witnessed thousands of conversions; a heightened sense of the presence of God that led to an increased devotion to prayer and Bible study; and an outburst of evangelistic activity. With time, however, the revival took on a distinctly Pentecostal character—Elton played the most important role in this shift.

Writing to Gordon Lindsay just before the beginning of the war, Elton said, "I have spent the last two weeks in Eastern Nigeria where there is no peace, and everyone is waiting with bated breath for the expected explosion and clash which could usher in another civil war and produce another 'Congo.' The region is full of police and military, and searches are carried out carefully every 50 miles or so. The whole region is an armed camp."[3]

During the first few months of the war, Elton started to scent a coming revival in this part of the country. He was convinced that the crisis would produce a longing for God in the hearts of much of the Igbo population. Writing in late 1967 he predicted: "We feel that 1968 will produce a situation where the people will hungrily turn to the Lord. We are preparing to take our part in a spiritual revival for this country. There will be tremendous need—and a great challenge to us all!"[4]

Elton himself became heavily involved in relief work and in evangelism throughout the region during this period. This necessitated many trips to the region. He had most likely just returned from one such trip when he sent a letter to the US, in which he wrote, "Greetings to you all once again in the Master's Name. At last I am able to devote some time to the office after trying to deal with the refugee and relief situation in Ibo land where conditions and problems are appalling."[5] Writing again in late 1968 to Gordon Lindsay, he noted with alarm: "There is little food, no Bibles, no church services, no clothes, no work, and no money. The war is nearly over officially, but the hatred and fear generated is terrible. I spent all last week with the man in charge of our newly liberated areas in Eastern Nigeria, and there are over 250,000 refugees in one district alone. Most of our evangelists are in camps. The need is tremendous and the frustration is nearly too much for us here. The war continues to take lives and whole towns are being razed to the ground; there is horrible misery and suffering."[6] In fact, so much time did Elton spend away from Ilesa that Osborn's magazine reported that Elton had had to abandon the project they were jointly coordinating in the West: "In time! Rev. S. G. Elton hands over the keys to the Osborn MEU in Nigeria to Nigerian Evangelists. Not long after, he was forced to leave his mission due to civil war."[7]

Almost from the beginning, Elton's battle strategy focused on moving loads of evangelistic tracts and revival magazines to the relief areas. Writing some months into the war, he said, "The prospect for literature in the future is enormous . . . I do not think it can even be gauged or guessed. . . . We are meeting with growing demands even now and as soon as postal facilities are restored in the former Eastern region, then we shall be inundated with demands."[8] In one letter to Lindsay, he reported that "the war continues to take lives and whole towns are being razed to the ground; and there are horrible tales of misery and suffering . . . and the whole country waits for revival. Fortunately we are aware of this, and we are preparing for the time when we shall get the chance to send in evangelists and literature to these war-torn areas."[9]

A report in *Herald of His Coming* noted, "While mail connections to the war devastated area are not fully re-established, doors are still open to reach the many Nigerians living in refugee camps by sending carloads of the vernacular heralds to evangelists who preach in these centres regularly. Disillusioned and destitute, these refugees are hearts prepared for the Gospel—or for seeds of atheistic propaganda. Who will reach them first? Our regular, sizable donations will enable Brother Elton to fill Christian workers' hands with the Gospel messages so greatly needed in this crisis time in Nigeria!"[10] Still in 1968, Elton wrote Lindsay:

We are still very much occupied with the war here, and now that the armies seem to be getting nearer to the final conclusion, then the tremendous task of resettling the country afterwards is taking much of our time. We have just spent a week with our Nigerian supervisor from the Efik-Ibibio area which has suffered so much during the war fighting. He himself had to carry his children on his back through the muddy creeks for eight miles to safety, and then his youngest child died in his arms.

We have been helping as much as we can and have now sent them 350 Bibles, because nearly all the Christians have lost everything, including Bibles. The task is all frustrating because there is so much misery . . . so much need . . . so many needy, and very, very few seem to realize the need or have any desire to get things moving. The apathy of the authorities is matched by the general apathy and hopelessness of the refugees. Even Christians are so weak and full of misery that it is a major task to revive their faith in the Lord. But we are getting more and more of the evangelists and church workers free from the refugee camps, and we have been able to provide them with Bibles and literature for the villages. But this task will take at least nine months, and until the next harvest is ready.

Strangely enough many of the Christians regard the recent war as a judgement from God because of the moral corruption of the area, and the indifference of the people toward the things of God. It is for this reason we believe that there is a big spiritual revival ahead for us in this area.[11]

By 1970 Elton was writing, "We are under heavy pressure here at this time. The relief areas are making very heavy demands upon us for magazines and literature, and we are doing all we can to meet these demands."[12] "There is a clear spirit of revival in Ibo land where there is no literature and where the people have mostly lost everything," he continued. "We have cleared all our stocks of magazines and tracts in Ibo and it is clear that we shall soon have to print at least one issue of the Ibo herald to try to meet the demand. . . . The needs out here now are greater than anything we have yet seen in Nigeria. The hunger in Ibo land is almost unbelievable and there is a tremendous demand for the Herald and its messages. It is highly appreciated."[13]

Speaking further about the pitiful situation in the war areas and the impact of *Herald*, Elton wrote, "They challenge one to do everything possible to meet the huge spiritual demands they are making. In several parts of Ibo land there is a big move of the Spirit of God, and it is satisfying and encouraging to note the big part that the *Herald of His Coming* is playing in this move. It is well-known and read avidly by many, and we have been unable to supply all who have asked for it. We are ready to go into print with an Ibo Herald as soon as we can secure enough newsprint paper. . . . We are all well here, still very, very busy but we now have the vision of Nigeria again being fully open to the Gospel and the demand and need is now greater than ever. We are doing all we can to pour literature into Ibo land where the demand is greatest."[14]

At another point during the war, Elton wrote to Lindsay: "The war in Nigeria is drawing to a close, and as we move into liberated areas, we are meeting with a tremendous opportunity for the Gospel and demands for good spiritual gospel literature. Most of the 'white' missionary staff had to leave, and the Nigerians are begging for books and papers for their people. No books are available in the liberated areas . . . and all property in bookshops has been burned or looted, and so we are starting from scratch in meeting the needs. Schools have been closed for fourteen months . . . colleges are not yet reopening but churches are starting to meet again, and the demand is tremendous. We have a good trained staff in Efik, Ibibio,

Ijaw and Ogoja provinces, and as soon as Ibo land reopens, then the demand will double again. We want to meet the need in these languages as quickly as possible, and there is still a huge demand for English. I know of no series of books which can meet the need as well as these Literature Crusade books. Please do not fail us."[15]

Elton's heavy involvement with relief work on one hand and with evangelism on the other during the war brought him into direct contact with many young evangelists whose ministries would shake the region just after the war and forever change its spiritual landscape. Even though Elton's ministry would become significant in shaping the future ministries of these young evangelists after the war, Bill Roberts' ministry as the travelling secretary for the Scripture Union in the eastern and mid-western regions of the country from 1964 to 1969, perhaps more than any other factor, created the evangelical fervour that laid the foundation for the post-civil war events.

Before coming to Nigeria in 1964, Roberts had first served in the country in the 1950s for two years immediately after college as a 2nd lieutenant in the Royal West African Force, to fulfil the compulsory British national service.[16] After this time, he went to Cambridge University, where he got a degree in geography. While at the university, he came in contact with the West Africa Prayer Group—an association within the Christian Union which focused on raising awareness among students about the opportunity for missionary work in West Africa after they finished from the university. Christians who were working in engineering, architecture, accounting, and in the other professions—especially schoolteachers—were as strategically positioned to be witnesses for the gospel as the traditional missionary.

Roberts later wrote that some of the happiest memories of his university days were of the visits to the school of such "missionaries" when they were on leave. This sowed the first seeds that would later lead to his coming to Africa. Upon graduation, he took up a teaching job and also became very active in the local Scripture Union group, but his colleagues knew he had a strong desire to work as a schoolteacher in Nigeria. One of them later suggested that he consider taking up the position of a travelling secretary for the Scripture Union in Nigeria. After a period of thinking and praying, he decided to do this and immediately sent a letter to the SU. Providentially, Ishaya Audu, who was then the president of the SU in Nigeria, was passing through England on business, and Roberts was called for an interview. His application was approved, and he was soon on his way to Nigeria.[17]

Roberts lived in the SU house just outside Umuahia, from where he travelled throughout the two regions "speaking to SU groups in the schools, sometimes to the whole school, offering advice to young people who cared to bring their questions and spiritual problems and . . . making Christian books available for them to buy."[18] An example of his influence in SU groups can be seen from a 1966 report by a member of the SU group at the University of Nigeria, Nsukka: "Mr Bill Roberts' visits have been such a blessing, for after each visit we receive new members and the old members are sort of revitalized. This is why we are all the more grateful to God that Bill Roberts is now stationed in the East. We are at least sure of more frequent visits from him. We pray God to guard and direct him in his difficult task."[19]

At the outbreak of war in 1967, Roberts decided to stay to help the students, when most expatriates were leaving because of the risk of staying behind in a war zone. There seems to have been a widespread fear of "another Congo" (a reference to the Congo Crisis of 1960–1966), because Roberts also makes reference to the Congo situation: "The whole world quickly began to refer to the people of this region as the 'rebels.' . . . We couldn't help wondering if these 'rebels' were going to treat us in the same way as the Congo 'rebels' had treated the white people within their area."[20] Even more frightening was the anti-British sentiment in Biafra because of the British government's stance of supporting Nigeria and rejecting any secession by Biafra. All British expatriates were advised to leave Biafra, but Roberts chose to stay at great risk to himself.

When the schools were closed shortly after the war began, Roberts' work was confined to the SU house in Umuahia, which played host to young people, mostly students (from secondary schools and tertiary institutions), week in week out, for many months. Initially the only meetings held were the Sunday Bible studies, but after a few weeks, specific activities were planned for an additional two days within the week. Such activities included Bible study, singing, intercessory prayers, evangelism, games (indoor and outdoor), and farming.[21] This schedule was kept up until the fall of Umuahia to federal troops eighteen months later. During this period, hundreds of students experienced a profound change in their spirituality. While many deepened their already existing relationship with Christ, others made their first commitment—but both categories were radically transformed at Umuahia. Speaking many years after the events, Cyril Okorocha, who worked closely with Bill Roberts at Umuahia, recalls, "At first, the meetings were held once a week, but quickly became daily—and there in the heart of a war zone, the Spirit of God broke in upon these students gathered for Bible study and prayer in an unprecedented, unplanned way. It was like a page from the Acts of the Apostles! This started a renewal which would eventually spread to the rest of Nigeria—even to other parts of West Africa."[22]

When Umuahia fell, the population moved to neighbouring towns and villages that were still under Biafran control. One of those closely associated with the fellowship remarked, "The Word of God was taken by the brethren to these areas, which proved athirst for it. It [was] spreading like wildfire and people [were] coming to a personal knowledge of the Lord Jesus Christ everywhere. One can look back now and thank the Lord for allowing Umuahia to fall."[23] The forceful evacuation from Umuahia came to be famously known in the SU family as the "Dispersion of Umuahia,"[24] reminiscent of the dispersion of the early church from Jerusalem.

Within six months of the dispersion, the number of SU groups had increased from twenty-five to eighty-five.[25] Roberts said that "these new groups were nearly all started by people who had come to know Christ, and been helped to grow as Christians, through the fellowship at Umuahia. Groups were now to be found here, there and everywhere, in villages, churches of all denominations, ammunition factories, hospitals, army camps and refugee camps. Hundreds more people were now hearing about Jesus Christ through the Scripture Union than ever before. . . . News of people coming into personal relationship with Christ was coming in from all points of 'Biafra.' "[26] Okorocha writes, "As the population fled from the advancing war, this revival was carried by the young people from village to village. These vast dislocations of population accelerated this spread of the Gospel."[27] These young people turned the East upside down with the message of the gospel which they preached to everybody, everywhere they went. "When hostilities ended with the demise of Biafra in January 1970, virtually every village and every refugee camp had become a centre of renewal."[28]

It was upon these young people who were already consumed by the passion for Christ that the Pentecostal fire fell after the war. Frances Lawjua Bolton, writing in *And We Beheld His Glory*, the most moving and intimate record of the revival till date, asked pointedly: "Did civil war break out in Nigeria because the Devil was trying to destroy the proposed move of God? Did revival come because we prayed? Did we pray because revival was coming?"[29] These questions have always been asked whenever a revival of historic proportions breaks out, and finding the answers has always been important to those who deeply long to see the glory of God perpetually manifested on the earth. Such release of glory leads to a great harvest of souls, brings about an increase in the miraculous, and causes the fear of God to come upon whole communities.

Stephen Okafor, one of three young men who were used to ignite the first spark of Pentecostal fire, became born again through Roberts' ministry.[30] The other two, Raphael Okafor and Arthur Oruizu, were won to Christ through the witness of Stephen. The three had been formerly very active in one of the hundreds of prayer groups scattered throughout the region at this time. These groups—which engaged in an amalgam of occultist and Christian practices—became popular just before the war and even more so at the outbreak of war. As Bolton observes, multitudes flocked to these pseudo-spiritual houses because the church was nowhere to be found. "The church was in exactly the same state as the nation. In darkness. There was virtually no life in the churches. Every Sunday morning for as long as I can remember, hundreds and thousands and even millions of Ibos flocked into the churches. . . . But most of them would have died and gone to hell. Most of them believed they were saved through being baptised and through being good. We all probably knew that Jesus died for 'our' sins, whatever that was, but it meant little or nothing. Liberal theology reigned. Very few people believed the Bible. And virtually everyone believed the age of miracles in the church was past. If one wanted spiritual power one became or consulted an occultist, spiritualist or a native doctor. And there were many of these. People wanted a reality and a spirituality that eluded them. But it certainly would not have occurred to them to look for this spirituality in the churches. The churches had a *form of religion but denied the power of it*. It was in this atmosphere of spiritual paucity and poverty that the prayer houses began."[31]

These prayer houses dominated the spiritual life of the region—with Christians and non-Christians alike patronizing them. When Stephen, who was twenty-eight years old, Raphael twenty-six, and Arthur thirty, saw the light, they published a letter denouncing the activities of these houses and calling people to come out of them. "The hour of freedom has come," they cried as they moved into the streets, villages, and towns, preaching the gospel and calling people to repentance. "With hearts full of joy we stand here today to make our stand known and ourselves clear to those who do not know and understand us. We plead that this letter should be looked into with love, seriousness and patience. We (Stephen, Raphael, Arthur) have been in the field together facing criticisms, appreciation, hatred from unbelievers and false brethren and love from brothers and sisters. We went into the field not with dogma, liturgy or man-made doctrine. Rather, we were driven out by passion for souls and we preach repentance and salvation through faith in Jesus," their letter began.

> Our intention has never been to destroy prayer houses but to put away the occult practices in them. And putting them out actually means: letting them know the error of the practices, pointing out their trust in them and not in Jesus. We three had been involved in occult practices until we met Jesus. . . .
>
> We must say here that the church up till now has not given official approval to these prayer groups. But only that it has been impossible for any formal church to even attack it. Only the gospel can do this and nothing more or less. Only the old time religion, as in The Acts of the Apostles, can go into the offensive and decisively win the battle. . . .
>
> They say we are trying to pull the church down. Wherever they say this we know that they are trying to protect themselves. We left our prayer group to revive and strengthen the churches; whichever church will welcome our yearnings for revival. They are ready to form new prayer houses but we are only out to form Jesus in the hearts of the people. The point is that they failed to understand us, for they refused to understand Jesus.[32]

The trio formed a group which they named "Hour of Freedom Evangelistic Association," and they began holding crusades, visiting schools, and printing and distributing tracts. Their activities gradually revolutionized Christian practice in the region. Never had groups of young men and women besieged Igbo towns and villages challenging the lukewarm state of the church, demanding that people consider their eternal prospects, and in the process literally hauling thousands of unsaved people into the kingdom. The first series of crusades were held at Awka Etiti, where Raphael's parents lived; Nnewi, Arthur Oruizu's hometown; Ojoto, Stephen's hometown; and also at Amichi and Oko.[33]

Ufuma, a town about forty-five kilometres from Onitsha, was the initial base of the three young men, but forced out by leaders of the prayer houses, they moved to Awka Etiti, which was farther away from Onitsha. In late 1970, the trio, having been separated for a while from their brethren at Umuahia and longing to see them, decided to visit. They had no money for the trip (money was scarce in those days as eastern Nigeria was just recovering from the war), so they decided to trek from Awka Etiti to Umuahia, a distance of about 280 kilometres (about 175 miles). The three men, speaking to Bolton about this time and the trek many years after the events, "without exception see this time as the high point of their ministry."[34] "They truly beheld His glory as they marched along, singing of heaven and salvation, preaching the gospel of Jesus in every town along their way. They sang as they trekked."[35] She continues this wonderful story: "They preached in market places, in the streets, in homes if they were invited in; they knocked on doors; they preached in season and out of season. They accosted anyone who would stop and listen to them. 'Where will you spend eternity?' they asked. 'Do you know Jesus?' they questioned. Many spoke to them and were converted. They prayed for the sick. They lived entirely by faith and the Lord, who takes care of the birds of the air and the flowers of the field, took care of His own children. In some towns they were not welcome and suffered the consequences. But undaunted and full of joy they pressed on till they got to Umuahia, a distance of some 175 miles."[36]

After seeing the brethren at Umuahia, they moved to Onitsha, settling at 22 Amobi Street, which had been Raphael Okafor's parents' home before the war; and it quickly became the centre of the revival that set Onitsha ablaze with Pentecostal fire. "Lord, send us revival. May it begin with me,"[37] they prayed frequently and fervently. Prayers were held every day almost without a break, and on many nights also.[38]

Thousands of young people, mostly between the ages of fifteen and twenty-five, attended the meetings over a period of about two years, where they were deeply affected by the prayers and preaching that went on all the time. These in turn went to towns and villages, to the streets and town halls, and to schools to tell of what they had experienced. Stephen, Raphael, and Arthur continually declared that the gift of the Holy Spirit had been promised to everyone, and followed it up by praying for the converts, who were filled to overflowing. This truth had previously been taught only within the confines of some of the older Pentecostal churches in the region, and even then it had become a mere formality. Now it was made "public" at 22 Amobi Street, and it revolutionized the lives of a whole generation of young people.

Raphael Okafor recalls that "people were in tears, some were falling down, and some were crying out, all kinds of things were happening. And people confessed to real healing and deliverance. . . . When people saw the things they were not seeing in churches, they had to believe God. . . . It was God's visitation, it was very clear to everybody."[39] Bolton recounts her own experience: "I began to invite my SU friends to the meetings at 22 Amobi Street. . . . As people accepted these Biblical teachings and were filled with the Holy Spirit, the fire of God was lit in every heart and we all became warriors. The Scripture Union became extremely active in organising meetings in the town and hundreds and hundreds of people came. Virtually every Sunday afternoon throughout the later part of 1970 and all of 1971, and beyond, was a 'crusade.' "[40] From 22 Amobi Street, the message that Jesus saves, heals, and delivers was taken all over eastern Nigeria.

SU groups across the region came in contact with the Pentecostal message in a variety of ways. One was through the ministries of preachers who had—prior to, or during the war—received the Holy Spirit baptism. Some of these were invited to the "guest services"[41] of these groups, where they emphasized the need for the empowerment brought about by the baptism of the Spirit and called out those who desired to be filled, to be prayed for. It was during one of such meetings in Umuahia in 1971 that Stephen, Raphael and Arthur received the Pentecostal experience of the baptism in the Holy Spirit. At that meeting the hearts of many were opened and their faith stirred: "People started to be filled in the Holy Spirit. And great was the joy! Stephen, Raphael and Arthur were also filled with the Holy Spirit at this time and their joy and zeal knew no bounds."[42]

Other SU members and groups came across the Pentecostal message through Pentecostal literature, especially by T. L. Osborn and Gordon Lindsay.[43] Also, the leaders of some SU groups were members of the traditional Pentecostal churches like the Assemblies of God—they gradually introduced teachings about the baptism of the Holy Spirit to their groups. Other SU groups, excited about the outpouring that was sweeping the region, felt compelled to open their doors to the ministry of the Hour of Freedom association, and went full swing with the revival.

The Hour of Freedom Evangelistic Association and their associates, as well as these SU members and groups, did not, however, have a smooth ride, as they were fiercely opposed by most church leaders, and also by the leadership of Scripture Union, because of their emphasis on the baptism of the Holy Spirit with the evidence of speaking in tongues and other Pentecostal manifestations. This opposition had started when Bill Roberts was around. When some of the SU members showed openness to Pentecostal influences, he frowned at it. Referring to some of the members' zeal for the things of God, Roberts wrote, "Everyone was talking about the Holy Spirit and longing to be filled with Him. Some were looking for a sudden 'filling' which would 'do the trick' once and for all: while others realized it had to be a continual, day by day, process. In their search, some went off at a tangent to make 'speaking in tongues' or fasting or miraculous healing their supreme aim as Christians."[44]

The SU leadership in eastern Nigeria generally took Roberts' position. As Anthony Nkwoka has noted, "The authorities of the Scripture Union were averse to Pentecostal and Charismatic manifestations. In their own view, the young believers must not be diverted from evangelical concerns to Pentecostal confusion."[45] Nkwoka cites the case of the Scripture Union National Conference at Awgu in eastern Nigeria in 1974, which "witnessed a doctrinal storm over Pentecostalism." At the conference, Tony Wilmot gave a testimony "of how his life got confused when he 'dabbled' into Pentecostal experience and strongly deplored Pentecostalism."[46]

The SU adopted (and issued) a statement on the doctrine of the Holy Spirit, which was written by Tony Wilmot: "The Scripture Union recognises that the Scriptures teach both the baptism of the Spirit and the gifts of the Spirit. We hold the person and work of the Holy Spirit to be subjects of great preciousness to the believer and we notice with regret that these subjects, which call for great reverence, have in recent times become increasingly matters of contention. It is our united resolution that preaching likely to stimulate contention about gifts such as 'tongues' or healing or miracles shall not be given at Scripture Union meetings or in association with the name of the Scripture Union. We counsel all staff workers, voluntary helpers and speakers at Scripture Union meetings to exercise restraint in this matter. Let everything be done decently and in order: make love your aim. The fruit of the Spirit is self-control."[47]

Raphael Okafor and his colleagues were summoned by SU leaders to a meeting where they were asked to renounce Pentecostalism. When it became obvious that they were resolute about preaching the baptism of the Holy Spirit with the evidence of speaking in tongues, they were

excommunicated from the SU.[48] Okorocha, in recollecting the origin of
the crisis, writes, "Spiritual euphoria did not last for too long. Those who
experienced renewal started picking up the reins of their lives, returning to
university or to work. As people settled back into a normal existence in the
following twelve months, tension quickly developed between the leaders
of the mainline churches, and the young revivalists whose interdenominational approach to the faith, charismatic style of preaching, and emphasis
upon personal holiness they found extremely threatening. Many of the
young were either expelled or frozen out of the mainline churches, leaving
to set up their own movements."[49]

Elton had been around throughout the period of the war and was well
aware of the beginnings of the revival and threw in his weight on the side
of the revivalists when they faced opposition from churches and many
leaders who did not understand what was going on. Elton was filled with
joy at what God was doing through these young men and women, and
decided to support their ministry with every resource at his disposal. He
wrote in excitement to Lindsay, "Revival is now so large that even present
supplies of books are totally inadequate. Three or four meetings daily with
a group of over 200 young people in attendance . . . not only hundreds
being converted daily, but outstanding healings. The war brought people
to the verge of despair, and now the Gospel is coming with hope and
power and thousands are being affected. . . . The books are invaluable . . .
nothing exists to compare with them."[50] Elton gave these young evangelists books by T. L. Osborn, Lindsay, and many other Pentecostal preachers for free and told them they could sell the books at a very minimal cost
to support their ministry. He was also paying them an allowance every
month for their upkeep.[51]

Raphael Okafor, speaking of Elton's influence on the revival, said,
"There were many people who were on his [Elton's] payroll, and this was a
great encouragement to many of the young evangelists in those days. . . .
We knew of his ministry and read some of his writings and some of the
things he was helping to bring in from T. L. Osborn, Gordon Lindsay, and
others. At that time, we were not talking of denominations, we were out
for truth, and Pa Elton was known for evangelism and missions; he was
known as a deep man of God with prophetic ministry. He was somebody
that emphasised the Holy Spirit and from my own background [SU] we
didn't have that kind of emphasis on the Holy Spirit. So his emphasis on
the Holy Spirit helped us a lot."[52] Stephen Okafor visited Ilesa a couple of

times to consult with Elton.[53] Bolton writes that "Pa Elton . . . was very much around. He became a father for all the great men of God that were coming out at this time."[54] Richard Burgess, a leading historian of the revival, notes that "Elton was an important influence during the Civil War Revival and an early mentor to Igbo neo-Pentecostal pioneers."[55] Godwin Nnaji, a participant in the revival, wrote, "In Ilesa from the West, Pa Elton . . . was there shepherding the . . . practising preachers."[56]

Elton was regularly travelling to the East to help out with the revival in every way possible—speaking at meetings, consulting with the leaders, and identifying the prevailing needs so he could find ways to meet them either on the spot or once he returned to Ilesa. An example of his involvement is seen in a letter he wrote, most likely in early 1973, to the publishers of *Herald of His Coming*: "It is harvest time here! I have just returned from another tour in the revival areas where we are seeing some wonderful results. The Lord is moving mightily in many ways."[57]

Elton was a guest speaker at a city-wide crusade organized by SU Onitsha in 1972.[58] "Our biggest difficulty is not to get souls saved . . . that is fairly easy in the present awareness of Nigeria to spiritual things," Elton wrote elsewhere, "but the problem of looking after the large number of converts which follow after every campaign. At this moment there are hundreds of souls being converted almost daily in Ibo land, and we simply do not have enough trained men at hand to stay and look after the converts. But they are eager to gather whenever they can for instruction. Brother Lindsay's books have been extensively used in these meetings and are of tremendous value."[59]

Pentecostal literature played a major role in the nurturing and development of this revival. Bolton notes that "contact was also made with groups and organisations outside Nigeria and the ministries of T. L. Osborn, Gordon Lindsay, and others as well as their books, were very helpful and supportive."[60] Paul Nwachukwu recalls that "we were excommunicated from the Anglican Church. . . . Osborn's tracts, like 'The Blood of Jesus,' 'The Purpose of Pentecost' booklets, *Join This Chariot*—a book on soul winning, were all armour in our hands, because it inspired us for soul winning and street corner ministries."[61] Burgess also writes, "I have noted the influence of books written by T. L. Osborn and Gordon Lindsay. Several former revivalists told me that Osborn's teaching helped to introduce an emphasis on Spirit baptism into the revival."[62] These tracts, booklets, and books were directly supplied by Elton. And he was also behind virtually all the contacts that the revivalists made with the foreign organizations that supplied literature.

Elton had been distributing Lindsay's literature in Nigeria from the mid-sixties under the Native Literature Crusade, a programme "closely allied with the Native Church Crusade." The Native Literature Crusade was started by Lindsay's organization to "put Full Gospel books into the hands of millions of persons overseas."[63] By the mid-1970s, the total number of Lindsay literature that Elton had distributed in the country must have run into many millions.

When Lindsay first intimated the missionaries representing his organization around the world about the literature plan in the mid-sixties, Elton's response was the most buoyant of all those published in *The Voice of Healing*:

> The communists have excellent booklets and magazines which are freely and carefully distributed. I think there is more Chinese than Russian literature here [Nigeria] at present. But that is even more dangerous. None of it is liked by the Nigerian Moslem government. There is a growing underground in this country and many school teachers and literates are being attracted by this subtle propaganda.
>
> We must, and we will deal with this by putting out the TRUTH. This is a battle for the mind which we can win if we do something about it. Daily we receive a large number of requests for booklets on Christian subjects and so your literature plan just fits into the whole pattern of things. We welcome it wholeheartedly and can assure you of our support . . . I believe the Lord will move and enable you to deal with the need for literature as you have so successfully dealt with the Native Church Programme. It is wonderful.[64]

By the late 1960s, Elton must have been routinely distributing hundreds of thousands of Lindsay's materials. We know this because Lindsay was writing in 1968 to his supporters to help raise the needed funds to help send more books to Nigeria: "We do not want to fail in extending a hand of the Gospel to these people. Brother Elton has requested an additional 115,000 Gospel books for immediate use."[65] According to a 1975 report by the Christ for the Nations office in Dallas, Elton was "responsibly" disposing of "52 boxes of books per month, and could use more."[66]

The following letter by one Francis Enyia from Nigeria, published in the October 1966 issue of *The Voice of Healing* under the caption, "Received Baptism While Reading Book," gives an example of the impact of Lindsay's books on Christians around the country: "I am now filled with the Holy Spirit through the help of your book, *The Baptism of the Holy Spirit*. I read 'Ten Reasons Why We Should Be Baptized,' and when I reached the point that says, 'If Jesus and the disciples need[ed] the Holy Spirit, how much more do we!' I remained on that point and promised never to go further until I was baptized in the Holy Spirit. And Jesus heard my prayer and now I am baptized. I am now pastoring two churches—one in Ekumtak and one in Odaji."[67]

Lindsay's twelve-booklet set on the fundamental teachings of the Pentecostal movement—with titles such as *Satan, Fallen Angels and Demons*, *The Baptism of the Holy Spirit*, and *The Nine Gifts of the Holy Spirit*—played a significant role in establishing the basic understanding of the workings of the movement. Osborn' books and Elton's *Herald of the Last Days* were also crucial in laying this foundation. Therefore, Elton, indirectly through Lindsay and Osborn, and directly through his *Herald of the Last Days*, played the most far-reaching role at the initial stage in laying the doctrinal foundation of the movement.

Elton's influence was again significant because, from the earliest days of the revival, he gave perspective to what was happening—he helped the key players to understand the implications of what they were doing—and how it fit into God's overall plan. This boosted their sense of belonging in the global advance of the charismatic movement. Paul Nwachukwu, one of the key actors in the revival, remembers that during his first meeting with Elton in the early 1970s, he (Elton) referred to the revival as the Latter Rain of God's Spirit.[68] Burgess corroborates this fact.[69]

After this wave of Pentecostalism swept over eastern Nigeria, resulting in resistance by the leadership of SU, many SU members who had embraced the revival formed groups which became parallel bodies to the SU township groups all over Igboland. These fellowships were usually led by the most zealous and charismatic leaders, and they encountered opposition from the SU because of the "Pentecostal emphasis and aggressive evangelistic style."[70] The members of these fellowships attended their respective local churches and only congregated for fellowship on specified meeting days—and the core activity of these groups was evangelism. Though SU as an organization was also committed to evangelism, it tended to restrict its evangelistic activities to its own groups and was reluctant to move beyond this boundary. Later, the Scripture Union, in its history, would accuse the pioneers of these fellowship groups as sheep stealers who jeopardized the work of the SU in their respective towns and cities: "As Scripture Union leadership tried to be 'mature' in handling the matter with the Pentecostals, one SU group after another was turned into a Pentecostal church. SU refused to protest, even when nearly the whole of SU in Umuahia was 'hijacked' . . . some left violently, but others . . . left quietly. In whatever form they left, they carted away SU members and used them to build their denominations."[71]

These Pentecostal groups were largely responsible for spreading the fires of Pentecostalism throughout eastern Nigeria. They comprised young and vibrant Christians who were ready to go to any length to get people saved, baptized in the Holy Ghost, healed, and delivered from all oppression. Over time, due to several factors,[72] most of these fellowship groups metamorphosed into full-fledged churches and parachurch organizations.

Some of the Pentecostal groups—churches and evangelistic associations—which emerged were Riches of Christ Mission, Master's Vessels Group, Holiness Evangelistic Association, and Christian Revivalist Missionary Team. Some other ministries which were at the forefront of the revival were founded independent of any links with the Scripture Union. Some of these were J. M. J. Emesim's Hour of Deliverance in Otuocha and Godson Ogbansiegbe's Christian Fellowship Group in Aba. Both the leaders of the independent Pentecostal groups (many of which went on to become full-fledged churches) which had their initial base in the SU and those of groups like Hour of Deliverance and Christian Fellowship Group were greatly influenced by Elton. Virtually every preacher that came out of the revival regarded Elton as a father. "He [Elton] is endearingly referred to as 'Pa Elton' by all those interviewed,"[73] wrote Ogbu Kalu, after listening to a wide range of reminiscences from the key leaders of the revival. Arthur Oriuzu (the Okafors' partner) recalls that virtually every preacher that was involved in the revival was connected to Elton: "He [frequently] travelled from Ilesa to [the] Eastern Region; he would get information and work with all the pastors. He distributed [resources] to every corner in Nigeria—tracts, salary, and gospel [literature]."[74]

Elton gradually became the backbone of the revival: theologically, spiritually, financially, and structurally. The movement was young; most of the leaders were in their early and mid-twenties; there were no clear structures; and Elton, like a midwife, stepped into the gap and guided the birthing process. Elton supported virtually every preacher who played a significant role in the emergence of the charismatic movement in eastern Nigeria.

Elton supported J. M. J. Emesim. Emesim, whom one scholar has referred to as the "Apostle of Pentecostalism in North West Igboland,"[75] founded the first major charismatic ministry in Igboland after the war—the Hour of Deliverance Ministry—which was established in Otuocha in October 1970. Jerry Anyaegbu, a scholar of Pentecostalism in Igboland, has noted, "Hour of Deliverance Ministry served as the forerunner of all the other Pentecostal/Evangelical churches or movements founded by the indigenes."[76] Emesim was initially based in Lagos, where he started his evangelistic ministry in 1968; he moved to the East in August 1970 with a team of evangelists to help in the spiritual restoration of the Igbos, an effort which he tagged "Spiritual Rehabilitation Programme." He became a mentor to many of those who became leaders in the revival through his Bible school, the Hour of Deliverance College of Evangelism.

Some of those who were trained there include[77] Benson Ezeokeke, one-time president of SU Onitsha, who founded Christ for All Mission in Onitsha in 1974; Obiorah Ezekiel, who founded the Christian Pentecostal Mission in Lagos in 1977; Chukwuedozie Mba, who co-founded Riches of Christ Mission in 1973; Wilson Uzumegbunam, who founded All Believers Fellowship Mission in Aba in 1978; Dominic Onuigwe, who co-founded National Evangelical Mission in Onitsha in 1975; Edward Ezenwafor, one of the leaders of the Grace of God Mission from the late 1970s; and Godwin Nnaji, who founded Revival Time Ministry in Enugu in 1980. These were some of the earliest and most influential indigenous charismatic churches in eastern Nigeria. (Even though some of these men only formalized their ministries as late as 1980, they had been actively involved in the revival from the early seventies.) Emesim was also a mentor to Paul Nwachukwu, Stephen Okafor, and scores of others.

As a student of Emesim's Bible school in the early seventies, Edward Ezenwafor also doubled as his driver. He recalls driving Emesim to Ilesa to see Elton at the end of every month: "We [usually] went to Ilesa every month end from Aguleri. Sometimes we would go to Lagos; while coming back from Lagos, we would branch in Ilesa to see Pa. And Pa would entertain us, give us some [books], mostly Lindsay books, Osborn books, and tracts of different titles. That was the first time I came to know him. As a young man by then and a student, most of the time I would stay in the car while he [Elton] was discussing with my principal [Emesim]."[78]

Elton supported Chukwuedozie Mba, Paul Nwachukwu, Augustine Nwodika, and Emeka Eze, the founders of the Riches of Christ Mission, the most successful of the indigenous Pentecostal churches in eastern Nigeria in the 1970s. (Riches of Christ Mission went through several transitions: it united with several other charismatic churches in eastern Nigeria in 1978 to become Jesus the Way Church. Later, it again experienced a division and was renamed Grace of God Mission; it is presently one of the largest charismatic churches in eastern Nigeria.[79])

Nwachukwu and Nwodika first met Elton on a visit to Ilesa in 1971. (At the peak of the revival, Raphael Okafor and Stephen Okafor consulted with Elton when they had an offer to study overseas. He counselled them that it was all right to get further education and helped them in securing visas.[80] It was at this point that Nwachukwu, who assumed responsibility for the Hour of Freedom work in Onitsha after the departure of the Okafors, and Nwodika travelled to Ilesa to see Elton.) Recalls Nwodika: "We (Paul Nwachukwu and I) visited him in Ilesa. We went there to visit him because we had been hearing about him and God had been using him mightily through his magazine in those days—*Herald of His Coming*—so we decided to see him face to face. When we got to Ilesa, he looked at us and said to us that the hand of the Lord was upon us. He just gave us a very powerful prophecy that God was with us, that people in the eastern side, this area, needed us badly, and that we should go to Bible school. Finally we took his advice and went to Benin, Church of God Mission Bible School; he was a lecturer there too. . . . He really wanted us to be in that school to see what was happening. Because in those days there was a great fire burning in Church of God Mission, a mighty move of God there, just like down here in the East."[81]

About a month into the Bible school programme, they felt God was calling them to return to the East. When they discussed the issue with Elton when he came around to teach at the Bible school, he told them to go and continue with their classes. But while speaking to the students that evening, he suddenly turned to them and said sharply, "Your people need you in the East."[82] That was the end of their Bible school programme. When they returned to Onitsha, they discussed with Mba and Eze, fellow SU Onitsha members, the idea of starting a church. Actually, Elton was the one who told Nwachukwu and Nwodika to go and start a church. "We were doing evangelistic work before; we told them we wanted to start a church; that we needed to have a base. Pa Elton told us that; he said we should start something."[83] The church started in Onitsha in 1973.

One of the most important marks Elton left on the formation of the charismatic movement in eastern Nigeria was his counsel to many of the Pentecostal evangelists who had formed evangelistic groups to plant churches in order to consolidate their work.[84] Elton warned that the movement would peter out if they didn't begin to plant churches. Richard Burgess corroborates the fact that Elton was the one who "initially introduced the church-planting concept in the East."[85] The church planting factor which Elton introduced into the equation was a turning point in the development of the charismatic movement in eastern Nigeria from the early seventies. As Matthews Ojo confirms: "The church planting concept promoted by Elton . . . changed the nature of the emerging Charismatic movements. Since most of the new churches planted were independent, this pattern soon became the norm for the rising Charismatic organisations. Hence, from the mid-1970s, many of the Charismatic organisations established by graduates and non-graduates adopted [a] similar independent and denominational character."[86]

"We went to Ilesa frequently because it [the revival] was a new thing, and we didn't know anything," says Nwodika. "Bible school did not teach us how to run a church, but Pa Elton kept on telling us about the church, about what to do; he was encouraging us, he was always coming [around]. He would travel from Ilesa to Onitsha to encourage us. That man was a prophet; he did a great work in our lives. He told us how to stand, how to fight the battle. He told us the road was narrow, that it was tough, hard, but that we should endure. He was just fortifying us as soldiers. . . . He taught us a lot and really trained us; then he helped us to stand, because that time it was not easy to preach the gospel; it was a confrontation between us and the Roman Catholic and Anglican, you know, in those days. We were almost the first indigenous Pentecostal church down here, and it was not easy, but thank God for that man; he was with us."[87]

Elton travelled to see the leaders of the Riches of Christ about thrice yearly, but they visited Ilesa more often, depending "on whatever came up." "If anything came up, we would travel. There was a time we had a quarrel—a big problem in the early seventies—and we went to him, and he told us such problems were not new in revival. Sometimes we had misunderstandings, but he kept on telling us, 'Don't hate yourselves; whatever you are going to do, no matter what they have done to you, don't hate. Learn to forgive and forgive early.' Those words were so strong in those days. . . . So we learnt from him how to forgive, how to tolerate, how to give. He really helped us to stand like good soldiers. In fact, that man made us into what we are today. . . . We strongly believed in him and he strongly believed in us. He would look at us and say, 'You are the one to carry this gospel.' When Riches of Christ was formed, he was there; we went to him, and he told us exactly what would happen. He called us and gave every one of us a specific prophecy; and all he said came to pass."[88]

Once, after giving Nwodika one of his notebooks, Elton told him, "Talk about the kingdom. Talk about the king." "If he [Elton] wanted to tease you, he would say, 'Talk about JC,' that is, Jesus Christ. Pa had a great honour and respect for Christ, and he imparted that to us. He really imparted to us the truth that there is nothing of this world that means anything. Papa would tell you there is nothing here. Pa would tell you how he left England and came down here. He left his job; Papa was working there and then God called him; he left it and lived down there at Ilesa. When he lived there, there was no house around that place. He talked about sacrifice, and he talked more about the reward; [that] after all is said and done, the best thing you want to hear from the Lord is 'Well done, my faithful servant.' . . . Papa was somebody that would tell you the Scripture as it is, not bending it to please you. Papa would preach and people would cry. . . . Papa warned us about what is happening now. About the false doctrines that would come up. He said, 'They will come out from your midst, from among you.' He said, 'You should be very careful.' He really warned about all these doctrines that are coming up. We honour that man; that man is our dad; he is our father."[89]

Elton loved the leaders of the Riches of Christ with all his heart, and he supported them with everything he had till he died. Edward Ezenwafor, who became one of the leaders of the ministry after it had metamorphosed into Grace of God Mission in the late seventies, recalls that he [Elton] was always "advising us and encouraging us, teaching us. I mean, what a father can be to a son—physically, spiritually and all—that was what he was to us. He *marketed* us in this country. Because the highest thing you can do for any preacher is to [give him a platform]. . . . He would tell us to go and plan a meeting in a place and say, 'I'm coming.' Our part was to plan, then invite him and take him around. He had meetings—Maiduguri, Kano, Kaduna. Sometimes he would open the meeting and sit down—we would be ministering; he would open the meeting and watch us minister."[90]

Elton was excited about their radical pursuit of God; he was deeply enthralled by the fact that they were willing to go all the way to see a release of the power of God in their day; he was moved by their determination in the face of great opposition. He loved the fact that they were non-conformists and took great pleasure in calling them rebels. "He called us rebels," recalls Ezenwafor. "One day, Nwodika asked him, 'Pa, why are you calling us rebels?' He replied, 'Don't you know that you guys are rebels against the devil?' He once asked us, 'Do you know why I move with the youths?' He said, 'The Holy Spirit. Remember that the Spirit will be poured upon the youths. I tap the anointing from you guys, and I give you people experience. You get from me; I get from you.' He was a good dad. He believed there was something you had [to offer]."[91]

Elton completely opened his heart—there were almost no inhibitions in his relationship with them. Except that he was white and noticeably elderly, he could have been mistaken for just one of their buddies. Ezenwafor fondly recalls a time when they had just finished a meeting at Onitsha and were on their way to another appointment. They were all huddled in the same car with Elton, and because the car was small, Elton offered to carry his wife on his lap (Hannah was in her eighties by this time!) so that there would be enough space. After she sat on his lap, to make light of the situation, Elton winked at them and said, "You are jealous of me?"[92] They all burst into laughter.

So much time and energy did Elton devote to mentoring the Riches of Christ leaders that at some point, fearing for his age and health, Ruth Elton complained that they were making her father overwork himself. As Ezenwafor recalls, "Ruth said we [were] dragging her father. I said, 'We are not the ones dragging your father; he is the one dragging us.' He dragged us everywhere, but somebody by the side would think we were the ones dragging him."[93]

Elton supported Tony Okeke, who co-founded Save the Lost Programme in Nnewi in 1971. Okeke first met Elton in 1972—even though he had known about him for a while—through correspondence with the publisher of a tract that was produced in England. After reading the tract, published by J. C. Hawkins, he became interested and wrote to him to order more copies for evangelistic outreaches. Hawkins wrote back to inform him that Elton was now responsible for printing the tract in Nigeria, and that he should contact him. "It was a very simple tract. I have forgotten the title, I think [it was] *Jesus Saves*," Okeke recollects. "I had no money on me. It was just two years after the civil war, and so I went to pray and said, 'God, well, I have received this letter from England to go to Pa Elton. I don't know him [personally], so what do I do?' I began praying, and I had only two shillings in my pocket. So I kept praying, and at a point, God said, 'Get up from there and go to Ilesa.' So I got up from my praying position and went down to Onitsha, and at Onitsha somebody gave me four shillings; I added the four shillings to the two shillings I had and took a vehicle to Agbor. I came down at Agbor and then took a loan of one pound that would take me to Ilesa. So I went to Ilesa with one pound."[94]

When he finally arrived in Ilesa, late in the night, Elton welcomed him and asked if he knew Stephen Okafor and Raphael Okafor; he then arranged a place for him to rest that night. When Okeke presented the letter from J. C. Hawkins the next day, "[Elton] just looked at me and looked at me. He asked me some questions which I answered. He said, 'Okay Tony, let me pray with you.' So he laid his hands on me and prayed for me, and then he wrote certain things on the paper and directed me to the warehouse. Instead of just getting tracts, he gave me a whole bunch of Gordon Lindsay's books; they were thirteen in the series. So it was not [just] a tracts thing. I got a whole bunch of books, and when I took it to his office, he prayed for me again and gave me five pounds. Five pounds in 1972! [This was] a journey I began with two shillings, and he said that I should regularly bring him reports of my activities. So that was it. From that time he began supporting me."

"He gave us the money to buy bicycles for some of the pastors that were working with me," recounts Okeke. "So from then on, every month end, I would go to Ilesa to receive sometimes three pounds, five pounds, seven pounds, to buy bicycles, and that was it for many years. I can't remember how many bicycles, but he sponsored bicycles, Bibles, books. In fact, at a point when T. L. Osborn finally came around in 1974 . . . he began giving me thousands of T. L. Osborn's books." When Elton gave Okeke Lindsay's books in 1972, he told him, "Tony, I am giving these books to you free of charge, but you can sell them, one for a shilling, and use the proceeds to support what you are doing." Okeke recalls:

This was apart from his own personal help. So I was selling these books one for a shilling, and it was fantastic. I can't finish telling Pa Elton's story. So every month's end, I travelled down to Ilesa, and after discussing with him, he would give me materials—Osborn's, Gordon Lindsay's books, magazines, *Herald of the Last Days* by their thousands—because he came to believe in me. He said I was doing a genuine work, so he gave me every support and every encouragement.

And, the other side of it was that, each time I was about to go, his wife would just come out of their room. She was old at that time, and she would say, "Tony, are you going now?" She would just be trembling and . . . she would say, "Kneel down, let me pray with you." So I would kneel down and she would . . . put her hands on my head and say, "Oh God . . . help this young man; direct him. God, keep him in Jesus' name." Each time I received their blessing, and it continued like that for many years, even into the eighties.

I got lingua tapes from him and horn speakers, then film projectors and films, the list goes on and on. . . . But in those early years most of us were dependent on him, not only for the financial support or moral support but because of his counsel. He imparted his life in me, and I will never ever regret [it]. Pa Elton is in heaven, but he is also here with us, and I have a part of him in me. And God used him to raise so many people in this country; we are all witnesses to it if we want to say the fact as it is.[95]

TWELVE

THE ENROLMENT OFFICE

On Friday, July 21, 1978, an unusual meeting was held at the Modakeke High School, Ile-Ife. It was the final day of a weeklong conference called by Elton for students in institutions of higher learning throughout western Nigeria.[1] He travelled from Ilesa to Ile-Ife daily to speak at the conference, which witnessed a very large turnout of students. At a point during the conference, he told his audience that he did not know how long he had before the Lord would call him home; therefore he wanted to pass the burden to the next generation.[2]

Speaking to the students on one of the days, he said, "May I remind you of what I said about Friday morning, and the old man holding the baby; he is going to pass it on to you on Friday morning—the vision. I am going to pass the vision on to you on Friday morning, and then I have done my job. I have done my job. But I am persuaded that my function and my work in this country have been in these last days, to bring you what I am bringing you this week. And when I finish that, amen, Lord. I hope to see it brought into being; I hope to see it come to pass. But I think I would have done my job—I think I would have passed it on. I hope to be spared many more years to tell it to many, many more, but if it's not so, it's enough here to-day to turn Nigeria upside down."[3]

He continued, "From Friday morning, you will cease to regard yourself [just] as a church member; that will be no glory in the future; [but you will begin to see yourself as] a warrior, a fighter . . . [with the] responsibility to carry a government in Nigeria. They are busy forming political parties in

Nigeria now. We are not going to form a political party, but on Friday morning, a new army will step out. That's what it means, carrying a responsibility, and the responsibility is what? Nigeria—to put it right."[4] "I want to put my hands on your hands . . . on that bow and arrow, and I want to say, 'Shoot and keep on shooting, don't stop' ", said Elton. "Don't stop. Go on and on and on and on, until it comes to pass. . . . I am passing on the vision; make quite sure you get it. . . . God will be here on Friday morning, and He wants to make a covenant with you."[5]

At the Friday meeting, he told the students that he had waited for twenty-five years for God to raise their generation and that he was there handing over the baton to them. Gbile Akanni, renowned Bible teacher and revivalist, who as a student of the University of Ibadan at the time attended the meetings, still had vivid recollections many years later of Elton speaking during that week: "[He] came and said, 'I have carried a burden for the past twenty-five years. I have been holding this burden in trust, waiting that there will be [young] men and young women whom I could lay it on before I die.' . . . On the final day, he said, 'Now, I have been speaking to you for five days; I am about to release [something] that will change your destinies. . . . All of you who have listened to me from Monday to Friday, and you are convinced you should carry this for your nation and for your generation. I will stand here, don't close your eyes; if you are sure about this, come out. If you are not sure, please sit down; don't come here.' "[6]

Akanni recalls, "I remember we were all filing out, trembling, trembling, trembling, and when we all filed out, he stood there, lifted his hands, [and] said, 'Father, like Simeon of old, I have carried this for these years; I have been waiting on you that you will give me men unto whom I could release this.' He said, 'This thing will change your lives; it will change your destinies; it will send some of you out of your base; it will locate you where you don't want to go; but I have carried it for twenty-five years, and I am convinced that there are men here whom I should lay it on.' Something that you cannot recover from fell on our lives. And he said, 'I may never see some of you again. . . . All I want to charge you is, do not disappoint God, and do not disappoint me his servant. I carried this in trust until you came. . . . Make sure it does not fail in your hands. God be with you.' And he finished and he walked away."[7] Many consider that meeting to be the single most powerful spiritual transaction Elton had with their generation.[8]

Reporting exultantly, the Christian Students' Social Movement (CSSM)—the group Elton had charged with organizing the conference—wrote in its newsletter:

Halleluiah! GOD, the Almighty God, the Infinite God, came down by the Holy Spirit into the midst of His people and did the things that were UNPRECEDENTED in this country ever. It was a week for which the man of God [Elton] had waited for 25 years to see.

It was the week when the changing of guards took place (a very serious matter.) The man of God FINISHED his work as far as NIGERIAN YOUTHS and UNIVERSITIES are concerned.

It was the week when the burden fell on the shoulders of NIGERIAN young men and women.

It was the week when God spoke by prophecy among other things: "My children, I have laid my cross on you, carry it. I have laid my cross on you, carry it."

It was the week when God gave us the Battle Cry of the Vision—"THE LORD REIGNETH," Psalm 97:1.

It was the week when the plan and strategy for the Battle for NIGERIA was explained from JOSHUA 6 and other Bible passages.

It was the week when the vision was restated.

The man of God requested prayer on the final day for himself and his wife that God would grant them life to see the vision . . . fulfilled.

As the prayer was about to be made, the Lord moving in a way never before experienced in the country in the same dimension spoke by the Holy Ghost through prophecy: "The two of you shall see the fruit of your work . . ."

The Lord specifically instructed us to pray for their daughter (which was done) and for the health of the wife.

It was the high point of a ministry that has lasted over 40 years.

It is significant that at the changeover point in this "relay race" to bring this vision to pass, the Lord began by telling the youths who are now doing the anchor leg: ". . . behold, I have set before thee an open door, AND NO MAN CAN SHUT IT . . ." (Rev. 3:8).

A message which the Lord has given over 40 years ago in WALES when He was speaking to the men who were coming to Nigeria with the gospel . . . and God added (that OUR HANDS) shall also finish it! Amen.[9]

The Modakeke meeting was the climax of many years of labour among Christian students in Nigeria's universities and colleges. When the door of ministry to the university campuses was first opened to Elton in the mid-sixties, his mission was clear: to raise an army of believers who would champion the plan and purpose of God for the last days, and who would take the responsibility for the prophetic destiny of their nation. He was arguably at his prophetic best when he early discerned the strategic role of the generation of students that were on the university campuses in the sixties and seventies in the execution of God's plan for Nigeria and decided to devote the rest of his life to mentoring them.

Elton moved into the universities at a most opportune time. The evangelical revival which had begun in the sixties was enjoying its finest hour. Hundreds of undergraduates were getting converted and catching the fire. They had come in contact with a profound revelation of Jesus Christ and were willing to put their lives at stake for it. It was common for many of them to stay back when a semester was over to seek God for His plan for their lives. There was a deep and widespread hunger on the campuses—an entire generation was on fire. One researcher has remarked that "through the work of the Scripture Union, SU, the Fellowship of Christian Students, FCS, the Nigerian Fellowship of Evangelical students, NIFES, and other students groups, there were stirrings in the Nigerian colleges and university campuses in the '70s which led to spiritual renewal among students. The love for the Lord and passion for souls that became evident among the students at that time is unprecedented in the history of the Nigerian Church's involvement in soul winning and has not been since that time."[10] Elton himself noted that "there is a move of the Holy Spirit among the young people in Nigeria . . . and can be indeed called a Jesus revolution."[11] He fully recognized the genuineness of this fire and the weightiness of the opportunity it presented; but he also knew they needed something extra—vision and direction. He declared that "the present move of the Holy Spirit, particularly among the young people, is not merely to get men and women converted, but also to train and prepare the Lord's Army for the coming contest."[12]

Elton had clearly mapped out a strategy for the schools from about the mid-sixties. In a letter to Gordon Lindsay in 1968, he discussed this plan: "We are also making every effort to reach the educated. It is amazing what steps and advances have been made in the last few years in education in this country. Nearly all the children over the age of 6 years go to school free, and most of them go on to higher schooling."[13] He continued, "There are now five universities in the country and these places are hotbeds for unrest and communism. So we made a plan of campaign last year to deal with these places of challenge. We felt that we must attack them and we did."

He went on: "One of our specially trained Nigerians—himself a graduate—took upon himself the task of starting special Christian witness classes in all these universities and of taking upon himself the task of giving them good literature and films, and all the sound books he could find. He also compiled a list of the elementary schools where English is spoken, and we sent a packet of magazines, tracts, and sample books to the headmasters. . . . It has proved a very profitable work, and there are groups of keen born again Christians gathering regularly in each of the universities for prayer and study and work among other undergraduates. . . . We feel that every possible effort must be made to reach these educated people and then they can influence others."[14]

In the early 1970s, he wrote, "The Lord will bring every dedicated recruit in touch with those he can deliver, if we are really determined to fight and deliver the captives of Satan. We are also sure that the Lord has His own representatives in every town and these are the men whom He will use, to advise . . . train . . . and direct the young people who are eager for service and battle experience. There are large numbers of student Christian groups in schools and colleges and the leaders of these groups should carefully consider their objectives for these young people. God desires they shall become fighters and active Christian workers. We are willing to send supplies of HERALD OF THE LAST DAYS for the training of such groups. Let us have the names, addresses, and details of such groups and we will gladly send lessons and magazines. It is our intention to publish instruction on the Baptism in the Holy Spirit and speaking in tongues in the next issues. Other articles on Healing and Demon possession and deliverance will follow, so that students can be trained for the future tasks."[15]

In an April 1973 letter to the publishers of *Herald of His Coming*, he again expressed his passion for students: "I shall be writing you after my return from a week's visit to the University of Ibadan where there are some good groups of the Lord's people, and some 500 students who are keen Christians. It is a privilege to be here at this time!"[16] Freda Lindsay reported in January 1975, "He [S. G. Elton] told us, 'God is on the move, especially among the educated young people. Many are forming active witnessing teams and Gordon Lindsay's books are in great demand among these groups to train young men and women in the Gospel.' "[17]

Elton envisioned a spiritual army of young Nigerian Christians that would boldly march through the nation, establishing God's government wherever they went. Battling not a few conservative forces on his way, he stopped at nothing to ensure that a generation clearly understood their place in God's plan and had the courage to pursue it. Beginning in the late 1960s, he embarked on an ambitious project of training the next generation; he sought them out wherever they could be found, especially in universities and colleges, and encouraged them with every resource at his disposal to lay hold of their destiny in God. This resulted in a massive spiritual shift that defined Christianity among young people in the sixties, seventies and eighties, and this later played a significant role in equipping a generation of Nigerian youth for the Christian ministry as church leaders and missionaries. Elton was a father, an apostle, to that generation.

Elton's ministry to the students reflects Bill Johnson's excellent description of the character of a true apostle: "Apostles are first and foremost fathers by nature. True fathers continually make choices for the wellbeing of their children with little thought to personal sacrifice. They are not jealous when their children succeed, but instead are overjoyed because of those successes. It is normal for a father to desire his children to surpass him in every way. Brothers compete, fathers do not. . . . The word coming from apostles is to bring clarification of the Father's focus for the church, and in turn strengthen our resolve to His purposes. . . . Apostles carry a blueprint in their hearts concerning the church and God's purposes on the earth. They are used to bring fresh revelation to the church."[18] One defining character of Elton's ministry, as one close protégé put it, "was a radical preparation of [young] Nigerians in a kind of parental way."[19] Elton was jealous over that generation in a way that is best captured by apostle Paul's words to the Corinthian church: "For I am jealous for you with a godly jealousy; for I betrothed you to one husband, so that to Christ I might present you *as* a pure virgin" (2 Corinthians11:2). Ogbu Kalu succinctly stated, "Elton lived as an apostle who discerned the new Christian temper of the nation and chose to rear these young firebrands."[20]

By the time Elton began mingling with students, he was already in his sixties. Many of the students, who were in their early and mid-twenties, were surprised that a man of his age and spiritual stature (having been used mightily for decades in making an impact on the church in Nigeria) would come to their level. "He was older than many of our grandfathers,"[21] one student would, years later, jokingly refer to the image their young minds had of the elderly Elton. Many were shocked at how "Pa Elton" believed in them and what God would do through them. He completely identified with that generation; he had a deep and genuine concern for them. He wrote, "It is clear that the Lord Jesus is seeking young men and women who are ready to serve Him and put Him first in their lives at any cost. It would seem also that the Lord is gathering this 'force' outside the organised churches, although many young people are still inside the churches. It is regretted that the churches are unaware of this call to battle and they are out of touch with the desires of the young to dedicate themselves to the Lord's service in this country today."[22] Here, he was clearly speaking as an advocate for the emerging generation.

Elton stayed very much in touch with the spiritual life on the campuses; he could usually tell what was going on with the fellowships. For instance, in 1980 he mourned the low spirituality that had set in at the Wesley Guild Hospital in Ilesa and in other institutions: "UCH is in a bad way . . . spiritually . . . likewise Unife."[23] But he had good words for some others: "But Uniben . . . ABU . . . Ibadan . . . Luth and Unilag are good."[24] In 1981 he wrote, "I was in LUTH 2 weeks ago . . . and they had a great time . . . 10 finalists [graduating students] and a good spiritual group there now."[25]

Elton never forced himself upon campus Christian groups—it is notable that he mostly never put together any meetings by himself. He patiently waited until he was invited, and then he created unforgettable experiences with those opportunities. After a while, it was clear to many of the Christian students that Elton was different from many of their other regular speakers. He had answers to their questions and had the spiritual capacity to equip them. He was, therefore, informally adopted as a spiritual father by many groups. Elton just seemed able to raise the students' spiritual vision like few others could.

He made them realize that they were responsible for the next phase of Nigeria's spiritual advance. "God is moving and calling out those whom He can trust to carry this revival . . . and most of those whom He is calling are laymen . . . and young people. Laymen will write the last victorious chapter of the church's history in Nigeria, in an outburst of surrender, dedication, and personal evangelism," were Elton's words in the twelfth issue of *Herald of the Last Days*, which was "dedicated to the young people of Nigeria who are stirred and excited by the prospect of tasting the wonderful life of a Christian; of realising the wonders of the New Birth and fullness of the Holy Spirit and of service of the Lord Jesus, in these wonderful but crisis days."[26]

Elton wrote, "There is a new move of the Holy Spirit among the young people in Nigeria and West Africa. It would seem that the Holy Spirit is deliberately choosing the young people of Nigeria to use them in these last days. There are hundreds of Christians in all the universities and colleges in Nigeria and they will increase in number and also in their understanding of the Bible and the Spirit in these last days. There are also a growing number of young people forming teams to evangelise their own communities and this is God on the move. What the churches have failed to do, God the Holy Spirit will accomplish through the Youth."[27]

Elton's prophetic message captured the heart of an entire generation. He remarked that it took both courage and a major paradigm shift to see and identify with the move of God among the youth: "Today in Nigeria, God is gathering an army and that I am sure of. What puzzles me and shakes me is that I go into groups and I look around and say, 'Lord, you mean to tell me that this is your army? Couldn't you find a better crew than this?' No! No! The big people are over there; and the big people are in the *head* and *shoulders* set up. There is an army, a company of young people, yet untried, ungoverned by tradition, willing to let customs go, willing to step out in a new way and with a vision to step forward. That's the army. We're not looking for clever men, we're not looking for big men, we are not looking for big names; we're looking for dedication, we're looking for people who will stand together with a vision. That's what God is looking for and the anointing will come on [them] to fight; to fight!"[28]

And also: "We are on active service . . . and our life business is WAR. We are in a spiritual warfare and Satan, the enemy, and his evil spirits are seeking to destroy our faith and prevent his slaves and captives being freed. . . . We cannot be independent in this battle; our strength lies in our unity. We need the encouragement, prayers and strengthening of all fighters to stand with us. We call upon ALL Christians, especially the young, no matter what their church may be, to join hands against the common enemy. There will be no armistice . . . and no peace treaty in this life. We at Herald of the Last Days are an enrolment centre. We are enlisting soldiers and warriors for the Lord from every state in Nigeria."[29]

After a profound encounter at a meeting where Elton preached (around

1977 at the University of Ibadan), Kole Akinboboye invited him to speak at the Christian fellowship at the Lagos University Teaching Hospital when he became president. "Those days, we had what we called 'Weekend of Deeper Teachings,' " recalls Akinboboye, "weekends that we dedicated for hearing things that ordinarily we would not hear at [the regular meetings]. He came for that programme; it was awesome; that was the beginning of the bonding."[30] "He was talking about things that I had not heard before; he wasn't speaking ABCs; he was talking kingdom things. . . . He spoke deep things and encouraged us to prepare ourselves to be vehicles for national transformation. To a large extent he brought relevance to Christianity. Christianity left the purview of the mundane or just trying to be religious."[31]

Okey Onuzo, a medical student at the University of Ibadan in the early seventies, remembers how one of Elton's teachings led to a turning point in his spiritual commitment. Elton was scheduled to preach at the Chapel of Resurrection by 7:00 p.m., but he invited "those who want to go deeper" to a meeting at 3:00 p.m. Onuzo was present at this "odd-hour" meeting, as the students called it. "When I became a Christian . . . they used to ask us to pray a total commitment to Christ. I didn't usually pray those prayers because I thought to myself that if you make a total commitment that means you have lost control. So Pastor Elton came one day. . . . And without knowing that I had that dilemma, Pastor Elton said, 'Young man,' and he wasn't talking to me in particular, 'let me tell you, you can never be better than God can make you.' That changed my life. So I made a total commitment, because I reasoned that if you cannot be better, you might as well just give your life to Him."[32] Either at Chapel of Resurrection or Trenchard Hall or at the Chemistry laboratory, Elton's teachings "made the Bible come alive," says Onuzo. He particularly remembers Elton speaking "about the tragedy of missed opportunities. That the human witnesses—Peter, James, and John—of the great conference [on the Mount of Transfiguration] between the law, the prophets, and grace, slept through it; it was very memorable."[33]

Steve Olumuyiwa remembers visiting the University of Ife in 1973, where he witnessed a heightened level of student Christian activity: "There were several groups of students praying, others witnessing, and still others organizing one meeting or the other. There was a beehive of spiritual activity; and the person behind it all was Pastor Elton."[34]

"We used to invite him over to speak in the campus chapel. At the time, there were few people who one could really seriously look up to, and he was elderly, and he was very knowledgeable in [the] Scriptures," recalls Peter Ozodo, who gained admission into the University of Ife in 1969, and became the president of the Evangelical Christian Union in 1971. "His ministry really was apostolic. He saw himself as an instrument that God had sent to bring Nigeria and particularly young Nigerians to the fore of ministry. And he was doing that with a very clear knowledge of not only the past of the evangelical movement in Nigeria, but the then present, and what struck me as unique was his way of pointing to the future of what was going to happen, which is what we are now living out in very clear terms. Pastor Elton was one of the first people I heard mobilizing for missions in the context of going to the world, the whole world, and insisting that Nigerians were called of God in a very special way to take the gospel to the whole world. . . . Those were the things he was saying, and they looked like just the ranting of an old man then. But having lived through it as a person, you see that the man was very prophetic."[35] Something else that struck Ozodo about Elton was "his gravitation towards young people, though he was old. You know . . . broadening his scope to accommodate young people, first in the universities, but not limited to the universities, because he embraced the young people coming out of the war in the East in Nigeria and was very instrumental to many of them being established in ministry; that was the second thing; that was very, very powerful about S. G. Elton."[36]

As a student of the University of Lagos in the late seventies, Francis Wale Oke recalls that "Pastor S. G. Elton affected my life through his personal counselling. I used to be with him regularly for personal counselling and discussion after I had known him; and his counsels were profound. He also affected me through his incisive teachings. He had a deep insight into the Word of God. His teachings were revolutionary at the time. He affected me through the prophetic grace upon his life. He prophesied so many things that looked and sounded weird in those days. For example, he prophesied that the move of God would be so strong in Nigeria there won't be enough church buildings to take the crowd. He prophesied that God [was] going to use Nigerians to spread the gospel all over the world. . . . In the seventies, it took only a prophet of the Lord to know these things. . . . Pastor Elton was very simple in his lifestyle. He was accessible. He loved to draw the younger generation to him and impart grace to them, though he was then over 70. He had a spiritual depth that is very rare. He truly walked with God. . . . His teachings were provocative and confrontational to traditional Christianity."[37]

Ikechukwu Utah, who met Elton in 1973 as an ECU member, recalls that "Pa Elton was an inspiration; his presentation of the gospel was prophetic; he believed he was preparing us for the future. He always foresaw a move of God in Nigeria and the need for mature men and women of God who would be able to manage what God was intending to do; so he was very passionate about it. His popular saying was that he would pray for revival, but that we were not ready if God would send revival. In other words, the people to manage the revival were not available. Therefore his focus in ministering to us was to raise men and women of God who would be used of God to impact the nation; [people] on whom God would place the responsibility of his move in Nigeria. . . . He saw the move of God in the campuses in the seventies as a prelude to a higher thing that God was intending to do."[38]

Niyi Beecroft, also an ECU member in the early seventies, remembers Elton's influence this way: "Our background then was purely evangelical, but here came this man who brought the prophetic spirit. He spoke often about the kingdom of God. He had a very clear vision about God's kingdom. What he had in mind was a Nigerian nation in which God's children . . . would make the fruits of the kingdom manifest in their work. His vision was of us going out [and] becoming professionals who were affecting our world. He preferred that most of us would remain . . . in our profession, which would give us a reach throughout the rank and file of the country. We would hold positions in which we would be affecting people. That was to him the vision of the kingdom; and it was a vision he espoused so much. [He believed] God's kingdom—heaven being brought to bear on earth—would happen as Christians arose, bearing the true testimonies [of the kingdom] in their various engagements in life. His emphasis was that the kingdom is here within us. He kept saying that again and again."[39]

Bunmi Oni, an ECU member in the early 1970s, recalls: "On one occasion I remember, we were desperate . . . there were a lot of pungent things happening in the [Evangelical] Christian Union. One of the things was that quite a few of the members failed their exams, and so we went to God and said, 'This cannot be, this is not the type of testimony [we should have],' and so on and so forth. It was a new thing for us at the time, and so we thought, maybe we didn't have enough faith. What was the problem? So the executives decided to go and see Pa Elton. We said, 'We want to increase our faith.'... And he would just sit down, the wise old man, [and say] 'What do you want?' We told him all of our stories and that, bottom line, 'How do we increase our faith?' He took one look at us and said, 'You don't know what you are asking for.' We said, 'What's wrong with this man? We want faith.' And he said, 'If I am going to pray for you for faith, then I am going to pray that God should send you trouble.' So we said, 'Wait, wait, wait.' He took us through to say, 'You know, if you want to increase your faith, your faith cannot be increased until it is tested; until you come into a situation that will demand faith and a situation that will demand faith has got to be an unusual kind of situation; it's got to be different, something that challenges you, something that you don't even like.' So he said again, 'Do you want to increase your faith?' I don't remember what our response was ... we hesitated; but bottom-line was that we left the place ... even more enamoured by the personality of this man."[40]

Joseph Olanrewaju, a president of IVCU in the late seventies, recounting the activities of the fellowship during his stay in the university, notes that "we also had additional weekend conferences sometimes coinciding with the commissioning of the IVCU executives. These special weekend conferences were always reserved for Pa Elton, the man of God from the UK who literally fathered us in the faith. Pa Elton performed all the commissioning of our executives every year, and we often travelled to his house in Ilesa for him to minister to us, pray for us, inspire us, or teach us prophetically. He was the one who gave me my first complete copy of 'Audio Bible Cassette,' containing the KJV [Bible]—Genesis to Revelation.... He was our father in the faith here below, who ministered to us without looking for any reward from man."[41]

Monica Jegede, two-time vice president of IVCU in the early eighties, also recalls, "[Pa Elton's] ministry work made a great impact on our campus ministry and even Pentecostalism nationwide. His coming to the fellowship was like Jesus appearing. His ministrations were always refreshing. He carried sincerity and authority. I later learnt he did not take money from us. He also paid for his own accommodation."[42]

Elton was always concerned about who would become the next president of the campus fellowships, of which there were then two or three on each campus. When a new fellowship president was chosen, he would be taken to meet Elton in Ilesa. He would pray and lay hands on the person and make the fellow see the import of what he had been called to do. "Whenever they were going to choose a new executive, either in IVCU or

LVCU, Pa Elton was the one who did the dedication service. He would usually have some input. [He did not] force it, but he would have some input, some influence, some advice for whoever was going to be chosen as president, because many of the truths that Pa Elton was bringing into the church . . . some of the new truths that were going to break away the shackles of legalism, of lack of revelation knowledge, [and bring the revelation of] the things of the Spirit, had to be channelled and championed by leaders who had the same vision."[43]

Fred Adegoke, president of IVCU in the 1980/81 set, recalls: "We used to have commissioning services—when a new executive was handing over to another set, we would commission them, and then our final-year graduates, every year we commissioned them and sent them forth—and traditionally it was Pastor Elton that came to minister and everybody was looking forward to Pastor Elton laying hands on you and commissioning you. You were in your final year, getting ready to leave the campus, and it was a very solemn and powerful service for us every year when the graduates were prayed for, and he usually brought a very powerful message about what God was doing, the army that God was raising, a new generation; and people would break down, and he would minister to every person personally. [He would] lay hands on us, lay hands on our hands, and commission us; he would commission the new executive and commission the [graduating students], sending them to the world—the commissioning service was Pastor Elton or nobody else. He would usually come for that. He taught us that leadership is actually service and used to make fun of the fact that the executives were called 'executive members'—that it shouldn't be 'executives,' it should be 'servants.' He used to make fun of that. He really had a tremendous impact. He was close to us. Each time he came, he checked into the guest house by himself; he wouldn't even let us pay; he wouldn't let us. . . . He never asked for [an] honorarium."[44]

Tunde Ajala, another president of IVCU in the mid-eighties, recalls, "He was very prominent in establishing the message of the Holy Spirit and His gifts in the church. At that that time, the message was so new and a lot of the young people in the campuses were excited about the message, so they always invited Pa Elton to the campus. We would always go to him—[all the] executives—about forty to fifty of us—and he would take us in and share with us. His wife was also always ready to serve us plantain and other refreshments. And as old as he was, anytime we were fasting, he would also fast along with us. There was a prophetic seminar that he usually organized at Camp Young [Ede] for all prayer secretaries and leaders from all campuses. They would gather at Camp Young and that weekend would be like being raptured into the very presence of God because of the level of impartation and the exposition of the word of God."[45]

Elton persistently and fervently preached that God was about to release an army of young men and women who would plant the gospel all over Nigeria, and in Europe and America, and he wanted them to be prepared, first by believing it, and then by receiving adequate training. "I was talking . . . two weeks ago . . . to about four thousand students and graduates. Those students held hands together—four thousand, one great crowd—and they said to Satan, 'Jesus Christ is Lord in Nigeria,' and we are one with Him,"[46] he remarked while preaching in August 1980.

Elton made it clear that the responsibility for Nigeria's missionary enterprise had passed on to Nigerians: "In the past, it was the overseas missionary societies who found both the personnel and the money to evangelise Nigeria and we are reaping today what they sowed. We are grateful for their sacrifice in bringing us the wonderful Gospel. But that is now changing, 'the day of the white missionary is finished.' God is changing that pattern and He is now putting the responsibility for taking that same gospel to the lost in our own country (as the 'white' missionaries brought it to us) on the heads of every Nigerian Christian of every denomination. In accepting the blessings of salvation, we made ourselves debtors to all men too. . . . We have acquired National Independence. We are attaining economic independence. We must also assume the spiritual responsibility for taking the Gospel to our own people."[47] He challenged the church in Nigeria in the early seventies:

> The vast areas of unreached souls in Nigeria today present us with a challenge to our faith, courage, and resources. This is a priceless treasure; . . . the souls of millions of Nigerians. The responsibility to invade these areas and possess this treasure demands unselfishness and sacrificial faith and devotion from us all. No single Nigerian Christian is excused . . .
>
> Yet it seems that such men are not in Nigeria! Can it be that Nigerian Christians are not willing to dedicate themselves in sacrificial devotion to the same extent as the missionaries who brought the Gospel to this land? Can it be that Nigerian Christians place a greater value on comfort, position, and money

than on the souls of the heathen? Reports are coming in from many parts of Nigeria where there are hundreds of villages and districts where the inhabitants have never heard of a man called Jesus. . . .

The church stands by in impotence. . . . Is it any wonder then that the Lord is turning to untrained men and women of faith who have learned of the miracle-working power of the Gospel and who know what the heathen need? God is raising up today, in Nigeria, groups of young men and women who are daring to take God at His word and step out in faith to move the Gospel and demonstrate to the heathen that the Gospel is still "the power of God unto salvation to everyone who believeth."[48]

Convinced that the future of God's plan for Nigeria rested with the youth, he prayed, "WE KNOW that it is the Lord's will for revival to cover the whole country. THEREFORE we claim a stirring in the hearts and lives of many young people now turning to the Lord."[49] Whenever Elton preached on the university campuses, the training of this generation was uppermost in his mind—the need to thoroughly equip them for service, especially after their university days.

He would encourage graduating students to be strong, as they would face greater challenges than they had ever experienced. During one year in the early seventies, he wrote concerning "many students, who are completing their studies this year" who had "surrendered themselves for the work of God and hands were laid on them, as hands were laid upon Paul and Silas in the [book of] Acts, and they were commissioned to go as the Holy Spirit had called them."[50] He declared emphatically that these students had been "called, chosen and commissioned by God" and that those who were left behind had the responsibility to "bring them daily before the Throne of Grace as they face the powers of darkness and win souls for Jesus Christ." These students were then given the following prophecy:

I am sending you away with a new deposit of My Word within you, because I have been working by the power of My Spirit, to leave within you a new deposit of Divine substance of My Word, so that as you go to your places, it will be a LIVING WORD, a creating Word, an enduring Word; and it must find its expression.

As you have received of the revelation and of the ministry of My Word by diverse operations, the effect will be in your own life, in your own home, and in your work, that the Word of God has come to you in a new and living way. The production of My dealing by My Spirit and Word is to the end that all of you face the enemy of yourselves, and know that My Word shall accomplish My purposes. I will not rest, my people, until I have accomplished all things I have promised concerning you.[51]

Elton made particular effort to demystify the work of ministry whenever he spoke to the students about fulfilling the call of God on their lives. He made sure they were not thinking of robes, collars, and stained glass windows when they considered being used by the Lord. "Christianity is not expressed in massive stone buildings, expensive organs, lavish stained-glass windows, but in human lives. . . . God is moving today in the hearts and lives of many of the young and many are yielding themselves up for the Gospel and we must join them,"[52] he would teach. He deliberately preached to liberate them from the organized church mentality: he was raising an army outside the organized church system from among the students. He had written, "There is a severe spiritual crisis in most countries. There is a lot of 'churchianity' . . . with large numbers of unconverted church members. But there is also a large growing group of soundly converted young people who are eager to leave the traditional 'church' methods and services and to step out in a wonderful desire to serve the Lord."[53]

While he talked about leaving traditional church methods and services, he quickly emphasized the necessity of "methods and services," knowing the tendency that could result from a misunderstanding of his teaching. "This is NOT a call for young people to forsake their churches but to remain where the Lord has found them. They should witness, testify, and join with other young people."[54]

For the first time in Nigeria's Christian history, hundreds of young university graduates without any denominational ordination or license became actively engaged in the work of the ministry as a result of the concept he engraved on their hearts, which promoted the empowerment of the Holy Spirit and the laying on of hands by an anointed leader over any formal denominational process or approval. In a radical departure from convention, Elton empowered an entire generation by commissioning them through the laying on of hands. While teaching on this, he declared without any ambiguity:

THE LAYING ON OF HANDS WAS A SIGN OF ORDINATION

"Separate me Barnabas and Saul to the work whereunto I have called them" (Acts 13:2). Both men had been called into the ministry many years before and had proved their ministry . . . they had made their calling clear and plain. Now they were being called into a larger ministry. Then, by the laying on of hands, they were confirmed in that calling again, strengthened and ordained.

Note those who took part in that ordination service . . . prophets and teachers . . . and one of them was undoubtedly a Negro . . . (Simon called Niger). Their authority came from the Holy Spirit and *that was all that was needed*. None of the Jerusalem apostles were there.

Every Christian consecrating themselves for the service of God should seek for a recognised servant of God to lay hands on them for the ministry and to see that the will of God should be made known, with confirmation.[55]

In consonance with his vision of a new missionary force of young men and women being raised to evangelize the remotest parts of the nation, Elton was always on the university campuses preparing students for mission work. In 1972 he was at ECU, where he trained them in preparation for their missions' week. He laid hands on them and sent them to preach the gospel with power in the neighbouring communities. One of the students remembers him saying, "My hands are ordinary hands, but when I lay it on you, I will connect you to heaven and then you will go and do the work."[56]

Whenever he preached on the campuses, he would prophesy that "a time is coming when the Nigerian Government [will] pay Nigerian youths to preach the gospel in all the nooks and crannies of the nation."[57] This prophecy was fulfilled in 1973. The administration of General Yakubu Gowon instituted the Nigerian Youth Service Corps (NYSC) scheme as part of his post-civil war programme of "rehabilitation, reconstruction, and reconciliation." This resulted in a lot of demonstrations on campuses. The students felt they were being used by the government as cheap labour. Christian groups from around the country turned to Elton for counsel, with many of the leaders visiting Ilesa several times. Peter Ozodo remembers Elton responding this way when he went to Ilesa to discuss the issue: "Are you foolish? Can't you see? This is God. This is God sending Nigerian students from the Southwest where there has been revival, to the North to preach the gospel. Many of you will find yourselves in the North and you will preach the Gospel there."[58]

Elton firmly believed the NYSC scheme was God's masterstroke in the penetration of northern Nigeria with the gospel. Elton had been deeply burdened for northern Nigeria for many years, and as early as 1971, he had started announcing to all who would care to listen that in terms of God's visitation the West had had its turn, the East was having its own (in the post-civil war revival), and that it was the North's turn.[59] Later, in a declaration of the things he believed God would accomplish in Nigeria, he wrote, "We know that the Lord wishes Northern Nigeria to hear the gospel, THEREFORE we claim more men and means to send them the gospel in the next two years."[60] Elsewhere he stated, "There is need for combined, united and organised prayer in order to open up many areas in northern Nigeria to the gospel."[61] And also: "The challenge of the Moslem and pagan northern part of Nigeria faces every born again child of God in the South. The North is our responsibility. There are too many evangelical groups playing around in the South trying to get propaganda results when God is waiting for them to attack Satan in other places."[62]

Elton expected young people to take up this challenge. An "advert" he placed in the sixth issue of *Herald of the Last Days* reads:

VACANCIES

Men and women are needed to take the Gospel of Jesus Christ to all parts of Northern Nigeria.

Qualifications: Certainty of personal conversion; Certainty of the ability of Jesus Christ to save, heal, and deliver all who trust Him.

Remuneration: Conflict with the enemy. The guaranteed peace of the Lord Jesus. Protection, blessings, and daily provision guaranteed by God Himself.

Interviews: Granted by God Himself to all applicants who desire to prepare themselves.

For equipment and assistance apply:

Enrolment Office in Nigeria,

Herald of the Last Days,

P. O. Box, 113, Ilesa.[63]

Around this period, in a section titled "Special Message for All Evangelists" in Nigeria, he began to shift the attention of the evangelists in the church towards northern Nigeria:

The Call of God today is to go out into unreached areas in Nigeria with the full Gospel, the message of deliverance which alone can meet the need of the masses in Northern Nigeria today. God will surely bless all who heed His call and seek the lost in the North. It will require great faith . . . faith that God can overcome the indifference of the pagans . . . the bigotry of the Muslims and save many of them.

It will need a working knowledge of the local language, and there are very many languages, and a certain amount of specialised training which will enable you to combat juju, witchcraft, and the powers of evil, and to deal with demons, disease and evil spirits and hostility.

If you are sure God has called you, then do not look to man, or wait for man to send you. We have no funds to finance you . . . and we do not call you . . . but if you are sure that God has called you, then He is waiting for you to prove and demonstrate your faith by stepping out in faith to obey this call . . .

Expect trials, they are God's methods and lessons to develop your faith. God will allow much tribulation . . . to deepen your faith and trust in Him. All God's vessels for ministering in the Muslim world must be full of faith and loyalty to God.[64]

Elton was clearly ready for a signal from heaven to invade northern Nigeria. When the NYSC programme was established, he knew heaven had spoken; it was time to mobilize God's forces for battle. Elton went round the university campuses to pass the message across that the scheme was a programme instituted by God to spread the gospel all over Nigeria, and that Christians were not to oppose it. It was God's strategy to spread the gospel to places it otherwise would not have gotten to in a long time.

Emiko Amotsuka, who was a student at the University of Ibadan, recalls that Elton "went all around all the university campus fellowships and told us that the scheme was God's agenda to evangelize Nigeria. He drove the message home powerfully that anywhere you were posted, 'know that you are sent there as an ambassador of the kingdom of God. Don't just go there as an ordinary person. You are sent there by God on assignment. Go there as an ambassador of the Lord Jesus Christ and establish the kingdom of God wherever you are sent.' That transformed the whole mind-set concerning NYSC. He told people not to bother to change their posting. 'Don't allow your parents to change your posting back to Lagos,' [he would say]."[65]

Christian youth corps members, already armed with a missionary mind-set, went with a specific mandate to evangelize the country, especially the Muslim-dominated areas of northern Nigeria. Reporting in 1977 about the pre-NYSC preparatory work on the campus, Elton wrote:

The final year students are busy with their final exams, and as they complete their academic work they have to go out for ten months' national service in remote and neglected areas chosen by the Federal government. This has been the government's plan for some years now, and we eagerly fit into it because the Christian students hope they will be sent to the Moslem north where they can witness and preach Jesus Christ. Thus the Federal government is actually paying for these young people to take the gospel into the areas sealed from missionary work.

They have done a wonderful job in past years and this is proved by many complaints received from the Muslim leaders against the federal government for sending Christians into their areas. But no one can forbid the Christians from witnessing and meeting with others in their own houses and residences. This year we laid hands on and sent out a large number—more than one hundred and twenty at Ife University, nearly two hundred in Ibadan, and large numbers in other universities as well.[66]

Niyi Beecroft recalls a remarkable experience with Elton in 1976. Elton was returning from a trip to the North, and Beecroft, who had remained in the North after his service year, travelled with him back to the South. As Elton drove, he shared some of the things on his mind. As Beecroft recalls, "He had way back then a very strategic vision of Nigeria and of what God was doing. He had a very clear understanding of where the country was headed, what role Christians would play by their being positioned in the North. The youth corps scheme, to him, was the hand of God keeping God's children there. He [Elton] was like a general actually presiding over the battlefield. He saw all of us who had been posted to various places not just as youth corps [members] serving the nation, but as foot soldiers in God's army, and each one of us bearing the gospel to all the places where we were [posted]. He spoke with excitement. He had a very grand strategic plan of what was happening."[67]

Amos Aderonmu met Elton in the early seventies through the leader of an evangelistic group he belonged to. He soon developed a close relationship with Elton and regularly visited him in Ilesa. At some point,

Aderonmu, who was a full-time evangelist, sensed that God wanted him to relocate to northern Nigeria for evangelistic work, so he went to Ilesa to discuss with Elton. "I told him I felt that the Lord wanted me to go to the North. [But] he said, 'Don't go yet.' "[68] So Aderonmu went back and continued his evangelistic work from his base at Ogbomoso. Later, Elton invited him to be a part of the pre-crusade team for Osborn's December 1974 crusade in Benin. A Land Cruiser jeep was assigned to him, along with a driver, and he toured many towns and villages in the mid-western state, preaching and advertising the crusade. On the last day of the weeklong school of evangelism that followed the main crusade, Aderonmu perceived the Lord was telling him it was time to go to the North. He immediately went to Elton to discuss the issue, and Elton replied, "Now you can go."[69]

Also attending the crusade and school of evangelism were scores of serving NYSC members who had been mentored by Elton while they were in school. They had carried the fire to their different fields and were doing exploits for God. One of them, Bayo Famonure, Aderonmu's very close friend, was serving in Zaria. When Aderonmu discussed his plans for evangelistic work in the North, Famonure was excited. He told Aderonmu that the Christian corps members serving in Zaria had been praying that God would send them an evangelist. Aderonmu's call was therefore an answer to prayer. During that week, Famonure and a couple of others who had come from the North, particularly from Zaria and its surrounding towns, informed Elton that they were planning a crusade in Zaria city, which was scheduled to hold about a week after the school of evangelism. Elton was excited about this. He gave them a Land Cruiser jeep for the crusade; the jeep was loaded full with evangelism tools—horn speakers, projectors, books, tracts, films, and so on. As Festus Ndukwe would tell the story of the crusade and its outcome years later:

Amos [Aderonmu] came to the north of Nigeria to meet some other zealous youths on Youth Service from Western Nigeria who had a burden for outreaches like himself. Amos, therefore, joined these young university graduates to go for many of these outreaches. As this was happening, these youths never knew that God was incubating something that would later influence the history of mission in Nigeria and Africa. The Zaria city crusade in 1974 was to be the trigger.

Some of these young graduates banded themselves together to lay siege on this Islamic city, a thing that had never happened before. You could preach in any other place, may be outside the city walls, that is, if you were courageous enough, but never inside the city, the Emir's fortress. This [is] a city that stands as one of the symbols of Islam in Nigeria. These young men began to meet every weekend to fast and pray for the crusade. They never expected what they saw. Naïve and not knowing the grave implications of the step they were about to take, these men with students from the nearby university and other high schools and colleges stormed the city.

Before the Islamic Hausa dwellers realized what was happening, a young man [Niyi Beecroft] dressed in white caftan had mounted the rostrum and preached. And surprisingly, some began to come out for altar calls, but it was followed by a hail of stones. They ran out of the city, bleeding. As they re-grouped to pray, a clear burden came upon them to reach out to these Islamic people.[70]

Many of those who participated in the crusade became the pioneer members of the group that would become known as Calvary Productions (CAPRO), a missionary organization founded in 1975, which has become the largest indigenous missionary organization in Africa. Famonure recalls the early days of this group: "This first crop of young people that formed this vanguard had nothing but God. They worked almost with bare hands. They lived by faith."[71]

Peter Ozodo, one of the founding members, recalls, "Elton was one of the major early supporters of the vision of CAPRO. He [Elton] encouraged ministry into the North because he believed the North was the next phase in the work of God and . . . when I found myself in the North I knew this was the fulfilment of what Elton had been telling us. Therefore, when we established CAPRO, it was natural for some of us to gravitate towards him again for support, assistance and guidance, and he didn't fail us."[72]

"What struck me about him [Elton] and would likely strike anyone who met him for the first time was the aura of holiness and authority around him," says Famonure, who first met Elton around 1969, while he was a student at the University of Lagos.

He [Elton] came across [to] anybody as a very serious man who knew his God. . . . His major teachings centred [on] holiness, [the] Holy Spirit, revival and the second coming of Christ. . . . He desired a deep revival for the church in Nigeria. He was a very good Bible teacher. He taught with authority and deep insight into Bible truths. . . . I had a very close personal relationship with him. He had a deep trust in me just as he had in many others. On sighting me enter his house, he would call on me to come right into his study. Maybe because I lived far away in the North, every visit of mine was a Bible school session. He was the chief custodian of a lot of evangelistic tools, including films, books, lingua [tape] units, and many others. All these he gave freely to anybody he discerned was genuine in winning souls. . . . He had a great impact on my life's ministry. He believed in me. . . . He took time off to teach and guide me. He was very supportive of my calling.[73]

Famonure, who led the pioneer leadership team of CAPRO, speaks of Elton's influence in the early days of the organization: "In the days when the church held suspect anybody with a calling outside the denominational settings, it was a great blessing to have Papa Elton on our side in CAPRO. He encouraged us and gave us a lot of gifts from his own ministry and from T. L. Osborn through him. The films he gave us went all over the North through CAPRO."[74]

At CAPRO's inception, Elton helped the group secure a Peugeot 404 pickup vehicle (with a driver) from the Osborn Foundation, and Aderonmu would usually travel once a month, from Zaria to Ilesa, to load the car with evangelism tools and also to give Elton a report of the work on the field. Elton also secured a stipend for Aderonmu, who became CAPRO's first full-time evangelist.[75] Aderonmu's recollections of his visits to Ilesa still stir deep feelings in him: "My times with him [Elton] were inspiring. . . . One thing that impressed me was his passion for evangelism, to see people know about Jesus at all cost. Mama would just sit down, listening to us. She would chip in once in a while; I enjoyed those times."[76] He remembers once telling Elton about how they were stoned during evangelism (this was after the December 1974 episode), hoping to get some sympathy. But he was shocked by Elton's reply: "That's good, that's good. Good job, good job. . . . You are hitting the enemy; he will fight back; he will fight back, that's good; keep it up."[77] Elton was a fighter (he loved to make statements like, "I like a fight. I have been fighting for years, and I don't like losing!"); he lived the life of a spiritual warrior, and he always sought to impart the same spirit to everyone who came around him. "The way [Hannah Elton] impacted my life was in the area of prayer. She was a praying woman. After we had finished talking, she would call me and just share her heart with me and [talk about] the principles of prayer. She would say, 'I am praying for you; I know you are in a difficult place.' And I know she did,"[78] says Aderonmu.

When the 1975 NYSC programme was rounding up, Elton and Hannah travelled to the North to speak to the graduating corps members. Speaking at the Ahmadu Bello University (ABU) chapel on a midweek evening, Elton challenged them that it was God who had brought them to the North and that they should see it as their mission field. "Those the Lord may call to stay back should stay back," he said. And indeed some stayed back. After speaking to the Kaduna state corps members, they drove to Kano and did the same thing with the outgoing Christian corps members. When it was over, they drove back to Zaria and then to Ilesa.

Elton visited again in 1976, to speak at a series of meetings put together by his protégés at his request. He spoke to different fellowship groups in Zaria: to a packed auditorium at the ABU chapel Sunday morning service; to a Fellowship of Christian Students (FCS) meeting; and to several fellowship groups scattered around Zaria city.[79] He then travelled to Kano, where he spoke at the Bayero University Kano (BUK) chapel and to a number of groups in Kano city. Aderonmu and others really believed Elton was going to die soon after, because of the things he said at the meetings. "The things he was saying to us wherever he went—it was like a farewell speech," he recalls. "I was at each meeting. The impression I got was that he was just giving his farewell message to the church in the North; in my mind I said, 'Maybe Papa is about to die.' But he lived beyond that time. He really encouraged us as a mission to keep doing that which we were called to do."[80]

Ozodo remembers Elton driving himself all the way from Ilesa to Zaria to preach at some of the early Last Days Gathering conferences (CAPRO's annual flagship conference), which began holding in 1976. Receiving Elton on arrival one particular year, Ozodo was "deeply, deeply touched" that he had driven such a long distance just to be with them and said, "Papa, you mean you drove yourself all the way from Ilesa to speak here?" "Yes, of course," replied Elton, "God provides strength."[81]

Elton's vision for stirring students for missions was not limited to northern Nigeria. He had a burden to reach every part of the country as well. Geoffrey Numbere, the founder of Greater Evangelism World Crusade, one of the largest charismatic ministries in the south-southern part of the country, first encountered Elton's ministry in his third year as a student at the University of Ife. Elton was the guest speaker at an ECU evening service. As he preached, he suddenly "paused and started pointing to someone in the auditorium saying, 'You there! You there!' "[82] Numbere recalled many years later. "Everybody started turning towards the direction of his finger to find out who it was. He kept on pointing and saying, 'That boy! That boy there!' " Most of the people sitting along that direction, frightened at the possibility of being singled out by Elton, "started eliminating themselves, each hoping he would not be the one." Interestingly, Geoffrey Numbere sat relaxed because the thought that Elton might be pointing at him was very far from his mind. When Elton eventually got to where Numbere was sitting at the back of the auditorium and said, "Youuuu!!" he almost jumped out of his chair with fright. As he came out to the front, Elton began to prophesy, "Yes, you are a young man from the Rivers State. You, the hand of the Lord is upon you. God is going to call you and send you to your people. His anointing is upon you, and you shall be a mighty instrument in His hand."[83]

Numbere did not immediately take to this prophecy and, therefore, did not visit Ilesa. However, after several personal encounters with God, he yielded to the call; then he travelled to Ilesa to see Elton. On seeing him, Elton laughed and said, "Have you finished running? I knew you would finally come, and I knew you were coming."[84] Numbere remembers that "the spiritual burden of this nation was so much on Pa Elton that he did not cease to call on God day and night for Him to raise up Nigerians that would carry the gospel to their own people."[85] Speaking of his own experience, Numbere writes, "He [Elton] seemed to have had a special burden for the old Rivers State (now Rivers and Bayelsa states). Talking about that burden several years later in the 1980s he [Elton] said, 'Each time I thought of Rivers State, the immorality there, the powers of darkness gripping the state and holding the people in bondage, there would be such a great burden on my heart. I cried and cried to the Lord to raise up a man for that land. . . . So when I met this young man [Numbere] and I got to know that he is from the Rivers State, I got interested.' "[86]

Elton counselled him and delivered what he said were instructions from the Lord as regards Numbere's ministry. Thus began a lifelong relationship that lent great support and solidity to Numbere's ministry. When Greater Evangelism World Crusade was founded, Elton placed Numbere and some of his first pastors on a monthly salary.[87] Once, when Numbere wrote to Elton during a very turbulent period in his ministry, he replied with words that are classic Elton:

Dear Brother Geoffrey,

Greetings once again in His (Jesus Christ) victorious Name.

Thank you for your letter; full of news and victories and problems and for your telegram, which came while I was away. But in any case there was little I felt I could do . . . except to claim victory on your behalf.

I rejoice with you for the persecution. It will work well in the end and it is just as we expected and it will continue to increase as you carry out the Master's wishes. This is the way He caused the Gospel to spread in the Book of Acts . . . persecution and scattering and it will be the same in Port Harcourt and Rivers. I am sure it is not pleasant for you personally but one thing it will surely do . . . it will teach you and strengthen you faster than anything else can in a very short time, and you will soon be expert in facing these problems. That is something to be envied!

I was speaking at the Evang. Union Sunday evening meeting in Ife University just after receiving your letter, and although I did not mention your name, I made mention of the pressure of certain servants of God . . . and many present would know and did know and they are aware of how the Lord is using you. They asked me to speak on "Christian Suffering" . . .!!! So I did with full illustrations (using you).

They are sheltered from your experience . . . and are missing a lot!!! So, please do not wilt or falter. Just take it all with the knowledge that He is with you and is doing a wonderful work in your life. I am thrilled to hear of the progress of the work there. It will spread and persecution is the fastest way to do it. So I hope to hear more of it from you. [88]

Numbere was only one of hundreds of students who were fired into fulfilling their ministries by coming into contact with Elton. While on campus, Elton's teachings had placed a burden on their hearts; many would never again be able to shake off this burden; it would weigh on them till they did something about it. Gbile Akanni, in dedicating one of his books to Elton, wrote: "To Pa S. G. Elton of blessed memory, whose life I was asked by God to watch closely (as a man who served in the pattern I would be called to walk in.) At the beginning of my stepping into the ministry, he graciously poured on me and several others a burden he had borne for twenty five years then. Under his hand I was commissioned into what has become my life burden today. . . . He also taught us and exemplified the principle of spiritual warfare in standing for God. His strong word on warfare was 'Do not turn back. There is no provision for those who turn their backs. Stand, having done all you know how to do, stand your ground.' "[89]

THIRTEEN

PAIN

Benson Andrew Idahosa's evangelistic ministry, which had been launched in the early 1960s, began to bud from the end of that decade. According to Ruthanne Garlock, Idahosa's first major biographer, while working as an accountant with the Bata Shoe Company, Idahosa started a little church which grew out of a Bible study group that met at Forestry Road, Benin City. When the congregation outgrew this storefront building, they managed to secure a land at the Iyaro district of Benin, behind the University of Benin compound. Construction began, and after a few months, though still uncompleted, the group moved into the new building.[1]

The membership of the church grew quickly, and at this point, Idahosa began praying about the need for a spiritual mentor. While at the storefront building, the congregation had submitted to the oversight of the Assemblies of God pastor through whom Idahosa had been converted, but he became wary of the possible future fallout that could result from being closely linked with a specific denomination.[2]

While praying about the situation in his bedroom, Idahosa was divinely instructed to go and find Sydney Elton.[3] Idahosa shared this vision with one of his elders and asked him to accompany him to Ilesa. When they arrived in Ilesa, they found a man who volunteered the address of someone who was in contact with Elton. When Idahosa finally met Elton, he greeted him with the following words: "You are the man God showed me. The Lord has called me to come and see you and ask you to be my father to lead me in the ministry." Elton welcomed him and told him that he had been receiving news about him for a few months before then and had been looking forward to meeting him. "I am so glad the Lord has brought you here,"[4] said Elton.

Recent research gives us further insight into the beginnings of Idahosa's church and his early relationship with Sydney Elton.[5] After about six years away from the country in the wake of the Latter Rain crisis, Edgar Parkyns, Elton's former colleague in the Apostolic Church, returned to Nigeria in 1960 as an independent missionary through Elton's platform.[6] While he was away from the country, he had been very active in the emerging charismatic movement in the UK.[7] Parkyns established a base in what was then a largely un-evangelized area in mid-west Nigeria.[8] Over time he built a vibrant team of young evangelists who travelled all around the mid-west evangelizing and planting churches. The network of churches was called "Apostolic Gospel Church."[9]

Through Parkyns' influence, "a prayer and Bible study group" that was called Calvary Fellowship was started at a shop in Ivbizua Street, on Mission Road, Benin, in 1962.[10] The group was officially inaugurated in 1965 by Parkyns, and later moved to Forestry Road, Benin.[11] (It seems Parkyns never really got involved in the running of the fellowship, only serving in the capacity of an adviser; he remained totally focused on working as a missionary.) In its early days, the fellowship "witnessed the coming together of young men and women hungry for the Word of God."[12] One of the young men was Benson Idahosa who was then a Sunday school superintendent at the Assemblies of God Church in Benin led by Udo Ukpo.[13] Idahosa was also a regular speaker at the fellowship.[14] British missionary Alan Macintosh, who ran a Bible school (West African Missionary Training Centre) in Ibadan in the mid-1960s, remembers meeting Idahosa a couple of times while visiting Parkyns. "He [Idahosa] was not [yet] known then,"[15] Macintosh recalls.

Over time the group metamorphosed into a church and was at various times led by N. O. Ojie and F. I. Ikpea.[16] Following Ikpea's departure in 1968 because of the civil war, Parkyns approached the leaders of the Assemblies of God to release Idahosa to oversee the church.[17] He officially took over the leadership of the group on October 26, 1968.[18] With numerical growth and Idahosa's dynamic leadership, the church began its upward climb to global fame. Idahosa wrote decades later, "When I left the Assemblies of God on October 24, 1968, in obedience to God's instruction, how could I figure a little prayer group would become the nucleus of a worldwide rallying point for believers."[19]

During Parkyns' final months in Nigeria—mid-1970 to early 1971—he made two significant decisions that would prove crucial to the future of the church that was growing under Idahosa's leadership. First, he handed over the network of churches—more than thirty—that had been established all over the mid-West through his missionary efforts to Idahosa.[20] From just one church, the work suddenly grew to almost forty churches. "That is actually what gave birth to the expansion of Church of God Mission,"[21] recalls one early member. Second, and perhaps more significantly, we know that at some point during this period, Parkyns linked Idahosa to his former colleague, Elton.[22]

During their first meeting, Idahosa discussed the church's building project (the Iyaro Church) with Elton. He told Elton how the church had sacrificed everything they had to erect the building, but that they would have to borrow money to put a roof on it. Elton promised to recommend him to Gordon Lindsay's Native Church Crusade programme. At the end of the visit, they decided to meet at least once a month (they were to alternate meetings between Ilesa and Benin) so that Elton could give advice and direction to the work.[23]

Gordon Lindsay visited Nigeria in March 1971 to see some of the churches which the Native Church Crusade had assisted. Elton sent a letter to Idahosa to inform him that Lindsay would visit Benin. In excitement, the church printed cards and invited non-members for the special meeting with Lindsay. About 250 people attended the programme. During the service, Elton turned to Lindsay and said, "I believe this man is going to be a key man in the work of God in Nigeria. I think we ought to ordain him to the ministry."[24] Elton stepped up to the pulpit and announced to the congregation that the two of them had agreed to ordain Idahosa to the ministry. He was called to the front of the gathering, and as he knelt at the altar, Lindsay and Elton laid hands on him and anointed him to the ministry. Lindsay, while reporting his visit to Benin, remembered the event this way: "Afterwards the local members requested that we should have a special ordination service for the young pastor, Benson Idahosa. We explained that we could only confirm what God had first done as we prayed and laid hands on him. We were convinced that God has His Hand upon this remarkable young man."[25]

During this visit, Idahosa expressed his desire for further Bible training, which led to Lindsay offering him a working scholarship to the newly opened Christ for the Nations Institute (CFNI) in Dallas, Texas. This was a dream come true for Idahosa. Freda Lindsay, commenting in 1973 on Idahosa's stay at CFNI, said, "Benson proved to be a very diligent student, and his praying was often with strong crying and tears. Both my late husband and I knew that the hand of God was upon this young man in an unusual way."[26]

Idahosa's comments on the "What Students Are Saying About CFNI" page of the January 1972 issue of *Christ for the Nations* magazine reveal the impact the school had on him: "As I wrote to my people in Africa, this is not the school you can describe, but 'come and see' for yourself. CFNI is where you can meet God and He meets with you through the Spirit-anointed instructors that God has raised to the glory of His name. All that I have experienced from the time of my conversion to the time I became a full-time preacher, I have gained more here than what I have for the past 11 years of my being a Christian and pastor. It has transformed me and made the Bible more real and true to me."[27] The exposure to world-renowned Bible teachers and preachers—like Charles Flynn, Loren Cunningham, Winkie Pratney, and Maxwell Whyte, who regularly taught at CFNI—was definitely an invaluable experience in the training of the then thirty-three year old Idahosa.

To make sure that he maximized his stay in the United States, Elton gave Idahosa the contacts of some pastors and churches that could provide some help to him.[28] During his time at CFNI, Idahosa came across a book by T. L. Osborn titled *Soul Winning*. He was troubled by the statistics in the book that "noted that the rate at which souls were being won to Christ was far below the [world's] population growth rate."[29] This led him to embark on a period of fasting and prayer, after which he decided to return to Nigeria, even though he was not through with his course. Seeing that his soul was impassioned, and knowing he could not be stopped, Lindsay accepted his decision and prayed for him.

Immediately he returned to Nigeria, burning with the vision in his heart, he called a meeting of all his church's elders, and also invited Elton, to discuss a plan to evangelize the whole nation.[30] Concurrently, he founded Christ for the Nations International Evangelistic Association. In stating the aim for founding the organization, Idahosa's fiery resolve, which truncated his studies in Dallas, is fully exhibited.[31] In this raison d'être, something deeply profound about Idahosa at this period of his life is revealed, and it is clear why Elton was excited about this young vision-ary. "Not only will Nigeria hear of this young man, Benson—I believe all of Africa will hear of him,"[32] Freda Lindsay remembered Elton saying in those early days.

Nigeria was divided into four sections, and an evangelistic crusade was scheduled for each region. The first of the crusades was held in Benin from February 25 to 29, 1972. In the following months, the crusade train moved to Warri, Ilorin, Agbor, Sapele, and Owerri. Elton, in addition to being Idahosa's primary adviser, was in charge of organizing the crusade follow-up efforts. Increasing numbers of crusades were conducted in various parts of Nigeria, and in a report dated March 15, 1976, Elton wrote, "We are fully committed to seeing that every soul who confesses the Lord Jesus as Saviour and Lord is also contacted again by a church leader or member and made to understand that it is only by continuing in the faith and growing in grace of the Lord Jesus that he can grow spiritually. This task is not as spectacular as the crusades, but just as essential and impor-tant, and we have a large force of young people who have been trained for the task. In the recent crusades in Calabar and Uyo, the estimated number of converts runs into thousands, and they came from many different towns and villages. We managed to secure the names and addresses of many of them and they are being contacted and sent literature. Also, suitable classes for converts are being arranged in each village or town where we can send a trained Christian."[33]

Idahosa's church experienced phenomenal growth throughout the 1970s: in 1976 it had grown to 317 churches, and by 1982 it had 712 churches in the country.[34] Freda Lindsay was around to dedicate Miracle Centre—the headquarter church in Benin in November 1975. She remarked, "So on Sunday morning I had the privilege of preaching the first sermon in the new building to about 2,000 people. What a time we had! The joy and the singing was like nothing I have heard anywhere in the world! . . . We sang and prayed and praised. Some danced for sheer joy!"[35]

Elton has left us some of the most fascinating vignettes of the early days in Benin. He wrote in 1973: "It is a thrilling sight to see senior government civil servants sitting close to the front with their Bibles and seeking for the Lord's blessing. One of the wonderful features of the growing church is the group of Christians who meet here regularly to plan and arrange for general crusades in mass evangelism, sometimes in pagan areas and now in Muslim areas. They are attacking the very strongholds of evil and getting results . . . hundreds definitely are being saved, changed and filled with the Spirit."[36] And in 1972: "God is moving in the mid-west state of Nigeria. It is a good sign to see the deep interest of the press . . . they have allocated a team of journalists and photographers to attend every crusade. In Agbor the press reported attendances of over 10,000. They also stated that over 500 testimonies of healing were received and they printed pictures of men and women who had been blind but who received their sight. Now we have the task of looking after the hundreds who wish to leave their idols and juju to become Christians. One noticeable feature in all these crusades is the large number of educated and trained young people who are moving forward and accepting Jesus Christ . . . some even leaving their work to go out preaching."[37]

Throughout the 1970s, Elton's glowing reports about the work in Benin gave Idahosa's ministry credibility with many international Pentecostal leaders who were in a position to help the young ministry achieve its dreams. Writing to Freda Lindsay in 1973, Elton stated, "I have recently been privileged to join the activities of the church in Benin City with our Brother, B. A. Idahosa, a former student of CFN Institute. I can testify that the Lord really is working there. The church is never empty and people are coming all the time with their problems and needs. There is always someone there to help them. The services sometimes are four and five hours long, but rarely boring because there is something being done all the time."[38] Freda Lindsay, writing in 1975, said, "Brother Elton also said that Benson Idahosa was the number one evangelist in Nigeria today. Wherever he goes, thousands of people assemble to hear him."[39]

These encouraging testimonials released favour in Idahosa's direction. These international leaders trusted Elton's judgement; they, therefore, could entrust resources into Idahosa's hands. The frequent references to Elton's testimonial—for example, "S. G. Elton, veteran British missionary in Nigeria for 38 years in Nigeria told us that 'at least 250 new full gospel churches have been started during the last two years, and large crusades with crowds of 15,000 to 25,000 are eagerly attended in many towns and tribes,' "[40] or "The Sunday morning I spoke, I helped receive an offering for the unfinished Christ for Nigeria Bible Institute. About $800 was given, which Brother Elton thought was terrific in light of the fact that . . ."[41] or "As we arrived 45 minutes early at Christ for Nigeria Institute with veteran British missionaries Rev. and Mrs S. G. Elton, we were . . ."[42]—in reports to supporters back in the US were definitely designed to reassure them of Idahosa's credibility. The reports were in essence saying, the Eltons believe in it, so you don't need to have any fear about its genuineness.

Referring to these early days in a 1995 documentary, Idahosa said, "Thereafter, Pa Elton and I began to work together when I went to look for him at Ilesa, he adopted me as a son to work with. . . . Then Elton introduced me to many ministries on planet earth."[43] Some of Idahosa's lieutenants from the early years recall that no matter how busy Idahosa's schedule was, he made sure he had a meeting with Elton once every month, to keep him abreast of developments in the ministry and to seek his counsel. Many close lieutenants recall several visits to Ilesa with Idahosa.[44] "No matter how busy he [Idahosa] was, he made a point of having a meeting with Brother Elton once each month to keep him informed, and to seek his counsel,"[45] writes Garlock.

Idahosa, once recounting one early example of this advisory role, said to Elton: "When I came here years ago to seek your advice and told you that I want[ed] to resign my job and go on full time, you advised me to hold on first. . . . [You said] I should come back and you would tell me [when] it was God's time. And I went back, and I was very, very disappointed because I wanted to go, and you just said, 'It's not time yet; the Lord will speak more to us.' I waited. Finally, before I could know where I was [*sic*], you sent a message to me to say, 'Now is the time,' and I left for the field."[46] Further speaking about the impact of the Eltons on his life, Idahosa said, "I gained most of all the things I have been teaching through these lives. They have taught me humility; they have told me, 'Pride goeth before [a] fall.' They have taught me that sticking to sin causes destruction and cutting short of life. They have advised me on money: not to pursue money, but pursue the gospel and God will supply the money. I have done all humanly I can to take their counsel as words from the mouth of the Lord."[47]

Throughout the seventies, it was considered a non-debatable fact among the leaders of the emerging charismatic ministries in Nigeria that Idahosa was Elton's special protégé. Many of these preachers and missionaries were also close to Elton, but it was generally acknowledged that Idahosa held a special place in his heart. Close observers of the Benin scene in the seventies all testify to the deep affection Elton had for "Benson," as Elton liked to call him. One leader put it this way: "Our big brother [Idahosa] got his attention, so at a point he faced Benin City with Benson Idahosa, so we the smaller [*sic*] ones would just sneak in from behind and get his fatherly blessing."[48]

Elton was also very influential in the early success of the Bible school in Benin. Indeed, Elton's role in the development of the school—which later became a full-fledged Bible institute called All Nations for Christ Bible Institute[49]—was one of his most important contributions to the success story and eventual international impact of Idahosa's ministry.[50] Throughout the 1970s, the Bible school was responsible for training many of the preachers and evangelists who became leaders in the charismatic movement in southern Nigeria.[51] Elton was influential in the enrolment of many of the students who attended the school in the early seventies, and who went on to become leaders in the movement. Elton wanted many of the budding preachers to attend the Bible school in Benin.

One early student, who was already an evangelist in eastern Nigeria before he came to the school, remembers that Elton "came there either once or twice in a month. He visited Benin more often than any other place I knew [of]. . . . I had been to Bible school before, but he [Elton] really wanted us to be in that school to see what was happening. Because in those days there was a great fire burning in Church of God Mission, a mighty move of God there, just like down here in the East."[52] John and Celia Valentine, a missionary couple who served in the Bible school in the seventies (John became principal of the school in 1975), recall that "Pa and Ma used to stay with us at Miracle Centre once a month when they came down from Ilesa to minister. We were fond of them and felt quite protective towards them as they were elderly. Ma was a very godly woman. . . . They furnished a bedroom [in our flat at Miracle Centre in Benin City]."[53]

Despite Idahosa's growing international reputation and influence by the end of the 1970s, Elton's role in his life and ministry did not diminish. In fact it increased. Elton was writing in 1980, "The Benin Convention was also good. . . . Things are moving well and fast there . . . and they start a new Graduate School of Theology in January . . . and the foundation of the new Christian University will be at Easter. . . . There [is a] big demand for me to move to lead the School of Theology in Benin . . . but I doubt if I will move . . . God sent me to Ilesa and he must speak again. Benson is under heavy pressure . . . but all is OK in Benin."[54]

A 1982 documentary film produced by Idahosa gave abundant testimony of the fruit of the decade-long protégé-mentor relationship. "You have prayed over my life and I have been privileged to pray for many, many, many millions through media of television," Idahosa began, and went on to tell Elton that "the prayer you thought was small . . . [that] you prayed a few years ago when I came here first,"[55] had gone on to bear great fruit, as evidenced by the wide and growing reach of his TV ministry. "As at today we are now in fifteen states in this country on television every week, including the northern part of this nation. We have just got Yola, Maiduguri, Bauchi, Ilorin, and so on in the North where the gospel is going on every day. Here in the western states, Ondo, Ibadan takes us occasionally now; they are planning to take us on full time; Cross River, Rivers State, Imo, Anambra . . . and Bendel State. I want you to pray because part of this tape will go around the whole nation. We are going to . . . put on tape how my life met with you."

Virtually all the questions asked by Idahosa were related to issues for which he perhaps wanted Elton's reassurance. For instance, when Idahosa asked what media, "in addition to face to face, mouth to mouth, and one on one," Elton would recommend for a ministry which wanted to extend the frontiers of its evangelistic outreach, he was obviously expecting Elton to speak to the controversy then raging over the engagement of Christians with television. Elton responded favourably that "everything that God has created has been created for our benefit. Man in sin has allowed the enemy to capture all these things. The mass media today in Nigeria is mainly under the control of Satan. TV, radio, are all created by God and created for us. And every one of them should be used. Literature plays an important part, TV plays an important part, radio plays an important part. The mass media must all be brought under the control of the Lord Jesus Christ."[56]

Idahosa easily moved on to the next question, which he must have been itching to ask: "What will you say to those who believe that radio and TV are Satan's box?"[57] William Kumuyi, founder of Deeper Christian Life Ministry, whose influence was then rapidly increasing across the nation, had called the television "Satan's Box"[58] and advised Christians not to watch it. In the face of such opposition to television viewing, Idahosa would have considered Elton's endorsement crucial to defending his television ministry's viewership and financial support. This was the case for many of the questions Idahosa asked.

Throughout the interview Idahosa continually emphasised how the Eltons had shaped and were shaping his ministry and spiritual outlook. At one point during the interview he hinted at how the demands of the rapidly expanding ministry had led to some decisions which he had now rescinded because of the Eltons' correction: "It is good news for me to pass to you today that as at April 2 1982 we have 712 churches in this country now which [were] given birth to since I met you and since you prayed for me, and 23 branches in Benin City. When two years ago mama [Hannah Elton] came to Benin she said something very quietly, she said 'If this work is of the Lord, the Lord will sustain it.' And since 1980 we stopped asking for pledges and vows and we just left everything like that."[59]

To be sure, Elton and Idahosa were as different as two persons could be: the one preferred to convey his teaching to small-to-medium sized groups with the hope of it spreading out in a concentric pattern; the other seemed to find his voice only before a sea of heads. Elton, even with his unmistakable Pentecostal flair, was still reserved, conservative, and self-effacing; Idahosa, on the other hand, was the master of style, flamboyance and charm, the poster child of glamorous Pentecostalism. Elton was the dutiful missionary in Ilesa who was always travelling to supervise the missionary-evangelists under his care in towns and villages around the country; Idahosa was the globetrotting evangelist whose appetite for taking the gospel to new cities and nations was matched only by his taste for ambitious projects.

They were different in style, but Elton loved him so dearly, and he was ready to give everything—anything—to make sure Idahosa succeeded. Whenever Elton talked about Idahosa and what was happening in Benin, there was a certain ring to his voice, the kind that only comes from the telling of a glad father about a successful son. Elton would not move out of Ilesa for any reason—that he even considered relocating to "lead the School of Theology in Benin" speaks volumes about his commitment to Idahosa.

• • •

IDAHOSA MADE A SURPRISE move in 1981 when in November of that year he stood for ordination in Benin City as bishop of the Church of God Mission. This was shocking to many Pentecostal/charismatic Christians in Nigeria—an ecclesiastical bishopric was antithetical to the spirit of the Pentecostal movement. As religion scholars Andrew Lyons and Harriet Lyons articulated the development, "Idahosa's career took some unpredictable, non-charismatic turns."[60]

The build-up to Idahosa's ordination began in the mid-seventies when David du Plessis was invited by Pope Paul VI to "create and mediate the

Sydney Elton in Ilesa, ca. 1960s.

A Christmas greeting card
sent out by the Eltons in
the early 1950s.

CHRISTMA: REE INGS.

& Mrs. S Elton.

P. O. Box 8,
Ilesha, Nigeria.

A classic photo of the Oke Oye congregation. Sitting in front are Hannah
and Ruth, with another missionary.

Ruth Elton, Ilesa, 1952.

Ruth with the students of the Women's Teacher Training College, Ilesa, 1957.
She was a tutor in arts and dress making.

Thomas Wyatt's Latter Rain crusades in Nigeria in 1953 and 1954 ushered in a fresh wave of Pentecostal revival around the country.

Elton in a vehicle donated by Thomas Wyatt for crusades.

Ruth (centre) with some missionaries during Thomas Wyatt's first crusade in Lagos, 1953.

The missionaries who were stationed at Oke Oye in front of the mission house when Cecil Cousen was visiting, ca. 1948. Standing (left to right): Pastors J. Kirkwood, A. H. Lewis, S. G. Elton, C. T. Morris, R. Brunt and Cecil Cousen. Sitting (left to right): Mrs Kirkwood, Miss V. Allen, Mrs Lewis, Mrs Elton, Ruth Elton, Mrs Rosser, Miss Anna Ungerman and Mrs Cousen. These missionaries, many of them close friends, were forced to take sides during the 1953 Latter Rain crisis.

What does the future hold? The Eltons on the veranda of the house they moved to after leaving the Apostolic Church in 1954.

Elton speaking in the United States, 1955.

Latter Rain evangelists from the United States having a meal with the Eltons in Ilesa.

Cecil Cousen and his wife (far right) at the Dean House Christian Fellowship in Bradford in the late 1950s. The Eltons don't appear in the photo but were present at the meeting. Cousen, one of the leaders of The Apostolic Church in Britain, was a major inspiration to those who embraced the Latter Rain revival within the denomination.

A team of Latter Rain evangelists on their way to Nigeria, 1954.

Elton with Glen and Lavenda Reeves in Caldwell, Ohio, in 1960. The couple came to Nigeria in 1963 as Latter Rain missionaries, serving in the Ikot Ekpene area for two years.

A team of Latter Rain evangelists getting ready to leave for Nigeria, 1954.

Dale Young seeing Elton off on a trip from Caldwell, Idaho, to Tulsa, Oklahoma, September 1960. Young sent Latter Rain missionaries to Nigeria and raised funds for others.

The Osborn Foundation team leading the recording of T. L. Osborn's sermons into Nigerian languages at the Eltons' compound in Ilesa, 1965.

The Eltons at their Ibala Road residence, Ilesa, ca. 1958.

The Eltons and Gordon Lindsay in Ilesa, during Lindsay's 1968 visit to the churches that had been sponsored by the Native Church Crusade.

Elton with Daisy Osborn (third from left) and the Osborn team in Ilesa, 1967. With them are evangelists that were being sponsored by the Osborn Foundation.

Royal treatment. Elton presents Daisy Osborn to the King of Ilesa, 1967.

Young Benson Idahosa.

Edgar Parkyns, Elton's friend and colleague from their Apostolic Church days. He was the one who introduced Benson Idahosa to Elton.

Idahosa, Elton and Daisy Osborn, planning for the Osborns' Benin Crusade, 1974.

The Idahosas and the Eltons in Benin.

Elton with some of the key figures in the post-civil war revival in eastern Nigeria. Standing (left to right): Paul Nwachukwu, Augustine Nwodika and one other person; squatting: Edward Ezenwafor.

The Eltrons, sometime in the 1970s.

The last photo of Hannah, taken February 28, 1983.

Elton in his office, ca. 1970s.

Cover of *Herald of the Last Days,*
Elton's flagship publication.

The family in the 1970s

Elton cooking!

Elton preaching at a Full Gospel Businessmen's International Fellowship programme in the 1980s.

Elton and Grace Delbridge, ca. 1985.

Final resting place of Sydney and Hannah Elton.

Roman Catholic-Pentecostal Dialogues."[61] The purpose of the dialogues was to stop the exodus of Roman Catholic Christians to Pentecostal churches in the wake of the Charismatic Renewal. The dialogues were to help Roman Catholic Christians who had embraced the renewal to feel more at home with expressing their spirituality within the Roman Catholic fold.[62] In 1976 du Plessis brought Robert McAlister, who was "leading a major Pentecostal reformation in Brazil among Roman Catholics and Pentecostals alike,"[63] into the dialogues.

While participating in the dialogues, McAlister "felt strongly that it was time for there to be a Pentecostal Bishop," and he proposed the idea to du Plessis, who then advised him to seek formal recognition from the Vatican. Even though the proposal was viewed favourably by those involved in the dialogues, the Roman Catholic leaders felt such a move would create a "precedence that could undo history and establish division within the Roman Church."[64] The Apostolic Counsel of the Roman Catholic Church advised McAlister to seek ordination with the Anglicans, after which the Vatican would be willing to authorize him to be "a special liaison to the Pentecostals." But when the Anglicans rejected the proposal because of McAlister's "emphasis on Pentecostal experience," du Plessis and John Meares created a presbytery and went to Brazil in 1978 to ordain McAlister as bishop.

When, in 1978, the pope heard of the ceremony, he believed it was "a gesture of genuine desire to identify with the historical church [Roman Catholic] and he defended the actions of the three Pentecostals and called for McAlister and du Plessis to be brought before him for commissioning as bishops of special recognition and rights, thereby establishing them both as direct descendants of apostolic succession."[65] Even though "this action and decision created much turmoil within the Roman Catholic-Pentecostal Dialogues, the Pope's decisive action and favourable response to the Pentecostals did indeed establish a historical tie to the papacy. . . . On that day in 1978, as a peace gift of the Roman Catholics to the newly recognized Pentecostal bishop, a purple stole was given to both Bishop du Plessis and Bishop McAlister. In the presenting of the stole it was stated that while Roman Catholic bishops wear Roman colours to identify with the history of the Church and the blood of the martyrs, the Pentecostals would wear the purple stole to identify with the blue of heaven and the blood of the martyrs combined, thus signifying the Pentecostals having experienced 'the heavenly sound.' "[66]

In 1981 McAlister consecrated John Meares and Benson Idahosa as bishops.[67] At Idahosa's ordination, McAlister stood in the office of primate, and Meares functioned as prelate.[68] (In fact, Idahosa was consecrated as both bishop and archbishop at the November 1981 ceremony in Benin.[69]) In 1982, these bishops formed the original college of bishops of the World Communion of Pentecostal Churches, which was later renamed International Communion of Charismatic Churches.[70]

After Idahosa's November 1981 consecration, he wrote a letter of appreciation to du Plessis, who was present at the occasion: "My heart is filled and overflowing with gratitude to you for coming and helping to make this a most memorable occasion in my life and in the life of Church of God Mission. Words fail to express my deep appreciation for you and your ministry in the body of Christ. I believe that God brought you on time to Nigeria and used you in a very special way."[71] Almost a year later, Idahosa was still basking in the euphoria of the consecration, as an October 1982 letter to du Plessis reveals: "I am still rejoicing at the goodness and mercy of God in my life. Perhaps the greatest moment in my life, outside of salvation, was God laying His hand upon me to make and consecrate me Archbishop and Bishop. Your participation in this ceremony meant so much to me."[72]

This was a complete about-turn for Idahosa who, just a few years earlier, had delighted in poking fun at ecclesiastical titles. In his inimitable way, he jokingly called archbishops "ashbishops,"[73] emphasizing the spiritual deadness, as he saw it, of ecclesiastical titles and structures.

Elton at some point became very disturbed about the new direction of Idahosa's message and ministry, and he expressed his fears in private conversations with many of his protégés. One of them recalls that Elton did not attend the annual convention of the Church of God Mission—which he never missed—in 1982, as a protest against Idahosa's consecration as bishop the previous year.[74] "He used to go to [Idahosa's] place every year. [But] I remember one particular year, I asked him; he said he was not going there. He [Elton] usually would talk. . . . If anything happened—particularly [for those of us] who were close to him—he would tell us. He had mentioned it to us that Idahosa was planning to 'go ecclesiastical,' that's the way he put it. [That] he was trying to structure; make himself archbishop. . . . He [Elton] also told us that he had discouraged him [Idahosa] and told him that he should not go that route. Elton [had] said this before the ordination took place. I guess he [Idahosa] shared this with Pastor Elton, and Pastor Elton said he disagreed and told him that that was unnecessary. . . . That very year . . . Pastor Elton did not go; [he] clearly denounced it. . . . Idahosa was a son. [But] they had to part ways. He said he wouldn't go, and he never went."[75]

Peter Ozodo remembers standing with Elton outside one of the auditoriums in the Department of Biological Sciences at the University of Ife in 1982, and Idahosa was coming from the opposite direction (he was also at the university to preach, but at a different meeting): "We were all walking towards each other, and Elton said to us, 'I regret sending this man to America; they have ruined him, and he is ruining the work here.' "[76]

Elton was convinced that Idahosa had become negatively influenced by a stream of the Pentecostalism movement in America that was unduly emphasizing materialism and fame. Elton believed that certain wrong influences were beginning to shape Idahosa's spiritual outlook—influences that would bring about a conversion to the American brand of Pentecostalism which Elton was wary of and had continually warned against.

Peter Ozodo relates an experience about a young lady who in the 1970s felt the call of God on her life and went to Elton for counselling. She discussed with Elton her plans of going to a Bible college in America for training, but Elton objected, "You will teach the Americans, not they teach you; they don't have anything to teach you."[77] He said that when she returned she would be speaking "America" more than the gospel. "He [Elton], for example, had earlier sponsored the late Pastor Idahosa to go to America and because of the outcome of that, Elton not only regretted having done that, but placed a blockade to other people who tried to do that, in a sense, and said, 'No, you don't do that; you don't go to America.' He said that America had brought a very bad colouration to Nigerian Christianity. Elton was always very sensitive about the possible negative influence of other cultures on the development of Pentecostal Christianity in Nigeria."

In a reply, in 1980, to the letter of a young Nigerian Christian living in the UK, he wrote: "Your views on the spiritual state of UK does not shock us . . . it will be so . . . they, as a nation, have left the right way and God has turned to other nations . . . (especially Nigeria) to do the job." He continued that "USA is even worse but they will return to the right way soon . . . but even so you will find a remnant in the UK."[78] Bayo Famonure recalls that Elton "was quick to point out the errors infiltrating the Pentecostal terrain in Nigeria and America. He warned me to avoid being polluted by the West."[79]

Such cautions were surprising, coming from a man who had played the leading role in introducing Nigerian Christians to the ministry of American Pentecostal leaders through magazines, books, audio and video tapes, and crusades in the country. He had written as late as 1981, with an obvious tone of approval, about the visit one of his protégés to the US: "He is planning a visit to U.K. & USA this year . . . plans to visit Hagin's camp mtgs and visit Osborns in Tulsa."[80]

What emerges from a thorough study of Elton's view on the subject is that he really wanted Nigerian Christians to get the best of what the West, particularly Britain and America, had to offer spiritually, and he personally did all he could to expose them to it; but he was always equally worried about the strong temptation posed by the many excesses, the razzle-dazzle, that was becoming the staple of certain streams of American Pentecostalism. "One of the reasons why we are so reluctant to let the Americans come into this country," Elton said in 1984, "is because they tend to promote for business purpose. We don't want Nigeria to copy America, because we want the blessings of God in Nigeria to be Nigerian. We want to know what God wants for us. What God wants for America is for them, and let them have it. We want the unadulterated blessing of God without any commercialism or promotions. Evangelism today is used for business purposes, for raising money and enabling a man to make a name as a big, well-known evangelist; and there are more failures than there are successes; and I can tell why."[81]

Elton never had any qualms about denouncing the practices in a movement that he believed had begun to stray from focusing on Jesus Christ to being man-centred, even if he had initially been a part of it. Elton's later view of some of the leaders of the Latter Rain revival of the early 1950s is a classic example. By the 1960s, Elton had surprisingly distanced himself from the direction in which the Latter Rain movement was headed. Writing many years later, he lamented what he regarded as the derailment of the movement: "In 1954, there was another attempt to establish through the Latter Rain [revival], the great kingdom teachings, and certain attempts were made particularly from America to go out to evangelise the Lord Jesus Christ and His gospel. . . . Then it became too commercialised, it became too much of a programme for various operators, not people who were dedicated to the glory of the Lord Jesus Christ but dedicated to the gathering in of dollars and the building up of individual churches and individual radio programmes. The motive was wrong and therefore the Holy Spirit was driven out of control of it."[82]

Elton was dismayed that a revival which he thought would usher in all the fullness of God's plans for man—and for which reason he invested everything in it—was so easily hijacked by man to fulfil his own ends rather than God's purpose. Elton fell out with Thomas Wyatt along the line. Elton regretted that Wyatt and some other leaders were exploiting the revival to promote their individual ministries.[83] Speaking many years after the events, Edgar Parkyns would also confirm Elton's stand: "It was a real move, but it was a move that was rapidly ruined by the greed and ambition of men."[84]

In the seventies and eighties, many Nigerian Pentecostal leaders, particularly the upcoming charismatic preachers, would have paid any price to have a relationship with the leading lights of the American Pentecostal scene. But Elton was raising a different cry; he wanted everybody to know that it was in Nigeria that God was doing a new thing. As far back as the sixties, Elton had begun preaching that God had initiated a move in Nigeria which was crucial in the plan of God for the last days and which was going to spread to the ends of the earth; it was therefore crucial that it be protected from any corrupting influence; and Elton believed he had the responsibility to guard the gates of the city.

Some keen observers like Peter Ozodo describe Elton as having an almost morbid fear that the hype and excess baggage of American Pentecostalism was going to corrupt what God was doing in Nigeria.[85] He feared that America's influence would be the ruin of Nigeria's Pentecostalism. Augustine Nwodika recalls that whenever he and some of his colleagues were travelling to America, Elton would give them some pocket money. "He would give us and say to us, 'Don't go there and learn their ways.' He would say, 'Go there, enjoy yourselves, say whatever you want to say, but don't allow their dollar to deceive you, and don't allow yourselves to be deceived.' . . . [He would] sometimes [give us up to] two thousand dollars in those days, in the seventies and eighties."[86]

But as much as Elton tried to stop the tide, from the early eighties, a shift began in Nigeria's Pentecostal movement that would significantly shape it along the lines of the American-style Pentecostalism that he greatly feared. Ironically, this shift was championed by no other person than Benson Idahosa, Elton's most visible protégé.

Mike Heathcote, Parkyns' successor as principal of the Bible school in Benin (he was there from January 1972 to November 1973), recalls that even in these early days Elton was already worried about America's influence on Idahosa: "Elton was bothered about American influence even in those early days. Elton was worried it might spoil the simplicity of Idahosa's message."[87] One protégé recalls Elton telling him and some others that he had "warned Idahosa about a number of things, but Idahosa would not [listen]. . . . Even though he would still go to preach for him, but he would tell us privately, 'Don't follow his example.' "[88] Another close protégé remembers Elton saying so many times, "Benson has missed the road."[89] Scores of Elton's protégés recall him saying the same thing. One recalls that Elton "was not happy about titles. . . . This idea of you calling yourself by a string of titles, he felt that wasn't the important thing."[90]

Another articulates Elton's thoughts on the issue this way: "Pa was always warning us about [the] dangers of the years that were ahead of us. . . . I remember one particular meeting, it was at the Polytechnic [Ibadan]—Pa preached on the Feast of Tabernacles and [on] rivers of living water that was going to come around the church with great miracles and everything, but he was always warning that not everybody was going to make it; that we should be very careful. He was always using examples—using people like Idahosa, that [he had] missed it, and that he was very disappointed in him; he said it publicly; Pa wasn't afraid of anything. He would say, 'Benson, God didn't ask him to build an empire; God asked him to take the word of God, but Benson has forgotten.' I think he finally —I can't remember particularly the details—he said he wasn't going to go to Church of God Mission again, because he had warned Ida-hosa about some of the mistakes that he was making—all [the] bishop and clothes and ecclesiastical things, which was where we were coming from and we said was wrong—how could we now go back to all those things? So, we younger ones, he kept advising us that we should not go in that path."[91]

Another protégé recalls Elton's words during one major meeting in Benin in 1981. "I was there at Miracle Centre, Benin, they gave the microphone to Pa Elton to speak, he said people were there, cars were there, but that the owner of the church—that's Jesus Christ—was not there. Pa said that openly. He said, 'You have people here, you have cars, you have money, but He is not here.' "[92]

One of Idahosa's closest lieutenants remembers Elton's last visit to Benin: "What I remember vividly . . . the day Pa Elton took me out; the service was on and Benson Idahosa was preaching at Miracle Centre and Pa Elton suddenly held my hand, so I followed him. And we went out; it was an evening service. And he said, 'Son, this is my last visit.' So I looked at him. He said, 'That man standing there [Idahosa] may not be the same man you see at home. Follow the man standing there, don't follow the man you see at home. I said, sir? He said 'Son, just take my word. Follow the man standing there. The man standing there has God's favour on him. He is going to make heaven. If you follow the one you see at home you will go to hell and the man will still go to heaven.' . . . He said there was something God had destined for Benin City, [but] God was taking it to the East. He said, 'Mark my words, it won't be long.' He said, 'You see those singing at the altar?' I said, 'Yes.' Then he said, 'Mark my words.' And he ended it there. He took my hands again and he said, 'The main part of the message is coming, let us go.' So I now followed him inside, he took me in. And that was the last time Pa Elton visited Benin."

He continues: "All we did or Archbishop Idahosa did to bring him back to Benin City did not work. All he did to persuade him to come, he didn't come. . . . That was about a year or two years before we moved to Faith Arena. I think it was about 1981 he came last. He was disturbed about some developments. He was disturbed. I think he just felt . . . peradventure he was noticing some things which did not conform with his own beliefs. It was during the period [that] the prosperity gospel actually started. We started laying more emphasis that God can prosper, God can prosper. It was as though the main issue of conversion was being relegated to the background."[93]

In a 1986 letter to John and Celia Valentine, Elton expressed his deep concern about Idahosa: "The work here is moving forward fast . . . but the main body of the churches is dividing and fighting and getting more and more involved in questionable operations etc etc. I am not going to give you details of B.A.I. [Benson Andrew Idahosa] . . . there is no need to do so . . . but you cannot believe what is in fact happening and it is bad. I watched him on T.V. recently and there was not a word of the gospel or the way of salvation in any of it. We shared the platform with . . . [Idahosa's assistants] in Jos . . . but were not impressed . . . but they do not realise their condition. You [the Valentines] did very well to get out when you did."[94] Celia Valentine recalls, "In the early days, Pa [Elton] was a mentor to Idahosa as he was to numerous other pastors in Nigeria and even beyond, but as time went on, there was a shifting to prosperity teaching and the celebrated American evangelists, so Pa's influence waned. . . . For various reasons we left Nigeria in 1980 and after that the Eltons' visits to Benin stopped."[95]

Elton was no longer at ease; his heart was breaking at what he considered a bad omen for the future of the church in Nigeria. Before the 1980s, Elton rarely expressed great fear about the future of the church in Nigeria. He had definitely warned time and again about the need for the church to be careful not to derail God's plan for Nigeria—about the need to fight for Nigeria's prophetic destiny. But these were simply warnings. Before the 1980s, Elton warned. But in the 1980s, he began to express fear. A certain foreboding pervades many of his messages in these last years. While he never lost his confidence in the glory that was coming, he became very anxious about the future. Many who were close to him in these closing years could feel his apprehension. Elton was grieving.

His disappointment over Idahosa's new direction gradually became representative of his fears about wider developments in the charismatic movement in Nigeria. Elton was convinced that a major erosion of the foundations of the movement was beginning to take place. He believed emphasis on the pursuit of true spirituality was becoming secondary and that the quest for materialism and fame was taking over the soul of the movement. Dreading that the corruption he deeply feared had begun to set in, he observed in 1983, "For years now I have been disgusted with the level at which evangelism has become a commercial project. . . . God is not in the promotion business."[96] Elton was never against the material prosperity of believers. In fact, he frequently preached that God wanted His children to prosper financially. But he also continually harped on the fact that the prosperity of the believer was not for self-aggrandisement, but rather for expanding the kingdom of God. "He warned about prosperity; like I said, the first [prosperity message] I heard was actually from Pa [Elton]; he believed in prosperity, but [was wary] of the way the Americans were teaching us. . . . He didn't have anything against prosperity, but he certainly warned us about it,"[97] one protégé recalls.

One of those who were really close to Elton in his final years remembers that so much did this shift affect Elton that it took a word from God to ease the tension in his heart. "The Lord had to speak a word. He said, 'My servant, you have mourned long enough over Saul; fill your horn with oil and go and anoint my David afresh.' I remember the time the Lord spoke that prophecy to him. And Pastor Elton mourned over Saul; he mourned over the degradation in the church, the problems. He kept mourning, and he kept wondering what would happen; he was longing for revival."[98] Another close observer recalls: "I remember Elton talking about an old order. I remember him talking about Saul; he talked about Saul and David. He told us that God was raising a Davidic order, a David company of people. . . . He said Saul represents an order, an old order that is fading. He warned us about the American kind of gospel; he said that people will begin to personalize ministries. He warned us about titles: that [a] title is not it, and that if this job [could] be done with titles, it would have been done [a] long time ago."[99]

It was in the early eighties that the "Saul and David" narrative became prominent in Elton's teaching. Saul was a metaphor for spiritual leadership which presently commanded great respect and influence (like Saul, who was "head and shoulders" [1 Sam. 9:2] above all Israel), but nevertheless had lost its way; and it was only a matter of time before the spiritual poverty of such leadership was exposed. David represented leadership that was completely dedicated to the purpose of God and which rejected any attempt to pursue its own ambition under the guise of the work of the ministry.

"In a way today in Nigeria, we've got a *head and shoulders* church governed by man's ideas, governed by man's organizations and governed in every way human," Elton said. "And God in many cases has left it. And that head and shoulders government, that head and shoulders vehicle, that head and shoulders church is there, and is going to oppose the Davidic, the David body that God is going to raise. For when Saul became king, he was all right for a time, but it was never recalled that Saul consulted God at all during the whole of his reign; he never consulted God. He could manage on his own, and he failed. And God could see that he had failed, and God's vessel and vehicle was ready. 'And God said to Samuel, fill your horn with oil and go' [I Samuel 16: 1]. . . . And God in these days is in the process of anointing a new body of people, followers and sons of King David spiritually, and not governed by *head and shoulders* government."[100]

Elton explained that one major challenge would be to discern the spiritual shift, to know that even though Saul was still on the throne, true spiritual authority had passed on to David. It would take the spiritually discerning to know that God had moved on. "The problem today is to discern the difference between the two bodies of people," Elton said. This crisis of discernment and subsequent choice was best symbolized by the life of Jonathan: "Jonathan was King Saul's son and Jonathan had vision, power, and revelation. Jonathan knew that God had left his father and that David was going to take his place as king. And Jonathan loved King David, the Scripture reveals. Jonathan and David formed one of the greatest love stories in the Bible; they loved each another. They were so close that they were closer than man and wife; they were one. Jonathan knew the future, and he said to David, 'When you're king, I'll be with you.' But it did not happen. Why? Because his revelation and his vision only stayed in his head and didn't go into action. He stayed with the 'head and shoulders' government and perished with it. He was slain with his father."[101]

Adapting the Saul-David typology to developments in the Pentecostal movement, Elton continued:

> I want also to say this, for those of you who are alive, the people who will head and lead the opposition and the persecution to that which God is doing in these days will be the Pentecostal churches. I know history will repeat itself. It's the leaders of the past revelation that always oppose the leaders of the new revelation. Always! And I had a little bit of it. I can tell you that Saul hated David and there is nothing that can be compared or measured like religious hatred.
>
> And the Pentecostal churches are going to hate us, because they'll say they've got what we are preaching. They taught it. I taught it. I know. They can't argue with me because I taught them; but they've lost it. They are only Pentecostals in name. They've lost it. But because we go and preach what they said they've got, and they've lost, we're exposing them. They'll lose their people and that's what they are afraid of. They'll lose their business and its money that's involved. But we're prepared for that.
>
> And I want you to be very careful of how you handle this situation. I'm warning you of the situation in Nigeria today. God is doing a new thing; He's bringing into light a manifestation of a new body of people altogether. That body will be God's church and they will win. That body will reach to the heights of purity, order, vision, and power. And we are nowhere near that level yet, but we are going there.[102]

Elton was concerned that many leaders, by reason of their impure motives, would become hindrances to the move of the Holy Spirit which the church so desperately needed. "If the priests won't do it, what then will happen?" he asked. "Then I am sorry, God is going to bypass the priests. That's judgement. God is not going to allow any body of men—however clever or clean or holy they call themselves—He is not going to allow any body of priests to take His place; He is going to brush them on one side."[103] Elton ever lamented over leaders who were still in the limelight even when it was clear that their hearts had been seduced by the enemy.

"I had a shock some years ago when I read Ezekiel 44. I had a problem on my hands," he began speaking about this concern. "I had been able in the permission of God to bring into existence a large number of men who have been used of God in Nigeria, and very, very few of them had made the grade. I won't tell you their names. They are a big sigh to me. We saw them born again; we saw them baptized in water; we saw them baptized in the Holy Ghost; we saw God use them in preaching the Gospel, in miracles—and I don't mean stomach ache, I mean raising the dead. I saw it happen—blind eyes [opened]. In a crusade this year, nineteen completely deaf and dumb people heard and spoke in one meeting. That's a miracle, because faith cometh by hearing, and how can a deaf and dumb person hear? That's a miracle when that happens . . . and nineteen in one meeting, but, somehow or the other something's gone wrong; some of those men are doing things I know are not righteous. They are becoming involved in the things of the world, the things of the flesh. They are becoming overambitious for money and position and property, cars, houses. What's gone wrong? The problem that I had to solve is this—God is still using them! And I asked the question, 'Lord, how can you do that? These men, I know they are not clean and you are using them.' "[104]

"Some years ago I found the answer," said Elton. He went on to talk about how God "still allows those men . . . [because of] grace," how "those men can still continue their sacrifices, how they can still minister in the outer court," but they can't come near the most holy place. In other words, their ministries, while glamorous and even sometimes confirmed by miracles, did not have the capacity to open the heavens and bring reawakening to the church. Their ministries lacked the capacity to cause men's hearts to burn and return to God. They could move men but not stir the heavens. To have this kind of ministry, Elton believed, was a great tragedy. The benchmark for true ministry was its ability to transform men into Christ's image and make them passionately committed to the plan of God. False ministry confined men to earthly desires even though this was pursued in a spiritual context—true spiritual ministry was heavenward, setting men ablaze for the kingdom of God. "We shall not be satisfied with seeing men and women accepting Jesus Christ only, but to go on and see that those converts are made into soldiers and fighters and not mere church members,"[105] he once declared.

"He warned us," recalls one protégé. "He spoke about the ten virgins; they went out in the night to receive the bridegroom. Five of them were wise; five of them were foolish. He said five is the number of ministry, that that parable was actually speaking about ministry. That at midnight there is going to be a separation: that a ministry will go up with the Lord, but another ministry will fade. And these were the five virgins that didn't have oil. Elton told us . . . that the days of one-man [show] are over. It's not about one man; it's about Jesus Christ. Elton was concerned [about these things]. He said it over [and over]; he fell out with a lot of people [because of it]."[106]

Whenever Elton talked about Saul in an emotional and direct way, his audience usually knew whom he was talking about. Saul had a general and also a specific connotation, a symbolic and a real reference.

The Elton-Idahosa relationship arguably had the most significant impact on the early development of the charismatic movement in Nigeria. When the decade-long collaboration ended, an era in the development of the movement was brought to a close.

One of Elton's greatest pains till his dying days was that he had lost one of his dearest sons to the "American gospel."

FOURTEEN

A REVOLUTIONARY CHRISTIANITY

The seventies were a socially turbulent decade in Nigeria's history. After the civil war ended in January 1970, the nation was trying to redefine itself, and an atmosphere of uncertainty prevailed in many spheres of national life; one crisis after another bedevilled the nation. The tension was particularly felt among students in the nation's institutions of higher learning who had come to distrust all forms of authority; they viewed almost every move by Nigeria's leadership with suspicion and tried to make their views known on practically every national issue. They were vigilant so as not to be short-changed in the unfolding Nigerian experiment; this would lead to several mass protests and repeated clashes with the government. As one historian of the period noted, "1971 to 1976 marked the years when Nigerian students graduated to a higher plane of struggle by demanding patriotic questions from the society. . . . Nigerian students within the period in question rose up in one body to fight . . . in order to ensure that the blood of the innocent Nigerians who died in the crisis years of 1966-70 was never shed in vain."[1]

On January 30, 1971, students of the Nnamdi Azikiwe Hall of the University of Ibadan embarked on a hunger strike to protest poor cafeteria services. By February 1—seventy-two hours into the hunger strike—the school authorities panicked and brought in the police to smash the demonstrations; one student died and many others were injured. As news from Ibadan travelled round the country, students expressed shock at the tragedy—police brutality on a university campus had been unknown in the country until this time. In solidarity with their colleagues, all the universities and other institutions of higher learning in the country organized protest marches. On February 3, the students of the University of Lagos carried a mock coffin and headed for Dodan Barracks, but they were stopped by antiriot policemen. In the fracas that ensued, many students were molested; the students in turn burnt two police stations. The next day, the students were allowed to present their demands to the head of state.

Similar demonstrations were carried out at the University of Ife; Ahmadu Bello University, Zaria; Advanced Teachers College, Zaria; Abdullahi Bayero College, Kano; Kaduna Polytechnic; and in several other campuses. On February 4, student leaders from all over the country gathered in Ibadan to plan the murdered student's burial arrangements, which was to take place two days later. At the meeting, "Messages of sympathy and solidarity were read. . . . Such messages came from student movements all over the world and the world university council based in Geneva."[2]

Yakubu Gowon, the head of state at the time, responded by setting up a panel of inquiry. The panel's report indicted the university's leadership, condemned the brutality of the police, and made recommendations for reforms. When the white paper released by the government generally disregarded the major recommendations of the panel, students were enraged. "Students' reactions to the useless report were spontaneous and immediate. . . . A press conference was addressed by the President of the National Union of Nigerian Students. . . . He told the press that Nigerian students had rejected the government white paper on the grounds that the white paper was 'unjust, inequitable and inconsistent with the spirit with which it was set up.' . . . That same day a delegation of Nigerian students all over the country converged at the Tinubu Square, Lagos, and made [a] bonfire of four copies of the government's white paper."[3]

On the first anniversary of the Ibadan mayhem, the National Union of Nigerian Students (NUNS) released its response to the government's white paper, titled "NUNS Black Paper."[4] In it, the students "made an eighteen point demand from the government," which captured the mood of Nigerian students about developments in the country, particularly with regard to the recklessness and rampant corruption in government. In his October 1970 Independence Day broadcast, Gowon had said: "I charge the youths of this country to demonstrate the virtues of resolution, dedication and faith. I call on particularly those who aspire to the future leadership of this country to be guided always by the highest ideals. You all have a special role to play in making Nigeria a great nation and a happier society. . . .This country needs the observance of more stringent moral standard. A new country cannot develop and attain greatness except its people are motivated by high ideals. The tone of the society must be changed if there is to be trust and confidence between the leadership and the people. Only then will people be happy to make the sacrifice necessary for achieving a faster rate of progress. This is why the military government will intensify the drive against corruption in whatever quarters it may exist."[5]

Gowon's takeover had initially been perceived as a harbinger of hope, but it was becoming clear to Nigerian students that his regime was a sham. The students' demands therefore went beyond the immediate Ibadan incident to the broader issues affecting the nation's progress. The black paper called for "the immediate removal of all civil commissioners from the Federal and State governments so as to enable the Nigerian people to identify clearly" those who were "responsible for the misfortunes of the country. The students called for a decree to limit the number of houses that a person could have in the country to two, adding that anyone found to have more than two should forfeit the rest to the state."[6]

The call by the students, which would be repeated in different forms throughout the decade, was an attempt to reclaim the promise of a great nation, which they believed was still attainable though the promise had suffered severe dents in the political upheavals of the sixties and the civil war that followed. The 1971 University of Ibadan crisis was, however, only a foretaste of what would happen in the succeeding years—the rest of the seventies would be marked by protests and demonstrations by Nigerian students.

The next major nationwide protests by students were sparked by Gowon's announcement in 1972 that the federal government had established a compulsory National Youth Service Corps programme. Again, in 1974, when the police tried to forcefully stop a peaceful procession for the third anniversary of the 1971 killing, violence erupted, leading to the arrest of many student leaders. Protests quickly spread round the country; four universities were immediately shut down and scores of student demonstrators were locked up by the police. The announcement by Gowon in October 1974 that the timetable for the transition to civilian rule was no longer feasible, and the Udoji Awards saga that December, revealed the complete bankruptcy of his government, which led to new levels of apprehension among students.

In July 1975, Gowon was overthrown in a coup d'état. Less than a year later, the new head of state, Murtala Muhammed, was killed in another coup. The seventies had begun with great hope for Nigerian students, but darkness now covered the horizon. Any previous hope about a great future was fast vaporizing. By the mid-seventies, the distrust that Nigerian students had for the nation's leadership reached unprecedented levels. Most university students and new graduates began to lose faith in the system and despaired about the future of the country.

In this atmosphere of distrust and disillusionment, many students, believing that democracy and military rule had failed in Nigeria, began to consider the communist (socialist) system as a viable alternative. Hundreds of students were open to indoctrination into socialist ideology, which at the time was being propagated through socialist literature that flooded the campuses. Words and phrases like "bourgeois," "neo-fascist," "progressive intellectuals," "Marxist," "native capitalist zombies," "reactionary bourgeois leaders," and "revolutionaries and peasantry" became popular. Many students proudly quoted leaders of communist nations like Mao Zedong of China and Fidel Castro of Cuba. Socialist ideology was thriving. At least six major socialist groups began enjoying some significant level of followership on the campuses: The Patriotic Youth Movement of Nigeria, The Progressive Youth Association (of Nigeria), The Black Nationalist Movement, Marxist Socialist Movement, Young Socialist Movement (of Nigeria), and The People's Society of Nigeria.[7]

Christian students were worried about the developments in the country. They were troubled not only by the corruption and general lack of direction, but also by anti-Christian trends, like the rise in occultism and reports of plots to Islamize Nigeria. Many Christian students interpreted the upheavals not only as a disruption of the social and economic stability and prosperity of the nation, but as assaults against the Christian subculture. From this perspective, the most serious threat of the seventies soon became the increasing trend towards socialism among students, many leaders, and many activists in the country.

Even though Christian students condemned the political, social, and economic decline, and believed, like most of their colleagues, that the military and democratic experiments had failed thus far, they vehemently opposed socialism as an alternative. They were alarmed at the rate at which their peers were embracing socialist ideology, which was at the time considered the number one adversary of Christianity all over the world. Many Christian students closely monitored the plight of Christians in communist countries, and books like Richard Wurmbrand's *Tortured for Christ*, which for a time was the most popular book about Christian persecution under communist regimes, were very popular among students.

By the mid-seventies, a prayer group, named "The World Prayer Band," had been started at the ECU (University of Ife) for the sole purpose of praying for the "communist Christians [Christians living in communist countries] and those in other parts of the world that are undergoing persecution."[8] The 1975 orientation edition of the ECU's monthly magazine dedicated about half the space to sensitizing students to "the evil and godless ideology called communism."[9]

One article (among many others) circulated among Christians in the country in the 1970s gives us a view into the temper of the times and the general Christian perspective of the socialist threat. The article, titled "Danger!! A Monster Rises against Nigerian Saints," published by a group called Jesus Revolution Voices (JRV), was "to be circulated strictly among 'born-again' Christians only."[10] The article began, "All through history, Christians have had challenges to their lives and faith. Today the Nigerian Christian is facing one of the greatest challenges of our time. As the nation passes through a period of uncertain ideological metamorphosis, people hold their breath for the unpredictable result of this ideological transition"; but the author wondered "how many Christians in this country are aware of our present spiritual condition as well as the nation's ideological position." It was a surprise that even though the debates on the Draft Constitution had "flared into nationwide debates over the TV, Radio and Press as to the best ideology for this country . . . we have not yet heard any true Christian speak on this topic."[11] Further disturbing was the fact that while the church was "at ease in Zion," "political adventurers" and "fanatics of socialism" were taking advantage of developments in the country and the debates about the Draft Constitution to argue for socialism as the best ideology for Nigeria.

The article rebuked Christians for their apathy and selfish motives and warned that there was impending danger if the church refused to wake up to the situation. The writer warned that the number of socialists in the country was increasing at an alarming rate. Many of the socialists were very determined people; many had already gone "underground"; others had "resigned their lucrative jobs for the sole purpose of working underground . . . for a Nigerian socialist state." Among their number were "lecturers, doctors, musicians and even old politicians who are using their positions to influence public on the new ideology." The socialists had many "student activists" on the campuses who "organise symposia and engage other students in brain washing discussions which are meant to indoctrinate them." They were dedicated and committed to their cause: "They are very ready to lose their jobs, live in rural areas, or even sacrifice their lives if need be, for the advancement of their goal."

The article concluded with a plea. "I am pleading with us to return to our first love, and become prayerful saints. We need a change of heart and attitude. This is a crisis-moment, a time of spiritual emergency, who will believe it? God needs dedicated and consecrated men and women who would stand in the gap. He needs intercessors of no mean degree who will catch the vision and take the burden, whom He will use to meet the challenge of this hour. Dear reader, you can be a volunteer in this crack squad. Our day is far spent in this country. Darkness is coming when no man can work. But we have JESUS, the SUN OF RIGHTEOUSNESS whose radiance can dispel this impending gloom."[12]

It was against this background—the confusion of the seventies—that Austen Ukachi, the president of Ibadan Varsity Christian Union, convened a meeting of leaders of Christian groups in Nigeria's institutions of higher learning, in May 1977, to share his burden about the challenges facing the country. At the meeting, which was held on May 6 and 7 of that year, Ukachi "explained in detail how the Lord burdened his heart" to bring the Christian groups together to discuss certain issues that needed urgent attention. The issues, as listed in the report of the meeting were "1) The threat of socialism, 2) The rate of growth of cults, 3) The rising demand for shrine worship by our intellectuals, 4) The alarming rate at which some brethren phase out spiritually as soon as they leave the institutions, and 5) The telling effects of the above on our country, our faith and the work of God."[13]

The atmosphere was charged with exhortations, singing, praying, and prophecy, and the attendees' response to Ukachi's presentation was unanimous: The report of the meeting noted that the representative from Kaduna Polytechnic said, "The same vision and burden have been caught by them over there in the North and they have started praying for the nation and for what line of action to follow. Therefore this meeting was an answer to prayers. He alerted us of the move by the Moslems to install a president for Nigeria by 1979 and subsequently wage a war of Jihad to turn the whole country into a Moslem nation. Plans for this have reached an advanced stage. He said that now is the time for action and we must be prepared to serve the Lord."[14]

The delegate from Adeyemi College of Education, Ondo, "confirmed the same burden and reiterated that our prayers and faith should be balanced now with action."[15] The representative from the University of Ife told the gathering that "the Professors at Unife have already started shrine worship, though they have not yet found a place to erect the shrine. . . . He reminded us that almost everything revolutionary has always originated from institutions of Higher Learning and God wants to use us Nigerian Christian students, to stop the menaces of the enemy and propagate the gospel of our Lord Jesus Christ."[16]

On the second day of the meeting, which was attended by seventeen representatives from thirteen institutions, it was decided that a new body be formed to address the concerns discussed at the meeting. The body was tentatively called Christian Students' Social Movement (CSSM). A central executive of seven members was chosen. A feeling of triumph pervaded the two-day meeting. The attendees felt a revolutionary movement that would seize the initiative and turn around the fortunes of the nation had been born. The conference acknowledged the role of NIFES in coordinating Christian groups on the campuses, but concluded that the vision of the new group was beyond the scope of NIFES. The report stated that "the issue of NIFES as a central body of the Christian Unions/Fellowships in the institutions of higher learning was raised and discussed. It was agreed that in as much as we would support and pray for the NIFES, this special assignment will not be coordinated by the NIFES though it should be involved."[17] The meeting ended with the adoption of specific strategies through which the group would tackle the challenges facing the nation and with a decision to reconvene the following month at the University of Ife.

A prayer bulletin circulated by the ECU after the May event, and before the June follow-up meeting, reveals a heightened level of spiritual activity on campuses—the resolution at the May meeting had released fresh energy to Christian groups around the country; for the first time in years, many believed there was indeed hope for the nation. Many were now beginning to think that they could do something, and that all hope was not lost after all. It was a call to battle, and Christian students across the nation responded well. Christian students across the land were ready for action. Many believed that something new was indeed happening, and more importantly, it was happening through Christian students.[18]

The June 29 to July 1, 1977 meeting of CSSM at the University of Ife produced the now famous "Ife Declaration" as a statement of the mission of the new movement. The declaration stated:

We, the Christian students of NIGERIA, meeting at the University of Ife by the grace of God on the 30th day of June, 1977 do make the following declaration:

1. As "the WORD (JESUS CHRIST) was made flesh and came to dwell among us and we beheld his glory," we believe that God has called us to bring down the gospel of Jesus Christ—from the clouds of theory to the ground of practice by using our talents, knowledge, vocations and skills to work and witness among our people in their everyday life situations in the towns, rural areas, farms, schools, places of work and in the homes.
2. We believe that Christian students, and indeed Christian workers and professionals, should play an active part in combating the evils and vices that abound in our country—NIGERIA. This we resolve to achieve through the Grace of God by practically demonstrating and faithfully propagating the principles of the gospel of the Lord Jesus Christ, in honestly and faithfully discharging our day-to-day duties in our homes, schools and places of work.
3. Knowing that there are forces of evil and corruption working to the moral detriment of this country, we call upon the leaders, students, workers, professionals—all and sundry in this country to examine their lives and rededicate themselves to the principles of honesty and moral uprightness set forth in the Word of God and befitting of this great Nation—NIGERIA....[19]

The Ife Declaration was signed by twenty-three Christian student leaders from seven higher institutions in the country. At this meeting, Austen Ukachi was elected as chairman; Emeka Nwankpa was elected as coordinating secretary; and Reuben Ezemadu from the University of Ibadan was chosen to be the general secretary.[20]

NIFES (whose position had been weakened by the earlier charismatic initiatives) was not favourably disposed to the emergence of CSSM; it raised accusations that the founding of the new body was selfishly motivated, and that it infringed on NIFES' role on the campuses. NIFES was threatened by the emergence of this new body because CSSM's message was popular among Christian students; many were actually concerned about the challenges facing the students on the campuses and also the nation at large, and there was a consensus that NIFES had been unresponsive to these developments. Many were willing to follow a new leadership if it could effectively mobilize evangelical students to action. There was debate after debate on the issue among evangelical students around the country. Questions were even raised in some quarters about the continued relevance of NIFES.[21]

While the leadership of NIFES admitted that it had not been responsive to the socio-political developments in the country, it was totally opposed to a new movement; and when NIFES realized that CSSM had the potential to rival its place on the campuses, it fought very hard to retain its constituency. It tried to persuade Ukachi to drop his plans of forming a new body and to instead incorporate his vision into NIFES' structure. But Ukachi and the leadership of CSSM rejected the offer. "The CSSM is not anti-NIFES, there is no reason why NIFES should not continue to exist—this country is wide enough to accommodate both of us,"[22] Nwankpa wrote in one reply to the leadership of NIFES.

On June 25, 1977, the NIFES executive committee met at the University of Ibadan; there it was decided that since Ukachi had refused the overtures of NIFES to incorporate CSSM into its structure, "the CSSM should be left on its own."[23] Even though NIFES sometimes painted the CSSM visionaries as self-promoting young men with misplaced zeal and was eventually able to convince a large part of its constituency, many of whom had initially embraced the CSSM vision, to abandon their support for the new movement, there continued to be an overwhelming response to the call by CSSM to mobilize. Just as the convulsions of the early 1970s had done, the CSSM/NIFES crisis caused major fissures among evangelical students around the country: sides were taken, relationships were broken. But as historian Simon Ifere wrote years later, NIFES was changed, even if momentarily, by CSSM's call to action: "It is, however, doubtless, to say that *The Ife declara-tion* at the wake of the charismatic revival was a catalyst to the whole initiative of making NIFES more relevant to the socio-political climate of the day."[24]

What NIFES did in the wake of the charismatic outpouring in the early seventies—being reactionary rather than taking the initiative—was repeated with the emergence of CSSM. (Matthews Ojo's commentary on the response of the Scripture Union to the beginning of the charismatic outpouring perfectly fits the attitude of NIFES throughout the seventies: "[The] Scripture Union was never prepared for the influence of the Charismatic Renewal that gripped the organisation from the early 1970s. Its response to the Pentecostal movement arose as a result of the opposition Scripture Union was encountering from a section of its member-ship and the public. Though interdenominational, Scripture Union made no effort to accommodate the Pentecostal experience of its members. Instead, any member who openly expressed his Pentecostal conviction and tried to teach it to others within Scripture Union was disallowed from active participation in the group. This inadequacy of Scripture Union was remedied with the establishment of alternative organisations."[25])

In defining itself and its mission, CSSM declared that "GOD, our Father, has given us a vision for our country NIGERIA. It is a MOMEN-TOUS and BIG vision. This vision is so exciting, that by it, God has put fire into our bones! God is on the move! . . . We make bold to declare that God's counsel shall stand and He will do all His pleasure in this country. . . . Our vision is that all Christian students, Youth Corpers, workers, professionals and businessmen/women use their God-given and acquired skills, talents, knowledge and vocations to WORK and WITNESS among our people in their everyday life situations in the rural areas, towns, farms, schools, places of work and in the homes."[26] CSSM clarified that the use of the word "student" in the movement's name did not make it "exclusive." Rather it was there to "give it identity because the vision came through students" and "the core of the movement is formed by students."[27] The word "social" may "raise eyebrows," it said, but "it is used because we are really going to interact with the people in every sphere of society." "Jesus Christ did so, and was called the friend of sinners—Great! We think it is a fitting word. We envisage that by putting ourselves on the spot every day we would always each time ask, 'What would Jesus Christ do in my situation?' . . . Social and political involvements are as much our duty as evangelism. . . . Our vision is that we all harness our talents and prayers to combat the negative influence and forces in NIGERIA."[28]

When Ukachi received the vision that became CSSM, one of the first things he did was to seek out "Pa Elton." According to him, he could think of no other interdenominational leader with experience, wisdom, and spiritual stature who would understand the vision. "Now, of course, I had just come from an SU background . . . I didn't understand what the Lord was fully saying. But Elton used to come to the campus . . . and he had been there a couple of times [after I got into UI] and he was a man who spoke with such authority as if to say he knew everything in the mind of God. So we went to him often for counselling,"[29] Ukachi recalls.

He visited Ilesa and shared with Elton that God had spoken to him to challenge Christian students about the social issues of the day. "I went to see him, and I told him all that God told me and he [just kept] looking at me. I was wondering, 'Why is this man looking at me?' Then he said 'Austen, who gave you this revelation?' " When Ukachi replied that it was the Lord, to his surprise, Elton said, "I have been waiting for this [vision] for twenty-five years." "I remember he made that comment several times. And he said, 'This thing is great,' " Ukachi remembers. Elton went on to talk to him about how it would affect the nations and said, "That's why I am alive."[30]

Ukachi says, "I went to him repeatedly, because again, many at times I would doubt, 'How do I know if this is from God?' More so [because we were] experiencing opposition; when the CSSM started, [there were] criticisms, oppositions. . . . I would always go back to Elton. And he would say, 'Austen, don't you worry. This thing, I tell you, is of God; it is of God. Take it from me, it is of God.' " "The one person who was there for us was Elton, whom we always ran to. He would encourage us, counsel us and say, 'Don't retaliate; keep on doing what you are doing. They will criticize you, but don't attack. But stay focused on what you are doing.' So, he . . . through that, taught us quite a lot."[31]

To the surprise of many Christian leaders (even several faithful to Elton), and against popular opinion, Elton stood firmly behind the CSSM vision. He saw it as the fulfilment of the vision the Lord had showed him for many years: the youth of Nigeria were being used as a prophetic voice to speak to issues concerning national life. A new breed was rising up, and Elton loved them with his whole heart. He saw in them the potential for the fulfilment of Nigeria's prophetic destiny. He declared:

Most young people are looking for a faith which is real and effective and related to their problems and the national situation. They see visions of what should be (Joel 2:28. Acts 2:17-18) and they turn away from counterfeits and empty words. They want action and they are not bound by tradition. With their new freedom in society they mean to make sure their faith is based upon more than tradition.

They have a national love, for their own country and its people and they mean to see they contribute towards a New Nigeria. . . . Young people are being sent all over the country and they realise they are called by God and have the means, in the gospel, to change Nigeria. *Let me advise all Christian youths*—when God calls He also enables, and He does not call you to do something you cannot do. He has called you and He will perform through you wonders for Nigeria.[32]

According to Elton, Jesus Christ was a revolutionary, a radical, and if the church was going to have any success in representing the gospel, it had to be the same. An irrelevant gospel was a useless gospel. "Christianity was never designed to be comfortable but revolutionary. It had to be completely revolutionary if it had to succeed in changing men, saving them, meeting their needs and thus changing conditions and nations. . . . Jesus used no violence but He was the true revolutionary."[33] Elton would preach frequently that the kingdom message was the most radical message. "Each time you pray the 'Lord's Prayer,' you are praying a revolutionary prayer," he said. "You are praying for a new kingdom, a new government, to be established on this earth. You are a radical . . . a revolutionary of a special kind."[34]

The Gospel is the only hope that the world has. Human governments are proving totally inadequate to meet the needs of men and women: politically, economically, and socially. Many of the people are suffering today because of the injustices and the corruption of the human governments.

The leaders of the world, the leaders of society and the great thinkers of the world have failed to produce a just and lasting society free from bribery, corruption and inequality. The solution is that they should accept the new king, the Kingdom of heaven, and *our gospel therefore has political implications; it therefore has economic implications, and social implications* as the solution of men have proved inadequate and insufficient, and their failure manifest. God is now setting up a kingdom and commanding us to go and preach that this kingdom will meet their needs.[35]

From its inception, Elton gave every resource at his disposal to CSSM. Elton printed their publications free with his printing press, and when it was not available, he paid for it to be printed elsewhere.[36] He was influential in the major decisions that determined the course of the movement. Elton was responsible for connecting some of the individuals who became the vanguard of the movement. Ukachi recalls that it was on one of his visits to Ilesa that Elton introduced him to Emeka Nwankpa and Steve Olumuyiwa. Nwankpa and Olumuyiwa had been protégés of Elton from their days on campus; they were both presidents (in succession) of ECU in the early seventies.

"Now, at some point, we came in contact with Emeka Nwankpa, because what happened was that Emeka Nwankpa also had [a] relationship with Elton, then once when I went there, Elton said, 'You must meet Emeka and Steve,' and that was how we came together. I had never known Emeka before . . . and that was how all of us came together. So we would always go to Elton to tell him what was being done and he would . . . explain to us what he thought God was saying. Because we were inexperienced. . . . And all these things were things we learned from Pa Elton, because he would always explain to us the principles of walking with God; that if you are walking with God, put His work first, and leave the rest in the hand of the Lord,"[37] says Ukachi. "Again, I would say he taught us what faith was, in the sense that he would always tell us that when it comes to money, 'It's God who funds His work. It is God who supports a man. So if you are going to walk with God, walk by faith and not by sight. Just trust the Lord.' Then he taught us this principle, 'When people criticize you, don't you ever say anything. Allow God to defend you.' Because I tell you, at some point, the criticisms were so much—from Christians and from the senior [friends] who had gone through the CU [Christian Union] and who were wondering, 'What is it you are doing? How is this Christianity different from ours?' "[38]

CSSM's travelling secretary, John Okposio, was stationed in Ilesa for the purpose of proximity to Elton.[39] Elton had been advocating the need for the gospel message to transform society much before CSSM began emphasizing it; it was therefore only natural that he became, according to CSSM, "very closely associated with the movement as a father, counsellor, and mentor. Indeed at a stage, the influence of Elton was so overwhelming."[40] Olanrewaju Phillips, a medical student who frequently functioned as Elton's driver for about the last three years of his life, remembers that he was always taking him to CSSM events in Ilorin, Ibadan, Ede, Ile-Ife, and several other towns.[41]

Elton became so close to the movement that he sometimes participated in the decision-making process. The minutes of one CSSM meeting in 1978 shows Elton's involvement in this direction: "The business [session] began with Bro. Emeka [Nwankpa] leading in choruses and words of exhortation. Later he called on Pastor Elton to give the guidelines of certain issues that will be discussed. These were his suggestions . . ."[42] In fact, the level of closeness became uncomfortable for one CSSM member, so much so that he complained to one of the leaders in a letter: "Pastor Elton is not playing the role (or rather playing more) than he should play. I cannot but put the blame squarely on our shoulders. He [Elton] may be thinking he's doing his best for us—perhaps."[43]

One of the founding members of CSSM recalls, "Pa Elton's message was different. . . . He wasn't a denominational person; he taught about the vision of the church; he talked about the kingdom. He also had a gospel that impacted society. He had a burden for establishing a righteous social order. He taught us that the gospel can change things, that we can change our society. He taught us to go to school; he told us to get higher degrees, and one of the reasons I went for my PhD was him. In those days you didn't need to do that. But he said we should get the best training because we [were] going to need it in the future to change our society. He taught a gospel that was relevant. He taught about integrity, righteousness; he also taught about prophetic insight, principles of the kingdom, and he supported prayers for the nation. He supported the CSSM. . . . He was tremendous."[44]

"He [Elton] made us understand in those early years that our mission here on earth was not [just] to prepare to go to heaven," one early CSSM member recalls.

Because it was the in thing that time that everybody must strive to make heaven—and that was all that mattered—[that] you have to live a holy life, you have to become born again so that you can go to heaven. So, here was somebody telling us that no, that's not what the Bible says, that the Bible is saying because you are born again, you already belong to the kingdom of God; and that you need to affect the people you are living with here on earth and establish that kingdom that you already belong to. [That you were expected to] make other people's lives better by preaching the gospel to them; and going beyond preaching the gospel, you make their life right by the use of your skill. If you are a Christian doctor and you have preached to people and they become born again, then you go further and make sure that their health [is OK], because that is part of the manifestation of the kingdom of God. . . . He used to tell us about the story of Elijah and Elisha—that the first miracle that Elisha did was to fix the water system of Israel.

At that time it was radical—it was new thinking. So we were just flocking to his meetings like packs of bees because somebody was telling me something that was entirely new, and he was talking with so much authority—he was talking it using so many Scriptures. So we began to see the Bible in a different light and Christianity in a different light, and being born again was much more than just preparing to go to heaven. It was affecting the earth, because the earth is the Lord's and the fullness thereof, the kingdom of God has come; the ultimate was heaven coming to earth, that the kingdoms of the world have become the kingdoms of God. Those things were very strange things; everybody was waiting for rapture, and he was saying, "Fine, the rapture will come, but you are coming back here to establish the kingdom of God."[45]

Elton regularly spoke of the need for Christians to be relevant in every field. He advocated that Christians get the best education and professional training they could, as it would be used by God to advance the cause of His kingdom. He believed the impact of Christians was to be felt in every sector of society—agriculture, education, politics, publishing, the economy, and every other area. Once, writing under the title "God's Plan for our Education," he noted, "We ought to realise that God expects the best from His servants and if the Lord opens the way for us to get a good education, then we are to take those opportunities and seek to use our training in the Lord's service."[46] It is important to understand that Elton wrote this at a time when many committed Christians regarded seeking secular positions and opportunities as worldly and a hindrance to the purpose of God. According to them, Jesus was coming soon, and there was no time to get entangled with "civilian affairs."

Victor Adegboye, a professor of medicine, recalls his experience: he wanted to leave the university while in his third year to pursue missions, but Elton told him it would make him irrelevant in the future.[47] Francis

Wale Oke narrates a similar experience: "When I was in the University of Lagos as an engineering and survey student, the hand of the Lord was so strong upon me and upon my life. I was so committed to the preaching of the gospel that I wanted to abandon my university education and go out to preach the gospel. If I had done that, it would have been a disaster. While I was still contemplating on this, we hosted Rev. Elton on our campus. As he stood to preach, he said, 'Some of you are under the mighty hand of the Lord. You are burning with a great passion to serve Him; that is why you want to abandon your university education. Don't do it. God has a purpose in bringing you here. When he begins a matter, He also finishes it. Even if you will not use your certificate at all, yet stay and finish your studies, God will use it to enhance your calling.' "[48]

Elton stressed the fact that whatever your profession was, it was a platform for preaching the gospel, for extending the influence of the kingdom of God.[49] He counselled Christians to get the best training so they could be strategically located in the key positions in the nation, where they could influence policy-making. He helped many Christians who wanted to pursue further educational training overseas to secure visas. Elton once preached, "It doesn't matter what qualifications you have, they will be needed in the future, so I advise you to get the best qualifications you can, so that your skills can then be dedicated and your talents can be dedicated to the Lord Jesus Christ for the benefit of establishing His kingdom over the visible people of the earth, dealing with the visible problems that are existing in commerce, in agriculture, and in the judiciary."[50] Femi Soetan, who knew Elton for about two decades, remembers that "Pa Elton told us to buy lands for agriculture. He told us to invest in farming."[51]

Giving one example of how to engage the society, Elton referred to an initiative that was launched in 1983 by "Dr Kennedy, who is the Secretary General of the National Association for the Rehabilitation of Prisoners (NARP)," and which he [Elton] was very much involved in and excited about. "We . . . are starting a move, and we hope this will be taken up by every part of the country, to attack prisons. Recently I had a crusade in Ilesa prison and in Benin prison; there's a church functioning regularly with thirty or forty properly converted men and women, and when they come out, what shall be done for them? Pray for them? Oh no! They are our brethren, and we've got to find how to rehabilitate and inject them back again into the society that had rejected them. It's our job and we've got to do something about it. Those are the sort of things we've got to attack; the strongholds of Satan, and that's the new evangelism that's coming."[52]

The church militant had the responsibility to unrelentingly attack Satan's strongholds, manifested as corruption in society. "In the place where you are and working; the government institutions in this country are in a terrible mess because you and I have failed to do our jobs. The corruption of the institutions today is because Christians are praying, 'Please Lord, bless me; please, I want a 504,' instead of attacking the enemy and stripping him of his powers, blocking his efforts in the factory, the office, the businesses, government departments where you work. I warn you, war will start the moment you stand there, and you'll either have to join in with them or they'll turn you out. Good! When they get you out, God will open a new door. Having succeeded in doing what He would have you do, He will look after you. Don't you worry! He won't let you be crushed by Babylon!"[53]

Elton became so deeply involved in CSSM that many who were close to him, but who were not a part of the movement, were awed by how completely Elton could be devoted to a group. So close did the relationship become that for those not a part of the core CSSM group, attempting to understand the relationship was like trying to understand the relationship between lovers. What drove Elton's commitment to CSSM? Elton believed the fulfilment of God's plan for Nigeria rested with Christians who could see that plan, and who were willing to stake everything to see it come to reality. That a group of young people were willing to dedicate themselves to that plan thrilled Elton; it rejuvenated his spirit; it made him young again; it made him pulse with new energy. He was determined to match their commitment to Nigeria's prophetic destiny by his commitment to them. If they were willing to lay down their lives for Nigeria, then he was willing to lay down his life for them.

Peter Ozodo, who was very close to Elton, but not a part of the CSSM, gives us an insight into Elton's devotion to the movement: "He believed the Nigerian youth had a very profound role to play in the reorganization of society. What I liked particularly about his views then was that this was supposed to be an outflow into society of Christian life and living; the SU concept at the initial stage was not very well defined as far as the extent to which a person could get involved in social work and in society as such. Elton sort of tried to bring that message in through the ministry of the

CSSM. . . . What he wanted was a very massive thing that would have affected a whole lot of young Nigerian students and graduates. In other words, what is now called discipleship in the marketplace was what Pa Elton saw way back then."[54]

From the early 1970s, Elton began articulating the theological framework that encouraged an engagement with all spheres of society. Elton believed the church was supposed to be a vehicle for national transformation. He wrote that "the gospel of Jesus Christ (now called Christianity) is designed for the market place rather than inside church buildings."[55] The church was to be held responsible if things went wrong in the society: "God has had a wonderful plan for our country since the world was made, but that plan is being hindered, not by Satan, but by the slowness and reluctance of the people of God to move forward with God into their spiritual inheritance and thus possess the promised land."[56] In an article, "The Developing Crisis in Nigeria," Elton spoke to the social crisis that led to the founding of CSSM:

While Christians gather inside "sanctuaries" to sing, "*He is able to deliver thee*" or "*Our God Reigneth*," the enemy laughs and increases his operations, and millions are still in bondage to poverty, ignorance, fear, and disease. Even some churches which received the blessings of the revival in Nigeria of 1930–1940, are now more interested in fighting to defend special doctrinal beliefs; others are more interested in internal societies and financial strength. All this is producing a harvest of sectarianism, bitterness, and divisions, pride and false piety resulting in powerlessness and an easy victory for Satan as he renders them ineffective in God's work.

Even among active evangelical Christian groups there is an attitude of indifference to the growing crisis and approaching harvest. Many adopt the attitude that nothing can be done because these are the signs of the last days. Some agree that prayer is necessary and after praying they feel they have done all they can. Others merely say that the second coming is near and that the Lord Jesus will deal with the problem.

All these explanations are mere excuses to cover laziness and to try to pass the responsibility for dealing with these problems back to God. We must awaken the church to realise that the Lord has given us the task of seeing that all men, all nations, have the chance to hear the gospel and the message that will change men and [historical] conditions. We must not be content to chant our hymns and say prayers while the crisis deepens and the masses are being prepared for the harvest. We cannot pass the responsibility back to God. There must be a change of thinking and attitude towards life and our responsibility for the condition of our nation and society. The great need of Christians in Nigeria is to realise that THEY ARE RESPONSIBLE for the present crises because of their indifference and inaction when they have the mighty GOSPEL TO SOLVE THE CRISIS.[57]

A few months after it was formed, CSSM held a national conference in Jos. Fred Adegoke, who was at the meeting where CSSM was formed, remembers the excitement and heightened sense of mission as students from all over the country flocked to Jos for the conference. On the train (most of the students from the South went by train) and on the buses, you could literally feel that something was about to burst forth. There was excitement in the air. "The meeting was tremendous. It was definitely an outpouring of God's Spirit. There was a great renewal among us; we flowed together. We forgot our differences. People just wanted God. That conference was really powerful; that meeting was the watershed," recalls Adegoke. "That was the beginning. . . . It was like a spark."[58]

Within a short time, CSSM became the most vibrant spiritual move-ment in the country—it became the rallying point for most of those who were seeking a fresh outpouring of the Spirit of God upon the church and the nation. "The work exploded and became very big," says Adegoke. A palpable sense of destiny descended on Christian students all over the country. A generation had suddenly come alive. The subsequent national conferences, which took place every December, witnessed some of the most intense moments in the history of Nigeria's Christian students; they were also the largest Christian students' meetings in the country in the late seventies and early eighties. "CSSM became *the* move, a powerful move, the Holy Spirit end time move; it was different. We were going round [the country]."[59] Speakers at the December conference—which was held in different parts of the country: Port Harcourt, Uyo, Lagos, Markudi, Asaba—included Benson Idahosa, William Kumuyi, Mike Oye, and many other leaders. There was also an annual Easter conference, which was usually held in Modakeke (Ile-Ife). The attendees at this conference were mainly students from the southwest, and Elton was usually the main speaker.[60]

CSSM's activities were spread nationally and were wide ranging. The work camps were among the most popular of the activities. CSSM members would go to a particular village, help out with the work on the villagers' farms, help with any other work in the community, and provide medical services and counsel. "We would help them during the day; we would go out, teach their kids, help them on the farm, do whatever they needed done in their community; [we] cleaned up their community. And then in the evening we invited them to a crusade."[61] The villagers were usually surprised that young men and women in the university could come to their level and participate in their everyday tasks. The first work camp was conducted in Aborisade, near Ile-Ife.

CSSM's prayer initiatives were also wildly popular: there was an annual end-of-year prayer meeting; there was fasting and prayer for the country on the first Saturday of every month, which was sustained for many years; CSSM also mobilized people to pray when there were any pressing national issues (CSSM mobilized prayer cells for the 1979 elections), or when the country was going through a rough patch. CSSM's activities were very popular with students and fresh graduates around the country. Many emerging leaders in the charismatic movement, like David Oyedepo and Christopher Tunde Joda, were regular faces at CSSM conferences.[62] CSSM had no members; it regarded itself as a movement, and participation in all its activities and initiatives were by those who embraced the vision of the movement. By the early eighties, CSSM had "transcended being a ministry to students, to include ministry to workers, businessmen and women, and churches in general."[63]

Immediately CSSM was formed, it began to boldly speak out on cultural, political, economic, religious, and social issues affecting the nation. In 1976, the constitution drafting committee submitted the Draft Constitution, which was to be debated by a Constituent Assembly. Among the issues which the drafting committee had left unresolved, to be debated by the assembly, were the inclusion of sharia law into Nigeria's constitution and the legalization of abortion. CSSM was disturbed that while other interest groups were sponsoring representatives to the Constituent Assembly, Christians were indifferent to the socio-political developments in the country.[64] CSSM believed the only way the outcome of the debates on the sharia and abortion issues could favour Christians was if Christians were in the majority in the assembly to "articulate the Christian viewpoint."[65] CSSM therefore embarked on enlightening, encouraging, and supporting Christians who were "interested in participating in politics."[66] They facilitated the formation of the "Christian

Action Committee" (CAC),[67] for interaction between Christian politicians and church leaders, and also to sensitize Christians to their political and social responsibilities.

When both the goals of a Christian majority in the Constituent Assembly and the failure of the sharia plan to go through were accomplished, CSSM believed it had scored a significant victory and immediately stepped up its campaign of national transformation, through newspaper articles, press conferences, and peaceful public demonstrations.[68] For instance, CSSM openly criticized Nigeria's hosting of the second world Black and African Festival of Arts and Culture (FESTAC) in 1977, because it believed the event committed Nigeria to idolatry. CSSM declared in one of its publications: "During the latter part of the first quarter of 1977, the kingdom of darkness unleashed its wild moves calculated at taking over completely the spiritual leadership of this nation; when there was increased tendency towards occultism and cult membership, agitation to turn this country into the hands of atheists through certain ideologies and deliberate attempts at eradicating the effects of the gospel and stop its further spread. The FESTAC, sort of threw wide the gates of Nigeria to those spirits from the kingdom of darkness and they all were offering our dear nation free tickets to hell and destruction."[69]

Concerning FESTAC '77, Elton said he could not comment because he was the *wrong* colour,[70] but made the church realise its responsibility in raising a lament against such a development. He had warned about "the revival of spirit cults and a call for a return to pagan culture in our nation."[71] CSSM also continued to campaign against the legalization of abortion in the country. Its vibrant women's wing staged peaceful anti-abortion marches in Ile-Ife, Ibadan, and Ondo, which attracted wide media attention.[72] A letter in this regard was sent to the head of state, Olusegun Obasanjo, who acknowledged it and assured them that the matter had been settled. They also campaigned against obscenity in the newspapers, particularly "the notorious 'page-three girl' in the Punch newspaper."[73] The page-three girl in the Punch was eventually dropped, and CSSM believed its campaign had been justified.

CSSM frequently made public statements on national issues through its prayer bulletin—to sensitize the populace and serve as a call for prayers. Elton gave Emeka Nwankpa, the coordinating secretary of CSSM, space at the back of *Herald of the Last Days* to write a column titled "Intercessors of Nigeria and Focus for Prayer." In the pursuit of its vision to transform the nation, CSSM facilitated or encouraged the formation of groups targeted at specific sections of society, such as The Association of Christian Teachers, Women Also, and Children Evangelism Ministry (CEM).

FIFTEEN

CALLING FORTH NIGERIA'S PROPHETIC DESTINY

Lton began one of his most extensive teachings on eschatology, a three-part sermon titled "The Kingdom of Heaven on Earth," by exploring the three questions that the disciples asked Jesus Christ on the Mount of Olives. In trying to answer these questions, considered by eschatology scholars as central to the Olivet discourse, Elton acquaints us with his thoughts regarding God's plan for Nigeria. He started the concluding part of the series, "Establishing the Kingdom of Heaven in Nigeria," by saying, "God is beginning to move in the world and arranging events for the final showdown of the future. Therefore, we are permitted to ask, 'What is going to happen in the future?' . . . The disciples asked this same question in Matthew 24. . . . I am going to be curious as the disciples were and ask my three questions."[1] He then asked his three questions: "When is the Lord Jesus Christ coming? When will the kingdom be set up on earth? How will we be involved in that kingdom?" He reemphasized the confidence the church should have in the Holy Spirit's role to "give us an insight and prepare our minds for the future,"[2] and then he surprisingly delved immediately into Nigeria's place in that future. This is a consistent pattern in almost all his teachings on the last days. What was the reason behind this Nigeria-focused eschatological outlook? The clearest argument favours the fact that Nigeria's role in God's end-time plan was central to Elton's vision of the future.

If anything evoked great excitement in Elton, it was Nigeria's role in God's end-time plan. At the back of all his books (actually booklets), he defined his ministry thus: "He [Sydney Granville Elton] now devotes most of his time to ministering the last days' messages and particularly the role of our nation in God's end-time plans for His world."[3] Speaking in 1985, he declared, "In my view, Nigeria is being selected by God for a very special purpose in His operations in the world. Nigeria has been specially favoured."[4] And, "God in these days is doing a new job, a much bigger job than you think, and God is revelling in it. God is shaking with delight! God is excited at this moment, as He prepares to carry out His last days' operation, particularly in Nigeria; because He has the rest of West Africa and possibly the whole continent in view. And He's going to take a great deal of time and care in developing what's here in Nigeria."[5]

At a time when he could have been taken for a babbler, he began emphasizing the potential of Nigeria's future role in world evangelization. He prophesied in the 1970s that Nigeria would one day become a leading missionary-sending nation, first to Africa: "One of the blessings we shall see in Nigeria will be the move of the Spirit to send the gospel to all places in West Africa from Nigeria, using Nigerians who have moved into this new blessing. . . . We must expand our prayer warfare to include Togo, Benin Republic, Cameroons, Ghana, Ivory Coast, Liberia, Sierra Leone, and every Central African nation. Having received the 'last days' blessing, Nigeria will be held responsible to pass it on to other nations."[6] And, "We must realise that the present revival and move of the Holy Spirit all over Nigeria is not only for Nigeria, but God has chosen Nigeria as the base from which He is going to invade other West African countries with the gospel of liberation and deliverance."[7] And then to the rest of the world:

We are on the edge of a mighty revival in the whole world, and particularly in Nigeria. I think it will begin in Yoruba land—and I may upset a few tribes—but I think it will begin in Yoruba land. I have been sowing the gospel for forty-five years in Yoruba land, and God is not a foolish farmer; He doesn't sow and not reap, and I am going to see the reaping, and the reaping is going to come very soon. There is going to be a mighty revival, and thousands—hundreds of thousands—are going to be converted every day, coming into the place where they can get food.

The reason why it is not taking place now is because God hasn't got enough men ready to take over and lead them. The prospect for evangelism is great, wonderful. But don't tie it down to ordained, trained workers. It will be done by ordinary men and women filled with the Holy Ghost, filled with the joy of the Lord and what God has done in their lives. The prospect is wonderful, and I am looking forward to seeing a great harvest.

It will cover the whole of Nigeria and Nigeria is God's instrument for the rest of West Africa. Many missionaries, Nigerians please, will go from Nigeria to the other countries and take the gospel with them, and Africa is going to be shaken more than any other continent has ever been shaken before. . . . This is the place where God is working; this is the place where the revival is going to be. This revival in this country will outshine, outmanoeuvre, and out-power any revival in any other country that I know of at the moment.[8]

He called Nigerian Christians in the 1970s to have a global vision. From Elton's teachings, it is abundantly clear that he believed in a special end-time role for the black race in God's plan. Emiko Amotsuka recalls, "He brought us into that awareness of the desire of God to use Nigeria in particular, and the black race in general. He brought us into an awareness of the fact that Nigeria occupied a very special place in the sight of God; [that Nigeria would play a prominent role in] global evangelism in the last days."[9] Speaking at the Ilesa fellowship in 1984, Elton used the history of the sons of Noah—Shem, Ham, and Japheth—as a picture of God's prophetic time line.

Each of these sons is the head of a complete race of people. Shem became the nation recognized by God as the nation of Israel. They were the custodians of the vision of God. . . . God chose them to display His glory and carry His message of deliverance and restoration. We know that they failed.

Japheth has now taken up the challenge. God in the Old Testament—through the Babylonian Empire, through the Medes and the Persians, through the various Gentile empires—propagated the system of Japheth. And Japheth has proceeded to govern the Gentile world until now. . . . Japheth has had charge of the whole purposes of God, particularly in the last two hundred and three hundred years, in the European race in Europe, and later in America. The Gentile world has failed to establish the kingdom of God on earth, so we are seeing the end of the Gentile rule, we are seeing the end of Japhetic rule, and there remains only one son, one head of a new race—the sons of Ham. And we are seeing some of them come to operation in these last days to bring in, finally, the kingdom of heaven on earth.[10]

Elton was calling Nigerians to see their specific role as the trigger of the "Hamitic movement." He once wrote, "It could also mean that the Lord will use this nation's Christians to 'kick open the doors' in other countries, especially West Africa."[11] By the mid to the late seventies, Elton began to impress upon his hearers the "map of Africa" vision. As far as we know, Elton was the first to give a spiritual connotation to Africa's map, or at the least, he popularized and imprinted its significance in the heart of a generation of Nigerian Christians. He told them the map of Africa is shaped like a gun and that Nigeria was in the position of the trigger. "There will be trouble in all the strategic points of the gun because the devil will not want God to use Africa as a weapon to shoot into the camp of the enemy. The horn of Africa is the loading point; the devil will trouble this region to prevent the gun from being loaded. The outlet of the bullet—South Africa, is bound by apartheid to prevent the bullet from being discharged, but the outlet will be opened. Nigeria occupies the position of the trigger, and the devil will do all he can [even if the gun is loaded] to stop the trigger from being released."[12] (One commentator has also written that "in the nineteen seventies, Sydney Elton . . . prophesied, he said, 'South Africa will be free, South Africa will partner with Nigeria in those days, and Africa will lead the world in various ways.' "[13]) This prophetic vision was an all-inclusive one, embracing the whole of the African continent. Over time, Elton's emphasis on the trigger became apparent—perhaps because of his own special role in preparing this part of the gun. "Pa Elton kept telling us that Nigeria was going to be the trigger of the next move of God,"[14] recalls Yinka Ayankogbe.

Elton preached that the knowledge of God's plan for Nigeria placed a burden on Christians—they could no longer excuse themselves from the responsibility of making sure that nothing stood in the way of that plan coming to fruition. In embracing his call to Nigeria, Elton envisioned the totality of the nation's life as his domain. Elton strongly believed that the battle for Nigeria's prophetic destiny could not be separated from the battle for Nigeria's soul. According to him, for Nigeria's prophetic destiny to be realized, Nigerian Christians had to fight to keep the nation stable in all spheres of national life. In a message preached in May 1984, Elton, perhaps in his most articulate presentation of issues related to the Nigerian state, made it clear that there was a battle to be fought for the soul of the nation. He declared:

Since the turn of Nigeria to civilian rule [a] few years ago, there has been great hopes and expectations that Nigeria will now go forward and develop and progress and become the leading nation in Africa that God plans for her. Those hopes are not being realized. Then after many years of prayers and many years of oil resources and internal wealth, we find a great instability. Threats are being made against our security; threats are being made and experienced against our standards of living, our standards of education, our standards of health and safety—threats which we are recognizing and realize will come upon us very soon.

There is political instability; there is social turmoil; there is economic instability, all threatening the progress of this nation and the development as God has planned it. There is also a spiritual apathy and an uncertainty. The Christians who should be the people who give hope and who can say an encouraging word and speak affirmatively concerning the future are puzzled. They have prayed; they have fasted; they expected God to answer their prayers. Instead of that, confusion and turmoil is increasing, and God seems to be silent; corruption seems to be rampant; the various department and government institutions are riddled with corruption, and it seems to the Christian that there is no hope for progress unless they are willing to take part in the corruption and exploitation that is going on.

There is extreme deficiency in all realms, and many of our large national institutions are not working and are a source of disgrace and shame to many of us. We had great hopes, we had great expectations, now those expectations have not been realized. There is a breakdown threatened in law and order, and [there is] immorality, and there are ecclesiastical leaders who are failing us all around, and we turn to ask, what is happening? What's the meaning of all this, and how are we to pray; what are we to pray for?[15]

He dedicated a chapter in *Demon Manifestations in the Last Days* to "The Battle for Our Nation," where he gave instructions on how to safeguard the soul of the country:

How often do you pray FIRSTLY for our nation? It is God's instructions that the problems and the needs of our country are more important than your own personal and family church needs. So we see that God is interested in the peace and welfare of this land and expects His people to claim this and to intercede and make war against evil authorities who are operating to create war, poverty, death and confusion, to hinder the will of God. . . . The first duty of Christians meeting in fellowship is prayer and the first topic of prayer is *"the government."* Most prayer meetings pray for the sick, the ministry, the unsaved, and especially our own special desires and needs, anything and everybody but the one group God puts first—*"the government."* When praying for the government what are we to ask for?—"that we lead a quiet and peaceable life in all godliness and honesty."

Good government maintains peace and order, it keeps communities open, it preserves civil liberty, it protects freedom of speech and freedom of assembly. This provides the means in which the gospel can be preached effectively. Bad government imposes unjust and arbitrary restrictions and suppresses the universal right of all men to believe in God and to express their faith by public worship and proclamation. . . .

The great majority of Christians never pray seriously for good government and this is a grave failing on their part. Christians get the kind of government they deserve and they have no rights to criticize or oppose if they are not prepared to pray for and get involved in the selection of a government.[16]

Then he went on to rebuke the church in Nigeria for the civil war: "The deadness, self-centred interests of the 1965–73 national church allowed the enemy to cause civil war in this country. Christians ought to have been able to control and prevent that. It is certain that the active prayer cells in 1979 contributed towards the successful peaceful outcome of the civilian elections."[17]

In a slight variation on this, written in 1978, he included a challenge to the church to be vigilant about the future: "The great spiritual revivals which covered Nigeria (between) 1930–1940, was a very very powerful movement and if the believers had realised their power and calling and had unitedly moved out and on with the Holy Spirit against the powers of darkness, it is likely the Nigerian civil war would never have happened and that Nigeria would be a great powerful Christian force in the world today and the whole of West Africa would have been evangelized. That did not happen, and we baptized-in-the-Spirit believers are to blame. It is not necessary to point accusing fingers at anyone now. We must learn by our mistakes and make sure that the plan of God for Nigeria does not spoil again in our hands."[18] "We must not become helpless onlookers of the scene in Nigeria," he wrote, "for we have the right and the power and authority to take part in shaping events and the future. It is dangerous to passively accept the worsening conditions in an attitude of 'What will be, will be,' and 'We are not part of this world and its problems.' Satan has appointed princes and powers set over various countries, including Nigeria, and we are called to challenge these powers."[19]

Elton, more than any other person, constantly emphasized that a fresh outpouring of the Spirit was going to sweep Nigeria; his greatest fear, however, was that there would not be enough mature and trained leaders to handle it. Prophesying about the coming revival ca. 1976, he said, "I will reveal many things to you, and as you find yourselves in the depths of MY WORD, you shall gather knowledge for you to be instruments in My Hand. The coming gatherings shall be so fruitful that you will not be able to cope with the vast preparation that you will be found in; you will have to cry for assistance, in mutual understanding and cooperation with others; then shall ye see the glory of your God."[20] But he then quickly expressed his fear: "The existing churches will not be able to accommodate this revival, and as yet God does not have enough trained 'deliverers' to deal with the crowds of seekers."[21] He drove home this point: "God is waiting to send another mighty revival to Nigeria but is looking for men and women who are prepared to sacrifice all, to seek this NEW REVE-LATION FOR THIS DAY."[22]

In the twenty-seventh issue of *Herald of the Last Days,* Elton invited all Christians in Nigeria to join him in a "pact of prayer."[23] "It is impossible to exaggerate the importance of real prayer for the expansion and progress of God's work in Nigeria and West Africa today," he wrote. "God is challeng-ing you to become a Christian of destiny. God needs your cooperation in prayer. You can change the situation in Nigeria, by your cooperation in prayer. . . . You are invited to become part of this great move of the Lord in Nigeria by joining with us as prayer partners in the Gospel."[24] To cham-pion the cause of this prayer movement, Elton started an organization called Intercessors of Nigeria.[25] He called on "ALL intercessors to join with us in attacking the forces of the enemy in every possible way and to cooperate with the Lord in carrying out this plan,"[26] and by 1976, he had begun to send out "a regular News Bulletin of World and West African events."[27] Interested persons were to write to "Intercessors of Nigeria, P. O. Box 113, Ilesa." Those who signed on to become prayer partners were going to be sent "free prayer bulletins and newsletter." According to Elton, the new prayer initiative was a product of prophecy:

The Lord has been speaking to us about the needs in Nigeria and we are giving here an extract from the message given in prophecy regarding the need for prayer.

"THOU shalt begin to pray and call upon my people throughout the nation that I want them to gather together in the places where they are to intercede and to pray with divine power and intercession.

For my people are not united; and I want them to be one. My Spirit shall come upon them to pray night and day, for I will have a prayer band in this country.

They shall pray alone, and they shall pray together, and there shall be thousands that pray daily.

They shall pray to the Lord of the harvest for many more of my chosen to be sent out into the nation before the end of the harvest comes. For you must know that Satan is building new strongholds in this nation and is ready to invade and cause much havoc. He has much power and he can do much damage except my people raise the standard against him.

Gather my people, call for them to set aside regular special times of prayer and intercession until I will move and deliver them and bring to pass all I have planned for your country."

So we call upon all Christians to believe in the call of the Lord and to personally and privately gather to take up this challenge of prayer for NIGE-RIA. This is the purpose of INTERCESSORS OF NIGERIA.[28]

Writing elsewhere, Elton tells of how prophecy shaped the call for intercession: "Some years ago the Lord spoke on this problem [the need to liberate Nigeria from the forces of darkness] and called for nationwide intercession. He said: 'Prove me, press into my presence, for the powers of darkness are against you. But I say that I will prove to you that I hold the world in my hand. My people shall pray and work and thousands, many thousands of souls shall be rescued. Ye shall pray for all nations and kingdoms and the people shall learn righteousness. Yet I will show this world that I am also a God of wrath. In a time when sins shall come forth, when it shall increase and when it shall destroy many people. I shall send forth the word of judgement. Therefore I shall call upon my people to pray.' "[29]

The roots of the intercessory/prayer movement in Nigeria and Africa can be traced to Elton's ground-breaking thoughts and actions in this direction.

It is significant how Elton connects prayer and an understanding of world events. By sending out a "regular bulletin of world and West African events," he was promoting an awareness of the need to understand what was happening in society. By following it up with a prayer bulletin and newsletter, he was advocating that the course of local and global events be influenced through prayer. "Today, God has set up a new channel to manifest His power and authority. . . . They are learning how to challenge Babylon and all its governmental powers and to restrict and curb its activities and also to attack Satan's strongholds of sin, sickness, demon oppression, ignorance, poverty and to deliver his captives. They know how to deal directly with God and to intercede with Him for the nation and thus shape events. No matter how great the darkness or the confusion; no matter how much the government tries to impose restrictions and make decrees controlling men's activities; this group of dedicated spiritual men are in touch with the throne and they are becoming the real power which shapes events."[30] And elsewhere: "We should now be influencing and controlling even national events."[31]

Elton frequently taught under such titles as "Spiritual Warfare in Prayer," "Guerrilla Warfare in Nigeria," "War with the Saints," and "Battle Plan for Nigeria." This was aimed at creating a theological foundation for the emerging prayer movement. "We are going to be allowed, invited, into the holiest place of all and I'm going to appear . . . and I'm going to say, 'Lord, I'm here on behalf of Nigeria,' " he once preached. "That's what we're trying to teach you, to minister in these days as priests, to teach the people and to stand in God's presence on behalf of our nation, this nation. . . . We are going to stand there before God and say, 'Lord, the sacrifice has been made for the whole world, and we're here to represent Nigeria.' Nigeria has sinned! Nigeria is making mistakes! Nigeria is wasting our inheritance, your inheritance. We're here, Father; spare Nigeria. And if we don't do that, a terrible judgement is coming upon Nigeria and the other nations. I want you to learn to do that, not only for your own family [but also] for your own town. We've got to be prepared to learn to stand before God on behalf of this nation as priests—as priests!"[32]

He also wrote: "We as saints of God ought to be prepared to stand before God as priests, high priests of a new order to confess the sin and failure, and the misrule and the mismanagement of our nation's rulers. We should stand before God on their behalf, confessing as Nehemiah did the mistakes of our leaders, and asking for God to spare this nation. God is ready to pour out His judgement upon Nigeria, and every other nation, but we His people in this country stand there to minister, blowing the trumpets to gather the people together, and spreading our words as words of hope for the whole nation, proclaiming the day of jubilee and proclaiming that we are prepared to call upon God for pardon for this nation. It is in our hands and as Moses and Aaron did so many times for the whole nation of Israel, let us stand before God on behalf of Nigeria to ask God to pardon Nigeria, and to hold back the judgement which she merits and which is due to fall upon her. Thus we prepare God's people, His church, His body for the final great Feast of Tabernacles."[33]

Elton was the one who introduced the teaching about spiritual warfare that recognized the activity of princes of darkness that influenced national policies and events in Nigeria. He was the one who introduced the revelation about the "Prince of Nigeria."[34] This first appeared in his writings on the Prince of Persia, as revealed in the book of Daniel. After quoting Daniel 10:12, he went on to explain that "this is one of the most amazing revelations of the operations in the spirit world. The 'Prince of Persia' is not the human ruler of Persia but a spirit prince under SATAN. This Scripture reveals the assistance of an evil spirit kingdom of powers of darkness which inhabits the heavenlies and that these powers determine the course of events in the gentile world (always of course within the limits of divine permission). We must assume that there is similarly a group of evil spirit powers assigned to control Nigeria."[35]

Elton clearly connected the activities of this prince to the socio-political history of Nigeria. He continued: "There was a nationwide rejoicing when Nigeria gained independence on October 1, 1960, but no one is deceived into thinking that we have solved all our problems or that we are fully free, even today. We still are in great bondage to corruption, immorality, drugs, and alcohol, and many other evils. We have thrown off colonial bondage but we still have our grave spiritual bondage. The truth is that Satan and the 'Prince of Nigeria' are still in control and daily increasing the number of his slaves in Nigeria."[36]

The church therefore had to realize that the battle for the control of the nation was first and foremost "a spiritual one and can only be won in the spiritual realm." "It cannot be won by edicts or democratic laws," Elton wrote, "but it can be won on our knees by Christians who have been born again and who realise that everyone must become involved, and who know how to reach the throne of God and defeat Satan." "Every new convert" had to be taught that "although salvation is free and gives internal peace with God and that with salvation comes many blessings, yet there is also an obligation towards fellow men who are still in bondage. When we have been freed and delivered we are responsible to take action to deliver others. We must teach every convert that they are soldiers, called to serve, called to arms, spiritually. We may not all be able to go out and evangelise or go to new evangelised areas. But we can all learn how to fight and win on our knees. When the Civil War started in Nigeria, no soldier had the right to decide where or when he wanted to fight or when he wanted to rest or sleep. He was under orders to fight for his country. No one spoke of hardship or inconvenience or complained about lack of food or money. It was war, and everyone had to endure hardship as a good soldier."[37] The church had to adopt a similar attitude.

Let us reassure ourselves that God has not handed Nigeria over to Satan or any of his forces and that Nigeria can be changed and won for Jesus Christ. All God needs is men and women who are ready to enlist in His army of volunteers, and are ready to give their time and money and talents to the task of winning this spiritual war.

It will mean making every man and woman know that only Jesus Christ has the answer to Nigeria's many problems. . . . Then it will take complete dedication to the task of fighting the enemy in prayer. There will be real all-night prayer meetings (not like many so called all-night prayer meetings held today for many reasons) and then there will be fierce enemy counter attacks. Every town and district will have its weekly prayer fighting meetings where Christians of all different denominations will gather to challenge the enemy and force him to release his captives and to stop holding up supplies of men and means for the war of real liberation for Nigeria.

Let us realise as we study these words that God looks for a man who will stand before Him and claim deliverance and forgiveness for our land. God actually waits for, and expects those of His people to accept the burden and responsibility for the continued freedom of Nigeria. God depends upon a man to represent Nigeria before Him, and that man can be YOU—and that man will be regarded by God as speaking for Nigeria. Let us not be general or vague in our praying but be very specific and realise and accept the burden and chance to represent our country before Him. If Nigeria goes more and more under the control of Satan and his forces, then we can truly say that there was no man found to stand before God for us.[38]

"Pastor Elton led us in spiritual warfare," says Kole Akinboboye, one of the leaders of the prayer movement in Nigeria. "Some of the things we know today about spiritual warfare, about battle, he taught us. He taught us how to pray; he taught us how to take authority; he taught us how to exercise kingdom dominion over situations in our land. Despite the problems we have in Nigeria today, I still know that by the grace of God, some of the things he taught us is what has kept the nation thus far. I remember during the 'Ali Must Go [crisis]' in 1978, there was crisis in the land . . . we prayed all kinds of prayers, fasted, did all kinds of things, and then we went back to Pastor Elton and said, 'What happened? Why did we have so much trouble?' And he said, 'The Lord is just teaching you a few lessons, how to take authority, how to take control of things.' "[39]

When Elton began espousing strategic prayers for the nation on such a massive scale, it was a completely novel idea. Up until the late seventies and early eighties, intentionally and actively praying for the nation was strange in most Christian circles. Austen Ukachi recalls visiting the University of Lagos to mobilize students to pray for the nation when CSSM's monthly "Prayer for the Nation" programme started. One of the executives of the Lagos Varsity Christian Union was confused: "Pray for Nigeria? What do you mean? What are we praying for Nigeria for?"[40]

"The prayer movement in Nigeria was one of the by-products of the Pentecostal/charismatic revival of the 1970s," Ukachi notes. "From the initial apathy to prayer at the beginning of the 1970s, to the present high level of consciousness of prayer, the movement has given rise to a massive explosion of churches and ministries. Since 1977, prayer has become one of the most visible and distinct ministries within the church community. The origin of the prayer movement can be traced to the 1970s, when the late Rev S. G. Elton sensitized some undergraduate youth to begin to intercede for Nigeria along the line of 1 Timothy 2."[41]

Elton's continuous exhortations on this issue were a call to arms for young people: "God seems to be calling upon His people in all times of national and spiritual crises to join with Him in dealing with those crises and that the power to deal with those crises can only be released when we fast. It is certain that God needs Holy Spirit-inspired prayer to force the powers of darkness to yield in some ways and that inspired prayer must often be accompanied by FASTING."[42] One CSSM member recalls, "Late Pa S. G. Elton is unforgettable. His prophetic message set the stage for programmes such as the first Saturday of the month 'Prayer for the

Nation,' which was zealously organized."[43] Fred Adegoke recalls, "Pa Elton was also very instrumental in the intercessory [initiatives of CSSM]. We had [these] special prayer meetings at Ife; first Saturday in the month was declared prayer and fasting for the nation, and it was rigorously adhered to. . . . We had prophetic words, strong prophecies; Pastor Elton also encouraged that. Some of the prophecies we took back to him, and he gave us his own interpretation. There were a lot of prayers for the nation. There was this awakening to pray for the nation. . . . Pastor Elton backed us, supported it and gave us his blessing in that direction."[44]

Elton trained a generation to become conscious of the spiritual implication of events and trends, and then to take appropriate spiritual action. One area in which this was visibly demonstrated was Nigeria's breaking of diplomatic ties with Israel—in concert with other African countries under the umbrella of the Organisation of African Unity—after the 1973 Arab-Israeli war. Drawing upon Elton's frequent exhortations about Nigeria–Israel relations (for example Elton preached, "It is good for us to seek and pray that the government of Nigeria shall recognise the state and government of Israel. Because whosoever is favouring Israel, whosoever is a friend of Israel, becomes a friend of God and the nation in the future will be judged on that basis."[45]), Elton's protégés concluded that Nigeria's severing of ties with Israel would be disadvantageous to the country's fortunes. For many, therefore, the restoration of Nigeria's diplomatic relationship with Israel became a matter of concern, and it demanded spiritual action. Emeka Nwankpa relates how they responded to this challenge: "The church in Nigeria prayed 18 years before an important event came to pass. In 1973 Nigeria broke diplomatic relations with Israel. Realizing how important it is that a nation stands with Israel, the church in Nigeria sought God, and relations were restored years later."[46]

Christ's Ambassadors Evangelistic Team (CAET), one of the pioneer charismatic organizations in Nigeria, which developed under Elton's mentorship (as one early member of CAET said, "Since inception, we were privileged to share ministry with Pa Elton. Some of the things we are holding onto today were from the understandings he passed to us."[47]), made a major public statement on the issue. In the Jan/Feb 1983 editorial of its then widely popular *Ambassador* magazine, titled "Nigeria-Israeli Relations—Whither?" it challenged the government on Nigeria's suspended relations with Israel:

It can be recalled that, in 1973 the Federal Military Government under the then Head of State, General Yakubu Gowon broke all links and diplomatic relations with the state of Israel. This was apparently a protest against her as a result of the "unfair" treatment she meted out to Egypt at that time. The protest action was basically not a Nigerian affair; it was in fact an O.A.U. decision against the state of Israel in sympathy with an O.A.U. member state—Egypt. So, all African states took the same action against the state of Israel.

But recent trends on international political events seem to give an entirely different indication, thus rendering Nigeria's present stand baseless and uncalled for. Egypt which had been the object and focal point of the protest action has since normalised relations with Israel sequel to Camp David accord. Zaire which was one of the protesting O.A.U. member states is now [on] good terms with Israel. Many more states, of course, will establish fresh relations with Israel in the very near future. But Nigeria seems to be at the cross-roads not knowing whither.

Among other reasons advanced in favour of the present break in diplomatic relations with Israel was the fear that Arab members of O.P.E.C may cause oil glut in the world market which will drastically affect Nigeria's economy since we depend solely on oil for our foreign reserve.

The association of Israel with apartheid South Africa, which Nigeria publicly denounced and leads other nations in the fight, is another reason for the continuation of the break.

While the first reason is baseless and the present economic situation renders it unfounded, the second is also hypocritical and confirms our policy of double standard since we have diplomatic dealings with Britain, America, France and other nations aiding Apartheid South Africa. The truth of the situation is that Nigeria needs to critically analyse situations in the Middle East and decide rather to take sides with God than to be against her creator.[48]

Once, when Nigeria planned to get an IMF loan, Elton encouraged young people to stand against it in prayer. In a later reference to the episode, Elton further encouraged them to be prepared for more of such battles in the future. "Who stopped the IMF loan?" Elton asked. "We did. We said no, we don't want your loan. You are not putting us in chains. The Lord will provide; keep your loans. Satan will come another way. . . . And not only that, we are not going to sit here inside the church waiting for you, we are going to come out. We are going to attack him in every department of government. We are going to attack you in every department where you are parading yourself as lord."[49]

To be identified with Elton was to be initiated into radicalness in social and political engagement. Elton taught that the church's isolation of itself from the ills of society was the product of a self-absorbed theology:

The Priest and the Levite were spiritual men. They desired to keep spiritual, but their idea of serving God was to keep spiritual and disassociate themselves from the problems of this world; they were isolated from the real needs of the people and that is not what God wants. The Lord Jesus came to minister to the poor, to minister to the needy. The Priest and the Levite have spiritual ideals, but the Samaritan had compassion. When he found the wounded man, he became involved. He laid aside his own plans, forgot his own schedule and his own interest, and didn't ask whether it was spiritually wise or necessary. There was a needy man and he became involved. It cost him and it meant that there had to be a continuing commitment to his care. I'll come back again; I'll minister to him again and again and continue to look after him until he is better.

The religious men were probably doing a good job in the temple, but they were not expressing the mind of God. They had isolated spirituality from problems in the world, and that's where we've got to sit down and study what we are going to do. We are men of another race, citizens of heaven, possessing divine life . . . we belong to God, we know him, and are rejoicing in our own relationship with Him. And many of us are selfishly resigned to occupying our time in whatever ways we like, until the Lord comes and takes us away, but we are not exercising care in our minds to the needy of this world. The illiterate, the outcasts, the drug addicts, the prisoner in prison, people in hospitals without anyone to care for them, the people who sleep in the market, the people who live in the villages, out of touch with civilization.[50]

Elton had scathing remarks for religious leaders who could not be bothered with anything outside the four walls of their churches. "Nowhere in the Bible are we commanded to hide ourselves inside church buildings merely to praise, pray or preach. We are hypocrites when we selfishly pray for ourselves and devote our efforts, time and money in building our own little kingdoms (either of business, vocation or church) and let the mass of the unevangelized go to hell without hearing the gospel. We believe the gospel of Jesus Christ is the only way to solve man's problems and the national crises, so we will be judged by God if we do nothing about this,"[51] wrote Elton. "I want to make a confession," he said. "The older I get, the more I have to do with the problems of people, and the more disgusted I get with religious leaders. They are not meeting the needs of the people. They are quite capable, some of them, of standing up in a very nice cloth on Sunday morning and preaching a cleverly arranged and cleverly dictated sermon and teaching people what they should do morally, but they are not coming down from their high pulpits and meeting the needs of the people."[52]

So, there is a ministry and a purpose for a believer to remain in the world today. A large number of born again [Christians] are merely existing and praying daily for the second coming of the Lord to take them out of this evil world. They are priding themselves that they are not of this world and they don't want to be associated with anything of the world. They're tired of this world, they're buffeted by the evils, and they are suffering, waiting for the second coming. That is not my view and that should not be yours either. The Lord Jesus Christ had no hesitations in coming into this world, it belonged to Him. He came to redeem this world, "For God so loved the world that he gave his only begotten son." God still loves this world and when He's speaking of that, He doesn't mean the trees, the rocks and the mountains; He means the people. God loves the people. And Psalm 2 reminds us that, "He's given the nations as an inheritance to his beloved son."

In John 17 the Master prays, "I pray that thou take them not out of the world." God is not interested in taking us out of the world; He's interested in keeping us in the world. We need protection from the evil one and the intercessory work of the Lord Jesus Christ is going on to prevent the evil one from overcoming us. He has a purpose in keeping us in this world and that purpose was outlined in Genesis 1:26-28, "Let us make man in our own image and let them have dominion," let them be governing, let them be our representatives on the earth, governing, ruling, reigning, exercising authority establishing the kingdom of heaven on earth. . . . He also said, "Ye are the salt of the earth."

We are the people who are keeping the world from growing more corrupt and if we stood our ground and maintained our witness, there will be less corruption in the world. The amount of corruption that we are grumbling about in governmental circles is largely due to the fact that Christians, who have been brought into the government are corrupted by the system and are not maintaining their light and are not the salt of the office, they're not the salt of the department or of the administration. They too are mingling with their colleagues who are ungodly and in darkness; they are insisting upon bribes, they are inefficient as workers; they are not salt, they are not cleaning up the system; and that is our responsibility. We are the saviours; the healers, the deliverers and those who are representing Jesus Christ on the earth.[53]

Elton always emphasized the great need for the church to be prophetic, so as to understand the timing of God's plans for the nation. A lack of prophetic perspective would be increasingly costly for the church and the nation. For instance, he believed that the revelation concerning the need to have an impact on the nation, which many young people received in the late seventies and early eighties, was a move of God. "About the 1980s, we saw God beginning to move nationally, and the people of Nigeria became aware of a new move of God which brought the nation into their reckoning,"[54] said Elton. Such prophetic awareness—sensitivity to the move of God concerning the nation at a given time—would be crucial to perpetually driving the nation in accordance with God's plan and also thwarting the enemy's plans.

The church's prophetic preparation would be crucial to God's move: "When we get into position, when we are right with God, then God can move. That's why God has had to keep the Lord Jesus Christ sitting on His right hand waiting for 1900 years: because He can't get His people into the right position. If God is now moving His people into a position where they're opening their eyes, where they are ready to commit themselves, where they are beginning to move forward, then God is saying, 'Get ready.' Come on, get ready, and God is going to move. And it's going to be a move of the Spirit of God throughout Nigeria, and we will wake up one night and it will start to move. And what has taken 1900 years, God will do in days."[55]

"There are men," he said, "upon whom God is putting His hand, and revealing them as prophets; men whose ears are in tune with the God of heaven, and He is speaking and speaking deep into their hearts, and they are revealing the mind of God in prophecy, particularly in regard to national and governmental matters."[56] "It is also clear that God must move in a special way in the next few years in Nigeria and that His move will affect and involve some of us. It is supremely important for the Lord's people to carefully study the 'signs of the times' and God's plans so that we may not miss His blessing and move in Nigeria."[57]

"It is also certain there will be a growing miraculous manifestation of prophetical guidance. The move of God will move so fast and be so big that special spiritual guidance will be given to protect as well as guide believers. . . . We can therefore believe and expect an increase in the operation of believers in national affairs as well as in the normal life of believers. This ministry will have to be learned under the guidance and control of the Holy Spirit and we can also expect an increase in the number of Christian Nigerians with leading national responsibilities and posts, so that the Lord's work and ministry will exercise a much greater influence in national life,"[58] Elton wrote.

SIXTEEN

"IT WILL BE WAR RIGHT TO THE GATES OF GLORY"

B ode Akintade met Elton for the first time when he returned to Nigeria in 1970, after training as a medical doctor overseas and taking up an appointment at the Wesley Guild Hospital, Ilesa.[1] Elton was then holding a weekly Bible study every Tuesday for the senior staff of the hospital.[2] This fellowship was at the instance of Andrew Pearson, Elton's close friend, who was the medical director of the hospital at the time. After the Wesley Guild Hospital was taken over by the government, Akintade opened a private clinic, Christian Health Centre (CHC), in Ilesa.[3] He soon began to long for the kind of fellowship and teaching he had enjoyed during the Wesley Guild days. (The fellowship had been discontinued after the government take-over.) He met with Elton to make an arrangement for his senior staff to meet in Elton's house for fellowship once a week.[4] They met every Thursday, starting in 1979; that was the beginning of the famous "Thursday fellowship," to which people came from far and near to learn at Elton's feet.

Elton once remarked concerning the fellowship, "CHC staff come for a meeting every Thursday p.m. and so we are involved in all they do. We act together in many ways."[5] Elton also noted concerning Akintade's clinic: "Christian Health Centre in Ilesa is OK. Lots of doctors with them at present but they face enormous problems because of the opposition from Wesley Guild and State because they (the latter) want CHC to go along with their corrupt practices . . . and when this is refused they decline all assistance."[6] When the Ilesa fellowship grew big, some people suggested putting up a shed within the compound to accommodate the growing population. Elton flatly rejected this idea; he said that he knew what the people would eventually make out of it: it would graduate from being a shed to being a church—and he was sent to build people only.[7]

It was at the Thursday fellowship that Elton, precept by precept, preached on the subjects which weighed most upon his heart; it was here that he freely communicated what he believed were his most important messages. The Thursday fellowship was a no-holds-barred kind of meeting. You attended only if you really wanted to listen to Elton. In these teachings, usually a blend of his teaching over many decades and material he was just developing, the essential Elton comes alive.

Many who attended the Thursday meetings confess that many of the teachings were difficult to understand: they didn't really get what Elton was saying. "Most of the things that he told us are all being fulfilled today, and it is now that I am truly understanding his messages,"[8] says one of those closest to him in the latter years. Elton knew some of the messages would be hard to take in; and perhaps in no other place does he better express this knowledge than in a 1984 message, in which he preached,

> Brethren, we have a wonderful message to give to the people of Nigeria. A message which speaks of the restoration, the re-establishing of God's authority on the earth through man in the establishing of the kingdom of heaven; and we are to aim high in our messages. We are to aim at the highest.
>
> It is possible that some of the people will not understand what we are saying, but we are to give the highest and those who are hungry will crave for it and will search for it until they find it. Those who want mere consolation on sin and what God can provide for them in Jesus Christ, let them go on their way.
>
> We will preach the highest, and the highest is that God is in the process of re-establishing on the earth, His authority, His dominion, His government in the restored kingdom of Heaven on earth; and wonder of wonders, he is going to use us . . . that is our hope for 1985 and 1986.[9]

A major focus of Elton's ministry in the final years was to stir the church to push for God's best: to set her sights on the highest that God had planned for her. Settling for less, being satisfied with little, was totally unacceptable to God; Elton, therefore, fervently decried the prevailing apathy in the church at every opportunity. There were great things the

Lord had in store for His church and it was her responsibility to press into it. "A large number of Christians," he said, "are content only to think of getting to heaven."[10] "I am constantly referring to this because it shows how unspiritual and how far out of the programme of God we are. They are concerned to get to heaven, leave this evil world, get to heaven, stay in heaven, where everything will be at peace and everything will be all right. That is their objective. [But] that is not the final plan of God. I am going to heaven; I am a heavenly subject; heavenly now. Being born again, I belong to God's eternal family; divine life dwells in me and in every person who is born again. . . . We therefore belong to a new race of people . . . not belonging to any tribe but belonging to the Lord Jesus Christ, sharing His nature and exhibiting His power. We should also manifest His character and His person. That's our objective. But a large number are content to really think of getting to heaven only and then sitting down and staying in heaven in eternal rest. That is not what the Bible teaches. The Bible teaches that the Lord has a plan for this earth, and He is going to revolutionise the earth."[11]

After once asking the question, "What is the Holy Spirit doing in these last days?" he went on to answer, "The aim, the object, the purpose, the programme of the Holy Spirit in these last days is this—He is going to recover one hundred percent testimony to the heavenly mindedness of God's programme, to the purity of the heavenly character of it, and to reproduce a body of people on earth who will accurately reflect the glory of the only begotten one full of grace and truth and holiness, light, power, everything. He is going to reproduce in a body of people all the character-istics of his wonderful partner, the Lord Jesus Christ. And that body will be hundred percent divinely created. It will be one hundred percent gold; and that means the elimination of all that is human. And God's purpose through the Holy Spirit today is to recover on earth His divine testimony through the Holy Spirit—one hundred percent pure. . . . The com-mander of the army [says], 'I am going to have it pure; I am going to have it purely divine.' That is the message."[12]

But then he mourned because "that is not the condition of the church today." "We may say we are going out in a blaze of glory—I believe it. We may say that we are going to go out all victorious, and I believe it. But facts in existence contradict me. . . . We are not righteous as God calls righteous-ness; I can assure you of that. There isn't a man or woman in this room, including the speaker, who has even grasped the early principles of what righteousness really is. That leaves an awful lot for some of us to put right. ... And I have said many times that when you see ministers falling over their pulpits and sobbing because of their failures, you can say the move is on. God's beginning to move because that's going to happen. Ministers first—let the priests [leaders] cry out, moan, howl, between the porch and the altar. And when the priests do it, the congregation will follow suit."[13]

Elton believed the church needed this kind of revival and reawakening if it was going to be shaken out of its lukewarm state and set on fire for God's purpose. He, therefore, put a lot of energy into promoting the cause of revival around the country. He was a firm believer in mass revivals where God moves in His sovereignty to turn around the fortunes of the church—he fervently preached this and encouraged believers to expect it. He was also, however, an advocate of the idea that the church could experience revival any time it met God's conditions:

> The Lord is moving in revival in many parts of Nigeria now and there is a great expectation among Christians that this will spread and involve the whole country. We believe that this is a real move of God for a special purpose of this time, but we also feel that there is a part for Christians to play in bringing that revival; ... make no mistake about it. The responsibility for revival rests with us. Billy Graham has stated, "I believe that we can have revival any time we meet God's conditions. I believe that God is true to His Word and that He will rain righteousness upon us if we meet His conditions." The question now is do we want revival? ... Are we ready to pay the price?[14]

He explored further: "Revival is the work of the Holy Spirit on the earth ... moving in the hearts and lives of His people. But revival also takes men into partnership. God's methods and instruments are men, and He has confined Himself to using men for revival. If we are ready to submit to God and conform to the stated conditions then He will bring revival. The very fact that there is a deep hunger and prayer in the hearts of so many Spirit filled people is a proof that God is moving again ... for it is only God who can create such hunger and He will not create it and then not fulfil it."[15] Then zooming in on Nigeria, he remarked: "God uses MEN ... and the coming revival will be brought by men, who are filled with the Holy Spirit and who are completely dedicated to God and revival in Nigeria in this day. He will not come through the church [denominational] system, but it undoubtedly will flow into the hungry churches and then meet the needs of thousands who will rush to seek salvation and deliverance . . . no matter the name of the church or the minister."[16]

While speaking to students at the Ibadan Polytechnic in January 1982, he elaborated on this revival, which he believed was about to engulf the nation: "A mighty move of God is on the way, and God is going to accomplish a mighty thing, and I will tell you how it will happen. There will be a sudden move of God spiritually in the hearts and lives of people and that which has been sown by the Spirit of God, of the word of God in the lives of men and women shall be quickened. The sowing, the witnessing that you have done with tract distributing and giving your testimony from house to house, meeting to meeting, God is going to pour out His Spirit upon that word, and it's going to come alive. . . . They're going to act in conviction and come running to men and women who know, who have got the answers. That's what's coming. Right throughout the country."[17]

Elton taught that the church was responsible for the establishment of the kingdom of God in all realms of human life, which required a radical departure from all forms of spirituality that could hinder it. "The Lord will speak to individuals [male and female] with the challenge to repent from dead works [our former unprofitable Christian service] and forsake all forms and appearances of worldliness and evil and to move forward with the Holy Spirit."[18] Leaving behind all that could stop her from entering into God's best, the church had to go right on to the peak of the spiritual journey—the revelation by the church to the world and the powers of darkness of the fullness of Christ as King and Lord; the church, through its character and power, revealing the peak of God's plan through the ages. The church could attain this and was responsible for seeking it.

The church's vision had to be lifted: "The great problem with Christians today is [that] they don't want to grow in vision. You have thousands of Christians who say, 'I am saved, I am baptized in the Holy Ghost, I am going to heaven, amen; finished.' That's not enough for me. That's not enough for God. God has got a bigger job for you than that. If God wanted to save you, baptize you in the Holy Ghost to take you to heaven, why didn't He take you when He saved you? Why did He leave you here? Because God has got a job for you to do, and without you, God cannot do that job! And I am going to tell you what that job is: that job is to establish Jesus Christ as Lord. That in the name of Jesus every knee in heaven, on earth, under the earth should bow. That's the vision."[19]

"God's got one big problem," Elton noted. "It isn't Satan—He is finished with Satan; it isn't sin—He is finished with sin; it isn't the world—He has dealt with the world; it isn't the nations—God is in charge of the world. God's got one big, big, big problem all over the world, in Nigeria . . . one problem, the same problem everywhere. I will tell you what it is—God can't get His people in the right place. God's problem is *us*. We are God's biggest problem. We have got a short vision. We want what we want for ourselves. We want naira; we want business; we want money; we want success; and God is saying, 'I have got something bigger than that.' And when you have got the vision that I have got, you won't want anything else."[20]

"God must move in an extraordinary way in these last days, and He will do a new thing, in a new way," Elton wrote. "But what will be God's aim and what will He seek to accomplish in these last days? Will He just move by His Spirit to save more people or has He a bigger purpose? We believe He has a great and wonderful purpose for these last days. . . . God's plan is to gather everything . . . in heaven and earth under Jesus Christ. God plans that His victorious Son will be the Head and the Master and the King over all authority and all power in heaven and earth . . . and that everyone shall know and realise the fact and accept that Cavalry was a glorious mighty victory and that God has laid every authority and power and judgement on Jesus Christ. That is the full meaning of Eph. 1:10. So we shall expect that God will direct attention solely in these last days to Jesus Christ, as the centre and head of everything."[21]

Any theology that placed man or even the church as the highest plan of God fell short of the mark—the revelation of Jesus Christ as God's perfect man was God's ultimate. The whole world had to see the "Victor of Calvary,"[22] as Elton frequently phrased it, in all His fullness, for the plan of God to be consummated on the earth. This would happen through the glorious ministry of the church, which would result in her uplifting on the earth; however, the uplifting of the church was not for the church's sake, but for Christ. "It is wise to be suspicious of any vision, or prophecy, or revelation, or message from anyone, which magnifies man or makes man the focus and centre of any ministry. It is a work of Satan to glorify man . . . it is the work of the Holy Spirit to glorify Jesus Christ. That is a test of true vision or prophecy."[23] Elton believed the church had begun to focus on herself as the end of God's plan to an extent which endangered its true ministry—the revelation of the fullness of Jesus Christ to the world.

Babatunde Ogunnaike, one of Elton's close protégés towards the end of his life, recalls a story that illustrates his stress on this point.[24] Like several other people that Elton mentored closely in the 1980s, Ogunnaike and his wife had a fellowship group in their house in Oshodi, Lagos, where they passed on to others what they had learnt from their years of interaction with Elton. On one of their trips to Ilesa, they walked through the door to meet a stern-looking Elton, who welcomed them with an equally strange question, "So where are the eagles?" "I had no idea what he was talking about, and I told him so," says Ogunnaike. "He [Elton] was astonished and asked if I had seen a particular article in one of the then-popular Christian magazines of the day, where, the writer, in promoting the fellowship group meeting in our house in Oshodi, had said something about 'where the carcase is there the eagles be gathered together' quoting from Matthew 24:28 in the King James Version. The writer then went on to imply that the Oshodi fellowship was the place to be if anyone wanted to know what God was truly doing those days. Ouch! My wife and I had nothing to do with the article, and did not know that it had been written, although we knew the writer well. Such was Papa Elton's concern for us; that we should not become careless, arrogant or to start to think too highly of ourselves; he was ready to reprimand me for such foolishness." He was adamant "that we should NEVER 'advertise' our home group meetings; that God Himself would bring to the meeting only the people that He (God) wanted to attend."

When Elton was sure that the couple had nothing to do with the article, he then told them, "You know what to do now, don't you?" "His point was that we would have to shut down that meeting, wait for a while and then reschedule a new meeting on a completely different day—start afresh. The 'advertised' meeting, especially because of the implied arrogance, was already compromised, and I needed to avoid the inevitable effect of the contamination that would come from having so foolishly glorified ourselves. Papa Elton was jealous for God's glory and was very strict in teaching us to be careful about promoting ourselves. He taught us that we are only effective to the extent that we allowed the Holy Spirit to work in our midst. The Holy Spirit will not work with a group of arrogant and self-absorbed ministers who think too highly of themselves. That event taught me a great lesson about the secret to Pa Elton's success in ministry."

Elton was worried that the charismatic movement was no longer motivated to push further in God. He was worried that the movement was showing signs of self-satisfaction. "There is a great and urgent need for all Pentecostal churches to awaken and repent and seek the Lord before He 'spits them out of His mouth' (Rev. 3:16)," Elton wrote. "They have been given the truth of the baptism of the Holy Spirit and have 'tasted of the power of the age to come' (Heb. 6:5), but have generally withdrawn into church buildings which have become their prisons, and they are now 'unprofitable servants' (Matt. 25:30, Luke 17: 10). When the Jews refused to accept Jesus' offer of the Kingdom of Heaven, He declared He was leaving them desolate (Matt. 23:37–39), and so judgment came upon them when the Romans destroyed Jerusalem. The Holy Spirit can do the same to those who misuse His gifts and blessings without putting them into action. We know the Holy Spirit has a full programme for these last days . . . a much bigger one than we have seen so far in Nigeria."[25]

God did not expect His children "to stand still or become static, but to grow and develop, in vision, spiritually, and doctrinally." Elton wrote, "As human beings we tend to stand and to feel that our great task is to hold on fiercely to the truths God revealed to us, and not to allow or accept anything new or fresh. We tend to fear anything new and this has caused denominations and sects who feel their call is to make sure they remain faithful to their original revelation. Each new revelation is fiercely opposed by the preceding groups, causing much bitterness and division. . . . There is every encouragement to keep looking forward for even more new light and revelations as we near the end of this dispensation."[26]

"There is need for a constant renewal of vision," Elton further wrote. "Yesterday's manna will not be suitable for today's needs and problems. . . . There must be a new vision of what God plans and is doing in these days in Nigeria. Without renewed fresh vision, the doctrines of the baptism of Holy Spirit and evangelism will be 'old order' and not accomplish God's purpose. Evangelical crusades are merely an exhibition of the power of God unless we are aware of God's plans for the outcome of each crusade which will produce 'soldiers' instead of mere church adherents. . . . There is a great need, even for 'Pentecostals,' to move on and forward in the experience and development of the growing ministry of the Spirit in these last days. We must never be satisfied with just speaking in tongues but to 'go on' to desire, covet and develop in deeper Spirit ministries for the deliverance of 'slaves' and the equipping of 'soldiers.' There will be greater and deeper manifestations of the Holy Spirit's power and ministry in the closing days of this Age and we MUST desire and covet the best gifts."[27]

We must realise that God never stands still but is constantly moving forward in revelation and the outworking of His plans and purposes for this world. God has NOT completed the revelation of Himself (that will take the whole of eternity) or His plans for Nigeria and the world. Man is only capable of understanding small doses of new revelations at one time and is constantly trying to declare that God has completed revealing His plans and purposes. This weakness of man has resulted in the creation of denominations which have been created to perpetuate and protect certain God-given revelations but those same denominations have also sealed themselves against any further new revelations and have therefore ceased to grow in the ways and revelation of God.

We shall only progress and develop as we "follow on to know the Lord" and to be open to more light. This principle is most vital in these last days when the Holy Spirit is moving so fast and God is revealing so many new plans for the future. . . . Obedience to any revelation of God will ensure further revelation from God. When we fail to act on revelation from God, then that closes the door to any further revelation.[28]

However, Elton taught, despite the many challenges the church had to deal with, God's unfailing commitment to her perfection would save the situation. God has an eternal commitment to the birth, growth and maturity of the church, just as He had for Israel, and even when the church failed to measure up to God's standard, He would find a way to restore her to the divine path and pattern. "God is going to perfect His church in the last days. He's not going to take us away in all our failures, in all our mistakes, in all our sin, that we are [committing] from day to day. He's going to bring a new conviction upon us by the Holy Spirit, which will cause us to repent, confess, and a new body will be born in us, among us; a body that will hate sin more than it has ever done. A body that will be pure and so ready for the Lord Jesus Christ as Ephesians 5:27 says: He's going to present to Himself a church, perfect, pure and holy, without blemish."

Using the typology of Israel's call to keep a Day of Atonement "in the seventh month, six months after the Passover," Elton preached that "so it will be in these last days, before the coming of the Lord, before the Feast of Tabernacles, there will be a great wave of repentance, a great wave of reconciliation with one another, a great wave of confession and putting right amongst ourselves that which has been done wrongly so that the Lord can bring to pass the last great feast of ingathering of the harvest."

He's coming for a perfect church, and although that may seem like a dream, yet God is going to accomplish it, and He's going to do it by bringing us under the power of the Holy Spirit into a state of repentance from dead works, into a position where we will be united, where we will be full of the Spirit and where we shall be governed in God's way and then as the whole body moves forward, perfected by the work of the Holy Spirit, into conflict, the final battle where we shall put our feet on Satan, and bruise him (that's Romans 16:10); we shall find that the perfect man shall come into being, shall come into sight for the whole world. The perfection of the saints is not something which God *might* do. It is something which God is committed to doing.[29]

To achieve this maturity in the church, the ministry gifts of evangelist, pastor, teacher, prophet, and apostle had to be restored to full functioning. "God's purpose in giving His gifts of men with ministries of apostles, prophets, evangelists, pastors and teachers was to perfect the saints, edify the whole body of Christ, and bring that body to a unity of the faith."[30] He continued, "We do not find this has happened, and so we can expect that the Holy Spirit will really reveal His own men whom He will equip and use to accomplish that plan of God."[31] Elton warned against the predisposition of many in leadership to equate titles with the spiritual authority of the ministry gifts. This, he declared, was the cause of much powerlessness in the ministry: "These five callings or gifts are not meant to be titles or even offices but MINISTRIES. In the past few years in Nigeria many have been given, or have taken for themselves, these titles, and think they are fulfilling Scripture. It is not a title that makes a man an apostle or prophet, but the MINISTRY of the Holy Spirit through him."[32]

The person and power of the Holy Spirit had to be restored to the forefront of church life for any significant corporate spiritual advancement in the last days. "There has been a big change in our knowledge of the Holy Spirit and ministry in the last few years,"[33] Elton said. "After being ignored for centuries, He is now coming to His rightful position and recognition. He is now recognized as being the divine executor and administrator and the commander-in-chief of all the Lord's forces. He is solely in charge of all spiritual operations in these last days, and His ministry will be increasingly emphasized as He prepares the Lord's people for the final conflict and victory over Satan as He demonstrates that redeemed men (and women) who are filled and subject to Himself can be as victorious as the Lord Himself."[34]

Elton was always emphasizing that a major outpouring of the Holy Spirit in the last days was not a luxury. The success or failure of the church's end-time ministry was dependent on it. He never stopped talking about his quest for such an outpouring: "We are preparing all the time for the big move that is coming. Very soon, Nigeria is going to experience a revival that it has never seen before, a mighty move of the Spirit of God."[35] "I believe there's going to be a last days revival; I believe there's going to be a last days outpouring of the Holy Spirit; I believe there's going to be a last days blessing that will produce a perfect church, a perfect body, a body working out covenant relationship with its head in heaven, manifesting the life, the character and the power of Jesus Christ, the head of the body on the earth in these last days—doing the works that Jesus Christ did when He was on earth and carrying out His promise, even greater works than He did, because He was restricted to one locality, geographically."[36]

The exercise of spiritual gifts also had to become a normal part of church life. "We have got to seek the fullness of the Spirit daily and to seek after and use the Spirit's gifts in dealing with all forms of evil, corruption and Satan's work. The Holy Spirit is God's highest authority on earth today and He needs a human channel to speak words of command to demon powers. That is why He needs us. The Spirit has declared final war on Satan and He must use us as His forces."[37]

One issue that was really dear to Elton's heart was the unity of the church. He believed the church could not finish its assignment as a divided and competing body. "The Lord's prayer, 'That they all may be one,' will be answered as the Holy Spirit draws all true believers into fellowship and service which will be part of the great spiritual revival of the last days," he preached. "Many regard that prayer as impossible, but the Lord's prayer MUST be answered, and we are already seeing a new coming together of the Lord's people brought about by the Spirit, which has nothing to do with the ecumenical movement and will not need a new organisation or denomination. There will be no time, or need, to form a denomination when the 'last day's move' flows through the churches. There will be so many seeking the Lord and deliverance that the church name will not mean anything. Let me ask, 'Are you more concerned with your own old ideas that you refuse to move on with the Spirit as he revives the church and brings salvation and deliverance to hungry souls?' There is only ONE LORD and ONE BODY."[38]

The "denominational spirit" always drew a direct and vehement attack from Elton. He believed it was a monster that stifled the creative expression of the life of God in the individual believer and, therefore, hindered Christ himself. Once, while doing an exposition of the book of Revelation, Elton took time out to express his views about denominationalism: "It [Revelation] records the conflict between the 'organization'—the 'system,'—and the 'organism,' which is the church. The organization is the large number of sectarian denominations which comprise 'churchianity' today, who have, like the nation of Israel before them, corrupted true spiritual worship and substituted ceremonies and religious rituals instead of the living Christ. Many denominational churches openly declare that God can only be reached through their own ceremonies and rituals, while others claim to be the only genuine 'Body,' but all are governed by men and not the Holy Spirit. They have left the true way and offer a counterfeit gospel. They are part of the 'system' and 'organization' called Babylon. But Satan is working with dying material. That is why he has an organization; he cannot create an organism like the church of Jesus Christ."[39]

As he would emphasize again and again, to avoid being misunderstood, Elton said this was not a call to believers to abandon their churches or leave their denominational fellowships; rather, he was attacking the spirit behind segregationist tendencies and denominational walls. "Sectarianism has no part in God's plan for this needy world. There is no place in this life from the Cross to the throne for a 'personality cult.' God will exalt only ONE MAN—His Son, Jesus Christ, and we should never seek a name or fame or fortune for ourselves."[40] He had observed the schismatic trend that was then beginning to plague the Pentecostal movement in Nigeria and tried to nip it in the bud. In what seems to be a prophetic exhortation, he warned,

> During the past few years in Christian work, a large number of men have felt they were called by God to step outside the government and leadership of their denominations and to set up independent assemblies and groups of their own. In some cases there is no doubt that this was a sincere move and forced upon them by circumstances which they could not avoid.
>
> But in too many cases men have started small independent works of their own in order to become leaders and independent of any authority or discipline . . . and to become the centre of their own work and group. These works have become places where the "personality cult" has made the leader or prophet the

centre of the worship and service, and the whole programme and church exists for his benefit. We feel this is not the will of God and not in accordance with the plan of God for His work. It is true that God never planned that any one man should be the master of another in His church. We only have ONE HEAD . . . ONE MASTER . . . The Lord Jesus. But it is also true that the Lord Jesus does not make every man a master independent of others. . . . He believes in cooperation in BODY functioning.[41]

For Elton, aiming for true unity of the faith among believers was aiming for the highest. In his understanding, if narrow denominationalism opposed the work of Jesus Christ on the earth, then true kingdom unity was the pathway to the restoration of true kingdom authority. Elton had no sympathy for leaders who walled their people in and made them believe that to be loyal to the denomination was equivalent to doing all the will of God—that the plan of God began and ended with their denomination. God's plans are big and require the whole body of Christ cooperating to be accomplished, he frequently preached.

Elton believed men, through denominationalism, were usurping the true spiritual authority that belonged to the kingdom, and that except that sectarian spirit was broken, the church would find it difficult to experience true kingdom authority. He noted, "In the Epistle to the Corinthians Paul had to deal with several manifestations of Babylon. 'There are contentions among you . . . every one of you saith, I am of Paul: and I am of Apollos: and I of Cephas: and I of Christ.' They had started different denominations even then, and sectarianism divides Christianity till today. This will increase in the last days as single men seek to set up their own kingdoms and churches all claiming to be led by the Holy Spirit. The Holy Spirit's work today is to unite (John 17:21) not divide or multiply sects. All denominations are guilty of sectarianism but we appeal to all Christians to truly unite in spirit as members of one family and one body, even the Body of Christ. As a result of sectarianism, there was a decline in the expression of spiritual authority in the church which allowed immorality of the worst kind to remain un-judged."[42]

In Elton's view, the challenge and battles of the last days required the whole body working together to establish the purpose of God. The denominational spirit prevented such cooperation among saints from different streams. As long as Satan could keep the church from fighting as one, then he could successfully stop it from laying hold of God's best and completely uprooting Satan's strongholds on the earth. The Holy Spirit was moving beyond the pettiness of denominationalism and calling the church to reach higher.

> These are days when the Holy Spirit is taking control, leading in His authority and demanding full submission; and rededication to His leadership and guidance. I'm afraid this inevitably may mean that many of the church organisations will not be prepared to fit into His programme. And although God has been so patient with many denominational leaders, I'm afraid the time has come when He's going to push them to one side, and turn to individuals who are not bound by tradition, who are not governed by church constitution . . . but who are obedient to the Spirit of God and who are brought into unity with one another, irrespective of denominational affiliation or loyalties.[43]

"It was and is God's plan for the church to be His vessel to bless the whole world and reveal the love and power of God to all peoples. It is feared that the church has developed the same sectarian attitudes as the Jewish nation at the time of Christ, and so the church has also become an internal self-seeking vessel instead of a means of general blessing to the whole world," said Elton. "God never intended His church to become a great human organisation concerned with its own welfare and programmes but an outward looking instrument which drew upon the power of the indwelling Holy Spirit for its life and power and which then went out into the world, with its Satan-controlled communities, with a divine life that flowed out and brought deliverance and blessing to all, even to unbelievers. In these last days 'MOVE' we shall see the believers resuming their TASK and moving out from inside the 'prison' walls of their churches out into the communities, with the gospel of deliverance which will bring life to many in liberating them from sin, sickness, Satan and circumstances."[44]

Many emerging leaders in the charismatic movement who were receiving a call to start church-based ministries and who went to Elton for counsel in his last years came back disappointed—God had spoken to them, but they felt Elton discouraged the idea of starting churches. As one protégé close to the Ilesa scene recalls, "Pa would always say, 'Don't start a denomination,' and they [young charismatic preachers] felt that the only way you could grow the church was by having branches, and so after a while they wouldn't just go [to Pa] anymore. . . . He didn't say we should not start churches, but he was always against this denominational thing, that we would wind up being like where we were coming from."[45]

The evidence from fifty years of ministry—devoted to building and supporting thousands of local churches—goes against the idea that Elton was against pioneering local churches. Elton had an unusual prophetic sensitivity to know when the denominational spirit was beginning to take over the soul of a movement. He had seen it repeatedly over the course of his ministry and in the many movements he had been a part of. Elton was afraid that the emerging charismatic movement in Nigeria was beginning to head in the same direction and was in danger of losing its purity and strength. He was concerned that if the focus shifted from spiritual development to maintaining a structure—more energy would be devoted to servicing the structure (the denominational machine) than to building up God's people to maturity and finishing the purpose of God on the earth. Elton was afraid that the movement would move away from the simplicity of devotion to Christ and become entangled in matters that had derailed previous movements. Elton feared that the movement was gradually moving away from the idea of simple but vibrant local churches to huge denominational structures. Elton was afraid that the movement would lose its vibrancy and, consequently, the ability to quickly respond to the instructions of the Holy Spirit. Elton was afraid that the movement would become man-centred rather than God-centred. He feared that the movement would get bogged down by human control and manipulation. He was afraid that the movement would become satisfied with itself and settle for less than God's best.

One of the early leaders of the 1970s revival in eastern Nigeria recounts a telling anecdote about Elton's fear concerning the emerging charismatic movement. "When we built our cathedral, he called us—he made it so plain—he said, 'You guys are going down there [the new cathedral], carry the fire here [the building where we started] to that place.' [He said] that those he had known that built cathedrals, all of them died [spiritually]. 'So be sure you carry the fire you have here—in this wood house—to that place,' he said. He gave us a serious warning; that they [those who had built cathedrals] were very zealous but when they built that thing, they thought they had reached their climax and then they sat down as kings. He told us again, so clearly, he said, 'Never you close your door to anybody, no matter how God has lifted you up, never; just be humble.' He said, 'A time will come when some ministers will not even see their members,' because they are so lifted up—so blessed that they have no more time for poor people. He said that that was not [true] Christianity; that we all are brethren. . . . He said, 'The master gave meat to the senior servant in Matthew 24, so that he would give food to other servants, but he decided to beat them and to eat the food.' He said, 'Beware, no matter how God has lifted you.' "[46]

The cathedral anecdote is significant in that Elton was not against the building of a "cathedral" as a physical place of worship, but he saw it as a metaphor of settling and becoming satisfied. He did not want a generation to have a cathedral mindset—to lose its initial fire and become complacent. But it is also possible that Elton was overreacting to his fears. Elton was always a very blunt person, and he sometimes expressed his fears in language that would have seemed hard, indeed too hard, for many. However, many observers of the Pentecostal/charismatic movement in Nigeria believe that Elton's fears have been confirmed and, in fact, surpassed.

The antithesis of having a denominational spirit was continually marching unto Zion, which represents a peak of the purpose of God's plan on the earth. "I want to examine exactly what Mount Zion stands for in this present age, particularly at this time as we move into the last few years of this dispensation, because it has very great meaning in these last days," Elton said in one of his teachings. "We are moving into a time when the great conflict of the church, inside the church, will be between that which has been built up by man, the earthly system, the buildings, the ceremonies, the liturgies, the church order and ceremonies and services, and that which has been built by God. All that has been built up has very little of New Testament significance, New Testament relevance, New Testament support, and very little of it has the blessing of God upon it. Much of it is not scriptural. We now come to that which is heavenly . . . those who are being governed by the Holy Spirit, who are worshipping by the Spirit, praying in the Spirit, being governed and led by the Spirit. All spiritual! Whose ambitions are all heavenly, who are not seeking to rush for naira and money, who are not seeking earthly possessions, earthly ambitions, earthly attainments, but heavenly attainments; that which is eternal, which is unshakable, and unmovable."[47]

In Elton's final years, the message of the kingdom, a theme which he had developed over time, became central to his ministry. He frequently dwelt on the fact that the period the Bible refers to as the end of the age had come upon the church, and you were either in or out; you were either prepared to take the battle to the enemy's gates or risked losing your place in God's end-time programme—there was not going to be any sitting on the fence. He declared during one conference in 1984: "Last night I warned you and told you of the great need for the church . . . to move on, press forward, [to] go on to perfection. The great disease of the Christian church in the world is that they are [seated] inside four walls enjoying anthems, enjoying their services and sermons and getting nowhere."[48]

Our attitude towards the last days, Elton stressed, is crucial to our successful engagement of this season in the church's history. The last days were going to witness the greatest battles of this present age, and the church had to develop a commensurate militant approach towards it. The church had to increasingly perceive itself as an army, and churches were to be recruiting and training centres for soldiers.

> We are to sound the trumpet, sound aloud the call for the people of God to waken. God wants His people to be aware of what He's doing in these last days. And let us not think that we are to accept the present defeated condition of the church. God does not want His church to be recognized as a defeated body. It is to be a victorious body, and we are going to be part of it. The church is now about to enter into a new phase of her existence—the phase where the Holy Spirit will move in glorious power and revival and bring her into a beautiful position. A new day is about to dawn, a new life is to be our portion, and a new inheritance in the Holy Spirit, a new experience of the power of God working through us. . . . We are tired of lukewarm Christianity which has been presented by the churches and the church leaders for 1900 years. We are wanting to fight. We are wanting to move into the realm of the Spirit and to be victorious, to execute on earth the judgement that God has given us, which is spoken of in Psalm 149.[49]

"What is the church doing in these days of crisis?"[50] he once asked. Much of the increase in chaos, nationally and globally, and the "break-down in moral standards in the family, schools, and institutions of higher learning" would be a direct result of an "increase in demon and evil spiritual powers from hell" and the "inspired operations of evil spirits who know their time is short and that a harvest is being prepared"; therefore the church had a major role to play in stemming the tide of this onslaught from hell and rescuing individuals and nations who were ignorant of the spiritual source of these troubles. The church had a priestly responsibility to stand in the gap to rescue the nations and save as many as possible. This would lead to the fiercest battles ever for the control of the destiny of nations. Satanic powers would have to be dislodged, leading to the greatest harvest of souls in history. But Elton often wondered whether the church was ready for this kind of battle:

> Why is it [the execution of God's plan for the last days] so slow? Because God has not got the men and women ready to carry it on. And I say, "Lord, look at them; they are all here." "Yes," the Lord says, "yes, they are all here. They are all here. They are singing and dancing and enjoying themselves. They are not ready to move out. They are not ready to go to the neighbours and the people in the town to say that Jesus is Lord."
>
> You like to enjoy church. And there is nothing wrong in singing and dancing . . . but remember those people out there who are not singing and dancing. . . . You are denying them the blessing you have gotten—God will judge you.[51]

Elton preached that the church which found itself between the end of the church age and the revelation of the kingdom age had to be "trained to reign." Living in a dynamic tension between the church age and the kingdom age required constantly existing in crisis mode; only the battle-ready Christian had any hope of surviving and thriving. Speaking about the peculiar characteristics of this period, he noted, "We are now actually in the period between the two Ages (GRACE AND KINGDOM) and so we can notice some of the principles ruling in the promised 'Kingdom Age' already beginning to show in the present age."[52] And, "The dispensation of grace—the church age, is almost complete, God is winding it up. Then He will usher in the next age—the kingdom age, when Jesus Christ will return to establish a visible kingdom of Heaven on earth, where He will reign together with His saints, together with His chosen body of people who have learned how to exercise power and authority, and they shall rule and reign with Him 1000 years."[53] Expatiating on this, he taught, "When God spoke to Simeon it was the end of the dispensation of LAW and the start of the new dispensation of Grace . . . the two periods overlapped in Simeon. He belonged to the old . . . but partook of the new. So today, we believe that the dispensation of grace is ending and will shortly give place to the new dispensation of the Kingdom . . . and Government . . . and the two periods are overlapping in these wonderful days."[54]

"As we move into the final years of this age, let us realize that our participation in this move will determine our responsibility and future ministry in the kingdom. The Holy Spirit is NOW calling new vessels and equipping them for the final conflict. Many, if not most, of the Christians will prefer to remain comfortably in their churches and businesses and be reluctant to step out into the conflict. Many others will be content to marry and give in marriage and enjoy life here now. But the Spirit is calling for OVERCOMERS. It is certain a great conflict lies ahead. It is certain Satan will succeed in many lives. But it is also certain that the Lord Jesus will also emerge triumphant with a people who have learned how to control themselves; overcome Satan, the flesh, and the world; and be likewise victorious, as He was victorious. They will have learned, on earth, the secrets of using His authority and establishing His government."[55] "It will be war right to the gates of glory," said Elton, "and everything will be done to disguise for Christians the real issues of the battle so that they can remain indifferent and absorbed in their personal and business worlds."[56]

"The Lord never intended that His church should become a sick hospital where weak and sick Christians can find rest and refuge," Elton wrote. "He planned that it would be a mighty ARMY, armed with the power of God (the Holy Spirit) and which would attack the forces of darkness and defeat them, and also which would become a body feared by all. The early church in ACTS demonstrated something of this power and unity and authority and the people and the authorities feared them. That was a spontaneous expression of the life of the Risen Lord and it caused people to think and become attached to it and to become part of that wonderful 'move of God' which swept all through the land."[57]

Under the direction of the Holy Spirit, the church was supposed to march in battle formation against the forces of Satan. The church was not supposed to be a haphazard and weak body; rather, a military spirit and structure, powered by the wisdom and direction of the Holy Spirit, was to be its driving force. "May I inform you that God is not gathering a mob, He's gathering an army, a trained army. They keep in step alongside each other; they march together. And when the one man who is in charge gives the order, everybody obeys. You watch an army—all the feet go in the right direction. They put their left foot forward first and then their right. They're all in step! All in step! And they are trained, trained to use their hands, trained to keep together. And as long as an army keeps together, there's no way the enemy can get it. There's no argument amongst the ranks as to who is chief. No argument! The captain is the boss and when he gives an order, they obey."[58]

The church at the end of the age had to increasingly embrace the message of the kingdom for it to walk in the fullness of the dominion that God intended for her. A kingdom mind-set was crucial to raising a church that had the capacity to bring the plan of God to consummation. End-time theology had to be first and foremost a "kingdom theology." The church had to see beyond herself—she had to see the kingdom. "There-fore there is the need to give a new vision and leadership to a new genera-tion. And this vision is the vision of the gospel of the kingdom,"[59] he said. "You have one word coming from our lips time and time again. That word is the kingdom. And you are puzzled in your mind as to really what it means. I have told you that the message of the kingdom of heaven is these last days' message and that is true."[60] Elton believed the church would always be limited in her impact if she didn't see herself as being only a part of a bigger plan—the kingdom plan. Elton preached in the early eighties:

I want to say this, which will upset some of your theology—the church is not God's ultimate. The church is God's vehicle, the same as the nation of Israel was, to bring in something better and bigger. Bigger than the church? Yes, yes. What is it? The kingdom. The Master came and He didn't say, the church is at hand, He said the kingdom is at hand. What does the kingdom mean? The restoration of the divine government on earth. . . . You pray it every Sunday morning . . . what do you mean? You are praying for something and you don't know what's coming? You might get into trouble. Thy kingdom come, and the kingdom will come.

And it will be that body that will bring in the kingdom. The body is not the kingdom. Shall I change the phraseology? The church is not the kingdom. The kingdom absorbs the church. The church is in the kingdom, but it is not the kingdom. The kingdom is very, very much bigger than the church. . . . The church age is about to be folded up. It is finished with; He is going to roll it up. It's a manifestation of the extreme wisdom of God. In what way? God taking slaves, converting them, putting a new nature into them, a new life into them, filling them with the same Holy Spirit that filled His Son and making them kings and priests to bust the entire principalities and powers of the kingdom of darkness. That's the wisdom of God."[61]

Elton's attempts at shifting his generation from a closed church mentality to a broad kingdom mind-set, were misinterpreted and often misunderstood by many as a direct attack on the church system. Though in trying to deliver a generation from what he termed "churchianity" and "churchmanship," he could sometimes sound extreme, his overriding goal was to make the kingdom life real and practical. "There is the doctrine of the kingdom. There is the present day manifestation of the kingdom and the full final restoration of the kingdom on earth. This is a practical teaching and refers to God's restoration of His authority and government over the earth. And that will be fully manifested and expressed through man in the future. Many people today are concerned with getting to heaven. We are going to heaven if we are born again, but it is God's plan to return us to the earth to reign with the Lord Jesus Christ, who will come again to the earth to take his rightful position as King of kings and Lord of lords over the whole earth,"[62] Elton preached. And also: "Today we find that most professing Christians think of a 'church' as a place or building. We need deliverance from this idea. I am not saying you should leave your present place of worship—but we must stop worshipping the 'church' as we see it. There is too much 'churchianity and churchmanship,' which has no part in the Lord's church or plan."[63] In one of his protégés' words, "Elton was a kingdom man."[64]

Our vision today is not merely to get men saved and baptized in the Holy Ghost and help them live godly lives; we are called to give the vision of the ultimate restoration of the government of God in lives, over nations and over the whole earth. We are born again and are destined to be rulers of the earth and God is going to re-establish that original Genesis 1:26–28, which was designed before the ages began and God is going to do it. We are going to see the kingdom established—"Thy will be done on earth as it is in heaven."

We are at the point where God is going to make the next big move and there's a possibility that the ages, the dispensations are overlapping. The old is running out and the new is coming in and we are seeing certain features of the new already being manifested, and the church is the vessel that God is going to use. The church is not the kingdom; the kingdom is the great overruling government of God and dominion over all men and the nations, over all creation and the universe. The church is inside the kingdom and designed and planned by God to be the governing vessel in the kingdom.[65]

Elton preached a literal catching away of the saints in the rapture, but he rarely emphasized it when dealing with the events of the last days. His eschatology was "dominion," as opposed to "escape." His emphasis was the coming kingdom and not the catching away of the church. In Elton's theology, the glory of the end was not in the fact that the church was going to *leave* this world, but that she was going to *reign* with Jesus Christ. Articulating this glorious vision, he stated, "The Lord Jesus Himself is coming again to be united with His triumphant body. That event draws near now. But the Bible leads us to believe that when He comes it will be to rapture a 'glorious' church, triumphant and victorious. . . . It is certain that the Lord's return will not be to remove a defeated church or even a disgraced church. So we can expect a wonderful future and experience soon for the church. . . . This is the final plan of God for His church. He is preparing her now for this gigantic task . . . the task of ruling the nations of this earth."[66]

Many Christians are crying to the Lord to return and rescue them. That is the cry of a defeated church. They are declaring that Satan and the world have won and are too strong for them. We declare this is NOT TRUE. No matter how much evil Satan brings, the Lord has a people who will stand and declare they are victors, and well able to handle it all. That is what God plans for the last days. A glorious, victorious, Spirit-filled church, clearly defeating Satan and proving the power of God is able to save, heal, fill and use redeemed men and women.[67]

There are many born-again evangelical Christians in today's world who act quite indifferently towards the rapid increase of Satan's kingdom and pray daily for the Lord to come to take them away before they succumb to him, instead of realising that God left us here to demonstrate the resurrection victory of the Lord Jesus and prove the power of the redeemed over a defeated Satan. It is dangerous for any Christian to be indifferent to conditions everywhere in all realms of public and national life wherever Satan holds sway. This shows Christians feel they have no responsibility for anything happening in the world today. God is interested and involved. It is wrong for believers to sit passively praying for the second coming while millions have never heard the gospel yet. [68]

The church had to boldly lay hold of the programme of God for the last days and refuse to be intimidated or curtailed by world events. The church had the responsibility to demand compliance to the plan of God. God's end-time move would not be a "rescue operation," to take the church out of the world, rather, "it's going to be a wonderful movement. . . . He is going to restore the power of the church. . . . The church is going to be a place where there is the power of God and God is going to restore the power to us."[69]

God is NOT going to rapture a weak, ineffective defeated church, whose witness in the world is negative and who has no power to effectively challenge, control and defeat Satan.

The church began in a blaze of glory at Pentecost and continued in a way which brought fear upon all and in a demonstration of power which produced thousands of converts daily, miracles of healing and deliverance and a challenge to the whole civilized world and even to the Roman Empire.

The church will complete the Age in a bigger and more powerful demonstration of God's power and glory. We are not to look back to Pentecost and pray for a repetition today. We are going to see a world-wide move of the Holy Spirit which will challenge the powers of earth and Satan, which will produce results far exceeding Pentecost and the Book of Acts, and the greatest miracles will be the complete victory over demon powers in individual lives, in towns and whole communities which will be radically changed.[70]

"We are gradually becoming aware of what power we have . . . and what God is doing in His church is moving towards dealing with the satanic majesty himself, dealing with Satan and his principalities—and that's what scares Satan. The gates of hell are not going to remain shut; we're going to kick them in and take over. And that's what Satan is scared of. We're not concerned so much with protecting ourselves; we've got protection, all right, and we'll move out. The best defence is in attack, and if you will look carefully in Ephesians 6, you will find there is armour for the head, armour for the breast, armour for the legs and the thighs, but nothing for the back. You turn your back on the enemy and you're exposed. He'll get you. Don't turn your back on him and run. Keep facing him and then you're protected, and you're all right,"[71] Elton preached.

God planned that [the church] should be the complete manifestation of the person, power and purposes of the Lord Jesus on earth during His absence. It should express the fullness of His power: to be completely triumphant at all times, undefeatable, and capable of meeting ALL the needs and solving all the problems of mankind, and to continue the earthly ministry of the Lord Jesus in restoring and re-establishing the rule and sovereignty of God. . . .

The Lord is not coming to rescue a defeated, dying, powerless church, but a living, powerful mighty Body which is feared by all and which is expressing the "fullness of Him who filled all things." . . . We feel that this newly empowered END TIME CHURCH will possess and demonstrate even greater operations of the Holy Spirit than we found recorded in the early church in the Book of ACTS.[72]

The church "is His masterpiece in this age. It's been here for nearly 2000 years, and I want to assure you without any doubts in my mind, it will not be a failure. And the Lord Jesus is saying, 'I will build my church and it is not going to be a failure.' Never! It will be a roaring success. It will be what the Lord Jesus Christ intended it to be on earth. There are no gates of hell in heaven; they are here, and here He's going to make it [the church] a success. He's going to make it the object of His purity, the object of His power, the object of His order, the object of His vision."[73]

Another theme to which Elton devoted much attention was the rise of a breed of Christians in the last days that would pursue the purpose of God with a courage and fierceness unprecedented in the history of the church. Their devotion to attacking and destroying all of Satan's strongholds in the earth and enthroning the life and principles of the kingdom of God would literally bring the age to a close. Elton believed the first stage of this plan would be the training and release of a special army that would walk in the character and power required to fulfil the demands of the times. He believed this would be a forerunner company, who would have the faith and courage to step into the waters of Jordan, even while it overflowed its banks, ahead of the rest of the church, to possess the Promised Land.

"God is raising up a people, and with His company of 'Overcomers,'

He will demonstrate His authority. We believe God is calling out and raising that group now; they are the 'Levites' of the last days who will stand in Jordan representing the whole Body, to secure protection, safety and deliverance for the Body and the great mass of seekers in the last days,"[74] he wrote. He believed the rest of the church could not be stirred if this forerunner company did not rise. His greatest quest, therefore, was to see this company emerge. Elton's vision was not of an exclusive company, but rather of an elite army, which he believed would challenge the rest of the church by its brilliance and power. "These are days when He's calling for His army to be prepared. We have sat down in this mountain long enough. It's time for us to cross over Jordan to possess our inheritance. And we are to begin to move. . . . The whole of the army of the Lord in the earth is waiting for men and women who will call the trumpets and use the trumpets, and who will call . . . to prepare for war."[75]

This drift towards what some considered spiritual elitism was a major issue that made him suspect in many circles as he came close to the end of his life, but Elton had no apologies for those who were uncomfortable with this teaching. He boldly declared, "It is therefore clear that in the church today, there is a select company of sincere dedicated believers who are determined to follow the Lord no matter what the rest of the congregation does. The idea of a 'select' chosen 'over-comer' group of Christians is often referred to in the Bible, but this does not give any authority for asserting separate rights or exclusive rights to the Lord's blessings, words or guidance."[76] Expressing this position more forcefully, he continued:

It is dangerous to separate ourselves and call ourselves by any special name or even "church," because we feel we have been specially chosen. This mistake leads to divisions and bitterness and sectarianism . . . which is a great sin in the Christian church today and has caused so much havoc and loss of spiritual power. The Lord Himself will know those who respond to His call and who seek to follow Him and He will deal with them and use them for His own purpose. This should never make anyone proud or feel specially called; or to separate themselves from the great move of the Holy Spirit today throughout the world. God loves *all* and wills that *all* should be saved and we deny this when we regard ourselves as specially selected for special purposes and that we have no connection with others whom we regard as less holy.

Yet once again, we affirm that it is clear the Lord does have a "select company." . . . And that He has to use this group to carry out His plans for today.

The church in general has refused to overcome self, the world and the devil. On the contrary, the church is overcome by them and thus her function for the Lord's purpose in the world today is foiled. But the Lord will have a "remnant" ... a group whom He can use to demonstrate His power and grace and ability to rule His own church and eventually the world.[77]

Here and in several other teachings, Elton reinforced the idea of this select company. "God himself is actually superintending the selection of His special 'army' as He did with Gideon's three hundred,"[78] he wrote. "Never in the history of the church have we faced such crisis, and conflict as we do now. The enemy is moving his hordes into a position where he can attack—attack, not the world, not the church, but those who are going to move forward. We must expect that if we dedicate ourselves to going forward with the Lord, the enemy will attack us. This is a call for war and we must recognize this call. The trumpets will blow, a trumpet calling for war, assembling the armed men to come together, calling God's army together and we are not to be surprised if that army turns out to be a very small army. God specializes in using few and using people who are of not much account as far as the world or the church is concerned."[79]

Elton repeatedly emphasized that the purpose of the forerunner company was to stir the rest of the church, to wake up and challenge the slumbering majority. As he explained, "It would seem today, universally, that God is anointing and using a ministry of Christians (mostly young people) to catch the vision of the kingdom in these last days, while the main body of the church sleeps on. This is not surprising. Even in the first century after Pentecost, the church was failing to follow her Lord but He had a group of 'overcomers' in each church, to whom He made special promises if they remained faithful. Even in the nation of Israel, God had to use a select body of people (the Levites) to protect and deliver Israel (Joshua 3:15–17). So today, God seems to be using a minority to save the majority and to fulfil His purposes."[80] God's ultimate intention, Elton preached, was for the whole church to engage in the last-days conflict and be a part of the Overcomer Company.

"Looking back now," Yinka Ayankogbe recalls, "most of what he [Elton] taught us were leadership concepts, drawing them from the Bible. I remember one of his major topics—it was the principle by which all of the children of Israel were led to the Promised Land. They were carrying the ark far in front and there were people carrying that ark; [he said] that is how the work of God is done. There are some people who would dedicate themselves to carrying the presence of the Lord; and it is that presence that they carry that parts Jordan, that parts the Red Sea. If that group of people are not there to carry that presence, the people of God cannot be led. Because there must be people in front who have dedicated their lives [to that purpose]."[81]

Because the final days of this present age would witness such an onslaught from hell as never before known in history, this "Special Forces" group had to be formed. "In the last days, there's going to be an all-out battle from hell. As I have mentioned, there will be revival in evangelism, a revival inside the church and there will be a great and mighty outpouring of the Holy Spirit. A revival in every aspect which will install Jesus Christ as the mighty saviour, install Him as the mighty deliverer, and install Him as the Lord of heaven and earth, in the hearts of His people. So also, there's going to be a mighty revival of the powers of darkness. Satan is going to gather all his available forces of demons, princes, principalities, powers, and he's going to have one great onslaught against—not against God, for Satan has already been defeated by Jesus Christ—the special company of people on the earth. That company of people is found inside the body of Jesus Christ and they will be the covenant relationship people. The people who are moving in conscious manifest relationship with each other—moving in conscious, visible relationship with the Father in heaven. The Father's nature and glory being seen in their lives and in their actions and they will be the object of the hatred of Satan and the objective of the battle in the last days."[82]

"God had the faith and the audacity to write the book of Revelation 1900 years ago and then said to Satan, 'Now read and study that. Your doom is in there.' And Satan has had 1900 years study of the book of Revelation, and he knows what's coming. He can interpret it, all right, and that's why he's trying to stop the emergence of that body of people who establish the kingdom of heaven on earth," said Elton. "A body of people who are going to step forward as kings and priests and say to Satan, 'Now listen to what I'm going to tell you; get out there and get down. I'm the boss now, not you.' And when that starts to happen, Satan's finished. And he's tried to stop it and has succeeded for 1900 years in delaying the emergence of that body of people who can exercise kingly authority and priestly ministry. But God is doing it now. In these last days the Holy Spirit is bringing together a body of people, one from here, one from there.

Not denomination. No! Men and women who are going to learn, having exercised kingly authority in their own lives and [who have] known how to govern themselves. . . . Who know how to exercise authority over Satan now, now, now, and tell him what to do! Exercising authority given to us by the man who has all authority in His hands."[83]

"DON'T CELEBRATE DEATH"

Hannah Elton died on March 25, 1983, at the age of eighty-nine. For fifty three years her all-round solidity had played a major role in Elton's success and her death was a huge loss. He had said of his relationship with her once while speaking on marriage, "There's a woman in my life that I cannot do without and that woman has been there for a long, long, long time. And I am happy and quite contented when I'm in her company. We don't need to talk, we don't need to touch; just there together. And what you think is necessary in marriage is not necessary in marriage. [What is necessary is] the joining of a soul with a soul, not a body with a body."[1]

Two factors perhaps added some uniqueness to their marriage—though it is difficult to measure how—the fact that Hannah was thirteen years older than him and that she led him to the Lord and witnessed the first stages of his spiritual growth. Elton would say in later years: "For your encouragement let me say this, I've been a Christian for many years, yet that young lady (my wife) there, was a Christian before I was. She saw me converted, she saw me baptized in water and I won't go any further. Oh yes, she saw me married."[2]

Hannah always made it clear that her first assignment was to look after her husband and to ensure that he succeeded in the ministry God committed to him, and she gave herself completely to this till the end. She was Sydney Elton's greatest human strength until her passing. Many of his protégés have referred to her as his spiritual thermometer. Whenever

Elton preached at a meeting, she sat in a particular way, and if she shook her head lightly, it meant there was no anointing on the sermon. Elton jokingly referred to this as "NGII"—no God in it. But if she nodded a little bit, it meant he was on track, and he would then go on full blast.[3]

Visitors to Ilesa were usually struck by two things about Hannah—her warmth and hospitality, and her godly disposition and devotion to prayer. She made everybody feel welcome and those who came to see Elton never failed to notice the grace that her presence engendered. Many would also remember several years later, the reassurance they felt about their ministries as she prayed for them.

For many years before her death, Hannah suffered from macular degeneration—a degenerative eye condition—which became really troublesome in her final years. On the day she died, she at first became unconscious; when the doctor suggested resuscitating her, Elton said, "No; let her go and rest."[4] A letter Elton wrote to John and Celia Valentine after Hannah's death also gives us some insight: "We [the Valentines] only heard from Pa again after Ma died. He told us that her degenerative eye condition had become much worse . . . and one night she said that she felt she could no longer look after Pa. They lay down on the bed and she quietly passed away."[5]

In the last years of his life, Elton lent his energy to as many initiatives as he thought could lead to a new wave of revival in the country. In a November 1980 letter to a Nigerian couple in the UK, Elton wrote, "We have been away from Ilesa for most of Oct – Nov . . . to BENIN twice . . . and then up to visit Ruth in Koto Karifi and then on to Zaria . . . and then to Kaduna . . . and then back to Koto. . . . We have been busy with Onitsha since then and leave for Port Harcourt on Dec. 4th for 5 days . . . and the Lord has been with us; and the journeys have been blessed. This country is indeed blessed and the Vision is moving. Zaria (ABU) was good and also Kaduna . . . and they accepted us in full and they are on the move spiritually. . . . CSSM are also moving forward and likewise NIFES. So we are busy . . . happy and occupied." He ended the letter on the same sanguine note he had started off with: "No news from Kano . . . . We expect to go to Nsukka and Enugu early in '81. That will cause an explosion towards the North."[6]

At seventy-three, the energy and excitement in Elton's voice is unmistakable—he showed no signs of slowing down—he was having the ride of his life furthering the cause of revival around the country. When he was asked in 1982, "How do you now spend your leisure?" Elton responded that he was not having a holiday and that he was not about to start one: "We are still continuing our ministry according to our strength. I have been preaching five times this week; five messages already this week, in this very week, and this is Thursday. . . . Then we are still writing, still writing articles, another new magazine is going to be produced, we are producing the articles for that. Letters? There is whole a pile of letters on my desk. There is no single day here without a number of callers and visitors from all over the country; for advice, for leadership. We are not able to travel as we would like to, but they are coming here instead of us going there. We are still very very busy indeed . . . and I haven't finished yet. The end is not in sight and the last few years of our lives will be much more glorious, much more fruitful than any years we have spent in Nigeria."[7]

Elton's teachings throughout the week of September 10 to 14, 1984, at the "Ministers, Leaders, and Christian Workers Conference" held in Port Harcourt reveal an Elton who was completely alive, his heart on fire, his voice clear and loud; he spoke like a general preparing his army for battle. "We have given you what God has given us," he began one of the teachings, "we have given you wonderful stuff; it has thrilled our souls; it has lightened our lives; it has given us a vision, and that vision keeps us alive. It keeps me alive."[8] He was writing in September 1986, at seventy-nine, "We have visited Maiduguri, Kano, Jos, Enugu, Onitsha, Owerri, Port Harcourt, [as] well as many places in the West this year alone. . . . The work here is moving fast. . . . Now we must get ready to leave for Enugu for five days mtgs."[9]

Around 1982 Elton had a minor heart attack during a trip to Ibadan: while driving, he had a sudden chest pain (angina), but he recovered and was able to drive himself back to Ilesa.[10] After he was examined by a doctor, it was discovered he had ischemic heart disease.[11] Unaware of its effect on his health, Elton had taken too many eggs over the years, which resulted in plaque building up along the inner walls of the arteries of his heart. "He had eaten too many eggs" says Ruth, "they are bad [for the health]; we didn't know then and that caused the trouble."[12] After the initial one, Elton suffered a number of other attacks, of which two were major.

The third occurrence was a major one. "It was in the night," Ruth remembers. "My mother came and called me and said, 'Dad wants to see you; he is not sleeping.' He didn't just want to tell my mother, I think. . . . When my mother said, 'Your dad's not feeling well,' I knew what it was but my mother didn't know, the doctor didn't tell her, but he had told me. So immediately I went to get another pillow . . . I set him up on it and then he said, 'Oh that's better . . . how did you know?' I knew what was going on but I didn't tell any of them."[13]

Ruth recalls that sometime after Hannah's passing Elton suffered another attack which led to his hospitalization at the University of Ife Teaching Hospital.[14] Referring to these bouts with heart trouble in a letter to the Valentines, Elton wrote: "First of all let me tell you of myself and my movements, etc etc, and give you chance to praise the Lord for what He has done for us. I slowly . . . very slowly survived after my heart attack and stroke which confined me entirely to the house and no travelling or meetings apart from our usual Thur. evening house meeting. When Ciss passed on, my condition got worse and eventually I was moved to Ife State Hosp. by Dr Andy the heart specialist . . . and it was felt I could be considered as a heart patient and an invalid."[15]

Sometime in 1983, thinking the end had come, Elton told some of his closest protégés at the time to go and seek the Lord to know if it was time for him to go home.[16] Five of them travelled to Osogbo to pray concerning the issue. They received in prayer that the Lord was going to heal him, and when they returned from Osogbo, they prayed for him and he eventually recovered.[17] Apart from the few occasions when Elton suffered the major heart attacks, he was generally healthy in his final years. "Unless you were told, you wouldn't know that there was anything wrong with him," Ruth recollects. He was still driving himself to meetings around the country in his late seventies. He only stopped at the insistence of his protégés.[18]

In the letter to the Valentines, Elton further noted that, "Ruth tried to combine looking after me and the house here with her own home and work . . . but it did not work . . . and eventually we persuaded Mrs. Grace Delbridge . . . with whom we stayed when we visited UK . . . to join me and look after me."[19] Grace Delbridge was Hannah Elton's chief bridesmaid when the Eltons wedded in 1930. Delbridge had known the Eltons since she was in her teens, and Hannah was the one who taught her dressmaking. She was also a member of the Brethren assembly the Eltons attended in Shrewsbury.[20] When the Eltons were leaving for Nigeria in 1937, Grace Delbridge's husband, Joseph, promised that he would always keep a place for them in their home where the Eltons could spend their furloughs.

"The first time that they returned to England [on furlough] after I was born became my earliest remembrance of them," recalls Elizabeth Metcalfe, daughter of the Delbridges. "They were our extended family and we were theirs. In subsequent years the pattern was the same. Our home was theirs whenever they had a furlough. During some of her teenage years Ruth remained with us and went to school in Shrewsbury. . . . Ruth and I shared a bedroom and spent some holidays together. I particularly remember staying with an aunt of mine in a village in the country. Ruth and I planned to climb to the top of a grassy hill, but I polished the bottom of her shoes so that she couldn't get a grip and would slide back down. As a little girl I was rather in awe of my Aunty Ciss and Uncle Syd (as they were known to me) as I was always told that, if I wanted to sit in their room with them I must be quiet and not talk. But I also loved them very much."[21]

Grace Delbridge visited the Eltons in Ilesa in 1960/61 and spent about twelve months in the country. As Elizabeth Metcalfe recalls, "A very close relationship continued and as the years rolled by, there had been an unwritten expectation or assumption that, as she [Grace Delbridge] was several years younger than Mrs. Elton, she would be a caring companion to whoever was bereaved first, be it Pa or Ma."[22]

Grace Delbridge became widowed in 1976. And soon after Hannah's passing, it was decided that she should relocate to Ilesa to look after Elton. In December 1983, Emeka Nwankpa went to England to bring her back to Nigeria "to be [a] companion to Pa." "[But] soon after she arrived in the country, they decided to get married," says Elizabeth Metcalfe. "My mother did not come to Nigeria knowing she was going to marry Ps. Elton, but the brother/sister relationship blossomed into love and they married [at] the Registry Office in Oshogbo on March 3, 1984. Emeka Nwankpa and Anna Ogunnaike were their witnesses."[23] "She came in Dec. '83 and decided to undertake the task and so we married in March '84 and she is still with me and doing a wonderful job,"[24] Elton wrote in 1986.

Elizabeth Metcalfe's recollections of the marriage, and of Elton's last years, leave us with some fascinating anecdotes. "Although the marriage sadly was to be quite short, it was a very happy marriage. They were both very young at heart and enjoyed each other's company immensely. Pa taught my mother to love the Nigerian people until she felt more at home in Nigeria than in England. But, because she was new to running a home Nigerian style, he would tease her a lot and they laughed together. It was always a real tonic to us and to all our family, who visited Ilesa in turn, to be with them."[25]

During their (Elizabeth Metcalfe and her husband) holidays in Nigeria, they would usually accompany Elton and Grace on preaching trips around the country. Elizabeth recalls "attending the annual convention in Onitsha where we saw hundreds of people praising and worshipping God and drinking in the word spoken by Pa. In complete contrast, Pa took us unannounced to a small village in the bush. We left the car when we could take it no further and walked the rest of the way to where we received a warm welcome from this small community. Pa explained that he had brought visitors to see them and that he would hold a service for them. The hub of a car wheel was banged as a means of summoning the people to worship and within a very short time people came out of their houses and assembled in the tiny church. Although we did not understand a word that was said or sung, it was wonderful to be part of that short service and to feel the love of those people. As we left they brought gifts of beautiful fruit for us to take back to Ilesha, very gratefully received."[26]

Grace returned to England when Elton died. On a number of visits to her home in Shrewsbury, Edward Ezenwafor remembers Elton's sermons always playing on her cassette player. She wanted to hear his voice all day. Her heart never left Nigeria and she wanted to die in Nigeria and be buried beside Elton in Ilesa. "She loved Elton; she loved him. She said to me [Ezenwafor], 'I have never seen a man like that.' "[27] She was making plans to return to Nigeria—a letter of invitation had been written on her behalf and she had applied for a visa—when she unexpectedly fell from the staircase and broke her leg. She passed away a few days later on September 10, 1987.[28]

When Elton was asked in 1982, "If Jesus doesn't come early and the Lord calls you home, would you rather want to be carried to England or buried in Nigeria?" he replied, "Oh no, we have left England, with no plan or desire whatsoever to go back again to England. This is our land; this is our country, and if the Lord doesn't come, okay, I will be buried on this land [his house in Ilesa] here."[29] When he was asked about who should be in charge of the burial services of himself and his wife when they eventually passed on, he responded with his characteristic bluntness: "We want no memorial services and no burial services. They will bury us; our bodies will be buried in a grave and we want no big fuss made whatsoever; that's not us going down into that grave. We've gone. If after that, the people with whom we have been connected want to gather themselves together, then God bless them; we have no objections whatsoever. I have an idea that those whom I leave behind will not want to be there for those [burial] services."[30] Four years later, as he neared his death, he gave instructions that whenever he died he was to be buried immediately. "Don't celebrate death," he said, "bury me immediately and carry on with the work of the kingdom!"[31]

On January 14, 1987, Sydney Granville Elton breathed his last.

"On the day of Pa's death, there had been no indication that the end was imminent," recalls Elizabeth Metcalfe. "The day had been normal and Pa retired to bed first. Very shortly afterwards my mother joined him but as she spoke to and touched him, there was no response. Quickly she realised something was very wrong, in fact feared that he had passed away. So, in the absence of a working telephone, she dressed and hurriedly walked alone in the dark through the streets of Ilesa to fetch the doctor."[32]

Elton had left instructions that whenever he passed on, Ruth had to be fetched from the mission field before he was buried. Someone was sent to Okene the morning of January 15, reaching there about noon. By 4:00 p.m. they had returned to Ilesa, where Ruth was met by a crowd that had gathered at the compound. Elton was placed in the coffin bought by Enoch Adeboye, the general overseer of the Redeemed Christian Church of God, and by 6:00 p.m. he had been buried.[33]

A titan had passed on.

• • •

In 2014, Ruth Elton celebrated her eightieth birthday in Ilesa, a town she first stepped into in 1937 as a three-year-old. Together, the Elton family—Sydney, Hannah and Ruth—have contributed about 160 missionary years to the development of Christianity in Nigeria—perhaps more than any other missionary family in Nigeria's history.

After arriving in Nigeria, Sydney and Hannah decided they were not going to have any more children so they could focus totally on the work. Speaking of this decision in later years Elton said, "As a white man my children would be expected to be trained in the UK, in English schools, and you can't be a missionary and have a large family. Because . . . I don't believe that a family should split up. I don't think children should go to school without their parents. So if there are children here, then eventually when they become school age, for education their parents have got to go back again to UK and live. That's the end of missionary life. We faced that problem in 1937, [and we decided] no more children, and there have been no more children. We had to sacrifice to get that."[34]

As she was only a child, Ruth's involvement in her parent's ministry in the early years in Nigeria was simply to travel with them as they moved from place to place overseeing the churches in the area under Elton's leadership. During this period, she was home-schooled by her mother, who taught her the basics of reading and writing. Before Ruth was four, Hannah regularly took time out to teach her about Jesus Christ—reading the Bible to her hearing every morning and then giving lessons from it. Memories of Hannah using a picture of Jesus hanging on the cross to illustrate the message of salvation remain vivid in Ruth's mind. Recalling her salvation experience at a tender age, Ruth remembers her mother talking about how Jesus was flogged, nailed, and crucified and how he died for the sins of humanity and then Hannah asked if she would accept Jesus as her Saviour and Lord.[35] Kneeling down at the stairs of her father's residence at that young age, Ruth made her first definite commitment to Jesus Christ.[36]

An interesting contribution Ruth made to her parents' ministry from an early age was interpreting for her mother. Ruth quickly picked up on the Yoruba language and often helped her mother in breaking the communication barrier in her interactions with the local Christian women. When the family travelled for its second furlough to the UK in 1944, she was registered in a private school in Shrewsbury—her first formal schooling—which she attended until 1946. Ruth recalls her father preaching at a night service during this furlough on the book of Revelation with the theme, "Behold I Stand at the Door and Knock." The message made another major impact on her heart, and she committed her life to Jesus Christ "in a more profound way."[37]

Ruth's quest for God continued to grow during her schooling in the UK from 1948 to 1952. She became dissatisfied with the prevailing standard of Christian living she observed around her and sought for a "genuine company of Christians with whom she could pursue the true life of faith."[38] When Cecil Cousen came to the UK in 1951 with the Latter Rain message, he provided the answer she had been searching for. During one of the meetings, she went forward to be prayed for and when hands were laid on her by Cousen, she felt something had been imparted to her. Sometime later, while praying before going to bed at night, she suddenly felt the presence of Jesus as if He was physically standing right beside her. When she opened her eyes to see, "it seemed a bright light filled the room,"[39] she recollected many years later. This experience proved to be a high point in her Christian experience. From that moment she "came to know Jesus Christ in a very deep way"; she committed everything to Him, and nothing else mattered any longer.

When she returned to Nigeria with her parents in 1952, she became heavily involved in the Latter Rain revival meetings around the country. It was about this time that she caught the vision of becoming a missionary. Most likely, her interest was first sparked by the many discussions around the table about taking the gospel to unreached places by the Latter Rain evangelists who frequented the Eltons' Ilesa residence during this period. To fulfil this vision, she began saving up money from her salary to buy a car for the mission field. At the time, she was employed as a dress making and art teacher at the government-owned Women's Teacher Training College, Ilesa.

Help soon came to actualize her dream when du Plessis visited. During the time he stayed with the Eltons in Ilesa he asked about her plans, and when he learned she was saving up to go to the mission field, he promised to recommend her to anyone who might be interested in sponsoring her. Shortly after his departure, Elton received a letter from du Plessis informing him that he had found somebody in Switzerland who was interested in supporting Ruth. Contact was made, and the money to purchase a vehicle was sent; she was also placed on a monthly allowance. She resigned her appointment with the government and became a full-time missionary.[40]

Ruth's missionary career began with an outreach to Oke-Eri (Igbaruku) near Egbe in Kogi State in 1959.[41] She was there until 1960 when her father travelled overseas for six months, and she had to return to Ilesa to oversee the work of the World Christian Crusade. This involved checking the reports which the evangelists on the various fields sent in monthly, paying their monthly allowance, and on-the-spot supervision of the work. In the course of this work, she visited Ebiraland, specifically Okene. She was disturbed by how un-evangelised the place was, by the large population of Muslims, and by how few churches were there. She returned to Ilesa, but the burden never left her.

After her father returned from his trip she returned to full-time mission work in Igbaruku. In February 1961, she moved over to Ebiraland, first settling in Oboroke Ihima. At the beginning of the work in Ebiraland her focus was on helping the evangelists that were being sponsored by her father; she also engaged the interpreters in Bible training sessions. Gospel campaigns were organized in several villages such as Oboroke, Ikuchi, Adavi, Obetura, etc, and churches were planted in these places.

After some years, through Ruth Elton's efforts, these churches were brought together to form the Gospel Assemblies of Ebiraland. Later it was renamed Gospel Assembly Church; this was again changed to Gospel Assemblies of Nigeria to accommodate the geographical spread of the church beyond Ebiraland. The Gospel Assemblies of Nigeria now has over a hundred churches with most of them in Ebiraland.[42]

For almost five decades Ruth has been involved in mission work to many unreached areas. Included are the Ebira Kato tribe, the Gwari tribe, the Bata Kwon people and several others. She eventually left Okene and established a mission base at Koton Karfi, from where she continued travelling extensively with other evangelists to establish the gospel in unreached places.

When her father died, she returned to Ilesa to oversee his work, but she continued to travel yearly to the mission field. She is presently involved in training and sponsoring missionaries, and creating awareness about the need to get involved in missions through her organisation, Coming Kingdom Outreach.[43]

Acknowledgements

From my first meeting with Ruth Elton—the only child of Sydney and Hannah Elton—until I concluded work on the manuscript in 2015, she was my biggest ally in the quest to rediscover her father's story and legacy. She patiently endured hours of interviews at her home in Ilesa and on the phone, and never failed to answer my many questions. I must have interviewed her—both formally and informally—close to forty times. She also provided me with the largest collection of memorabilia— photographs, copies of the now classic *Herald of the Last Days* magazine, the complete collection of *Special Ministers' Course for Nigeria*, and her father's sermon tapes. She was also crucial in gaining access to many of Elton's associates and protégés. Thank you Baby Ciss!

Joyce Lee, Catherine McGee, Lauren Brooks, Michelle Yarborough and the rest of the staff of the Flower Pentecostal Heritage Centre, Springfield, Missouri, USA—thanks for responding to my numerous requests with patience, promptness and enthusiasm; you guys are really wonderful.

Andrew Saunders of the Apostolic Church Archives, Wales, went beyond my requests to locate publications whose existence I was unaware of, and which proved crucial to understanding Elton's story; thanks, Andrew, for your generosity. Alf Russell and Karen Davies of the Wolverhampton City Council Archives; Alison Healey and Liz Young of the Shropshire Council Archives; Rhydian Davies of the National Library of Wales; David Morris and Andrew Dulley of the West Glamorgan Archive Service, City and County of Swansea; Nancy Gower, archivist at the David Allan Hubbard Library, Fuller Theological Seminary; staff of the Jacob Ade-Ajayi Library, Ibadan; staff of the National Archives, Ibadan; and staff of the National Archives, Enugu—thanks for all the research, for answering my enquiries promptly, and for pointing me in the right direction.

I am also grateful to many individuals and organisations that facilitated my research in various ways: the staff of the Gospel Revivals Inc., Seelyville, Indiana, publishers of *Herald of His Coming* magazine, helped in digging out the invaluable issues of the magazine that featured Elton's letters; Laura Premack of the University of North Carolina generously included my request in her PhD thesis research at the Swansea Archives; after about three years of searching, Olu Amure of the Church of God Mission media department, Benin, was finally able to track down the video documentary on Sydney Elton produced by Benson Idahosa.

Temidayo Adeyemo's initiatives towards reviving interest in Sydney Elton's story among many of his protégés—especially through the 2004 edition of *Essence Restored* magazine dedicated to Elton's life, and the 2007 special commemoration service to mark twenty years of his passing— are a great resource to any Elton researcher; his personal encouragement on this project has also been very helpful. Elizabeth Metcalfe—daughter of Grace Delbridge—was really generous in walking me through the details of her mother's marriage to Sydney Elton and stories about his final years. Muyiwa Longe and Demilade Ogundele spent about a year transcribing a large collection of Elton's taped sermons—I am more than grateful for your labours.

The personal collections of a number of individuals enriched my Elton memorabilia: a major collection of sermon tapes from Kunle Kehinde of the Obafemi Awolowo University, Ile-Ife; a collection of Elton's letters from Femi Soetan, Imole Ayo Eye Hospital, Ile-Ife; *Herald of the Last Days* magazine from Olanrewaju Phillips, Mount Zion Hospital, Ile-Ife; sermon tapes from John Ladega, Kingdom Gospel Church, Ilesa; and an invaluable ECU (University of Ife) magazine collection from Olubunmi Oni, Lagos.

I deeply appreciate all those who granted me interviews. I am also grateful to all those who read the manuscript and offered suggestions that have greatly improved the overall quality of the book: Ruth Elton; Adam Mohr, University of Pennsylvania; Richard Burgess, University of Roehampton; Afe Adogame, the University of Edinburgh; Allan Anderson, University of Birmingham; and Gary Maxey, West Africa Theological Seminary, Lagos.

I was a scholar-in-residence at the West Africa Theological Seminary (WATS), Lagos, during one two-year period of the research work, and this provided me with ample time and resources to focus on the project. I am grateful to Gary Maxey, founder of the seminary, and his wife, Emma Lou, for facilitating my access to this superb programme for scholars and researchers. The provost, William Udotong; the director of communication, Femi Martins; and the entire staff of the seminary, were also very supportive.

The enthusiasm, encouragement and all-round support of the following friends and leaders was crucial in carrying the project through many critical phases: Matthews Ojo (Obafemi Awolowo University, Ile-Ife), Fred Adegoke (University of Ilorin), Christine Ajike-Nzenwata, Olugboyega Alaba (University of Lagos), Oluyemi Osinbajo (Simmons-Cooper Partners, Lagos), Debo Adesina (WaterGate Church, Sango-Ota), Paul Nwachukwu (Grace of God Mission, Onitsha), Ehi Duke Ekoh, John Daukoru, Koyejo Alaba, Richard Ikiebe (Pan Atlantic University, Lagos), Adeyemi Akisanya (Adeyemi-Akisanya Associates, Lagos), Yomi Kasali (Foundation of Truth Assembly, Lagos), Taiwo Odukoya (Fountain of Life Church, Lagos), and Olubi Johnson (Scripture Pasture Christian Centre, Ibadan).

I had a super amazing editor in Ibukun Omojola—I owe you one! Also, many thanks to my proofreader, Uche Okonkwo.

Ladi and Taiwo Thompson—Living Waters Unlimited Church (LWUC), Lagos—I am truly blessed to call you my pastors. Thank you for always caring so deeply about God's people, and labouring diligently to see His kingdom come. I love you dearly.

Tunji and Christiana Osinulu—thank you for being a great blessing to my wife and I.

I am privileged to serve alongside a great pastoral team at LWUC—your passion for God's kingdom deeply inspires me.

Being a part of a great local church can be one of the most exciting adventures on earth, and I am honoured to call LWUC home. Thank you all for your love and support. I am glad to be on this journey with you.

My family has proven time and again that one of the greatest assets anyone can have in life is a loving and supportive family. Dad and Mum—Akinyele and Alice Abodunde—you are the greatest parents in the world; your example of love and sacrifice will resound to generations. My siblings—Akinwumi, Oladapo, and Funmilola—thanks for the great friendship, and the spiritual and intellectual contribution. My parents-in-law—Olugboyega and Olubisi Alaba—your support has been massive; thank you! My brothers-in-law and sisters-in-law—you have always been a great source of encouragement; thank you.

My son, Semilore, thank you for understanding when daddy had to lock the door to focus! I am confident that you will grow up to be the warrior you were born to be.

My daughter, Tamilore, you are welcome!

My lovely wife, Dupe, you sacrificed the greatest to see this book through. Now you can breathe! I love you and I will always be grateful for you. Thank you, love.

Notes

ABBREVIATIONS USED IN THE NOTES

CFTN	*Christ for the Nations magazine*
DAHL-DDPA	David Allan Hubbard Library, Fuller Theological Seminary, Pasadena, David du Plessis Archives
DOP	David Odubanjo Papers
ER	*Essence Restored*
FD	*Faith Digest*
GRO	General Register Office (England and Wales)
HHC	*Herald of His Coming*
HOLD	*Herald of the Last Days Magazine*
MF	*March of Faith*
NCF-BCC	Nigeria Christian Fellowship Bible Correspondence Course
NNAE	Nigeria National Archives, Enugu
NNAI-AMAC	Nigeria National Archives, Ibadan, Aladura Movement (Apostolic Church)
NNAI-ACA	Nigeria National Archives, Ibadan, Apostolic Church and Aladura
NNAI-BFT	Nigeria National Archives, Ibadan, The Faith Healer – Babalola and the Faith Tabernacle
PE	*Pentecostal Evangel*
ROG	*Riches of Grace*
REP	Ruth Elton Papers
TAH	*The Apostolic Herald*
HOG	*The Herald of Grace*
VOH	*The Voice of Healing magazine*
TACA	The Apostolic Church Archives, Wales
CSSMA	Christian Students' Social Movement (CSSM) Archives
ECU	Evangelical Christian Union, University of Ife
IVCU	Ibadan Varsity Christian Union

1937 Diary   Sydney Elton's 1937 Diary
Sermon   Sydney Elton's sermons
Rev. S. G. Elton Interview   Interview with Rev. S. G. Elton, April 2, 1982.
Church of God Mission Publication, Benin

Selected Interviews

1. Emmanuel Onofurho. General Overseer, Soul Harvesters Mission, Warri. October 26, 2012.

2. Niyi Beecroft. ECU (University of Ife) member during the early 1970s; member of the Board of Regents of Covenant University, Ota. March 5, 2012.

3. Olubunmi Oni. ECU (University of Ife) member during the 1970s; former CEO, Cadbury Nigeria, Plc. April 7, 2012.

4. Olubi Johnson. Senior Pastor, Scripture Pasture Christian Centre, Ibadan. May 11, 2012.

5. Austen Ukachi. President of the IVCU, 1977; pioneer chairman of the CSSM; Senior Pastor, He's Alive Chapel, Lagos. May 5, 2012.

6. Fred Adegoke. ECU (University of Ife) member during the 1970s; professor in the Department of Guidance and Counselling, University of Ilorin. April 10–11, 2012.

7. Stanley Ikechukwu Utah. ECU (University of Ife) member during the 1970s. Pastor of Foursquare Gospel Church, Victoria Garden City Lagos. February 24, 2012.

8. Okey Onuzo. ECU (University of Ife) member during the 1970s; founder, Life Support Medical Centre, Ikeja Lagos. February 2012.

9. Amos Aderonmu. Former International Director, CAPRO International. March 23, 2012.

10. Peter Ozodo. President of ECU, University of Ife, 1973; one of the pioneers and one-time president of CAPRO International. September 2006; February 17, 2012.

11. Biola Adeniran. President of the IVCU, 1977 and one of the founders of the Tuesday Group; presently one of the leaders in the Deeper Life Bible Church founded by W. F. Kumuyi. February 29, 2012.

12. Geoffrey Numbere. ECU (University of Ife) member during the 1970s. Founder, Greater Evangelism World Crusade. Port Harcourt. February 25, 2011.

13. Sam Olofin. IVCU (University of Ibadan) member during the early 1970s;

professor in the Department of Economics, University of Ibadan. April 6, 2011.

14. John Valentine. Principal of the All Nations for Christ Bible School, Benin, 1975–1976 and 1979–1980. April 16, 2012.

15. Ruth Elton. Daughter of Sydney and Hannah Elton. Scores of interviews between March 2003 and 2013.

16. Kola Ejiwumi. First travelling secretary of the NIFES. October 8, 2007 and August 28, 2012.

17. Raphael Okafor. One of the founders of Hour of Freedom Evangelistic Association; one-time general secretary of Scripture Union in Nigeria; Bishop of Ihiala Diocese, Anglican Communion of Nigeria. August 19, 2006.

18. Paul Nwachukwu. Scripture Union leader in Onitsha in the early 1970s; General Overseer of Grace of God Mission, Onitsha. August 14, 2006.

19. Bola Sani. Founder, Advertisers for Jesus, Ilesa. November 2006.

20. Andrew Daniels. Principal of the All Nations for Christ Bible School, Benin, 2006–2015. November 26, 2008 and November 21, 2013.

21. Matthew Owojaiye. IVCU (University of Ibadan) and Tuesday Group member during the early 1970s. General Overseer, Food for Total Man Ministries, Kaduna. December 2006.

22. Steve Olumuyiwa. ECU (University of Ife) member during the mid-1970s; Board of Trustees member, Intercessors for Nigeria, Abuja. December 2006.

23. Emiko Amotsuka. IVCU (University of Ibadan) member during the mid-1970s; founder, Koinonia Ministries, Ibadan. 2003 and August 2008.

24. Kole Akinboboye. LVCU (University of Lagos) member during the late 1970s; founder, Adonai Ministries, Akure. 2006.

25. John Okposio Marshall. Director, Crown Financial Ministries, Port Harcourt. 2006.

26. S. O. Ogedengbe. Founder, Ogedengbe Chambers, Ilesa. December 16, 2006.

27. John Ladega. General Overseer, Kingdom Gospel Church, Ilesa. Several interviews, 2003, 2011, and 2013.

28. Victor Adegboye. Professor in the Department of Surgery, University College Hospital, Ibadan. 2006.

29. Tunde Adesida. Founder, Christian Embassy International, Akure. 2003.

30. Felix Omobude. Founder, New Covenant Gospel Church, Benin; president of the Pentecostal Fellowship of Nigeria, 2013 – date. 2006.

31. Tony Chukwudili. Founder, Children Evangelism Ministry, Ilorin. 2006.

32. Emeka Nwankpa. Founder, Intercessors for Africa, Ghana; founder, Sundolos African Leadership Training Program. October 20, 2006.

33. Olufemi Soetan. Founder, Imole Ayo Hospital, Ile-Ife. 2006.

34. Mike Oye. First Nigerian Travelling Secretary, Scripture Union in Nigeria; minister in the Methodist Church of Nigeria, Osogbo. 2006.

35. Olanrewaju Phillips. Founder, Mount Zion Hospital, Ile-Ife. 2006.

36. Bode Akintade. Founder, Christian Health Centre, Ilesa. 2006.

37. John Dean. First Travelling Secretary, Scripture Union in Nigeria. October 29, 2009.

38. Elizabeth Metcalfe. Daughter of Grace Delbridge. May 31 and June 13, 2012.

39. Beverly Wells. Latter Rain missionary to Nigeria, 1961 to 1962, and, 1967 to 1970. March 12, 2010.

40. Isaiah Oke. Founder, Last Days Evangelical Ministry, Ilesa. June 11, 2010.

41. Joseph Ojo. Early member of the Church of God Mission, Benin; General Overseer, Calvary Kingdom Church, Lagos. December 12, 2012.

42. Godwin Nnaji. One of the leaders of the post-civil war revival in eastern Nigeria; General Overseer, Revival Time Ministry, Enugu. August 2006.

43. Augustine Nwodika. One of the leaders of the post-civil war revival in eastern Nigeria; General Overseer, Throne of Grace Church, Enugu, December 12, 2012.

44. Edward Ezenwafor. One of the leaders of the post-civil war revival in eastern Nigeria; General Overseer, Throne of Grace Church, Enugu, December 12, 2012 and April 1, 2013.

45. Tony Okeke. Leader of Scripture Union, Nnewi, in the early 1970s and one of the leaders of the post-civil war revival in eastern Nigeria; General Overseer of Save the Lost Mission, Nnewi. December 18, 2012.

46. Dele Olowu. ECU (University of Ife) member during the early 1970s; Regional Coordinator of the Redeemed Christian Church of God, Mainland Europe. December 19, 2012.

47. Arthur Oriuzu. One of the leaders of the post-civil war revival in eastern Nigeria and one of the founders of Hour of Freedom Evangelistic Association. December 24, 2012.

48. Bayo Famonure. One of the founders of CAPRO International and its first Chief Executive Secretary. January 17, 2013.

49. Emmanuel Ajao. Deputy General Overseer, New Covenant Church. March 5, 2013.

50. Yinka Ayankogbe. IVCU (University of Ibadan) member during the mid-1970s; Associate Professor at the College of Medicine, University of Lagos. March 15, 2013.

51. Bill Isaacs-Sodeye. Formerly professor in the Department of Haematology and Chemical Pathology, Obafemi Awolowo University, Ile-Ife; founder, the

Healing Love of Christ Ministry, United Kingdom. March 21, 2013.

52. Peter Obadan. Early member of the Church of God Mission, Benin; former Deputy Governor, Edo State. July 2, 2013.

53. Mike Heathcoate. Principal of the All Nations for Christ Bible School, Benin, January 1972 – November 1973. November 25, 2013.

54. Alan Macintosh. Missionary to Nigeria in the 1960s and founder of West African Missionary Training Centre, Ibadan. December 13, 2013.

55. Oyiba Ogbuoji. Founder, Open Christian Centre, Abuja. February 14, 2014.

56. Dejo Akande. One-time president, Christ's Ambassadors Evangelistic Team, Ibadan. March 2008.

57. Joseph Ali. General Overseer, Christ Assembly, Ilorin. February 25, 2014.

58. Omadeli Boyo. One-time NIFES president; founder, Pinecrest Specialist Hospital and founding Senior Pastor of Chapel of His presence, Lagos. February 22, 2014.

59. Olugu Orji. ECU (University of Ife) member during the early 1980s. March 10, 2014.

60. Sunday Isehunwa. Professor in the Department of Petroleum Engineering, University of Ibadan. Faculty of Technology. February 26, 2014.

61. Babatunde Ogunnaike. LVCU (University of Lagos) member during the late mid-1970s; Professor of Chemical and Biomolecular Engineering at the University of Delaware. January 3, 2015.

62. A. I. Edosonwan. Early member of the Church of God Mission, Benin; founder, Christian Missionary Church, Aduwawa, Benin. May 5, 2015.

63. Cosmas Ilechukwu. One of the founders of the National Catholic Charismatic Students (NCCS); founder, Charismatic Renewal Ministries, May 7, 2015.

Prologue: A Most Unusual Exit

1. Sermon, *Divine Government.*
2. Lindsay, Gordon. "Nigeria," *CFTN*, August 1971, p. 8.
3. Chernow, *Alexander Hamilton*, p. 6.

Chapter One: "From Shrewsbury to Africa"

1. 1861 Census—Household Transcription, Elton Daniel, Albert Terrace Willenhall, www.findmypast.com (The National Archives of the UK).
2. "An extract from Post Office Directory of Staffordshire 1850," Willenhall History Society Website, http://jshercliff.demonweb.co.uk/willen-hallhistory/aboutwillenhall.htm. Accessed 29/4/2012.
3. 1841 Census—Household Transcription, Elton Daniel, Lee Street, St Margaret, Leicester, www.findmypast.com (The National Archives of the UK).
4. 1861 Census, Elton Daniel.
5. 1891 Census—Household Transcription, Elton Ernest, No. 2, Court 3, Stafford Street, Willenhall, www.findmypast.com (The National Archives of the UK).
6. 1861 Census, Elton Daniel.
7. "Willenhall," *from History, Gazetteer and Directory of Staffordshire, William White, Sheffield, 1851*, http://www.antonymaitland.com/parkapdx.htm. Accessed 03/12/12.
8. "Willenhall in History," from Walsall Local History Centre, http://www.antonymaitland.com/parkapdx.htm. Accessed 03/12/12.
9. 1881 Census—Household Transcription, Elton Daniel, K, 3, Court Stafford St., Willenhall, www.findmypast.com (The National Archives of the UK).
10. 1891 Census, Elton Daniel.
11. 1881 Census, Elton Daniel.
12. 1891 Census, Elton Ernest.
13. Certified Copy of an Entry of Marriage—Ernest Elton and Edith Annie Baker, GRO, 2282447/5.
14. Certified Copy of an Entry of Birth—Sydney Granville Elton, GRO, 2346204-1.
15. 1911 Census—Household Transcription, Elton Ernest, 43 Sherwood Street, Wolverhampton, www.findmypast.com (The National Archives of the UK).
16. Certified Copy of an Entry of Death—Edith Annie Elton, GRO, 2282447-7.
17. Ibid.
18. Certified Copy of an Entry of Birth—Ronald George Elton, GRO, 3720073-1.

19. Interview with Ruth Elton, daughter of Sydney Granville Elton, May 2010.

20. Certified Copy of an Entry of Death—Ernest Elton, GRO, 2282447-6.

21. Ruth Elton, May 2010.

22. Ibid.

23. Alf Russell, Wolverhampton Archives & Local Studies.

24. Ruth Elton, May 2010.

25. "Shropshire," http://en.wikipedia.org/wiki/Shropshire. Accessed 3/12/12.

26. Allen, Garland E., and Bird, Randy. "Charles Darwin." Microsoft® Encarta® 2009 [DVD]. Redmond, WA: Microsoft Corporation, 2008.

27. Rev. S. G. Elton Interview.

28. Sermon, *The Tabernacle.*

29. Lindsay, Carole. "Nigerian Notebook," *VOH*, August 1966, p. 3.

30. Alison Healey, researcher, Shropshire Archives, October 14, 2009.

31. Ibid.

32. Ruth Elton, 2003.

33. Ibid.

34. Alison Healey, October 14, 2009.

35. Certified Copy of an Entry of Marriage—Sydney Granville Elton and Hannah Catherine Elizabeth Cartwright, GRO, 2282447-4.

36. Rev. S. G. Elton Interview.

37. Lindsay, Carole. "Nigerian Notebook," p. 3. In the county borough of Wolverhampton where Elton grew up, many school children were encouraged to choose the teaching profession. Young boys and girls usually left elementary school and entered secondary school between the ages of ten and eleven. At age fourteen, they could qualify for the Intending Teachers Exhibition – a form of scholarship – if they showed interest in pursuing a career in teaching. The award of an "exhibition" was made upon a special recommendation by a pupil's head teacher as to the suitability of the candidate "by character, aptitude and attainment for the Teaching Profession." The intending teacher stage lasted for two years, when the pupil, now sixteen, would qualify for the bursar stage. "Bursarships" were awarded "upon the recommendations of the Head Teachers of the respective Secondary Schools . . . that the candidate is suitable in every respect, and is likely to pass the Training College Qualifying Examination during the year of Bursarship." The candidates and their parents were also required to sign a declaration of "*bona-fide* intention to become a teacher in an elementary public school, and to give an undertaking that at the end of the year of recognition as Bursar, he (or she) will, if required, accept an engagement as a Student Teacher . . . for a period of one year. At the end of the bursar year, when each

candidate was expected to have passed an examination that qualified them for admission into a recognized teacher training college, they were appointed as student teachers for one year. In 1922 the annual grant for a boy intending teacher was ten pounds for the first year and twelve pounds for the second year; fifteen pounds for the bursar year, and forty pounds for a student teacher. After a successful year as a student teacher, a candidate would then proceed to a two-year course at a teacher training college of his choice. Elton would have qualified to be an intending teacher in 1921; a bursar in 1923; and a student teacher in 1924. If he trained as a teacher locally after his student teacher year, he would probably have attended teacher training college in Dudley, which is several kilometres south of Wolverhampton (there was a dearth of teacher training institutions in the 1920s, and the one in Dudley was the closest), and he would have qualified about 1926, when he was nineteen. However, in a search of the Wolverhampton Education Committee Minute Books, November 1918 to October 1929, there is no mention of any Sydney Granville Elton, even though literally hundreds of names of teachers and trainee teachers are listed in these volumes, as well as those of the pupils awarded bursaries and scholarships. The list is incomplete, however. "Proposed Secondary School," Education Committee of the County Borough of Wolverhampton, WOL-C-EDU/18, 192-1921, pp. 10-12; "Particulars of Scholarships to be offered during the year ending 31st July, 1922," Wolverhampton Borough Education Committee Minute Book 20, 1922-1923, p. 16; "Preparation for Teachership—General" Wolverhampton Education Committee Minute Book 23, Nov 1925 – Mar 1927; Information supplied by Alf J. Russell, Archives & Local Studies Assistant, Wolverhampton City Council, October 27, 2011; letter from Alf J. Russell, November 2, 2011.

38. Ruth Elton, 2003.

39. Lloyd, *Shrewsbury: Historic Centre of Beautiful Shropshire*, p. 49.

40. Ibid.

41. Sermon, *Your Inheritance*.

42. In fact, it seems Elton inherited so much that he continued to draw from it decades later. He said in August 1980, "When my father died he left a will and in that will was stated clearly my inheritance. It was all written in the will for me, and no one could take it from me. It was mine; it was willed to me by my father. And when he died, I entered into my inheritance. It was mine. I claimed it, I enjoyed it, to this day I am enjoying it," Sermon, *My Inheritance in Jesus Christ*.

43. Certified Copy of an Entry of Marriage – Sydney Elton and Hannah Catherine.

44. 1901 Census—Household Transcription, Cartwright Hannah, Butlers House, Coldra, Christchurch, www.findmypast.com (The National Archives of the

UK).

45. Ruth Elton; and Certified Copy of an Entry of Birth—Hannah Catherine Elizabeth, GRO, 2282447-2.

46. Ruth Elton, 2010. Elizabeth Angela Marguerite Bowes-Lyon (August 4, 1900 – March 30, 2002) historically known by the title "Queen Elizabeth the Queen Mother" was the wife of King George VI and the mother of Queen Elizabeth II. She was queen consort of the United Kingdom from her husband's accession in 1936 until his death in 1952, after which she was known as "Queen Elizabeth the Queen Mother," to avoid confusion with her daughter, the present Queen Elizabeth. Hannah's mother served her while she was yet Elizabeth Bowes-Lyon, when her family was visiting a house where she served as cook and housekeeper.

47. Certified Copy of an Entry of Marriage—Sydney Elton and Hannah Catherine.

48. http://www.shropshire.gov.uk/factsfigures.nsf/viewAttachments/HHAY-8SVB3P/$file/1931-census-england-and-wales-country-report-herefordshire-and-shropshire.pdf.

49. Newspaper cutting from Ruth Elton.

50. "Shropshire," http://en.wikipedia.org/wiki/Shropshire.

51. Certified Copy of an Entry of Birth—Ruth Elton, GRO, D 614949.

52. Lindsay, Carole. "Nigerian Notebook," *VOH*, August 1966, p. 3.

53. Okey Onuzo, February 2012.

54. Sermon, *Fellowship with God*.

55. Sermon, *The Tabernacle*.

56. Sermon, *The Meaning of the Kingdom*.

57. Sermon, *The Outline of the Kingdom as Given in the Old Testament*.

58. Ibid.

59. Sermon, *The Tabernacle*.

60. Sermon, *God's End-Time Army's Confrontation with the Enemy*.

61. Sermon, *Relationship with the World*.

62. Alison Healey, Shropshire Archives.

63. Turnbull, *What God hath Wrought*, pp. 13–21.

64. Llewellyn, *A Study of the History and Thought of the Apostolic Church in Wales in the Context of Pentecostalism*, p. 20.

65. Ibid., p. 23.

66. Ibid., p. 25.

67. Worsfold, *Subsequence, Prophecy and church Order*, pp. 6–13; Llewellyn, *A Study of the History and Thought of the Apostolic Church in Wales in the Context of Pentecostalism*, p. 30; "History of the Apostolic Church in the United Kingdom," http://www.apostolic-church.org/index.php?history. Accessed 3/12/12.

68. Malcomson, "Pentecostal Pioneers Remembered," http://pentecostal-pioneers.org/DPWilliams.html.

69. Llewellyn, *A Study of the History and Thought of the Apostolic Church in Wales*, p. 31.

70. Worsfold, *Subsequence, Prophecy and church Order*, pp. 139–140.

71. Ibid., p. 21; Llewellyn, *A Study of the History and Thought of the Apostolic Church in Wales*, p. 31.

72. Turnbull, *What God hath Wrought*, pp. 15–18.

73. Llewellyn, *A Study of the History and Thought of the Apostolic Church in Wales*, pp. 22–23.

74. Turnbull, *What God hath Wrought*, pp. 22–26.

75. Weeks. "History," http://www.apostolic-church.org/index.php?history.

76. "Answering Nigeria's Call for Help," *TAH*, September 1931, p. 3.

77. Ruth Elton, 2010.

78. Sermon, *Let Us Go On*.

79. REP, Letter from T. O. Davies to Sydney Elton, April 25, 1935.

80. Sermon, *The Ministry of Laying on of Hands*.

81. Emeka Nwankpa, 2006.

82. Rev. S. G. Elton Interview.

83. Sermon, *Divine Government*.

84. Sermon, *Let Us Go On*.

85. Ibid.

86. Sermon, *Divine Government*.

87. Ibid.

88. Ibid.

89. Ruth Elton, 2003.

90. Livingstone, W. P. *Mary Slessor of Calabar: Pioneer Missionary*. Doran: New York, 1916.

91. Rev. S. G. Elton Interview.

92. Sermon, *God's Last Days Move*.

93. Sermon, *MIZRAH: Government of God*.

94. Sermon, *The Ministry of Laying on of Hands*.

95. 1937 Diary.

96. Ibid.

97. Ibid.

98. "Elder Dempster Lines," http://www.elderdempster.org/. Accessed 3/12/12.

99. 1937 Diary.

100. Ibid.

101. Deduction from *The Apostolic Herald* and TACA, Minutes of Missionary Committee Meetings.

102. TACA, Minutes of Missionary Committee Meeting, Bradford, May 24, 1937.

103. REP, Bible "Presented to Ruth Elton from the Superintendent Teachers of the Shrewsbury Apostolic Sunday School," December 1937.

Chapter Two: The "Wretched Tabernacles"

1. Ademakinwa, *History of the Christ Apostolic Church*, p. 13.

2. Ibid.

3. Ibid.

4. Ibid., p. 14.

5. Ibid.

6. Ohadike, Don C. "Diffusion and physiological responses to the influenza pandemic of 1918–19 in Nigeria." *Social Science & Medicine* 32, issue 12, 1991, Abstract.

7. Ibid.

8. Ibid.

9. Mitchell, *Religious Change and Modernization: The Aladura Churches among the Yoruba in Southwestern Nigeria*, p. 102.

10. Ademakinwa, *History of the Christ Apostolic Church*, pp. 14–15.

11. Ibid.

12. Mitchell, *Religious Change and Modernization: The Aladura Churches among the Yoruba in Southwestern Nigeria*, p. 101.

13. Ademakinwa, *History of the Christ Apostolic Church*, p. 15.

14. Ibid., p. 15.

15. Turner, *History of an African Independent Church: The Church of the Lord Aladura,* Vol. 1, p. 9.

16. Mitchell, *Religious Change and Modernization: The Aladura Churches among the Yoruba in Southwestern Nigeria*, pp. 101–102.

17. Ademakinwa, *History of the Christ Apostolic Church*, p. 11.

18. Ibid.

19. Ibid.

20. Ibid., pp. 11–12.

21. Ibid., p. 12.

22. Ibid., p. 16.

23. Ibid.

24. Mitchell, *Religious Change and Modernization: The Aladura Churches among the*

Yoruba in Southwestern Nigeria, p. 136.

25. Peel, *Aladura,* pp. 62–63.

26. Adegboyega, *Short History of the Apostolic Church in Nigeria,* pp. 4, 6.

27. Mohr, Adam. "Out of Zion into Philadelphia and West Africa: Faith Tabernacle Congregation, 1897–1925," *Pneuma* 32, 2010, pp. 56, 64–69.

28. Mitchell, *Religious Change and Modernization: The Aladura Churches among the Yoruba in Southwestern Nigeria,* pp. 105–106.

29. Ibid., p. 106.

30. Ibid., p. 107.

31. Ibid.

32. Ademakinwa, *History of the Christ Apostolic Church,* pp. 21–22.

33. Mitchell, *Religious Change and Modernization: The Aladura Churches among the Yoruba in Southwestern Nigeria,* p. 108.

34. Mohr, Adam. "Out of Zion into Philadelphia and West Africa: Faith Tabernacle Congregation, 1897–1925," *Pneuma* 32, 2010, p. 73.

35. Ademakinwa, *History of the Christ Apostolic Church,* p. 19.

36. Ibid., p. 26.

37. Adebanjo, *Christ Apostolic Church: Sixty Years of its Existence, 1935–1995,* p. 4.

38. Ibid.

39. Ademakinwa, *History of the Christ Apostolic Church,* pp. 50-51; Mohr, "Out of Zion into Philadelphia and West Africa: Faith Tabernacle Congregation, 1897–1925," *Pneuma* 32, 2010, pp. 75–77.

40. Ademakinwa, *History of the Christ Apostolic Church,* p. 52.

41. Ibid., p. 51.

42. Ibid.

43. DOP, letter from Ambrose Clark to David Odubanjo, April 26, 1921.

44. Adegboyega, *Short History of the Apostolic Church in Nigeria,* pp. 10–14.

45. Peel, *Aladura,* p. 69.

46. Adegboyega, *Short History of the Apostolic Church in Nigeria,* p. 15.

47. Turner, "Pentecostal Movements in Nigeria," *Orita,* Vol. 6, no. 1, p. 44.

48. Olowe, *Great Revivals, Great Revivalist,* pp. 116–119; Oshun, Christ Apostolic Church of Nigeria, p. 113; Alokan, The Christ Apostolic Church, p. 49. Several accounts exist of the beginnings of this revival. According to another eyewitness account, Babalola was called to Osogbo on Thursday, July 10, 1930, where he was already known as an "aladura"—a man of prayer—to attend to a sick man, after which he returned to Ilesa the following day. The same account mentions the case of one Dick Taiwo who had suffered constant harassment from witches and who received complete deliverance after Babalola had prayed for him. This

account is recorded in Oshun, *Christ Apostolic Church of Nigeria*, p. 112.

49. Vaughan, *The Origins of Apostolic Church Pentecostalism in Nigeria, 1931–52*, p. 31.

50. Peel, *Aladura*, pp. 91, 98.

51. Alokan, *The Christ Apostolic Church*, p. 36; Olowe, *Great Revivals, Great Revivalist*, pp. 115–122; Adegboyega, *Short History of the Apostolic Church in Nigeria*, pp. 21–26.

52. Ade Aina, *Twenty-five Years of the Aladura Churches in Ibadan*, p. 1.

53. Oshun, *Christ Apostolic Church of Nigeria*, p. 107.

54. Ibid., p. 37.

55. Ibid., p. 107.

56. Oshun, *Aladura Revivals: Apostle Babalola's Challenge to Christian Missions*, p. 9.

57. Abodunde, *A Heritage of Faith*, p. 337.

58. NNAI-BFT, Oyo Prof/736/2, letter from the Assistant District officer, Ilesa, to the District Officer, Ife, August 13, 1930.

59. Ward-Price, *Dark Subjects*, p. 241.

60. Dallimore, Henry. "The Aladura Movement in Ekiti," *Western Equatorial Africa Church Magazine*, XXXVI, January 1931, pp. 93–94.

61. Mitchell, *Religious Change and Modernization: The Aladura Churches among the Yoruba in Southwestern Nigeria*, p. 160.

62. "Africa," *TAH*, February 1935, p. 7.

63. "A Wonderful Revival in Nigeria," *TAH*, October 1932, p. 5.

64. NNAI-BFT, Oyo Prof/736/9, letter from the Assistant District officer, Ilesa, to the Senior Resident, Oyo Province, March 25, 1932.

65. Ibid.

66. NNAI-BFT, Oyo Prof/662/32-33, letter from secretary of Southern Provinces, Enugu, to the Resident, Oyo Province, August 31, 1931.

67. Peel, *Aladura*, p. 100.

68. Abodunde, *A Heritage of Faith*, p. 343.

69. Ibid.

70. Ibid.

71. Adegboyega, *Short History of the Apostolic Church in Nigeria*, p. 38.

72. Ibid., pp. 37–38.

73. DOP, letter from Ambrose Clark to David Odubanjo, December 11, 1922.

74. Mohr, Adam. "Out of Zion into Philadelphia and West Africa: Faith Tabernacle Congregation, 1897–1925," *Pneuma* 32, 2010, p. 79.

75. Adegboyega, *Short History of the Apostolic Church in Nigeria*, p. 39.

76. Ibid., p. 48.

77. Ibid.

78. "What a Native Pastor says about the Big Revival in Nigeria, West Africa," *TAH*, December 1931, p. 12.

79. Ibid.

80. Ibid.

81. Ibid., p. 11.

82. Ibid., p. 10.

83. Williams, D. P. "The African Tour Triumph!" *TAH*, January 1932, p. 9.

84. Turnbull, *What God hath Wrought*, p. 73.

85. Adegboyega, *Short History of the Apostolic Church in Nigeria*, pp. 52–61.

86. NNAI-BFT, Oyo Prof/662/61–62, letter from Assistant Commissioner of Police, Oyo-Ondo Province, Ibadan, to, the Resident, Oyo, October 29, 1931.

87. NNAI-BFT, Oyo Prof/662/67, letter from Assistant Commissioner of Police, Oyo-Ondo Province, Ibadan, to, the Resident, Oyo, November 3, 1931.

88. NNAI-AMAC, Oyo Prof 1/28/C111/4, letter from the District Officer, Ife-Ilesa Division, Ife, to, the Resident, Oyo Province, Oyo, October 10, 1932.

89. Ibid.

90. Williams, D. P. "The African Tour Triumph!" *TAH*, January 1932, p. 9.

91. Adegboyega, *Short History of the Apostolic Church in Nigeria*, p. 56.

92. Adegboyega, *The Adoption of the Apostolic Church as a Denominational Name in Nigeria*, p. 17.

93. Turner, *History of an African Independent Church*, p. 31.

94. "Nigeria," *TAH*, February 1932, p. 4.

95. Adegboyega, *Short History of the Apostolic Church in Nigeria*, p. 68.

96. Ibid., p. 69.

97. Odunaike, *The Path of a Master Christian*, p. 55.

98. Ibid., pp. 51–52.

99. Perfect, George. "The Nigerian Revival," *TAH*, October 1940, p. 78.

100. Ibid., pp. 78–79.

101. Ibid., p. 78.

102. Perfect, George. "Nigeria's Spiritual Awakening Spreads," *TAH*, December 1933, p. 9.

103. Perfect, George. "God Consolidating His Great Work in Nigeria," *TAH*, November 1933, p. 6.

104. Rosser, C. H. "Africa," *TAH*, August 1935, p. 8

105. Ibid.

106. Weeks, *Chapter Thirty Two: Part of a History of the Apostolic Church*, p. 159.

107. Ibid., p. 168.

108. Elton, *Black Magic and Jungle Prophets*, p. 2.

109. Perfect, George. "The Travelling Problem in Nigeria," *TAH*, May 1937, p. 61.

110. Sermon, *Kingdom Provision*.

111. 1937 Diary.

112. Elton, "Acting Black," *TAH*, May 1938, p. 34.

113. Ibid.

114. 1937 Diary.

115. Allan, Vera. "The Late Pastor Babatope," *TAH*, January 1951, p. 431.

116. Babatope, J. A. "Nigeria," *ROG*, September 1937, p. 104.

117. Vaughan, *The Origins of Apostolic Church Pentecostalism in Nigeria*, p. 30.

118. Perfect, George. "Who is this Babalola?" TAH, December 1937, pp. 126–127.

119. Ibid. p. 127.

120. Perfect, George. "The Nigerian Revival," *TAH*, October 1940, p. 79.

121. NNAI-BFT, Oyo Prof/662/32-33, letter from Assistant Commissioner of Police, Oyo-Ondo Province, Ibadan, to, the Resident, Oyo, August 31, 1931.

122. NNAI-AMAC, Oyo Prof 1/28/C111/4, letter from the District Officer, Ife-Ilesa Division, Ife, to, the Resident, Oyo Province, Oyo, October 10, 1932.

123. Ositelu, *The Words of Prophecies of Things to Happen From the Year 1931 Onwards*, 1931.

124. NNAI-BFT, Oyo Prof/662/48, letter from Assistant Commissioner of Police, Oyo-Ondo Province, Ibadan, to, the Resident, Oyo, October 20, 1931.

125. Ibid. NNAI-BFT, Oyo Prof/662/34.

126. NNAI-BFT, Oyo Prof/662/31, letter from Assistant Commissioner of Police, Oyo-Ondo Province, Ibadan, to, the Resident, Oyo, October 23, 1931.

127. Vaughan, "Nigeria," ROG, September 1937, p. 108.

128. NNAI-ACA, Ekiti Div/1/1/41a/143, letter from George Perfect to the District Officer, Ekiti Division, Ado-Ekiti, July 23, 1937.

129. Adegboyega, *Short History of the Apostolic Church in Nigeria*, pp. 89–90.

130. Ibid., p. 90.

131. 1937 Diary.

132. NNAI-ACA, Ekiti Div/1/1/41a/275, letter from the District Officer, Ekiti Division, to George Perfect, February 18, 1935.

133. NNAI-ACA, Ekiti Div/1/1/41a/142, letter from the District Officer, Ekiti Division, to George Perfect, June 30, 1937.

134. NNAI-ACA, Ekiti Div/1/1/41a/275, letter from the District Officer, Ekiti Division, to George Perfect, February 18, 1935.

135. Dallimore, Henry. "The Aladura Movement in Ekiti," *Western Equatorial Africa Church Magazine*, XXXVI, January 1931, p. 94.

136. NNAI-ACA, Ekiti Div/1/1/41a/42-43, letter from Wright to the Resident, Akure, May 12, 1932.

137. NNAI-ACA, Ekiti Div/1/1/41a, letter from Assistant District Officer, Ado Ekiti, February 18, 1935.

Chapter Three: Healing Wars

1. Turnbull, *What God hath Wrought*, p. 25.

2. Evans, Noah. "How I heard and Answered God's call to Nigeria, *TAH*, June 1934, p. 3.

3. Turnbull, *What God hath Wrought*, p. 36.

4. Turnbull, *What God hath Wrought*, p. 29; "Nigeria – West Africa," TAH, August 1936, p. 58.

5. Sermon, *Let us Go On*.

6. Ibid.

7. "Africa," *HOG*, May 1942, p. 38.

8. The Apostolic Church, *Floods upon the Dry Ground*, p. 172.

9. Sermon, *Divine Government*.

10. NNAI-ACA, Ekiti Div/1/1/41a/148, letter from Sydney Elton to the District Officer, Ado Ekiti, October 13, 1937.

11. Abodunde, *A Herald of the Last Days*, p. 26.

12. Emmanuel Ajao, 2013.

13. "Other men of God Speak on Elton – Enoch Adejare Adeboye," *ER*, Vol. 1, No. 1, Oct – Dec, 2004, p. 40; Adegboye, Victor. "Faith Works," *ER*, October 2004, p. 45.

14. Adegboye, Victor. "Faith Works," *ER*, October 2004, p. 45.

15. Ibid.

16. Sermon, *God's Last Days Move*.

17. Sermon, *God's Army*.

18. 1937 Diary.

19. Ibid.

20. Ibid.

21. Ibid.

22. Ibid.

23. Ibid.

24. Ibid.

25. Adegboyega, *Short History of the Apostolic Church in Nigeria*, p. 40.

26. Ibid., p. 44.

27. Ibid.

28. Ibid.

29. Mitchell, *Religious Change and Modernization: The Aladura Churches among the Yoruba in Southwestern Nigeria*, p. 116.

30. Ademakinwa, *History of the Christ Apostolic Church*, p. 52.

31. Adegboyega, *Short History of the Apostolic Church in Nigeria*, pp. 11, 13.

32. Ibid., p. 14.

33. Turner, *History of an African Independent Church*, p. 14.

34. Adegboyega, *Short History of the Apostolic Church in Nigeria*, p. 95.

35. Ibid.

36. Ibid., p. 96.

37. Ibid., p. 1o1.

38. Ibid. p. 102.

39. Ibid.

40. Ibid., p. 106.

41. Ibid., pp. 102–110.

42. Turner, *History of an African Independent Church*, p. 33.

43. Adegboyega, *Short History of the Apostolic Church in Nigeria*, p. 113.

44. TACA, Supplement to Agenda of Missionary Committee Meeting, pp. 5–6.

45. Adegboyega, *Short History of the Apostolic Church in Nigeria*, p. 6.

46. DOP, letter from Ambrose Clark to David Odubanjo, April 30, 1923.

47. Ibid., letter from Ambrose Clark to David Odubanjo, April 26, 1921.

48. Ibid.

49. Ibid., letter from Ambrose Clark to David Odubanjo, March 5, 1923.

50. Adegboyega, *Short History of the Apostolic Church in Nigeria*, p. 1o1.

51. Peel, *Aladura*, p. 111.

52. Perfect, George. "The Nigerian Revival," *TAH*, October 1940, p. 79.

53. TACA, Supplement to Agenda of Missionary Committee Meeting, February 7, 1939, p. 6.

54. Ibid.

55. Ibid., p. 7.

56. TACA, Supplement to Agenda of Missionary Committee Meeting, June 26, 1939, pp. 1–12.

57. Ibid., p. 1.

58. Ibid.

59. Ibid., p. 2.

60. Ibid., pp. 4–5.

61. Ibid., p. 5.

62. Ibid.

63. TACA, Supplement to Agenda of Missionary Committee Meeting: Matters for Discussion with Pastor George Perfect, p. 8.

64. Ibid.

65. TACA, Minutes of Missionary Committee Meeting, Bradford, March 31, 1939, p. 68.

66. Ibid.

67. Adegboyega, *Short History of the Apostolic Church in Nigeria*, p. 122.

68. TACA, Minutes of Missionary Committee Meeting, Bradford, March 31, 1939, p. 71.

69. Adegboyega, *Short History of the Apostolic Church in Nigeria*, pp., p. 125.

70. Ibid., p. 130.

71. Ademakinwa, *History of the Christ Apostolic Church*, p. 101.

72. Oshun, *Christ Apostolic Church of Nigeria*, pp. 48–49.

73. Ademakinwa, *History of the Christ Apostolic Church*, p. 101.

74. Peel, *Aladura*, p. 111.

75. Adegboyega, *Short History of the Apostolic Church in Nigeria*, p. 130.

76. Vaughan, *The Origins of Apostolic Church Pentecostalism in Nigeria*, p. 30.

77. Babatope, J. A. "Welcome back to West Africa!" *TAH*, March 1940, p. 20.

78. NNAI-ACA, Ekiti Div/1/1/41a/195-196, letter from Sydney Elton to the District Officer, Ado Ekiti, January 18, 1940.

79. Adegboyega, *Short History of the Apostolic Church in Nigeria*, pp. 134–135.

80. Ademakinwa, *History of the Christ Apostolic Church*, pp. 89–90.

81. NNAI-ACA, Ekiti Div/1/1/41a/195-196, letter from the District Officer, Ado Ekiti, to Sydney Elton, March 4, 1940.

82. NNAI-ACA, Ekiti Div/1/1/41a/195-196, letter from Sydney Elton to the District Officer, Ado Ekiti, March 27, 1940.

83. "Warning to Pastor S. G. Elton," Report of the Meeting of the G.E.C. held at Ibadan on 16/6/49, p. 2.

84. The Apostolic Church, *Floods upon the Dry Ground*, p. 172.

Chapter Four: "Why the Halo?"

1. Wells, *Weavings from My Nigerian Journal*, p. 25.

2. Ibid.

3. Ibid., p. 26.

4. Ibid., p. 27.

5. Ibid.

6. Ibid. p. 30.

7. Bode Akintade, 2006.

8. Sermon, *God's Last Days Move.*

9. Wells, *Weavings from My Nigerian Journal*, p. 29.

10. Ibid. p. 31.

11. Ibid.

12. Vaughan, *The Origins of Apostolic Church Pentecostalism in Nigeria*, p. 79.

13. Turnbull, *What God hath Wrought*, p. 76.

14. Rev. S. G. Elton Interview.

15. Peel, Ijesha and Nigerians, p. 168.

16. Ibid.

17. Ruth Elton, 2006.

18. Elton, Sydney. "Why the Halo?" *HOG*, August 1946, p. 177.

19. Ibid.

20. Ibid., p. 178.

21. Ibid., p. 179.

22. Ibid.

23. Ibid., p. 180.

24. Ibid.

25. The Apostolic Church, *Floods upon the Dry Ground*, p. 172.

26. Elton, Sydney. "Kings Shall Fall Down Before Him," *TAH*, August 1937, p. 88.

27. Elton, Sydney. "Africa Appeals," *TAH*, October 1939, p. 109.

28. Elton, Sydney. "Kings Shall Fall Down Before Him," *TAH*, August 1937, p. 88.

29. Elton, Sydney. "Africa Appeals," *TAH*, October 1939, p. 109.

30. "Africa," *HOG*, June 1942, p. 50; "Africa," *HOG*, August 1942, p. 74.

31. Elton, Sydney, "The Fight for Peace," *TAH*, p. 39.

32. Elton, Sydney. "Progress in Ilesa," April 1944, p. 45.

33. Elton, Sydney. "The Privilege of the Home Church," *HOG*, February 1946, pp. 43-44.

34. Elton, Sydney. "The Harvest Truly is Plenteous But!" *HOG*, January 1945, p. 9.

35. Elton, Sydney. "Studies in Black and White," *TAH*, July 1938, p. 51.

36. Babatope, J. A. "Nigeria," *ROG*, September 1937, pp. 105–106.

37. Elton, Sydney. "Studies in Black and White," *TAH*, July 1938, p. 51.

38. Rosser, C. H. "Studying and Studious," *HOG*, August 1946, pp. 174–175.

39. Ibid.

40. "An Appeal," *HOG*, February 1946, p. 31.

41. Elton, *Black Magic and Jungle Prophets*. pp. 2–3.

42. "An Opportunity Occurs," *TAH*, July 1950, p. 229.

43. Parkyns, E. F. "A Call at Our College," *TAH*, April 1951, p. 89.

44. NNAI-AMAC, Oyo Prof 1/28/C111/16, letter from the Chief Inspector of Education, Ibadan, to, the Resident, Oyo Province, April 2, 1946.

45. "Ilesa Training Centre, Nigeria," *Pentecost*, June 1953, p. 3.

46. Parkyns, E. F. "A Call at Our College," *TAH*, April 1951, pp. 88–89.

47. Elton, Sydney. "Progress in Ilesa," April 1944, p. 48; McGill, D. H. "First Impressions of Nigeria," September 1942, p. 96; Elton, Sydney, "the Challenge of our work in the Ilesa Area, Nigeria," *HOG*, June 1946, p. 139.

48. Sermon, *God's Last Days Move*.

49. Rosser, C. H. "Reflections," *TAH*, July 1950, p. 219.

50. Sermon, *Let Us Go On*; TACA, Minutes of Missionary Committee Meeting, Bradford, August 25 and 29, 1949.

51. UK Incoming Passengers Lists, 1878–1960 – Sydney G. Elton, March 16, 1944, www.ancestry.co.uk (The National Archives of the UK).

52. Ruth Elton, 2003.

53. Ibid.

54. UK Incoming Passengers Lists, 1878–1960 – Sydney G. Elton, March 4, 1948, www.ancestry.co.uk (The National Archives, UK).

55. UK Incoming Passengers Lists, 1878–1960 – Sydney G. Elton, April 17, 1950, www.ancestry.co.uk (The National Archives, UK).

56. TACA, Minutes of Missionary Committee Meeting, Bradford, July 14, 1949.

57. TACA, Minutes of Missionary Committee Meeting, Bradford, October 15 & 16, 1951.

58. Rutland, *Obeying His Call*, p. 69.

Chapter Five: Rain

1. Morris, Cecil. The Art of Assessing Spiritual Values," *TAH* January 1951, p. 425.

2. Ibid.

3. Ibid.

4. Sermon, *The Establishment of the Kingdom in Nigeria*.

5. Derry, E. L. "Revive Personal Evangelism," *TAH* January 1951, p. 438.

6. Wood, Vernon. "Concerning the Convention," *TAH* February 1952, p. 30.

7. Allan, Vera. "Rain on Mown Grass," *TAH* December 1951, p. 285.

8. Morris, Cecil. "We Want another Pentecost," *TAH* February 1953, p. 25.

9. Rutland, *Obeying His Call*, p. 59.

10. Riss, Richard. "The New Order of the Latter Rain," *Assemblies of God Heritage*, Fall 1987, p. 15.

11. Llewellyn, *A Study of the History and Thought of the Apostolic Church in Wales*, p. 53.

12. Riss, *Latter Rain*, p. 54.

13. McIntyre, *E. W. Kenyon and His Message: The True Story*, p. 145.

14. Warnock, *The Feast of Tabernacles*, p. 3.

15. Ibid.

16. "The Latter Rain Reformation," http://www.cityatthecross.com/reformation/latterrain.html.

17. Riss, *Latter Rain*, p. 12.

18. Ibid., p. 11.

19. "The Latter Rain Reformation," http://www.cityatthecross.com/reformation/latterrain.html.

20. Hocken, *Streams of Renewal*, p. 25; Riss, Richard. "The New Order of the Latter Rain," *Assemblies of God Heritage*, Fall 1987, pp. 15–16; "The Latter Rain Reformation," http://www.cityatthecross.com/reformation/latterrain.html.

21. "The Independent Assemblies of God International Canada," *The Canadian Mantle*, October 2008, p. 8.

22. Ibid.

23. Hocken, *Streams of Renewal*, p. 25.

24. Ibid.

25. Hamon, *The Eternal Church*, p. 225.

26. TACA, Minutes of Missionary Committee Meeting, Bradford, 1945–1949.

27. REP, Photograph.

28. Ruth Elton, 2003.

29. Hocken, *Streams of Renewal*, pp. 30–37.

30. Ibid., p. 25.

31. Althouse, *Spirit of the Last Days*, p. 49.

32. Ibid.

33. Llewellyn, *A Study of the History and Thought of the Apostolic Church in Wales*, p. 61.

34. Althouse, *Spirit of the Last Days*, pp. 49–50.

35. Llewellyn, *A Study of the History and Thought of the Apostolic Church in Wales*, p. 58.

36. Hocken, *Streams of Renewal*, p. 26.

37. Ibid.

38. Wallis, Arthur. "Springs of Restoration: Origins of the New Charismatic Churches in the UK," http://www.revival-library.org/pensketches/charismatics/springs.html.

39. TACA, Minutes of Missionary Committee Meeting, Bradford, May 24, 1951, p. 329.
40. Rutland, *Obeying His Call*, p. 19.
41. Minutes of Missionary Committee Meeting, Bradford, April 29, 1952.
42. Rutland, *Obeying His Call*, pp. 20-21.
43. Ibid., p. 38.
44. Ibid., p. 55.
45. Ibid., p. 77.
46. "Names and Descriptions of British passengers embarked at the port for Liverpool," www.findmypast.com (The National Archives, UK).
47. Ruth Elton, 2003.
48. Ibid.
49. Elton, *Black Magic and Jungle Prophets*. p. 3.
50. Ruth Elton, 2012.
51. Ibid.
52. Sermon, labelled "Pa Elton." No title and no date.
53. Ibid.
54. Sermon, Edgar Parkyns, *Reminiscences*.
55. Ruth Elton, 2012.
56. Jennings, *Pastors According to Mine Heart*, pp. 7–9. His name features in many Latter Rain narratives.
57. Ruth Elton, 2012.
58. Rutland, *Obeying His Call*, p. 97.
59. Ibid., p. 99.
60. Riss, Richard. "The New Order of the Latter Rain," *Assemblies of God Heritage*, Fall 1987, p. 17.
61. Ibid.
62. "The Latter Rain Reformation," http://www.cityatthecross.com/reformation/latterrain.html.
63. Elton, *Black Magic and Jungle Prophets*. p. 3.
64. Wyatt, *Wings of Healing over Africa!*, p. 21.
65. Elton, *Black Magic and Jungle Prophets*. p. 3.
66. Rutland, *Obeying His Call*, p. 103.
67. Elton, *Black Magic and Jungle Prophets*. pp. 3-4.
68. Ibid., pp. 4–5.
69. Ibid., p. 4.
70. Rutland, *Obeying His Call*, pp. 104-105
71. "Apostolic Church Delegates Arrive in Lagos from U.S.A.," *Nigerian Tribune*,

February 17, 1953, p. 7.

72. Elton, *Black Magic and Jungle Prophets.* p. 5.

73. Wyatt, *Wings of Healing over Africa!*, pp. 26–27.

74. Elton, *Black Magic and Jungle Prophets.* pp. 5–6.

75. Wyatt, *Wings of Healing over Africa!*, p. 23.

76. Ibid.

77. Lindsay, Gordon. "Nigeria," CFTN, August 1971, p. 15.

78. "Evangelists Work Wonders in Efik Land," *The Nigerian Daily Standard*, February 23, 1953.

79. Elton, *Black Magic and Jungle Prophets.* p. 6.

80. Sermon, *The Ministry of the Holy Spirit in These Last Days.*

81. "Dr Poole and team invited to Christ Church Cathedral," *Daily Times*, March 5, 1953, p. 16.

82. Elton, *Black Magic and Jungle Prophets.* p. 7.

83. "Blind For 5 Years Healed Last Night," *Nigerian Tribune*, Friday November 20, 1953, p. 1.

84. "Erskine Holt," Erskine Holthttp://en.wikipedia.org/wiki/Erskine_Holt.

85. "Revival Fires Burn Bright in Africa," *MF*, February 1954.

86. "Pentecostal Revival in West Africa: Crowds Average over 15, 000," *Pentecost*, June 1954, p. 11.

87. "Brief History of Christ Gospel Church of God Inc.," http://www.cgcng.org/about-us.php.

88. "Pentecostal Revival in West Africa: Crowds Average over 15, 000," *Pentecost*, June 1954, p. 11.

89. Ibid.

90. Peter Ozodo, 2006.

91. "Pentecostal Revival in West Africa: Crowds Average over 15, 000," *Pentecost*, June 1954, p. 11.

92. Ibid.

93. Sermon, *Let Us Go On.*

94. Ukachi, *The Best is Yet to Come*, p. 53.

Chapter Six: Crisis

1. Llewellyn, *A Study of the History and Thought of the Apostolic Church in Wales*, pp. 51–53.

2. Ibid., p. 51.

3. Riss, *Latter Rain*, p. 106.

4. Ibid., p. 137.

5. Larbi, *Pentecostalism: The Eddies of Ghanaian Christianity*, p. 212.

6. Leonard, *A Giant in Ghana*, p. 138.

7. Llewellyn, *A Study of the History and Thought of the Apostolic Church in Wales,* p. 62.

8. Leonard, *A Giant in Ghana*, p. 138.

9. Ibid.

10. Riss, *Latter Rain*, p. 139.

11. Llewellyn, *A Study of the History and Thought of the Apostolic Church in Wales,* p. 60.

12. Ibid., p. 62.

13. Larbi, *Pentecostalism*, p. 213.

14. Ibid., p. 214.

15. Ibid.

16. Ibid.

17. Walker, Daniel. "The Shaping of a New Form of Missionary Initiative from Africa," University of Birmingham Research Project. http://www.glopent.net/-Members/dwalk/research-project-the-shaping-of-a-new-form-of-missionary-initiative-from-africa. Accessed 5/12/12.

18. TACA, Minutes of Missionary Committee Meeting, Bradford, March 22 and April 5, 1955.

19. Ibid., January 17, 1955.

20. Sermon, Edgar Parkyns, *Reminiscences.*

21. Wellings Vivian and Rosser Cyril. "Sailing! Seeing! Settling!" *TAH*, September 1953, p. 136.

22. Ruth Elton, 2012.

23. Ibid.

24. Rutland, *Obeying His Call*, p. 117.

25. Ibid., p. 118.

26. Ibid., p. 122.

27. Ibid.

28. Ibid., p. 125.

29. Ibid., pp. 126-127.

30. Ibid., p. 127.

31. Ibid., p. 130.

32. Ibid., p. 132.

33. Rosser, Cyril. "Progress Toward Perfection," *TAH*, March 1954, p. 35.

34. Elton, Sydney. "Africa Awakes," *MF*, October 1955, p. 12.

35. Sermon, *The Establishing of the Kingdom in Nigeria.*
36. Rutland, *Obeying His Call*, pp. 109–111.
37. Turnbull, *What God hath Wrought*, p. 80.
38. Vaughan, *The Origins of Apostolic Church Pentecostalism in Nigeria*, pp. 102–103.
39. TACA, Minutes of Missionary Committee Meeting, Bradford, June 16, 1954.
40. Ruth Elton, 2012.
41. Ibid.
42. Ibid.
43. TACA, Minutes of Missionary Committee Meeting, Bradford, February 3, 1953.
44. Ruth Elton, 2012.
45. The Apostolic Church (LAWNA), *A Brief Biography of Late Pastor Samuel Gbadebo Adegboyega*, p. 16.
46. Ibid.
47. Ibid., p. 17.
48. Sermon, *Divine Government.*
49. Sermon, *Restoration: All Things New.*
50. Sermon, *Let Us Go On.*
51. Sermon, *untitled.*
52. Rutland, *Obeying His Call*, p. 180.
53. Ruth Elton, 2012
54. Ibid.
55. Ibid.
56. Ruth Elton, 2010.
57. Sermon, *Kingdom Provision.*
58. Ibid.
59. Sermon, *The Vision: Effects on Life and Church Government.*
60. Ibid.
61. Olowe, *Great Revivals, Great Revivalist*, p. 227.
62. Ibid., p. 228.
63. Ibid., p. 229.
64. Oshun, *Christ Apostolic Church of Nigeria*, p. 139.
65. Rutland, *Obeying His Call*, p. 217.
66. Ibid., p. 219.
67. Ibid., p. 224.
68. Larbi, *Pentecostalism: The Eddies of Ghanaian Christianity*, p. 412.
69. Ruth Elton, 2012.

70. Ibid; Rutland, *Obeying His Call*, p. 219.

71. Rutland, *Obeying His Call*, p. 222.

72. Sydney G. Elton. Ancestry.com. *New York Passenger Lists, 1820-1957* [database on-line]. Provo, UT, USA. Ancestry.com Operations, Inc, 2010.

73. Elton, *Black Magic and Jungle Prophets.* p. i.

74. Ibid., pp. 15–16.

75. Hocken, *Streams of Renewal*, p. 27.

76. Ruth Elton, 2006.

Chapter Seven: There is a Responsibility upon Me

1. NNAE, AHODIST 234/14/1/357, letter from G. G. Danby George, Aba, to the District Officer, Ahoada District, February 16, 1935.

2. Timeline of The Apostolic Faith Church, http://www.apostolicfaith.org/-aboutus/Timeline.asp.

3. NNAE, AHODIST 234/14/13/357, letter from the Senior Education Officer, Owerri Province, to the District Officer, Ahoada District, February 2, 1946.

4. NNAE, AHODIST 2234/14/5/357, letter from G. G. Danby George, to the District Officer, Ahoada District, July 30, 1942.

5. Dayhoff, *Living Stones in Africa*, p. 237.

6. Synan, *The Holiness-Pentecostal Tradition*, pp. 48–49.

7. Dayhoff, *Living Stones in Africa*, p. 237.

8. NNAE, ABADIST 9/1/1544/5, letter from Rev. I. O. Uruakpa, Rev. E. E. Brown and Rev. D. W. Woyo, to Officer in Charge, Immigration Office, Lagos, November 26, 1952.

9. NNAE, ABADIST 9/1/1544/7, letter from Senior District Officer, Aba Division, to The Senior Resident, Owerri Province, February 6, 1953.

10. Ruth Elton, 2010; stationeries of the ministry.

11. Ruth Elton, 2010.

12. Ibid.

13. NNAE, RIVPROF, "Report on Christian Activities."

14. Ibid.

15. Ibid.

16. DAHL-DDPA, Africa – box 85: David du Plessis' Regional Subject Files-Pentecostal Adherents, "Nigeria: East, West and North," pp. 5–6.

17. Ibid.

18. Ibid., p. 2.

19. "Dr Wyatt in Africa," *MF*, April – May 1955, p. 8.

20. "World Mission Training Centres Established in Gold Coast and Nigeria," *MF*, February 1954; "Four More Recruits to Africa," *MF*, December 1954, p. 3.

21. "Brief History of the Wings of Healing," http://www.thomasrwyatt.org/brief-history.

22. "News from Nigeria," *MF*, January 1955, p. 6.

23. "News from Nigeria," *MF*, February 1955, p. 6.

24. "News from Nigeria," *MF*, January 1955, p. 7.

25. Hammond, Stanley. "Iwaraja, Nigeria," *MF*, November – December 1955, p. 9.

26. "Other Satanic Stronghold Falls," MF, March 1956, p. 9.

27. Beverly Wells, 2010.

28. Ibid.

29. Wells, *Weavings from My Nigerian Journal*, p. 87.

30. Ibid.

31. Ibid., p. 150.

32. Ibid., p. 151.

33. Ruth Elton, 2010.

34. Ibid.

35. NNAE, CALPROF 17/1/352/1, report of visit of missionaries of World Christian Crusade, Calabar, December 17, 1955.

36. NNAE, CALPROF 17/1/352/3, report of visit of missionaries of World Christian Crusade, Calabar, January 6, 1956.

37. NCF-BCC, lesson one.

38. Ibid., p. 9.

39. "Our Freedom," *MF*, September 1955, p. 6.

40. Letter from Sydney Elton to Thomas Wyatt, *MF*, June 1955, p. 12.

41. Letter from Solomon Akintola to Thomas Wyatt, *MF*, June 1955, p. 12.

42. Letter from S. U. Ekpo to Thomas Wyatt, *MF*, June 1955, p. 12.

43. "How to Deal with Sickness," NCF-BBC, p. ii.

44. "Pentecost, 1947 – 1966," http://shop.revival-library.org/Product-Details.asp?ProductCode=011_pen.

45. "Nearly 200,000 Pentecostal People in Nigeria," *Pentecost*, December 1957, p. 11.

46. Du Plessis, David. "World Awakening," *World Wide Revival*, March 1958, p. 18.

47. Ibid., p. 19.

48. DAHL-DDPA, Africa – box 85: David du Plessis' Regional Subject Files-Pentecostal Adherents, "Nigeria: East, West and North," p. 2.

49. "Indigenous Church in Nigeria," *Pentecost*, March 1956, p. 11.

50. Ibid.

51. Squire, Fred. "My Most Terrific Pentecostal Meeting," *Pentecost*, December 1959, p. 5.

52. "The International Camp Meeting," *Pentecost*, December 1955, p. 8.

53. "Said at the I.M.C. Ghana," *Pentecost*, March 1959, p. 3.

54. "Grant's Faith Clinic," *VOH* July 1962, p. 10.

55. Elton, Sydney. "Africa Awakes," *MF* October 1955, p. 13.

56. Ibid.

Chapter Eight: Partnerships

1. Williams, F. H. "Nigeria Honours Her Benefactors," *Pentecost*, March 1961, p. 6.

2. Lindsay, Carole. "Nigerian Notebook," *VOH*, August 1966, p. 3.

3. Ruth Elton, 2010.

4. Sermon, *Let Us Go On.*

5. Rev. S. G. Elton Interview.

6. *Kaduna 1962: Record of the Thirteenth Assembly of the Christian Council of Nigeria.*

7. Ibid., p. 50.

8. "Native Church Crusade!" *VOH*, November 1961, pp. 6–7.

9. Ibid.

10. Ibid., p. 6.

11. Ibid.

12. Ibid.

13. Ibid.

14. "Missionaries learning of the Native Church Plan agree that it meets the Need of the Hour" *VOH* January 1963, p. 6.

15. "Gordon Lindsay's Report of His Round-the-World Tour in Interest of World Missions,"*VOH* May 1963, p. 10.

16. "The Call from Mohammedan Area of Nigeria," *VOH*, August 1963, p. 4.

17. Ibid.

18. Sermon, *Kingdom Provision.*

19. Ibid.

20. "Native Church Crusade!" *VOH*, November 1961, p. 6.

21. Elton, Sydney. "Upogoro, Nigeria," *VOH*, June 1966, p. 9.

22. "Go Ye into All the World," *VOH*, November 1965.

23. Elton, Sydney. "Africa: It is not too Late," *VOH*, February 1965, p. 10.

24. "From the Editor's Desk," *VOH*, August 1966, p. 2.

25. Lindsay, Gordon. "Nigeria," *CFTN*, August 1971, p. 8.
26. Ruth Elton, 2006.
27. Letter from Gospel Revivals Inc. Seelyville, Indiana, USA to author, November 1, 2010.
28. Ibid.
29. NCF-BCC, lesson six, p. ii.
30. Ruth Elton, 2006.
31. Letter from Gospel Revivals Inc. to author, November 1, 2010.
32. *HHC*, May 1963.
33. *HHC*, April 1964.
34. "Nigerian Herald," *HHC* (July 1963).
35. "Nigerian Herald," *HHC* (October 1963).
36. Ibid.
37. "Nigerian Herald," *HHC* (March 1964).
38. *HHC*, April 1964.
39. Ibid.
40. Ibid.
41. Ibid.
42. Ibid.
43. Ibid.
44. *HHC*, November 1964.
45. *HHC*, October 1964.
46. Ibid.
47. "Testimony from Nigerian Herald," *HHC* (January 1965).
48. *HHC*, June 1964.
49. "Letter From S. G. Elton," *HHC* (March 1965).
50. "Nigerian Herald" *HHC* (February 1966).
51. *HHC*, April 1966.
52. *HHC*, September 1966
53. Ibid.
54. Ibid.
55. "Nigerian Herald," *HHC* (April 1971)
56. Letter from Gospel Revivals Inc. to author, November 1, 2010.
57. Ibid.
58. Osborn, Daisy. *The King and I*. Tulsa: T. L. Osborn Evangelistic Foundation, n.d.
59. Ibid.
60. Ibid.

61. Ibid.

62. Ibid.

63. Ibid.

64. Osborn, T. L. "Revival in Lagos, Nigeria," *FD*, March 1957, pp. 2–3.

65. Osborn, *We Found Black Gold*, n.p.

66. Osborn, T. L. "Galilean Crowds repeated in Ibadan," *Pentecost*, June 1957, p. 8.

67. "West Africa's Largest Cities Stirred by Pentecostal Evangelist," *Pentecost*, March 1959, p. 15.

68. Osborn, *We Found Black Gold*.

69. Ibid.

70. Ibid.

71. Isaiah Oke, 2011; Ruth Elton, 2010

72. Osborn, *We Found Black Gold*.

73. Ibid.

74. Ibid. "Afterwards, he [Osborn] told that Jesus promised to heal the sick when we would lay our hands on the suffering in Jesus' Name. When I heard the revivalist tell us to lay our hands where we suffered, and to pray and expect the living Jesus to cure us, I removed the rubber pads from [my] knees, dropped the wood blocks and laid my hands on my legs during the prayer. During the prayer, something lifted me up from the ground so that I did not feel that I was sitting as before. It was such that I opened my eyes to see if someone was lifting me up but no one was. It was so real that I next thought I was sitting up on something that was holding me up in the air. I felt and there was nothing at all. It was a strange feeling. A power was actually lifting me and holding me. A friend of mine standing by saw me being raised up, and he thought I was trying to get up; but I was not. This power was just lifting me by itself. My friend came near me and helped me more and raised me up on my feet. I held him fast by the neck for full 15 minutes. Then I asked him to leave me and I began to take steps by myself. As I realised I was healed, I started to the platform to tell the Revivalist and to give glory to God. My heart was so happy. I could not help shouting out and rejoicing. As I came up to the platform, someone shouted: 'This is Karimu!' I cried back: 'No, I am not! Do not call me Karimu any longer because I am no longer Moslem. I am going to follow Christ and these Christians and they will give me a new Christian name!' "

75. Ibid.

76. Ibid.

77. Osborn, T. L. "World Missions Crusade: Evangelising with the Natives," *VOH*, July 1953, p. 10.

78. Ibid.
79. Osborn, T. L. "World Missions Crusade: Evangelising with the Natives," *VOH*, July 1954, p. 9.
80. Ruth Elton, 2010.
81. Ibid.
82. "Biafra/Nigeria M.E.U. Report," *FD*, December 196, p. 19.
83. Sermon, *Relationship with the World.*
84. "Biafra/Nigeria M.E.U. Report," *FD*, December 196, p. 19.
85. Peter Daniels, 2006.
86. Mike Oye, 2006.
87. "Soulwinners Unlimited Nigeria," *HOLD* No. 13, p. 12.
88. Ibid.
89. "Soulwinners Unlimited Nigeria," *HOLD* No. 16, p. 12.
90. "Soulwinners Unlimited Nigeria," *HOLD* No. 18, p. 12.
91. Ibid.
92. Ibid.
93. Garlock, Ruthanne. *Fire in His Bones.* Tulsa: Harrison House, 1981, p. 153.
94. "Soulwinners Unlimited Nigeria," *HOLD* No. 24, p. 12.
95. Ibid.
96. "Soulwinners Unlimited Nigeria," *HOLD* No. 14, p. 12.
97. Ibid.
98. "The Ripening Harvest," *HOLD* No. 34, p. 4.
99. "Now is the Time for Action," *HOLD* No. 8, p. 12.
100. Sermon, *Divine Government.*
101. "Now is the Time for Action," *HOLD* No. 2, p. 12.
102. "Soulwinners Unlimited Nigeria," *HOLD* No. 17, p. 12.
103. "Now is the Time for Action," *HOLD* No. 8, p. 12.
104. "Greetings to Our Nigerian Partners, 1974," p. 2.
105. "Nigeria," *FD*, February 1963, p. 24.
106. "Letters Pro and Con," *FD*, May 1963, p. 14.
107. "Victory in Nigeria," *FD*, OctOber 1963, p. 29.
108. "Mail Call," *FD*, December 1966, p. 28.
109. "Lighting the World through OF Literature," *FD*, March 1970, p. 20.
110. "Nigeria: Osborn Cares," *FD*, December 1967, p. 20.
111. "Osborn Ministries Global Impact," www.osborn.org, p. 3.
112. "Osborn Team Sparks Nigeria 'Tools Invasion,' " FD, August 1965, p. 3.
113. Ibid., p. 4.
114. "Soulwinners Unlimited Nigeria," *HOLD* No. 25, p. 12.

115. "The Unbeatable Outreach," *FD*, July 1971, p. 11.

116. Ibid., p. 12.

117. Ibid.

118. "Nigeria: Osborn Cares," *FD*, December 1967, p. 20.

119. "Now is the Time for Action," *HOLD* No. 8, p. 12.

120. "Nigeria: Osborn Cares," *FD*, December 1967, p. 20.

121. "Just in Time: Nigeria/Biafra M.E.U. Report," *FD* December 1967, p. 21.

122. Ibid., p. 19.

123. Emmanuel Ajao, 2013.

124. Isaiah Oke, 2011.

125. Amos Aderonmu, 2012.

126. "Christmas in Africa," *FD* December 1974, p. 3.

127. Ibid., p. 4.

128. "Christmas in Africa," *FD* December 1974, p. 4.

129. Ibid., p. 3.

130. Amos Aderonmu, 2012.

131. "7,000 Nigerian Soul-winners can't be Wrong," *FD* April 1975, p. 3.

132. Letter from Pat Lovern, Executive Assistant, OSBORN Ministries International, to author, January 2, 2013.

Chapter Nine: Last-Days Messenger

1. Letter from Gospel Revivals Inc. to author, November 1, 2010

2. Ibid.

3. "What is the Time?" *HOLD* No. 1, p. 2.

4. "What is God saying Today?" *HOLD* No. 4, p. 1.

5. "God's New Move Today in Nigeria," *HOLD* No. 2, p. 1.

6. "What is the Time?" *HOLD* No. 1, p. 1.

7. Sermon, *Feasts of End Time.*

8. "God's True Church in Nigeria" *HOLD* No. 6, p. 11.

9. "Now is the Time for Action," *HOLD* No. 8, p. 12.

10. Nwankpa, Emeka. "Editor's Note," HOLD No. 40, p. 2.

11. "The Land of Ham," *HOLD*, No. 40; and "A New People of God," *HOLD* NO. 41.

12. "Editorial," *HOLD* No. 37, p. 2.

13. "Editorial," *HOLD* No. 34, p. 2.

14. "What is the Time?" *HOLD* No. 1, p. 2.

15. Ibid.

16. "What is God saying Today?" *HOLD* No. 4, p. 1.

17. "What is the Time?" *HOLD* No. 1, p. 2.

18. "God's New Move Today in Nigeria," *HOLD* No. 2, p. 2.

19. Ibid., pp. 1–2.

20. "By What Authority?" *HOLD* No. 15, p. 2.

21. "The Power of Vision," *HOLD* No. 3, p. 11.

22. "God's New Move Today in Nigeria," *HOLD* No. 2, p. 2.

23. "The Power of Vision," *HOLD* No. 3, pp. 2, 11.

24. Ibid., p. 11.

25. Ibid.

26. "God's True Church in Nigeria," *HOLD*, No. 6, pp. 1–2.

27. "What is the Time?" *HOLD* No. 1, p. 2.

28. "The Power of Vision," *HOLD* No. 3, p. 2.

29. Ibid.

30. Ibid.

31. "God's New Move Today in Nigeria," *HOLD* No. 2, p. 2.

32. Ibid.

33. "What is God saying Today?" *HOLD* No. 4, p. 1.

34. Ibid., p. 2.

35. "Now is the Time for Action," *HOLD* No. 4, p. 12.

36. "God's True Church in Nigeria," *HOLD*, No. 6, p. 7.

37. Ibid.

38. Ibid.

39. Ibid., p. 6.

40. "By My Spirit," *HOLD* No. 34, p. 6.

41. "What is the Purpose of the Healing Ministry?" *HOLD* No. 5, pp. 6-7.

42. Ibid., p. 7.

43. "The Gospel of the Kingdom," *HOLD* No. 6, p. 8.

44. "What is the Time?" *HOLD* No. 1. p. 11.

45. "Can these Bones Live Again?" *HOLD* No. 12, p. 1.

46. "Now is the Time for Action," *HOLD* No. 8, p. 12.

47. "The Coming World Ruler," *HOLD* No. 8, p. 11.

48. "Is Your God too Small?" *HOLD* No. 11, pp. 1-2.

49. "The Coming World Ruler," *HOLD* No. 8, p. 2.

50. "Lift Up Thy Rod," *HOLD* No. 22, p. 11.

51. "They Shall Do Exploits," *HOLD* No. 23, p. 11.

52. "Satan's Church in Nigeria," *HOLD* No. 7, p. 11.

53. "They Shall Do Exploits," *HOLD* No. 23, p. 11.

54. "The Authority of the Believer," *HOLD* No. 25, p. 8.

55. "Spiritual Growth," *HOLD* No. 13, pp. 6-8.

56. "God's Will – God's Time," *HOLD* No. 32, p. 1.

57. Elton, *The Coming Kingdom*, pp. 42–43.

58. Ibid., pp. 3–4.

59. "Chosen Vessels of Honour," *HOLD* No. 9, p. 6.

60. "The Power of the Age to Come," *HOLD* No. 9, p. 2.

61. "Guerrilla Warfare in Nigeria," *HOLD* No. 10, p. 6.

62. Ibid.

63. "The Coming World Ruler," *HOLD* No. 8, p. 11.

64. Ibid.

65. "Profession or Passion?" *HOLD* No. 21, p. 1.

66. "Can These Bones Live Again?" *HOLD* No. 12, p. 2.

67. "Profession or Passion?" *HOLD* No. 21, p. 2.

68. "Lift Up Thy Rod," *HOLD* No. 22, p. 1.

69. "Fight," *HOLD* No. 26, p. 1.

70. "The Crime in the Church," *HOLD* No. 5, p. 4.

71. "Lift Up Thy Rod," *HOLD* No. 22, pp. 2, 11.

72. "Fight," *HOLD* No. 26, p. 2.

73. "God's End-Time Move," *HOLD* No. 28, p. 2.

74. Ibid.

75. Ibid.

76. Sermon, *Feasts of End Time*.

77. "Operations of the Holy Spirit in the Last Days," *HOLD* No. 39, p. 8.

78. "God's End-Time Move," *HOLD* No. 28, p. 1.

79. "Do Not Let the Foolish Virgins Steal Your Oil," *HOLD* No. 10, p. 9.

80. "The Coming Revival," *HOLD* No. 21, p. 3.

81. Ibid., p. 4.

82. Ibid.

83. Ibid.

84. "Do Not Let the Foolish Virgins Steal Your Oil," *HOLD* No. 10, p. 9.

85. "By My Spirit," *HOLD* No. 34, p. 5.

86. "As it is in Heaven," *HOLD* No. 29, pp. 1-2.

87. Ibid., pp. 2, 11.

88. "The Cost of A Vision," *HOLD* No. 32, p. 5.

89. Sermon, *God's Demands and Promises Regarding Prophecy for the Last Days*.

90. "The Cost of A Vision," *HOLD* No. 32, p. 6.

91. REP, 1974 Greeting Card, p. 2.

Chapter Ten: "We are at War"

1. Lowman, *The Day of His Power*, p. 242.
2. Ibid.
3. Ibid., p. 243.
4. Adesogan, *Faith, Politics and Challenges*, p. 28.
5. Ojo, *The Growth of Campus Christianity and Charismatic Movements in Western Nigeria*, pp. 176–177.
6. *UCH Chapel Handbook*, pp. 2–3.
7. *The Fellowship of Christian Students Handbook*, p. 2.
8. "Lagos University," *SPAN*, 1967, No. 2, p. 15.
9. "University of Nigeria, Nsukka," *SPAN*, 1966, No. 3, p. 16.
10. "University of Nigeria, Nsukka," *SPAN*, 1967, No. 2, p. 14.
11. "Lagos University," *SPAN*, 1967, No. 2, p. 15.
12. "University of Ibadan," *SPAN*, 1966, No. 1, pp. 18-19.
13. "University College Hospital, Ibadan," *SPAN*, 1966, No. 1, p. 19.
14. "University of Nigeria, Nsukka," *SPAN*, 1966, No. 3, p. 16.
15. Lowman, *The Day of His Power*, p. 241.
16. Adesogan, *Faith, Politics and Challenges,* p. 37.
17. Ifere, *God's Response to Nigeria*, p. 42.
18. McMahan, *Safari for Souls*, p. 35.
19. "Ahmadu Bello University, Zaria," *SPAN*, 1966, No. 3, p. 15.
20. Sam Olofin, 2011.
21. Lowman, *The Day of His Power*, p. 79.
22. Ibid., p. 243.
23. Adesogan, *Faith, Politics and Challenges*, p. 40.
24. "Lagos University Medical School and Teaching Hospital," *SPAN*, 1966, No. 1, p. 18.
25. Ifere, *God's Response to Nigeria*, p. 29.
26. "University of Ibadan," *SPAN* 1966, No. 3, p. 15.
27. Ojo, *The Growth of Campus Christianity and Charismatic Movements in Western Nigeria*, p. 195.
28. Ifere, *God's Response to Nigeria*, p. 28.
29. Ibid, pp. 28, 38.
30. Ojo, *The Growth of Campus Christianity and Charismatic Movements in Western Nigeria*, pp. 195–196.
31. John Dean, 2009.

32. Ojo, *The Growth of Campus Christianity and Charismatic Movements in Western Nigeria*, p. 196.

33. Ibid.

34. Sam Olofin, 2011.

35. Peter Ozodo, 2006.

36. Ibid.

37. Sermon, *Let Us Go On*.

38. Ojo, *The Growth of Campus Christianity and Charismatic Movements in Western Nigeria*, p. 196.

39. Ibid., pp. 196–197.

40. Ibid. pp. 199–201; Biola Adeniran, 2012.

41. Ojo, *The End-Time Army*, pp. 40–41.

42. Ojo, *The Growth of Campus Christianity and Charismatic Movements in Western Nigeria*, pp. 199–201.

43. Sam Olofin, 2011.

44. Ibid.

45. Porter, Ray. Obituary: David Bentley-Taylor, Missionary leader in China. *The Guardian*, Saturday 16 April 2005, http://www.guardian.co.uk/news/-2005/apr/16/guardianobituaries.

46. Oye, Mike. "Those S.U. Days," *Essence Restored*, Vol. 1, No. 1, Oct – Dec, 2004, p. 58.

47. Sam Olofin, 2011.

48. "Power for Today," *HOLD* No. 14, p. 3.

49. "Progressive Christianity," *HOLD* No. 35, p. 1.

50. "Ministry of the Holy Spirit," *HOLD*, No. 8, p. 6.

51. Ibid.

52. Ibid.

53. "Do Not Let the Foolish Virgins Steal Your Oil," *HOLD* No. 10, p. 9.

54. "Ministry of the Holy Spirit," *HOLD*, No. 8, p. 6.

55. Ibid.

56. Biola Adeniran, 2012.

57. Ibid.

58. Ibid.

59. Yinka Ayankogbe, 2013.

60. Ibid.

61. Biola Adeniran, 2012.

62. Ojo, *The End-Time Army*, p. 44.

63. Yinka Ayankogbe, 2013.

64. Bunmi Oni, 2012.

65. Letter from the president of the ECU to fellowship members, July 3, 1973.

66. Ojo, *The Growth of Campus Christianity and Charismatic Movements in Western Nigeria*, p. 206.

67. Letter from the president of the ECU to fellowship members, July 3, 1973.

68. Ikechukwu Utah, 2012.

69. Bill Isaac-Sodeye, 2013

70. Okey Onuzo, 2012.

71. Lindsay, Freda. "Nigeria Is Ripe," *CFTN*, January 1975, p. 7.

72. Niyi Beecroft, 2012.

73. Ibid.

74. Yinka Ayankogbe, 2013.

75. Ifere, *God's Response to Nigeria*, p. 60.

76. Ibid.

77. "PAFES Training Course, University of Ghana, Sept 7th – 28th, 1968," *SPAN*, 1969, No. 1, p. 14.

78. "Across Africa," *SPAN*, 1972, No. 3, p. 10.

79. Lowman, *The Day of His Power*, p. 250.

80. Fred Adegoke, 2012.

81. Hall, *Fasting: Atomic Power with God*, p. 2.

82. Harrell, *All Things Are Possible: The Healing and Charismatic Revivals in Modern America*, p. 81.

83. Ibid., p. 214.

84. Fred Adegoke, 2012; Biola Adeniran, 2012.

85. Hall, Franklin, *The Return of Immortality*. Phoenix: Hall Deliverance Foundation, Inc., 1976.

86. Hall, Franklin. *The Body-Felt Salvation*. n.d.

87. Ibid.

88. Hall, *The Return of Immortality*, p. ii.

89. Emiko Amotsuka, 2008.

90. Lowman, *The Day of His Power*, p. 251.

91. Ikechukwu Utah, 2012.

92. Hall, *The Return of Immortality*, p. 57.

93. Ibid., p. 38.

94. Ibid., p. 57. According to Hall: "When the author [Hall] made a trip to Nigeria, West Africa, many came in attendance to the great open air crusades to hear him. The author told the crowds to get their heads up and eyes open and they would see the beautiful IHO descend and appear to them. With simple, believing

obedience they did look up and the Immortality Heavenly Object did come forth. Hundreds saw the IHO come forth. They described the heavenly object as a golden light with beams of light coming from underneath. When the streamers of light touched any person they became healed instantly of any ailment that they wanted to leave them. Beams of white tongues of light, cloven towards the upper elongated area, and stretched downwards towards certain individuals looking upward. Repeatedly the cloven wings flashed downwards at people's bodies. When the lightening phenomena touched the people (many were touched simultaneously by the IHO flames like fire) they had a new energetic well refreshed feeling. It was beautiful to behold and experience. Many claimed to be freed from sickness and tiredness. Many told us that they had such an exhilarating feeling of regeneration and lightness that it seemed they had no legs at all. They just felt weightless and it seemed at times they were ready to take off and be raised above the earth."

95. Ojo, *The Growth of Campus Christianity and Charismatic Movements in Western Nigeria*, p. 214.

96. Ibid.

97. Numbere, *A Man and A Vision*, pp. 153–162.

98. Ibid.

99. Ikechukwu Utah, 2012.

100. Emiko Amotsuka, 2008.

101. Ikechukwu Utah, 2012; Okey Onuzo, 2012; Yinka Ayankogbe, 2013.

102. Ikechukwu Utah, 2012.

103. Yinka Ayankogbe, 2013.

104. Liardon, *God's Generals: Why they Succeeded and Why Some Failed*, pp. 299–306.

105. Numbere, *A Man and A Vision*, p. 158.

106. Yinka Ayankogbe, 2013.

107. "SCRIPTURE UNION NIGERIA," *Daily Times*, August 6, 1973, p. 25.

108. Ojo, *The Growth of Campus Christianity and Charismatic Movements in Western Nigeria*, p. 460.

109. Ibid., p. 444.

110. Abodunde, *A Heritage of Faith*, p. 576.

111. Ibid., 577.

112. Ibid.

113. Ibid.

114. Lowman, *The Day of His Power*, p. 251.

115. "What Next?: Challenge to Nigerian Christians to 'Go On'," *HOLD* No. 39, p. 2.

116. Matthew Owojaiye, 2006.

117. "Speaking in Tongues," *HOLD* No. 15, p. 3.

118. "The Cost of A Vision," *HOLD* No. 32, p. 6.

119. Sermon, *God's Demands and Promises Regarding Prophecy for the Last Days*.

120. Matthew Owojaiye, 2006.

121. Emeka Nwankpa, 2006.

122. Biola Adeniran, 2012.

123. Fred Adegoke, 2012.

124. Peter Ozodo, 2012.

125. Yinka Ayankogbe, 2013.

126. Fred Adegoke, 2012.

127. Ibid.

128. "Guerrilla Warfare in Nigeria," *HOLD* No. 10, p. 8.

129. Ikechukwu Utah, 2012.

130. Okey Onuzo, 2012.

131. Sam Olofin, 2011.

132. Ibid.

133. Babatunde Ogunnaike, 2015.

134. "Weapons of Our Warfare," *HOLD* No. 17, p. 7.

135. Sermon, *Divine Government*.

136. "Power for Today," *HOLD* No. 14, p. 5.

137. "What Next? Challenge to Nigerian Christians to 'Go On'," *HOLD* No. 39, p. 3.

138. Emeka Nwankpa, 2006.

139. Sermon, *Divine Government*.

140. Ibid.

141. Adedayo Adeyemo, 2013.

142. Abodunde, *A Herald of the Last Days*, pp. 83–84.

143. Elton, *Nine Gifts of the Holy Spirit*, p. 60.

144. Sermon, *Prepare for War*.

145. Sermon, *Covenant Relationship in the Epistle to the Ephesians*.

146. Elton, *Nine Gifts of the Holy Spirit*, p. 37.

147. Paul Nwachukwu, 2006.

148. Sermon, *Divine Government*.

149. "Other men of God Speak on Elton – Enoch Adejare Adeboye," *Essence Restored*, Vol. 1, No. 1, Oct – Dec, 2004, p. 40.

150. S. O. Ogedengbe, 2006.

151. Abodunde, *A Heritage of Faith*, pp. 592–594.

152. Emiko Amotsuka, 2003.

153. Emiko Amotsuka, 2006.

154. Olubi Johnson, 2012.

155. Ibid.

156. Alabi, *Prophet in the House: A Biography of Rev. (Dr.) Francis Wale* Oke, p. 51.

157. Abodunde, *A Heritage of Faith*, p. 597.

158. Ruth Elton, 2012; Emmanuel Ajao, 2013.

159. Ruth Elton, 2013.

160. Ojo, *The Growth of Campus Christianity and Charismatic Movements in Western Nigeria*, pp. 284–285. In fact, it was while Oyedepo was on a trip to Ilesa to see Elton, and while lodging in a hotel for the night because Elton was out of town, that he received the vision: "The hour has come to liberate the world from all oppression of the devil, by the preaching of the Word of faith and I am sending you to partake in this."

161. Ikechukwu Utah, 2012.

162. Emmanuel Ajao, 2013.

163. Raphael Okafor, 2006; "EFAC History," http://efaclz.org/us/history/, accessed 7/5/2015.

164. Elton, *Nine Gifts of the Holy Spirit,* p. 63.

165. Fred Adegoke, 2012.

166. Raphael Okafor, 2006.

167. Sermon, *God's Army.*

168. Ukachi, *The Best is Yet to Come*, p. 146.

169. Ibid., p. 147.

170. Ibid., p. 155.

171. Ojo, *The Growth of Campus Christianity and Charismatic Movements in Western Nigeria*, p. 499.

Chapter Eleven: Rebels

1. Burgess, *The Civil War Revival and its Pentecostal Progeny*, p. 130.

2. Kalu, Ogbu. "Doing Mission through the Post Office: Naked Faith People of Igboland, 1920-1960," *Neue Zeitschrift fur Missionswissenschaft* 56, No. 4, 2000, p. 14.

3. Elton, Sydney. "Biafra: A Report Direct from Nigeria," *CFTN*, November 1968, p. 10.

4. "Nigeria," *HHC* (January 1968).

5. "Nigerian Heralds," *HHC* (September 1970).

6. Elton, Sydney. "Biafra: A Report Direct from Nigeria," *CFTN*, November 1968,

p. 10.

7. "Just in Time: Nigeria/Biafra M.E.U. Report," *FD*, December 1967, p. 19.

8. *HHC*, October 1969.

9. Elton, Sydney. "Biafra: A Report Direct from Nigeria," *CFTN*, November 1968, p. 11.

10. "In Nigeria," *HHC* (April 1970).

11. Elton, Sydney. "Biafra: A Report Direct from Nigeria," *CFTN*, November 1968, pp. 11–12.

12. Elton, Sydney. "Nigerian Herald," *HHC* (August 1970).

13. Ibid.

14. "Nigerian Heralds," *HHC* (September 1970).

15. Elton, Sydney. "Biafra: A Report Direct from Nigeria," *CFTN*, November 1968, p. 12.

16. Roberts, *Life and Death among the Ibos*, pp. 7–8.

17. Ibid., p. 18.

18. Ibid., pp. 19-20.

19. "University of Nigeria, Nsukka," *SPAN*, 1966, No. 3, p. 16.

20. Roberts, *Life and Death among the Ibos*, p. 21.

21. Ibid., p. 33.

22. Kew and Okorocha, *Vision Bearers*, p. 87.

23. Roberts, *Life and Death among the Ibos*, p. 79.

24. Ibid.

25. Ibid.

26. Ibid.

27. Kew and Okorocha, *Vision Bearers*, p. 87.

28. Ibid.

29. Bolton, *And We beheld His Glory*, p. 2.

30. Ibid., p. 12.

31. Ibid., pp. 4–5.

32. Ibid., pp. 11–20.

33. Ibid., p. 34.

34. Ibid., pp. 43–44.

35. Ibid., p. 44.

36. Ibid.

37. Ibid., p. 86.

38. Ibid., p. 87.

39. Raphael Okafor, 2006.

40. Ibid., pp. 72-73.

41. Burgess, *The Civil War Revival and its Pentecostal Progeny*, pp. 233–234.

42. Bolton, *And We beheld His Glory*, p. 29.

43. Burgess, *The Civil War Revival and its Pentecostal Progeny*, p. 235.

44. Roberts, *Life and Death among the Ibos*, p. 69.

45. Anthony Nkwoka, "Interrogating the Form and the Spirit: Pentecostalism and the Anglican Communion," in *Creativity and Change in Nigerian Christianity*, David Ogungbile and Akintunde Akinade, ed., Lagos: Malthouse Press Limited, 2010, p. 82.

46. Ibid. pp. 82–83.

47. Burgess, *The Civil War Revival and its Pentecostal Progeny*, p. 233.

48. Raphael Okafor, 2006.

49. Kew and Okorocha, *Vision Bearers*, pp. 87-88.

50. Lindsay, Gordon. "Nigeria," *CFTN*, August 1971, p. 8.

51. Raphael Okafor, 2006.

52. Ibid.

53. Ibid.

54. Bolton, *And We beheld His Glory*, p. 99.

55. Burgess, *The Civil War Revival and its Pentecostal Progeny*, p. 130.

56. Nnaji, *Looking Beyond the Night*, p. 12.

57. *HHC*, April 1973.

58. Anyaegbu, *The Growth and Development of Pentecostal/Evangelical Movements in Igboland*, p. 35.

59. "Nigeria: Revival again in Nigeria after the War," *CFTN*, August 1972, p. 5.

60. Bolton, *And We beheld His Glory*, p. 99

61. Paul Nwachukwu, 2006.

62. Burgess, *The Civil War Revival and its Pentecostal Progeny*, p. 235.

63. "Native Literature Crusade," *VOH*, February 1966, p. 6.

64. "We Must Put Out the Truth!" *VOH*, May 1965, p. 3.

65. Elton, Sydney. "Biafra: A Report Direct from Nigeria," *CFTN*, November 1968, p. 12.

66. Stevens, Stevens. "What Will They Read?" *CFTN*, February 1975, p. 8.

67. "Received Baptism While Reading Book," *VOH*, October 1966, p. 14.

68. Paul Nwachukwu, 2006.

69. Burgess, *The Civil War Revival and its Pentecostal Progeny*, p. 349.

70. Ibid., p. 163.

71. Maduako, *Flame of Fire: The Story of Scripture Union (Nigeria)*, pp. 98–99.

72. Chukwuka, *Looking Beyond the Night*, pp. 21–22.

73. Kalu, *The Embattled Gods: Christianization of Igboland, 1841–1991*, p.

74. Arthur Oriuzu, 2012.
75. Anyaegbu, *The Growth and Development of Pentecostal/Evangelical Movements in Igboland*, p. 210.
76. Ibid., p. 51.
77. Ibid., p. 209.
78. Edward Ezenwafor, 2012.
79. Anyaegbu, *The Growth and Development of Pentecostal/Evangelical Movements in Igboland*, pp. 53–61; Burgess, *The Civil War Revival and its Pentecostal Progeny* pp. 281–282; Augustine Nwodika, 2012.
80. Raphael Okafor, 2006.
81. Augustine Nwodika, 2012.
82. Ibid.
83. Ibid.
84. Paul Nwachukwu, 2006.
85. Burgess, *The Civil War Revival and its Pentecostal Progeny*, p. 281.
86. Ojo, *The End-Time Army*, pp. 61–62.
87. Augustine Nwodika, 2012.
88. Ibid.
89. Ibid.
90. Edward Ezenwafor, 2012.
91. Ibid.
92. Ibid.
93. Ibid.
94. Tony Okeke, 2012.
95. Ibid.

Chapter Twelve: The Enrolment Office

1. Emeka Nwankpa, 2006.
2. Ibid.
3. Sermon, *Let Us Go On.*
4. Ibid.
5. Ibid.
6. Sermon, Gbile Akanni, *Advancing the Kingdom.*
7. Ibid.
8. Emeka Nwankpa, 2006.
9. "God's Doings at the C.S.S.M, Training Conference, July 17th – 21st, 1978," *The Alarm*, No. 8., pp. 1–2.

10. Ndukwe, Festus, and Famonure, Bayo. "A Mustard Seed Beginning," http://www.capromissions.org/mustardseed.html.

11. "By What Authority?" *HOLD* No. 15, p. 2.

12. "Prepare for War," HOLD No. 13, p. 2.

13. Elton, Sydney. "Biafra: A Report Direct from Nigeria," *CFTN*, November 1968, p. 11.

14. Ibid.

15. "Prepare for War," HOLD No. 13, p. 11.

16. *HHC*, April 1973.

17. Lindsay, Freda. "Nigeria is Ripe," *CFTN*, January 1975, p. 8.

18. Johnson, Bill. "Apostolic Teams," http://www.bjm.org/articles/12/apostolic-teams.html.

19. Niyi Beecroft, 2012.

20. Kalu, *African Pentecostalism*, p. 91.

21. Abodunde, *A Herald of the Last Days*, p. 100.

22. "The Invincible Few," *HOLD* No. 12, p. 7.

23. Letter from Sydney Elton to Dr. & Mrs. Femi Soetan, November 28, 1980.

24. Ibid.

25. Letter from Sydney Elton to Dr. & Mrs. Femi Soetan, February 16, 1981.

26. "Can these Bones Live Again?" *HOLD* No. 12, p. 2.

27. "Features of the Ministry of the Holy Spirit in the Last Days," *HOLD* No. 39, p. 12.

28. Sermon, *God's Army*.

29. "Now is the Time for Action," *HOLD* No. 6, p. 12.

30. Kole Akinboboye, 2006.

31. Ibid

32. Okey Onuzo, 2012.

33. Ibid.

34. Steve Olumuyiwa, 2006

35. Peter Ozodo, 2012.

36. Ibid.

37. "Other men of God Speak on Elton – Francis Wale Oke," *Essence Restored*, Vol. 1, No. 1, Oct – Dec, 2004, pp. 36–37.

38. Ikechukwu Utah, 2012.

39. Niyi Beecroft, 2012.

40. Bunmi Oni, 2012.

41. Adesogan (ed.), *A Fountain of Life: The Story of Ibadan Varsity Christian Union*, p. 159.

42. Ibid., p. 176.
43. Olubi Johnson, 2012.
44. Fred Adegoke, 2012.
45. "Other men of God Speak on Elton – Tunde Ajala," *Essence Restored*, Vol. 1, No. 1, Oct – Dec, 2004, p. 41.
46. Sermon, *A God Given Vision*.
47. "The Crime in the Church," *HOLD* No. 5, pp. 3–4.
48. "Our Inheritance – The Heathen," *HOLD* No. 6, pp. 9–10.
49. "Give Me this Mountain," *HOLD* No. 16, p. 11.
50. "Special Message and Challenge To all Students – Teachers – Graduates," *HOLD* No. 19, p. 12.
51. Ibid.
52. "The Crime in the Church," *HOLD* No. 5, p. 4.
53. "Prepare for War," HOLD No. 13, p. 1.
54. Ibid., p. 11.
55. "Laying on of Hands," *HOLD* No. 18, p. 10.
56. Bola Sani, 2006.
57. Interviews with several Elton protégés.
58. Peter Ozodo, 2006.
59. Ibid.
60. "Give Me this Mountain," *HOLD* No. 16, p. 11.
61. "By My Spirit," *HOLD* No. 34, p. 6.
62. "Lord, Increase our Faith," *HOLD* No. 32, p. 9.
63. "Our Inheritance – The Heathen," *HOLD* No. 6, p. 10.
64. "Special Message for All Evangelists," *HOLD* No. 10, p. 12.
65. Emiko Amotsuka, 2008.
66. Garlock, *Fire in His Bones*, pp. 152–153.
67. Niyi Beecroft, 2012.
68. Amos Aderonmu, 2012.
69. Ibid.
70. Ndukwe, Festus and Famonure, Bayo. "A Mustard Seed Beginning," http://www.capromissions.org/mustardseed.html.
71. Ibid.
72. Peter Ozodo, 2012.
73. Bayo Famonure, 2013.
74. Ibid.
75. Amos Aderonmu, 2012.
76. Ibid.

77. Ibid.
78. Ibid.
79. Ibid.
80. Ibid.
81. Peter Ozodo, 2012.
82. Numbere, *A Man and A Vision*, p. 32.
83. Ibid., pp. 32-33.
84. Ibid., p. 52.
85. Ibid., p. 32.
86. Ibid.
87. Ibid., p. 54.
88. Ibid., p. 53.
89. Akanni, *The Price, Plight and Perils of the Anointed*, p. 5.

Chapter Thirteen: Pain

1. Garlock, *Fire in His Bones*, p. 95.
2. Ibid., pp. 98–99.
3. Ibid., p. 99.
4. Ibid., p. 101.
5. Emeka, *Benson Idahosa Factor in Nigerian Pentecostalism*, pp. 197–202; A. I. Edosonwan, 2015; Peter Obadan, 2015.
6. Sermon, Edgar Parkyns, *Reminiscences*.
7. Wallis, Arthur. "Springs of Restoration: Part 1," *Restoration*, July – August, 1980, pp. 21–24.
8. Sermon, Edgar Parkyns, *Reminiscences*.
9. Obadan, *The Legend*, p. 13.
10. Ibid., p. 3.
11. Ibid., p. 4.
12. "Historical Overview," http://cgmglobalconvention.com/about-cgmi/.
13. Emeka, *Benson Idahosa Factor in Nigerian Pentecostalism*, pp. 197–202.
14. Obadan, *The Legend*, p. 5; Emeka, *Benson Idahosa Factor in Nigerian Pentecostalism*, p. 188.
15. Alan Macintosh, December 13, 2013.
16. Obadan, *The Legend*, pp. 3–5; Steward, *Historical Background of Churches in Nigeria*, p. 66; Emeka, *Benson Idahosa Factor in Nigerian Pentecostalism*, pp. 185–188.
17. Obadan, *The Legend*, pp. 4–5; Emeka, *Benson Idahosa Factor in Nigerian*

Pentecostalism, pp. 187–188.

18. Obadan, *The Legend*, p. 4.
19. Ibid., p. 5.
20. Peter Obadan, 2013.
21. Ibid.
22. A. I. Edosonwan, 2015; Peter Obadan, 2015; Emmanuel Onofurho, 2012; Emeka, *Benson Idahosa Factor in Nigerian Pentecostalism*, p. 187.
23. Garlock, *Fire in His Bones*, p. 104.
24. Ibid., p. 104.
25. Lindsay, Gordon. "Nigeria," *CFTN*, August 1971, p. 15.
26. Lindsay, Freda. "Nigeria Is Ripe," *CFTN*, January 1975, p. 6.
27. "What Students are Saying about CFNI," *CFTN*, January 1972, p. 7.
28. Garlock, *Fire in His Bones*, p. 115.
29. Ibid., p. 115.
30. Ibid., p. 125.
31. "Presenting Christ for the nations International Evangelistic Association," *Christ for the Nations – Nigeria Magazine*, June – August 1973, p. 2.
32. Lindsay, Freda. "Special World Report," *CFTN*, January 1976, p. 12.
33. Garlock, *Fire in His Bones*, pp. 151–152.
34. Rev. S. G. Elton Interview.
35. Lindsay, Freda. "Nigeria Is Ripe," *CFTN*, January 1975, p. 7.
36. Elton, Sydney. "Nigeria," *CFTN* April 1973, p. 8.
37. "500 Testimonies of Healing Received," *CFTN* December 1972, p. 11.
38. Elton, Sydney. "Idahosa (CFN Student) Having Great Success," *CFTN* April 1973, p. 8.
39. Lindsay, Freda. "God is on the Move," *CFTN* January 1975, p. 8.
40. Ibid.
41. Ibid.
42. Lindsay, Freda. "What I saw in Israel and Nigeria," *CFTN* January 1976, p. 11.
43. *From Glory to Glory.* A documentary on the History of the Church of God Mission International, 1995.
44. Felix Omobude, 2006; Joseph Ojo, 2012.
45. Garlock, *Fire in His Bones*, p. 155.
46. Rev. S. G. Elton Interview.
47. Ibid.
48. Tony Okeke, 2012.
49. Idahosa, *From Zero to Surplus*, p. 10; "All Nations for Christ Bible Institute," http://cgmglobal.org/ANFBII.htm.

50. Ibid; Abodunde, *A Heritage of Faith*, p. 552–553; Ojo, *The End-Time Army*, pp. 61–63.

51. Abodunde, *A Heritage of Faith*, p. 552–553.

52. Augustine Nwodika, 2012.

53. John Valentine, 2012.

54. Letter from Sydney Elton to Dr. & Mrs. Femi Soetan, November 28, 1980.

55. Rev. S. G. Elton Interview.

56. Ibid.

57. Ibid.

58. Ibid.

59. Ibid.

60. Lyons, Andrew and Lyons, Harriett. "Religion and the Mass Media," in *Religion and Society in Nigeria: Historical and Sociological Perspectives*, Jacob Olupona and Toyin Falola ed., Ibadan: Spectrum, 1991, p. 115.

61. "Historical Perspective of the I.C.C.C.," http://www.theiccc.com/history.html.

62. Ibid.

63. Ibid.

64. Ibid.

65. Ibid.

66. Ibid.

67. Ibid; Garlock, *Fire in His Bones*, pp. 189–190.

68. "Historical Perspective of the I.C.C.C.," http://www.theiccc.com/history.html.

69. Obadan, *The Legend*, pp. 120–121.

70. "Historical Perspective of the I.C.C.C.," http://www.theiccc.com/history.html.

71. DAHL-DDPA, Letter from Benson Idahosa to David du Plessis, November 17, 1981.

72. Ibid., October 1982.

73. Ikechukwu Utah, 2012.

74. Fred Adegoke, 2012.

75. Ibid.

76. Peter Ozodo, 2012.

77. Ibid.

78. Letter from Sydney Elton to Dr. & Mrs. Femi Soetan, November 28, 1980.

79. Bayo Famonure, 2013.

80. Letter from Sydney Elton to Dr. & Mrs. Femi Soetan, February 16, 1981.

81. Sermon. *Prepare for War.*

82. Sermon, *The Establishing of the Kingdom in Nigeria.*

83. Ruth Elton, 2012.

84. Sermon, Edgar Parkyns, *Reminiscences.*

85. Peter Ozodo, 2006.

86. Augustine Nwodika, 2012.

87. Mike Heathcote, 2013.

88. John Okposio Marshall, 2006

89. S. O. Ogedengbe, 2012.

90. Kole Akinboboye, 2006.

91. Anon. 2012.

92. Augustine Nwodika, 2012.

93. Peter Obadan, 2013.

94. Letter from Sydney Elton to Rev. and Mrs. John Valentine, September 14, 1986.

95. Celia Valentine, 2006.

96. Sermon, *Prepare for War.*

97. Olubi Johnson, 2012.

98. Kole Akinboboye, *Ancient Landmarks: Special Commemoration Service for Late Pa S. G. Elton*, 2007.

99. Fred Adegoke, *Ancient Landmarks: Special Commemoration Service for Late Pa S. G. Elton*, 2007.

100. Sermon, *God's Last Days Move.*

101. Sermon, *God's Army.*

102. Sermon, *God's Last Days Move.*

103. Sermon, *The Ministry of the Holy Spirit in These Last Days.*

104. Ibid.

105. "Operations of the Holy Spirit in the Last Days," *HOLD* No. 39, p. 8.

106. Fred Adegoke, *Ancient Landmarks: Special Commemoration Service for Late Pa S. G. Elton*, 2007.

Chapter Fourteen: A Revolutionary Christianity

1. Babatope, *Student Power vs. Militarism (1971–1975)*, p. vii.

2. Ibid., p. 14.

3. Ibid., p. 20.

4. Ibid., p. 23.

5. Ibid., p. 24.

6. Ibid., p. 23.

7. "Danger!! A Monster Rises Against Nigerian Saints," n.d., p. 3.

8. The Newsletter: Evangelical Christian Union, University of Ife, Ile-Ife, September – October, 1975, p. 4.

9. "Titbits about Communism," *Unshackled*, 1975, pp. 13–23.

10. "Danger!! A Monster Rises Against Nigerian Saints," n.d., p. 1.

11. Ibid.

12. Ibid., pp. 5–6.

13. "Report of the Meeting of the Presidents/Representatives of Christian Organisations in the Nigerian Institutions of Higher Learning held at University of Ibadan, Ibadan on 6th and 7th May '77," p. 1.

14. Ibid.

15. Ibid.

16. Ibid.

17. Ibid., p. 2.

18. "Prayer Requests," ECU, n.d., p. 1.

19. "The Ife Declaration," *The Battle Axe*, n.d., p. 1.

20. Austen Ukachi, 2006.

21. Ifere, *God's Response to Nigeria*, pp. 62–63.

22. Ibid., p. 63.

23. Ibid., p. 62.

24. Ibid., p. 64.

25. Ojo, *The End-Time Army*, p. 160.

26. "Our Vision," *The Battle Axe*, n.d., p. 1.

27. Ibid., p. 2.

28. Ibid., p. 3.

29. Austen Ukachi, 2012.

30. Ibid., 2006.

31. Ibid., 2012.

32. "Features of the Ministry of the Holy Spirit in the Last Days," *HOLD* No. 39, p. 12.

33. "Revolutionary Christianity," *HOLD* No. 36, p. 3.

34. "As it is in Heaven," *HOLD* No. 29, p. 1.

35. Abodunde, *A Herald of the Last Days*, p. 111.

36. Austen Ukachi, 2006.

37. Austen Ukachi, 2012.

38. Ibid.

39. Emeka Nwankpa, 2006.

40. Ikoh and Ukachi, *The Story of the Christian Evangelical Social Movement of Nigeria*, p. 9.

41. Olanrewaju Phillips, 2006.

42. CSSMA, Minutes of the C.S.S.M. meeting on the 22nd July 1978 at the

University of Ibadan, Ibadan, p. 3.

43. CSSMA, Letter from one CSSM member to Austen Ukachi, November 7, 1979.

44. Adegoke, Fred. "God is Raising an Army," *ER*, October 2004, pp. 49–50.

45. Yinka Ayankogbe, 2013.

46. "Practical Christian Living," *HOLD* No. 12, p. 8.

47. Victor Adegboye, 2006.

48. "Other men of God Speak on Elton – Francis Wale Oke," *ER*, Vol. 1, No. 1, Oct – Dec, 2004, pp. 36–37.

49. Emiko Amotsuka, 2003.

50. Sermon, *The Establishing of the Kingdom in Nigeria.*

51. Femi Soetan, 2006.

52. Sermon, *Prepare for War.*

53. Ibid.

54. Peter Ozodo, 2012.

55. "Revolutionary Christianity," *HOLD* No. 36, p. 3.

56. Elton, *Demon Manifestations in the Last Days*, p. 65.

57. "The Ripening Harvest," *HOLD* No. 34, p. 3.

58. Fred Adegoke, 2012.

59. Ibid.

60. Ibid.

61. Ibid.

62. Ibid.

63. Ojo, *The End-Time Army*, p. 109.

64. Ikoh and Ukachi, *The Story of the Christian Evangelical Social Movement of Nigeria*, pp. 13–14.

65. Ibid., p. 14.

66. Ibid.

67. Ibid.

68. Ibid., pp. 13–15.

69. Ojo, *The Growth of Campus Christianity and Charismatic Movements in Western Nigeria*, p. 267.

70. Emeka Nwankpa, 2006.

71. Elton, *Nine Gifts of the Holy Spirit*, p. 61.

72. Ikoh and Ukachi, *The Story of the Christian Evangelical Social Movement of Nigeria*, p. 14.

73. Ibid.

Chapter Fifteen: Calling Forth Nigeria's Prophetic Destiny

1. Sermon, *The Establishing of the Kingdom in Nigeria.*
2. Ibid.
3. Elton, *Nine Gifts of the Holy Spirit,* back cover.
4. Sermon, *The Establishing of the Kingdom in Nigeria.*
5. Sermon, *God's Last Days Move.*
6. "Features of the Ministry of the Holy Spirit in the Last Days," *HOLD* No. 39, p. 14.
7. "Lord, Increase Our Faith," *HOLD* No. 32, p. 9.
8. Rev. S. G. Elton. Interview.
9. Emiko Amotsuka, 2003.
10. Sermon, *The Outline of the Kingdom as Given in the Old Testament.*
11. Elton, *The Coming Kingdom,* p. 43.
12. Adesida, Babatunde, 2003.
13. "The Changing face of Africa," http://neuafrika.com/wp/?p=28#comment-561, June 18, 2008.
14. Yinka Ayankogbe, 2013.
15. Abodunde, *A Herald of the Last Days,* pp. 120–121.
16. Elton, *Demon Manifestations in the Last Days,* pp. 57, 59, 61–62.
17. Ibid., p. 63.
18. "What Next?: Challenge to Nigerian Christians to 'Go On'," *HOLD* No. 39, pp. 1–2.
19. "Fight," *HOLD* No. 26, pp. 1–2.
20. "Prepare for War," *HOLD* No. 13, p. 11.
21. Ibid.
22. "We are the Master Race," *HOLD* No. 4, p. 9.
23. "The Ministry in the Holiest," *HOLD* No. 27, p. 8.
24. "Intercessors of Nigeria," *HOLD* No. 27, p. 12.
25. Ibid.
26. "Intercessors of Nigeria," *HOLD* No. 28, p. 12.
27. Ibid.
28. "Intercessors of Nigeria," *HOLD* No. 29, p. 12
29. "The Prince of Persia," *HOLD* No. 36, p. 9.
30. Elton, *Babylon the Kingdom of Satan,* p. 19.
31. Ibid., p. 40.
32. Sermon, *Kingdom Lifestyle.*
33. Sermon, *Feasts of End Time.*

34. "The Prince of Persia," *HOLD* No. 36, p. 8.
35. Ibid., p. 7.
36. Ibid., p. 8.
37. Ibid.
38. Ibid., p. 9.
39. Kole Akinboboye, *Ancient Landmarks: Special Commemoration Service for late Pa S. G. Elton*, 2007.
40. Austen Ukachi, 2012.
41. Ukachi, *The Best is yet to Come*, pp. 341–342.
42. "Stewardship of Fasting," *HOLD* No. 20, p. 9.
43. Adesogan (ed.), *A Fountain of Life: The Story of Ibadan Varsity Christian Union*, p. 170.
44. Fred Adegoke, 2012.
45. Sermon, *Restoration: All Things New*.
46. "Emeka Nwankpa: Intercessors for Africa," The 700 Club, http://www.cbn-.com/700club/features/emeka_nwankpa.aspx.
47. "Your Success Call," *Essence Restored*, Vol. 1, No. 1, Oct – Dec, 2004, p. 28.
48. "Nigeria-Israeli Relations – Whither?" *Ambassador* Vol. XI, No. 1, Jan/Feb 1983, p. 2.
49. Sermon, *Vision*.
50. Sermon, *Relationship with the World*.
51. "The Ripening Harvest," *HOLD* No. 34, p. 4.
52. Sermon, *Relationship with the World*.
53. Ibid.
54. Sermon, *The Establishing of the Kingdom in Nigeria*.
55. Sermon, *God's Last Days Move*.
56. Sermon, *The Church: His Body III*.
57. "The Next Few Years in Nigeria," *HOLD* No. 38, p. 4.
58. "Greater Works," *HOLD* No. 32, p. 14.

Chapter Sixteen: "It will be War Right to the Gates of Glory"

1. Bode Akintade, 2006.
2. Ibid.
3. Ibid.
4. Ibid.
5. Letter from Sydney Elton to Dr. & Mrs. Femi Soetan, November 28, 1980.
6. Ibid.

7. John Ladega, 2006.

8. Edward Ezenwafor, 2012.

9. Sermon, *The Meaning of the Kingdom.*

10. Sermon, *The Kingdom of Heaven on Earth: New Jerusalem and Mount Zion.*

11. Ibid.

12. Sermon, *The Ministry of the Holy Spirit in These Last Days.*

13. Ibid.

14. "God's Pattern for Revival in Nigeria," *HOLD* No. 16, p. 6; "Greater Works," *HOLD* No. 32, p. 12.

15. "Can these Bones Live Again?" *HOLD* No. 12, p. 2.

16. Ibid.

17. Sermon, *God's Army.*

18. "The Next Few Years in Nigeria," *HOLD* No. 38, p. 4.

19. Sermon, *A God Given Vision.*

20. Ibid.

21. "God's End-Time Move," *HOLD* No. 28, pp. 2, 11.

22. "The Coming Revival," *HOLD* No. 1, p. 10.

23. "Woe, Lo, Go," *HOLD* No. 27, p. 4.

24. Babatunde Ogunnaike, 2015.

25. "What Next? Challenge to Nigerian Christians to 'Go On'" *HOLD* No. 39, p. 4.

26. "If My People will Grow," *HOLD* No. 37, pp. 1&3.

27. Ibid., p. 3.

28. "Progressive Christianity," *HOLD* No. 35, p. 1.

29. Sermon, *Feasts of End Time.*

30. "God's Chosen Spiritual Leaders for the Last Days," *HOLD* No. 39, p. 19.

31. Ibid.

32. Ibid.

33. "Features of the Ministry of the Holy Spirit in the Last Days," *HOLD* No. 39, p. 12.

34. Ibid.

35. Sermon, *A God Given Vision.*

36. Sermon, *Covenant Relationship in the Epistle to the Ephesians.*

37. "Power and Authority Today for All Believers," *HOLD* No. 39, p. 18.

38. Ibid., p. 13.

39. Sermon, *Covenant Relationship in the Epistle to the Ephesians.*

40. Elton, *Babylon the Kingdom of Satan,* pp. 23–24.

41. "Independence or Partnership," *HOLD* No. 5, p. 10.

42. Elton, *Babylon the Kingdom of Satan,* pp. 36–37.

43. Sermon, *The Establishing of the Kingdom in Nigeria.*

44. "Community Deliverance," *HOLD* No. 37, p. 16.

45. Olubi Johnson, 2012. Francis Wale Oke, one of the budding charismatic leaders of the 1980s, personally experienced this: "Towards the latter end of his life, Pastor Elton exhibited a bias against organized church system. As a matter of fact, he strongly discouraged me and several other now-prominent men of God from starting [a] "new" ministry or church. On four occasions after his counsel, I called off the idea of starting our ministry, but the Holy Spirit would not just let me rest, until one day, after discussing with him, I had to settle down with God, and with a heavy heart, prayed through to victory. . . . It was several hours of agonizing prayer. Then came a breakthrough and a season of laughter in prayer. And the Sword of the Spirit Ministry was born, contrary to Pastor Elton's counsels. "Other men of God Speak on Elton – Francis Wale Oke," *Essence Restored,* Vol. 1, No. 1, Oct–Dec, 2004, p. 37.

46. Augustine Nwodika, 2012.

47. Sermon, *The Kingdom of Heaven on Earth: New Jerusalem and Mount Zion.*

48. Sermon, *The Ministry of the Holy Spirit in these Last Days.*

49. Sermon, *Feasts of End Time.*

50. "The Ripening Harvest," *HOLD* No. 34, p. 3.

51. Sermon, *God Given Vision.*

52. "God's End-Time Move," *HOLD* No. 28, p. 1.

53. Sermon, *The Ultimate Restoration of the Kingdom on Earth.*

54. "The Power of Vision," *HOLD* No. 3, p. 11.

55. "The Next Few Years in Nigeria," *HOLD* No. 38, p. 4.

56. Elton, *Babylon the Kingdom of Satan*, p. 56.

57. "Community Deliverance," *HOLD* No. 37, p. 17.

58. Sermon, *God's Army.*

59. Sermon, *The Meaning of the Kingdom.*

60. Sermon, *Restoring the Church.*

61. Sermon, *Kingdom Lifestyle.*

62. Sermon, *The Meaning of the Kingdom.*

63. "God's True Church in Nigeria," *HOLD* No. 6, p. 2.

64. Emiko Amotsuka, 2008.

65. Sermon, *Restoration of the Kingdom of His Son.*

66. "God's True Church in Nigeria," *HOLD* No. 6, p. 11.

67. "The Conflict of the Last Days," *HOLD* No. 39, p. 6.

68. Elton, *Babylon the Kingdom of Satan*, p. 46.

69. Sermon, *Restoring the Church.*

70. Elton, *Demon Manifestations in the Last Days*, p. 66–67.

71. Sermon, *God's Last Days Move.*

72. "The End Time Church," *HOLD* No. 37, p. 12.

73. Sermon, *God's Last Days Move.*

74. Elton, *Babylon the Kingdom of Satan*, p. 45.

75. Sermon, *Feasts of End Time.*

76. "A Chosen Company," *HOLD* No. 18, p. 1.

77. Ibid. pp. 1–2.

78. "The Invincible Few," *HOLD* No. 12, p. 7.

79. Sermon, *Feasts of End Time.*

80. Elton, *The Coming Kingdom*, p. 35.

81. Yinka Ayankogbe, 2012.

82. Sermon, *Covenant Relationship in the Epistle to the Ephesians.*

83. Sermon, *Kingdom Lifestyle.*

Epilogue: "Don't Celebrate Death"

1. Sermon, *Spiritual Marriage.*

2. Sermon, *The Revelation of John the Beloved about the End.*

3. Emeka Nwankpa, 2006.

4. "Mama Elton: Single and Still Searching," *Essence Restored*, Vol. 1, No. 1, Oct – Dec, 2004, p. 51.

5. John Valentine, 2012.

6. Letter from Sydney Elton to Dr. & Mrs. Femi Soetan, November 28, 1980.

7. Rev. S. G. Elton. Interview.

8. Sermon, *It is Finished, It is Done.*

9. Letter from Sydney Elton to Rev. and Mrs. John Valentine, September 14, 1986.

10. Ruth Elton, May 2010.

11. Ischemic heart disease (also known as Coronary artery disease), is the most common type of heart disease and cause of heart attacks. The disease is caused by plaque building up along the inner walls of the arteries of the heart, which narrows the arteries and reduces blood flow to the heart. While the symptoms and signs of coronary artery disease are noted in the advanced state of disease, most individuals with coronary artery disease show no evidence of disease for decades as the disease progresses before the first onset of symptoms, often a "sudden" heart attack, finally arises. "Coronary artery disease," https://en.wikipedia.org/wiki/Coronary_artery_disease.

12. Ruth Elton, 2012.

13. Ibid.
14. Ibid.
15. Letter from Sydney Elton to Rev. and Mrs. John Valentine, September 14, 1986.
16. Emeka Nwankpa, 2006.
17. Ibid.
18. Ruth Elton, 2006.
19. Letter from Sydney Elton to Rev. and Mrs. John Valentine, September 14, 1986.
20. Elizabeth Metcalfe, 2012.
21. Ibid.
22. Ibid.
23. Ibid.
24. Letter from Sydney Elton to Rev. and Mrs. John Valentine, September 14, 1986.
25. Elizabeth Metcalfe, 2012.
26. Ibid.
27. Edward Ezenwafor, 2013.
28. Elizabeth Metcalfe, 2012.
29. Rev. S. G. Elton Interview.
30. Ibid.
31. Ruth Elton, 2006.
32. Elizabeth Metcalfe, 2012.
33. Ruth Elton, 2006.
34. Rev. S. G. Elton Interview.
35. Ruth Elton, 2010.
36. Ibid.
37. Ibid.
38. Ibid.
39. Ibid.
40. Ibid.
41. Ruth Elton, 2006.
42. Ibid.
43. Ibid.

Bibliography

Books, Dissertations and Articles

Abodunde, Ayodeji. *A Herald of the Last Days*. Ibadan: Complete House Publishers, 2007.

Abodunde, Ayodeji. *A Heritage of Faith: A History of Christianity in Nigeria*. Ibadan: Pierce Watershed, 2009.

Ade Aina, J. *The Present-Day Prophets and the Principles upon which they Work*. University of Nigeria, Nsukka edition, 1964.

Adebanjo, S. A. *Christ Apostolic Church: Sixty Years of its Existence, 1935–1995*. Ijebu Ode: Christ Apostolic Church, 1996.

Adegboyega, S. G. *Short History of the Apostolic Church*. Ibadan: Rosprint Industrial Press, 1978.

Ademakinwa, J. A. *Iwe Itan Ijo Aposteli ti Kristi*. Lagos: CAC Publication, 1971.

Adesogan, E. K. *Faith, Politics and Challenges: A Christian's First-Hand Account*. Ijebu Ode: Heinemann, 2006.

Akanni, Gbile. *The Price, Plight and Perils of the Anointed*. Gboko: Peace House Publications, 2002.

Alabi, Soji. *A Prophet in the House: A Biography of Rev. (Dr.) Francis Wale Oke*. Ibadan: Caltop Publications, 1998.

Alokan, J. A. *The Christ Apostolic Church, 1928–1988*. Ibadan: Ibukunola Printers, 1991.

Althouse, Peter. *Spirit of the Last Days: Pentecostal Eschatology in Conversation with Jürgen Moltmann*. New York: Continuum International Publishing Group, 2003.

Anyachor, Monday. *History of the Apostolic Church in Igboland*. Owerri: Ihem Davis Press, 1988.

Anyaegbu, J. O. "The Growth and Development of Pentecostal/Evangelical Movements in Igboland: A Case Study of North-West Igboland, 1965–1990," Master's thesis, University of Nigeria, Nsukka, 1991.

Ayegboyin, D. and Ishola, S. A. *African Indigenous Churches: A Historical Perspective*.

Lagos: Greater Heights Publications, 1999.

Babajide, D. O. *The Founding of the Ministries of Prophet Joseph Babalola and Prophet Daniel Orekoya in 1930.* Ilesa, 1980.

Babatope, Ebenezer. *Student Power vs. Militarism (1971–1975).* Ibadan: Deto Deni Productions, 1976.

Benjamin, Steward. *Historical Background of Churches in Nigeria.* Lagos: Interwale Press, 1984.

Burgess, Richard. "The Civil War Revival and its Pentecostal Progeny: A Religious Movement among the Igbo People of Eastern Nigeria, 1967–2002," PhD thesis, University of Birmingham, 2004.

Chernow, Ron. *Alexander Hamilton.* USA: Penguin Books, 2004.

Christian Council of Nigeria, *Kaduna 1962: Record of the Thirteenth Assembly of the Christian Council of Nigeria.* Ibadan, 1962.

Dayhoff, Paul. *Living Stones in Africa.* Iowa: Unpublished Manuscript, 2011.

Elton, Sydney. *Black Magic and Jungle Prophets.* Portland: Wings of Healing Publications, n.d.

Emeka, Paul. "Benson Idahosa Factor in Nigerian Pentecostalism," PhD thesis, University of Nigeria, Nsukka, 2001.

Emeka, Paul. "Benson Idahosa Factor in Nigerian Pentecostalism," PhD thesis, University of Nigeria, Nsukka, 2001.

Ezemadu, Reuben. *The Mandate: How Far and How Much More?* Ibadan: Christian Missionary Foundation Inc., 2007.

Ezemadu, Reuben. *The Vision So Far: A Story of the Christian Missionary Foundation.* Ibadan: Christian Missionary Foundation, 1993.

Fafunwa, Babatunde. *A History of Education in Nigeria.* London: George Allen and Unwin, 1974.

Fellowship of Christian Students. *The Fellowship of Christian Students Handbook for FCS officials, Staff Advisers/Senior Friends and Branch Executive Committees.* Jos, 1992.

Floods upon the Dry Ground: A Report of the Apostolic Church International Convention, August 5–13, 1939. Penygroes: Apostolic Publications, 1939.

Garlock, Ruthanne. *Fire in His Bones: The Story of Benson Idahosa.* Plainfield, New Jersey: Logos Books, 1981.

Hackett, Rosalind (ed.). *New Religious Movements in Nigeria.* Lewiston, New York: E. Mellen Press, 1987.

Hackett, Rosalind. *Religion in Calabar: The Religious Life and History of a Nigerian Town.* Berlin: Mouton de Gruyter, 1989.

Hall, Franklin. *Atomic Power with God with Fasting and Prayers.* Phoenix, 1946.

Hall, Franklin. *Faith Treatments*. Phoenix, 1967.

Hall, Franklin. *The Body-Felt Salvation*. Phoenix, 1968.

Hall, Franklin. *The Return of Immortality*. Phoenix, 1976.

Hamon, Bill. *The Eternal Church: A Prophetic look at the Church: Her History, Restoration and Destiny*. Pennsylvania: Destiny Image, 2003.

Harrell, David Edwin. *All things are Possible: The Healing and Charismatic Revivals in Modern America*. Bloomington: Indiana University Press, 1979.

Hocken, Peter. *Streams of Renewal: The Origins and Early Development of the Charismatic Movement in Great Britain*. Devon: Paternoster Press, 1995.

Holt, Bradley. "Healing in the Charismatic Movement: The Catholics in Nigeria," *Religions*, Vol. 2, No. 2, December 1977.

Idahosa, Benson. *From Zero to Surplus*. Benin: Idahosa World Outreach, 1993.

Ifere, S. E. *God's response to Nigeria: The Story of NIFES*. Jos: NIFES Press, 1995.

Ikoh, C. and Ukachi, A. *The Story of the Christian Evangelical Social Movement of Nigeria*. Lagos: CESM Publication, n.d.

Intercessors for Nigeria. *Intercessors for Nigeria Information Brochure*. Lagos: Intercessors for Nigeria, 2004.

Isichei, Elisabeth. *Varieties of Christian Experience in Nigeria*. London: Macmillan, 1982.

Jenkins, Philip. *The Next Christendom: The Coming of Global Christianity*. Oxford: Oxford University Press, 2011.

Jennings, Charles. *Pastors According to Mine Heart*. Owasso, OK: Truth in History, 2008.

Kalu, O. U. *The Embattled Gods: Christianization of Igboland, 1841–1991*. Lagos: Minaj Publishers, 1996.

Kalu, Ogbu (ed.). *The History of Christianity in West Africa*. United Kingdom: Longman, 1981.

Kalu, Ogbu. "Doing Mission through the Post Office: Naked Faith People of Igboland, 1920-1960," *Neue Zeitschrift fur Missionswissenschaft* 56, no. 4, 2000.

Kalu, Ogbu. "The Third Response: Pentecostalism and the Reconstruction of Christian Experience in Africa, 1970-1995," *Journal of African Christian Thought*, 1, no. 2, 1998.

Kalu, Ogbu. "The Wind of God. Evangelical Pentecostalism in Igboland, 1970-1990," in Pew Charitable Trust Lecture (ed.). Centre for the Study of Christianity in the Non-Western World. Edinburgh: University of Edinburgh, 1992.

Kew, Richard and Okorocha, Cyril. *Vision Bearers*. Pennsylvania: Morehouse Publishing, 1996.

Larbi, Kinsley. *Pentecostalism: The Eddies of Ghanaian Christianity*. Accra: CPCS,

2001.

Leonard, Christine. *A Giant in Ghana*. Chichester: New Wine Press, 1989.

Liardon, Roberts. *God's Generals: Why they Succeeded and why Some Failed*. Tulsa: Albury Publishing, 1996.

Lindsay, Gordon. *The Gordon Lindsay Story*. Dallas: Christ for the Nations, 1992.

Llewellyn, Henry Byron. "A Study of the History and Thought of the Apostolic Church in Wales in the Context of Pentecostalism." Master's thesis, University College Cardiff, 1997.

Lloyd, L. C. (ed.) *Shrewsbury: Historic Centre of Beautiful Shropshire*. Shrewsbury: Shrewsbury & District Chamber of Commerce/Wilding & Sons Ltd, 1957.

Lowman Pete. *The Day of His Power*. England: Inter-Varsity Press, 1983.

Lyons, P. A. And Harriet, L. D. "Religion and the Mass Media," in Jacob K. Olupona and Toyin Falola (eds.), *Religion and Society in Nigeria: Historical and Sociological Perspectives*. Ibadan: Spectrum Books, 1991.

Madeibo A. A. *The Nigerian Revolution and the Biafran War*. Enugu: Fourth Dimension Publishing, 1980.

Maduako, D. (*et al*). *Flame of Fire: The Story of Scripture Union (Nigeria)*. Ibadan: Scripture Union Press, 2005.

Malcomson, Keith. "Pentecostal Pioneers Remembered,"http://pentecostalpione-ersorg/DPWilliams.html.

Marshall, R. "Pentecostalism in Southern Nigeria," in Paul Gifford (ed.), *New Dimensions in African Christianity*. Ibadan: Sefer Books, 1993.

Marshall, Ruth. *Political Spiritualities: The Pentecostal Revolution in Nigeria*. Chicago: University of Chicago Press, 2009.

Mitchell, Robert. "Religious Change and Modernization: The Aladura Churches among the Yoruba in Southwestern Nigeria," PhD thesis, Northwestern University, Evanston, Illinois, 1970.

Mitchell, Robert. "Religious Protest and Social Change: The Origins of the Aladura Movement in Western Nigeria," in Robert Rotberg and Ali Mazrui (eds.), *Protest and Power in Black Africa*. New York: Oxford University Press, 1970.

Mohr, Adam. "Faith Tabernacle Congregation and the emergence of Pentecostalism in Colonial Nigeria, 1910s–1941," *Journal of Religion in Africa* 43, No. 2, 2013.

Mohr, Adam. "Out of Zion into Philadelphia and West Africa: Faith Tabernacle Congregation, 1897–1925," *Pneuma* 32, 2010.

Ndubuisi, C. I. "Evangelical Pentecostalism in Southern Igboland, 1930–90," Master's thesis, University of Nigeria, Nsukka, 1991.

Nnaji, Godwin. *Looking Beyond the Night*. Enugu: SNAAP Press, 1997.

Numbere, Nonyem. *A Man and A Vision*. Port Harcourt: Greater Evangelism

Publications, 2008.

Nwosu, L. Ugwuanyi. "Christianization of South-West Igboland, 1902–1967." PhD thesis, University of Nigeria, Nsukka, 1989.

Obadan, Peter. *The Legend*. Benin: Glopet Limited, 2006.

Ojo, J. O. *The Life and Ministry of Apostle Joseph Ayodele Babalola, 1904–1959*. Lagos: Prayer Band Publications, 1988.

Ojo, Matthews. "Charismatic Movements in Africa," in Andrew F. Walls and Christopher Fyfe (ed.), *Christianity in Africa in the 1990s*. Edinburgh: University of Edinburgh, 1996.

Ojo, Matthews. "Deeper Christian Life Ministry: A Case Study of the Charismatic Movements in Western Nigeria," *Journal of Religion in Africa* XVIII, 2, 1988.

Ojo, Matthews. "The Dynamics of Indigenous Charismatic Missionary Enterprises in West Africa," *Missionalia* 25, no. 4, 1997.

Ojo, Matthews. "The Growth of Campus Christianity and Charismatic Movements in Western Nigeria," PhD thesis, King's College, University of London, 1986.

Ojo, Matthews. *The End-Time Army: Charismatic Movements in Modern Nigeria*. Eritrea: Africa World Press Books, 2006.

Olusheye, E. H. L. *Saint Joseph Ayo Babalola: Africa's foremost Religious Revolutionary Leader, 1904–1959*. Ibadan: Christian Overcomers Publishers, 1998.

Osborn, Daisy. *The King and I*. Tulsa: T. L. Osborn Evangelistic Foundation, n.d.

Osborn, T. L. & Daisy. *The Gospel According to T. L. & Daisy*. Tulsa: OSFO Books, 1985.

Osborn, T. L. *The Purpose of Pentecost*. Tulsa: T. L. Osborn Evangelistic Association, 1963.

Osborn, T. L. *We Found Black Gold*. Tulsa: Faith Digest Publications, 1957.

Oshun, C. O. "Christ Apostolic Church of Nigeria: A suggested Pentecostal consideration of its historical, organizational and theological developments, 1918–1975," PhD thesis, University of Exeter, 1981.

Oshun, C. O. *Aladura Revivals: Apostle Babalola's Challenge to Christian Missions*. Inaugural lecture delivered at the Lagos State University, Ojo, Lagos, July 2000.

Oshun, Olubunmi. "The Spiritual Standard of the Nigerian Faith Tabernacle Pioneers (1918–30)." Paper presented to the 19th Annual Conference of the National Association for the Study of Religions, Jos, 1998.

Oshun, Olubunmi. *Oba Sir Pastor Isaac Akinyele: an Example of Integrity in Service*. Lagos: Pierce Watershed, 2014.

Ositelu, Josiah. *The Words of Prophecies of Things to Happen From the Year 1931 Onwards and for about the Next Six Years*. Ibadan: Ilare Press, 1931.

Oyebamiji, I. O. "A Historical Study of the Missions Strategy of Calvary Ministries

(CAPRO), 1975–1995." Master's thesis, Theological College of Northern Nigeria, Jos.

Parkyns, Edgar. *His Waiting Bride: An Outline of Church History in the Light of the Book of Revelation.* Wheatcorn, 1996.

Peel, J. D. Y. *Aladura: A Religious Movement among the* Yoruba. London: Oxford University Press, 1968.

Peel, J. D. Y. *Ijesha and Nigerians: The Incorporation of a Yoruba Kingdom.* Cambridge: Cambridge University Press, 1983.

Peel, J. D. Y. *Religious Encounter and the Making of the Yoruba.* Bloomington: Indiana University Press, 2000.

Riss, Richard. *Latter Rain: The Latter Rain movement of 1948 and the Mid-twentieth Century Evangelical Awakening.* Canada: Honeycomb Visual Productions, 1987.

Rutland, Joy. *Obeying His Call.* Australia: Copyhouse, 1995.

SCM. *Student Christian Movement of Nigeria: Silver Jubilee Souvenir Publication 1940–1969.* Ibadan: Abiodun Printing Works, 1965.

Synan, Vinson. *The Holiness-Pentecostal Tradition: Charismatic Movements in the Twentieth Century.* Michigan: William B. Eerdmans, 1997.

The Apostolic Church LAWNA Territory. *A Brief Biography of Samuel Adebayo Adegboyega M.O.N, J.P. 1897–1979.* Lagos: The Apostolic Church LAWNA Territory Publication, n.d.

The Apostolic Church Nigeria. *The Apostolic Church Nigeria 50th Anniversary Souvenir Brochure.* Ilesha, 1981.

Turnbull, T. N. *What God hath Wrought: A Short History of the Apostolic Church.* Bradford: The Puritan Press, 1959.

Turner, H. W. "Pentecostal Movements in Nigeria," *Orita,* Vol. 6, no. 1.

Turner, H. W. *History of an African Independent Church: The Church of the Lord Aladura, vols. I & II.* London: Oxford University Press, 1967.

UCH Chapel Handbook. Ibadan: UCH Chapel Committee, n.d.

Ukachi, Austen. *The Best is yet to Come: Pentecostal and Charismatic Revivals in Nigeria, 1914–1990s.* Lagos: Summit Press, 2013.

Ukah, A. F. "The Redeemed Christian Church of God (RCCG), Nigeria. Local Identities and Global Processes in African Pentecostalism," PhD thesis, University of Bayreuth, 2003.

Vaughan, I. J. *Psychology of a Pilgrim with a Limp.* Great Britain, 1983.

Vaughan, I. J. *The Origins of Apostolic Church Pentecostalism in Nigeria, 1931–52.* Ipswich: Ipswich Book Company, 1991.

Warnock George. *The Feast of Tabernacles: The Hope of the Church.* North Battleford: Sharon Publications, 1951.

Watt, E. S. *The Quest for Souls in Qua Iboe.* London: Marshall, Morgan & Scott, 1951.

Westgarth, J. W. *The Holy Spirit and the Primitive Mind.* London, 1946.

Wogu, E. A. *The Origin and Growth of the Assemblies of God Church in Nigeria.* Lagos, 1973.

Worsfold, Luke. "Subsequence, Prophecy and Church Order." PhD. thesis, Victoria University of Wellington, New Zealand, 2004.

Sydney Elton Sermons

1. *We Beheld His Glory,* Port Harcourt, September 12, 1984.
2. *Training in the Wilderness,* Lagos University Teaching Hospital, January 1, 1981.
3. *Oyo State NYSC Commissioning of Christian Corpers,* Ibadan, July 3, 1983.
4. *We Have Come to Mount Zion,* Ilesa, December 1983.
5. *Who Controls Nigeria,* Ilesa, May 1984.
6. *The Elect Remnant,* Ile-Ife House Fellowship, April 17, 1985.
7. *Fellowship With God,* Ilesa, August 8, 1983.
8. *Things Soon to Come (I),* Ibadan Varsity Christian Union (IVCU), October 8, 1978.
9. *Things Soon to Come (II),* IVCU, October 8, 1978.
10. *Things Soon to Come (III),* IVCU, October 8, 1978.
11. *Things Soon to Come (IV),* IVCU, October 8, 1978.
12. *Authority of the Believer,* CSSM Meeting, University of Ibadan, October 7, 1978.
13. *Enthroning the King,* January 20, 1986.
14. Survey of Prophecy in New Testament and Last Days, Ede, October 1984.
15. *MIZRAH – Government of God,* Ilesa, December 1984.
16. *Feasts of the LORD,* Ilesa, September 1983.
17. *Bringing the Church to Fullness (I),* 1983.
18. *Bringing the Church to Fullness (II),* 1983.
19. *Anointing of the Body,* Ilesa, 1983
20. *Things Which Cannot Be Shaken,* January 1983.
21. *We Beheld His Glory,* Ilesa, August 1984.
22. *The Trumpet's Call,* July 1985.
23. *The Gospel of the Kingdom,* Ilesa, February 10, 1983.
24. *God's Last Days Move,* Ibadan Polytechnic, January 30, 1982.
25. *Origin of Satan and Demons,* Ilesa, 1982.
26. *God's Army Confronts Enemy,* Ilesa, March 10, 1983.
27. *God's Move Today,* Ibadan, January 30, 1982.

28. *His Inheritance and Ours*, Ilesa, May 1984.

29. *The Church – His Body (III)*, Ilesa, n.d.

30. *Government of His Body*, Ilesa, n.d.

31. *It Is Finished*, Ilesa, September 1984.

32. *The Tabernacle*, September 1983.

33. *Entering into Rest*, Ilesa, May 1984.

34. *Job: The LORD Reigneth*, Ilesa, October 1983.

35. *Church of the First Born*, Ilesa, December 1983.

36. *Divine Government*, Ibadan Polytechnic, January 30 1982.

37. *God's Army*, Ibadan Polytechnic, January 31, 1982.

38. *Priesthood of Believers*, Ilesa, August 1983.

39. *The Kingdom and the Church*, Ilesha, March 24, 1983.

40. *Spiritual Marriage*, Ede, March 7, 1986.

41. *Our Inheritance*, Onitsha, August 22, 1981.

42. *My Inheritance in Jesus Christ*, Onitsha, August 10, 1980.

43. *The Anointed Over the Anointing*, Onitsha, Friday 21, 1981.

44. *Authority of the Believer*, Onitsha, August 25, 1979.

45. *The Battle for Nigeria*, Onitsha, August 8, 1980.

46. *Christian Relationship with Church*, Onitsha, August 8, 1980.

47. *Restoring the Church*, Onitsha, August 9, 1980.

48. *God-Given Vision*, Onitsha, August 7, 1980.

49. *Relationship with the World*, Ilesha, June 16, 1983.

50. *Prepare for War*, Ede, March 16, 1984.

51. *Kingdom Provision*, Ilesha, June 23, 1983.

52. *The Kingdom of Heaven*, January, 1984.

53. *Let us Go On,* CSSM Training Conference, Modakeke, July 1978.

54. *The Ministry of the Holy Spirit in these Last Days*, Port Harcourt, September 11, 1984.

55. *It is Finished – It is Done*, Port Harcourt, September 13, 1984.

56. *The Revelation of John the Beloved about the End.*

57. *Covenant Relationships in the Epistle to the Ephesians.*

58. *Behold I set before You an Open Door*, August 23, 1981.

59. *Kingdom Series: The Meaning of the Kingdom (I)*

60. *Kingdom Series: The Outline of the Kingdom as Given in the Old Testament (II).*

61. *Kingdom Series: The King Comes to His Kingdom – Unveiling the Person of the King Himself (III).*

62. *Kingdom Series: The Citizens of the Kingdom in the New Testament (IV).*

63. *Kingdom Series: The Establishing of the Kingdom in Nigeria (V).*

64. *Kingdom Series: The Ultimate Restoration of the Kingdom on Earth (VI), February 10, 1983.*

65. *Restoration of the Kingdom in Nigeria.*

66. *Restoration of the Kingdom of His Son.*

67. *The Lifestyle of the Members of the Kingdom of Heaven on Earth.*

68. *Kingdom Lifestyle.*

69. *Establishing the Kingdom of Heaven.*

70. *The Kingdom of Heaven on Earth: New Jerusalem and Mount Zion.*

71. *The Fellowship Inside The Kingdom,* February 10, 1983.

72. *The Christian and His Profession.*

73. *Hebrews and the Body.*

74. *Anointing the Body.*

75. *The Ministry of Laying on of Hands,* June 1985.

76. *God's Demands and Promises Regarding Prophecy for the Last Days.*

77. *The Vision: Effects on Life and Church Government,* October 1, 1986.

78. *Restoration: All Things New.*

79. *Vision,* February 12, 1986.

Other Sermons

1. Parkyns, Edgar. *Reminiscences.* n.d.

2. Akinboboye, Kole. *Ancient Landmarks: Special Commemoration Service for Late Pa S. G. Elton, 2007.*

Magazine Collections and Video Documentaries

1. *The Voice of Healing Magazines,* volume 2. United Kingdom: John Carver Ministries and Revival Library, 2013.

2. *Pentecost: The Voice of the Pentecostal World Movement, 1947–1966.* United Kingdom: Revival Library, 2008.

3. *Black Gold*: Osborn Crusades in Yaba and Ibadan, Nigeria, in 1957. Tulsa, OK: OSFO International, ca. 1957.

4. Idahosa, Benson. *Interview with Rev. S. G. Elton.* April 4, 1982. Benin: Church of God Mission International, 1982.

5. Akanni, Gbile. *Advancing the Kingdom*: Last Days Gathering 2011. Lagos: CAP-RO, 2011.

6. *From Glory to Glory:* A Documentary on the History of the Church of God Mission International. Benin: Church of God Mission International, 1995.

Illustration Credits

All images, with the exception of those listed below, are from Ruth Elton.

1. **David Odubanjo**. Christ Apostolic Church Archives, Ibadan.
2. **Joseph Ayo Babalola**. Alokan, J. A. *The Christ Apostolic Church, 1928–1988*. Akure: Ibukunola Printers, 1991.
3. **Ambrose Clark**. "Testimony of Pastor Clark." First Century Gospel Church (Headquarters), 3 Palatine Road, Califon, NJ. http://0350-2f1.netsolhost.com/word press/wpcontent/uploads/2011/12/-fcg_church_founder3.pdf.
4. **Noah Evans, George Perfect and Idris Vaughan**. *The Apostolic Herald*, December 1934.
5. **D. P. Williams, W. J. Williams and A. Turnbull**. *The Apostolic Church Nigeria 50th Anniversary Souvenir Brochure*. Ilesha, 1981.
6. **Thomas Wyatt**. Personal collection of Thomas Randolf Wyatt
7. **Elton speaking in the United States, 1955**. *March of Faith*, October 1955.
8. **A team of Latter Rain evangelists boarding a plane for Nigeria, 1954**. *March of Faith*, December 1954.
9. **A team of Latter Rain evangelists getting ready to leave for Nigeria, 1955**. *March of Faith*, November–December, 1955.
10. **The Osborn Foundation team leading the recording of T. L. Osborn's sermons into Nigerian languages at the Eltons' compound in Ilesa**, 1965. *Faith Digest*, August 1965.
11. **Royal treatment. Elton presents Daisy Osborn to the King of Ilesa, 1967**. Osborn, Daisy. *The King and I*. Tulsa: T. L. Osborn Evangelistic Foundation, n.d.
12. **Edgar Parkyns**. Personal collection of Andrew Daniels.
13. **Elton with some of the key figures in the post-civil war revival in eastern Nigeria**. Personal collection of Elizabeth Metcalfe.

14. **Elton and Grace Delbridge in Enugu, ca. 1985.** Personal collection of Elizabeth Metcalfe.

Index

Made in United States
Cleveland, OH
01 August 2025

19041831R00308